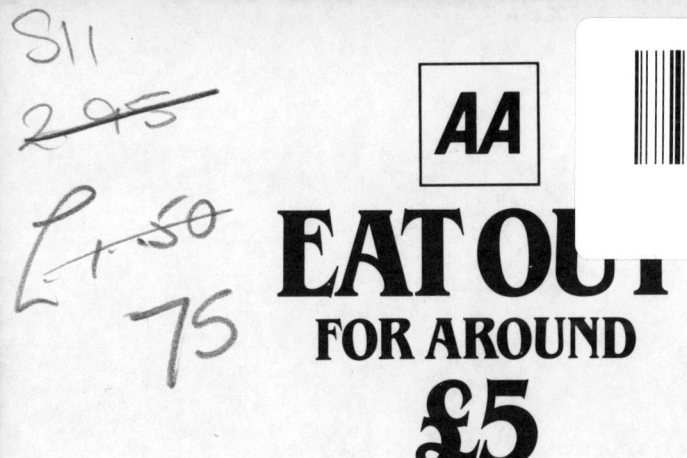

Editor: Barbara Littlewood
Designer: Andrew Haughton
Consultant: Ian Tyers, Manager, Hotel and Information Services
Gazetteer editor: Pamela Stagg
Maps: prepared by the Cartographic Services Unit of the Automobile Association
Cover photograph: prepared with the assistance of The Bodega, Alresford

Advertisement Production: Christopher Heard, tel. 0256 20123 (ext 2020)
Advertisement Sales Representatives:
North of England and Scotland, Brian Nathaniel, tel. 061-338 6498
Wales and Midlands, Arthur Williams, tel. 0222 60267
South-west England, Bryan Thompson, tel. 027-580 3296
London and South-east England, Melanie Mackenzie-Aird, tel. 0494 40208
Central Southern England, Edward May, tel. 0256 20123 (ext 3524) or 0256 67568

Filmsetting by Vantage Photosetting Co. Ltd., Eastleigh and London
Printed and bound by William Clowes (Beccles) Ltd., Beccles and London

The contents of this book are believed correct at the time of printing. Nevertheless the Publisher can accept no responsibility for errors or omissions or for changes in the details given. Prices in particular may vary. While every effort is made by the Publisher to ensure that the information appearing in advertisements is correct, no responsibility can be accepted for inaccuracies.

© The Automobile Association, January 1983/56614

All rights reserved. No part of this publication may be reproduced, stored in a retrieval system, or transmitted in any form or by any means – electronic, mechanical, photocopying or otherwise – unless the written permission of the Publisher has been given beforehand.

ISBN 0 86145 143 0

Published by the Automobile Association, Fanum House, Basingstoke, Hampshire RG21 2EA

Contents

Inside cover		Symbols
4		Introduction – Counting the Costs
5		English Wine
		Eating Places:
		England
12	1	The South-West Peninsula
42	2	Wessex
62	3	The South-East
70	4	Cotswolds and Chilterns
82	5	London
98	6	East Anglia
108	7	East Midlands and Peak District
118	8	The Heart of England
140	9	The North-West
154	10	Yorkshire and Humberside
166	11	The North and the Lakes
		Scotland
174	12	Edinburgh and the Border Regions
184	13	Glasgow and the West
194	14	Central, Tayside and Fife
202	15	Highland and Grampian
208	16	**Wales**
223		**A to Z of towns**

Counting the Costs

There is no doubt that a good three-course meal is one of the simplest yet most profound pleasures life can offer, but 'paying through the nose' for it at an uncaring restaurant can sometimes take the edge off that pleasure. That's why the AA Hotel and Restaurant Inspectors have again taken to the road to bring you an even more comprehensive and far-reaching guide to low-price, yet high-standard eating places. Although eating out is becoming more expensive generally, we are pleased to report that most of the establishments in this book are holding their prices down as far as possible. As this book demonstrates, there are restaurants in Britain where excellence and economy are combined to provide opportunities for good eating out on a budget in congenial surroundings. It is not at all difficult to have a really good three-course meal, whether of traditional English fare, Continental or Asian cuisine, without spending the equivalent of the week's housekeeping money. The AA Hotel and Restaurant Inspectors have visited and recommended all these places – a seal of approval from a group of established eaters-out! My Inspectors are not peak-capped grading machines with slide rules, but professional men and women with a profound appreciation of what is best and worst in hotels and restaurants. The guide is divided into England, Scotland and Wales and subdivided into sixteen touring regions. Each region is introduced by a map which indicates the location of the towns listed. In certain cases it may be advisable to use a road atlas where an inn is out of town.

All prices quoted are the latest available before going to press in autumn 1982, but care has been taken to exclude places where prices for a three-course meal are likely substantially to exceed £6 during 1983. As far as possible VAT and service charges have been included in the calculation.

Ian Tyers

Ian Tyers
Manager, Hotel and Information Services

English Wine

First of all, do not confuse 'English Wine', made in England from wine-grapes grown in the open-air in English vineyards, with 'British Wines', made commercially in Britain from imported grape-juice concentrate and marketed as sherry-type, port-type etc. Do not confuse it either with the 'wine' made all over Britain by members of amateur wine-making societies from apricots, parsnips, tea-leaves, nettles – indeed anything fermentable.

The Germans who make wine from wine-grapes grown at about the same latitude as much of southern England call their white wine by names familiar to most people in Britain – Mosel and Riesling. For the white table wine of comparable quality made in this country there is as yet no generic term other than 'English Wine'. Although a new appellation on the wine list for the present generation, English wine has as old and distinguished an ancestry as any of the German 'classics'.

The First Vines

The first vines to grow in Britain were brought over from Gaul by the Roman soldiers and administrators who occupied this most northerly province of the Roman Empire for 300 years up to AD 400. As the period of conquest lengthened into occupation the new Romano-British population made vine-growing and wine-making part of a lifestyle which at last was civilised and cultured. After the Romans departed, the activity was taken to Wales and the West Country by those who were lucky enough to escape the invading barbarians from across the North Sea who overran the island in the Dark Ages. According to the chronicler, William of Malmesbury, no county in Anglo-Saxon England had so many or so good vineyards as Gloucester either for fertility or for sweetness of grape. The wine made from those grapes had 'no unpleasant tartness or eagerness, and is little inferior to the French in its sweetness'. By the time the Normans, with their wine-drinking tradition, became the new ruling class, English wine was to be found all over the southern counties. As the new conquerors moved north across the Thames they found so many vineyards around Ely that they called the area 'L'Isle des Vignes'. When the new king, William I, ordered his Domesday Survey in 1086, his commissioners recorded 45 vineyards in 14 counties.

Medieval Vineyards

It is a myth which dies hard that vine-growing and wine-making ceased in England when Eleanor of Aquitaine married King Henry II, and the vineyards of the Bordeaux region became part of his realm. Our Plantagenet kings drank the flinty, white English wine made of grapes from the Windsor Castle vineyard as well as the lush, red wine which came in such large quantities from Aquitaine. The medieval Archbishops of Canterbury had big vineyards at Teynham and Northfleet in Kent, and English wine from their grapes filled the cellars of their palaces. The small vineyard cultivated by the archbishop's bailiff at Sevenoaks is remembered today by the famous Vine Cricket Club, one of the oldest in England, formed in 1734. The bishops of Rochester had vineyards at Rochester, Halling and Snodland.

Equally untrue is the belief that no more English wine was made after Henry VIII dissolved the monasteries in the middle of the 16th century. He closed the religious communities for lack of spirituality, not lack of vine-growing and wine-making expertise. It is likely that the lay lords to whom establishments such as Battle Abbey and Pershore Abbey passed, made sure that the vineyards and wine presses were handed over in good order. With fewer monks who had the time and the discipline to tackle the difficult craft of viticulture and wine-making, both would have suffered a set-back, but neither were eclipsed. There was no shortage of English vine-growers and wine-makers in the centuries that followed. In the view of John Rose, author of *The English Vineyard Vindicated* (1666) the strange decay of vines among the English was due not to the climate but to 'our own neglect and the common vicissitude of things'. It was a question then – and still is – of fitting the vine (of which there are a vast variety) to the climate. The error lay in thinking it was *vice versa*, confusing dessert-grapes with wine-grapes, and jumping to the conclusion that the English climate was not 'suitable' for the vine.

In *The Compleat Vineyard* (1670) William Hughes pointed proudly to the vineyards of England which produced 'a great store of excellent good wine' and that in spite of the fact that 'we are no nearer the pole than well-known German wines'. The anonymous author of *The Vineyard* (1727) pronounced that the lack of wine in England 'was not owing to the unkindness of our soil or the want of a benign climate, but to the inexperience of our natives or a want of curiosity in such as are capable of convincing themselves by an easy experiment of the practicableness thereof'.

Vineyards of the Nobility

In 1610 Robert Cecil, first Earl of Salisbury, sent the famous botanist, John Tradescant, to Flanders to find vines to start a vineyard on the banks of the river Broadwater at Hatfield House. The following year the French ambassador in London had 30,000 vines sent over to Hatfield, with a promise that another 10,000 would follow. John Evelyn paid the vineyard a visit in 1643 and noted it in his diary. The vineyard was well looked after when Charles I was a prisoner there in 1647; Samuel Pepys walked in it after dinner one July evening in 1661.

John Evelyn helped design the Italian garden which Henry Howard, grandson of the Earl of Arundel, built at Albury Park near Guildford in 1666, which included a vineyard laid out in terraces above a broad expanse of water (which is still unbuilt on today). John Aubrey describes the vineyard at Albury as being of twelve acres. The layout was similar to that which the Hon Charles Hamilton, youngest son of the sixth Earl of Abercorn, con-

ceived for the 10-acre vineyard he planted leading down to the artificial lake on the estate he acquired at Cobham, Surrey, called Painshill, in 1738. With the aid of a French vigneron, David Geneste, whom he paid to leave the family vineyard at Beziat in Clairac, Guienne, Hamilton was soon making hogsheads of 'still champagne', and later red wine, from the 35,000 vines he planted overlooking the river Mole. It sold readily in the inns of Cobham until 1773 when he disposed of the estate to pay his debts. The vineyard was maintained however until the beginning of the 19th century. The site, though overgrown, is still open ground, and the Friends of Painshill are planning to clear it and replant the 18th-century vineyard beside the mock ruined chapel which still stands at the water's edge.

Even larger was the walled vineyard which James Oglethorpe laid down at Westbrook Place in Godalming, Surrey in 1720. Oglethorpe, a prominent social reformer and Member of Parliament, went out to America in 1732 and founded the city of Savannah, Georgia. When he returned, he married and went to live on his wife's estate in Essex, but wine-making continued at Westbrook at least until 1754 when the vineyard was visited by Dr Richard Pococke who noted of Godalming in his *Travels Through England* (1754), that here was 'General Oglethorpe's, where there is a vineyard out of which they make a wine like Rhenish.' The vineyard was mentioned in the sale particulars when the estate came on the market in 1823. As at Painshill, the site, though overgrown, is still open ground and most of the vineyard wall is still standing.

The vineyard in the park of Arundel Castle in Sussex from whose grapes the Duke of Norfolk made 60 pipes (6,300 gallons) of 'burgundy' in 1763 is not only still open ground in 1983, but is once more yielding wine-grapes – Harry Evans has been growing Chardonnay and other varieties on the 18th-century site (now outside the park) since 1970. In his book *Vine-Growing in England* (1911) H. M. Tod, FRHS, said the Arundel wine was 'not equal to the best of Beaune but better than ordinary'. The commune of Beaune grew at least three classes of wine, 'and there is nothing to prevent Sussex growing wine equal to the second of these as well as the ordinary'. In 1884 Andrew Pettigrew remembered having a talk with Lord Howard of Glossop about vines and vineyards when his lordship had remarked that his father had tasted some of the Arundel wine 'which he said was very good and resembled Burgundy'.

Experiment in Wales

Andrew Pettigrew was responsible for planting the most remarkable English vineyard of all – in Wales. In 1873 the young and wealthy Scot, Patrick Crichton-Stuart, third Marquess of Bute, took it into his head to reconstruct his South Wales property Cardiff Castle, and the nearby ruined Castell Coch, according to his idea of a medieval castle. Part of the transformation scene of the latter was an extensive

vineyard; and in 1875 he and Andrew Pettigrew planted several thousand Gamay Noir and Mille Blanche vines on a three-acre site overlooking the river Taff.

It was good enough for *Punch*. If ever wine produced in Glamorgan was to be drunk, quipped the humorous weekly, it would take four men to do it: the victim, two others to hold him down and a fourth to force the wine down his throat. *Funny Folks* remarked 'Lord Bute had, it appears, a Bute-iful vineyard at Castell Coch near Cardiff where it is hoped much wine will be produced that in Future Hock will be superseded by Coch and the unprounounceable vintages of the Taff. Coch-heimer is as yet a wine *in potentis*, but the vines are planted and the gardener Mr Pettigrew excepts no petty growth'.

But in spite of the mockery, it worked. They took the abundant supply of grapes, mostly black, in a horse and cart down to Cardiff Castle and made wine, both red and white, in the cellars. The 'still champagne' of Castell Coch sold at £3 a dozen in the bar of the Angel Hotel opposite. In 1884 they made 1,500 bottles, in 1887 3,600. The mayor of Cardiff bought three crates. The 1893 vintage, which produced 12,000 bottles, was bought at the usual 60s a dozen but fetched 115s a few years later. The third marquess died in 1900, but the making of Castell Coch Wine continued until the sugar ration was withdrawn on the outbreak of war in 1914. Pettigrew's son maintained the vineyard however until 1920.

The English Wine Revival

There was then a break – the first – of some 25 years in which there is no evidence that any English wine was made at all. It was long enough for its impressive history to be forgotten. Any mention of the making of it as a serious activity was met with derision and disbelief. It was patronisingly relegated to the realms of folklore, to be rescued in 1946 by Ray Barrington Brock who for the first time applied scientific market-research methods to determine which of the 2,000 varities of vine plant would grow and ripen in the conditions of the English climate. It was his findings, and Edward Hyams's book *The Grape Vine in England* published in 1949, which encouraged Major-General Sir Guy Salisbury Jones to plant a vineyard at Hambledon in Hampshire in 1952, which set in motion the great English wine Revival which is still gathering momentum.

In less than thirty years the number of acres under vines in England has increased from the general's single plot to more than a thousand. In the twenty-seven counties stretching from Derbyshire to the Isle of Wight and the Channel Islands where the 230 vineyards of more than half an acre are to be found, there are 70 whose owners welcome visitors anxious to see for themselves what hitherto they had believed possible only 'on the continent' – rows of vines in the open air with bunches of grapes hanging from them and wine (made from them commer-

cially) on sale as they go out. Yes it works. Today some 800,000 bottles of English Wine are sold every year, with a retail value of £4 million, most of it white, but with some red from vignerons like Bernard Theobald and Graham Barrett.

Vineyards to Visit: East Anglia

The English Vineyards Association publishes a 'List of English Vineyards Open to the Public' – you can write for one from its secretary Diana Hibling, Ridge Rarm, Lamberhurst, Kent (tel: Lamberhurst 890734). The settings of many of these English vineyards themselves make a visit worthwhile. The winery where 'Elmham Park' wine is made at Dereham in Norfolk is in a fine old, pantiled 18th-century building of mellow red brick which stands across one side of the courtyard of Elmham House. The proprietor, Robin Don, Master of Wine, planted his first vines experimentally in 1966 and made his first commercial vintage in 1974. His main variety, as elsewhere, is Muller-Thurgau. North Elmham was the seat of the Bishops of East Anglia from 631 to 1071, and the cathedral vineyard stood close beside the well-preserved ruins of the Anglo-Saxon cathedral, the only pre-Norman cathedral still visible above ground in England. Part of the old graveyard lies under a corner of the cathedral vineyard, and the roots of many of the vines are among Christian Saxon bones.

Anyone attending a September Open Day at Boyton Vineyards planted at Hill Farm, Halstead in Essex in 1977 will find themselves in a farm dating from the 15th century (and listed under Grade 2). The buildings once used as barns have been converted to take the machinery of a well-appointed winery. For parties of more than ten, a wine-tasting is arranged. From the Wine Lodge off-licence, visitors can buy the estate-bottled wine by the bottle or case – and those inspired to have a go and start their own vineyard can get rooted vine cuttings.

Kent

At the 32-acre Lamberhurst Vineyard in Kent, which Kenneth McAlpine started with eight acres in 1972, visitors can take the Vineyard Trail, and for 70p a time wander through England's largest vineyard on any day of the week without giving notice. Serious oenologists, who must give notice, are shown round the modern winery between 1 May and 30 October, and can see the cellar in which the juice is fermented and tanks able to hold 210,000 litres, and the press room with the automatic screw press which can squeeze juice out of five tons of grapes in four and a half hours. Any bottle removed from the big Bonded Bottle Store is liable to Excise Duty of 67p a bottle plus 15 per cent VAT. With £1–18 (but perhaps more by the time this is printed) going to the British Government from each bottle, no wonder English Wine is expensive.

Typical of the young professional English Vignerons of today are Stephen and Linda Skelton who, before planting five-and-a-half acres of vines at

Spots Farm, Small Hythe, near Tenterden in Kent, devoted two years to studying the business in the Rheingau wine-growing area of West Germany. It was time well spent, for their 'Spots Farm Seyval Blanc' won them the coveted Gore-Brown Trophy of 1981 awarded by the English Vineyards Association for the Best English Wine of the Year. The Skeltons welcome visitors on conducted tours of their vineyard and winery between June and September (Tenterden 3033). Theirs is part of the 175 acres of vines in South-East England, where four vineyards within an eight mile radius – Biddenden, Carr-Taylor, Lamberhurst and Spots Farm – between them took more than 77 per cent of the awards of the main category of the 1981 Gore-Brown trophy.

Sussex

When the Ferdinand Pieroth Weingut–Weinkellerie GmbH bought Willie Ross's five-year-old vineyard at Barnsgate Manor, Herons Ghyll near Uckfield in Sussex for £250,000, their managing director Kuno Pieroth announced that they hoped to enlarge it to 50 acres to give an eventual output of 150,000 to 250,000 bottles of English wine a year. For visitors to Barnsgate there is not only the vineyard to see but a wine Information Centre with a wine library and museum. A barrel cellar houses old equipment used by vintners and cellar masters. Tasting wine on the terrace overlooking the Ashdown Forest is quite an experience, but first contact Pieroth Ltd on 01-965 3538.

Christopher Ann has a well organised tour for anyone who looks in on his English Wine Centre at Drusilla's Corner near Alfriston, Sussex, where he has a small experimental vineyard nestling in the side of the South Downs. His wine cellar is in an old Sussex Barn where collections of early corkscrews, cider-making equipment, cigar rolling pieces and other early bits of wine making paraphernalia are on show: contact him on 0323 870234. Christopher also runs an annual 'English Vineyard Wine Festival' at Alfriston each September – 1983 will be the ninth year. With their grape-treading and wine-tasting competitions, these festivals, where most leading English wine makers have stalls, have attracted large crowds, keen to have the opportunity of sampling the whole spectrum of English wine.

Where to Buy

The largest stocks of English wine are held by such firms as Valley Wine Cellars at Alfriston, the Merrydown Wine Shop at Horam, Sussex, and at Mainly English, 14 Buckingham Palace Road, London, SW1, which has 'London's Largest Selection of English Wine'. The wine departments of Harrods, Fortnum & Mason and Searcys sell at least half a dozen brands, most with the English Vineyards Association 'Seal of Quality', such as 'Felstar', 'Pilton Manor', 'Cavendish Manor', 'Adgestone', 'Wootton' and 'Barton Manor'.

Though the quantity of English wine available leaves much to be desired, there is nothing to deplore about its quality, as blind tastings by authoritative 'experts' testify. English wine is neither plonk nor *vin ordinaire*. For the time being its official status is Table Wine. The EEC decided in 1973 not to give it 'quality' status – equal to German *qualitätswein* – until ten years' production had been subjected to official scrutiny. The English Vineyards Association applied for a Government-approved certification trade mark for English Wine in 1971, which though not necessarily a mark of quality was at least a guarantee for both producer, distributor and consumer that the wine to which it referred was both properly made and palatable. It took seven years for the British Government to make up its mind, but acceptance of a Certification Trade Mark was finally achieved in 1978. It was only granted to wine which had undergone stringent laboratory tests and had been approved by a tasting panel of experts. Unofficially this gave English Wine the cachet of a regional wine on a par with German *Landswein* or French *vin de pays*.

English Wine Weekends

Those who want to get better acquainted with English wine could not do better than spend an English Wine Weekend at one of the two hotels who have had this enterprising idea. Iain Hatfield's English Wine Weekend at Belstead Brook Hotel, Ipswich is a £39.95– a-person package which starts on Friday evening with an English Wine Tasting in the Garden Bar. On Saturday morning there is a conducted tour of Bruisyard Wine Centre near Framlingham with its vineyard and winery; and on Sunday visits to Basil Ambrose's Cavendish Manor vineyard and Mike Crisp's at Boyton. Telephone 0473 684241 for more information.

Never tasted any English wine? Well here's your chance to have a go. It's the smart thing to do in the 1980s. Don't get left out.

HUGH BARTY-KING
September 1982

GRANADA

Your welcome to the motorways for fast and friendly service 24 hours a day 365 days a year.

Petrol at competitive prices

Wholesome food freshly prepared and served

Take away food and beverages

Variety and value

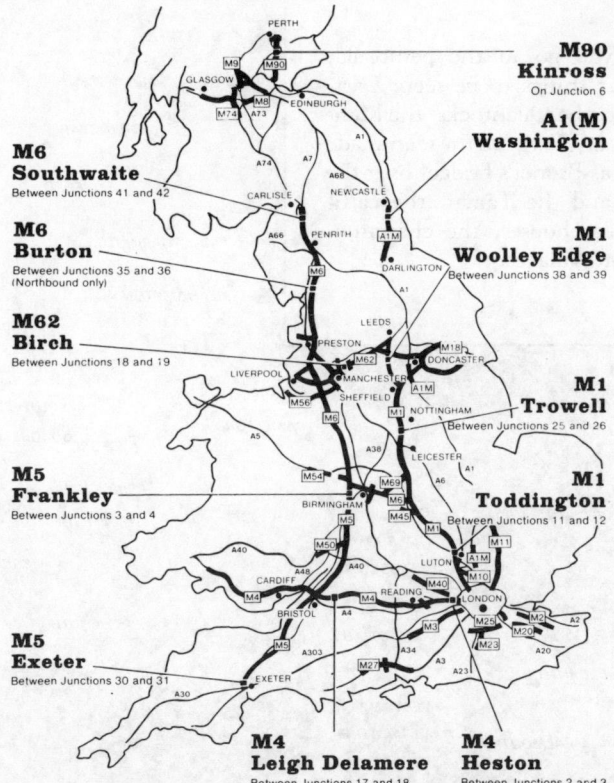

M90 Kinross On Junction 6

A1(M) Washington

M6 Southwaite Between Junctions 41 and 42

M6 Burton Between Junctions 35 and 36 (Northbound only)

M1 Woolley Edge Between Junctions 38 and 39

M62 Birch Between Junctions 18 and 19

M1 Trowell Between Junctions 25 and 26

M5 Frankley Between Junctions 3 and 4

M1 Toddington Between Junctions 11 and 12

M5 Exeter Between Junctions 30 and 31

M4 Leigh Delamere Between Junctions 17 and 18

M4 Heston Between Junctions 2 and 3

Choose Granada – you are very welcome

THE SOUTH-WEST PENINSULA

Cornwall, Devon, Somerset and Avon, commonly known as the West Country, comprise the south-west peninsula. It – and the rest of England – come to a stop at Land's End where the Cornish granite yields to the mists and storms of the Atlantic.

Most visitors come for the seaside – and Cornwall, Devon and Somerset are famed for their tall cliffs, with inaccessible, bird-haunted niches, and for the long stretches of sand where surfers lie in wait for the Atlantic rollers. Avon is less well endowed with coastline, but it has two of the most beautiful cities in Britain – Bath and Wells, and one of the most interesting, Bristol.

Wherever you go in the peninsula, there are great things to be seen: Dartmoor, Exmoor, the Quantocks, the Mendips, Glastonbury Tor; and the man-made wonders such as Brunel's bridges over the Avon Gorge and the Tamar, the cathedrals and great houses, the charming, picture-postcard villages.

Each of the four counties has its own selection of local dishes. Some have spread to the rest of the country – for example, Cornish clotted cream and the ubiquitous cream tea – while others have almost died out. You can, for instance, buy what passes for a Cornish pasty almost anywhere – though few would known what you meant if you called it by its proper name: 'tiddy oggy'. A mixture of meat and potatoes and onions wrapped in pastry, it provided a convenient way for a Cornish tin miner to take a sustaining meal to work – and that is how it originated.

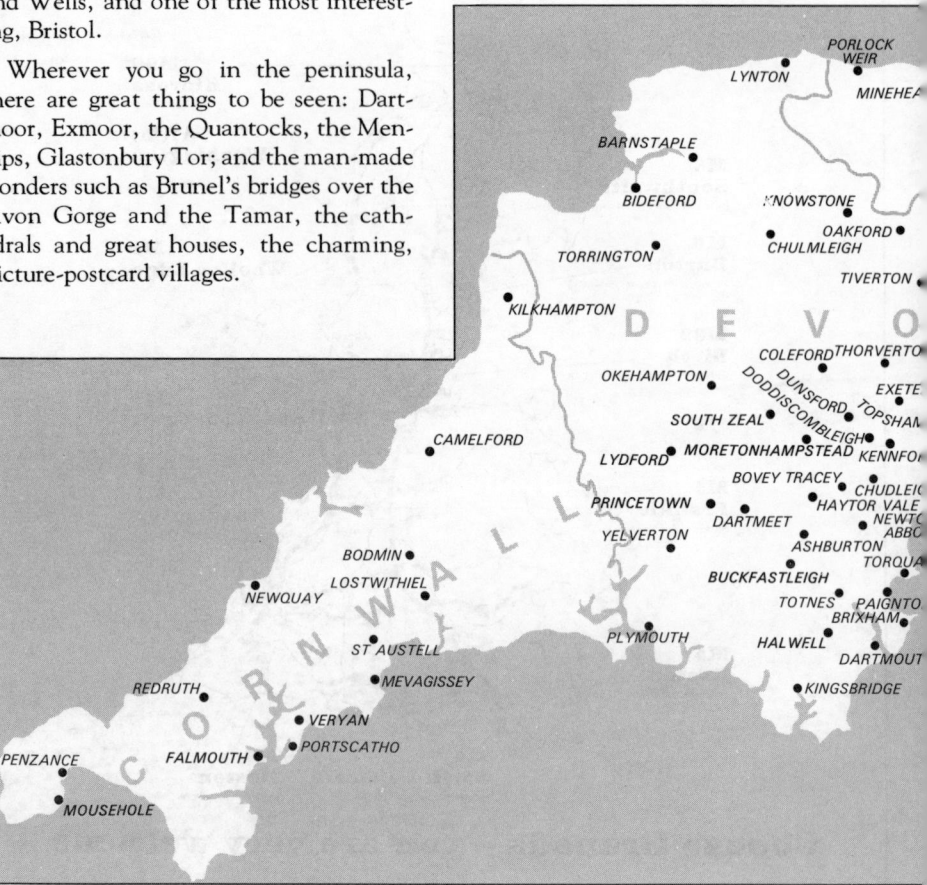

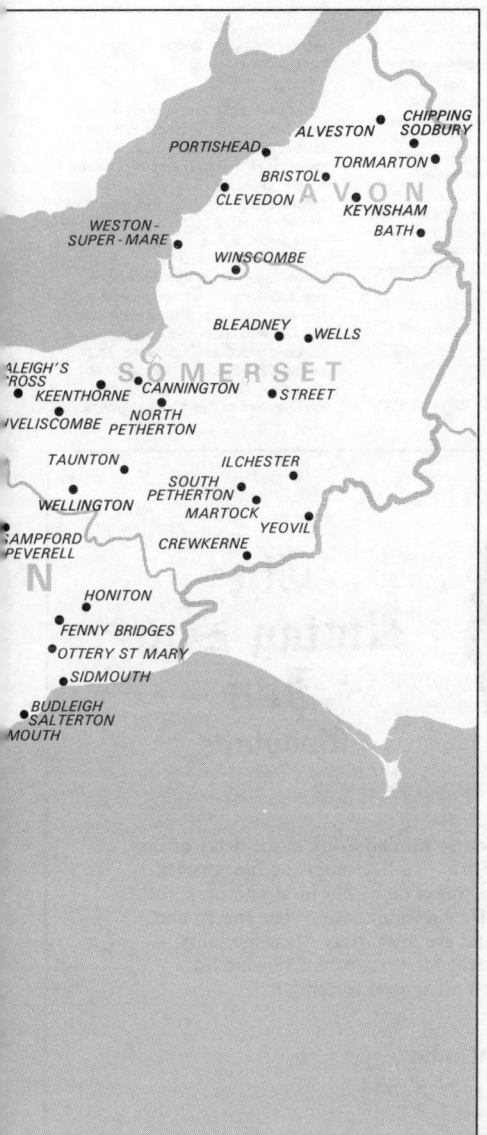

Pig's head and star gazy pie are two Cornish specialities that are less easy to find. The former involved soaking half a pig's head in brine for two weeks, boiling it for $2\frac{1}{2}$ hours, and then, with other ingredients, putting it through a mincing machine. It seems hardly worth the effort. Nor would a star gazy pie evoke much of an appetite at first sight. The pie-crust is pierced with six holes through which the heads of herrings (or mackerel or pilchards) gaze balefully at the diner – each with a sprig of parsley in its mouth. Somerset rook pie sounds scarcely more appetising, but at least you couldn't see the birds.

At Kingsteignton in Devon, they used to celebrate Whitsuntide by slaughtering a young ram. On the Monday, it was taken alive though the streets on a cart – decorated with lilac and laburnum. Next day, it was killed and the meat was sold cheaply to the poor.

Bath has always had a talent for baking things: it did, after all, give its name to the Bath bun, and to a biscuit, the Bath Oliver. Each biscuit, if you look carefully, shows a picture of its maker, with the words 'Oliver Inventor' beneath it. The city also produces Sally Lunn teacakes. Sally Lunn baked them and sold them in the streets during the 18th century when Bath was at the zenith of its fortunes. Her house, in Paradise Alley, still stands.

All these survive. The elver cakes, which Defoe used to enjoy on his visits to Keynsham near Bristol, do not. Anybody wishing to imagine them should contemplate the idea of small eels, covered with pastry, and baked.

Alveston — Barnstaple

ALVESTON

The Ship, Post House Hotel ☆☆☆
Thornbury Road
(0454 412521)
Open: Mon–Sun 12noon–2pm
[P] [♿]

The Ship Inn at the Post House Hotel provides all the charm, character and history of an inn dating back to the 16th century. Available on the bar menu are home-baked hot and cold pies from £1.65, salads from £1.75 and French stick rolls at 85p. Gâteaux and fruit pie and cream are from 65p, and a cup of coffee 45p.

ASHBURTON

The Dartmoor Motel ★★
(Ashburton 52232)
Open: Mon–Sun 12noon–2pm, 7–9.30pm
[C] [P] [♿]

The three-course set lunch at this pleasant, family-run modern motel close to the A38 offers a good choice of main courses for around £3.50. The à la carte menu is extremely tempting, with an emphasis on fish and grills. Seafood special – scampi, prawns, mussels and cockles cooked in sherry and cream – is a delight, but you will have to choose a lower priced starter and sweet to keep within your budget when you sample it. Children are offered a half-portion lunch at around £2.

Rising Sun Inn, Woodland
(Ashburton 52544)
1½m off southbound A38
Exeter–Plymouth.
Open: Mon–Sun 11.30am–2pm, 7–10.30pm
[C] [♫] [P] [♿]

Once used by sheep drovers as an overnight stop on the road to Dartmoor, this rustic old inn houses an interesting collection of prints dating from the early 1920s. Some of the people depicted still form a faithful band of locals who meet and drink here. A sumptuous cold buffet, which includes home-cooked cold meats, fresh salmon, salads and pies, is very reasonably priced, and there are grills and basket meals for those who like it hot, all freshly prepared on the premises. Children can enjoy a meal on the covered verandah or in the pleasant garden to the rear. This is an ideal place from which to see the Devonshire countryside; Torbay and Plymouth are both nearby.

BARNSTAPLE

Barnstaple Motel ☆☆☆
Braunton Road
(Barnstaple 76221)
Open: Mon–Sun 12.30–2pm, 7–10pm
[C] [♫] [P]

The restaurant and bar of this pleasant motel are ideal places to break a journey and enjoy good food. Hot and cold bar snacks include cottage pie, chips and peas. A three-course lunch in the restaurant is around £4. Choices include grapefruit and mandarin cocktail, roast lamb or gammon and pineapple and sweets from the trolley. A similar three-course dinner is £6, with a slightly larger selection of main courses, including beef chasseur.

Roborough House, Off A39 1m N of Barnstaple, down lane signed Hospital.
(Barnstaple 72354)
Open: Mon–Sun 12noon–2pm, 7.30–9.30pm
[C] [P] [♿]

Set in 14 acres of well-kept gardens and woodlands in a secluded position above Barnstaple, it's worth stopping here for more than a snack. The former private house was built in 1800 on a south-facing hillside overlooking the Taw estuary. Now a family hotel run by the Sneddon family, you can get breakfast, morning coffee, afternoon tea, bar snacks, and a table d'hôte lunch and dinner. Miss Fiona Sneddon runs the kitchen, specialising in home-made fare such as Devon-style chicken with apple, cider and cream sauce, or devilled lamb cutlets, tasty soups and pâtés, and her own fresh fruit cream ice. All these may be on the special tourist three-course lunch menu

The Rising Sun Inn
Woodland

Barry and Maureen Johnson welcome you to eat and drink in the heart of the countryside. On a direct route from Torbay to Dartmoor the Inn, once a stop-over for sheep drovers, has a fine collection of old rural photographs and a bar full of interesting keys. It offers a wide range of bar snacks and grills, superb buffet table, lunchtime and evenings. Real Ale a speciality — taste the local brew and cider, draught Madeira, extensive wine list.
Ample parking. Large garden area, ideal for children.

Reservations:
ASHBURTON 52544

Bath

for £4.95. Snacks range from egg mayonnaise salad £1.10 to 8oz sirloin steak and chips at about £4.50. Dinner is nearer the £8.50 mark.

BATH
Clarets Wine Bar, 6–7 Kingsmead Square
(Bath 66688)
Open: Mon–Fri 10am–2.30pm,
6.30–11pm, Sat 11.30pm,
Sun 7–10.30pm

C F P S

Clarets is a beautifully converted white-walled cellar, with teak furniture. In fine summer weather, chairs and tables are set out under the large plane tree in the cobbled square outside. The owner Liza Tearle is a thoroughly experienced restaurateur and serves tasty dishes prepared from good fresh food. Choose from starters, casseroles (including a vegetarian vegetable and cheese version) with bread and butter and green salad (about £2.75–£4.50) and home-made sweets, with filter coffee to complete a very pleasant meal. Snacks are available at reasonable prices and wine is 70p a glass.

Danish Food and Wine Bar
Pierrepont Place
(Bath 61603)
Open: Mon–Sat 11am–2.30pm

F P S

The Fernley's Danish Food and Wine Bar (behind the hotel), although small and simple, is both stylish and comfortable, and well worth a visit for the variety of its delicious open sandwiches of meat, fish and cheese (around 95p). To these you can add salads (for a small extra charge), and finish with pastries and cream and good filter coffee. As an alternative try the

"...CLARETS? THE FOOD IS SMASHING – REAL COFFEE; FANTASTIC SELECTION OF WINE. IT'S NOT A PUB AND NOT A RESTAURANT; IT'S JUST CLARETS..."

GET TO KNOW CLARETS.
GOOD FOOD, GOOD WINE, GOOD COFFEE.

CLARETS
KINGSMEAD SQUARE, BATH.

Telephone: Bath (0225) 66688

LA CRÊPERIE
BATH

OPEN 7 DAYS A WEEK

Here you can enjoy an imaginative selection of freshly prepared dishes in comfortable and friendly surroundings.
Bureau de Change.
Private parties catered for.

Telephone: BATH (0225) 65966

Bath

cold table where, for from about £2.75, you can help yourself to as much cold meat and salad as you can heap on your plate.

Julius Geezer, 31 Barton Street
(Bath 63924)
Open: Mon–Thu 12noon–2.30pm, 6–11.30pm, Fri & Sat 12noon–2.30pm, 6–12mdnt, Sun 12noon–2.30pm, 7–11pm

This newly-opened restaurant has a Roman theme to its menu, and a three-course meal with wine comes to around £6. Brutus' Brew (French onion soup), Christian Pie (braised beef and mushrooms) and a sweet with coffee will cost around £5.30. There is a cheaper lunch menu with two or three daily specials usually under £3.

KT's Restaurant, 4–5 Grand Parade
(Bath 61946)
Open: Mon–Sun 12noon–3pm, Mon–Thu & Sun 5.30–10.30pm, Fri & Sat 5.30–11pm

Close to the city centre and adjacent to the market, this restaurant has a simple, bright décor and the cheerful, efficient staff provide a speedy service. Starters (25p–95p) can be followed by one of the popular range of char-grilled burgers served with mixed salad and baked potato or chips at around £3. A variety of other main meals are available from £3–£4.50. The delicious home-made waffles 85p–£1.25 and profiteroles, £1.45 are popular desserts with regular customers. A fascinating selection of cocktails is available and a number of New World wines.

La Crêperie, Janes Hotel, 7 Manvers Street
(Bath 65966)
Open: Mon–Sun 7.30am–11pm

La Crêperie, in Janes Hotel just off the city centre and close to the railway station and bus station, is bright and freshly decorated, with a relaxed and informal atmosphere. Crêpes are the speciality of the house and there is a large range to chose from, both sweet and savoury, from 85p–£2. Highly recommended are the chicken and asparagus, or the apple sizzle (spiced apples topped with cinnamon sugar and nuts soaked in Calvados). Char-grilled burgers, steak and lamb cutlets complete the main-course menu, while soup at 50p makes an appetising starter. The Crêperie is licensed and has a selection of cocktails £1.40–£1.85, or try Normandy cider at £1.60 for 75cl.
See advert on p. 15

The Laden Table, 7 Edgar Buildings
(Bath 64356)
Open: Mon–Sat 12noon–3pm, Mon–Sun 6–11.30pm

A fully-licensed wholefood restaurant seating about 18 in a pleasant, relaxed atmosphere with soft background music. Proprietor Peter Slotter stays in the kitchen, concocting wholefood creations such as samosa (a crispy, deep-fried, filled Indian pastry at 35p) millet balls (millet mixed with fresh vegetables at 40p) or stuffed pitta bread at around £1. His partner, Valerie Tranter, waits at table, and she will draw your attention to the constantly-changing blackboard menu which lists dishes such as cauliflower cheese, chef's salad or curry, all under £2. Sweets include fresh fruit cheesecake and honey baked apple.

Peaches, 14 Pierrepont Street
(Bath 330201)
Open: Mon–Sun 12noon–2pm, 6pm–11pm

This cheerful cellar restaurant, close to the city centre, is within a few minutes walk of the Roman baths and the Pump Room. Starters range from 60p–95p and there is a good choice of main courses including a variety of casserole dishes priced from £2.20–£2.65 served with baked potato, crusty bread or chips.

PEACHES IS FOR EATING AT

14 PIERREPONT ST., BATH. Tel: 330201
WE HAVE A CHANGING DAILY MENU — SOMETHING FOR EVERYONE —
Relax in the cosy friendly atmosphere of our cellar alcoves and enjoy yourselves.
Open for suppers: Monday to Sunday 6pm - 11pm
Lunch: Tuesday to Saturday 12pm - 2pm
Large bookings welcome!
SEE YOU SOON

TRY US

SPORTSMAN STEAK HOUSE

Converted Stone Barn, 11 miles south of Bath

Open Monday to Friday 12 noon - 2.30 p.m. 6.30 - 11 p.m.

Enjoy a drink in the first floor bar, in an open-plan area, while your meal is prepared.

Credit Cards   Car Parking   Children catered for

Rode Hill, Rode, Bath. Telephone 0373 830249

Salads, burgers and steaks are also included in the menu. Sweets priced at 75p–90p include chocolate bombe and cheesecake. There is a 'special' for all three courses and a vegetarian dish is available. A jug of real ale or a glass of country wine go well with the food.

Sportsman Steak House
Rode Hill, Rode
(Frome 830249)
11m S of Bath on B3109 Rode–Bradford-on-Avon road
Open: Mon–Fri 12noon–2.30pm, 6.30–11pm
C P S

This converted stone barn has a copper-topped bar on the first floor, in an open-plan area where you can enjoy an aperitif while Philip, the resident chef, prepares your meal. Starters include fruit juices, prawn cocktail, and Strasbourg pâté with fingers of hot toast. Main dishes are unfussy but good, with two lamb chops, a pork chop or gammon steak at about £2.80, or a luscious, tender T-bone steak at twice the price. Not only do those prices include freshly-cooked chips, peas and mushrooms, but also ice cream or cheese to follow. Even with wine, you can keep around the £5 mark.

BIDEFORD
Rose of Torridge, The Quay
(Bideford 2709)
Open: Mon–Sun 9am–10pm, Winter Mon–Sun 10am–10pm
P

This licensed restaurant is named after the daughter of the first Mayor of Bideford. It is open for morning coffee, lunches, afternoon tea and dinner. At lunch-time, a range of light meals and salads is available, all priced at under £3. Toasted sandwiches and snacks cost less than £1, and there is a good choice of sweets, also at around £1. The steak-bar menu provides a choice of grilled and fried dishes and a three-course meal will cost under £6.

BLEADNEY
The Stradlings, Bleadney
(Wells 73576)

Bideford
—
Bristol

On B3139 near Wells
Open: Mon–Sat 11am–2.30pm, 6.30–11pm, Sun 12noon–2pm, 7–10pm
P

This Somerset pub and restaurant has fine views over the moors and Mendip Hills. The blackboard menu lists about 30 dishes including steak and kidney pie £1.50, pizzas £1.80 and pâté £1.25, all home-made. The more exotic snails in garlic butter and mushrooms Valenciennes are also under £2, while steaks are from £4.10. The separate restaurant is open in the evenings but a three-course meal is outside our budget.

BODMIN
Castle Hill House Hotel ★★
(Bodmin 3009)
Open: Mon–Sat 7–8.30pm, Sun 12.30–2pm
P

Ken and Sylvia Flint's Castle Hill House Hotel is an elegant Georgian mansion set in two acres of lawns and gardens. Delicious home-produced food such as soup, pâté and steak and kidney pie proves popular with guests and locals alike, and it's as well to book in advance for dinner. The table d'hôte menu offers a three-course meal and coffee for about £5.25, and some items on the small à la carte menu are within our price range. A good selection of freshly-made sweets, including gâteaux and home-made fruit pies is served with clotted Cornish cream.

BOVEY TRACEY
Riverside Inn, Fore Street
(Bovey Tracey 832293)
Open: Mon–Sat 11am–2.30pm, 6–11pm, Winter 10.30pm, Sun 12noon–2pm, 7–10.30pm
P

This large inn by a stream enjoys a picturesque situation in the centre of Bovey Tracey, a popular touring area within a stone's throw of Hay Tor. On display is the sword, broken in two, which

is said to have been used by the knight, De Tracey in the murder of Thomas à Becket. There are two eating places to choose from; the Cavalier Restaurant offers a substantial à la carte menu of grills, while the King Charles Buttery has a more budget-priced selection, such as basket meals, pizzas, sandwiches or salads. A choice from the à la carte of chef's own pâté, the Moorland grill (which includes kidney, egg, sausage, chop, gammon) with vegetables of the day and lemon sorbet, accompanied by wine and coffee would come just within our limit. On Sundays a set three-course lunch with coffee can be had for around £3.

The Rock Inn, Haytor Vale, 4m W of Bovey Tracey off B3344
(Haytor 205/305)
Open: Mon–Sun 11am–2pm, 6.30–10pm
P

This late Georgian inn nestles below Haytor, the best known of the Dartmoor Tors. The proprietors Mr and Mrs Deane spent 20 years in Nigeria before taking over the Rock Inn 4½ years ago, and they were joined by their son Adrian. There is a good choice of bar snacks, including smoked mackerel pâté 80p, West African groundnut stew and side dishes £2.50, fish pie £1.75, and a range of sweets at 65p. A three-course table d'hôte dinner at £4.95 is served between 7.30 and 8.30pm, but it is essential to book in advance. Try French onion soup, followed by pork chop cordon bleu, your choice of sweet and coffee.
See advert on p. 30

BRISTOL
Arnolfini, Narrow Quay
(Bristol 299191)
Open: Tues–Sat 11am–8pm

Presenting new developments in music, dance, theatre and cinema, the Arnolfini public arts complex boasts this airy and spacious bistro-style restaurant with its taped background music and blackboard menu, with salads, cold meats and cakes on display on long counters. There is always an exhibition of works of art on the walls. Once a docks

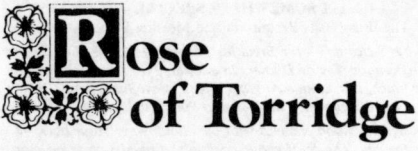

LICENSED RESTAURANT
The Quay, Bideford, Devon.
Telephone: Bideford (02372) 2709
John and Andy Fletcher-Cullum

Light Meals   Toasted Snacks
Children's Menu   Beverages
Salads   Afternoon Teas
Toasted Sandwiches   Sweets

17

Bristol

warehouse, the restaurant overlooks St Augustine's Reach. Soups, pâtés and a hot dish of the day are all reasonably priced, and a three-course light meal can be enjoyed for around £2.50. Salads are particularly interesting, and a special mixed salad of new potatoes, beetroot onion and mackerel costs 65p.

Le Château Wine Bar, 32 Park Street
(Bristol 28654)
Open: Mon–Sat 9.30am–2.30pm, 5.30–9pm
F S

This informal, busy city centre wine bar brims over with business people at lunchtime – a tribute to good food and unpretentious but relaxing surroundings, with wooden furniture and lighting from candles in wax-encrusted bottles. Behind the Victorian bar a blackboard proclaims the range of hot lunchtime dishes – pork fillet kebabs in lemon garlic sauce, moussaka, chili con carne, kidneys Java at prices around £1.60–£2.20. Also at lunchtime and in the evening a selection of cold meats, pâté, cheeses, mackerel and attractively-prepared salads is on offer at about £1.85–£1.95. Interesting desserts include peaches in brandy, and blueberry pie – both around 75p, as well as cheesecake, ices and sorbets.

The Chequers Inn, Hanham Mills, Hanham
(Bristol 674242)
Open: Mon–Sat 12noon–2.30pm, 6.30–11pm, Sun 12noon–2.30pm, 7–11pm
C F P

This riverside haven, close to the city, offers an 'economy lunch' which is likely to include a casserole or joint of the day for around £3.70. No wonder The Chequers is a popular haunt, attracting not only local business people but family parties, particularly for Sunday lunch, and even yachtsmen taking a spot of shore-leave. Apart from the restaurant offering a comprehensive choice of grills or 'Fisherman's Choices', the self-service bar has a carvery specialising in 'Roasters' – succulent rare beef or roast pork with vegetables for around £3 or

cold ham off the bone for about £2.50. Lasagne, steak and kidney pie or turkey and ham in white sauce are also available for around £1.50 including vegetables. Snacks run from 50p and pastries and gâteaux are on offer at give-away prices.

Circles Restaurant, Dingles, Queens Road, Clifton
(Bristol 215301)
Open: Mon–Sat 9am–5.30pm
C F S

This comfortable, modern, self-service restaurant displays cold meats, salads, pâtés and a variety of sandwiches, all at very reasonable prices. Staff are on hand to help you to the various permutations of interesting salads which range in price from around £1–£2. Hot quiches and meat loaf are around 80p and soup costs about 40p. With cream gâteaux on offer at around 55p to complete the menu, this is a much sought-after filling station for shoppers.

Dragonara Hotel ☆☆☆☆
Redcliffe Way
(Bristol 20044)
Open: Captain's Cabin Bar: Mon–Fri 12.30–2pm
Garden Room: Mon–Fri 6.30–10pm, Sat–Sun 12.30–2pm, 6.30–10pm
C F P S

The Garden Room is a bright and pleasant restaurant within Ladbroke's Dragonara Hotel. A typical meal here might consist of pâté in the pot, followed by chicken breast provençale, with ice-cream to finish, at a cost of around £5. However, take care, as several of the main dishes will take you over the budget. At the recently introduced Cabin Bar though, you can choose from a variety of hot and cold dishes (e.g. moussaka or salad of the day) after a bowl of soup, for as little as £1.50.

Giovanni Pizzeria, 15 Union Street
(Bristol 22731)
Open: Mon–Thu 11.30am–12mdnt, Fri–Sat 11.30am–2am, Sun 5.30–12mdnt
C F S

Home-made pizzas are the speciality here. You can buy a simply-dressed tomato, oregano and garlic version, or go for a more elaborate one like pizza Giovanni – an extravagance of mozzarella cheese, tomato, oregano, salami and black olives, costing about £2.50. The skilful preparation of these and other dishes is on view to diners, providing interesting 'while-you-wait' entertainment. A more conventional form of entertainment is the nightly disco dancing and, occasionally, there is a live band at weekends.

Grand Hotel ★★★★
Broad Street
(Bristol 291645)
Open: Brass Nails Restaurant 'Any Time Menu' Mon–Sun 7.30am–10.30pm
C P

For the purpose of this guide we recommend the 'Any Time Menu' which is served by professional uniformed waiters in the bar area of the Brass Nails restaurant. This menu offers light meals all day and includes a 'Breakfast Platter' at £2.75, morning coffee with home-made cookies at £1, and traditional afternoon tea at £2.50. Other dishes, whitebait, vegetarian meals, omelettes, etc are priced between £1.75 and £4. There is also the main restaurant adjacent but the prices come outside the limit for this guide.

The Guild Restaurant, Bristol Guild, 68–70 Park Street
(Bristol 291874)
Open: Mon–Fri 9.30am–5pm, Sat 9.30am–4.30pm (no hot meals on Sat)
S

The small Guild Restaurant, with its attractive extension on to a terrace, covered in winter, but opened in summer to allow patrons to eat in the sun, is a part of the smart Bristol Guild store in the city centre. Under the capable direction of Jean O'Malley and Julie Gregory, inexpensive lunchtime meals of good quality include a selection of home-made soup, quiches or pâtés chalked on a blackboard menu. Soup is around 75p–90p, quiches are around £1 and pâtés with salad about £2.50–£2.70. A

AT LAST SOMEWHERE SPECIAL —
The Brass Nails Restaurant and Meeting Place

You are always welcome — for Breakfast, Morning Coffee, Luncheon, traditional Afternoon Tea or Dinner. In addition, for those too late for breakfast or lunch, our unique Anytime Menu is available from 7.30am to 10.30pm each day (8am to 9pm Sunday).

In the evening, the mood changes with our Sundowner Hour between 6 and 7 pm for your choice of exotic cocktails, a pianist plays on most evenings, and an imaginative a la carte menu to tempt you to stay awhile.

The Brass Nails Restaurant and Meeting Place
next to the Grand Hotel, 57 Broad St., Bristol 1.
Telephone Adrian Portlock on 291645 for table reservations.
— SOMETHING SPECIAL AT ANYTIME OF THE DAY.

hot main dish of the day could be spaghetti bolognese, moussaka, a roast or a casserole, all served with vegetables at around £2.80. Creamy desserts are delicious and modestly priced at around 90p.

Llandoger Trow, 5 King Street
(Bristol 20783)
Open: Mon-Fri 12noon-2.30pm, 6-11pm, Sat 11.30, Sun 12noon-2pm, 7-10.30pm
C ♫ P S ♣

King Street boasts a number of impressive 17th- and 18th-century buildings, including the long-running Theatre Royal, first opened to the public in 1766. But none is more interesting, or has attracted more legends, than Llandoger Trow, built in 1664, one of the oldest inns in the city and now run by Berni. Duckling and T-bone steaks are specialities of the house here and the steak and duck restaurant does an extremely good local trade. In the smaller steak and sole restaurant, prices range from about £3 for fillets of place to just over £6 for fillet steak. Half a duckling costs around £6.

Marco's Trattoria, Queen Road
(Bristol 28508)
Open: Mon-Sat 12noon-3pm, 6-10.30pm, Fri 11pm, Sat 11pm
S

Down a short flight of steps, below the busy shopping street of Queens Road, you will find the quiet haven of Marco's Trattoria. This intimate little restaurant is simply-furnished with comfortable chairs and polished-wood tables in a cellar-type décor, complete with the original flagstone flooring. Your needs will be attended to by one of the charming waitresses. A satisfying meal can be based on the traditional English steak at around £5 or, for a little less, one of the Italian specialities such as bistecca al pizzaiola or scaloppine milanese for £4 or so. All meals are served with French fries (or spaghetti with the Italian dishes), garden peas, roll and butter, and include in their price ice cream for dessert, a selection of Italian cheeses with buscuits or apple pie.

Brixham
—
Buckfastleigh

Parks, 51 Park Street
(Bristol 28016)
Open: Mon-Sun 12noon-11pm
♫ P ♣

Although the restaurant itself is only four years old Parks, situated in Bristol's busy Park Street and close to the city's lovely university and museum is housed in a Georgian listed building. It is fresh and bright, bedecked with attractive plants, grand mirrors and fans from the once-far flung Empire. Specialities here are savoury pancakes made with buckwheat and filled with such things as chicken in mushroom and white wine sauce, smoked haddock in cream sauce, or cheese with spinach and nutmeg, all at about £3, including salad and teas such as Earl Grey and jasmine served with milk or lemon, at around 45p per person. Main-course dishes, served with vegetables or salad, and jacket potato with butter or sour cream, include 8oz sirloin steak and chicken sauté with Madeira sauce at £3.95. In addition there is a Chef's Special. Desserts include gooseberry and elderflower ice cream at around £1.15. House wine is about 75p.

Trattoria Sorrento,
239 Cheltenham Road
(Bristol 45879)
Open: Mon-Thu, Sun 6pm-2am, Fri-Sat 6pm-3am
P

This spacious, modern trattoria, bedecked with Chianti flasks, is noted for its home-made pastas and pizzas. Freshly made for each customer, the pizzas are rated by gourmets as 'the finest this side of Mount Vesuvius', and the Chef's Special is a particularly praiseworthy specimen - brimming over with Italian cheeses, tomatoes, bacon, salami, corn, peppers, mushrooms and anchovies! Pizza and pasta dishes cost around £2 but the steak and chicken dishes, English or Italian style, are more expensive. So generous are the main courses that the luscious sweets, Italian cheeses and speciality coffees prove to

be quite a challenge. Whatever your choice, dishes will be served to you in true Italian style by cheerful (and sometimes singing) Italian waiters who look as though they have just been plucked from the sunshine of Italy.

BRIXHAM

The Elizabethan, 8 Middle Street
(Brixham 3722)
Open: Summer Tue-Sun 12.15-2pm, Wed-Sat 7-9.30pm, Winter Tue-Sun 12.15-2pm
C P S ♣

Small-paned windows, stuccoed walls and ceiling beams lend an air of cosy antiquity to this small restaurant in the town centre. Fresh flowers are a complement to the fresh, home-made fare. The lunch menu offers a choice of main courses and desserts for around £2.75. Roast chicken, pork or fillet of plaice could be followed with apricot crumble or Devonshire junket with clotted cream. An appetiser such as home-made soup of the day, pâté or scampi, will set you back from 50p-£1.90. Dinners are served during the season and it would be easy to exceed the limit here, but soup, followed by strips of beef in wine sauce with peppers and mushrooms and fresh cream chocolate puffs can be savoured without fear of overspending. The restaurant is conveniently situated opposite Brixham bus station and near to the multi-storey car park in the town centre.

BUCKFASTLEIGH

Dart Bridge Inn, Totnes Road
(Buckfastleigh 2214)
Open: Mon-Sun 12noon-2pm, 7-10pm
♫ P ♣

Just across the road from the River Dart, this mock Tudor inn has pleasant gardens, a sun terrace and a family room. It is less than 100 yards away from the A38 Exeter-Plymouth road. The interior is furnished in pub lounge-bar style. Hot and cold meals are served, the former consisting mainly of grills with chips and peas from £1.90-£5. A cold buffet with salads and meats costs £2.75.
See advert on p. 20

THE GUILD RESTAURANT
68-70 Park Street, Bristol
Tel: 291874

This busy cafe — restaurant forms part of the well-known Bristol Guild shop. Adjacent to a secluded terrace garden it is a haven of peace and quiet only a few yards from the traffic of Park Street.

The wide selection of home-made cakes makes coffee and teatime something special. At lunch you are spoilt for choice — delicious home-made soups, quiches, pâtés, casseroles and imaginative salads. Typical desserts include the superb chocolate brandy mousse, lemon cheesecake and apple crumble.

BUDE

Red Post Restaurant, Launcells (3½m E of Bude on A3072)
(Bridgerule 305)
Open: Summer Mon–Fri & Sun 9am–10pm, Sat 6.45am–10pm, Winter Mon–Wed 9am–5pm, Fri–Sun 9am–10pm

P ♿

The restaurant is housed in a converted stable attached to a former coaching inn where there is also an authorised Tourist Information Bureau. A substantial breakfast costs around £2, a large range of snacks cost less than £2. Cream teas are also served and, with the exception of some of the steak dishes, you can get a three-course meal within our budget.
See advert on p. 27

BUDLEIGH SALTERTON

The Lobster Pot, 16 High Street (Budleigh Salterton 2731)
Open: Summer Mon–Sun 10.30am–5pm, 7–10pm, Winter Tue–Sun 10.30am–2pm, evening by arrangement

C 🍴 S ♿

Near the sea front you will find this bright, white-painted restaurant with its small-paned windows and gay red canopy. Renowned for its fresh seafood specialities, you can enjoy an array of other dishes too in the comfortable, Georgian-style interior. A three-course

Bude
—
Chipping Sodbury

set lunch is available for around £3, and the à la carte menu gives a good choice for under £5. Particularly recommended are the pâté with salad garni and mixed seafood and salad. Dinner offers specialities such as scallops à la crème (scallops cooked in white wine sauce), and vegetables are included in the price of the main course. A three-course dinner rounded off with coffee can cost around £5.

CAMELFORD

Lanteglos Farmhouse Hotel
Lanteglos, 1½m south-west off the A39
Open: Easter–end Oct,
Mon–Sun 11am–2pm, 7–10.30pm

C P ♿

Set in its own grounds, this attractive small hotel offers delicious snacks. They are available in the elegant hotel bar, or in the garden in good weather, at lunch times and in the large cellar bar at night. There is a good range of dishes up to £3.95. Try pizza at £1.20, cottage pie £1.30, lasagne £1.50 or spaghetti bolognese £2.20. A table d'hôte and an à la carte menu are available in the evening but are generally outside the limits of this guide.

CANNINGTON

Blue Anchor Inn, Brook Street, Cannington
(Combwich 652215)
Open: Mon–Sun 12noon–2pm, 7–10pm

🍴 P

This long, low, wisteria-clad inn was built in the 1600s. Rebuilt and greatly modernised in 1948, the Blue Anchor has enjoyed constant popularity for as long as anyone cares to remember. Proprietors David and Anne Rees provide an extensive range of bar snacks starting from soup, sandwiches and pâté and building up to steak and all the trimmings, and food is reasonably priced and well-prepared. There's a choice of two house wines.

CHIPPING SODBURY

The Lawns Inn, Church Road, Yate (Chipping Sodbury 314367)
Open: Bar snacks:
Mon–Sat 12noon–2pm
Restaurant: Mon–Sun 12.30–2pm, 7.30–11pm

P

Part of the Lawns is genuine Tudor-built in 1625. It is a popular eating place in lovely surroundings. The restaurant boasts authentic period plasterwork which complements the comfortable modern furniture. A bright little buttery offers a wide range of hot or cold snacks. The

---

Dart Bridge Inn
TOTNES ROAD, BUCKFASTLEIGH
Telephone: 2214

A picturesque Inn on the river Dart near Buckfast Abbey and the famous Dart Valley Railway.

Family room.

Mine Hosts: Beryl and Gordon

The Lobster Pot
Licensed Restaurant
16 High Street, Budleigh Salterton, Devon.
Luncheons ● Dinners
Seafood specialities and grills
Open March to December
Reservations Tel. 2731

former, in the 80p–£1.45 price-range, include curry, cottage pie, lasagne and chili con carne. A three-course meal in the restaurant costs from £5.50. Accent is on grills.

CHUDLEIGH

The Wheel Craft Centre, Chudleigh Mill (Chudleigh 853255)
Open: Mon–Sun 10am–6pm
[P] [&]

Created on the site of the original Town Mills which were used to grind corn, the Wheel Craft Centre has a restored watermill complete with working wheel. Visitors can watch the group of craftsmen and women at work and browse around the wholefood and craft shops which form part of the centre. The 'Tea Shoppe' provides much more than cream teas. Home-made soup with a hot roll costs 45p, and you may follow this with one of the Special Hot Lunches – farmhouse stew at £1.25 and chicken in red wine at £1.65 are examples. Home-made desserts served with clotted cream cost from 65p. Lighter snacks include 'Things on toast' for 65p, omelettes with salad at 90p and vegetarian dishes from 95p. As yet The Wheel is unlicensed, though one has been applied for.

Chudleigh — Coleford

CHULMLEIGH
Fox and Hounds Hotel ★★
Eggesford
(Chulmleigh 80345)
Open: Bar: Mon–Thu 11.30am–1.45pm, 6–9.30pm, Fri–Sat 11.30am–1.45pm, 6–10pm, Sun 7–9.30pm
Restaurant: Mar–Sep, 7.30–9pm
[P]

The Fox and Hounds Hotel, close to the River Taw, halfway between Exeter and Barnstaple, is a rambling country hotel, the mecca of fishermen. The Eggesford Bar offers a wide range of snacks at a reasonable price. A salad bar in summer offers an impressive choice from £1.80. A Fox's lunch, consisting of French bread, ham and cheese, garnished with tomato and pickle, costs £1.40. In the tourist season, a four-course dinner may be had for around £6 in the hotel dining room.

CLEVEDON
Mon Plaisir Restaurant
32–34 Hill Road
(Clevedon 872307)
Open: Mon–Sat 12noon–2pm, 7–10pm
[P]

For Mr Luis Moran and his staff 'Mon

Plaisir' is certainly the operative phrase, for here nothing is too much trouble and with their warm, friendly welcome they hope to make eating here 'your pleasure' too. You will dine in comfort at this Victorian house, set just off the sea front, where well-prepared food is served in generous portions. The three-course set lunch (with a choice of five main courses) is excellent value at around £2.25. In the evening a three-course dinner with a choice of sweets and starters, and a main course such as steak chasseur, gammon or sirloin steak and all the trimmings will cost around £5.
See advert on p. 22

COLEFORD
The New Inn, 4m north-west of Crediton on A377
(Copplestone 242)
Open: Mon–Sat 11am–2pm, 6–11pm, Sun 12noon–2pm, 6–10.30pm closes ½hr earlier winter evenings Mon–Thu
[P] [&]

This 13th-century residential free-house with a thatched roof and old beams offers the unique charm of a country inn. It is set in an unspoilt Devonshire village. Lunchtime bar snacks range from 65p–£3.50. Soup followed by sirloin steak then cherry cheesecake will cost under £5. But if you want something more simple try the ploughman's lunch at 80p or ham salad with chips at £1.75. In fine weather the

The Wheel
CRAFT CENTRE

Chudleigh Mill,
Clifford Street.
Tel: Chudleigh 853255

Health Food Shop

Mill Tea Shoppe
(everything home made)

Working Water Wheel

Craft Shop

Skilled Craftsmen at work

A selection of Dennis Holland's collection of Vintage Cycles and Farm Equipment, as seen on Westward Television

21

food can be eaten outside while watching the ducks on the stream, which runs through the gardens.

CREWKERNE

The Old Parsonage ★★
Barn Street
(Crewkerne 73516)
Open: Mon–Sat 12noon–2pm, 7–8.30pm, Sun 12noon–2pm

C P &

On the corner of a quiet lane you will find this charming old rectory, personally run by Kenneth Mullins. Home cooking is the big attraction here. Interesting dishes such as cockles in cheese sauce and grilled rainbow trout with almonds and Pernod, are scattered liberally throughout the à la carte menu (most of which are unfortunately outside our price limit). The table d'hôte menus for lunch and dinner are reasonably priced at around £5. A traditional Sunday lunch of three courses plus coffee and cream costs approximately £3.50, with a special children's version at 50p less.

DARTMEET

Badger's Holt
(Poundsgate 213)
Open: Mon–Sat 9.30am–6pm, Sun 10.30am–6pm. Closed: Nov–Apr

C & &

Crewkerne
—
Doddiscombleigh

The tumbling waters of the boulder-strewn river flow past this white-painted timber restaurant nestling in the shadow of Dartmoor. Rare birds such as the strange silver pheasant from the Far East are on view in the garden. The food is not exotic, but is very good for all that. Table d'hôte lunch at £3.30 is outstandingly good value. A choice of starters includes home-made chicken and tomato soup served with fresh home-made bread, and smoked mackerel salad. Hot main course dishes such as roast turkey, loin of pork with pineapple or fried scallops with tartare sauce are served with ample portions of well-prepared vegetables. Home-cooked gammon or roast lamb with a mixed salad are two of the cold alternatives. Desserts include a delicious almond-flavoured trifle, apple pie or junket.

DARTMOUTH

The Steam Packet, 3 Duke Street
(Dartmouth 3886)
Open: Mon–Sun 12noon–2pm, 6.30–10.30pm (Sun 7–10.30pm)

F S

Everything is shipshape in this neat little glass-fronted wine bar situated just 300yds from the river front, and as one might expect from such a nautical name, seafood is a speciality. As seating is limited to 18 people you may have to wait for a place or book in advance – either way you'll be well justified in paying the Steam Packet a visit. Young owner David Hawke has a background of hotels and catering in this country where he did his training, and in the West Indies. Brazil and Switzerland where he worked. So you can be sure that when you taste his home-made quiches, pizzas or steak and kidney pie you're tasting some of the best around – and the price is right too!

DODDISCOMBLEIGH

The Nobody Inn ×
(Christow 52824)
S of Exeter, 2m E of Christow
Open: Restaurant:
Tue–Sat 7.30–9.30pm
Bar snacks: normal licensing hours

P

At one time weary travellers would stop at this inn in vain. An unknown purchaser had refused hospitality by locking the door, causing them to continue on their journeys in the belief there was 'nobody in'. Now, in the heavily-beamed bar with its imposing stone fireplace, a varied range of bar meals awaits you, and more substantial fare in the charming 'character' restaurant. The menu here includes some comparative rarities – 'Nobody' soup, lamb sweetbreads and

32-34 Hill Road, Clevedon, Avon
Telephone: Clevedon 872307
(entrance in Copse Road)

Mr. Luis Moran and his staff look forward to welcoming you to MON PLAISIR. It will be a memorable occasion for you with superb cuisine which comes at a very moderate charge.

Please note that we close on Sundays and Mondays.

New Inn

The interior of this 13th Century inn has been extensively and tastefully renovated and great care has been taken to maintain the original character and charm of the building, while combining the best of modern comforts and facilities.

The charming restaurant has established a considerable reputation for it's small but exclusive a la carte menu, serving English and Continental specialities. The wine list includes a fine selection of French, German and Italian wines.

NEW INN, COLEFORD.
Telephone: Copplestone 242

Coleford

Dunsford — Exeter

DUNSFORD

Royal Oak Inn
(Christow 52256)
6m SW of Exeter, just off B3212 to Moretonhampstead
Open: Mon–Sat 11am–2.30pm, 6–10.30pm, (11pm Fri & Sat), Sun 12noon–2.30pm
[F][P][&]

A charming village inn in a rural setting, the Royal Oak offers sustenance either in the comfortable bar or in the dining room. An extensive menu includes home-made soup, prawn cocktail and chicken-liver pâté as 'beginners' from around 55p–95p. A selection of grills such as gammon and peaches or English steaks ranges in price from about £2.50–£4. Fish, chicken or steak and kidney pie are around £1.95 and a selection of salads about £1.50–£2.25 (prawn salad). Desserts include gâteaux with cream, or black cherries with meringue and cream and vary in price from around 65p–85p.

EXETER

Clare's, 13 Princesshay
(Exeter 55155)
Open: Mon–Sat 9.30am–5.30pm
[P][S][&]

There are some classy shops in Princesshay, a pedestrian area just off the High Street and not far from the Cathedral, and Clare Dowell and Simon Shattock's brightly modern counter-service restaurant is just the place for a snack or lunch when you tire of looking in the gift shops and boutiques. It's justly popular with office workers, too, who have to find the quickest and cheapest good food around. 'Country style' hot dishes such as lasagne with rice and salad garnish, steak and kidney pie and gammon and courgettes in a cheese sauce cost around £1.95. A salad with quiche, pizza or meat costs about £1.95. Clare's is licensed to sell wines, beer and cider.

also with duck à l'orange, but they will prepare your favourite dish on request.

Coolings Wine Bar, 11 Gandy Street
(Exeter 34183)
Open: Mon–Sat 12noon–2.15pm, 5.30–11.30pm
[P][S]

Tucked away in one of the older, interesting streets behind the main shopping area is this stylish, family-run wine and food bar where all the food is freshly-prepared on the premises. Beams and checked tablecloths create a welcoming interior and you can also dine in the converted cellars. An excellent range of meats, pies and salads is displayed on the long self-service bar, including such delights as chicken Waldorf salad, tuna and rice salad and sugar-baked ham and salad, all around £1.70–£2.25. Hot dishes such as lasagne (about £1.70) and cottage pie are chalked up on the blackboard. There is a choice of about six sweets for around 60p–75p.

Hole in the Wall, Little Castle Street
(Exeter 73341)
Open: Restaurant: Mon–Thu 12noon–2.30pm, 6–10.30pm, Fri–Sat 12noon–2.30pm, 6–11pm
Wine bar: Mon–Sat 12 noon–2.30pm, Fri, Sat 7–11pm
[C][F][S][&]

One of the nationwide Berni Inn chain of restaurants, the Hole in the Wall is an old building of character. It provides an attractive, well-appointed restaurant, offering steak, fish and chicken dishes. Those familiar with Berni Inns will know that included in the price of each main dish are potatoes, vegetables, roll and butter, and to follow, ice cream or cheese and biscuits. Other desserts, such as apple pie, cheesecake or sorbet, are available for an extra 50p–60p. The perfect finishing touch is the coffee, served in a glass with a generous topping of cream for about 30p.

The Red House Hotel ★
2 Whipton Village Road, Whipton
(Exeter 56104)
Open: Mon–Thu 12noon–2.30pm,

7–10pm, Fri–Sat 12noon–2.30pm, 7–10.30pm, Sun 12noon–1.30pm, 7–9.30pm
[C][P][&]

This imposing red brick building about a mile from the city centre has a warm comfortable décor with oak refectory tables and settles. There is an excellent bar menu from which one may select a snack or a satisfying three-course meal. A crock of delicious home-made soup served with French bread may be followed by a cold platter (a variety of cold meats, pâtés, pies and fish with self-service salad) from around £1.95–£2.75, or a bar grill such as minute steak, chicken or scampi for about the same price. Large steak platters are £3.95. There is always a good selection of sweets including gâteaux from around 60p–70p.

The Ship Inn, Martin's Lane
(Exeter 72040)
Open: Mon–Sat 12noon–2pm, 6.30–10.30pm
[C][F][S][&]

Sir Francis Drake wrote in a letter dated 1587 'Next to mine own shippe I do most love that old 'Shippe' in Exon'. Today, good wine and victuals are still there to be enjoyed, and at quite reasonable prices. The upstairs restaurant is perhaps a little dark and cramped, with deep red wallpaper and upholstery, high-backed settles, and windows within a few feet of the building across the lane, but the atmosphere is right and service is very quick and cheerful. All food is à la carte — the same menu for lunch and dinner. Starters include Scott's pâté at 80p and — a speciality of the house — whitebait, at about 85p. Fresh Torbay sole is the most popular fish dish — around £3.20. Roasts and grills are equally reasonable, the most expensive being fillet steak garni which costs over £5. All dishes include peas or tossed salad, fried or croquette potatoes, roll and butter. Sweets include vanilla ice with cream and meringue Chantilly.

The Swan's Nest, Exminster
(Kennford 832371)
4m S of Exeter on the A379 to Dawlish

THE STEAM PACKET
3 Duke Street, Dartmouth.
Telephone: Dartmouth 3886

SEAFOOD OUR SPECIALITY
also
Home made quiche, pizzas, steaks and steak and kidney pie.
Open: Monday - Sunday 12 noon - 2pm, 6.30 - 10.30pm. Sunday 7 - 10.30pm.
Wise to book

Exmouth

Open: Mon–Sat 12noon–2pm, 6–10pm, Sun 12noon–1.30pm, 7–10pm

P

Mervyn and Joan Ash have run the Swan's Nest for 15 years, and in that time they have managed to create a delightful and popular inn. Lots of rich, dark oak – and a fresh flower for every table – make for a warm welcome. The menu is simple but very good value – help yourself to crisp, green salads, cold meats, pâtés, sandwiches and fresh filled rolls; plus a superb selection of gâteaux, cheesecakes and fruit flans. Such a meal will cost you around £4.75 including coffee.

EXMOUTH

Nutwell Lodge, Lympstone (Topsham 3279)
3m N of Exmouth on the A376
Open: Mon–Sat 12noon–2.30pm, 6–11pm, Sun 12noon–1.30pm, 7–10pm

P

The vast lounge of this rambling Georgian hotel with its massive, dark wooden bar, glowing pink-shaded lamps, antiques, oil-paintings and intimate sunken area with soft upholstered settees serves a selection of snacks to tempt anyone's palate. Garlic and red wine pâté with salad, chutney and toast is a meal in itself at about £1.50, and there is always a hot dish of the day, served in an earthenware pot and accompanied by a side-salad, chutney, hot roll and butter, for around £1.85. Platters of cold meats, crab and prawn are also available. Sweets such as apple strüdel with cream, gâteaux and cheesecake vary from about 70p–80p.

Ye Olde Saddler's Arms, Lympstone (Exmouth 72798)
2m N of Exmouth on the A376
Open: Mon–Sat 12noon–2pm, 7–10pm, Sun 12noon–2pm

C P

Nestling in the picturesque village of Lympstone is this charming cream-painted inn, with tables and gay umbrellas in the pleasant garden when the sun shines. Bar meals are well worth sampling, but so is lunch or dinner in the

Exmouth
―
Honiton

Manger Restaurant. An extensive à la carte menu offers some eight starters, including home-made soup at around 50p and mushrooms in batter at about £1.05. Grilled fish, poultry and steaks feature as main courses, varying in price from around £3.65 for stuffed trout to £5.15 for 12oz rump steak. A selection of sweets at about 80p includes delicious meringue glacé and banana split.

FALMOUTH

Crill House Hotel, Golden Bank (Falmouth 312994)
Open: Mar–Oct Mon–Sun 11.30am–3pm, 7–8pm

P

This attractive, peaceful, small country hotel lies just west of Budock Water Village and personal service is provided by the owners, the Fenton family. Morning coffee, cream teas and snack lunches ranging from sandwiches at 50p to scampi and chips at £2.20 are all available. There are three dinner menus priced at £3.50, £4.75, and £6.50 which includes coffee and mints. Snacks can also be served in the evening.

Greenbank Hotel ★★★
Harbourside
(Falmouth 312440)
Open: Mon–Sun 12.30–2pm, 7–10pm

C P

Officers and passengers would leave their full-rigged packet ships and tea clippers at anchorage just off the pier of this attractive harbourside hotel before unwinding with a good meal. The names of ships and their captains and other nautical memorabilia adorn the walls of the Greenbank. Today this traditional hotel offers good honest food to a different clientele. The lunch is especially good value at about £4.50 offering a fair choice. And how could one better complement a main course of fresh grilled fillet of mackerel meunière than to sit before spectacular views of the mouth of the River Fal?

FENNY BRIDGES

The Palomino Pony, 3m W of Honiton on the A30
Open: Mon–Sat 10.30am–2.30pm, 5.30–11pm, Sun 12noon–2pm, 5.30–10pm, closes 10.30pm in Winter

P

This 17th-century thatched inn, originally an old coaching house, oozes with charm and character. The proprietor breeds Palomino ponies (hence the name of the inn) and they can be seen in the stables at the rear. A lunch-time bar menu is available. The triple-decker club sandwiches at 75p or a meal in themselves, or try home-made pasty at 65p or turkey or duck pie at 95p. Real ale is served at the bar and there is a large selection of knock-out cocktails. There is a children's room and families are always welcome.

HALWELL

The Old Inn
(Blackawton 329)
On A381 6m from Totnes
Open: Mon–Sat 12noon–1.35pm, 7–10pm, Sun 12noon–1.30pm, 7–9.45pm

C P

There's an emphasis on home-cooked meats, soups and sweets at this old country inn. Choose from a wide range of grills and salads (the cold meat platter is particularly good value at £2.40) and eat from a refectory table in the wood-panelled bar or, weather permitting, in the well-kept beer garden. A 1-lb T-bone steak with chips, peas etc, costs over £5, but you'll be well within the budget with the popular honey-roast gammon steak, fish, or basket meals. Sweets with clotted cream are all under £1.

HONITON

Knights, Black Lion Court, High Street (Honiton 3777)
Open: Mon–Sat 12noon–2.30pm, Tue–Sat from 7pm. Closed Sun and Bank Hol

C P S

Good, wholesome, home-made dishes are the order of the day at Knights. Try the

---

Ye Olde Saddlers Arms
Large Car Park

Lympstone, Devon. Telephone Exmouth 72798.
Very attractive restaurant with a varied menu. Good range of bar snacks, including home made sweet & savoury pies available, in the large lounge bar.
A pleasing, flowering garden with running stream. Other attractions being an aviary, and swings for the children.

Opening times
Restaurant: Lunchtimes and every evening (except Sunday).
Bars: 11am-2.30pm and 6pm-10.30pm Monday-Thursday (till 11pm Friday & Saturday).
12pm-2.00pm and 7pm-10.30pm Sunday.

cauliflower soup with cream and a slice or two of fresh cracked wheat bread for starters, followed by cider-baked ham, salad and foil-wrapped jacket potato with yoghurt and mint dressing – and, if you feel there's room under your belt for more, you can top the meal off with home-made sherry trifle or spicy rhubarb crumble with cream for a mouth-watering finale.

Monkton Court Inn, Monkton Honiton 2309)
On A30 2m N of Honiton
Open: Mon–Fri 10.30am–2.15pm, 5.30–10.15pm, Sat 10.30am–2.15pm, 5.30–10.45pm, Sun 12noon–2pm, 7–10.30pm
C P

This imposing stone-built 17th-century inn with distinctive mullioned windows has a comfortable, welcoming interior – all dark polished wood and soft seating. Appetisers include pâté and toast for 80p and prawn cocktail for 95p. Hot main courses come from the charcoal grill – all served with coleslaw or fresh side salad and a choice of potatoes. Try German bratwurst (meaty pork sausage), American ranch steaks or ground steak hamburgers from the hot selection, or help yourself from the cold buffet (around £2.50). 'Afters' (you're in Devon now!) such as Dutch apple pie served with clotted cream are about 85p.

Ilchester
Kennford

ILCHESTER
Ivelchester Hotel, The Square (Ilchester 220)
Open: Mon–Sun 12noon–2pm, 7–9.15pm
P

Bang in the centre of this sleepy Somerset town, which is a through-route to the West Country, you'll find this unpretentious hotel-restaurant where orders are taken at the bar for the excellent table d'hôte meals both at lunchtime and in the evening. A three-course lunch can cost as little as £4–£5. Appetisers include home-made soup or fruit juice and there is a choice of five main courses, including roast duckling and apple sauce. A home-made sweet or ice cream completes the meal. For around £5–£6, a three-course dinner offers four choices of starters, including rollmop herring, five main courses and a wide selection of sweets.

KEENTHORNE
Apple Tree Cottage Hotel, Keenthorne, Nether Stowey
(Spaxton 238)
Open: Mon–Sun 10.30am–2.30pm, 6.30–10pm
C P

This restaurant has a 1930s style dining room and a contrasting, olde-worlde beamed bar with a stone inglenook. Menus and meals are planned and produced by owner Manfred Krombas, who served his cooking apprenticeship both here and on the continent. Chili con carne, cottage pie, steak and kidney pie or speciality boeuf bourguignon are typical hot dishes, while meat salads, sandwiches and assorted ploughmans supplement the cold collation. A three-course table d'hôte lunch, with the choice of five starters and five main courses, a selection of fresh vegetables and a sweet from the trolley costs just £4.25 in the restaurant.

KENNFORD
Haldon Thatch, Bottom of Telegraph Hill, on A38 4m S of Exeter
(Exeter 832273)
Open: Mon–Sun 10am–11pm
C P

As you'd expect from the name, the restaurant is housed in an attractive thatched property, perched high above the road commanding fine views of the surrounding countryside. Décor is predominantly red with well-spaced tables and Ercol chairs. There are over a dozen starters ranging from 40p–£1.10. Of the main courses, you can sample a medium sirloin steak for £2.90 or deep-fried scampi at £2.20, and the Haldon

---

THE IVELCHESTER HOTEL
Ilchester, Somerset.
Telephone: Ilchester 840 220

The House of Good Fayre

The 'Ivelchester' is the home of the famous Ilchester Cheeses, and is known for a wide choice of food and, in particular, for the grills, roast duckling and Fondue Bourguignon which are special features of the attractive menu. There is a well-stocked wine cellar with a noteworthy variety to suit most tastes, and the 'Dog House' Bar is one of the attractive features of this pleasant West Country establishment.

Apple Tree Cottage Hotel
Keenthorne, Nether Stowey, Nr Bridgwater
Telephone: Spaxton 238

Enjoy your pre-dinner drinks in our Olde Worlde Bar with log-burning Inglenook fireplace. In contrast, our dining room is decorated in simple but elegant 1930's style. We offer Traditional English and French Cuisine. Watercress Soup or Baked Eggs with Shrimps and Mushrooms, then choose perhaps Partridge cooked in Sherry & Grapefruit or Beef Bourguignon. Excellent selection of Sweets.

mixed grill (8oz hamburger, sausage, fred egg and bacon) is excellent value at £1.60. Desserts fall in the 35p–65p range, so you should see some change from £5. Traditional Devon teas are served during late afternoon and there is an à la carte evening menu, but choices under £5 are rather limited.

KEYNSHAM
The Grange Hotel ★★
42 Bath Road
(Keynsham 2130)
Open: Bar snacks:
Mon–Sun 11.30am–2.30pm
Restaurant: Mon–Fri 6.30–9pm,
Sat–Sun 7–9pm

P

Once the main farmhouse in the area, this Georgian building in the centre of Keynsham has a comfortable air. A collection of Cries of London prints and medallioned cartoon prints adorn the restaurant walls. Lunchtime bar snacks range from 45p–£1.55, and include paté, chicken drumsticks and traditional pastries. Dinner in the restaurant may be selected from an à la carte menu, where you will have to restrict your choice, but at lunchtime a meal of tasty soup, fillet of plaice and all the trimmings, followed by wholesome apple pie and cream should leave change from a fiver.

KILKHAMPTON
The Coffee House, Kilkhampton, Nr Bude
(Kilkhampton 484)
Open: Whitsun–Oct Mon–Sat 10am–9pm, Sun 10am–6pm. Out of season by prior arrangement only

P &

Set in a small square in the centre of Kilkhampton this restaurant was recently converted from a derelict cottage. In warm weather meals can be taken in the garden at the rear. The lunch and dinner menus are similar, mainly fried dishes, pies and salads, with a range of snacks and sandwiches available at lunch-time. A three-course meal of melon cocktail, fried chicken, fruit pie and cream, with coffee and a glass of wine will cost around £4.

Keynsham
—
Lostwithiel

Penstowe Manor ★
Penstowe Road
(Kilkhampton 354)
Open: Mid May–mid Sep, bar menu
Mon–Sat 12noon–2.15pm, 7–9.30pm,
Sun 12noon–1.45pm, 7–9.30pm
Restaurant Mon–Sun 7–9.30pm

C ♪ P &

A pleasant granite building, in a secluded spot, yet just a short distance from the A39. The large bar overlooking the gardens serves a variety of normal bar meals from soup at 40p to rump steak at £4.25. The attractive dining room, with cheerful friendly staff, offers good cooking and most three-course meals are within the limit of this guide. There is a good choice of fish, meat and poultry dishes. The 'Sunday Special', roast beef, is £3.50.

KINGSBRIDGE
Globe Inn, Frogmore
(Frogmore 351)
Open: Mon–Sat 11am–2.30pm,
6–11pm, Winter 10.30pm,
Sun 12noon–2pm, 7–10.30pm

C P

Brian and Janet Edmond have given this 17th-century free house a complete face-lift since they took over in 1979. Emphasis is on local produce and home cooking, with starters, including a paté of the day, ranging from 55p–N2£1. Devonshire lamb, baked in cider, tops the list of about 10 main dishes, which are all under £2.50 (except rump steak £4.50), and none of the delicious desserts is over 80p. Simple arithmetic will reveal that there's no need to forego coffee to stay under a fiver.

Woosters, The Quay
(Kingsbridge 3434)
Open: Mon–Sun 12noon–2pm,
7–10pm, Winter open only Tue–Sat)

C P S &

Woosters – housed in a two-storey cottage – specialises in fish, which is not surprising since it is situated right on the quay. If you choose one of the superb dishes prepared from locally-caught fish

you're likely not to be able to run to three courses within our limit. Nevertheless, the blackboard menu lists inexpensive dishes such as prawn and pork chow mein at £2.85 or steak and kidney pie at £2.95, which with a starter of seafood soup at 80p and a sweet such as chocolate fudge cake with Devonshire cream at around 95p will not break the bank.

KNOWSTONE
The Mason Arms, Knowstone, near South Molton
(Anstey Mills 231)
Open: Summer Mon–Sat 11am–2.30pm,
6–11pm, Sun 12noon–2pm,
7–10.30pm, Winter Mon–Thu
Sun 12noon–2pm, 7–10.30pm,
Fri–Sat 12noon–2pm, 7–11pm

S

Beside the foothills of Exmoor a truly rural 13th-century picture-postcard inn is the delightful location of this warm and intimate restaurant. Here in the evenings an à la carte menu offers much fine fare at around the £5 mark, whilst at lunchtime across in the bar there's a plethora of pies, prawn salad (£2.25) and ploughman's (£1) on offer, with soup and paté as starters.

LOSTWITHIEL
The Tawny Owl Restaurant,
19 North Street
(0208 872045)
Open: Summer Mon–Sat 9am–9pm,
Sun 11am–5.30pm, Winter
Mon–Sat 9am–5pm closed Wed. Closed New Year

P S &

This informal, licensed restaurant in the centre of historic Lostwithiel has softly coloured walls adorned with the work of local artists. Emphasis is on home cooking which characterises the whole range of delicious dishes, savouries, gâteaux and pastries. Home-made soups are about 60p and the lunch-time hot 'dish of the day', served with fresh vegetables, costs less than £2. Specialities include beef provençale, steak and kidney pie or casserole of beef in Guiness. Quiches, omelettes and

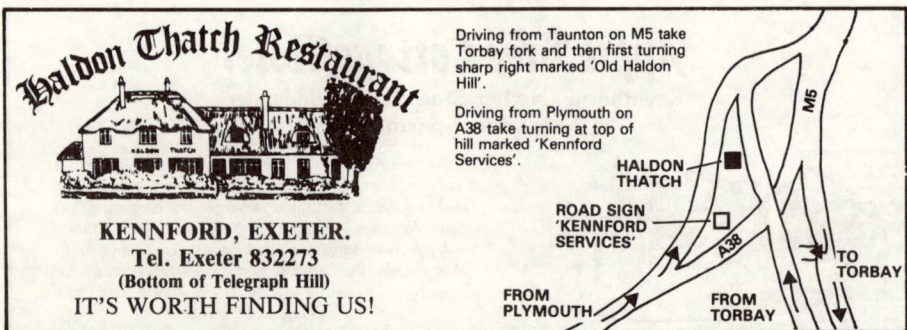

KENNFORD, EXETER.
Tel. Exeter 832273
(Bottom of Telegraph Hill)
IT'S WORTH FINDING US!

26

salads are available and there are home-made Cornish pasties at lunch-time served with plain or savoury-filled jacket potatoes for around £2.50. In high season evening meals for under £6 could feature oak-smoked mackerel (£3.25), pork chop braised in ginger beer (£3.50 with vegetables) or beef goulash and fresh vegetables at £3.25.

LYDFORD

The Castle Inn, Lydford
(Lydford 242)
Open: Mon–Sun 12noon–2pm, 7–9.30pm (last orders)
C P

Close to the beautiful Lydford Gorge and next to the castle ruins is this superb example of a 16th-century English pub. The Foresters' Bar, where meals are served, has low lamp-lit beams and a great Norman fireplace ablaze with vast logs in winter or with a profusion of flowers in summer. At lunchtime, apart from a selection of soups, pâtés and basket meals, a sumptuous help-yourself buffet luncheon table is available which includes soups, roast chicken, duck, beef, home-cooked ham, crab, mackerel, smoked salmon, smoked trout, hot home-made steak and kidney pie, cold meat pies, salads, cheeses, sweets and coffee. The extensive à la carte evening menu could exceed our budget, but careful selection could give you a feast for around £5.

The Manor Inn Hotel ★
Lydford Gorge
(Lydford 208)
Open: Mon–Sun 12noon–2pm, 7.30–9.30pm and normal licensing hours
C P

French-style cuisine is the hallmark of this pleasant old inn, where Richard Squire prepares an enormous variety of fare. Satisfying bar snacks include curry, scampi or a variety of omelettes for around £1.60 or Manor Hot Pot for 95p, but if you catch a whiff of the sumptuous aroma wafting from the restaurant you will find it difficult to resist. A four-course table d'hôte dinner could comprise ravioli Milanaise or Chef's chicken liver pâté, boeuf bourguignon or crepinette of

Lydford
—
Minehead

seafood Mornay, a choice of sweets from the trolley, cheese and biscuits and coffee – all for £6. The à la carte menu includes 18 starters and main course Manor Specialities such as Devonshire pork cooked with sliced apples and local cider, finished with cream and served in apple cases or boned chicken legs stuffed with creamed chicken and herbs.

LYNTON

The Blue Ball Inn, Countisbury Hill, Countisbury
(Brendon 263)
A mile E of Lynton on the A39
Open: Mon–Sun 11am–2.30pm, 6–11pm
F P ⚐

The Blue Ball Inn stands amid some of North Devon's most beautiful countryside, just over a mile from the picturesque villages of Lynton and Lynmouth. The inn still retains the charm and character of its 17th-century hostelry days with beams, real ale and a welcoming open log fire. In the evening familiar bar snacks such as ploughman's, ham sandwiches and salads are served, along with a selection of more substantial meals like rump steak or breaded plaice, rainbow trout, all at reasonable cost.

MARTOCK

The George Inn
(Martock 822574)
2m off the A303
Open: Mon–Sat 10.30am–2pm, 6.30–11pm, Sun 12noon–2pm, 7–10.30pm
C P ⚐

The George first appeared in church records way back in 1512 and there's a list of licensees dating from 1677 on display. However, most people will be more concerned with the food, of which there is a wide selection at reasonable prices. At the bar, try the 'George Special' of tender steak with onions and mushrooms in a butter bap for about

£1.65, or alternatively you might prefer a modest cheese and pickle sandwich or the venerable ploughman's. The small restaurant, adjacent to the bar, was once the local bakery. It has been converted into a cosy eating place where you can enjoy a three-course meal during the day and choose from the extensive menu available in the evening. A three-course Sunday lunch is available for £3.30 (half price for children).

MEVAGISSEY

Mr Bistro
(Mevagissey 842432)
Open: Mon–Sun 12noon–2pm, 7–12mdnt
C ⚐

This pleasant, family-owned bistro is located at the harbour's edge in what used to be an old 'bark house' (where a preservative for coating fishing nets was made from crushed bark and resin). Hence, an old local expression for strong tea is 'like bark water'. Such tea would not be served at Mr Bistro, which caters for everyone's palate and pocket. Lunchtime fare starts with cook's own soup or freshly pressed orange juice for around 45p, followed by an interesting range of home-produced main dishes, with emphasis on seafood, all at about £2 with salad; examples are, seafood platter, fried squid, smoked salmon pâté and prawn quiche. A selection of desserts is available in the region of 75p and a children's menu for under £1 should satisfy any beefburger fan. The evening menu, whilst appealing to the most discerning diner, is generally beyond the bounds of this book.

MINEHEAD

The Good Food Inn, 34 The Avenue
(Minehead 4660)
Open: Summer Mon–Sun 10am–10pm, Winter closed Mon
C S ⚐

Very few restaurants can boast of a service to equal the Good Food Inn: a staggeringly comprehensive menu of à la carte family fare offered for 12 hours a day and all extremely good value for money. Starters, ranging in price from

---

𝓡ed 𝓟ost 𝓡estaurant

Launcells, Bude, N. Cornwall, EX23 9NW.
Reservations: Bridgerule (028-881) 305
BREAKFAST, MORNING COFFEE, LUNCHEON,
CREAM TEAS, DINNER.

Summer Season open 7 days a week
Easter to end of October
9 a.m. to 10 p.m. (Saturday 7 a.m.)

Winter
Monday to Wednesday 9 a.m. to 5 p.m.
Friday, Saturday, Sunday 9 a.m. to 10 p.m.
Closed Thursdays

Junction of the A3072 and B3254 roads

35p to over £1 include speciality gourmet soups. Steaks, seafood and poultry are offered in many guises, from around £2–£6 and all may be served in an appropriate wine sauce for another 50p. A numerous variety of pizzas, omelettes, burgers and salads is on offer. Sweets include a vast range of fancy pancakes, some served with liqueurs, prices around £1–£1.35. Special two- and three-course simple grills are available for children at around £1.15, including a soft drink. As a special bonus, if you order and complete a three-course meal between 2.30–4pm, soup and sweet are offered free.

Northfield House Hotel ★★★ HL
Northfield Road
(Minehead 5155)
Open: Mon–Sun 12.45–1.30pm, 7–8.30pm
C P

Built at the turn of the century as a tea planter's mansion, this splendid hotel has spectacular views of the sea and the Brendon Hills to the south. The magnificent three acres of garden were designed by Sir Edwin Lutyens and Miss Gertrude Jekyll – the ideal setting for a lunch to remember. At £5.20 the four-course lunch is exceptional value, with choices for each course. After a meal of cream of vegetable soup, roast chicken and salad, lemon layer pudding and fresh fruit or cheese, what better than a stroll around the tranquil gardens?

Moretonhampstead
—
Mousehole

A bonus to non-resident guests is the 9-hole putting green.

MORETONHAMPSTEAD
Ring of Bells, North Bovey
(Moretonhampstead 375)
Open: Mon–Sat 11am–2.30pm, 6–11pm, Sun 12noon–2pm, 7–10.30pm
P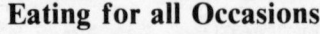

Just off the tree-studded village green in the pretty, moorland hamlet of North Bovey is this delightful 13th-century pub. A thatched roof, three-feet thick walls and low ceilings supported by time-blackened beams are features that attract moorland holidaymakers to the inn's door, but it's the quality of the food that has them returning year after year. A three-course dinner with coffee will cost just over £6 in the restaurant, where corn on the cob, followed by pheasant with bread sauce and vegetables of the day, and a sweet from the trolley might be your choice. Bar meals for lunch or dinner include filled jacket potatoes, Stilton ploughman's, chicken quiche and fresh fruit and cream or gâteaux.

White Hart Hotel, The Square
(Moretonhampstead 40406)
Open: Mon–Sun 12noon–2pm, Sun 1.30pm, 7–8.30pm

C P

During the Napoleonic Wars, French officers on parole from Dartmoor Prison met at the White Hart. By then, this 300-year-old building was already established as a coaching inn. Its simple, elegant exterior is distinguished by the figure of a hind above the portico. The interior is unpretentious and comfortable. Lunchtime bar snacks are excellent and reasonably priced (chef's steak and kidney pie at £1.95). As part of the 'Taste of England' scheme, the restaurant menu offers some good basic English dishes (including Devon apple cake) and an excellent value, three-course tourist menu at £6. An effort is made to use fresh local produce wherever possible. Afternoon teas are served to non-residents in the hotel's charming lounge.

MOUSEHOLE
Cairn Dhu ★★
Raginnis Hill
(Mousehole 233)
Open: Mon–Sun 12noon–2.30pm, 7.30–9.45pm. Closed: Oct–May
C P

A crow's nest view of Mount's Bay, from Penzance, past St Michael's Mount to the Lizard, can be enjoyed from Cairn Dhu. Donald and Angela Sibley's hotel and restaurant, perched about two hundred feet above the bustling village of Mousehole, exudes warmth and

---

Eating for all Occasions
☆ AUTUMN WINTER SPRING SUMMER ☆

INN MINEHEAD
THE GOOD FOOD INN
Family Licensed Restaurant

34 THE AVENUE, MINEHEAD
OPEN THROUGHOUT THE YEAR
Offering a Warm and Happy Atmosphere
Serving SNACKS, GRILLS, STEAKS, POULTRY, SEA FOODS

and a Salad Bar
and a Speciality
Pancake and
Sweet Menu
Takeaway Service   **Minehead 4660**

friendliness. Excellent value table d'hôte lunch or dinner offers three courses for £6. Typical dishes are crab pâté or potted tongue, followed by skate with black butter, lamb Louise or home-made steak and kidney pie. Delicious desserts include strawberry shortcake, orange sorbet or peach and brandy ice cream. A wide range of international cheeses and a glass of French house wine round off an enjoyable meal. Bar food is available on the bar and on the sun terrace, where coffee and cream teas are served.

Newquay

NEWQUAY

Cross Mount Hotel ★★
Church Street, St Columb Minor
(Newquay 2669)
Open: Mon–Sun: normal licensing hours.
Restaurant: 12.30–1.30pm, 6.30–9.30pm
Bar: 12noon–2pm
C P S

The Cross Mount Hotel is just on the outskirts of Newquay but enjoys a village environment. The building is basically 17th century and combines a small residential hotel with restaurant and bar. Burnt orange, toning with the mellow natural stone walls, is the basic colour in the dining room, giving a warm and cheerful setting for a well presented meal. Table d'hôte dinner (available 6.30–7.15pm) at about £4.50 is good value, as is the traditional Sunday roast at around £3.50. The 'tourist menu' all-in à la carte dinners for around £6 give a wider choice, and orders are taken until 9.45pm. Bar snacks include basket meals at about £1.70, garnished sandwiches priced at around 50p, omelettes 80p or so, and soup with roll and butter at about 55p. There are also salads at about £2.

The Lower Deck, 26 Fore Street
(Newquay 6520)
Follow signs for Fore Street and Harbour
Open: Summer Mon–Sun 12 noon–3pm, 5.30–10.30pm, Winter, weekends only
C ♫ ⌂

A Pugwash character in a boat – the restaurant's distinctive logo – indicates your arrival at the Lower Deck. The seaside theme is continued inside the part pine-panelled, open-plan restaurant, slung with fishing nets and adorned with prints of old Newquay. The Lower Deck's a place for the family on holiday, with a children's menu and a good basic choice of food. Try a ploughman's, fisherman's lunch, fish and chips, home-made pies and quiches, followed by one of the home-made sweets (around £1) will renew your holiday energy. The evening menu consists of steak, chicken, gammon, chops and a roast dinner and a selection of the chef's specialities. You can enjoy a three-course meal within our budget. The Upper Deck, open in the evenings, offers a more expensive à la carte menu.

The Ring of Bells
North Bovey
(1 mile from Moretonhampstead)

You step back into history when you enter the 13th century
RING OF BELLS
What's more, you'll enjoy really Good traditional English Food. An open fire and candelit dining room will add to the pleasure of your visit.
Superb accommodation is available, all bedrooms having private bathrooms. Booking is advised.

Telephone: Moretonhampstead 375

On Dartmoor   MORETONHAMPSTEAD   Open every day all year

Peter Morgan's
White Hart Hotel
& Restaurant

FULLY LICENSED
Breakfast — Excellent Bar Lunches
A la Carte Dinner
Tourist Menu Dinner
(Local fresh foods, meat butchered daily. Farm cream)

Reservations tel: 0647 40406
A taste of England

NEWTON ABBOT

The Dartmoor Halfway, Bickington
(Bickington 270)
Open: Mon–Sat 11am–2.30pm,
6–10.30pm, Sun 12noon–2pm,
7–10.30pm
C P

A 'change' house in coaching days, this 17th-century cob and stone inn, three miles west of Newton Abbot, has a garden and patio where one may enjoy a meal on hot days. The large, open-area bar is furnished in oak, with wood panelling and hessian-covered walls. Here you may sample one of nine starters, a particular favourite being 'grotti nosh', a meal in itself for around 60p. Follow this with seafood risotto or steak and kidney pie at around £3, and complete the treat with fruit pie and cream washed down with fresh coffee and cream with a Turkish delight or mint chocolate.

NORTH PETHERTON

Walnut Tree Inn
(North Petherton 662255)
Open: Mon–Sat 11am–2.30pm,
6–11pm, Sun 12noon–2pm, 7–9pm
C P ☕

A 19th-century coaching inn, this hotel has recently been renovated by its owners, Richard and Hilary Goulden, to make it a welcome overnight stop for the modern traveller. Prices are surprisingly

Newton Abbot
—
Okehampton

low – from around £1.80 for an omelette to £4.30 for a steak. Snacks and light meals are available in the bar and there's a very accommodating children's menu, featuring all the old favourites.

OAKFORD

Higher Western Restaurant, Oakford
(Anstey Mills 210)
On the A361, 1½m W of Oakford
Open: Tue–Sun 12noon–2pm,
3–5.30pm, 7–10pm
P

This small, attractive restaurant is recommended mainly for its good lunch-time bar snacks, from a range of open sandwiches (such as chicken, prawns, salami from around £1.25) to pâté and salad, lasagne, home-made steak and kidney pie or lamb chops and chicken escalope. You can have a three-course meal, including soup and roll and a sweet, for anything from £4–£5.50 depending on your choice. There is a set Sunday lunch for around £4.95. Dinner is rather more expensive. Many a motorist will be relieved to find a good pull-in at such a remote spot.

OKEHAMPTON

Bearslake Restaurant, Lake, Sourton,
5m south-west of Okehampton on the A386
(Bridestowe 334)
Open: Tue–Sun 10am–2pm, 7–10pm
C P ☕

The choice of bar food at lunch-time ranges from an open prawn sandwich at £1.30 to spicey beef casserole with baked potato at £1.95. A three-course meal with coffee will cost around £3.80 and a traditional Sunday roast just a few pence more. After your meal you can enjoy a stroll in the fresh air (weather permitting) as the restaurant has open access to the moor. The à la carte menu offered in the dining room is rather beyond our price limit.

The Countryman, Beacon Cross, Sampford Courtney
(North Tawton 206)
5m N of Okehampton on the B3215
Open: Mon–Sat 11am–2.30pm,
7–10.30pm, 11pm Fri–Sat,
Sun 12noon–2pm, 7–10.30pm
P

This sophisticated, unusual inn in the heart of Devon is frequented as much for its excellent bar food as for its draught

LOOK FOR THE LITTLE MAN IN HIS BOAT...

Dine in the comfort of our well appointed restaurant. An excellent variation of tasty snacks, lunches and evening meals are readily available. Our Daily Specials are provided to suit your pocket. Children are also catered for with a special menu and while the adults are deciding the children are given crayons to colour the picture printed on the reverse of the menu, which can be taken away as a reminder of your visit.

**Lower Deck Restaurant, 26 Fore Street, Newquay.
Telephone: Newquay 6520.**

The Rock Inn
Fully Licensed

HAYTOR VALE
NEWTON ABBOT, DEVON
Telephone Haytor 205 and 305

Late Georgian Inn situated in small village on the edge of Dartmoor.

Extensive array of bar snacks.

3 course table d'hote dinner.

*Open 11am-2.30pm and 6.30pm-10pm
Dinner only 7.30pm-8.30pm*

beers. A three-course meal from the à la carte menu will just about come within the £6 limit if carefully selected. A choice of ten starters, including pâté à la volaille (chicken pâté with Cognac) may be followed by one of six main fish courses, a grill, poultry, curry or home-made steak and kidney pie. Most of the home-made desserts, served with cream, will price the meal above £5, but an ice cream is an alternative. The cold buffet table includes a host of salads, ploughman's lunches and sandwiches.

OTTERY ST MARY
King's Arms Hotel ★
Gold Street
(Ottery St Mary 2486)
Open: Mon–Sun 12noon–2pm, 7–9.30pm
C P S

Built in 1756, the King's Arms Hotel was originally an old coaching inn. Now the cream painted building commands a central position in this picturesque little town. The oak-decorated Tar Barrel Bar offers an excellent range of food – either snacks or a full three-course meal. Following soup of the day, steak pie, plaice fillets, chicken or beef curry, cider-baked Devon ham, and ham or beef salads are some of the choices for a main course, ranging in price from about £2.50–£3.50. Vegetables are included. A good choice of sweets is available for

Ottery St Mary
—
Paignton

around 60p. The à la carte dining room menu is more pricey, but still good value and children are catered for.

PAIGNTON
Chez Michel, 107 Winner Street
(Paignton 556100)
Open: Mon–Sun 12noon–2pm, 7–12mdnt (11.30pm Sun)
C ♫ S

The atmosphere is very continental at Chez Michel, when you dine by candlelight in the central courtyard at scrubbed pine tables bedecked with fresh flowers. The restaurant offers an impressive menu with a European flavour but for our budget-conscious readers the wine bar is the place. Charcoal-grilled chicken, steaks, rainbow trout or porc en brochette range from £1.50–£3.50 and this includes a jacket potato and self-serve salad. For a little over £1 extra you can have fruit salad or cheese and biscuits with coffee. Go along on Monday evenings if you enjoy live folk music.
See advert on p. 32

Laikin, 33 Hyde Road
(Paignton 551005)
Open: Mon–Sun 12noon–2pm, 5.30–11.30pm
☐ P S

The unusual marble-look frontage and smoked glass, 'porthole'-style door is an incongruous entrance to this Chinese restaurant in the main shopping area. Inside, the décor is more appropriate, with Chinese lanterns illuminating black chairs, white cloths and sparkling cutlery. Chicken with cashew nuts and fried rice followed by apple, banana or pineapple fritters and syrup cost around £5.25 from the à la carte menu, and a business person's lunch is always available at just about £2.50 for three courses – terrific value. Chinese or Russian tea is served, as well as coffee.

La Taverna, 53 Torbay Road
(Paignton 551190)
Open: Summer Mon–Sat 10.30am–2.30pm, 5.30–11pm, Sun 12noon–2pm, 7–10.30pm, Winter Mon–Thu 10.30am–2.30pm, 5.30–10.30pm, Fri–Sat 10.30am–2.30pm, 5.30–11pm, Sun 12noon–2pm, 7–10.30pm
S

A bit of the Mediterranean on the English Riviera. The canopied front is set back from the road far enough to allow tables and sunshades to be placed outside in

---

WALNUT TREE INN
North Petherton, Somerset
On A38 (Exit 24 M5 One Mile)
Telephone: North Petherton 662255
A comprehensive bar menu with snacks, starters, platters and desserts always available during opening times, with extra à la carte dishes for evening dining pleasure. Good local country hospitality with the added attraction of comfortable, modern accommodation, all rooms having private bathrooms, television and teasmaids. Well worth a visit.
Children are very welcome. *Open all year round*
**FOOD AVAILABLE: Weekdays 12am to 2.30pm and 7pm to 10pm
Sundays 12 noon to 2pm and 7pm to 9pm**

Higher Western RESTAURANT

Intimate old world residential restaurant, situated on the A361 Taunton-Barnstaple holiday route 1½ miles west of Oakford. Ideal for Exmoor and coast.
You can be assured of a warm welcome and superb food.
Open for Lunch — Cream Teas — Dinner — Bed & Breakfast.
NEAR OAKFORD, TIVERTON, N. DEVON EX16 9JE
Telephone Anstey Mills (039 84) 210

Penzance — Plymouth

fine weather; wrought ironwork, white-rendered walls with painted murals and Italianate tiled floor in the dining area complete the illusion that the Italian sun shines outside. The family of the owner, Ernest Pelosi, has lived in Paignton since 1903, so it may be with a sense of nostalgia that the Mediterranean scene has been so carefully created. Small portions of pasta dishes are served as starters, or you can choose spaghetti bolognese at about £1.95 as your main course. Pizza specialities cost near enough the same. Other bar snacks (about £1.10–£1.50) include sausages, egg, beans and chips, and ploughman's lunch. There is a short list of other main dishes, including steaks, chicken, fish and salads.

PENZANCE

Admiral Benbow, Chapel Street
(Penzance 3448)
Open: Mon–Sun 12noon–2pm, 7–10pm

C &

In the early 18th century, bands of smugglers known as the 'Benbow Brandy Men' made the Admiral Benbow Inn their headquarters. Here it was that the surplus tea, 'baccy, perfume, silk and brandy were hidden. Today, it boasts an equally desirable list of goodies to be chosen from the 'Vittals Chart', such as Cornish lobster, smoked mackerel pâté, roasts, grills and various curries. Ice creams are the speciality – try the 'gooseberry lagoon' (coffee ice, gooseberries and iced fruit syrup) or the Southern Star (banana, paw-paw, peach and iced fruits), and wash it all down with a shot of finest rum. Buffet lunches are available in the bar upstairs at around £2.60.

Smuggler's Hotel and Restaurant
Newlyn Harbour
(Penzance 4207)
Open: Mon–Sun 6.30pm–12mdnt

C &

This 270-year-old character restaurant overlooks picturesque Newlyn Harbour, choc-a-bloc full of fishing boats, nets and weatherbeaten fishermen. Legend has it that there was once a secret tunnel direct from the restaurant's cellar bar to the harbour side, and the one-eyed smuggler whose sinister portrait acts as the restaurant's sign certainly looks as though he once drank his fair share of boot-legged brandy. Freshly caught mackerel makes a tempting starter at £1.15, followed by piping hot lamb barbecue, port Marsala or Mexican chicken, all under £3. Sweets are generously served from the trolley at around £1. David and Ann Reeve, resident proprietors, are always at hand.

PLYMOUTH

The Khyber Restaurant ××
44 Mayflower Street
(Plymouth 266036)
Open: Mon–Sun 12noon–2.30pm, 6–11pm

C P

Pass the Khyber and you will miss the chance of enjoying a friendly, well-established Indian restaurant run with family pride since 1960. Décor and furnishings are very Indian, cuisine is authentic and of a high standard. Table d'hôte lunch includes a starter such as shami kebab (delicious round pats of finely chopped meat with spices and onions), a selection of curries and English dishes, and a sweet – try guavas and clotted cream – to follow. Several dinner menus are also around £6, and the reasonable prices also allow you the pick of the à la carte menus.

Merlin's Restaurant ★
2 Windsor Villas, Lockyer Street
(Plymouth 28133)
Open: Mon–Sat 12noon–2pm, 6.30–9.30pm

C ♪ P S &

There's often something extra going on in this small hotel close to the city centre. Barbecues, Hallowe'en night parties, French or Greek evenings and beggar's banquets are Anne and Bill Proudman's

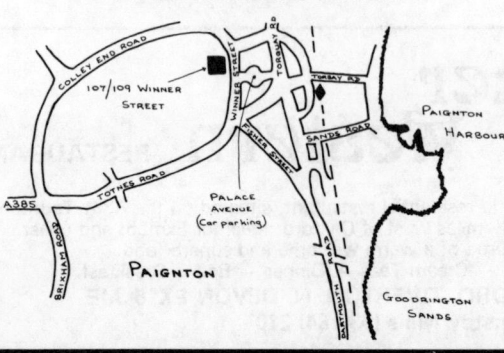

CHEZ MICHEL

107 WINNER STREET, PAIGNTON, DEVON

—

WINE BAR AND RESTAURANT FRANCAIS

—

EXTENSIVE RANGE OF WINES STOCKED

—

RESERVATIONS & ENQUIRIES:—

—

PAIGNTON (0803) 556100

Polperro — Ralegh's Cross

specialities, but a no-nonsense lunch or dinner is always readily available. You'll be pleasantly surprised at the low prices of the well prepared dishes, served in an atmosphere of intimate friendliness. The à la carte menu offers, for example, delicious home-made soup, chicken chasseur with fresh and tender vegetables, and a sweet from the trolley for under £5; and much of the more exclusive à la carte menu is also within our budget – bar the lobster!

POLPERRO

Crump's, Crumplehorn (¾m N on A387) (Polperro 72312)
Open: Mon–Sun 10.30am–5.45pm, 7.30–10pm
P

Mike and Wendy Costello's tea room and bistro, in this most picturesque of Cornish fishing villages, is a low-beamed 250-year-old farmhouse, furnished in the late Victorian/Edwardian style and offering a range of cuisine to suit all tourist tastes. Daytime meals are pâtisserie-style; snacks, light dishes and set lunches. Freshly prepared salads with crab or duck or home-made pizza and quiche cost around £2.75, including soup, fruit juice or melon as appetisers. The bistro atmosphere is enhanced in the evening with white tablecloths and candles. In addition, the Family Wine Bar serves light dinners, similar in choice to the daytime menu.

PORLOCK WEIR

The Pantry, Cottage Hotel and Restaurant
(Porlock 862749)
Open: Mon–Sun 12noon–6pm
C P

This attractive buttery, whose entrance is located by the Cottage Hotel garden, serves a good selection of meals and snacks throughout the day. A satisfying three-course meal can be had for a price well within our budget. For starters you could choose prawn cocktail or home-made chicken liver pâté served with French bread, both around £1.50 and a main course of home-made cottage pie with garden peas costs about £2. With a dessert of fruit salad with cream for around 65p and a coffee at 25p you have a full meal for well under £5.

PORTISHEAD

The Peppermill Restaurant
3 The Precinct
(Portishead 847407)
Open: Mon–Wed 9.30am–3pm, Thu–Sat 9.30am–10.30pm
C P S

Enterprising female proprietors occasionally give cookery demonstrations at this bright, clean restaurant in Portishead's town-centre precinct, and the results of their endeavours go on sale to the public for about £5.50 for a full supper. At mid-day, the business lunch costs around £2.95 with grills from £1.75–£1.95, omelettes around £1.30 and home-made sweets at 70p. A lunch and dinner 'speciality' three-course meal costs £6.50.

PORTSCATHO

Smugglers Cottage of Tolverne
King Harry Ferry, Roseland Peninsula
(Portscatho 309)
Open: May–Oct: Mon–Sun 12noon–2pm, 3–5.30pm, 7.30–10pm
P

Sailing and boating enthusiasts can drop anchor and pop into sample the delicious home-made cuisine offered by Elizabeth and Peter Newman at this picturesque thatched cottage nestling close to King Harry's Ferry. Part of the cottage and the beach were used by the Americans in the preparation and planning of D-Day in the last war. At lunch-time there's an attractive cold buffet of home-produced quiches, fish mousses and meats, accompanied by original fresh salads. Barbecue evenings at the Boathouse Bar-B-Q are ideal for the children. Informal suppers are superb value. Starters include stockpot soup at around 75p or smoked trout for about £1.75. For your main course your selection could be savoury pancakes or omelettes for around £3.50. Gooseberry fool or apple pie are a couple of the tempting desserts.

PRINCETOWN

Fox Tor, Two Bridges Road
(Princetown 238)
Open: Apr–Oct: Mon–Fri, Sun 9.30am–5.30pm, later times by arrangement
P

Just a little more than a stone's throw from the famous Dartmoor prison, this licensed restaurant specialises in fresh, home-made fare ranging from scones and Devon cream to full three-course meals. Appetisers at 60p and under, include egg mayonnaise or soup of the day with home-made bread. For your main course you can enjoy sirloin steak with mushrooms, tomatoes, peas and buttered new potatoes for as little as £4. Sweets such as fruit tart or Devonshire junket are served with cream for 70p or less.

RALEGH'S CROSS

Ralegh's Cross Inn, Brendon Hills, Watchet
(Washford 40343)
Open: Summer Mon–Sat 10.30am–11pm, Sun 11am–10.30pm
C P

Following recent full-scale alterations, this old Exmoor inn now has one large bar (which serves a variety of snacks and light meals), and a charming olde worlde restaurant for the discerning diner. Nearly everything is home-made, including soup served with a wheatmeal roll for around 90p, and liver pâté at about £1.90. Ham with egg and French fries costs around £2.70, while Brendon Hill Bobtails (rabbit casserole) and local pheasant casserole are about £3.50 each. Desserts, at around 85p, include peach cheesecake, lemon soufflé and coffee gateau. The Cordon Bleu restaurant is, alas, outside our price limit.
See advert on p. 34

The Khyber Restaurant

44 MAYFLOWER STREET, PLYMOUTH
Telephone: Plymouth (0752) 266036/663707

Premier Indian restaurant famous for its cuisine. Family business established since 1960. Listed by British Tourist Authority, Touring Club Royale de Belgique and many others. Ample parking space. Open all year for lunch and dinner except Christmas and Boxing Day. Licensed. Credit cards. Private parties. Last Order 11 p.m.

REDRUTH
Penventon Hotel ★★★
West End
(Redruth 214141)
Open: Mon–Sun 12noon–2pm,
7–9.30pm

C L P

This haven just off the A30 is set in 11 acres with ample parking. Lunch is available in the 'Top Bar' which has a range of bar snacks and the hotel restaurant which provides three-course meals. The bar snacks range from sandwiches at 85p to fresh Newlyn crab Thermidor with roll and salad at £2.75. In the summer the restaurant provides a three-course lunch with coffee and petits fours for under £5.50, and there is a free glass of wine (there is a charge of 70p for the wine in the winter). In the evening the small cellar bistro provides starters from 75p, a choice of seven main courses, curry, steak and fish dishes £1.25–£3.35, and a range of sweets under 75p.

Redruth
—
St Austell

ST AUSTELL
Hicks Wine Bar, Church Street
(St Austell 4833)
Open: Mon–Sat 11am–2.30pm

The Tudor frontage of Hicks gives way to a small, intimate wine bar of simple design with wooden tables and stools, and wine racks against the walls. Food is attractively displayed at one end of the bar and dishes can be chosen from a blackboard menu. Main meals are served with a selection of three salads such as curried rice or tomato, cucumber and onion, and an apple and celery mixture. These accompany various salamis, home-made quiche, gala pie or chef's home-made pâté – all around £1.20. There is a range of tasty hot dishes such as cottage pie and chicken and ham pie at £1 and £1.50. For dessert choose from Stilton, apple and biscuits, gâteau or cheesecake all at around 50p.

Ralegh's Cross Inn
EXMOOR NATIONAL PARK, SOMERSET

Locally caught and shot food, served by friendly staff in this old inn, 1,250ft up on the Brendon Hills in Exmoor National Park. Near the new Wimbleball Reservoir and Clatworthy Reservoir.
Pheasant, salmon and trout also locally shot rabbit are but a few of the fare offered on an extensive snack menu. A Cordon Bleu Restaurant is open in the evenings for which you will require a reservation.

Brendon Hills. Telephone Washford 40343
Open Monday-Saturday 10.30am-2.30pm and 6pm-11pm
Sunday 11am-2pm and 7pm-10.30pm

Penventon Hotel
REDRUTH CORNWALL
Telephone REDRUTH 214141

CORNWALL'S LATEST NIGHT SPOT
TRUMPETS
Now 1am on Fridays and Saturdays
DISCO, BISTRO and 2 BARS
Free entrance for parties etc.
Tel. Redruth 214141 for details
OPEN TUESDAY TO SUNDAY
Champagne given away each evening
Adults only

Pier House Hotel ★★
Harbour Front, Charlestown
(St Austell 5272)
Open: Summer Mon–Sun 8–10pm
P

The Pier House Hotel, magnificently located right at the harbour's edge at the picturesque Georgian village of Charlestown, is well worth a visit though you must choose your dishes with care to keep within budget. The small harbour still exports china clay, and from the split-level restaurant of the charming, period hotel, adorned with masts, riggings and other nautical relics, one can view the complex manoeuvring of ships, laden with china clay, in the outer basin of the tiny docks. A la carte dinner offers good choices of French and English cuisine, such as Charlestown smoked mackerel (about £1.15), followed by fresh local sole or rágout of seafood (both around £4), rounded off with fresh strawberries or crème caramel (both about £1), or a good choice of cheeses. Fresh seafood salads are also available.

SAMPFORD PEVERELL
The Farm House Inn, Leonard's Moor
(Tiverton 820824)
Open: Mon–Sat 7am–12mdnt,
Sun 12noon–10.30pm
C F P ☼
This restaurant is a conversion of two cottages and set back off the road in its

Sampford Peverell
—
Sidmouth

own grounds. Cooking is predominantly of the wholesome English variety and all meals from breakfast through morning coffee, lunch, afternoon tea, dinner and supper are served here. At lunch-time, as well as the à la carte choice, there is a special 'dish of the day' which costs from £1.50–£2, and the three-course Sunday lunch, featuring traditional roast beef, carved in the restaurant, is around £4. If you prefer a lighter meal, a cold buffet is set out in the attractive bar.

SIDMOUTH
Applegarth Hotel ★
Sidford
(Sidmouth 3174)
Open: Mon, Wed–Sun, 12.30–1.30pm,
Mon–Sat 7–9.30pm
C P S ☼
The Applegarth dates back to the 16th century when it was used as a staging post for monks who transported salt from the mines of Salcombe Regis to

Exeter. The 'olde-worlde' character pervades the building to this day, not least in the restaurant with its beamed ceiling. The cuisine is always new and exciting – Barbara being a Cordon Bleu cook. For lunch, her array of dishes such as pâté Strasbourg, veau a la crème flambée and trout Applegarth will tempt the most discerning palate. More conventional dishes such as braised steak and chicken with honey and lemon sauce (both including starter, vegetables and sweet) cost around £3.75 but a two-course meal costs only £2.50 – one-course as little as 75p. Desserts are the responsibility of young chef Tracey, who produces tasty concoctions with the aid of fresh cream, sherry, brandy or liqueurs.

Bowd Inn, Bowd Cross
(Sidmouth 3328)
On A3052 2m from Sidmouth seafront
Open: Mon–Thu 11am–2.30pm,
6–10.30pm, Fri–Sat 11am–2.30pm,
6–11pm, Sun 12noon–2pm, 7–10.30pm
P
Strategically placed at Bowd Cross en route to Sidmouth is this attractive 12th century inn, set in a welcoming shrub and flower garden. Low ceilinged, beamed bars are cosy and inviting and the choice of food is excellent. Starters such as whitebait at 95p, melon frappé at 75p or home-made soup at 50p are on offer. Main courses include home-made

Applegarth Hotel
and Restaurant

Sidford, Sidmouth, Devon.
Tel. Sidmouth 3174

Open: Monday, Wednesday-Sunday 12.30pm-2.00pm.
Monday-Saturday 7pm-9.30pm

16th century Applegarth, with all its natural charm will enchant you. Excellent food, prepared with great care and imagination in our kitchen. Exciting main courses. Cost includes all vegetables freshly cooked and served in heated covered dishes. Starters and puddings are a speciality using simple farm fresh ingredients and local produce. Ample and popular wine list.
No dogs in Restaurant. Large free car park.

Bowd Inn

Proprietors: Mr and Mrs D Plowman
SIDMOUTH · DEVON
Telephone Sidmouth 3328

BAR FOOD — OUR SPECIALITY
A picturesque thatched 12th-century building with an abundance of antique brass and copper. Enjoy succulent food:– Angus Steaks, Duckling l'Orange, Ossobuco, Lemon Sole, Steak and Kidney Pie and many more home made specialities prepared in our kitchen. Don't forget your Starters and Sweets. Relax by a pre-drink by the fireplace in either the "Duck or Grouse" or the "Bulverton" bars with the Magnificent carved settles.

Large Visitors' Garden and Car Park   BTA Recommended Inn

quiche Lorraine at £1.70, tongue, ham or beef platters at £2.10 and crab platter at £2.40. Fish dishes, roast duckling and steak are also available. All dishes include potatoes or French fries and salad or vegetables of the day. Home-made sweets are at 85p.

Tudor Rose, High Street
(Sidmouth 4720)
Open: Mon–Sun 10am–10.30pm (bar, usual licensing hours)

[S][&]

Situated in the main shopping street next to Woolworths, the restaurant has been here for many years, but the tastefully decorated Tudor Lounge Bar is a new addition. Hot and cold fork dishes are available in the bar priced at around £1. The afternoon tea menu lists a range of starters, fish dishes, salads and fried dishes for under £3, as well as cakes, pastries and cream teas. Full meals are served in the Tudor Rose Restaurant and a meal of soup, lemon sole, banana split, coffee and a glass of wine would cost around £5.25.

SOUTH PETHERTON

The Pump Room, Oaklands Palmer Street
(South Petherton 40272)
Open: Mon–Sun 12noon–2pm, 7–10pm

[C][P]

This attractive little food and wine bar lies at the back of Oaklands Restaurant (a good à la carte AA-appointed restaurant with menus above our limit). A variety of tempting dishes ranges from brandy and fish pâté, gammon steak with pineapple or home-made turkey and herb pancakes, and with a sweet and coffee the price should not exceed £5 at the Pump Room.

SOUTH ZEAL

Oxenham Arms ★★
(Sticklepath 244)
Open: bar snacks
Mon–Sat 12noon–2pm, 7–9pm,
Sun 12noon–1.30pm, 7–9pm

South Petherton

Taunton

Restaurant: Mon–Sun 12noon–1.30pm, 7.30–9pm

[C][P][&]

'The stateliest and most ancient abode in the hamlet' is how Eden Phillpotts described this beautiful, beamed inn, which was first licensed in 1477. The hamlet quoted is South Zeal, a cluster of houses found by taking a slight detour off the A30 east of Okehampton. Bar snacks offer an array of fish and seafood – from rainbow trout with potatoes and vegetables for around £2 to plaice and French fries for £1.50. Home-made fruit pie and cream is about 75p. On Sundays cold meals only are served in the bar – salads include roast beef or chicken for £1.65 and cheese for just over £1. Three-course meals served in the cottagey restaurant are excellent in both choice and value for money. Lunches are priced by the main course and vary from £3.85 for home-made steak, kidney and mushroom pie to £5 for rump steak.

STREET

Greylake, Greinton
(Ashcott 210383)
Open: Tue–Fri, Sun 9am–11pm,
Sat 7am–11pm

[C][P][&]

Greylake is all things to all men, women and children, but it is not one of your brash modern complexes, for the restaurant is housed in a 17th-century whitewashed stone cottage, full of charm and character. There is a wide choice of food at painless prices. At midday, 11 different main courses are on offer (including deep-fried scampi and a mixed-grill), and with starter, dessert and coffee, only the dearest steak dishes will take you over the £5 mark. A 'Sunday special', with roast pork as the main course, is around £3 (half-portions are available for children). Various salads and light meals can be had throughout the day.

Knight's Tavern ★★★
Wessex Hotel
(Street 43383)
Open: Mon–Sat 10.30am–2.30pm, 7.30–10pm, Sun 12noon–2pm, 7.30–10pm

[C][♬][P][&]

With direct access from the car park, there's no need to go through the hotel to reach the Knight's Tavern, so it is a good place to know about, especially for families with children. Pleasant cheerful service and comfortable modern surroundings make it a worthwhile stopping place. Rest awhile in the King Arthur Bar – aptly named in this Camelot Country, where at lunchtime you can choose from a wide variety of bar snacks, and there are joints from the carvery, charcoal grills, omelettes, curries, fish and many other favourites at budget-prices. You could choose a good dinner in the grill room/restaurant under the limit too, though you could bust the budget if you ignored the menu prices. Fruit juice, followed by fillet of plaice and a sweet from the trolley would come within our limit, leaving plenty over for a glass of wine at 50p and a tip – and there are a number of other permutations under our price limit.

TAUNTON

Heatherton Grange Hotel ★
Bradford-on-Tone
(Taunton 46777/8)
On A38 1m from M5, junction 26
Open: Mon–Sat 12noon–2pm, 7–10.30pm, Sun 12noon–2pm, 7–9pm

[C][P][♬][&]

This former coaching inn, dating from 1826 or earlier is easily accessible from Taunton or the M5. A wide variety of bar meals cost around the £1.50 mark and include Madras curry, steakburgers, home-made pies and salads (including fresh lobster and crab in season). Most of the à la carte menu presented in the small dining room is within our three-course budget. Basic favourites are supplemented by sweetbreads in sherry sauce, Swiss pork chop (stuffed with oregano, cheese, onions and mushrooms) or breast of chicken in a lovely lemon sauce.

the wessex hotel and knights tavern

STREET, SOMERSET
Telephone Street 43383
Open: Monday–Saturday
10.30am–2.30pm and 7.30–10pm
Sunday 12 noon–2pm and 7.30–10pm

A grill room/restaurant set in King Arthur country, with Wells, Glastonbury and Cheddar all within easy reach. Snacks all reasonably priced are available at the King Arthur Bar at lunchtime as well as "Ploughmans" and an admirable assortment of charcoal grills, salads or home-made steak & kidney pie.
In the evening, our à la carte menu contains a mouth watering selection of fish poultry and steak dishes. What could be more enjoyable than Stuffed Escalope of Veal with Mushroom and Tomato Sauce. Our bar is stocked with local beers and a good selection of medium priced wines.

THORVERTON
Dolphin Inn
(Exeter 860205)
Open: during licensing hours. Meals:
Mon-Sun 12noon-1.45pm, 7-10pm

P &

This two-storey inn enjoys a central position amid a picturesque village setting. Décor and furnishing in the Victoria Lounge bar would have pleased even the most discerning Victorian, and the deep-seated armchairs offer a place to relax with an after-dinner coffee. An archway leads through the bar to the attractive Gueridon Restaurant, romantically illuminated with oil lamps to produce a complementary atmosphere in which to enjoy some of the homely fare offered on the extensive menu. House specials include lemon sole with prawns and mushrooms, and home-made steak and kidney pie with Mackeson. Try the soup (also home-made) to start with, and for dessert there is a choice of cold sweets or ice cream – all reasonably-priced. Traditional bar snacks are available every day – the locally-produced pasty with gravy sounds like a tempting and cheap filler at about 45p. Lunch can also be taken in the wisteria-clad beer garden or in the separate real ale and wine bar.

Thorverton
Torquay

TOPSHAM
Amadeus Restaurant, 62 Fore Street
(Topsham 3759)
Open: Tue–Sun 12.30–2pm, 6–10pm

P &

The recorded music of Amadeus Mozart, after whom the restaurant is named, provides a relaxing atmosphere for meals in this attractive little restaurant in the town centre. Tom and Jose Williams serve a selective luncheon for £4.25 (children under 13 yrs £2.25). Starters include soup and home-made pâté and there is a good range of main courses such as seafood pilaf with lemon garni, sauté lamb's kidneys on a bed of rice, and a roast. Excellent home-made sweets with rich clotted cream and coffee (50p extra) complete a first-class meal. In the summer months cold buffet lunches with salad and potatoes are served and may include delicious local salmon. To avoid disappointment table reservations are essential. The evening meals are à la carte, but at an average price of £9 are beyond the scope of this guide.

TORMARTON
The Vittles Bar, The Compass Inn, Tormarton
(Badminton 242)
Off the A46 Stroud–Cheltenham road,

and a few minutes from junction 18 of the M4.
Open: Mon–Sat 10am–2.30pm,
Sun 12noon–2pm,
Mon–Thu 6.30–10pm,
Fri–Sat 7–10.30pm, Sun 7–10pm

C P &

This pleasant old country inn has four bars to choose from, but we suggest hungry travellers make straight for the Vittles Bar, where a tempting cold buffet is on display. Hot dishes are listed on a blackboard, and can often include rabbit pie, hot seafood casserole (both £2.55) or ham and asparagus in cheese sauce with salad at £2.45. Starters include prawns with mayonnaise or pâté about £1.55. Various home-cooked meats with salad and sandwiches are also on offer, and sweets cost from 80p. Full meals can also be taken in the restaurant. Leading off the Vittles Bar is the Orangery, a pretty, glass-enclosed garden which draws families in the summer.

TORQUAY
The Copper Kettle, Ilsham Road, Wellswood
(Torquay 23025)
Open: Summer
Mon–Sun 9.30am–10.30pm, Winter
Tue–Sat 10am–5pm

♫ P S &

This 'copper kettle' brews up not only for guests enjoying a refreshing cuppa after

---

Heatherton Grange Hotel
Bradford-on-Tone. Tel: (0823) 46777
FULLY LICENSED   **FREE HOUSE**

Serving morning coffee, luncheon and dinner, table d'hôte or à la carte menus.
French cuisine available.
Dancing and cabaret most evenings.
We also serve a comprehensive range of bar snacks both lunchtime and evening.
Children catered for.
We cater for all tastes. Conferences, private parties, wedding receptions etc.

DOLPHIN INN
THORVERTON, EXETER

Bar meals available every day, from the not so humble pastie to the T-Bone steak.
Dining room open every day, morning and evening. A la carte menu, and special table d'hôte Sunday lunch.
Families welcome with children.
Accommodation. Fishing.
LARGE CAR PARK
BEER TERRACE
Tel: Exeter 860205

37

Torquay

a meal but also for the picnicker on his way to the beach some yards away. Later in the day, day trippers about to make the long drive home are catered for. This is a special service offered by Leslie Bentham at his neat little Georgian restaurant in the heart of hiis holiday town. Many a thirsty tourist has had his flask filled to the brim with piping hot tea or freshly-percolated coffee by the enterprising Mr B. His wife, Elaine, specialises in high-standard home cooking – and the well-cooked roast lunch (with a starter) at around £1.95 and a Devonshire cream tea (with home-made scones) at about £1.10 is very popular. Salads are the house speciality; egg mayonnaise, chicken, fresh crab, salmon and many more – all from around £2 with special reduced prices for children.

The Epicure. 34 Torwood Road (Torquay 23340)
Open: Summer Mon–Sun 10am–10pm, Winter Mon–Tue, Thu–Sun 10am–5pm
🅵🅿🆂♿

With some 30 years' experience in hotels and catering behind him, proprietor Gary Dowland runs his attractive little restaurant with the emphasis on personal service and quality grill-style fare. Situated some 600yds from the harbour, in a row of shops, The Epicure is one of Torquay's oldest restaurants and instantly recognisable by its green stucco exterior with green woodwork and sun canopy. The deceptively small frontage leads into a long, brightly-decorated dining room. The cool exterior colouring is echoed inside with lush green plants. Best china and cutlery is used here and the walls bear framed prints of old sheet music. An extensive menu of fish dishes and grills is available, with home-made soups a starter speciality. Parents please note the special children's menu with main dishes less than half the standard price.

Homestead, 40 Tor Hill Road (Torquay 23210)
Open: Mon–Sat 12noon–2.30pm, 5.30–9.30pm, Winter
Mon–Sat 12noon–2.30pm,
Mon–Wed 5.30–7.30pm,
Thu–Sat 5.30–9.30pm
🆂♿

This bistro-style eating place has a mixture of English and American dishes on the menu. Choose from salads, fish dishes, American-style burgers, steaks, grills, house specials and a good range of sweets. The steaks may take you over our price limit, but with careful choice you can have a good three-course meal with coffee and wine within our budget. A range of bar snacks are available at around £1.

Livermead Cliff and Livermead House ★ ★ ★
Torbay Road
(Torquay 22881 – Livermead Cliff, Torquay 24361 – Livermead House)
Open: Lunch 1–2pm, dinner 7–8.30pm
🅲🅿♿

The big attraction here is the marvellous view afforded by these sea-front hotel restaurants. Cream leatherette seats and velour drapes make for a very comfy inside setting and the uniformed staff are keen to ensure that everything is to your satisfaction. A set luncheon menu at £5.25 offers soup or fruit juice as a starter, with a choice of four hot main courses (grilled mackerel, fried lamb's liver, grilled pork chop or prawn omelette) plus a wide range of salads – the pressed ox tongue is delicious. Desserts include apple pie with cream and coupe Andalouse. There are special children's portions. A four-course dinner is served for £7. On the seafront you will find Livermead House – a sister hotel run along almost identical lines.

Pizza-King, 2 The Terrace, Fleet Street (Torquay 24365)
Open: Summer
Mon–Sun 12noon–12mdnt, Winter
Mon–Sat 12noon–2pm, 6–11pm
🅵🆂♿

A cheerful, bright red canopy invites you into this rustic-style restaurant with wood-panelled walls and oak refectory tables.

Roy & Staff Welcome you to

ḦOMESTEAD

GOOD FOOD

licensed eating house

40 Tor Hill Road, Torquay.
Tel. 23210

Our policy, of offering a varied and interesting, carefully prepared menu, at very reasonable prices, combined with a unique relaxed atmosphere and good service, has rewarded us with a regular clientele from all walks of life . . . all with an eye for something different.

(Situated near Castle Ciscus, opposite the New Central Church).

LIVERMEAD HOTELS
TORQUAY
"Two Ideal Holidays"

Livermead House HOTEL ★★★   *Livermead Cliff* HOTEL ★★★

When in Torquay a warm welcome awaits you at these two privately owned and run independent hotels, with a wide range of catering facilities to suit all tastes.
Enjoy the peace and quiet of Livermead Cliff Hotel, with it's panoramic views over Torbay, or the sporting facilities of Livermead House Hotel, 300 yards along the road. Both Hotels on the sea front at sea level.
*140 Bedrooms over 100 with Bath *Restaurants enjoy panoramic views over Torbay *Value for money Table d'hôte Menu with à la Carte available for Lunch or Dinner *Imaginative Bar Snacks at reasonable prices *Private Rooms for that special Lunch or Dinner Party. Open for meals evenings as well.
Member of Best Western Hotels

Livermead House 0803 24361   Livermead Cliff Hotel 0803 22881

AA ★ ★ ★ Merit Award

Red-painted chairs add warmth and colour to the simple yet attractive décor. There are 20 really substantial pizzas to choose from. You can make a feast out of the Pizza-King Special which is topped with cheese, tomato, salami, onion, mushroom, ham and pimentoes. It costs about £2.30 and if your appetite can take it, 50p or so will add a baked potato and, at around 55p, a green salad. An extensive salad bar offers an exciting range of salads for around £1.50 (try apple, orange and celery or chicken Waldorf). Home-made soup, quiches and curries are also available. A special lunch for children costs around 80p. Wine is sold by the glass at about 70p.

TORRINGTON
Castle Hill Hotel ★★
South Street
(Torrington 2339)
Open: bar: Mon–Sat 11am–2.15pm, 7–10.30pm, Sun 12noon–2pm, 7–10.30pm
Restaurant Mon–Sun 12noon–2pm, 7.30–9pm
C ♫ P ❧

Magnificent views over the Torridge Valley and the hills beyond can be enjoyed from the garden of this delightful old hotel. A wide range of snacks is available in the bar, including a hot dish of the day such as curry, cottage pie or pork chops. The table d'hôte three-course lunch, served in the restaurant, is only around £2.75, with four or five choices of starter, three hot main courses – a roast and fish dish are always avaialable – and a salad. There is also a generous selection of sweets from the trolley. Cheaper portions are available for children. The extensive evening à la carte menu features grills of all descriptions, and a three-course meal can be achieved for around £6.

TOTNES
Casa Doro, 67 Fore Street
(Totnes 863932)
Open: Mon–Sat 12noon–2.30pm, 7.15pm onwards
C P S

Torrington
—
Totnes

Catch the distinct Spanish flavour of this small restaurant on the ground floor of a three-storey listed building. Heliodoro Lopez runs the place with the aid of his wife and mother-in-law, and together they produce a marvellous list of goodies. Tasty starters such as 'tropicanas' (layers of grilled ham, cheese and pineapple served on bread) or barquitas de apio (celery boats filled with tuna fish, peppers and olives) make interesting appetisers, with paella, chicken Espanol or a host of imaginative, cosmopolitan main courses to follow. Vegetables of the day are included in the price. Sweets, including delicious figs in brandy, are around £1. A glass of wine is 65p.

The Cott Inn, Dartington
(Totnes 863777)
Open: Mon–Sun normal licensing hours
C P ❧

A charming 14th-century building – long, low and warmly lit. The split-level, stone floor and timbered ceiling create a fine, olde-worlde atmosphere. Meals here nowadays are all home-made and presented buffet-style. Examples from the excellent daily spread are pork escalop (£3.25) and apricot meringue (80p). So successful has the operation become, that owner Mr Shortman has recently added an extension to accommodate the growing number of diners.

Cranks Health Food Restaurant
Dartington Cider Press Centre, Shinners Bridge, Dartington
(Totnes 862388)
Open: Mon–Sat 10am–5pm
P S

Cranks have made a name for themselves by serving appetising whole-foods while at the same time encouraging crafts by displaying specially-commissioned articles and equipping their restaurants with craftsman-made furniture and pottery. This branch, in the interesting Cider Press Centre, which is dedicated to the encouragement and display of traditional crafts, is run on the

usual Cranks lines with a buffet service counter serving soups, salads, and vegetable-based savouries, the accent being on compost-grown vegetables and unchemicalised (their word!) ingredients. All food, including wholemeal bread, is baked on the premises. A substantial three-course meal with coffee is unlikely to cost more than £5 or so, and includes soup, a hot savoury such as mushroom stroganoff and vegetable crumble, a sweet and coffee. There's outside seating for 30.

The Sea Trout Inn ★★
Staverton
(Staverton 274)
Open: Mon–Sun 12noon–2pm, 7–10pm
C ♫ P ❧

The à la carte menu is rather expensive and would surely take you beyond our limit, but you need not deny yourself the pleasure of eating in this attractive old inn, for they also serve a comprehensive list of bar meals. A typical meal would be grapefruit cocktail, home-made quiche Lorraine with chips and veg, gâteau or cheesecake and coffee for around £4. The bar occupies the original part of the building, and with oak furniture, white-washed walls, beamed ceiling and stone fireplace it retains a certain 'olde worlde' look. Bar meals are limited on Sundays when a full lunch is provided in the restaurant, and in fine weather meals can be taken on the patio.

The Waterman's Arms, Bow Bridge, Ashprington (3m S of Totnes off the A381) (Harbertonford 214)
Open: Mon–Sat 11am–2pm, 6–10.30pm, Sun 12noon–2pm, 7–10pm
P ❧

Standing adjacent to the old Bow Bridge, deep in the lovely Devonshire countryside lies the 'picturebook' Waterman's Arms Inn. Polished brassware adorns the bar where at lunchtime, for £3.10, you can order excellent and very substantial salads with fresh crab, turkey, ham or beef all served with crusty bread and butter. Home-made soup, cottage pie and a few sweets are also available. In the summer you can enjoy your lunch at the tables on the

The Cott Inn

Is recognised by The Automobile Association as a listed Inn. There is a fine selection of food to choose from:—
Hot dishes like tender pork escalope, barbequed lamb and crab and avocado flan come and go whereas cold cuts like prime Scotch beef are always on. Paricularly good sweets include a superb raspberry pavlova and lemon Jamaican tart.
The management promises that not only will it endeavour to maintain its standard both for food and accommodation but satisfy its customers needs.
We are pleased to accept Diners Club International, American Express, Barclaycard and Access.

The Cott Inn, Dartington, Devonshire. Tel: (0803) 863777

39

banks of the pretty River Harbourne. More expensive meals are served every night in the restaurant, but they are outside the scope of this guide.

VERYAN
Polsue Manor Hotel ★★
Ruanhighlanes
(Veryan 270 or may change to Truro 501270)
Open: Etr–Oct Mon–Sun 7.30–8.30pm
[P][&]

Dinner at this spacious, elegant manor house, secluded beyond a tree-lined drive, is a peaceful and enjoyable experience. You'll find it midway between Tregony and St Mawes just off the A3078. Rex and Diana Dufty will make you very welcome in the gracious, country house-style restaurant. A typical table d'hôte three-course meal of home-produced, quality cooking could include Coquilles St Jacques, followed by tenderloin of pork, rounded off with liqueur gateau at a cost of £6.

WELLINGTON
Beam Bridge Hotel ★★
Sampford Arundel
(Greenham 672223)
Open: Mon–Sat 11.30am–2.30pm, 6.30–11pm, Sun 12noon–2pm, 7–10.30pm
[C][♪][P][&]

This small hotel on the A38 is an ideal stopping off place for the motorist. If you are in a hurry, the bar snacks are the thing – jacket potaoes with cheese, prawn or curry filling cost only 95p. Bill of fare in the peaceful restaurant offers a very wide choice, with a good range of starters. Deep fried breaded mushrooms with tartare sauce are delicious and cost less than £1. Chicken Kiev or lambs kidneys with herbs and wine sauce are interesting main courses. A host of sweets include crème caramel and black cherry and kirsch ice cream, which cost between 40p–70p.

Matilda's, 9 South Street
(Wellington 4124)
Open: Mon–Fri 9am–5pm, Sat 9am–4.30pm, 8–10pm
[S][&]

The traditional female touch is immediately apparent in this small, ground-floor, shop-fronted restaurant serving mainly breakfasts, lunches and teas. And no wonder, for the fresh, pretty atmosphere, with green print wallpaper and matching curtains offsetting pine furnishings is created by a mother-and-daughter partnership. The food selection is café, rather than restaurant fare (although Matilda's is licensed) – simple but definitely homespun, with vegetables, salads and fruit fresh from Mrs Stirling's garden. Fresh fish is ordered, daily, from Brixton. Children's meals are available. Full breakfast is £2; lunch may be Matilda's broth (75p), chicken with salad and potatoes (£1.95)

Veryan
—
Wiveliscombe

or omelette (£1) and a chocolate or ginger sundae (75p). The quality reflects Mrs Stirling's experience in the catering world – until two years ago, she and her husband ran the red star hotel, Winter's Tale, in Burford. Matilda's is her retirement occupation!

Poachers Pocket, Burlescombe
(Greenham 672286)
6m S of Wellington on the A38
Open: Restaurant: Mon–Sat 12noon–2.30pm, 6–10pm, Sun 12noon–2.30pm
Bar: Mon–Sat 11am–2.30pm, 6–10pm, Sun 12noon–2pm, 7–10pm
[P][&]

This 17th-century inn gives you the choice of a pleasant bar or a peaceful restaurant. The bar offers a wide range of snacks, including chicken or prawn curry, scampi or chicken in the basket, gammon and pineapple, rump steak, giant pasties, salads and sandwiches. In the restaurant, the à la carte menu gives excellent value and you can feast on terrine provençale (a rough, spicy pâté), pheasant cooked in Madeira wine, and apfel strudel with Devon cream for around £6. All main courses include vegetables. Children are welcome and can eat food from the bar menu in the restaurant if their parents wish to eat à la carte.

WELLS
Riverside Restaurant, Coxley
(Wells 72411)
3m S of Wells on the A39
Open: Mar–Sep Mon–Sun 10am–11pm, Oct–Feb Tue–Sun 11am–2.30pm, 6–10pm
[♪][P][&]

This 10-year-old family-run restaurant was originally an 18th-century cottage which housed the local wheelwright in an adjoining barn. Nestling alongside the River Sheppey, it has retained its simple charm, not least because it is run very much as a family concern with Mrs Gorizia Reina looking after the kitchen, daughter Lucy the restaurant, and her father Angelo Reina supervising the business as a whole. Children are particularly welcome with a menu to suit their tastes; dishes like egg and chips or sausage and chips cost around £1. Main courses offer two house specialities: pollo al cacciatore (chicken with a sauce of wine, tomato, mushrooms and pimento) at about £3.75 and bistecca alla Siciliana (rump steak in a slightly hot red wine sauce) at around £4.25 – all include croquet or chipped poatoes plus vegetable of the day or mixed salad. Coffees include a rum, coffee and fresh cream concoction. Any dishes on the menu may be taken away at slightly less than the normal charge and you can place your order by telephone.

WESTON-SUPER-MARE
Chris's Restaurant, 8 Alexandra Parade
(Weston-super-Mare 23481)
Open: Mon–Sun 12noon–2pm, 6–11.30pm
[C][♪][P][S]

Chris's Restaurant, formerly known as the Regent Steak House and under the same management, is a small, attractive, fully-licensed eating place with 16 tables in polished dark wood, red/gold-patterned upholstered chairs with elegant green carpet and plush curtains, all of which add warmth to the room. Charcoal-grilled steaks are the house speciality, but, as these are priced at around £4.50 (including French fries and peas), care must be taken when choosing accompanying courses. Other grills, salads or omelettes are plain but less pricey. The 'chef's specialities' are more ambitious creations with tempting sauces, but these are likely to be outside our budget. For the grand finale there are six special coffees, including monk's coffee with Benedictine liqueur.

WINSCOMBE
Sidcot Hotel ★★
Sidcot
(Winscombe 2271)
Open: Tue 7.30–9.30pm, Wed–Sat 12.30–2pm, 7.30–9.30pm, Sun 12.30–2pm
[P]

Set high in its own grounds and overlooking the beautiful Winscombe Valley, this imposing stone-built mansion has a pleasant dining room offering excellent-value three-course table d'hôte lunches and dinners to non-residents for about £5. Home cooking is the norm here, and house specialities include fresh cream Pavlovas. An extensive and reasonably-priced à la carte menu also operates.

WIVELISCOMBE
Country Fare, 4 High Street
(Wiveliscombe 23231)
Open: Mon–Wed & Fri 9am–5.30pm, Sat 9am–5pm, Sun 12noon–2pm
[P][&]

Use Wiveliscombe's free parking and stroll down the High Street to Country Fare! This small 18th-century family restaurant has an extensive range of good, fresh basic food, including home-made cakes and pastries. The Paskin family regard the comfort and satisfaction of their guests as of prime importance; home cooking is prepared and served to high professional standards. The daily 'bargain bite', consisting of dishes such as home-made sausage, apple and chutney pie or two beefburgers and chips will set you back only £1.15, ham, egg and chips £1.50. A set lunch for under £3 might include soup, pork chops in cider (locally-brewed, naturally) or a roast, followed by fruit pie and cream.

40

YEOVIL

Bountiful Goodness, 5 Union Street
(Yeovil 73722)
Open: Mon–Sat 9.30am–5pm,
6–10.30pm

⬚S⬚ ⬚P⬚ ⬚♿⬚

Situated in Yeovil town centre Bountiful Goodness is a wholefood restaurant enthusiastically run by Liz Morris and Margaret Bentley. Décor is clean and bright with pine tables and pretty tablecloths in the evenings. Coffee with home-made cakes are available mornings and afternoons. At lunch-time the quiches, pizzas and salads are all under £2 and there is a range of sweets under 75p. In the evenings the 'tonights specials' could be spaghetti bolognese or seafood pancakes and the menu (similar dishes to the lunch menu) has starters and sweets under £1 and main courses under £3. The restaurant is licensed, a glass of wine is 70p and a pint of real ale 70p. There is also a take-away next door which is popular with business people.

The Pen Mill Hotel, Sherborne Road
(Yeovil 23081)
Open: Restaurant Fri–Sat 12noon–2pm,
7.30–10.30pm
Buttery Mon–Sun 12noon–2pm,
7–10pm

⬚C⬚ ⬚♫⬚ ⬚P⬚ ⬚S⬚ ⬚♿⬚

The weekday cold buffet consists of cold meats or pie with a selection of help-yourself salads from £1.95 or so. There is a hot daily special at about £1.95. Other bar meals include sausage, egg and chips at around £1 to a variety of steaks with all the trimmings from about £4.35. The restaurant serves a table d'hôte three-course meal for around £3.95 with a limited but good choice for all courses, and on Sundays this price buys a four-course meal featuring a traditional roast main course.

The Stradlings
~ The Country Pub of Character ~

We offer a range of exciting bar food, some traditional and some unusual. Our attractive bars offer a large range of wines, real ales and beers, open every day of the year.

For that special dinner try our Character Restaurant, open Tuesday to Saturday — excellent menu and fine wines at reasonable prices.

The Stradlings, a free house, is on the B3139 Wells to Wedmore Road.

Telephone: Wells 73576

WESSEX

One searches for a phrase that will sum up Wessex, but there isn't one. The region is much too varied to be pinned down, and if it is hard to describe Wessex briefly, it is no less difficult to define its boundaries. The name comes from 'West Saxon' whose most famous king, Alfred the Great, made Winchester his capital. Afterwards, the size of Wessex waxed or waned, according to who won what battle. For present purposes, Wessex includes only Dorset, Wiltshire, Hampshire and the Isle of Wight, but it could have included several other neighbouring counties without distorting history.

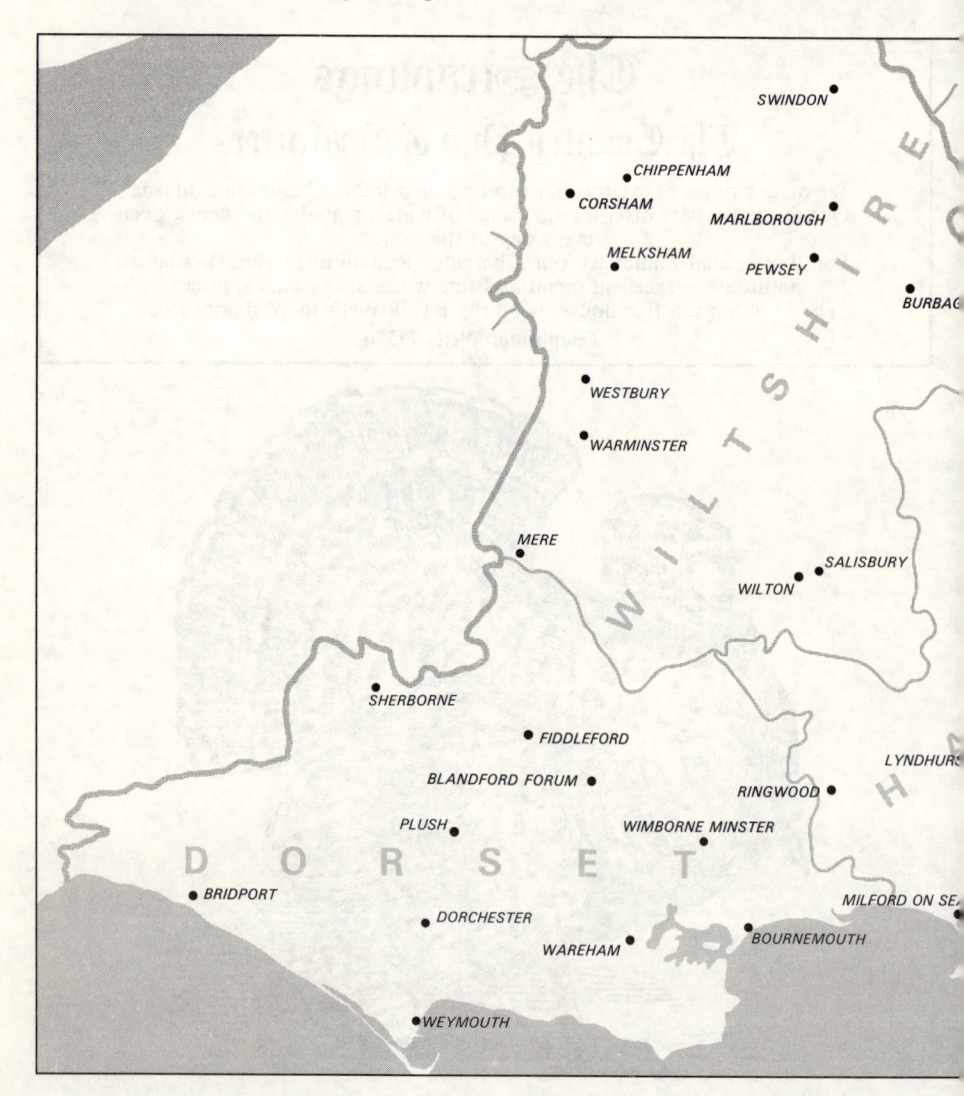

Much of Wessex is unspoiled, providing you don't look too closely at the area between Bournemouth and Portsmouth, and ignore the proliferation of caravans on the Dorset cliffs: all that has not been defiled is beautiful. In all of Britain there are few, if any, regions that contain so much dramatic evidence of the past. The most obvious instance is, of course, Stonehenge – that strange assembly of giant stones on Salisbury Plain. It was built between 1800 and 1400BC. The elements are arranged in such a way as to suggest a remarkable knowledge of astronomy. How the builders achieved it, and how they transported these enormous stones from the Prescelly Hills in Pembrokeshire, are both unsolved mysteries.

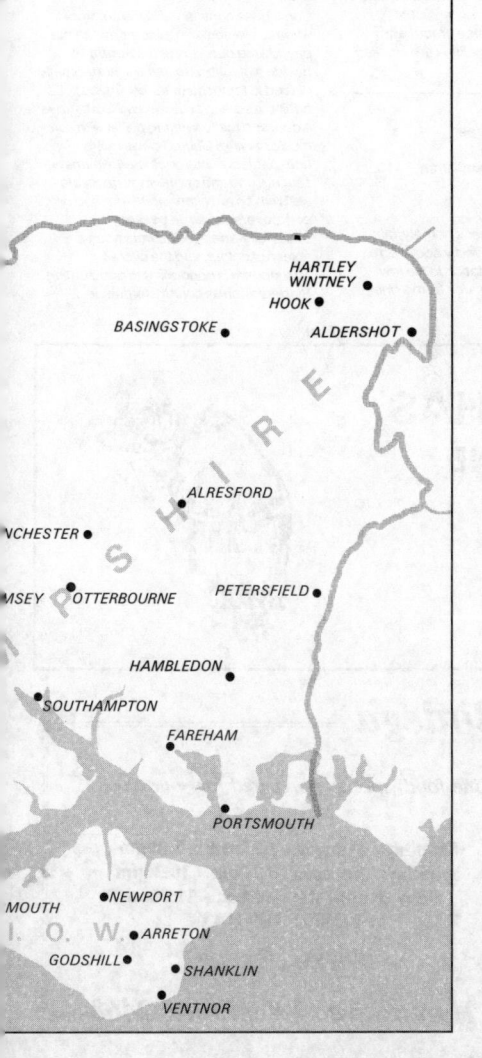

Carving outlines or silhouettes on chalkland seems to have been an occasional obsession of the southern English. Wessex has more than its fair share, and Wiltshire is famous for its white horses, while Dorset has the great Cerne Abbas giant.

Wessex is Hardy Country, though, in Dorset, one sometimes has to ask *which* Hardy: Thomas Hardy, the writer, whose study is preserved in Dorchester Museum, or Vice-Admiral Sir Thomas Hardy, Nelson's flag-captain in the *Victory* at Trafalgar. Dorchester is the novelist's Casterbridge, and in *The Mayor of Casterbridge* Hardy describes an age-old country dish – furmity, sometimes called frumenty, a '... mixture of corn in the grain, milk, raisins, currants, and what not, that comprised the antiquated slop in which she dealt ...' Hardy obviously thought poorly of it and his character, Michael Henchard, can only relish it when laced with rum, getting so drunk on four bowls of the concoction that he auctions his wife and child.

Dorset was once famous for one of the rarest of English cheeses, the Blue Vinney. Although something by that name is sometimes found in shops, experts say that it is not the true, old farmhouse cheese but a modern imitation of the real thing.

Wiltshire has a reputation for curing fine hams, and for making good mustards to go with them. The Hampshire rivers are as famous for their trout as the New Forest was for its venison, which might well be on a menu of traditional dishes in Wessex, as might poacher's pie. Had the deer been taken from the New Forest in the reign of one of the Norman kings, and had the poacher been caught, one of his hands would have been cut off. If you find venison on the menu these days in any of the restaurants listed here, it is unlikely to have come from the New Forest.

Aldershot — Basingstoke

ALDERSHOT

Johnnie Gurkha's ✗
54 Station Road
(Aldershot 27736)
Open: Mon–Sat 12noon–2.30pm,
5.30–11.30pm

[S]

Aldershot is better known as 'Home of the British Army' rather than a hunting ground for gourmets, but when engineer Hari Karki left the Gurkhas four years ago, where better to start his own restaurant than... Aldershot. He and his wife Meera have not only introduced the town to the rarities of genuine Nepalese food but have attracted much praise from Eat Out for Around £5 readers. Behind its unpretentious exterior in the 'downtown' area the restaurant is decorated with trinkets from Nepal, photographs of the Himalayas, Gurkha regimental memorabilia and a standard of service of which Kipling himself would have been proud. First-time visitors hardly need to move from the 'Nepali Special Thal' at £4.50 for three courses including a starter of mamocha – a soup with meat filled dumpling – well worth the time it takes to prepare. Evening booking is advisable.

ALRESFORD

The Bodega, 32 Broad Street
(Alresford 2468)
Open: Mon–Sat 10.30am–2pm,
7–10.30pm, 11pm Fri & Sat

[F][P][S]

The Bodega is a smart and sophisticated wine bar in picturesque Alresford – a small town which with its quaint shops, steam engines and watercress beds, attracts tourists from all parts of the globe. Interior décor is unobtrusive, with cream-painted panels and dark wood tables and chairs, but on summer evenings many patrons prefer to sit in the pretty covered courtyard, hung with the works of local artist Neville Paine. Start your meal with a home-made soup of the day and move on to a tasty Dutch speciality known as saté – a kebab of grilled pork in a piquant sauce, served on a wooden skewer at around £2. Sweets change daily, but could consist of chocolate mousse or ice cream with Grand Marnier. Specialities are chalked on a blackboard.

BASINGSTOKE

The Bistro, 1 New Street
(Basingstoke 57758)
Open: Mon–Fri 12noon–2pm, 7–10pm,
Sat 7–10pm

[C][P][S]

Doug and Suzy Palmer's homely little restaurant has deservedly acquired a very good local reputation in the few years since its conversion from a one-time doctor's surgery. Simple décor and furnishing create a typical bistro atmosphere. At lunchtime the à la carte menu is supplemented by a variety of salads and home-made hot dishes offering excellent value with good choice and quick service. A typical lunch consisting of fresh asparagus soup, coq-au-vin, followed by strawberries and cream cost £3.65. The full menu offers several choices within the budget including house specialities like Porc Dijon and marinated lamb kebabs.

Corks Food and Wine Bar
25 London Street
(Basingstoke 52622)
Open: Mon–Sat 10am–2.30pm,
6–10.30pm

[F][S]

Corks goes continental in the summer when customers can 'take a pew' on the paved area outside the restaurant, beside a blackboard menu – strategically placed to tempt passers-by. Inside, behind a screen of brown half-curtains, is a dark and mellow eating place with soft music playing. Church pews make unexpectedly comfortable and intimate seating, and fine engravings decorate walls which are either white-washed or cork covered. A large basket of beautifully-arranged flowers adds a splash of colour, and the overall atmosphere is conducive to good eating. Starters such as country terrine or

---

JOHNNIE GURKHAS
NEPALESE CUISINE
54 Station Road
Aldershot
Hampshire

Tel. Aldershot 27736

The Bodega

Fine food, specially prepared for your delight

Open:
Monday - Saturday 10.30am - 2.30pm
Monday - Thursday 7.00pm - 10.30pm
Friday & Saturday 7.00pm - 11.00pm
CLOSED SUNDAY

SUPPER LICENCE

- 32 Broad Street, Alresford, Hampshire. Telephone: 2468 -

smoked mackerel for £1, plus hot casserole-type main courses with rice or jacket potato at £2.40 are always available. There are three or more scrumptious puds to choose from (all under £1) and an excellent array of cold meat salads (at less than £3). for £1.30 the special lunch of filled jacket potatoes, savoury crumble or meaty pasta with a glass of house wine is good value. There is a special three-course menu in the evenings for £3.75, and live folk music two nights a week.

The Light of Shahzalai, 11 New Street, Joice's Yard
(Basingstoke 3509)
Open: Mon–Sun 12noon–2.30pm, 6–12mdnt
C S ♪

Tucked away in an older part of the town, this Indian restaurant offers a wide range of food at surprisingly low prices. Service is the keynote here, with all staff genuinely anxious that you should enjoy your meal. A plethora of curries (marked hot, medium and mild on the menu to avoid burnt palates!) are available from £2– to £4, and Tandoori chicken costs uner £3. Of the other specialities, chicken tikka, kabab or onion bhazia make delicious starters. For the less adventurous, English dishes, such as steak with mushrooms and chips at £2.50, are excellent value. Desserts cost from 60p to about £1.

Perrings Coffee Shop and Wine Bar
Seal House, Seal Road
(Basingstoke 66266)
Open: Tue–Sat 9.30am–4.30pm, lunch 11.30am–2.30pm
♪ S ♪

Nothing but the best is available at Perrings furniture store and lunch is no exception. A trellis-work ceiling with wicker-globed lighting and subtle exposed brickwork behind the serving counter complete a décor which is both relaxed and tasteful. A tempting array of food awaits you. Start with nourishing ham soup at around 55p, then choose from a wide selection of cold dishes, or a hot dish of the day such as chicken fricasée with peppers served on a bed of

Blandford Forum
Bournemouth

rice (this costs less than £2.50). Cold meat salads, including beef, chicken or ham are priced a little more, but the choice of salads is excellent – one example is rice with walnuts and sultanas. Delicious desserts such as feathery-light Black Forest gâteau or blackcurrant cheesecake are only around 60p.

Tundoor Mahal Restaurant
4 Winchester Street
(Basingstoke 3795)
Open: Mon–Sun 12noon–3pm, 6pm–12mdnt
♪ S

Once the Midland Bank, this listed building retains its original stately exterior while the inside is transformed into a smart restaurant with warm red décor, wood-effect walls, Indian-style arches and nicely-positioned alcoves with hanging lights. Fresh flowers, candle-lit tables and soft background music complete the pleasant atmosphere. Cuisine is basically Bangladesh and Indian specialities with some Malayan, Persian and English dishes. A special three-course lunch costs around £1.75, with three choices for the main couse including prawn, meat or chicken pillau. The à la carte menu includes a selection of original dishes – dhal soup with orange (around 50p) and beef Bangla curry served with fresh cream are worth sampling (at around £3). Sweets are fairly standard Indian dishes. A three course dinner is generally available under £6.

BLANDFORD FORUM
Anvil Hotel & Restaurant ★★
Pimperne
(Blandford 53431)
Open: Mon–Sun 12noon–2.30pm, 6–10.30pm, 11pm Fri–Sat
C ♪ P ♪

Real wood fires are a feature of the Anvil, and the only restaurant between Blandford and Salisbury is housed in a beautiful, thatched 16th-centruy building, reputed to have originated as

an Elizabethan farmhouse. Satisfying snacks may be taken in the newly extended and cleverly restored bar. Home-made fare such as cottage pie £1.50, coquille St Jaques (made from fresh local scallops – £2) or beef curry with rice at £2 are the order of the day. Salads, soup, pâté and basket meals are also available. The beamed restaurant, with its brick floor has an à la carte menu which could easily break the budget. Soup, chicken à la crème (poached in a white wine and mushroom sauce) and a sweet is just within the limit.
See advert on p. 46

BOURNEMOUTH
Ann's Pantry, 129 Belle Vue Road, Southbourne
(Bournemouth 426178)
Open: Summer Tue–Sat 10.30am–2pm, 6–10pm, Sun 10.30am–2pm, Winter Fri–Sun 10.30am–2pm
S ♪

This corner-sited restaurant, only 100 yards from the seafront, has an exterior reminiscent of a superior Victorian pub. At lunchtime there is an extremely reasonable à la carte menu with starters below 50p, and main courses, including pork chop and apple sauce and gammon with pineapple, range from £2 to £3. Children's choices at around 90p include the well-loved bangers, beans and chips. A three-course set lunch is priced by the main dish – starting at about £1.95 for cottage pie or curry to around £2.25 for roast beef and Yorkshire pud. A three-course Sunday roast lunch costs around £2.50. Excellent table d'hôte three-course dinners are also served for around £3.50, and there is a slightly more expensive à la carte evening menu. Home-cooking is a speciality of the restaurant.

La Fontaine, 141 Belle Vue Road, Southbourne
(Bournemouth 420537)
Open: Tue–Sat 12noon–2pm, 6.30–9.30pm, Sun 12noon–2pm
S

Tucked away in a residential suburb of Bournemouth, this cosy restaurant has

---

Perrings SALAD AND WINE BAR

★ Excellent Salads, Sandwiches, and Pastries.
★ Selection of Hot Meals.
★ Superb Fresh Coffee or a Glass of Wine.
★ Catering for Children.
★ Open Tuesday to Saturday 9.30 a.m. - 4.30 p.m.

Seal House, Seal Road, Basingstoke. Tel: 66266

Bournemouth

attractive pine-panelled walls and ceiling. Ivor Jones and his wife June assure you of a warm welcome. There is a regularly-changing chalked-up menu and an average three-course lunch costs just under £3. In the evenings prices rise only slightly to £4.50. Coffee is 25p extra.

Fortes, The Square
(Bournemouth 24916)
Open: Florentine Restaurant Mon–Sun 12noon–10.30pm, Coffee Shop: Mon–Sun 8am–6pm. Self Service Restaurant: Mon–Sun 10am–10.30pm, Opening times may change in winter

C♬P S☼

This is a typical Trusthouse Forte operation, providing everything from takeaway snacks for the beach to three-course à la carte dinners in an elegant setting, at prices that represent very good value for money. The ground floor self-service restaurant serves an excellent lunch, high tea or supper at prices from little more than £1 to £2, as well as cakes and pastries, sandwiches, bowls of mixed salad, ice creams and beverages. The Coffee Shop serves hot snacks and grills throughout the day, with soup, hotdogs, hamburgers and pizzas as just some of its attractions. The Florentine offers a choice of three-course lunches at prices from about £4 to just under £6, including various Italian dishes and a traditional weekend lunch at around £5.50. The à la carte menu is also reasonably priced.

The Old England, 74 Poole Road, Westbourne
(Bournemouth 766475)
Open: Mon–Sun 9.30am–3pm, 6–10.30pm

C♬P S☼

A warm welcome awaits you at this delightful olde worlde restaurant. Cuisine, though, is 20th century and well-cooked with fresh vegetables. A set three-course meal costs £4.25 (with big reductions for children), alternatively an extensive à la carte menu includes a range of starters from chilled tomato juice at 35p, to crab cocktail at around £1.75. Numerous main dishes are available, typical options being Dorset chicken £3.95 and pan-fried gammon with pineapple £4.10. Steak, unfortunately, should be avoided if you're to stay within the budget. Tempting home-made desserts such as crème caramel or fruit crumble cost around 80p. For light snacks try the Dickens Wine Cellar.

Planters, 514 Christchurch Road, Boscombe
(Bournemouth 302228)
Open: Mon–Sat 12noon–2.30pm, Sun–Thu 6.30–11pm, Fri, Sat, 6.30pm–mdnt

C♬P S☼

This modern restaurant with its Hollywood movie theme and lively background music boasts a New Orleans-style cocktail bar with over fifty cocktails running from 95p for apricot sour to £2.35 for wild jaffa. The food is American, with a range of unusual specials such as prawn jambalaya (£4.10) and steak in schlitz (£4.20). Spicy chili con carne with pitta bread and side salad costs around £2.40. For dessert there is an all-American line up of spiced apple pie, chocolate fudge cake, hot waffle with maple syrup and fresh cream and various sundaes for just over £1.

The Salad Centre, Post Office Road
(Bournemouth 21720)
Open: Mon–Fri 10am–8.30pm, Winter 10am–5pm, Sat 10am–2.30pm

C P S

This family-owned-and-run Salad Centre encourages and caters for sensible health-food, vegetarian-style, eating. Patrons are invited to refrain from smoking and family pets are definitely not admitted. The décor is clean and bright and the staff charming and most helpful. Everything is home cooked and made of the freshest, purest ingredients, with no artificial additives of any kind. There is a brave display daily of more than a dozen different salads, with quiches, nut roasts, savouries and – in the winter – various hot dishes. Fruit juices include apple, lemon,

---

Anvil Hotel
Pimperne, nr. Blandford, Dorset.
Tel: Blandford 53431

Thatched hotel and restaurant, parts 400 years old. Beamed restaurant serving home-made soups and pate, table d'hote set lunch and Sunday lunch. Woodfires.

Scallops speciality and Bar snacks. Outside eating in summer on the patio or in the garden. Heated outdoor swimming pool. Family run.

Bridport — Corsham

grapefruit and beetroot and there is a good range of beverages, though the Salad Centre is unlicensed.

Trattoria Tosca, 12 Richmond Hill (Bournemouth 23034)
Open: Mon–Sun 12noon–2.30pm, 6–11.30pm
C A P S &

The cuisine at Edward Cobelli's charmingly informal Trattoria Tosca in The Square is, not suprisingly, Italian but not expensively so. There is a good range of starters at prices from 45p to £1.85, spaghetti dishes at about £1.55 to £2.10, and Italian specialities, including the romantically named filleto Casanova, at around £3 to £5.50. Service is friendly, willing and speedy, but do book at the weekend if you want to be sure of a table.

BRIDPORT
Bistro Lautrec ✗
53 East Street
(Bridport 56549)
Open: Mon–Fri 12noon–2pm, Mon–Sat 7–10pm
A P S &

Food and environment go together in this typical French-style bistro. Candles in bottles, check tablecloths, Lautrec posters and chalked-up menus make just the right setting in which to enjoy a lunch of terrine provençale at about £1, followed, perhaps, by stuffed green peppers with vegetables or salad for just over £1. Evening meals, in a more sophisticated yet still informal atmosphere, cost around £6.

Bull Hotel ★
34 East Street
(Bridport 22878)
Open: Mon–Sat 12noon–2pm, 7.15–9.15pm, Sun 7.15–9.15pm
P

The Terleski family have restored their 16th-century coaching inn. They are keen to offer good hospitality at a very reasonable price and succeed. There's a wide range of bar meals, including a choice from the daily speciality menu costing between £2.50 and £4 for three courses, and hot or cold snacks from

50p–£4. It can all be washed down with a glass of real ale. The daily speciality choice offers unfussy dishes such as fresh seafood, and the usual range of grills is available. For dessert try crème caramel or apple strudel.

BURBAGE
The Savernake Forest Hotel ★★
Savernake
(Burbage 810206)
Open: Mon–Sun 12noon–2pm, Tue–Sat 7–9pm, Sun 7.30–9pm
C P &

On the fringe of the beautiful Savernake Forest, this charming old hotel specialises in home-prepared dishes. The Buttery Grill menu offers soup (70p) or home-made pâté (£1.20) as starters. Main dishes include quiche, chili con carne, pizza, shepherd's pie, smoked mackerel, fish pie, lasagne, interesting salads and an ever-changing hot dish of the day, all under £3. Traditional Sunday lunch costs around £5.50. An ambitious à la carte menu is available in the restaurant – unfortunately beyond the scope of this guide. Last orders 9pm.

CHIPPENHAM
The Rowden Arms, Bath Road
(Chippenham 3870)
Open: Mon–Thu 12noon–2pm, 7–10pm, Fri–Sat 12noon–2pm, 7–10.30pm, Sun 12noon–1.30pm, Summer only Sun 7–10pm
C P &

On the main Bath Road out of Chippenham is this attractive, modern pub with a low rake, chalet-style roof and a colourful painted farmhouse wagon in the forecourt. You can sip cocktails in the comfortable lounge bar while surveying the very extensive menu offering freshly-prepared food. A selection of 14 starters ranges from soup of the day for about 48p to more substantial hors-d'oeuvre at around £1.65. Fish dishes, grills, salads and specialities, such as loin of pork Marsala £3.85 and rump steak (around

£4.50), are available for the main course and there is an impressive choice of sweets at a variety of prices. Among the more expensive (around £1) are banana split and rum baba.

White Hart Inn, Ford
(Castle Combe 782213)
Off A420 Bristol/Chippenham on slip road to Colerne
Open: Mon–Sun 12noon–2pm, 7.30–9.30pm
P

Idyllically situated beside a trout stream and overlooking the lush Weavern valley, this 16th-century stone-built pub is the epitome of Olde Englande. Low, beamed ceilings, log fires and suits of armour set the scene, while Ken Gardner, Fleet Street journalist and writer, personally attends to the food preparation. Home-cooked ham-on-the-bone or braised beef, served with vegetables cost around £2.50 in the bar, and for less than £3 you can savour locally-caught trout. Some dishes from the à la carte menu could be sampled within the budget, but venison in port wine or creamed pheasant cost around £5.50, so you would have to forego a starter or sweet course.

CORSHAM
Methuen Arms Hotel ★★
(Corsham 714867)
Open: Mon–Thu, Sat 12noon–2pm, 6–10.30pm, Fri 12noon–2.30pm, 6–11pm, Sun 12noon–2pm, 7–10.30pm
C P &

Situated midway between Chippenham and Bath on the A4, the hotel is in close proximity to Corsham Court, the country seat of Lord Methuen, whose heraldic arms are displayed above the entrance portico. In fact, the building is steeped in history and Winter's Court, where lunch and dinner are served, retains the oak beams and Cotswold stone of a grandiose bygone age. A midday three-course businessperson's meal is a bargain at £5 (especially as minute steak is on the menu), but unfortunately the candlelit dinners are just beyond our range. However, there are further options in the Long Bar such as sandwiches, basket meals, and a cold table, all

---

THE ROWDEN ARMS

Spacious restaurant and plush lounge bar in modern house, situated on the A4 one mile south-west of Chippenham.
Extensive menu in Grill Room and snacks at the bar.
Small parties catered for, including wedding receptions.
Lunch served from 12pm until 2pm, Monday to Saturday and 12 until 1.30pm Sundays.
Dinner served from 7pm until 10pm, Monday to Thursday,
7pm until 10.30pm, Friday to Saturday.
Sunday dinner 7pm until 10pm, June to September inclusive.

BATH ROAD, CHIPPENHAM, WILTSHIRE
For reservations telephone Chippenham 3870

Dorchester — Hambledon

reasonably priced. Liquid refreshment includes a glass of house wine at about 75p.

DORCHESTER
Judge Jeffrey's Restaurant
High West Street
(Dorchester 64369)
Open: Summer Mon–Sat 10am–5.30pm, 7–9.45pm, Sun 12noon–2pm, Winter Fri–Sat only

[F][S][⚬]

Viewed as a building, Ann and Anthony Coletta's Judge Jeffrey's restaurant is of great historical and architectural interest. It was sympathetically restored and put to its present use in 1928, but had been first monastery property and then a private house for something like five centuries before. Judge Jeffreys lodged here in 1685 while making his mark in the town with orders for 74 executions. Today, the restaurant which bears his name is a friendly place, full of atmosphere, providing morning coffees, bar snacks, lunches, afternoon teas and dinners at prices which could hardly be accounted a trial to anyone. You can buy a substantial lunch for about £5 or eat à la carte for very little more. The evening à la carte menu is very English, listing scampi, veal, gammon steak and Dorset pork fillet all reasonably priced.

FAREHAM
Gabbies, 30–32 West Street
(Fareham 284853)
Open: Mon–Sat from 10am until late

[C][F][P][S]

This smart hamburger restaurant in the older pedestrian shopping area boasts far more than weighty burgers on its menu. You can enjoy a good three-course meal here or just catch a snack – filled jacket potatoes, French bread sandwiches, pancakes, pizzas, etc. Sweets include gâteaux, cheesecakes, and ice cream sundaes. If you have a taste and appetite for burgers, Gabbies special is excellent – a ¼lb or ½lb lean beefburger topped with mushrooms, peppers, tomato and melted cheese served in a toasted roll with French fries or salad for around £2.55 to £3.45.

FIDDLEFORD
Fiddleford Inn
(Sturminster Newton 72489)
Open: Mon–Sat 12noon–2pm, 7–10pm, Sun 12noon–1.30pm, 7–9.30pm

[P][⚬]

This creeper-clad inn makes a welcome stopping-place on the beautiful, but remote A357 – the Sturminster

Newton/Blandford road. Informality is the keynote and your hosts Geoffrey and Jill Fish ensure that there's a warm and cosy atmosphere. A lunchtime blackboard menu offers regularly changing speciality dishes.

HAMBLEDON
The Bat and Ball Inn, Broadhalfpenny Down, Hambledon Road, Clanfield
(Hambledon 692)
Open: Mon–Sat 12noon–2.15pm, 7–10.30pm, 10pm Winter, Sun 12noon–1.45pm, 7.30–10pm

[C][F][P]

Even in the mid-18th century, when the cricket club at Hambledon became the strongest team in England and turned a rustic pastime into a national sport, the Bat and Ball was a hit with the locals. The inn overlooked the pitch on Broadhalfpenny Down and the players (wise chaps) would repair to it after, and sometimes even during, a match to indulge in 'high feasting'. Today the inn is even more popular despite being way out in the country, so it's always advisable to book a table. Hosts Frank and Katherine Rendle (Katherine does the cooking) have retained a cricketing atmosphere in the front bar; curved cricket bats, two-stump wickets and all, while the other bar is decorated in the more traditional beams-and-brass style. Order food at the bar and eat here if you like, or have your meal

---

THE METHUEN ARMS HOTEL
CORSHAM, WILTS.
Telephone Corsham 714867

Partly dating from the 15th century, with oak beam and stone wall atmosphere, this character inn's restaurant offers a three course business lunch and a full à la carte menu. Whilst the Long Bar provides cold table and bar snacks.

Three Lounge Bars and skittle alley.

Car parking for 100 cars.

Resident Proprietors:
Mr. & Mrs. T. R. D. Stewart, FHCIMA

The Fiddleford Inn

Sturminster Newton, Dorset
Telephone:
Sturminster Newton (0258) 72489

Free House serving real ale. Extensive Bar meals, all home cooked food specialising in seafood and steaks. Garden. Children welcome.

Geoffrey & Jill Fish

Hartley Wintney — Mere

waitress-served in the cosy restaurant which overlooks an attractive garden. You really have to be something of a glutton to bust our £5 budget because prices are very reasonable. All five starters (from soup to a generous prawn cocktail) are under £1 and eight main courses range from about £1.10 for a Jumbo sausage, through mouth-watering meat pies (around £1.50) to grilled sirloin steak at about £4 – great value, considering that all the main dishes are served with chips, peas, mushrooms, onions and salad garni. Salads and ploughman's are also available. If you're not stumped when it comes to the sweet course, try an apple pie (40p) or gâteau (80p) or finish off with cheese and biscuits. No children or dogs allowed except on the front patio.

HARTLEY WINTNEY
Whyte Lyon
(Hartley Wintney 2037)
Open: Mon–Sat 12noon–2.30pm, 6–10.30pm, Sun 12noon–2pm, 7–10.30pm

C P

East of the picturesque village of Hartley Wintney, nestling in a hollow beside the A30, is the rambling, historic one-time coaching inn now owned by Schooner Inns. Peter Cole, who assists the manager, claims that part of the building dates back to the 14th century. At present two grill bars, heavily beamed and partitioned in the usual Schooner manner, offer a range of old favourites at competitive prices. The Portcullis Restaurant has a salad counter from which you can serve-yourself to as much side salad as you want. Ice creams or cheeses are included in the price of the main course, which could be rump steak (around £5), half a roast chicken in barbecue sauce (around £4) or plaice and lemon (about £3.50). A starter will add about £1 to your bill. Apart from a bigger selection of starters, Dover sole and duckling, the Cromwell Bar boasts the ghost of a girl who hanged herself in that very room. So popular is the Whyte Lyon with the locals that a third restaurant – the Hartford Grill has been opened upstairs.

HOOK
White Hart, London Road
(Hook 2462)
Open: Tue–Sat 12noon–2pm, 7–10pm, 10.30pm Fri & Sat

P

On the old coach road from London to Exeter stands the White Hart, one of the oldest pubs in the country. Entrance from the car park is through an out-of-the-past courtyard, by a row of old cottages which were once the stable boys' quarters. The dining room, with its dark-wood fittings and a lattice work of beams, has one wall etched with the ghostly outline of a coachman and his horses. Fruit juice, pâté or soup followed by a mixed grill served with chips or new potatoes and the vegetable of the day will cost around £4. A sweet such as apple pie and cream or cheese and biscuits complete the meal. Bar snacks are of a high standard, and a three-course meal of cream of chicken soup, a veal or pork dish or sausage and mash and strawberry gâteau can cost as little as £3.

LYNDHURST
The Bow Windows Restaurant
65 High Street
(Lyndhurst 2463)
Open: Summer Mon–Sun 10am–10pm, Winter Mon–Wed 10am–6pm, Thu–Sun 10am–10pm

P S

The little town of Lyndhurst is on a major holiday route in the heart of the New Forest . . . and gets very busy in the tourist season. With this in mind, Bow Windows is particularly conveniently placed opposite a large free car park. Behind those bow windows is an interior decorated with mirror tiles and large murals of forest scenes. The menu is extensive and conventional.

MARLBOROUGH
Attilio's Wine Bar, 13 New Road
(Marlborough 52969)
Open: Mon–Wed, Fri–Sat 12noon–2pm, 7–10.30pm, Sun 7–10.30pm (closed Bank Hols)

C P S

A cheerful aura of Italy in a corner of rural Wiltshire, Attilio's interior is simple and attractive, with an emphasis on natural textures – rush, cane, brick and wood. The excellent pizzas – with fresh tomatoes and oozing with cheese – can form a filling base for a within-the-budget three-course meal. Lunchtime meals and snacks range in price from 60p–£3. Our inspector was impressed by the home-made crusty rolls, served with a large dish of creamy butter. You'll need a bit of mental juggling to keep the price of an à la carte selection down.

MELKSHAM
The West End, Semington Road
(Melksham 703057)
Open: Mon–Sun 12noon–2pm, Sun 1.30pm, 7–10pm

C P

This attractive mellow stone and tile hostelry has an interior with a farmhouse look – beamed ceiling, open-stone fireplace and scrubbed table tops. A limited menu offers simple but well-prepared dishes with emphasis on succulent steaks, all with interesting names. You may wrap your lips around the 'Farmer's Daughter' (a 8oz sirloin for around £4) or perhaps you'd prefer a Ploughboy's lunch or Hungry Horse? Three courses including a village pâté for a starter and Emmerdale apple pie with cream will cost around £6.50 with coffee. **See advert on p. 50.**

MERE
Magpie Granary, Castle Street
(Mere 860263)
Open: Mon–Sat 9am–5.30pm, Sun (Etr–Sep only) 11.30am–5.30pm

ATTILIO'S Trattoria & Wine Bar

13 New Road
Marlborough
Telephone 52969

For that special occasion and evening meal try a traditional Italian meal in pleasant informal surroundings.
All food freshly prepared on the premises.
Business lunches at special low prices.
Personal service always.
Excellent wine list.
Telephone for reservation.

|P|S|&|

This coffee shop and adjacent bakery offers home-made bread, cakes, pastries and pies. There is a restricted hot lunch menu and a special two-course table d'hôte lunch priced between £1.50 and £2. A carefully selected children's menu for the under 12's is available and there is a Salad Bar in the summer to accompany the turkey and ham pie and the chicken pie. A good range of snacks are available throughout the day.

MILFORD-ON-SEA

Bay Trees, 8 High Street
(Milford-on-Sea 2186)
Open: Tue–Sat 12noon–2pm, 7–9pm, Sun 12noon–2pm

|C|P|&|

This charming restaurant has a patio and beautiful gardens where you can enjoy your pre-meal drinks. The lunch menu at £3.60 (£4.75 on Sundays) provides traditional British fare (roast beef is a speciality of the house). The food is fresh and carefully cooked to ensure excellent value. The evening à la carte menu can provide a three-course meal within the price limit of this guide. The restaurant is very popular with the locals and it is advisable to book in advance or arrive early to be sure of getting a table.

Milford-on-Sea
—
Pewsey

OTTERBOURNE

The Tyrol, Winchester Road on the A31 between Winchester and Southampton (Twyford 712220)
Open: Mon–Sat 12noon–2.15pm, Mon–Thu 6–10.30pm, Fri 6–11pm, Sat 6–11.30pm, closed Mon in Winter

|C|P|P|

Step inside this Tyrolean bar and restaurant run by Austrian proprietor Gunther Kampichler and you could be hundreds of miles away in the heart of Austria. The traditional décor and furnishings provide a genuine Alpine atmosphere which is enhanced by the traditional costumes worn by the staff in the evenings. The speciality dishes on the menu include Wienerschnitzel (£4.25 including vegetables), Torten from £1.05 and Apfelstrudel at 85p. Careful selection from the range of starters will keep you just within our limit. Try the Austrian beer served in stone mugs and wine in traditional wrought-iron dispensers.

PETERSFIELD

The Punch and Judy Restaurant
High Street
(Petersfield 2214)
Open: Mon–Sat 8.30am–5.15pm

|C|P|S|&|

This attractive olde-worlde building dating from 1613 has plenty of charm and combines a bakery, coffee shop and small restaurant. A set menu of good basic English fare could include smoked mackerel, roast beef and apple pie for £5.40 or prawn cocktail, chilli con carne and gâteau for £5.25. There is also a dish of the day on offer such as roast loin of pork served with a good selection of well-prepared vegetables.

PEWSEY

The French Horn, Marlborough Road (on A345)
(Pewsey 2443)
Open: Mon–Sat 10am–2pm, Sun 12noon–1.45pm,
Mon–Thu 6–10pm, Fri & Sat 6–10.30pm, Sun 7–10pm

|P|&|

This attractive inn, which lies adjacent to the Kennet and Avon Canal, was converted from old cottage and a smithy. The menu is not over-elaborate, but large portions of good, wholesome dishes are provided. For starters, try a tasty home-made soup at 60p or prawn cocktail at £1.25. For your main course, steaks are from £4.50, home-made steak and kidney pie with vegetables is £1.50 and scampi £2. Salads range in price from £2–£2.50. The home-made fruit pies are excellent value at 75p. A set Sunday lunch (which includes a glass of wine) is available at £4.75.

The West End Inn
Semington Road, Melksham, Wiltshire.
Tel: Melksham 703057

Open Mon-Sat 12 noon-2.00pm, 7pm-10pm.
Sunday 12 noon-1.30pm, 7pm-10pm
Large Car Park — Fully Licensed.
Farmhouse fayre offers you simple good food and wine at reasonable prices. Our menu is limited but all our food is freshly prepared.
Very old established inn once a farmhouse. Ushers fine traditional ales, wines and spirits.

THE FRENCH HORN

THE PUB FOR FOOD

3 Course Sunday Lunch £4.75 (inc. glass of wine)
Lunch and Evening Meals always available.
Excellent Wadworths Ales
Log fires.

MARLBOROUGH ROAD, PEWSEY, WILTSHIRE, SN9 5NT
Telephone: Pewsey 2443

PIDDLETRENTHIDE

Brace of Pheasants, Plush, 2m north-east of Piddletrenthide off B3143 (Piddletrenthide 357)
Open: Mon–Sat 11.30am–2.30pm, 7–10.30pm, Sun 12noon–2pm, 7–10.30pm

[P][&]

This thatched free house dates from the 16th century. The proprietor Joan Chandler has a wide experience of catering and provides an excellent choice of meals in the Buttery Bar, well within the price range of this guide. The blackboard menu lists, amongst other dishes, home-made soup 55p, home-made pâté £1.60, cold meat platter with a range of salads £3.75, smoked salmon platter £3.95 and a range of hot dishes under £4. Sweets are 75p and coffee 40p. A children's menu is available.

PORTSMOUTH

The Hungry One, 15 Arundel Way, Arundel Street
(Portsmouth 817114)
Open: Mon–Sat 9.30am–5pm

[♫][P][S][&]

For the very best kind of snack bar, in clean, comfortable, purpose-built surroundings, try Michael See's Hungry One. Fresh salads are a speciality of the house and range in price from Cheddar cheese at just over £1.60 to red salmon at around £2.30. There is a good selection

---

Piddletrenthide
–
Romsey

---

of substantial snacks from about £1.80 for chicken or plaice and chips to nearly £2.20 for scampi and chips. There is a range of delicious desserts from around 50p. No alcohol, but finish with the locally-esteemed coffee with fresh cream.

RINGWOOD

Peppercorns Restaurant
9 Meeting House Lane
(Ringwood 78364)
Open: Tue–Thu 10am–2.30pm, Fri–Sat 10am–2.30pm, 7.30–9.30pm, Sun 12noon–2pm

[P][S][&]

Hanging flower baskets, bright against the whitewashed walls, pick out Peppercorns. Exposed beams and hunting prints create a relaxed atmosphere, enhanced by displays of fresh flowers. Appetisers range in price from soup of the day at 65p to prawn cocktail at £1.25. Main courses, served with vegetables of the day, include a variety of roasts from £2.25–£2.50 and fish from £2.10. Cold buffet items cost from £1.85–£2.50 – home-cooked ham, roast beef, and chicken are included. Daily specials such as cottage pie at £1.65 or braised liver and onions at £1.90 change daily. Desserts, for example

---

Bakewell tart, home-made fruit pies or gâteau are in the 75p–£1 range. Sunday lunch is a special feature, with a choice of four starters, two roasts or fish, two hot sweets or a selection of desserts. Home cooking with the maximum use of fresh vegetables is a speciality.

ROMSEY

The White Horse, Ampfield
(Braishfield 68356)
Open: lunchtime licensing hours

[♫][P][&]

Nestling at the foot of a wide curve of the A31 is the welcoming sight of the picturesque, black-and-white-timbered White Horse pub. Inside, the large lounge bar is all beams and comfort, with a cavernous brick fireplace. Cindy and Ron Bagley offer astonishingly good bar lunches and you will find it difficult to spend as much as £5 for three courses, wine and coffee. Cindy does all the cooking and even the generous cottage pie, which comes in an individual dish, is full of surprises – with peppers and sweetcorn it only costs 95p! Beef curry, chicken supreme or sweet and sour pork are all under or around £1, and salads are available. Start with pâté and finish with delicious, light Black Forest gâteau or fruit flan bursting with fruit – both served with cream and costing just 60p. Coffee costs 30p a cup.
A recent addition is the delightful

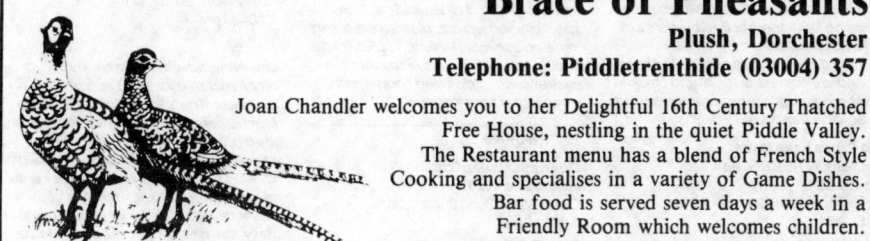

Brace of Pheasants
Plush, Dorchester
Telephone: Piddletrenthide (03004) 357

Joan Chandler welcomes you to her Delightful 16th Century Thatched Free House, nestling in the quiet Piddle Valley. The Restaurant menu has a blend of French Style Cooking and specialises in a variety of Game Dishes. Bar food is served seven days a week in a Friendly Room which welcomes children. Charcoal Grills are available every day. Real Ales.

Ron and Cindy welcome you to the White Horse Inn Ampfield

A fine selection of beers are available and bar snacks are offered Monday-Friday between 12.00 and 2.00pm

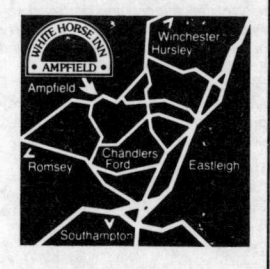

Nr. Romsey, Hampshire.
Tel. Braishfield 68356

Salisbury — Southampton

children's garden, where kids can choose dishes such as sausage and chips or fishfingers and chips from their own special menu.

SALISBURY

The Baron of Beef, Endless Street (Salisbury 28937)
Open: during normal licensing hours. Mon–Sun 12noon–2pm, 6–10.30pm

C F P S

The Baron of Beef, opened in February 1978, is a timber and brick transformation of a much older pub. Its lunchtime bar menu includes steak and kidney pie or Cornish pasty, both served with chips and peas, as well as home-made cold dishes such as egg, cheese and onion flan for around £1 and prawn salad for under £2. A ploughman's lunch costs around 65p. The main menu includes excellent home-made soup or pâté as appetisers. Plaice, chicken, lamb or gammon are typical main courses, served with vegetables and trimmings, at around £3 each. Steak dishes are between £3.45 and £4.75. Most desserts are around 75p.

Claire's Upstairs Restaurant
7–9 The Market Place (Salisbury 3118)
Open: Mon–Sat 12noon–2.30pm, 6.30–10.30pm

C F P S ♦

Very handy for shoppers, this is a pleasant rendezvous for a quick break or a substantial lunch. Claire's offers good food at very reasonable prices and (with its children's meals offering two courses including fish fingers or beefburgers at just £1.30) is excellent for families. Evening dishes include casserole of beef cooked in Guinness at £2.70 and chicken cooked in tarragon, brandy and cream at £3.30, or thereabouts.

The Cross Keys Hotel
Shaftesbury Road, Fovant (Fovant 284)
Open: Mon–Sun 12noon–2pm, 7.45–9pm

C P ♦

The famous highwayman Jack Rattenbury enjoyed the victuals prepared at the Cross Keys. This charming, stone-built hostelry was built around 1485, and can be found in the heart of beautiful countryside. Snacks available in the Buttery Bar include curry or chicken and chips for between £2 and £5, and very modestly-priced ploughman's lunches and freshly-cut and toasted sandwiches. Pauline Storey prepares more elaborate dishes for the evening meal.

The Greyfisher, Ayleswade Road (Salisbury 27511)
Open: Mon–Sun, 10am–2.30pm, 6–10.30pm

F P ♦

Once a very small pub. The Greyfisher has been turned, like the ugly duckling, from a coot into a heron. Wooden beams and bare brickwork give this two-year-old inn, hard by both cathedral and shops, a character which merges well into the rest of Salisbury. There is a wide range of dishes, from a good home-made steak and kidney pie at about £1.80, beef or chicken curry and rice at around £1.90, to sirloin steak garni at around £4. For a snack, or a first course, Wiltshire ham, home-made soup, or prawn cocktail cost about £1 or less, and for dessert, fruit pie and cream or bread pudding and cream at 65p make a worthy ending to the meal. Seating is very comfortable and the service friendly and fast.
See advert on p. 54

Michael Snell, 8 St Thomas's Square (Salisbury 6037)
Open: Mon–Sat 9am–5pm

P S ♦

No-one should go to Salisbury without trying Michael Snell's superb Black Forest gâteau. In these old, part millhouse premises, the Swiss-trained Mr Snell makes and sells his own chocolate and cakes, besides specialising in the sale of fine teas, coffees, jams, chutneys and local honey. His light lunch menu contains a great variety of dishes, all at under £3, including smoked mackerel fillet with carrot and coleslaw, and cheese flan or home-made pizza with salad. Children's portions are available. Appetisers include soup for about 60p and a selection of torten and pastries or speciality sorbets completes a satisfying three-course meal for around £5. Michael Snell is unlicensed. This restaurant has easy access for disabled people, with some tables on street level.

SHERBORNE

Swan Inn, Cheap Street (Sherborne 4129)
Open: Mon–Sun 12noon–2pm, 6.30–10pm

C P S ♦

The Swan Inn is to be found through an archway from a pedestrian short cut, leading from the main car park close to the town centre. This quaint hostelry offers a selection of satisfying grills, including scampi £4.20, half duck and rump steak (both under £5), all served with garni and French fries or jacket potato. Grills may be supplemented with appetising starters (50p–£1.20) such as pâté, whitebait and prawn cocktail, and sweets such as home-made apple pie.

SOUTHAMPTON

Golden Palace ×
17 Above Bar Street (Southampton 26636)
Open: Mon–Sat 11.45am–12mdnt, Sun 12noon–12mdnt

C F P S ♦

Slap in the middle of Southampton's modern shopping area, this colourful Chinese restaurant oozes Eastern calm. Prettily decked out with coloured lanterns, tiles, high archways and pillars to give a 'palatial' effect, it is immensely popular with the local orientals, and every encouragement is given to Western diners to use chopsticks. Dishes from the Tim Sum menu such as prawns Cheung Fun or meat rolls and duck's webs (available from 12noon–5pm only) prove to be the best loved and are all, unbelievably, around £1.65 each. A three-course à la carte dinner works out at about £6.

La Margherita, 4–6 Commercial Road (Southampton 333390)
Open: Mon–Sat 12noon–3pm, 6pm–12mdnt, Sun 7pm–12mdnt

C F P ♦

A popular nightspot, particularly with theatre and cinema folk from the nearby Gaumont, is Franco Fantini's La Margherita. 'Let's go Marghereating' is the house motto, with a choice of starters ranging in price from about 50p for hot garlic bread to around £2.25 for Parma ham and melon. There are made-to-order pizzas, from £1.75 upwards, and main dishes such as fresh fish, a significant proportion of which, except sole Meunière, cost less than £3.95.
See advert on p. 55

Mr C's, Park Lane, off Cumberland Place (entrance along lane on the left of the Southampton Park Hotel) (Southampton 332442)
Open: Mon–Sat 12noon–2pm, 6.30–11pm

C P ♦

This lively, fun-eating place is not recommended for those with small appetites. The full range of starters from farmhouse soup (75p) to fresh prawns on shell (£1.75) can all be served with salads, baked potato or chips for an extra £1.45. The main course specialities and pies range from £3.25–£6.25, and desserts from 75p. A blackboard menu of daily 'specials' gives extra choice in the cheaper price range. Cocktail prices start at £1.95.

Piccolo Mondo, 36 Windsor Terrace (Southampton 36890)
Open: Tue–Fri 10am–8pm, Sat–Mon 10am–7pm

F S

Very handy for top-of-the-town shopping and the Hants and Dorset bus station, Salvatore La Gumina and Domenico Bibbo's Piccolo Mondo incorporates bakery and snack bar. A good cup of coffee costs 30p, freshly-baked cheesecakes and cream cakes around 60p, and freshly-cut sandwiches are available. Hot snacks include home-made lasagne alla Romana and the cooked-to-order pizzas both priced at £1.60. Fried chicken is £2.25.

The Baron of Beef

Endless Street, Salisbury
(Next to main Bus Station)
Telephone: 28937

Bar:
Local and national beers,
Bar snacks, Lunches.

Restaurant: (Supper Licence)
Open during all licenced hours

GRILLS

SPRING CHICKEN (Half)
Garden Peas or Toasted Salad, Fried or Croquette Potatoes, Roll and Butter

PRIME GRILLED LAMB CUTLETS
Mint Sauce or Redcurrant Jelly, Garden Peas, Tossed Salad,
Fried or Croquette Potatoes, Roll and Butter

GRILLED PORK CHOP, APPLE SAUCE
Garden Peas or Tossed Salad, Fried or Croquette Potatoes, Roll and Butter

GRILLED GAMMON STEAK with Fried Egg or Pineapple
Garden Peas or Tossed Salad, Fried or Croquette Potatoes, Roll and Butter

GRILLED RUMP STEAK GARNI
Garden Peas or Tossed Salad, Fried or Croquette Potatoes, Roll and Butter

GRILLED T-BONE STEAK GARNI
Garden Peas or Tossed Salad, Fried or Croquette Potatoes, Roll and Butter

GRILLED FILLET STEAK GARNI
Garden Peas or Tossed Salad, Fried or Croquette Potatoes, Roll and Butter

Fine selection of wines.   Sweets & Coffee.

THE GREYFISHER

Newbridge Road, Harnham.   Tel: Salisbury 27511

TWO ELEGANT BARS, LOCAL & NATIONAL
BEERS, COLD BUFFET COUNTER
GRILLS & HOT BAR MEALS
OUTSIDE PATIO
LARGE CAR & COACH PARK

La Margherita
Restaurant

6 Commercial Road, Southampton
Telephone (STD 0703) 333390

GOOD

MARGHEREATING

Enjoy GOOD Home Made food in a lively Italian atmosphere.

Our inexpensive Menu offers an extensive choice — 16 appetisers, 30 Main courses, 16 delicious desserts, plus a wide selection of excellent wines.

COME MARGHEREATING!
— An enjoyable experience

Pizza-Pan, 28A Bedford Place
(Southampton 23103)
Open: Mon–Sun 10am–3pm, 6pm–1am

C F P S

This enterprising bistro-cum-restaurant has boldly-written outside menus and an eye-catching window display of bottles to tickle the palates of passers-by. Inside (where a personal welcome awaits you), Ercol-style tables and chairs, with check tablecloths, fill the large eating area. Most appetisers here tend to be rather expensive (around £1.30), but this is compensated by the pasta prices (e.g. cannelloni ripieni – £1.85, pizza Napolitana – £1.55).

Simon's Wine House, Vernon Walk,
Carlton Place
(Southampton 36372)
Open: Mon–Thu 11.30am–2.30pm,
7–10.30pm, Fri–Sat 11.30–3pm,
7–11pm, Sun 7–10.30pm

F P S

This simple Simon wine house, with its dark wood, bare bricks and bowls of shiny green palms is located in Southampton's bohemian back-street area. Dishes chalked on a blackboard include home-made pâté or chicken curry at under £2, and Simon's pie (a speciality of the house), with sweets such as gâteau, cheesecake and trifle all for around £1.

Swindon
—
Wareham

SWINDON
Sheraton Suite, East Street
(Swindon 24114)
Open: Mon–Sat 12noon–2pm

C P S

If ornate surroundings are what you look for in a restaurant, you could do no better than to eat in the red and gold dining-room of the Sheraton Suite. Sit back amidst the chandeliers, velvet-upholstered chairs and flock wallpapers and enjoy the table d'hôte lunch, priced at about £3.50. This includes a starter of soup or fruit juice, and eight choices of main dishes such as roasts, steaks, chicken chasseur or fish plus a daily special such as devilled kidneys followed by cheese or a sweet from the trolley. You may, if you prefer, order from the à la carte menu; most dishes obviously fall outside our price range, but three courses such as melon, scampi and gâteau are still within reach. Snacks are available from the bar.

WAREHAM
The Anglebury Coffee House
15 North Street
(Wareham 2988)
Open: Mon–Sat 9.30am–5pm, lunch served 12noon–2pm

C P

This coffee house, situated in an attractive 16th century building in Wareham town centre, offers home-made cakes and light lunches prepared by the proprietors Anne and Rodney Goodhand. Lunches represent good value for money with tasty home-made pies (made with feather-light pastry) quiche and a savoury pizza served with a crisp salad, all at under £2. Start your meal with soup at 35p and finish with home-made fruit pie and fresh cream at 55p. The beamed interior is bright, attractive and clean and it is said that the Anglebury was once the haunt of Lawrence of Arabia.

The Old Granary, The Quay
(Wareham 2010)
Open: Mon–Sat 12noon–2pm, Sun 12noon–3pm, Mon–Fri & Sun 6.30–9pm, Sat 6.30–10pm

C P

This picturesque restaurant, situated on the banks of the River Frome, dates from 1770 and was converted from a grain store. The choice of dishes is extensive, a two-course lunch is priced from £1.50–£3.20 and includes seafood platter, home-made pâté, hot country pie, all served with mixed salad and potatoes or granary roll and butter. The à la carte menu provides a three-course meal for lunch or dinner and with careful selection you can keep within the price limit.

Armando RESTAURANT
· THE PIZZA PAN ·

**A GRAND PLACE
never-ending food and fun!**

*Renowned for fish and selective cuisine specialities.
Melodic music, singers or accordian everynight.*

**28a BEDFORD PLACE SOUTHAMPTON
Telephone 36688 — 32604**

The Anglebury Coffee House

15 North Street, Wareham, Dorset.
Telephone Wareham 2988
Proprietors: Mr and Mrs Goodhand

MORNING COFFEE
★★★
LIGHT LUNCHES
★★★
AFTERNOON TEAS
★★★
Home Cooking — Licensed
Open 6 days a week (Closed Sundays)

Red Lion Hotel ★
Town Cross
(Wareham 2843)
Open: Mon–Sat 12noon–2.15pm,
Sun 12noon–2pm, 7–9.15pm
C P S

In the centre of this small country town, this brick hotel with dormer windows and colourful hanging flower baskets is a find for travellers en route to Bournemouth or Weymouth. Interesting bar snacks are available from 60p–£1.25 and a good table d'hôte three-course meal can be had in the restaurant for around £4 at lunchtime or around £6 in the evening. Choices for lunch could be spaghetti bolognese, fricasée of veal à la crême and strawberry meringue. The dinner menu offers a more imaginative selection of desserts such as profiteroles. A wider choice is available on the à la carte menu, but three courses could break the budget.

WARMINSTER
Chinn's Celebrated Chophouse
Market Place
(Warminster 212245)
Open: Mon–Sat 12noon–2pm,
7–10.45pm (except mid-Oct)
S

Rabbits, or rather the lack of them, are the reason that this charming little eating place exists today. The Pickford family had for many years carried on a Butchers'

Warminster
—
Weymouth

and Fish, Game and Poultry business in Warminster, and if it hadn't been for a devastating outbreak of myxomatosis in 1965, they would still be using these cellars for their once well-established trade in rabbits and rabbit skins which were graded and dispatched from here. Braving their misfortune the Pickfords decided to convert the cellars into a restaurant. So, today you will be welcomed by staff dressed in the traditional straw boaters and striped aprons of that original business. With their knowledge of meats, fish and poultry you are assured a good, reasonably-priced meal. Chops themselves cost around £2.50, whilst all steaks are English and, with the fresh fish, are bought whole to be made ready for the menu at prices ranging from about £2.50 for cod fillet to £5 or so for fillet or T-bone steak. Salmon, mackerel and herring, too, are smoked on the spot and all pâtés are home-made (sold as starters at 90p–£1.20).

WESTBURY
Whalley's, 35 Warminster Road
(Westbury 822551)
Open: Mon–Sun 12noon–3pm, Fri & Sat 7.30–11pm
P ♿

This modern shop-fronted restaurant is on the main Warminster Road through town. The selection of snacks, including pizza, cottage pie, cauliflower cheese and pâté are all under £1. Main dishes, roast lamb, braised beef in ale, steak and kidney pie, fish dishes and salads are under £2, sweets are around 50p. There is an evening à la carte menu on Friday and Saturday but most of the meals are just outside the limits of this guide. Cream teas are also served.

WEYMOUTH
The Clarendon Restaurant
52/53 The Esplanade
(Weymouth 786706)
Open: Mon–Sun 9am–11pm
C S ♿

A seafront restaurant near the shopping area which provides day-long refreshment for flagging shoppers and sunbathers. A three-course meal for £2.95 offers a range of starters, grills, roasts, cold buffet and sweets – excellent value! Fresh seafood is available daily and the local crabmeat salad for just £3.75 is a treat. Prime rump steak is £4.50. Children's portions of most à la carte dishes can be ordered but the Pirate's Delight or Cowboy's Brunch at 80p are established favourites. An ideal place to take a hungry family of holidaymakers.

CHINN'S
CELEBRATED CHOPHOUSE
MARKET PLACE, WARMINSTER.
Telephone: Warminster 212245. (Closed Sundays).

A cosy family run grillroom situated in the centre of Warminster in an old world cellar.

We offer an unpretentious menu at reasonable cost, served in a friendly, informal manner.

It is not necessary to book but please do if you so desire.

Wilton — Winchester

WILTON

Ship Inn, Burcombe
(Wilton 3182)
Open: Mon 10am–2.30pm, 6–10.30pm,
Tue–Sat 11.45am–2pm, 6.30–10pm

[F][P][&]

An old inn of great character, The Ship is run by Ken Price who was once a chef on the Cunard liners, the Queen Mary and the Queen Elizabeth. If the day is sunny, sit at one of the tables set out in the garden and enjoy your meal out in the open air. The garden also has a trout stream running by it. There is a good menu to choose from and the choice is varied. Starters include country pâté served with hot toast at 95p and melon in a boat also at 95p; main courses include, at one end of the price-range, mushroom or cheese and tomato pizza, with chips and garni for £1.40, to lobster thermidor at £7, and there are plenty of dishes in the intermediate range.

WIMBORNE

Horton Inn, Horton
(Witchampton 840252)
Open: Mon–Sat 12noon–2pm, 7–10pm,
Sun 12noon–2pm, 7.30–9.30pm

[P]

Good bar snacks are a feature of this attractive 18th-century free house. There's a paved patio where you can savour your food when the sun shines. Dorset pâté or smoked mackerel pâté are tasty snacks, both just over £1, and a range of attractive salads is available at around the £2 mark. The restaurant has an à la carte menu, avocado and prawns, beef carbonade, and Dorset Apple Cake cost £5.50, though some meals may go over our budget.

Quinneys, West Boro'
(Wimborne 883518)
Open: Tue–Sat 9.15am–5.15pm (lunch served 12noon–2pm)

[P][S][&]

Quinneys is a delightful old cottage near to the town's main square and the Minster. Various one-course economy meals include avocado pear with prawns and salad (£1.75) and grilled lamb cutlets with three veg (£2.75). The three-course lunchtime meals on offer range from £3.75–£4.50 and examples are roast chicken, lamb and gammon, plus the local speciality – Wimborne trout. Quinneys has its own bakery producing home-made gateaux (65p), cream cakes (40p) and a host of original recipe confectionery. There is also an extensive tea menu. Wine is 60p a glass.

WINCHESTER

The Cart and Horses Inn, Kingsworthy
2m N of Winchester off the Winchester by-pass
(Winchester 882360)
Open: during licensing hours Mon–Sun,
hot food 12.15–1.45pm, cold food 12noon–2pm, hot food 7–9.45pm, cold food till later

[C][P][&]

Built in 1540, the Cart and Horses is a traditional beams-and-brasses type of pub. The furnishings are simple, staff friendly and there is a good range of bar food to choose from. Salads, hot dishes and snacks range from 85p–£2.50 and the daily 'specials' are chalked on the blackboard. Sweets start at around 75p. The à la carte menu served in the restaurant is beyond our price range, but a carvery is due to open soon, which should be within our limit. There is garden seating for children and if the weather is poor they may use the restaurant (though not the bar).

Minstrels Restaurant
18 Little Minster Street
(Winchester 67212)
Open: Mon–Sat 10am–6pm

[&]

Situated just off the High Street this friendly restaurant in farmhouse style with pine tables and chairs is a popular venue

Whalley's of Westbury

35 WARMINSTER ROAD,
WESTBURY, WILTS BA13 3PD
Telephone Westbury 822551

Proprietor: Janice Blackham

Licensed Restaurant

- **O** MONDAY to SATURDAY 10am-5pm for coffe, lunch and tea
- **P** SUNDAY from 11am-3pm for traditional Sunday roasts
- **E** FRIDAY & SATURDAY EVENINGS from 7.30pm for evening meals
- **N** — also open any other weekday evening by reservation only

Coach parties by arrangement

HOME MADE PIES
GATEAUX
CHEESECAKES
OUR SPECIALITY

The Horton Inn

Horton, Wimborne
Telephone: Witchampton 840252

An attractive 18th-century free house where good bar snacks and an interesting selection of main dishes from the à la carte menu are available. In the fine weather you can enjoy the sun while you savour your food on the paved patio.

Open: Monday - Saturday 12 noon - 2pm & 7 - 10pm
Sunday 12 noon - 2pm & 7.30 - 9.30pm

THE SHIP INN

BURCOMBE, WILTON, SALISBURY.
Telephone 743182

This Old Inn by the banks of the river offers
a selection of traditional ales, local and national
keg beers.

In summer a pleasant seat on the lawns leading
to the river and winter an open log fire,
giving a very pleasant atmosphere.

Snack bar catering to the highest quality.

Restaurant

À la carte menu

Grills

Sunday lunches

Children welcome

Large car park

Winchester

for shoppers and tourists alike. A delicious range of home-made cakes, sweets and patisserie are on display to accompany your morning coffee or afternoon tea. Hot dishes available throughout the day are quiche, pizzas, savoury pancakes and jacket potatoes at around £1 each. Salad side dishes are 35p or a selection of these can be formed for a meal around £1.50. Other dishes include ratatouille, fisherman's pie and moussaka at £1.75–£3.

Mr Pitkin's Wine Bar & Eating House
4 Jewry Street
(Winchester 69630)
Open: Restaurant
Sun–Thu 12noon–2pm, 7–10pm,
Fri–Sat 12noon–2pm, 7–10.15pm
Bar Mon–Thu 11am–2.30pm,
6–10.30pm, Fri–Sat 11am–2.30pm,
6–11pm, Sun 12noon–2.30pm,
7–10.30pm

C F S ⌂

When Tony Pitkin left the hubbub of Fleet Street advertising, he brought a little of the London life to Winchester with him. His wine bar is now one of the busiest rendezvous in the city, with live music (often jazz) two nights a week and a pleasantly trendy, Edwardian-style atmosphere. The long, narrow bar with gas-lamp-style fittings and enlarged prints of wine labels; Mr Pitkin blends into the atmosphere well with his bow tie and colourful shirts. Three courses from the appetising slabs of cold meats and smoked fish, hot dishes of the day (about £1.75) and good range of starters and sweets will cost £3–£4. A chef presides over the bar's Sunday roast and Yorkshire pudding (about £2.50). The upstairs restaurant, elegant and intimate with its marble fireplace and russet walls, serves a daily lunch for around £5, but beware of the enticing items with a budget-breaking surcharge in brackets. Dinner is now less expensive if chosen from the new Menu Touristique, which offers three good courses at £5.95.

Splinters × ×
9 Great Minster Street
(Winchester 64004)
Open: Mon–Sat 11am–2.30pm

C S

Mike and Fiona Sherret's tastefully Victorian restaurant, with its dark gold wallpaper and 'ball' lights, offers predominantly French cuisine – its à la carte lunches are mainly outside our price range, but it earns a well-deserved place in the guide for the excellent-value lunches served in the brasserie, where soup is 95p, hot or cold ratatouille 95p, fresh crab au gratin £1.65 and a range of meat dishes around £2.60. Desserts are under £1, and coffee 50p. If the ground floor is full, you can order the brasserie menu upstairs in the restaurant.

The Wykeham Arms
75 Kingsgate Street
(Winchester 3824)
Open: Restaurant Tue–Sat 7–9.15pm,
Sun 12noon–2pm
Bar Mon–Sat 10am–2.30pm, 6–11pm,
Sun 12noon–2pm, 7–10.30pm

C P ⌂

Stroll from the city centre through Cathedral Close to this pub in the shadow of Winchester College. In the bars, the stripped pine, country house atmosphere is complemented by customers from the college, cathedral and cricket pitch. The back room restaurant (dinner little over £6) is pleasantly like a private living room. The warm welcome from Stanley and Mary Wright adds to this impression. Diners are surprised by a free bowl of salad between starter and main course. Good solid food is elevated from the ordinary – steak and kidney pie, prepared with Guinness or poacher's pie (rabbit and venison in cider). In the bar, try the excellent value nourishing soup (60p), herby cottage pie (95p) or hot tuna and sweetcorn quiche (£1.35). Sweets range from home-made apple pie to gâteau.

The Cart & Horses Inn
KINGSWORTHY — NEAR WINCHESTER

Carvery
A choice of
Beef, Pork, Lamb, Chicken, Duck, Venison and Pheasant in Season
Fresh Vegetables and Roast Potatoes

Bars
SUPER COLD BUFFET — WIDE RANGE OF HOT BAR SNACKS/MEALS
REAL ALE TRADITIONALLY SERVED — CHILDRENS GARDEN
TWO LARGE CAR PARKS — LOG FIRE IN WINTER

Isle of Wight

ISLE OF WIGHT

ARRETON

The Fighting Cocks
(Arreton 254/328)
Open: Mon 12noon–2pm,
Tue–Sun 12noon–2pm, 7–9.30pm

Built on the site of an inn that had stood for three centuries, and using much of the original stone, The Fighting Cocks boasts a smart restaurant specialising in grills and seafood, but also offers pork chop or grilled gammon at about £3.80. Bar snacks feature at 40p or so, hot dishes at around £1.50 and cold meat salads starting at around £1.90.

GODSHILL

Essex Cottage Restaurant, High Street
(Godshill 232)
Open: Etr–Oct Tue–Sat (out of season Sat and Sun only) 12.30–5.30pm, 7–9pm

[C][hotel][P][S][knife/fork]

Godshill is cream tea country with more tea gardens to the square inch, probably, than any other part of the British Isles. The Essex Cottage does a very good cream tea at just over £1, as well as an excellent table d'hôte lunch at around £3.50. Dinner from the table d'hôte menu will cost only around £5.45 for four courses. The lunch menu is basic English fare including roast beef or chicken and cherry pie and cream.

NEWPORT

Bugle Hotel, 117 High Street
(Newport 522800)
Open: during normal licensing hours

[P][S]

The origins of the Bugle Hotel are a little obscure. It served as the Parliamentary headquarters for the Island meeting between Charles I and the Parliamentary Commissioners. Table d'hôte lunches are around £5, a three-course table d'hôte dinner at about the same and other meals can be chosen from the à la carte menu.

SHANKLIN

Cliff Tops Hotel ★★★
Park Road
(Shanklin 3262/3)
Open: Restaurant Mon–Sun 1–2pm, 7–9pm
Coffee Shop Mon–Sun 10am–6pm (summer only)

[C][P][S]

Cliff Tops calls itself the 'good food' hotel and takes a great pride in its English and French cuisine. The three-course table d'hôte lunch here is not expensive and dinner is reasonably priced also.

The Tudor Rose Restaurant
59 High Street
(Shanklin 2814)
Open: Tue–Sun 10am–9pm

[C][hotel][S][knife/fork]

A long, mock-Tudor building originally a bakery and tea-rooms, in which proceedings are supervised by proprietor John Barrymore Simpson. Lunchtime fare consists of mainly traditional English roasts, but fresh salmon, cold meats and flans are also available, and can be followed by a choice from the sweet trolley. With a starter such as pâté or home-made soup, the whole meal is excellent value at less than £4.

VENTNOR

The Royal Hotel (THF) ★★★
Belgrave Road
(Ventnor 852186)
Open: Mon–Sun 8–9.30am, 12.30–2pm, 7–9pm

[C][P]

The Royal does a limited but reasonably priced à la carte menu, a three-course buffet lunch at around £4 and a four-course table d'hôte dinner at about £6 as well as a menu of children's favourites priced below £1. Dinner is a particularly appetising affair, with such dishes as devilled whitebait or egg Mornay for a starter followed by rack of lamb rosemary and then perhaps fresh strawberries for dessert in season.

YARMOUTH

The Bugle Hotel ★★
St James's Square
(Yarmouth 760272)
Open: Mon–Sun 12.15–2pm, 7.15–9pm

[C][hotel][P][S][knife/fork]

The 300-year-old Bugle, with its panelled dining room, complete with ancient stone fireplace, has a great deal of character and charm. The cuisine is international and the menu table d'hôte, with a three-course lunch at about £4.50 (£5 on Sunday) and dinner at around £6. Dinner is an excellent meal, offering a good choice of dishes including prawn cocktail, followed by lamb's kidneys bourguignon with delicious Black Forest gâteau as dessert. The recently-enlarged Galleon Bar, with décor on a nautical theme, has cold meat salads and various snacks available from 50p–£2.

The George Hotel ★★
Quay Street
(Yarmouth 760331)
Open: Mon–Sun 8.30–10am, 12.30–2.15pm, 7.30–9.15pm

[C][P][knife/fork]

Built by the Governor of the Island, during the reign of Charles II, the George is now a comfortable family-owned and run hotel, popular with yachties and locals. A table d'hôte lunch in the panelled dining room costs around £4.35, but dinner is now a little above our budget. The food is English traditional, with fresh vegetables and is very good. For lunch you can enjoy cucumber salad, nutty fillet of plaice, and apricot trifle. Bar snacks include hot dishes ranging in price from £1.55 for sausage and chips to about £4.75 for steak and salad. Sandwiches and lighter snacks are also available. A large glass of French house wine costs around 70p in the restaurant – a welcome accompaniment to your meal.

THE COFFEE SHOP AT CLIFF TOPS HOTEL

Shanklin, Isle of Wight
Telephone: Shanklin 3262

Opposite lift to the beach. A very popular meeting place.
Excellent choice of meals with a special cold buffet for light luncheons.
Hot dish of the day with vegetables available at lunchtimes.
All pastries, Danish pastries, gâteaux and scones freshly made each day.
Open every day 10.30 a.m. – 10.30 p.m. May to September.

THE SOUTH-EAST

Three counties – Kent, Sussex and Surrey – make up the South-East – the Garden of England. Kent is where they make and grow things and where, from the Cinque Ports, sailors used to defend the realm. Sussex is buttressed against the sea by the line of the South Downs, which reaches from Beachy Head into Hampshire. It also contains Ashdown Forest – once the property of John of Gaunt, more recently the playground of Christopher Robin and Pooh.

Sussex tends to conjure up a picture of gentlemen in expensive tweeds shooting expensively reared pheasants in expensive woods. The Bluebell Line, that splendid reminder of branch lines and trains that looked like trains, somehow enhances the impression. In places, one feels that time stopped one day in the reign of Edward VII. But this is a very subjective impression. A visit to one of the resorts, say Brighton, will haul one back smartly into the 1980s. Both counties – and Surrey, too – are in commuterland: that residential world where the breadwinners cram themselves daily into railway carriages, travelling to and from their offices in London.

Whatever else Kent may produce in the way of fruit in its innumerable orchards, its most widely appreciated commodity is hops. Before machines took the job over, hop picking provided paid summer holidays for innumerable families in the East End of London: they even ran special trains for them from Charing Cross station. The Kentish landscape has benefitted from the industry by the small oast houses in which the hops were dried. Nowadays, many of them have been converted into private houses, but they still look pretty.

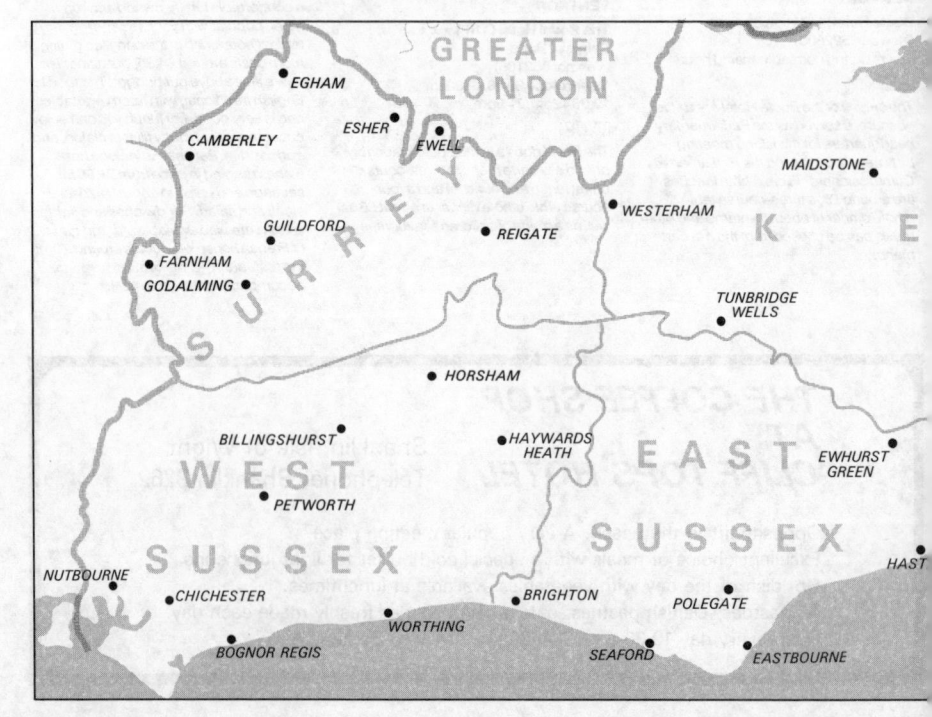

In view of its hop gardens, one might imagine that the beer in Kent would be better than anywhere else in Britain. In fact, the county has no more breweries than anywhere else, nor is the bitter any better than that brewed in Sussex – or, to go farther away, Rutland or Yorkshire.

At Lamberhurst, a village near that erratic line which separates Kent from Sussex, a south-facing hillside is covered with vines. The wine they produce is bottled on the estate, and compares very favourably with good German vintages – notably Moselle and Riesling. Nearly all English wine is white – largely on account of the climate, which only provides enough sun to ripen a white-wine grape.

Obviously one can expect good Dover sole in Kent, and Whitstable, at the mouth of the Thames, is rightly proud of its oysters. These are available in most places, though one would have to look more carefully to find a Biddenden cake. What is more, one would have to be in the right place on the right day.

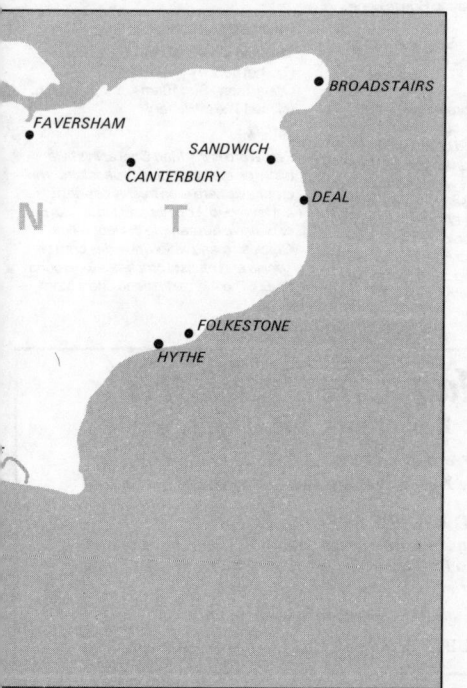

The Biddenden Twins were Eliza and Mary Chulkhurst who lived in the village for all their lives. When they died, they made provision for the poor of the parish to receive bread and cheese on Easter Monday. Visitors were to be offered little cakes – ginger breads, brandy snaps and ginger nuts, and the fund that paid for them was named the 'Biddenden Dole'.

Alas, you will probably search the bakeries and teashops in vain for Huffkins (oval cakes, half an inch thick with a hole in the middle of each) and Oast Cakes. The recipe for the latter included currants and parsnip wine. No doubt there is not enough parsnip wine available to achieve anything approaching mass production. Nor do they seem to keep well. The instructions contain the advice 'Eat without delay'.

In Sussex, local dishes include Ashdown partridge pie (the partridges shot by those expensive gentlemen?), which is not a commonplace of restaurants. It might, however, be amusing to go into a bar and ask for a glass of Huckle My Buff. If the barman knew what he was about, he would give you an egg flip well laced with brandy.

Although Windsor Castle is in Berkshire, Surrey folk named a dish after it: Broad Windsor Beans. It does not sound particularly appetising. Perhaps, if Windsor had been in their own county, they might have thought up something better. But what you are likely to find in Surrey teashops – the better ones, anyway – are Maids of Honour. These cakes were a great favourite of Anne Boleyn. Henry VIII is said to have given them their name when he happened upon one of Anne's maids of honour eating one.

BILLINGSHURST

The King's Head, High Street
(Billingshurst 2921)
Open: Mon–Wed, Sun 12noon–2pm,
Thu–Sat 12noon–2pm, 7–10pm

C P S

This delightful 500-year-old coaching inn in the centre of the village boasts a restaurant extension with a separate entrance from the bar – though you can partake of the cold buffet or snacks there if you are in a hurry. Fresh, home-made fare is the hallmark of the restaurant, where you could start with soup or pâté at around 55p. Main dishes include steak and kidney pie and delicious lasagne and form the basis of the set lunch. In winter good old treacle pudding helps you keep the cold weather at bay.

Old House, Adversane
(Billingshurst 2186)
Open: Mon–Thu & Sun 10am–6pm, Fri & Sat 10am–9.30pm

C P

Manager Jeremy Steward supervises proceedings throughout the day in this quaint, 14th-century restaurant, its two rooms with low oak-beamed ceilings displaying an abundance of antiques – some for sale. Basic English fare includes a special lunch served at any time of the day for around £3.25. Soup of the day, home-made steak pie or home-made quiche and a sweet of the day – fruit pie, ice cream or fruit salad – is a typical menu. The à la carte menu includes grills at about £2.95 and the special farmhouse meals include home-made pies and casseroles at around £2.50.

BOGNOR REGIS

Tudor Rose, 55 London Road
(Bognor 23682)
Open: Summer Mon–Sat
10.30am–10.30pm, Winter closed Mon

The restaurant is split into two sections and has olde-worlde wooden-beamed ceiling and walls. A daytime menu offers starters (such as chilled melon) from 50p–£1.50, followed by various fish, roasts and salads at sensible prices (leg of lamb £2, fillet of plaice £1.80,

Billingshurst — Broadstairs

farmhouse grill £2.90). In the evening prices rise, but it is still possible to stay within the budget. For example, a grapefruit cocktail plus grilled gammon with cheesecake to finish will cost you about £4.65. Of the specials, chicken Maryland is good value at £3.30. Coffee is 40p.

BRIGHTON

The Cypriana Steak House and Greek Restaurant, 22 Preston Road
(Brighton 202661)
Open: Mon–Sun 12noon–3pm,
6pm–1am

C P S

This small, intimate restaurant specialises in Scotch beef and authentic Greek food. English dishes consist of about 11 appetisers, fish, poultry, grills, flambés and omelettes. Greek specialities include as appetisers houmous or taramasalata, both at around £1. Main courses such as moussaka or stifado (beef cooked with shallots and served with rice and potatoes) cost about £3.40. Sweets from the trolley are around 75p. For a real treat, try a Meze – 'a full two-course meal consisting of 14 delicious Greek dishes to satisfy the most discerning palate'. This is served for two or more people and costs around £4.50 per person.

Meeting House, Meeting House Lane
(Brighton 24817)
Open: Summer Mon–Sun 8am–6pm,
Winter Mon–Sat 8am–6pm

P S

Tom and Sean Wall preside over their modern coffee shop-cum-snack bar with its wooden tables and bench seats, bright décor and counter service. Hot and cold dishes are available, including quiche lorraine and salad or steak and kidney pie at around £2, and there is also a good selection of cold meats. Starters include minestrone or French onion soup for about 40p and you can finish with a delicious Danish pastry or a slice of apfelstrudel at about 50p.

Richards' Restaurant, 102 Western Road, Hove
(Brighton 720058)
Open: Mon–Sun 12noon–2.30pm,
Mon–Thu 6–10.30pm,
Fri–Sat 6–11.30pm, Sun 6–10pm

C P

This garden-style restaurant has wooden trellis with hanging plants and wicker chairs, and is open from 10am for coffee and light snacks. Starters include Stilton and onion soup and home-made pâté, main courses range from various fish dishes to devilled chicken, lasagne, and steak, oyster and Guinness pie. There is a good selection of sweets on the trolley. A satisfying three-course meal is available for around £5. Coffee is from 35p and a glass of wine 70p.

Tureen Restaurant, Upper North Street
(Brighton 28939)
Open: Tue–Sat 12noon–2pm,
7–9.30pm, Sun 12noon–2pm

C P

This unpretentious bistro-style restaurant features a large Japanese tureen in the window and floral-patterned banquettes along the walls. Cuisine is English with French influence and the à la carte menu offers a host of delights. However, we suggest our readers stick with the £3.75 set lunch, which offers three courses such as egg mayonnaise, sweet and sour pork, and summer pudding. On Sundays a traditional English roast with starter and sweet will cost £5.95. Coffee is 50p and a glass of wine 80p.

BROADSTAIRS

The Mad Chef's Bistro, The Harbour
(Thanet 69304)
Open: Mon–Sun 10am–3pm, 6–11pm, (closed Tue in Winter)

C P

Paul Ward is the Mad Chef at this little bistro on the harbour at Broadstairs. The emphasis here is on freshly caught fish and seafood. Lobster and turbot can be expensive but sample the lunch-time Quickies menu which includes crab or cockle and mussel omelettes for around £1.50. The à la carte menu offers other

---

The Mad Chef's Bistro

The Harbour, Broadstairs. Tel. Thanet 69304

Why not come for a quick cheap Lunch? Evening Booking essential. Kent's leading fish restaurant.

MAD CHEF'S SPECIALITIES
★ Crab & Shell fish Soup. ★ Fried Shelled Prawns Provencale. ★ Oysters.
★ Lobster Thermidor. ★ Devilled Crab. ★ Grilled Dover Sole. ★ Scampi.
★ Curries. ★ Steaks. ★ Plus a lot more
Vegetarian and Wholefood at reasonable prices.

BRING A BOTTLE NO CORKAGE   ACCESS   DINERS CLUB   BARCLAYCARD   AMERICAN EXPRESS

specialities such as pheasant and turkey pie or mixed meat kebabs, both at around £4. Starters include gazpacho, and there is a huge list of tempting sweets. Lovers of Dickensian memorabilia will be interested to note that the Mad Chef's is situated between Dickens' House Museum and Bleak House. Booking is essential on summer evenings.

CANTERBURY

Alberry's Wine and Food Bar
38 St Margarets Street
(Canterbury 52378)
Open: Mon – Thu 11.30am – 2.30pm, 6 – 10.30pm, Fri – Sat 11.30am – 2.30pm, 6 – 11pm, Sun 6 – 10.30pm

C P S

A genuine Roman pavement in the basement bar is the talking point of this establishment, where for the price of a simple meal you buy a whole evening of entertainment. Jazz and rock musicians often play beneath the arched ceilings. A good selection of wholesome food includes beef braised in Guinness, chicken chasseur, or pork and apples in cider, all for around £2 and the very popular steak sandwiches served with salad for about £3. Sweets cost around £1 or less and there is a choice of about 10 ice-creams.

CHICHESTER

The Coffee House, 4 West Street
(Chichester 784799)
Open: Mon – Sat 10am – 5.30pm, (half day Thu during Winter months)

S

Emphasis here is upon simple, no-nonsense food made from fresh ingredients and cooked on the premises. Plats du jour, including shrimp or chicken salads cost from £1.80 upwards. Three-egg plain omelettes are also available, as is Welsh rarebit at around 75p. The licensed restaurant menu is restricted but is excellent value, particularly the cold buffet dishes at around £1.80 – £2.20.

Canterbury
—
Egham

Jason's Bistro, Cooper Street, off South Street
(Chichester 783158)
Open: Mon – Sun 12noon – 2pm, 7 – 10.30pm

🍴 S

Tucked away in Chichester's Cooper Street is Jason's Bistro, where a team of staff run by Gerhard and Enid Boesser serve bistro-style lunches and dinners in this spacious and imaginatively-modernised old outhouse building. Starters, including home-made soup with hot garlic bread range from about 60p – £1.50. The 'Chef's Dish of the Day' is usually an excellent buy at around £2; other main courses cost between £2 and £5.75, including vegetables.

Micawber's Kitchen, 13 South Street
(Chichester 786989)
Open: Mon – Sat 11.30am – 3pm, 6 – 10.30pm, Sun 11.30 – 3pm, closed Sun in Winter

P ♿

Named after the character in Charles Dickens' novel, David Copperfield, this restaurant has a warm and friendly atmosphere. The dinner menu differs very slightly from the luncheon menu and on both there is a good range of dishes to choose from. Starters are at around £1, main dishes from £1.95 and desserts are under £1. Try home-made soup, chicken chasseur and cheesecake, all for £3.50. Coffee is 30p and a glass of wine 60p.

DEAL

The Hare and Hounds, Northbourne
(Deal 65429)
Open: Mon – Sun 12noon – 2.30pm, 6 – 11pm

C 🍴 P

Here's a charming country pub where everyone is catered for; you can have a quick nibble at a bar snack or enjoy a leisurely restaurant meal at a modest price. There are three or four 'specials' which are changed daily, one of which could be mussels in garlic butter, cod

steak in prawn and scallop sauce and lemon cheesecake at £5.45. Alternatively you can sample one of a wide variety of home-made quiches or a succulent steak and kidney pie with vegetables for about £1.50. Finish with a slice of home-made cheesecake or Black Forest gâteau.

EASTBOURNE

New Lounge, 4 Cornfield Terrace
(Eastbourne 31309)
Open: Tue – Sun 11.45am – 2pm

P ♿

Joyce Ellis prepares good, plain English fare in this family-run restaurant. Although at weekends a more exotic, à la carte menu is offered, the workaday table d'hôte lunch offers a choice of soup or fruit juice followed by fish, roasts, steak and kidney pie, liver and bacon or cold buffet. Puddings include home-made fruit pie and custard or various sponges for an all-inclusive price of around £3.20.

EGHAM

Maggie's Wine Bar, 2 St Judes Road, Englefield Green
(Egham 37397)
Open: Mon – Thu 11am – 2.30pm, 7 – 10.30pm, Fri – Sat 11am – 2.30pm, 7 – 11pm, Sun 12noon – 2pm, 7 – 10.30pm

C P S ♿

If you are energetic enough you can 'do' the Runnymede Memorial, the Kennedy Memorial, the RAF Memorial, and still be in time for Sunday brunch at Maggie's. If you wrongly feel that Sunday brunch at under £2.50 is not filling enough, enjoy a traditional three-course roast meal at around £4.50. Afterwards you can watch Prince Charles play polo at nearby Windsor Great Park, or you could stay with the Sunday papers that are provided. John Barnikel creates daily menus which include unusual soups such as egg and prawn at around 70p, home-made pâtés at around £1, moussaka and lasagne at around £2.50, and for the trencherman, an English sirloin steak platter at around £5.
See advert on p. 66.

Micawber's Kitchen

13 South Street, Chichester. Tel. 786989

★ A la Carte menu, Dishes of the Day, Selection of Salads, Vegetarian quickies.
★ Seafood Cellar Bar
★ Select wine list and top quality house wines at reasonable prices
★ Strong lager and local Chidham Real Ale stocked
★ Party bookings of up 25 welcomed in our upstairs function room
★ We are ideally situated for pre-theatre or after-theatre dinners

LUNCH 11.30 a.m. - 3.00 p.m. DINNER 6.00 p.m. - 10.30 p.m. (11.00 p.m. Sat.)
FRESH LOCAL FISH AND SEAFOOD OUR SPECIALITY

Esher — Guildford

ESHER

Julie's Bistro, 10 High Street
(Esher 66681)
Open: Mon–Sun 10am–4.30pm,
Tue–Sat 6–10.30pm

🎵 P 🍴

This tastefully-decorated bistro is situated in the centre of Esher, near the race course and on the main A3. There is a good range of starters mainly around £1. Burgers with salad or jacket potato or chips are under £3, and boeuf bourguignon, chicken supreme and sauté turbigo are just a few of the main dishes and are also under £3. Sweets at 85p and coffee 30p–50p.

EWELL

The Loose Box, 2 Cheam Road
(01-393 8522)
Open: Mon–Sat 11am–2.30pm,
Mon–Thu 5.30–10.30pm, Fri,
Sat 5.30–11pm

🎵 P S

This stylish wine bar is a hub of activity in this suburban Surrey village. One attraction is the dazzling array of bargain-priced food – game pie and salad at only around £1.50, a selection of home-made quiches with salad and lasagne both around £1. Cheesecakes, gâteaux or home-made apple pie are all about 60p.

EWHURST GREEN

The White Dog Inn, Ewhurst Green
(Staplecross 264)
Open: Mon–Sat 12noon–2pm, 6–10pm,
Sun 12noon–1.30pm, 7.15–10pm

P 🍴

This part 17th-century village inn, with recent additions, is set in 11 acres of gardens and woodlands in a peaceful Sussex village. Mine hosts are Tim and Pat Knowland. While Pat prepares the meals Tim looks after the bar and restaurant. The menu is chalked on the wall and features mainly English dishes. You could try home-made soup, home-made steak and kidney pie with fresh vegetables, and tipsy cake for just over £4. For an extra 45p you can have all the freshly-made coffee you can drink.

FARNHAM

Sevens, 7 The Borough
(Farnham 715345)
Open: Mon–Sat 12noon–2.30pm,
6.30–10.30pm, Fri–Sat 11pm

C 🎵 P S 🍴

Sevens has an intimate atmosphere – from the crowded wine bar at the front to the low-ceilinged bistro at the rear and on the first floor. Starters range from about 75p–£1.50 and include a delicious mushroom pâté. Main courses start at around £3 for lasagne or chili con carne to about £4.30 for rump steak with dishes like coq au vin, barbecued beef and sweet and sour pork in between at around £3.50. Sweets and cheeses are all about 90p. Very popular with business people and shoppers, it is wise to get to Sevens early!

FAVERSHAM

The Recreation Tavern Restaurant
16 East Street
(Faversham 6033)
Open: Mon–Sun 12noon–2pm, 7–10pm

C 🎵 P S 🍴

Once a 17th-century, square oast house this small tavern has been tastefully restored by the present owner. You can choose from a hot or cold buffet including over a dozen salads, meats cut from the bone and a variety of dishes accompanied by salad plus coffee for around £2 upwards. You may also be tempted by one of Chef Andrew Leach's delectable sweets. Interesting hot dishes are always available at around £5.

FOLKESTONE

Pullman Wine Bar, 7 Church Street
(Folkestone 52524)
Open: Mon–Sat 12noon–2pm,
7–9.30pm

🎵 P S 🍴

The Tudor-style building housing Michael and Janet Barnwell's wine bar is thought by some to be the most beautiful in Folkestone. Hot and cold dishes are presented buffet style. Soup is around 60p and a main dish such as oven-fresh pizzas are £1.15–£2.25, home-made casseroles and pies from £1.25, curries £1.25 and scampi from £1.95. Sweets such as gâteaux and flans are about £1. In fine weather, meals may be enjoyed in the attractive garden.

GODALMING

Maigrets Bistro, 78 High Street
(Godalming 29191)
Open: Tue–Sat 12noon–2pm,
3–5.30pm, 7–10pm

C 🎵 S 🍴

You won't find any trench-coated French police inspector in this quaint olde-worlde restaurant. Maigret, in this case, is the name of the pleasant lady owner Maigret Bricusse. The interior is a cosy low-ceilinged, beamed and half-panelled room which is all the more romantic in the evening, by candlelight. Bay windows overlook the main shopping street of Godalming. A blackboard menu offers a selection of well-cooked dishes at reasonable cost. A sample meal might include starters of avocado viniagrette or taramasalata at around 85p, main dishes such as chicken Somerset cooked in cider with celery and vegetables for about £2.75 or a selection of salads with prices starting at £1.90. Sweets cost 90p and there's as much coffee as you can drink for 35p. Cream teas and light snacks are available in the afternoon.

GUILDFORD

The Castle Restaurant, 2 South Hill
(Guildford 63729)
Open: Tue–Sat 12noon–2pm,
5.30–11.30pm (last orders 9.30pm),
Sun 12noon–2pm

C P

The older part of this restaurant blends well with the garden effect of the extension, with its stone floor and brick walls. Table d'hôte lunches cost around £4 for two courses or £4.50 for thee courses. Seafood pancake is one of eight interesting starters on offer, and of 11 main courses, kidneys with mushrooms in red wine sauce is recommended. The

---

John and Frances Barnikel

Maggie's Wine Bar

Fine Wines and Superb Food
Pates and Quiches Our Specialities . . .

2 St. Judes Road, Englefield Green, Surrey.
Telephone: Egham 37397

list of sweets is impressive, chestnut ice cream sundae being one of the more unusual examples. Dinner is around £2 extra.

Pews Wine Bar, 21 Chapel Street (Guildford 35012)
Open: Mon–Sat 12noon–2.30pm, 6.30–11pm

[🎵][S][♦]

David Allen runs Pews with flair and a friendly smile. Formerly an old ale house, the building's split-level rooms have dark beams and wood panelling, but are bright with log fires in their proper season and fresh flowers all the year round. The blackboard menu has a choice of hot dishes, from around £2, for example chicken Portugaise and chili con carne and a variety of curries. There is a large selection of wines (house wine 60p a glass or £3.30 a bottle).

Yvonne Arnaud Restaurant, Millbrook (Guildford 69334)
Open: Mon–Sat 12.30–2pm, 6.15–11pm

[C][🎵][P][S][♦]

You won't go far in Guildford without seeing mention of the Yvonne Arnaud Theatre. A set lunch in the curved Theatre Restaurant costs about £3.95 for two courses and around £4.75 for three. The menu is constantly changing, as a high percentage of patrons are regular playgoers. Evening meals are excellent, but alas, out of our league.

HASTINGS

Crossways, Lower Pett Road, Fairlight (Pett 2356)
Open: Tue–Sun 12.30–2.30pm, 7.30–9.30pm (last orders)

[P][♦]

Well-prepared, good-value English cooking is the keynote of this small restaurant, looking very like a modern village home at the crossroads in Fairlight. A three-course lunch costs only about £3 and offers such old favourites as home-made steak and kidney or chicken and mushroom pie, roast beef with Yorkshire pud or roast chicken. Sweets, also home-made, include blackcurrant

Hastings — Nutbourne

and apple pie or rhubarb crumble. The dinner menu is à la carte and more exotic fare such as rainbow trout with almonds (around £3.25) is available. With starters ranging from 32p for soup of the day to 90p for prawn cocktail and desserts from 60p, you will still have change from a fiver.

HAYWARD'S HEATH

Country and Wine, 124 South Road (Haywards Heath 458040)
Open: Mon–Sat 10am–10pm

[C][🎵][P][S][♦]

This modern bistro specialises in home-cooked fresh food and choice wines and real ale. Décor is rather exotic, with plush wall-to-wall seating, bamboo cane divides, and fresh flowers on every table. Salads and other dishes are on show in a large display cabinet. The menu includes various cold meat salads and a hot dish such as chicken casserole at about £2.95. Home-made soup and pâté are tasty starters at around £1.40 and sweets include huge fresh cream meringues. A thriving take away service also operates.

HORSHAM

Pilgrim's Halt, 24 West Street (Horsham 63281)
Open: Mon–Sat 12noon–2.30pm, 6–9.30pm, 10pm Sat

[P][S][♦]

A sister restaurant to last year's 'thousandth entry' winner in Maidstone, this first-floor premises in a 13th-century building is run along the same lines as its now-famous twin by Ruth and Dennis Treadaway. Home-made soup or pâté are typical starters at 66p–£1.04, main dishes include Southdown lamb chops at £3.41. Sweets from the trolley are £1.10.

HYTHE

The Butt of Sherry, Theatre Street (Hythe 66112)
Open: Mon–Sun 10.30am–2.30pm, Tue–Sat 6–10.30pm

[S][P][♦]

This cosy wine bar is housed in a part 17th century building and an intriguing feature is the millstone which is set into an internal wall. You can be sure of a warm welcome from Mary Freeman – try her home-made steak and kidney pie at £2.75, or a plate of ham off the bone, roast beef or ham and tongue all at around £2. Starters are available at 40p–£1.25 and sweets at around £1. The Butt of Sherry is well-known for its good wine. French beer is also available.

MAIDSTONE

The Pilgrim's Halt, 98 High Street (Maidstone 57281)
Open: Tue–Sat 12noon–2.30pm, 7–10.30pm, Sun 12.30–3pm

[C][🎵][♦]

Winner of our 1981 thousandth entry competition, The Pilgrim's Halt remains excellent value for those who will join the search for imaginative meals served in pleasant surroundings throughout the coming year. Daily specials such as old English casserole represent best value for money, but fillet of North Sea plaice or Wiltshire gammon won't break the bank at under £2.50. Finish with vanilla ice cream with hot chocolate fudge sauce.

NUTBOURNE

Cedar Tree Restaurant, On A27 near Bosham
(Bosham 573149)
Open: Tue–Sun 12noon–2.30pm, 7–10.30pm

[S][♦]

David and Sue Ullah have successfully converted a one-time transport café, on the main Emsworth–Chichester road, into a thriving little restaurant. The set three-course lunch is £2.80 and includes roast of the day and home-made steak and kidney pie, plus salads as a lighter option. During the evening the five-course set dinner is £6 (available Tue–Fri) and a one-course evening meal costs from £4. A large coffee is around 40p a cup.

CROSSWAYS RESTAURANT
Corner of Waites Lane, Near Hastings.
Tel: Pett 2356

Fully licensed

Len & Babs welcome you to their intimate Country Restaurant for good home cooked food.

Open all year round — (closing day Mondays).

For lunches and Evening Meals.

Afternoon Cream Teas a speciality.

PETWORTH

The Lickfold Inn, Lodsworth, 3m W of Petworth off A272
(Lodsworth 285)
Open: normal licensing hours

P

Real ale fanatics will feel at home at this old hostelry and free house, serving a wide selection of beer from the wood. To soak up their liquid intake, they might also be interested in the lunchtime menu of home-made steak and kidney pie, lasagne and other hot dishes, plus a good range of snacks and sandwiches for under £2.50. Evening meals include a wide table d'hôte selection for around £4.50, in which chicken kiev, sole ma facon and Lickfold skillet might figure. Add a starter (whitebait?) and a sweet such as chocolate rum gateau to make a really memorable meal.

POLEGATE

The Wishing Well, Wilmington, 2m W of Polegate on the A27
(Polegate 5956)
Open: Mon–Sun 10am–6pm (hot food is served 12noon–2.30pm)

P

Teas have been served in the gardens for over 100 years. The Wishing Well is now under the personal supervision of Fay Steadman, who is assisted by her mother. In the afternoon you can enjoy Sussex cream teas, mini teas and a variety of snacks in the attractive gardens (prices range from 30p–£1.15). Lunches are served in the restaurant and include fillet of haddock at £1.95, burgers from £1.95 and a range of salads. Home-made soup is a tasty starter at 50p and a range of desserts is available. The restaurant is licensed.

REIGATE

Home Maid, 10 Church Street
(Reigate 48806)
Open: Mon–Sat 6.45am–6pm, Sun 10am–3pm

As the name suggests, the atmosphere is homely, the food simple. The staff have a warmth and courtesy that is almost old-fashioned. Black beams offset cool white walls and checked tablecloths. Two three-course lunch menus, served from 11.30am, at £2.15 or £3.75 are of the grill, roast or fried variety, with fresh vegetables when available. Traditional puds follow, including steamed sponges and rice pudding. Individually-priced grills and snacks are also available throughout the day, giving a café-style service, although Home Maid is licensed.

RYE

The Peacock Wine Bar, Lion Street
(Rye 3161)
Open: Summer Mon–Sun 12noon–2.15pm, Mon–Thu &
Sun 6.45–9.30pm, Fri & Sat 6.45–10pm, Winter Mon–Wed, Fri–Sun 12noon–2pm, Fri–Sat 7–9pm

C P

This period, cottage-style restaurant/wine bar has a small separate bar and is under the personal supervision of the owner, Jane Edgar, who does most of the cooking. For starters, try the excellent home-made soup at 70p or the pâté at £1.05. Light snacks range from £1–£1.60, but for those wanting something more substantial, home-made steak and kidney pie, pork and turkey pie, moussaka and chili con carne are all priced at around £2. The desserts are under £1 and coffee is 50p.

SANDWICH

16th Century Tea House
9 Cattle Market
(Sandwich 612392)
Open: Mon–Sun 9am–6pm, 7–11pm

P S

Set in the market square of the picturesque old town is this historic 16th century building with a quaint, beamed restaurant. A three-course lunch is served here for around £4.20. Appetisers include Normandy pâté with toast or hors d'oeuvres. Home-made steak and kidney pie or sweet and sour chicken with special fried rice are two of the five main courses on offer, and desserts such as chocolate nut sundae or baked lemon curd roll complete the meal. A suggested evening dish is grilled gammon steak Hawaiian style which, with starter and sweet costs around £4.85.

SEAFORD

Regency Restaurant, 20 High Street
(Seaford 895206)
Open: Summer
Tue–Sun 12noon–2.15pm, 6.30–9.30pm, Winter 12noon–2.15pm, 6.30–9.30pm, Sun 12noon–2.15pm

S

Head for the daily special three-course menu served on the ground-floor of this two-floor restaurant, and you'll be well within budget. Upstairs there is an à la carte menu, ideal for party bookings. All the cooking is masterminded by Andrew Robertshaw, the restaurant supervised by his partner Eric Rolton. Special main courses may include plaice or cod, home-made steak and kidney pie, roast chicken or chicken leg cooked with wine and mushrooms, all served with fresh vegetables. The set price of £3.95–£4.50 includes soup or fruit juice starter and choice of sweet. In addition, a better quality three-course menu, for lunch or dinner, is available at £5.95.

Petworth
—
Worthing

TUNBRIDGE WELLS

Bruin's Bar and Ristorante Orso,
5 London Road
(Tunbridge Wells 35757)
Open: Mon–Sat 12noon–3pm, 7–11pm

C P S

Good food, good wine, good ale and great company are what Randy and Gill Brown, owners of Bruin's, view as life's 'bear necessities'. All three are taken care of in the bar, decorated in shades of brown and adorned with an assortment of teddy bears that give the restaurant its name. The first-floor restaurant (orso means 'bear' in Italian) offers a wide choice of Italian specialities, very reasonably priced. In the bar, snacks range from onion soup with bread for under £1 to steak and kidney pie for around £2.

WESTERHAM

The Henry Wilkinson, 26 Market Square
(Westerham 64245)
Open: Mon–Thu 12noon–3pm, 7–10.30pm, Fri–Sat 11.30am–3pm, 7–11pm

S

This new wine bar has a pleasant restaurant with pine tables and a good choice of home-made casseroles and soups, fresh salads, savoury flans and pies. The blackboard menu displays the special hot dish of the day for lunch and supper, which is usually served with potatoes or rice and a green salad. Desserts include meringue glacée and a pudding of the day for around 75p and a three-course meal may cost from £4.50 upwards.

WORTHING

Happy Cheese, Liverpool Buildings, Liverpool Road
(Worthing 201074)
Open: Mon–Sat 8.30am–5pm

S

Two floors are devoted to this modern eating place and bar. A wallboard menu offers such dishes as home-made soup, roast chicken with vegetables, pizzas and salads. A three-course meal with coffee and wine need not cost much more than £5.

TELEPHONE NUMBERS

In some areas telephone numbers are likely to be changed by British Telecom during the currency of this publication. If any difficulty is experienced when making a reservation it is advisable to check with the operator.

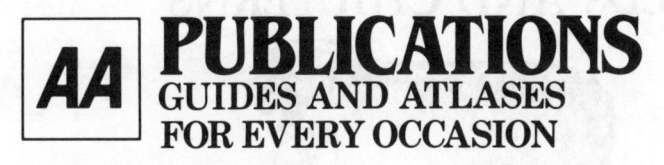

AA PUBLICATIONS
GUIDES AND ATLASES FOR EVERY OCCASION

SUPERGUIDES

HOTELS AND RESTAURANTS IN BRITAIN
Impartially inspected and updated annually, this guide lists 5,000 AA approved places to stay or wine and dine in comfort.

CAMPING AND CARAVANNING IN BRITAIN
1,000 sites around Britain, checked for quality and maintenance of facilities are graded accordingly. A special colour feature compares tent, trailer tent and caravan holidays.

GUESTHOUSES FARMHOUSES AND INNS IN BRITAIN
Thousands of inexpensive places to stay, selected for comfortable accommodation, good food and friendly atmosphere. Special colour feature on best Guesthouses, Farmhouses and Inns in the book.

SELF CATERING IN BRITAIN
A vast selection for the independent holiday-maker — thatched cottages, holiday flats, log cabins and many more, all vetted by AA inspectors.

STATELY HOMES, MUSEUMS, CASTLES AND GARDENS IN BRITAIN
An unlimited choice for all the family, including zoos, wildlife parks, miniature and steam railways, all listed with opening times, admission prices, restaurant facilities etc.

TRAVELLERS' GUIDE TO EUROPE

CAMPING AND CARAVANNING IN EUROPE

GUESTHOUSES, FARMHOUSES AND INNS IN EUROPE

ATLASES

COMPLETE ATLAS OF BRITAIN
Superb value for the modern motorist. Full colour maps at 4 miles to 1 inch scale. 25,000 place name index, town plans, 10-page Central London guide, distance chart and more.

MOTORISTS' ATLAS OF WESTERN EUROPE
AA atlas covering Europe at 16 miles to 1 inch scale. 10,000 place name index, route planning section, town plans of capital cities.

All these publications and many more are available from AA shops and major booksellers.

COTSWOLDS AND CHILTERNS

Gloucestershire, Oxfordshire, Buckinghamshire, Bedfordshire, and Hertfordshire are the area covered by the two ranges of hills, the Cotswolds and the Chilterns. The Cotswolds, many of which are about 600 feet above sea level, are the more austere. Farmers earn most of their incomes from sheep and, here and there, there's a discreet dab of industry: a brewery, perhaps, or, as at Chipping Norton, a little factory that manufactures gloves. On the other hand, the Cotswolds have what must surely be the prettiest collection of villages anywhere on earth. Everything is built from that golden stone, so distinctive to this part of the country.

By contrast the Chilterns are wooded, and their beechwoods were used in the chair-making industry which still persists at High Wycombe. There is lovely countryside in the Chilterns, but development has spoilt the scenery somewhat in Hertfordshire and Bedfordshire.

In between the two, there is a kind of no-man's land created by the River Thames. Having ambled from its source in the Cotswolds as far as Oxford, it (like so many graduates of the University) suddenly becomes more self-assured.

Gastronomically, Oxford seems to favour the gown rather than the town – or so novelists would have us believe. Rotund academics regale themselves with over-ripe pheasant, washed down with fine claret and followed by gallons of vintage port – possibly needing a visit to the spa at Cheltenham (also in the area) to reduce their blood pressures.

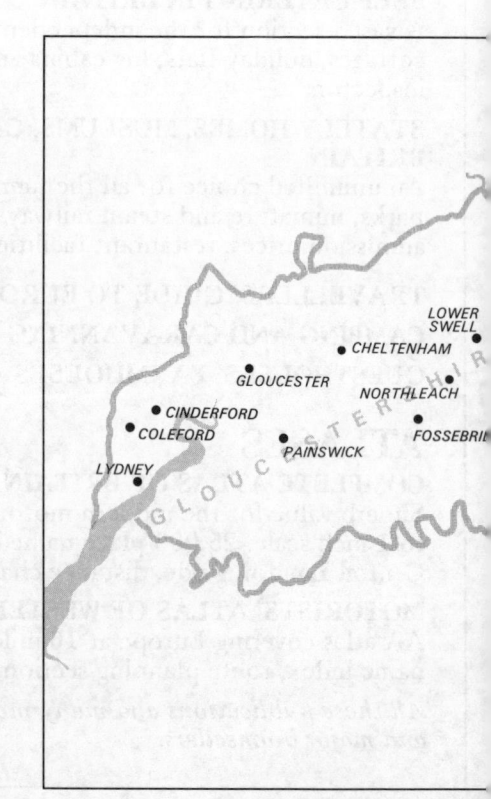

If you thumb through old recipe books, you will find that Oxford Colleges have given their names to a number of things – notably Brasenose Ale (which sounds delicious) and New College Pudding (well ...). The older inhabitants of the Cotswolds can cook a very passable dumpling – just as, in Buckinghamshire, somebody once hit upon the happy idea of sprinkling beef with brown sugar instead of salt. It produces a richer gravy and a more succulent flavour.

In Gloucestershire, they make Double Gloucester cheese which, apart from its excellence, is remarkable for the fact that nobody seems able to recall what happened to Single Gloucester. The cheeses used to be made in the Vale of Berkeley, and 'single' referred not to the quality but the size of the cheese.

As for the more bizarre (and consequently unobtainable) dishes, this portion of Britain seems to have had a talent for creating them. Gloucester Royal Pie, for example, was a one-off sent each year by the corporation of Gloucester to the king. It weighed 20lbs. The ingredients were lampreys (fish rather like eels – Henry I died after he had eaten too many of them) caught in the River Severn. All the decorations were made from gold, and these included a crown and sceptre on top and four lions around the base – plus the city's coat of arms.

At Painswick Feast, which takes place on 19 September, they excelled in bad taste by cooking a pie of 'puppy dogs'. Nowadays, more sensibly, they bake a cake covered with almond paste and place a china dog on top of it.

Paddy Lambtail Pie was, of course, made from lambstails. According to the instructions, the most arduous part of its creation was removing the wool.

AMERSHAM

Bear Pit Bar and Bistro
Whielden Street
(Amersham 21958)
Open: Mon–Sun 12noon–2.30pm,
Sun–Thu 7–10.30pm, Fri–Sat 7–11pm

C 🍴 ♿

A bear-baiting pit can still be seen inside this delightful, period bistro which is almost concealed in the courtyard of the 16th-century Saracen's Head pub. 'Beginnings' include 'Bloody Mary' soup (70° proof – B. marvellous!) or grilled smoked mackerel, both around £1. Main courses are from around £2.50. Particularly recommended is a spicy chili con carne served with a crisp salad and hot pitta bread. The French dressing is outstanding. Alternatives include marinated beef kebab, gammon, trout, steak, crab salad Louis or Bear Pit Burgers. 'Endings' offer a good choice and chocolate gâteau with whipped cream is about £1.

The Elephant and Castle, High Street
(Amersham 6410)
Open: Summer Mon–Sun 12noon–2pm, 7–9.30pm

C P ♿

This historic pub, covered with climbing roses, offers good-value, well-prepared meals for the hungry public. Steak pie and two veg or Spanish omelette are popular choices costing around £2.50. You can take lunch in any part of the low-beamed, olde-worlde pub that takes your fancy, and in addition, there's a small-budget à la carte menu offering mostly grills. Children are welcome in the pleasant beer garden.

The Hit or Miss Inn, Penn Street Village
(High Wycombe 713109)
Open: Mon–Sun 12noon–2pm, 6.30–10pm. Closed last week in Jul, first week in Aug

P

Within range of six from its own cricket ground across the road – any customer can join the club and play – this aptly-named wisteria-covered 17th-century inn is a big hit with the locals and visitors alike. In the Cricketers Bar, they can also enjoy an excellent selection of home-cooked fare available every day for lunch or dinner. Chef's pâté and toast is about £1, chicken a la king £1.80, and strawberries when in season about 45p, or try a 'steak butty' – sirloin steak grilled with onion and garlic, sandwiched in French bread and costing around £2. In addition, the restaurant serves an excellent three-course budget menu at lunchtime for about £5.75. Choice is wide – pâté stuffed mushrooms in batter, sauté of beef paprika and peach fool is a good example.

Paupers, 11 Market Square
(Amersham 7221)
Open: Mon–Sun 12noon–2pm, 7–10pm

C P ♿

Situated close to the parish church of St Marys, Paupers is housed in an attractive cottage with its black and white Tudor-style exterior gaily decorated with brass coach lamps and striped awnings. Inside is a warm 17th-century room which retains much of the period atmosphere with an inglenook fireplace, exposed beams, polished oak tables and pew seating. The menu offers two set dinners, two courses for less than £6 and three courses for just over £6. Appetisers include mushroom pâté or prawn salad with seafood sauce and a choice of six main dishes includes lemon chicken or baked bream. Finish with a home-made sweet and a cup of freshly-ground coffee.

AYLESBURY

The Bodega Wine Bar, The Market Square
(Aylesbury 27582)
Open: Mon–Sat 10am–2.30pm, 7–10.30pm

🍴 P S

The Bodega from the 18th century is all that remains from the days of the historic George Hotel, which boasts a tunnel, used by Roundheads, under the Market Square. This sophisticated, well-decorated wine bar offers food cooked to perfection. A blackboard lists a hot dish of the day such as chili con carne, lasagne or beef curry at around £1.50 and cold meats such as turkey breast or ham off the bone with salad at around £2, topside of beef for about £2.50 (including kouskous or coleslaw) and American cheesecake for around 70p. Some interesting German dishes are also available.

The Hen and Chickens at Aylesbury
Oxford Road
(Aylesbury 82193)
Open: Mon–Sat 12noon–2pm, Tue–Sat 7–10pm

C P S ♿

This popular pub with its attractive ship-boarding stands on the Oxford Road roundabout close to the original 'Aylesbury duck' pond. Manager Richard Stretton welcomes you to the pleasant buttery bar. Soup, home-made pies with vegetables and potatoes, and a sweet will cost around £4. The main restaurant menu offers you a three-course meal from around £5.

BALDOCK

The Vintage Wine Bar, 31 Hitchin Street
(Baldock 895400)
Open: Mon–Sat 10.30am–2.30pm, 7–11pm

C 🍴 ♿

This old timber-frame house near the centre of Baldock has been converted into an attractive wine bar. Husband-and-wife team Barbara and Peter Clarke cook and wait at table. A choice of hot and cold dishes are available. You might start with stuffed mushrooms or prawns in soured cream (both at 80p), followed by lasagne (£2) or trout studded with prawns cooked in garlic butter (£3). There is a good range of sweets to finish your meal. The cellar bar serves draught real ale and ploughman's and toasted sandwiches.

BISHOP'S STORTFORD

The Swan Restaurant, 88 South Street
(Bishop's Stortford 52007/59439)
Open: Mon–Sat 9am–9.30pm, Sun 12noon–2.30pm

C 🍴 P S ♿

A delightful Regency-style frontage with attractive half curtains on brass rails tempts you to explore further into this

Amersham — Bishop's Stortford

HOT and COLD LUNCHES and SNACKS

THE BODEGA WINE BAR

The Market Square, AYLESBURY, Bucks.
Telephone Aylesbury 27582

Monday-Saturday
10.00-2.30pm. 7-10.30pm. (11pm Fri. & Sat.)
Closed all day Sunday

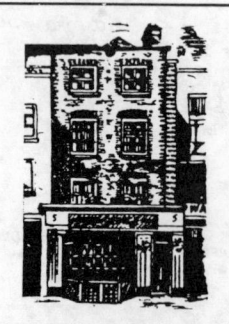

72

Burford — Coleford

restaurant. On the à la carte menu, the home-made soups and selection of omelettes are to be recommended, although more exotic dishes such as melon liqueur and Porterhouse steak garni are offered at prices coming close to our limit. A daily lunch menu costs around £4 for three courses plus coffee, with Sunday lunch at around £5 for adults, half price for children.

BURFORD

Windmill Restaurant, Asthall, 3m E of Burford off the A40 (Burford 2594)
Open: Mon–Sun 12noon–2pm, Mon–Sat 7–10pm

C P S

This recently-opened restaurant, situated in a six-acre site overlooking the Windrush Valley, is a useful stopping place for travellers. The park offers picnic facilities, and packed meals are available from the restaurant and can either be eaten in the park or taken away. If you prefer to eat in the lovely 18th-century, Cotswold-stone building, the restaurant offers a cold buffet at £2.50 and a reasonably priced à la carte menu featuring simple dishes. Morning coffee (10am–noon) is available as well as afternoon tea. In the evening the menu is more expensive but represents good value for money.

CHELTENHAM

Forrest's Wine Bar, Imperial Lane (Cheltenham 38001)
Open: Mon–Sat 10.30am–2.30pm, 6–10.30pm

F P S

Forrest's is tucked away in Imperial Lane just behind Habitat and is a useful venue at lunchtime or during the evening with the cinema nearby. The large, high-ceilinged ground-floor premises was formerly a bakery but has been cleverly adapted, with low-slung pendant lights and intimate eating areas cordoned off by waist-high walls. There are over 20 wines sold by the glass here at prices from about 60p–90p. The menu changes daily but a typical one might well include a choice of soups at around 40p, a continental ploughman's (with sausages) or cheese pancake with tossed salad, both at about £1 and a choice of three enticing plats du jour such as lamb kebabs with spiced rice and salad, or grilled rump steak from just £2 to around £5.

Mister Tsang ✗
63 Winchcombe Street (Cheltenham 38727)
Open: Mon 7–11.30pm, Tue–Fri 12noon–2pm, 7–11.30pm, Sat 12noon–12mdnt

C S

Food 'to indulge the palate and encourage good health' is what Mister Tsang and his family aim to provide. We were impressed by the nutritious and tasty house hors d'oeuvres at about £1.60, beef in black bean sauce (around £2.70) and king prawns with ginger and spring onions. To keep within the budget and do justice to the extensive menu, go with a friend or three! The seafood pot (a secret recipe, costing about £4.50) is very tasty, and Mister Tsang's 'Introduction to True Cantonese Cuisine' for two or more people works out at about £4 a head for a good variety. Desserts include Chinese toffee apples and are around £1.

Montpellier Wine Bar and Bistro
Bayshill Lodge, Montpellier Street (Cheltenham 27774)
Open: Mon–Sat 12noon–2.30pm, 6–10.30pm, 11pm Fri–Sat, Sun 7–10.30pm

C P S

This imposing Regency building behind the Montpellier Rotunda has been converted from a long-established grocer's shop into a ground-floor wine bar and cellar bistro. You can buy 10 or so wines by the glass for about 55p upwards. Notice boards display the daily menu, which includes hot soup at around 35p among the dozen or so starters, a hot speciality dish of the day, a variety of pies, smoked meats and fish from around £1.50–£2.50, interesting salads, and tempting sweets from 75p.

CINDERFORD

The White Hart Hotel Restaurant and Bistro, St White's Road, Ruspidge (Cinderford 23139)
Open: Mon–Sun 12.15–2pm, 7.30–9.45pm

P

Meals can be taken in the restaurant or bistro. An extensive à la carte menu features the popular Forester's Grill for around £3.95. Dishes such as pork tenderloin, steaks and chicken Kiev are about £5, so if you want a starter and a sweet you will have to choose carefully to stay around £6.50. The cold table in the bistro has meats and interesting salads which you serve yourself – as much as you want for around £2.50. A snack menu includes Californian salad (chicken, sweetcorn and home-cooked ham with lightly curried mayonnaise) at about £2.50 and hot dishes such as chili con carne at £2. Traditional Sunday lunch is served at around £5.

COLEFORD

White Horse Inn, Staunton (Dean 33387)
Open: Mon–Sat 12noon–2pm, 7–10pm, Sun 12noon–1.15pm, 7–10pm

P

This early Victorian pub, strategically sited 'twixt Coleford and Monmouth on the A4136 in the beautiful Forest of Dean, was built on top of a much older hostelry which now forms the inn's Cellar Restaurant. Prices are a little above our limit here, but the Saddle Room Grill, complete with beams and stable paraphernalia, offers well-prepared food which is both economical and interesting. Home-made liver pâté is about £1.20 and home-made soup 60p. Smoked mackerel or local trout served with vegetables are both around £3. Dish of the day could be lasagne, coq au vin or home-made chicken and mushroom pie at around £1.75.

White Hart Hotel and Bistro

CINDERFORD — Telephone Dean (0594) 23139

Large selection of tasty starters such as —
Fresh melon, curried prawns, prawn or crab cocktail, home-made soups.
Various main courses —
Hearty Forester's grill, smoked gammon, pineapple and cider sauce.
Charcoal grilled —
Steaks, chops, fresh salmon; also our old favourites:
Special omelettes, chillis, curries, pizzas — all home-made.
And then, if you've got room, enjoy one of our sumptuous sweets. All accompanied by your choice from our wine list.
Traditional Sunday lunches. Open every day lunchtimes & evenings.
We also do a large selection of sandwiches plain or toasted.

The Wyndham Arms ✕
Clearwell
(Dean 33666)
Open: Tue–Sat 12noon–2pm, 7–10pm,
Sun 12noon–2pm, 7–9.30pm

C P &

Built in 1340, in the centre of the ancient Dean Forest village of Clearwell, this picturesque inn has long been renowned for the excellence of food served in the à la carte restaurant. The Wyndham Arms has also gained an enviable reputation for satisfying bar snacks and for appetising meals in the Grill Room. Whitebait or mushrooms tartare cost about £1.95 in the bar, while egg and prawn mayonnaise or chicken liver pâté are a few pence less. An extensive range of grills includes fresh local trout, pork chop, gammon steak and fillet steak, served with all the trimmings and costing from around £4–£6. Home-made desserts are around £1.

COOKHAM

The Two Roses, High Street
(Bourne End 20875)
Open: Wed–Mon 12.15–2.15pm,
(closed 2 weeks mid-Feb and 1 week mid-Nov

S P &

A delightful 400-year-old cottage restaurant where Marian Smith excels with her home cooking, using only fresh ingredients. The steak and kidney pie is £2.85, chicken curry £2.55 and home-made pâté, crême brulée and bread-and-butter pudding are all at 70p. There are always five 'specials' on offer daily as well as traditional grills. Cosy wooden pew seating and period décor complete the scene. The restaurant is licensed and open in the evenings, but the menu is more expensive and elaborate.

DATCHET

Chez Petit Laurent, Country Life House, Slough Road
(Slough 49314)
Open: Mon–Thu 11am–2.30pm,
6–10.30pm Fri–Sat 11am–2.30pm,
6–11pm

Formerly The Upper Crust, Chez Petit Laurent is run by Steven Winter. Good food at moderate prices is offered in typically French surroundings.

ETON

The Eton Buttery, 73 High Street
(Windsor 60914)
Open: Mon–Sun 9.30am–10.30pm

C ♪ S &

Alongside the Thames and next to the bridge joining Windsor to Eton is this bright, modern buttery with its smart French cane chairs and elegant pot plants. Take a tray and make your choice from the cool and colourful salads, cold meats and poultry on display, or try a hot dish such as chicken and ham vol au vent

Cookham
—
Hungerford

at around £2.75. Find a window seat and watch the boats on the river below, with Windsor Castle in the background. Evening suppers are also served.

Eton Wine Bar, 82–83 High Street
(Windsor 55182/54921)
Open: Mon–Thu 11.30am–2.30pm,
6–10.30pm, Fri–Sat 11.30am–2.30pm,
6–11pm, Sun 12noon–2pm, 7–10.30pm

S

Within earshot of the famous College, this attractive wine bar is the place to go for good wholesome food and a folksy atmosphere. Décor is simple, with scrubbed wooden floors, church-pew seating and stripped-pine furniture. Alternatively you can sit out in the small garden. Mike and Bill Gilbey and their wives do the cooking, producing such delights as mushrooms à la Grecque, smoked salmon and cucumber flan, and spicy cinnamon cream and nut roll, all for £6.20.

FOSSEBRIDGE

Fossebridge Inn ★★
(Fossebridge 310)
Open: Mon–Sun 12noon–2pm,
Sun 1.30pm, 7–9.30pm

P

Ideally-placed in a wooded valley and beside a small river is this part-Georgian, part-Tudor inn, with its roaring log fires, stone walls and beautiful antiques. At around £1 you can sample starters such as mushrooms à la Grecque or spicy crab pâté, and a main course of home-made cottage pie or fresh local trout costs from around £2 upwards. The selection of home-made sweets may include a light and fluffy lemon meringue pie or a crispy bread and butter pudding.

GLOUCESTER

The Comfy Pew, College Street
(Gloucester 20739)
Open: Mon–Sat 9am–5.30pm

C S

On the main approach to the cathedral, The Comfy Pew lives up to its name with some entirely appropriate seating. David Spencer's food is home-cooked and wholesome; it's reasonably priced too, with soup, roll and butter at around 60p, a variety of meat or fish salad platters from £1.80, pâté with salad and toast, curried prawns and snacks on toast all under £1.50.

Tasters Wine Bar, 22 London Road
(Gloucester 417556 and 23536)
Open: Mon–Thu 12noon–2.30pm,
7–10.30pm, Fri–Sat 12noon–2.30pm

C &

This cheerfully decorated bar, close to the city centre features hot and cold dishes such as Stilton and spring onion quiche or mackerel pâté (at about 90p)

cider-baked gammon or Spanish pork may be the hot dish of the day, both at around £2 and extremely tasty. Boston aubergines or curried prawn and melon balls cost around £1. Crisp, fresh salads and potato dishes are in demand and sweets cost 70p–£1.

HATFIELD

Corks and Crumbs, 23 Park Street, Old Hatfield
(Hatfield 63399)
Open: Mon–Sat 10am–11pm,
Sun 11am–3pm, Summer 4pm or later

P &

This wine bar and coffee house, with pretty patio and terrace, in the old part of Hatfield, is run by a husband-and-wife team. It's small, attractive, and imaginative, with a menu to match. Corks and Crumbs wins points for offering a vegetarian pie, hot cheesy pepper, or courgette and tomato gratin (none much over £1). For the meatier-minded, the daily special main courses from £3–£5.50 may feature Mexican lamb with savoury rice and vegetables, or kidneys in red wine sauce. Wines are imaginatively chosen too, the restaurant is not afraid to offer lesser known varieties from Chile or Bulgaria.

HEMEL HEMPSTEAD

The Old Bell Hotel, High Street
(Hemel Hempstead 52867)
Open: Mon 12noon–2pm,
Tue–Thu 12noon–2pm, 7–9pm,
Fri–Sat 12noon–2pm, 7–10pm

C P S

Built in 1580, and an inn since 1603, the Old Bell is a fine example of a 17th-century hostelry. Here you can dine by candlelight in the original Tudor dining room with its intriguing 19th-century French wallpaper. Appetisers include melon with orange segments and curaçao for just over £1. Main courses include lamb kebab at around £3 or pepper steak, cooked in butter and finished with brandy and cream at £4. A special three-course menu at £5.50 is available for both lunch and dinner.

HUNGERFORD

The Tutti Pole, 3 High Street
(Hungerford 2515)
Open: Mon–Fri 10am–5.30pm, Sat & Sun 10am–5.45pm

S P &

Open for morning coffee, luncheons and home-made afternoon teas this cosy cottage tea-shoppe is very popular especially on the 2nd Tuesday after Easter when the 'Tutti-Men' come to collect their dues. Ask the manageress, Val, about this fascinating local tradition. Good home-cooking is the order of the day and the lunch menu includes omelettes, sandwiches, quiche and salads at under £1.80. There is a special hot dish of the day which is priced from £1.60. Sweets are 60p.

Leighton Buzzard — Maidenhead

LEIGHTON BUZZARD
The Cross Keys ×
The Market Square
(Leighton Buzzard 373033)
Open: Mon 10am–2.30pm,
Tue–Sat 10am–2.30pm, 7–10pm,
Sun 12noon–2.30pm

[C][P][S][◆]

Opposite the famous 15th-century Market Cross, this pub food bar serves a selection of hot and cold snacks at budget prices. On fine days you can bring the children and enjoy food on the paved forecourt. A special children's menu operates – including egg salad at 50p to half-portion scampi and chips at about 70p. Hot snacks for adults are either served with chips or vegetables and potatoes – plaice, curried chicken, veal escalopes or hot dish of the day such as hot-pot or beef stew are examples, all in the £1–£1.50 range. Cold buffet meats, fish, pâtés and salads are reasonably priced and desserts such as gâteaux with fresh cream cost 60p.

LITTLE CHALFONT
The Copper Kettle, Cokes Lane
(Little Chalfont 3144)
Open: Tue–Sat 9.30am–5pm

[P]

Simplicity is the keynote here, with polished tables and wheel-backed chairs for about 20 people. The lunch is home-cooked, just as mother used to make it and, astonishingly, below £3 for three courses. Soups or fruit juices are offered as appetisers. Main dishes served with a variety of fresh vegetables include steak or chicken and mushroom casseroles, roast pork and apple sauce or home-baked pies or flans. Cherry and apple sponge is a typical sweet.

LYDNEY
The Old Severn Bridge Hotel, Purton
(Dean 42454)
Off A48 between Lydney and Blakeney
Open: Mon–Sat 12noon–2.30pm,
6–11pm, 10.30pm in Winter, Sun
12noon–2pm, 6–10.30pm

[C][P][◆]

It is said that Sir Walter Raleigh did his courting here – and small wonder – for the pleasant rural scene encompasses the River Severn and the Cotswold Hills. Now parts of this country inn date back only to 1835, but the setting is as romantic as ever; with lawns and terrace laid out with umbrella'd tables – and a fish pond. There are a selection of bar snacks (home-made pâté salad at £1) and a larger selection of bar meals including local trout at £2.50. Fresh vegetables are used whenever possible. Home-made soup is 65p and sweets are 95p.

MAIDENHEAD
The Bacchus Swiss Restaurant
St Mary's Walk
(Maidenhead 36638)
Open: Mon–Sat 12noon–2.30pm,
Tue–Sat 7–10.30pm

The restaurant is decorated in the style of a Swiss chalet, with sloping wooden ceilings. A selection of cheese, meat and fish fondues are available ranging from £2.75–£4.95. Other Swiss specialities include Raclette Valaise at £3.25 and Veal Zurichoise at £3.95. Starters are from 95p and sweets from £1.25. All prices are subject to VAT.

Bumbles, Bridge Avenue
(Maidenhead 36724)
Open: Mon–Sun 12noon–2.30pm,
7–10.30pm

[C][S][◆][P]

Maidenhead's 'first American restaurant' is a friendly place with a bright attractive décor. An imaginative list of grills, steaks and burgers grace the menu and starters include Iowa corn chowder soup and spare ribs with barbecue sauce, both around £1.30. Spare ribs are also served as a main course (with a finger lickin' good Bumbles special sauce) for about £3 or, for the same price you might prefer a cadillac – a 6oz beefburger served on a bun with crisp back bacon and deep fried onion. Sweets include pan-fried pancakes with maple syrup at around 95p.

THE COPPER KETTLE

Little Chalfont, Tel. Little Chalfont 3144

Morning Coffee, Luncheons, Afternoon Teas, Home Made Cakes

Closed Sunday & Monday
Open Tuesday - Saturday 9.30 am - 5.00 pm
LUNCHES SERVED BETWEEN 12.15pm - 2.00pm

The Old Severn Bridge Hotel

PURTON, Nr. LYDNEY, GLOUCESTERSHIRE
Telephone DEAN (STD 0594) 42454

Morning Coffee — Luncheon — Dinner — Accommodation

Ray, Hazel and Edward would like to welcome you to their beautiful Hotel pub, to enjoy freshly cooked meals in the bar or restaurant, and see the most magnificent scenery looking across a wide expanse of the river.
Any turning on the right between Lydney and Blakeney on the A48 will bring you to us, on the banks of the River Severn.

MARLOW

Burgers, The Causeway
(Marlow 3389)
Open: Mon 9am–12noon,
Tue–Sat 9am–5.45pm

[P][S][⌖]

Opposite Marlow Park, this 17th-century building has been in the Burger family since 1942. The restaurant is on two levels. A simple, homely menu offers well-cooked food at very reasonable prices. Dishes include liver pâté or egg mayonnaise as a starter, steak and kidney pie or chicken and ham vol-au-vents with potatoes and vegetables, plus fruit pies and custard or Black Forest gâteau and cream to finish. A three-course meal costs around £3.60.

NEWBURY

Cromwell's Wine Bar, 20 London Road
(Newbury 40255)
Open: Mon–Sat 10.30am–2.30pm,
6–10.30pm, 11pm Fri–Sat

[C][P]

Though a Courage Brewery-owned wine bar, Cromwell's avoids any big business anonymity, thanks to friendly table service from Colin and Jo Maddock and a relaxed, warm interior. Bare floorboards, pew seating and checked tablecloths are the setting for 'no frills' fare. There's a good selection of hot and cold dishes on display, including pizza and salad (£1.50), daily specials from £1.60, and grilled rump steak with salad (£4.25). A choice from the sweet flans and gâteaux or cheeseboard, will keep you well within budget.

The Hatchet, Market Place
(Newbury 47352)
Open: Mon–Sat 12.30–1.45pm,
6.30–9.45pm, Sun 7.30–9.45pm
Newbury Race Days: Open 12noon

[C][♫][P][S]

By the Corn Exchange in this attractive market town, you'll discover this interesting restaurant, with its unique ceiling of wattle sheep-pen fencing. Emphasis is on grills and roasts at competitive prices. Rump steak is around £4.50, lamb cutlets or shallow-fried

Marlow — Oxford

rainbow trout about £3.25. A good selection of starters includes seafood cocktail and there are tempting sweets from the trolley to complete the meal.

The Sapient Pig, 29 Oxford Street
(Newbury 44867)
Open: Mon–Fri 12.30–2pm,
Tue–Sat 7.30–10pm

[C][♫][P][S][⌖]

This sophisticated bistro is steeped in Laura Ashley. The cosy atmosphere is an ideal setting for the delicious home-cooked fare. Hot dish of the day is around £3 and could be anything from sauté of pork provençale to Olde English steak and kidney pie – both served with three vegetables. Coronation chicken is an appetising cold dish costing around £2 and salads are available from 40p. Desserts, including such delights as strawberry Pavlova or apfel strudel cost around £1.50.

NORTHLEACH

Country Friends ✕
Market Place
(Northleach 421)
Open: Tue–Sat (lunch by appointment only), 7–9.30pm, Sun 12.30–2pm

[C][P]

The table d'hôte at this charming Cotswold-stone restaurant is excellent. For around £5.40 on weekdays and about £5.60 on Sundays, you can enjoy an imaginative meal which offers a choice of starters – a soup, perhaps a fish pâté – and a main course served with potatoes and fresh vegetables. On Sunday the choice of main course includes a roast and weekday menus include such things as chicken breast with a cream and curry sauce; sweets might include chocolate roulade.

OLNEY

The Olney Wine Bar, 9 High Street South
(Bedford 711112)
Open: Mon–Sat 12noon–2pm,
7–10.30pm, Fri–Sat 11pm

[♫][P][S]

The charming Georgian shop front of this wine bar leads into a room with an attractive open fireplace. The original bakehouse ovens are still to be seen in the back room. Bill of fare is on a blackboard and includes prawn pil pil and pâté with bread, both at around £1.20, lasagne, spaghetti bolognese and chili and rice at £2.65. Desserts are at around £1. Live music on Wednesdays.

OXFORD

Burlington Bertie's Restaurant and Coffee House, 9a High Street
(Oxford 723342)
Open: Mon–Sun 10am–12mdnt

[S][⌖]

Look above the covered market in Oxford High Street, and there's Bertie's – all plants, pub mirrors, cane-bottomed chairs and highly-polished tables with wrought-iron pedestals. You can get a meal or any kind of drink here at any time. The cuisine is English and Continental, the service fast and efficient, the welcome warm and friendly. Salads are priced at under £3.85, moussaka and pasta dishes at under £3, and meat and fish main courses at under £5.50. Desserts include 'specials' such as pancake delight.

Maxwell's, 36 Queen Street
(Oxford 42192)
Open: Mon–Sun 11.30am–12mdnt

[♫][S][⌖]

A bright and breezy first-floor restaurant where the high ceiling, iron girders and steel supports give an aircraft-hangar effect. American-style food is efficiently served in an informal atmosphere. Specialities such as lamb kebab, chili and chicken (around £2.75) supplement the hamburgers, which come with French fries, tossed salad and a choice of dressings. Ice cream sodas and milk shakes continue the American theme.

The Nosebag, 6–8 St Michael's Street
(Oxford 721033)
Open: Mon–Sat 10.30am–5.30pm,
Fri–Sat 6.30–9.30pm,
Sun 12noon–5.30pm

[♫][S]

The Hatchet

**Market Place, Newbury.
Telephone: 47352**

The building is nearly 200 years old, and situated in the market place in the centre of Newbury. Comfortable bar, with seating in stalls along one side. Restaurant has an old world effect, with rustic ceiling and old cartwheels for centre lighting.

There is a function room with a separate bar, for large parties.

Painswick — Reading

Inelegant its name may be, but this upstairs, split-level restaurant, with its oak-beamed ceiling and bright and homely décor, has a certain charm all of its own. The lunchtime hot dish of the day for around £1.95 is likely to be moussaka, chicken à la crème or herrings in oatmeal. A tempting choice of original salads costs around 80p. With soup at about 60p and hot garlic bread at about 40p, the three-course lunch must be a bargain, even after ordering delicious ice cream or sorbets. And on Friday and Saturday evenings the Nosebag offers an excellent three-course meal for just under £5 with exciting main courses such as mackerel with gooseberry sauce and a glass of wine and coffee.

Opium Den ✕
79 George Street
(Oxford 48680)
Open: Mon–Sat 12noon–2.30pm,
6–12mdnt, Sun 1–2.30pm, 6–12mdnt
C F P S

Don't let the name discourage you, but the only addictive thing sold at the Opium Den is the food. Cantonese with a few Pekinese dishes, the specialities of the house are the sizzling dishes brought piping hot to your table on wooden platters. Lunchtimes are always busy, with a table d'hôte menu available at around £2.50. The à la carte is extensive, with prices to suit all pockets. Set dinners are particularly reasonable at around £6–£7 for two people.

PAINSWICK

The Painswick Hotel, Kemps Lane
(4m N of Stroud on A46)
(Painswick 81160)
Open: Mon–Sun 12.30–2pm
C P

This elegant hotel with a country-house atmosphere is recommended here for its buffet luncheon and traditional Sunday lunch. The buffet is laid out in an anteroom to the comfortable bar lounge which overlooks the garden. You can choose from the hot dish of the day (which could be lasagne, canelloni, boeuf bourguignon or steak and kidney pie) with vegetables at £2.50 or cold meats and salads also at £2.50. Dessert with fresh cream is 65p and coffee 35p. The buffet is not served on Sunday. The three-course Sunday lunch is £5.45 (children under 12 £4).

READING

Beadles Wine Bar, 83 Broad Street
(Reading 53162)
Open: Mon–Sat 10.30am–2.30pm,
5.30–10.30pm
C F S

This popular basement wine bar is situated on the one-time site of Simmonds Brewery and the original globe lights are still a splendid feature. An interesting selection of food includes 'snacks for the peckish or starters for the starving' such as taramasalata at around £1.40. Main courses served with salad could be roast beef, turkey, chicken, dressed crab or prawns, depending on their availability or a hot dish such as prawn risotto (£1.60) or pork in a cream and mushroom sauce, served with courgettes and potatoes at around £2.45. Delicious home-made sweets follow.

The George Hotel ★★
King Street
(Reading 53445)
Open: Mon–Sun 12noon–2.30pm,
6–11.30pm, Sun 7–11pm
S

The historic, timbered George Hotel complete with cobbled courtyard and stagecoach has obscure origins, but appears in a rent roll dated 1578. Today it boasts four steak bars of distinctive character. The Cocked Hat, Pickwickian and Cavalier Grills and Rib Room offer an excellent selection of grills and roasts. Half a roast duckling with apple sauce and jacket potatoes is very good value at around £5.50–£6 – this includes a choice of sweets or cheeses.

Heelas Restaurant, Broad Street
(Reading 55955)
Open: Tue–Sat 9.30am–5pm, 6.30pm, Thu, 5.30pm Sat
P S

Still a haven in one of Reading's most popular department stores, but now relocated and newly built on the second floor. Heelas' licensed restaurant offers a relaxing break from the hustle of a busy day's shopping. Predominantly green and white décor with lots of leafy green plants is complemented by the classy contemporary prints which line the walls. Smart waitresses provide swift service and the food tastes all the better for being served on modern Wedgwood bone china. There are meals to suit everyone, from a half portion of fish and chips for children and a Danish open sandwich, piled high with meat or cheese and salad, for the weight-conscious to the Chef's choice roast beef and Yorkshire pudding. This meal is the most expensive but even with three courses and coffee you could still have change from £5.

Mama Mia, 11 St Mary's Butts
(Reading 581357)
Open: Mon–Fri 12noon–2.30pm,
6–9.30pm, Fri 10pm, Sat 12noon–10pm
C F P S

The trattoria Mama Mia serves only Italian food and wines in an almost operatic setting of rough-cast, white-painted walls, crowned by rafters hung with clusters of Chianti bottles and strings of onions and other vegetables. Home-made soups at around 85p, pastas and pizzas from around £1.90, offer excellent value, although penny- and weight-watchers are advised to resist the entrées.
See advert on page 78

Sweeney and Todd, 10 Castle Street
(Reading 586466)
Open: Mon–Sat 11am–3pm,
5.30–10.30pm, Fri–Sat 11pm
P S

Through the Victorian pie shop, up sawdust-strewn steps, is this small saloon-type restaurant, with church-pew seating, copper curtain-rails and gilt globe lighting. Meals are also served below in the cellars. Lunchtime specials such as roast suckling pig cost around £2.50, with fresh vegetables from 40p. Imaginative home-made pies about

---

6-8 St. Michael's Street
Oxford OX1 2DU

*Famous for good food.
A lunch under £5.*

Salads, fruit tarts, cakes made on the premises.

The Nosebag

*Open daily 10.30-5.30
Except Sunday 12.00-5.30
and Fri/Sat Evening
6.30-9.30*

Your pre-theatre meal

Oxford 721033

77

£1.20–£1.60 include steak and oyster, kidney and fennel and poachers (mixed game). 'Vicars' lunches consist of a plate of cold meat with French bread, pickles and salad and they set you back around £2. Home-made treacle tart, apple pie and crumble and fresh fruit with cream are some of the home-made desserts on offer for 65p–80p.

REDBOURN
Aubrey Park Hotel ☆☆☆
Hemel Hempstead Road, Redbourn,
St Albans
(Redbourn 2105)

Redbourn
—
Rickmansworth

Open: Ostler's Room Sun–Sat
12.30–2pm, 7–10pm, Sat 7–10.30pm
C F P ♠

The warmly-glowing Ostler's Room, with its glazed brickwork and low-beamed ceilings, is dedicated to the serving of traditional English dishes in an atmosphere of medieval jollity. A wholesome three-course meal can be picked from a choice of kitchen-garden broth or Whitby mix (prawns, crabs and mussels in a cocktail sauce), followed by deep dish steak and kidney pie, braised beef in stout, or Studham spatchcock (whole baby chicken in a piquant sauce) and finishing with pastries and puddings from the cook's pantry.

RICKMANSWORTH
The Chequers Restaurant
21 Church Street
(Rickmansworth 72287)
Open: Mon–Sun 12noon–2pm,
7–10.30pm
C ♠

The Chequers Restaurant, built in 1580, is the oldest building in this old town.

You must come to
Mama Mia
The authentic Italian Restuarant — Pizzaria
Has a relaxing atmosphere which lets you enjoy the specialities of typical Italian cuisine rich in tradition and fantasy.
A little bit of Italy in the very heart of Reading.
All dishes prepared in front of you.
Only Italian wines.
Excellent choice of menus from Pizza to Pastas from Scampi to Steaks.
11 ST MARY'S BUTTS, READING. Telephone 581357

COTSWOLD CAFE & RESTAURANT
THE GREEN, BROADWAY, WORCS.
Telephone: Broadway 85 3395
Enquiries: Mrs. SUSAN WEBB

Morning Coffee - Luncheons - Afternoon Teas - Grills
Parties Catered For - Home-Made Ice Cream - Suppers
(In Summer Season - Sat. & Sun Only) Table Licence.

SWEENEY & TODD

famous pies
fine cuisine
real ale

Retail Shop
8.30a.m. - 5.30p.m.
Restaurant
12p.m. - 3p.m. and 5.30p.m. - 10p.m.
Bar
10.30a.m. - 2.30p.m. and 5.30p.m. - 10.30p.m.
Extra ½ hour Friday/Saturday p.m.

10 Castle St., Reading.
Tel: 586466

Another Four Pillars Group venture, the menu and prices are comparable with those at the Pinner restaurant, though during any particular week the actual dishes available are different. There is a separate, more expensive steak menu. A table d'hôte lunch is available at about £2.50 a head.

ST ALBANS

Black Lion Hotel, Fishpool Street
St Michaels Village
(St Albans 51786/64916)
Open: Mon–Fri 12noon–2pm, 7–10pm,
Sat 12noon–2pm, 7–10.30pm,
Sun 12noon–2.30pm

C P &

Modernisation has not stripped the interior of its character and old beams and brickwork abound. In the bar an impressive cold buffet is on display for £2.50 and a hot dish of the day such as Irish stew costs around £2. A table d'hôte menu in the restaurant is priced by the main dish – from about £5 for lamb sweetbreads with banana or fillet of plaice bonne femme to nearly £6 for escalope of chicken Viennoise or roast pork. Appetisers include corn on the cob, ham and cottage cheese coronet and a selection of home-made soups. Choice from the sweet trolley is good.

St Albans
—
Theale

Tudor Tavern, 28 George Street
(St Albans 53233)
Open: Mon–Sun 12noon–2.30pm,
6–11pm

C ♫ P &

The special thing about Berni is that it restores and preserves some of this country's most attractive old buildings. The Tudor Tavern is the oldest complete half-timbered building in the ancient city of St Albans. Many main-dish prices here include tomato soup to start, roll and butter, and ice cream or cheese and biscuits to follow, so an 8oz rump steak with chips, tomato and peas at about £5 is just in our price range.

STOW-ON-THE-WOLD

Old Farmhouse Hotel, Lower Swell 1½m
W of Stow-on-the-Wold on A436
(Stow-on-the-Wold 30232)
Open: Mon–Sat 12.15–2pm,
Sun 12.30–2pm

C P &

A charming and personally run small hotel noted here for its bar lunches and 'Swell Suppers' and also for Sunday lunch at £6. The bar lunches include a range of fried fish dishes, omelettes, salads and sandwiches all at under £3.

The 'Swell Supper' menu has some similar dishes and also includes trout at £3.75 and sirloin steak at £6 which is the most expensive dish. There are a selection of sweets at 75p, coffee and mints are 60p.

THAME

The Coffee House, 3 Buttermarket
(Thame 6302)
Open: Mon–Tue, Thu–Sat 10am–5pm

♫ P S &

This charmingly decorated restaurant with its pine furniture, white walls, large open fireplace and green plants was opened in 1979. Appetisers include home-made pâté with brandy, served with French bread (the most expensive starter at around £1.50), main courses include spaghetti bolognese made with wine, pizza and a daily special such as cottage pie or chicken and ham pie all for around £2.50. Desserts include chocolate rum mousse for around 85p.

THEALE

Red Peppers, 21 High Street
(Reading 303408)
Open: Tue–Thu 12noon–2pm,
7–9.30pm, Fri & Sat 12noon–2pm,
7–10pm

C P S &

---

198 Fishpool Street, St Michaels Village, St Albans.
Telephone: St Albans 51786/64916

Superb cuisine in a charming setting . . .

Ideally situated in the peaceful old Roman area of St Albans, the Black Lion Hotel on Fishpool Street — noted for its charm and wealth of Georgian architecture — offers the best of comfort, together with a varied cuisine of an unusually high standard, maintained by a well trained and friendly staff.

Old Farmhouse Hotel
Lower Swell, Cheltenham.
Telephone: Stow on the Wold 30232

Sixteenth century Cotswold farmhouse set in the centre of the picturesque village of Lower Swell, 1 mile west of Stow on the Wold. Full central heating, individually furnished bedrooms with colour TV. Choose from dinner menu or à la carte suppers. Weekday bar lunches in the lounge bar and garden.

We had a very enthusiastic report from the AA inspector who visited Red Peppers. Things start looking good from the moment you sit down and are offered crudités. The atmosphere created by proprietors Guy and Lynne Symons is spontaneous and warm, the food is freshly cooked, home-made and generously apportioned. The hot stuffed mushrooms at £1.15 are a house speciality and highly recommended as a starter. There is something about a well-prepared lamb cobbler at £3.50 that beats any fancy foreign dish, but do save space for the rather special banana split at £1.25, or a choice from the selection of pies and puddings at 90p. House wine is 70p a glass.

TURVEY

The Chicery, The Laws Hotel, on the A428 from Bedford to Northampton
(Turvey 213)
Open: Mon–Thu 12noon–1.45pm, 7–9.30pm, Fri–Sat 12noon–1.45pm, 7–10pm

A new concept in eating-out, the Chicery offers a limited menu based on gas-fired lava-brick grilling of chicken, cooked with various home-made sauces including Tandoori, Barbecue, Sunshine and Piri-Piri. Plain grilled pork chop, rump steak and chili con carne are also available. The décor is a garden theme of white and green, with metal garden chairs, paving-

Turvey
—
Windsor

stone-type lino, green garden trellis round the walls with tablecloths to match help to give it an outdoor atmosphere. Start off with pâté, soup or grapefruit cocktail at under £1, chicken tandoori, or chicken piri-piri at £2.75 and, if you have a sweet tooth, chocolate fudge cake or meringue glacé at 75p.

WALTHAM CROSS

Sour Grapes, 41b High Street
(Lea Valley 718633)
Open: Mon–Thu 11am–2.30pm, 7–10.30pm, Fri–Sat 11am–2.30pm, 7–11pm, Sun 7.30–10.30pm

P S

Situated close to the 'cross', this attractive wine bar has maps of French vineyards on the walls and distinctive wooden tables and chairs making it a relaxed and casual rendezvous for lunch or dinner. The blackboard menu offers a hot 'dish of the day', pizzas and salads all for about the £2 mark, and a sweet to finish with costs around £1. Service is friendly and efficient and in fine weather you can enjoy your food in the peaceful garden at the rear.

WELWYN GARDEN CITY

Toby Food and Wine Bar, 49 Wigmores North
(Welwyn Garden City 26663)
Open: Mon–Sat 11.30am–2.30pm, Wed–Sat 6.30–11pm

C F P S

Striking artwork and an attractive brown awning identify Toby's, where Eric and Elsa Norris both do the cooking for their popular wine bar. Dishes may include smoked mackerel at about £1.25, beef casserole for around £2.45 and home-made apple pie and fresh cream for about 75p. The Victorian décor of this first-floor, split-level bar, with its genuine mahogany bar front is an ideal background for enjoyment of both food and excellent wine. Downstairs, the Toby Grill serves breakfast.

WINDSOR

The Drury House Restaurant, 4 Church Street
(Windsor 63734)
Open: Tue–Sun 12noon–5.30pm

In this charming 17th-century setting, within a stone's throw of the guardsmen at the gate of the Castle, Joan Hearne serves good, plain English food at no-nonsense prices, with a choice of salads from around £2.50 and of main dishes from £2.50 for grilled lamb's liver and

AA TAKE THE SCENIC ROUTE EVERY TIME

- 26 major routes covering England, Scotland and Wales
- More than 5,000 miles of planned alternative routes
- Easy-to-follow maps and route descriptions
- Approx 400 colour photographs showing the best of 'unknown Britain'
- Illustrated features on beautiful countryside areas

On sale at AA shops and major booksellers

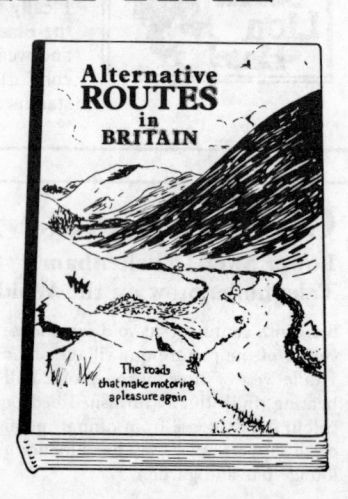

bacon, to around £5 for three courses. Omelettes cost around £1.50. Home-made gâteaux are on sale.

London Steak House, 10 Thames Street (Windsor 66437)
Open: Mon–Sat 12noon–3pm, 6–11pm, Sun 12.30–3pm, 6.30–10.30pm
C S

Handily placed for a visit to Windsor Castle, this busy restaurant, although small, has refreshingly uncluttered floor space. Traditional-style wall-lights interspersed with framed prints make for a pleasant enough décor. A well-cooked meal such as onion soup (75p), lamb cutlets (£2.95) and ice-cream (75p) sounds reasonable, but you'll need to add about £1 for vegetables.

WINGFIELD

The Plough Inn, off the A5120 near Toddington
(Toddington 3077)
Open: Mon–Sat 12noon–2pm, 6–10.30pm, Sun 12noon–2pm, 7–10.30pm
P

A good place to stop when the weather's good, this Whitbread pub dating from the early 17th century is in pleasant countryside between Houghton Regis and Toddington, and has a garden. A fairly conventional choice of lunches is available Monday to Saturday (roasts,

Wingfield — Woolhampton

steak, fish, etc), but excellent value. Apart from peas, only fresh, local vegetables are served. Interesting specialities such as venison pie make filling main courses.

WINSLOW

The Bell Hotel, Market Square (Winslow 2741)
Open: Mon–Sun 11.30am–2pm, 6–9.30pm
C P S

Musical church bells provide an authentic background to the peaceful, historic atmosphere of the heavily-timbered and balustraded Claydon Restaurant of this 17th-century hotel. The table d'hôte menu in the restaurant offers three courses plus coffee for around £4. Tournedos Val Prais is an enterprising main course, and fresh strawberries and cream are served as a dessert when in season. The Wineslai Bar serves a good selection of grills including steak garni at about £3.25 or lamb chop, pork chop or plaice for around £2.50. French fries and chips are included. A lunch special with vegetables of the day costs about £1.75.

WOOLHAMPTON

The Rowbarge, Station Road (Woolhampton 2213)
Open: Mon–Sun 12noon–2pm, 7–9pm
P

Character actor Lawrence Naismith presides over this low-ceilinged inn. The menu changes every day, but excellent examples are home-made rissoles in wine gravy with sauté potatoes or haddock Monte Carlo (served with parsley and egg sauce, poached egg and sauté potatoes). Prices range from around £2, and a good meal should not cost much more than £5.

TELEPHONE NUMBERS

In some areas telephone numbers are likely to be changed by British Telecom during the currency of this publication. If any difficulty is experienced when making a reservation it is advisable to check with the operator.

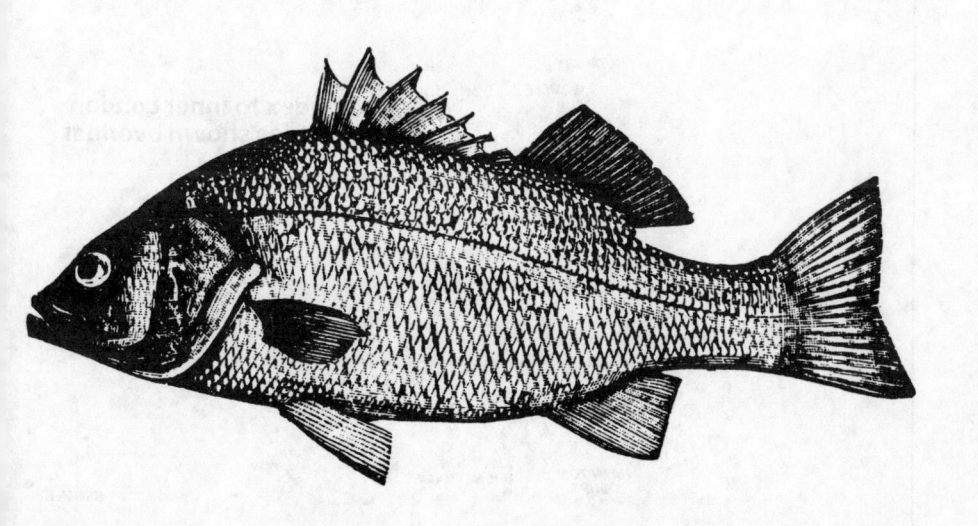

LONDON

A newcomer to London may find it helpful to realize that it used to be two adjacent cities: the City of Westminster and the City of London itself. They were surrounded by villages. Indeed, as recently as a couple of centuries ago, you could set off from what is now the West End and walk to Chelsea along a footpath with fields on either side. The tide of building has, of course, overwhelmed the countryside, and the result is a metropolitan colossus about ten miles from one end to another.

Nevertheless, if you look for them, you can still discern traces of the villages: the urban sprawl has simply welded them together. Each has its own characteristics, its own little shops, and its own eating places. Hampstead people call a corner of what is almost a town in its own right 'the village'. Neighbouring Highgate makes no bones about it: the pretty part on top of the hill is commonly referred to as 'Highgate Village'. Even in Soho, you can find such homely touches as a local ironmonger amid the more exotic retail outlets.

Soho, apart from its slightly sinister reputation, is widely regarded as the cosmopolitan centre of the capital: the place where you are most likely to find foreign

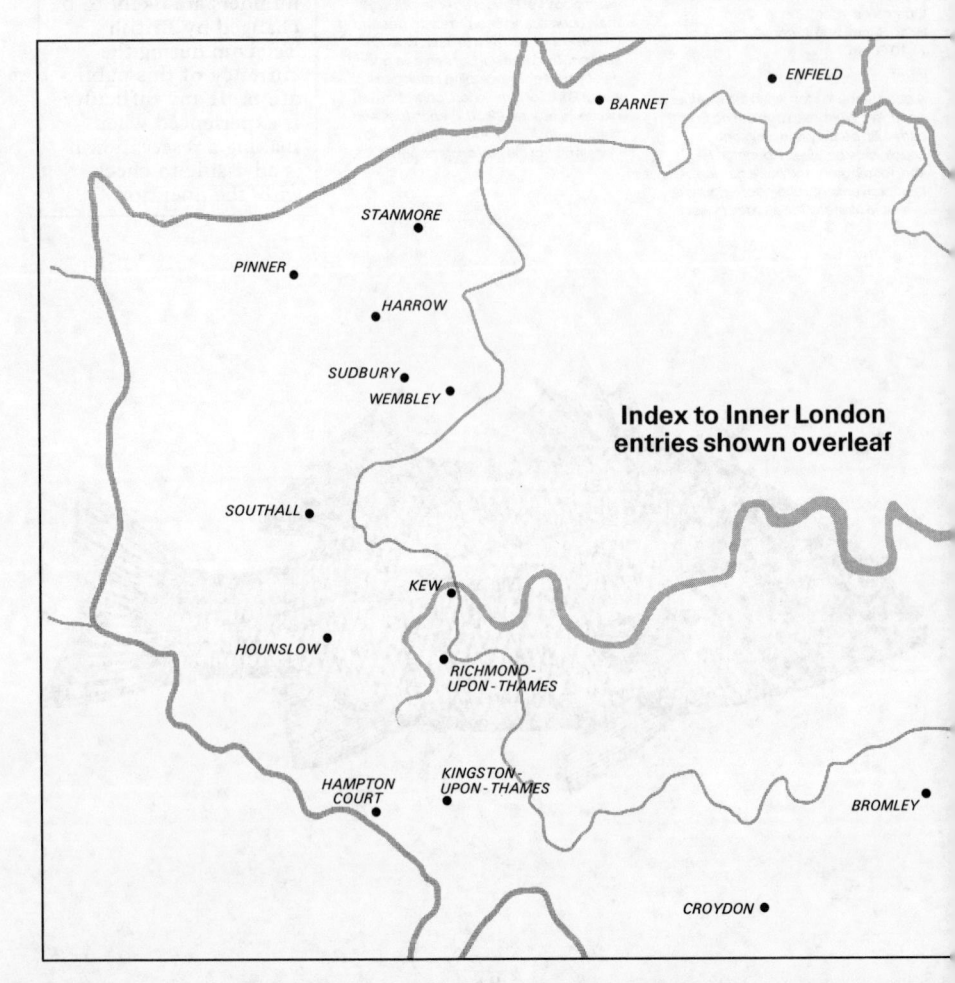

Index to Inner London entries shown overleaf

restaurants. This dates back to the end of the 17th century, when Huguenot refugees from France settled in the fields and built homes for themselves.

London, like everywhere else, undergoes changes from time to time. When they are first mooted, conservationists are apt to decry them vociferously, and when, for example, it was decided to move the fruit and vegetable market away from Covent Garden, many observed that London would never be the same again. Well – it wasn't. In this respect, it was rather better. Not the least of the new enjoyments are cafés where you can sit out of doors in pleasant surroundings.

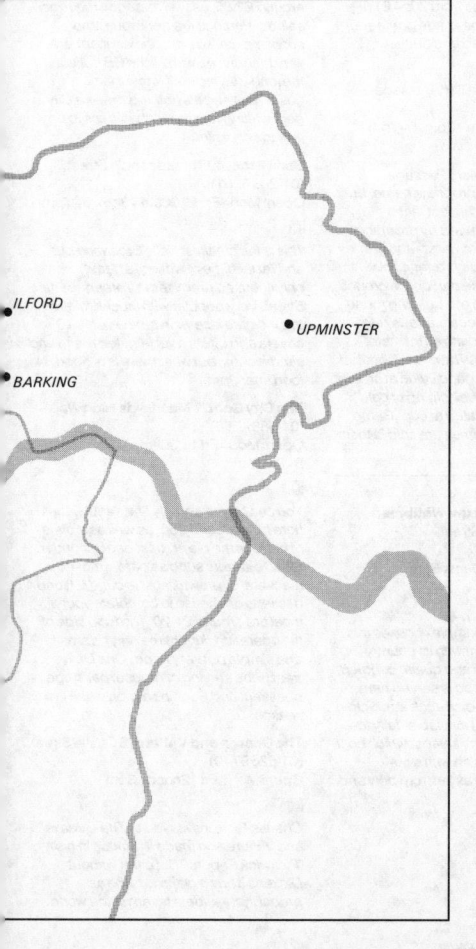

Over on the eastern side of the metropolis, Greenwich – with the National Maritime Museum, the Royal Naval College, the Royal Observatory, and the *Cutty Sark* – is the storehouse of knowledge concerning the sea, ships, and the meridian. Indeed, according to our calculation, it is possible in one bar to buy your drink in the eastern hemisphere, cross over longtitude 0°, and consume it in the western. This particular tavern, the Trafalgar, used to be a gathering point for Members of Parliament who, once a year, travelled down the Thames to indulge themselves at a whitebait (baby herrings) feast. The fish were caught in the river a few yards away.

Nowadays, they have been expelled by pollution, but don't be too disappointed. They are still alive and well at Southend near the mouth of the estuary. March to August is the season if you prefer it fresh (like almost everything else, it comes frozen all the year round). Other shellfish much loved by Londoners are cockles and winkles – and stalls still sell them. Jellied eels are hard to come by, but these, too, survive, particularly in the East End.

Since somebody once wrote a music hall song entitled *Boiled Beef and Carrots*, we must assume that this dish used to be a favourite with Londoners, though you will find little evidence of it today. Roast sucking pig was also much enjoyed. Again, if you ask the average waiter whether it is available, the answer is likely to be 'No'. As for swan pie, you can forget all about it. Queen Anne, admittedly, was very fond of it – especially when the birds were larded with bacon. But the attitude to swans has changed since them.

Of the West End clubs, the Reform has given its name to a lamb cutlet dish; Bootles – so *very* exclusive – to a cream pudding. At a slightly lower social level, you can always settle for sausages and mash (and probably find them).

Greater London Index

		Page
Inner London	E1	84
	EC1	84
	EC2	84
	EC4	85
	N1	86
	N6	86
	N8	86
	NW1	86
	NW3	86
	NW8	86
	SE1	86
	SE3	87
	SE9	87
	SE10	87
	SE19	88
	SW1	88
	SW3	88
	SW6	89
	SW7	89
	SW8	89
	SW11	89
	SW15	89
	SW16	90
	SW19	90
	W1	91
	W2	92
	W3	92
	W4	92
	W5	92
	W8	92
	W9	92
	W11	93
	W12	93
	WC1	93
	WC2	93
Outer London		94

Inner London
E1 – EC2

E1

Nick's Place, 137 Leman Street
(01-488 9908)
Open: Mon–Fri 10am–11pm,
Sat 6–11pm, Sun 12noon–3pm,
6–10.30pm

C🍴

You have heard of French and Italian bistros, and here is the first English bistro which offers good home cooking using traditional British recipes. The lunch menu offers a variety of hot and cold food from substantial snacks to full meals. The evening menu offers a choice of 10 pies, all very different and four other dishes. All the main courses are £4 (including vegetables) except for royal venison pie at £4.50. Try the John Bull pie, a mixture of steak, mushroom and onion with a soft suet crust, or Fish Porters' pie, a fascinating Billingsgate fishmarket recipe. Starters range from 70p–£1 (we recommend the home-made game soup) and to finish, try bread and butter pudding at 75p.

Grapeshots, 2–3 Artillery Passage
(01-247 8215)
Open: Mon–Fri 11am–3pm, 5–7pm

C P S

For a wine bar in Artillery Passage Grapeshots is an appropriate name, but put out of your mind the fact that grapeshot was produced by dropping lead from a height into water – the grapes here are of a more fruity variety. This Davys of London wine bar, on the ground and basement floors of a building round the corner from Petticoat Lane, is rather on the small side but with an intimate, relaxed atmosphere. The menu is limited and largely cold but good value at around £2.20 for an enormous helping of cold meat, with a mixed salad at 60p. Game, salmon and strawberries are sold in their proper seasons.

EC1

The Coffee Shop at the Whitbread Brewery, Chiswell Street
(01-606 4455)
Open: Mon–Fri 8.30am–5pm
Sat 10am–5pm

🍴

The large brewery complex houses this bright little restaurant with its country-kitchen atmosphere and quaint cobbled courtyard. Simple food is served here, with at least one hot dish such as chicken à la king (around £2) available daily to supplement the many salads, which cost between £1–£2. Finish with a no-nonsense pud such as jam roly-poly and a cup of coffee.

EC2

Balls Bros, 6–8 Cheapside
(01-248 2708)
Open: Mon–Fri 11.30am–3pm, 5–7pm

C P S 🍴

This is a typical Balls Bros City outlet, with food at lunchtimes only, but an excellent wine list including some very reasonable half-bottles. The ground floor bar and basement restaurant serve satisfying snacks and sandwiches, a range of good salads and one hot dish daily, all from around £2–£3.50. This is a friendly and comfortable little bar, with a faithful following among City folk.

Balls Bros, Moor House, London Wall
(01-628 3944)
Open: Mon–Fri 11.30am–3pm,
5–7.30pm

C P

Don't look for an evening meal here, because you won't find it. The lunchtime menu is a typical one for the Balls Bros chain, with hot and cold dishes from around £2.85, as well as sandwiches and salads. Portions are generous, and service excellent, and the atmosphere very friendly. As with all the BB outlets, the long-staying staff know their customers and it's nothing to see a City gent waiting for 'his own' waitress to be free to serve him.

Balls Bros, 42 Threadneedle Street
(01-283 6701)
Open: Mon–Fri 11.30am–3pm, 5–7pm

C

This is the smallest Balls Bros wine bar and (at the time of writing, at least) the only licensed premises in Threadneedle Street. Very popular with stockbrokers, this intimate little wine bar has only 16 covers and offers a very limited menu and sandwiches, but what there is is good. No food after 3pm.

The City Boot, 7 Moorfields High Walk
(01-588 4766)
Open: Mon–Fri 11.30am–3pm,
5–8.30pm

C

You can buy extremely fine sandwiches here from around 95p, as well as a plate of ham, game pie or roast beef for under £2.50. Starters such as pâté, smoked mackerel or prawns cost around £1, and desserts or cheese to complete your meal are around £1.20. The food side of the operation (lunchtime only) is small and simple but very good. One Davys treat is the serving of grouse, partridge, pheasant and Scotch salmon when in season.

The George and Vulture, 3 Castle Street
(01-626 9710)
Open: Mon–Fri 12noon–3pm

C 🍴

Charles Dickens stayed at The George and Vulture and made it famous in his 'Pickwick Papers'. But even without Dickens it has a claim to fame as probably the oldest tavern in the world,

Inner London
EC2–EC4

for it is known to have existed in 1175 although only one wall remains of the old structure. The present building retains the Pickwickian aura and is almost a museum in its own right. You can't stay there now, but you can have a substantial lunch at a very reasonable price. There is a good selection of starters, most of them around £1. Fish and main courses (a good mixed grill, for example) are from £2.50, with vegetables extra. For a sweet there is, in season, fresh strawberry flan, and a variety of other items. Stilton cheese is recommended, but there is plenty of choice from the cheese board. The restaurant is available in the evening for private functions – just telephone for menu details.

EC4

Bow Wine Vaults, 10 Bow Churchyard
(01-248 1121)
Open: Restaurant Mon–Fri 12noon–3pm
Wine bar Mon–Fri 11.30am–3pm,
5–7pm

The minimum charge of £4 for lunch at the Bow Wine Vaults would buy you baked Scotch salmon with mayonnaise or perhaps you would prefer smoked poussin salad for around £3.50. Starters are priced from £1.20 for chilled watercress soup to £1.50 for smoked salmon mousse. Main courses include daily specials at around £2.90 – £3.90 and for a sweet you might choose chocolate and strawberry surprise or strawberry fool, at £1 or so. The restaurant is a converted warehouse with whitewashed walls, but a Victorian atmosphere is created by the furnishings and bric-à-brac. There is a good range of wines.

Corts, 33 Old Bailey
(01-236 2101)
Open: Mon–Fri 11.30am–3pm,
5–8.30pm

[C][♬][S]

Rub shoulders with lawyers (and possibly criminals too!) in this comfortable wine bar near the Central Criminal Court. Food at lunchtime is straightforward and enjoyable, with soup at about 80p, a selection of quiches, pies and cold meats for around £2 (potatoes and salad could add about £1), and cheesecake, chocolate gâteau or apple pie at £1 or so.

Mother Bunch's Wine House
Old Seacoal Lane
(01-236 5317)
Open: Mon–Fri 11am–3pm,
5.30–8.30pm

[C][P][S]

Under the railway arches in Old Seacoal Lane, hard by Ludgate Circus, this Davys of London wine bar does a nice line in Buck's Fizz at £2.50 a tankard. Food (do book for the place is extremely popular) is mostly cold but very tasty and good value. A generous plate of finest ham off the bone or game pie with mixed salad or hot potatoes can be had for under £2.50. Seafood is a speciality here. Starters and sweets are around £1.

Oodles, 31 Cathedral Place
(01-248 2559)
Open: Mon–Fri 11.30am–7pm

[P]

Although it's in a new building, this Oodles has succeeded in retaining the character of all the others, even though this branch is unlicensed. See under Marble Arch W2 for full description.

Slenders Wholefood Restaurant and Juice Bar, 41 Cathedral Place
(01-236 5974)
Open: Mon–Fri 8.30am–6.15pm

[♬][P][S]

Situated in a quiet backwater of the City, and with an equally quiet décor of natural brick, wood and hessian, Slenders is tremendously popular. There is seating for over 100 in separate booths. At lunchtime it is extremely busy. The menu is vegetarian and you can obtain a good wholesome meal for about £2. Everything is prepared on the premises, including the wholemeal bread. A good mixed

---

𝕹ick's 𝕻lace
FULLY LICENSED RESTAURANT

WE SPECIALISE IN BRITISH PIES MADE FROM OLDE TRADITIONAL RECIPIES
FULL TAKE-AWAY SERVICE AVAILABLE

Open: Monday to Friday from 10am. Last orders 11pm. Saturday from 6pm. Last orders 11pm.
Sunday from 6pm. Last orders 10.30pm.
Outside catering for 5 to 500 people

137 Leman Street London E1 8EY
Telephone: 01-488 9908
"It is wise to book"

In the shadow of St. Paul's overlooking the Paternoster Square

SLENDERS
WHOLEFOOD RESTAURANT AND JUICE BAR
41 CATHEDRAL PLACE, E.C.4

Delicious soups, salads, savouries, fresh fruit juices and home-baked wholemeal rolls and cake.
Fresh yogurt and farm produce daily. Quick self-service. Strictly vegetarian.
Seating for over 100 and all items to be taken away. One minute St. Paul's Underground.
Large car park nearby.

Open Monday till Friday 8.30am-6.15pm

01-236 5974

Inner London N1–SE1

salad or a hot dish such as vegetable and cheese flan or stuffed peppers costs about £1.30 for a portion, and sweets – chocolate mousse or fresh fruit salad are around 70p each.

N1
Grapes Wine Bar, The Mall, Camden Passage, Islington
(01-359 4960)
Open: Mon–Tue, Thu–Fri 12noon–3pm, 6pm–1am, Wed & Sat 12noon–1am
🎵 P

This sophisticated wine bar spills out on to a pretty verandah and subtle décor including cushioned 'milk churns' make it a most original haunt. On Saturdays you can enjoy live folk music or even a Noël Coward evening! Original dishes include aubergine Charlotte at around £2, chili con carne garnished with fresh apple for about £2, home-made desserts such as cheesecake and summer pudding.

N6
The Flask Tavern, 77 Highgate West Hill, Highgate Village
(01-340 3969)
Open: normal licensing hours
C P S 🍴

Built in 1663, The Flask Tavern has been the haunt of many interesting characters, including the legendary highwayman Dick Turpin and distinguished painters Hogarth, Morlane and Cruickshank. During the summer the natural wood tables, set out in the large stone courtyard, are constantly in use. You may eat a snack in one of the three popular bars, but if something more substantial is preferred, a good three-course meal can be had in one of the bars for around £3. Starters include soup or grapefruit, main course sauté kidneys, fried plaice, fried rock salmon or cod and shrimp Mornay. Dessert is a choice of ice creams or banana fritters.

N8
La Cresta Restaurant, 18 Crouch End Hill
(01-340 4539)
Open: Mon–Fri 12noon–3pm, 5.30–11.30pm, Sat 5.30–11.30pm
C P S

A family-owned-and-run restaurant, where a warm welcome is assured. The menu is mainly Italian, with a few English fish and steak dishes thrown in for good measure. Highly recommended is the house speciality of veal escalope valdostana – a marvellous concoction of ham, cheese, spaghetti and veal at about £3, and the freshly-baked poppy seed bread which complements every dish.

NW1
Sea Shell, 33–35 Lisson Grove
(01-723 8703)
Open: Tue–Sat 12noon–2pm, 5.30–10.30pm

Here is a fresh fish restaurant par excellence, where portion control has been abandoned in favour of customer satisfaction. A Rolls-Royce parked outside while its owner queues for a take-away cod and chips, or enjoys a quick sit-down meal in the small restaurant, is not an uncommon sight. Apart from the fried chicken, the menu is devoted entirely to fish such as plaice, cod, halibut, skate, lemon sole and Dover sole. An extremely satisfying meal can be had for around £3.50, including soup and sweet.

NW3
Cosmo, 45–46 Northways Parade, Finchley Road
(01-722 1398)
Open: Restaurant Mon–Sun 12noon–11.30pm, last orders, 10.45pm
Coffee shop Mon–Sun 8.30am–11pm
S

Mainly Continental food is served at this uncluttered restaurant with its large shop-front window. Try chilled fruit soup with macaroons for starters, then move on to Hungarian beef goulash with continental dumpling, or sweet and sour braised beef in a raisin sauce with red cabbage. The unadventurous might be relieved to know you can get good old egg, sausage and chips here too. Sweets include real Viennese apple strudel with whipped cream or crème caramel chantilly. Many well-known personalities can be seen here.

Pippin Restaurant, 83–84 Hampstead High Street
(01-435 6434)
Open: Mon–Sun 11am–12mdnt
C P 🍴

An enticing selection of vegetarian specialities in the shop window draws you into this interesting restaurant. Self-service operates – just collect a tray and have it laden with your choice from the list of items displayed on the wall menu. Everything is reasonably priced – salads, hot risotto, cauliflower cheese and delicious nut roast.

NW5
Edward's Bistro, 323 Kentish Town Road
(01-267 6956)
Open: Mon–Sat 6.30–11pm
C P S 🍴

Edward's Bistro was built around an old shop and the old shop front has been preserved inside the entrance. Wood panelled walls hung with paintings, a dark ceiling and gingham-covered lamps hanging over each table complete the effect. Dinner here is pricey but excellent value, including specialities such as pork and pineapple kebabs, ragoût of beef and pepper or garlic steak. An imaginative three-course dinner can be enjoyed for about £5. All desserts are served with lashings of cream.

SE1
Archduke, Concert Hall Approach, South Bank
(01-928 9370)
Open: Mon–Fri 10am–12mdnt, Sat 5.30pm–12mdnt
C 🎵 P 🍴

A skilful conversion of a railway arch, with the trains still rumbling along overhead. Elizabeth, Philip, and Colin Richmond have created a lively wine bar and restaurant, very popular both with local office workers and South Bank culture lovers. On the lunch menu, starters are around £1. The main courses are under £4: try the home-made pie, usually steak and kidney, or fisherman's pie at £2.85. There is also a daily 'special' and a cold table. Sweets are from £1.05 and coffee is 45p. Three-course meals are available in the evening, but for something different try the sausage dishes at under £4.

Royal Festival Hall Cafeteria South Bank
(01-928 3246)
Open: Mon–Sun 12noon–10.30pm
🎵 P

Good places to eat are few and far between once you're south of the river, so it's worth knowing that you can use the Festival Hall cafeteria whether you're attending a performance or not. Quite near to Waterloo Station and not far from Waterloo Bridge, the South Bank complex is aesthetically pleasing even to those who are not too keen on modern architecture. The uncrowded cafeteria overlooks the busy and perennially interesting Thames, and provides a pleasant place to relax and enjoy a meal. Each day there are two hot dishes costing around £2.50 as well as cold meats and salads, and home-made sweets and good coffee are served.

RSJ, 13A Coin Street
(01-928 4554)
Open: Mon–Fri 12noon–3pm, 7–11.30pm, Sat 7–11.30pm
C 🎵 P 🍴

Once a stable but for the last 30 years a cycle warehouse, this newly-converted restaurant occupies a prime position near to the West End and Covent Garden, as well as the South Bank. Decorated in smart brown and white, it is deservedly popular with business-people from the nearby offices. Starters include watercress soup and haddock mousse and main courses offer cold salmon-trout and calf's liver with avocado. For sweets, try Dutch apple pie, strawberries and cream or various sorbets.

Skinkers, 40–42 Tooley Street
(01-407 9189)
Open: Mon–Fri 11am–3pm, 5.30–8.30pm
C

Inner London SE3–SE10

Built into the railway arches under London Bridge, next door to the London Dungeons horror museum, Skinkers is beautifully cool in summer, very spacious and relaxed, and enormously popular with City folk and local business people. Décor, menu and wine list are in Davy tradition. The buffet offers starters from about £1, a plate of finest smoked ham, roast beef or game pie (all around £2), with a mixed salad at 60p or so. If you're going on the off-chance, get there early.

SE3

The Barcave Wine Bar, 7–9 Montpelier Vale, Blackheath
(01-852 0492)
Open: Mon–Sat 12noon–3pm, 5.30–11pm, Fri–Sat 12mdnt, Sun 7–10.30pm

Special feature of this wine bar is the pretty walled terrace garden on two levels with fountains, a fish pond and hanging plants – very restful on a summer evening. Listed on a blackboard are Today's Specials such as minute steak with chasseur sauce and new potatoes at £2.95, curry or cold chicken and salad at around £2.90. A printed menu offers a choice of eight starters from melon (about 60p) to pâté maison (about £1). Cold buffet includes excellent rare roast beef for around £1.70. Quiche or lasagne are examples from the hot buffet at about £1.50. Cheesecakes, gâteaux, trifles or fresh fruit salad are served, and cost from 90p.

Kate 2 Bistro, 121 Lee Road
(01-852 3610)
Open: Mon–Sat 12noon–2.30pm, Tue–Sat 7–10.30pm

The food at this simple bistro presided over by Kate Lee and Diana Willis was described as the 'most enjoyable meal tasted in over 30 years of eating out' by one of our inspectors. A varied menu includes mackerel fillets in sherry sauce as an appetiser at about £1.20, home-made quiche and mixed salad for around £3, scampi served with mixed salad at £3.85, or steak pizzaiola at around £4.60 as main courses, and a selection of delicious desserts which change daily as shown on the blackboard. Special portions are offered for children.

SE9

Bistro 22, 1 West Park, Mottingham
(01-851 2233)
Open: Mon–Sat 7–11.30pm

French posters, bright tablecloths and candles lend an authentic air to this unpretentious bistro, where the menus are written in French and English. A host of interesting dishes are on offer, but care will be needed if you are to pick three courses for around £5, since vegetables are individually priced. Try apple stuffed with cream, celery and nuts at less than £1, hot garlic bread (only about 25p), cocktail de fruits de mer – seafood in wine and cheese – around £3.85 with vegetables and syllabub au citron – about 85p.

Mellins Wine and Food, 90 Eltham High Street, Eltham
(01-850 4462)
Open: Mon–Sat 12noon–2.30pm, 7–11pm, Sun 7–10.30pm

Mellins the apothecary stood here for about 200 years and the wine bar has retained the signs, labels and display cases. An interesting menu offers hot or cold platters such as ham ratatouille or fish pie for about £2, chili con carne or moussaka for about £2.15, and goulash, chicken basquaise or pork'n peppers for close on £3.50. Banana mousse is one of the many tasty desserts.

SE10

Bar du Musee, 17 Nelson Road, Greenwich
(01-858 4710)
Open: Mon–Sat 12noon–3pm, 6.30–11pm, Sun 12noon–2pm, 7–10.30pm

This wine bar is on two levels with a cellar bar reached by a spiral staircase. Coats of arms and Dickensian prints enhance the décor. There's a good choice of starters but try the soup of the day, with French bread, at around 95p. Hot dishes such as pizza and salad (around £2.50) or a 6oz pure beefburger with salad and French fries (about £2) are recommended. Beef or ham salads at around £2.75 are particularly good. Desserts include cheesecakes, gâteaux and profiteroles.

Davy's Wine Vaults, 165 Greenwich High Road
(01-858 7204)
Open: Mon–Fri 11.30am–3pm, Mon–Thu 5.30–10.30pm, Fri 5.30–11pm, Sat 12noon–3pm, 7–11pm

Under Davy & Co's head office building in Greenwich the old wine cellar is now used as a wine bar and eating house. Victorian touches add to the out-of-the-past aura and help to make this a most popular place. Davy's offer 'fine foreign wines' and 'rare ports of the finest vintages' to wash down their specialities such as avocado pear with prawns at just over £1.45, cold chicken cooked in red wine and spices at about £3.80, or the tempting fresh salmon salad at around £5.95. If you're looking for something slightly less expensive, why not try the cold buffet?

Diks, 8 Nelson Road, Greenwich
(01-858 8588)
Open: Mon, Wed–Sat 12noon–2pm, 7–11pm, Sun 12.30–3pm

Value for money is guaranteed at this delightful restaurant. Proprietor Dik Evans cooks all the food, even the bread rolls and mint fudge served with the coffee. The soup and pâté are served in terrines from which you help yourself to as much as you like. At lunch, three courses are priced by the main dish – veal scaloppini Viennoise with fruit juice and meringue glacé at £4.50.

Gachons, 269 Greek Road, Greenwich
(01-853 4461)
Open: Wed–Mon 10.30am–5pm, Thu–Sat 7–10.30pm

Kate 2 Bistro

121 Lee Road, Blackheath, London SE3 9DS

Proprietors: Kate Lee & Diana Willis

French-style candelit bistro —
Friendly and informal atmosphere —
Serving genuine home-cooked food at excellent value —
Licensed.

Reservations: Tel. 01-852 3610

Inner London
SE19–SW3

Young chef/proprietor Marc Gachon-Dyer says his cooking has been greatly influenced by his French mother, and he produces a Cordon Bleu Chef's Special (such as kidney sautéed in wine with fresh vegetables) every day to prove it. In fact, this quaint little coffee house, with its bright pine furniture, caters for the majority of tastes by offering a selection of pastries and salads (about £1.75) to supplement the substantial hot meals, such as home-made quiche and chicken vol-au-vent.

The Source, 106 Blackheath Road
(01-691 1010)
Open: Mon 12noon–3pm,
Tue–Sat 12noon–3pm, 7–11pm

[V][&]

Enthusiastic vegetarians, Keith and Norma Perry ensure that you enjoy wholesome, unadulterated food in pleasant surroundings – pine tables, a Welsh dresser and an old kitchen range set the scene for a gastronomic experience in healthy eating. Appetisers include stuffed vine leaves or mushrooms à la Grecque, both around 95p. The list of main dishes is no less interesting, with stuffed pepper and ratatouille costing about £2.50 and quiche with salad and potatoes at around £2. All the desserts, such as cinnamon apple cake, are around £1 and are served with fresh cream or yoghurt.

SE19

Joanna's, 56a Westow Hill, Upper Norwood
(01-670 4052)
Open: Mon–Fri 12noon–2pm,
6–11.15pm, Sat 6–11.30pm

[C][F][P][S][&]

Very appealing décor, with hanging plants, large photographs of film stars and smart check tablecloths, is complemented by an atmosphere kept fresh by two huge ceiling fans. Burgers are a speciality of the house – 100% beef served in a toasted sesame bun plus potatoes and fresh salad. There are six varieties – 'Gourmet' is dressed in wine and mushroom sauce. You can have a 6oz burger for around £2.95. There is also a good selection of prime steaks and 'specials' such as grilled jumbo shrimps at £3.95 and fried chicken with plum sauce at £3.65 (served with side salad and french fries). Starters and delicious desserts such as 'Joanna's Special' – hot waffle with maple syrup and whipped cream or ice cream sundaes are available at around £1.

SW1

The Green Man, Harrods, Knightsbridge
(01-730 1234)
Open: Mon–Sat 11.30am–3pm

[P][S]

They say that there's nothing you can't buy at Harrods – at a price, and that's true even when it comes to finding a tasty meal. Located next to the Men's Department, the air is distinctly pubby and masculine in the Green Man restaurant. Pleasant and fast service is one bonus to the excellent food, with seafood platter at around £5.25 the most expensive item on the menu. A cold buffet displays a choice of salads, cold meats and a very good game pie for about £3.90. Apple pie or cheesecake are examples of desserts.

Knightsbridge Spaghetti House,
77 Knightsbridge
(01-235 6987)
Open: Mon 12noon–3pm,
Tue–Fri 12noon–3pm, 5.30–10.30pm,
Sat 12noon–3pm, 5.30–11pm

[F][P][S][&]

This is the most famous of the Spaghetti Houses – six Italian restaurants specialising in pasta dishes. The menu is nearly the same throughout the group, with all the pastas and pizzas costing about £2 a portion. Also on the menu are fish and meat dishes, served with potatoes and another vegetable, or spaghetti, or rice, or salad. There's a good selection of starters, sweets and cheeses.

The Scallop Restaurant, Central Hall, Westminster
(01-222 3222)
Open: Mon–Sat 12noon–2.30pm,
3.15–5.30pm

Occupying the whole of the basement under the vast Central Hall, The Scallop caters for large numbers yet manages to present well-cooked, appetising food at modest prices. The à la carte menu includes grills and omelettes, all (except steak) priced around £2, fish and chips or salad for under £2, and a selection of sweets priced around 70p. The special lunchtime menu offers soup or fruit juice at around 40p, a choice of five main courses such as a roast, steak and kidney pie or a pasta dish (costing in the region of £1.70, and a sweet at about 65p. There is also a three-course set lunch for around £3 which is very good value.

Strikes, 124 Victoria Street
(01-834 0644)
Open: Mon–Sun 11.30am–11.30pm

[C][S][&]

Just why a group of American-style eating houses should be named after a British general strike is hard to fathom, but arrive at Victoria Station feeling hungry and you may be glad to see a Strikes restaurant opposite the main exit. Inside, you'll find a long narrow room with tables along one side, decorated with pictures of the 1926 strike, and there's a staircase twisting down to a second dining area. Starters vary from soup at 60p to avocado pear and prawns at £1.45 and you may choose a main course from a wide selection of hamburgers (£1.65–£3.50), platters (fish and chips at £1.95 to minute steak, egg, mixed salad and chips at £3.15), steaks (up to £4.50), salads (£1.95 for tuna, or ham and cheese). Whichever you choose you'll be offered a choice of relishes and sauces at your table. Desserts are all variations on the theme of ice cream, and magnificent concoctions some of them are.

SW3

Le Bouzy Rouge, 221 King's Road, Chelsea
(01-351 1607)
Open: Mon–Sat 11.30am–3pm,
5.30–11pm, Sun 7–10.30pm

[F][S]

A wine and spirits shop on the ground floor and a wine bar in the basement is an excellent combination, and a useful place to find a few yards from Chelsea Antique Market (if you've any money left). Simple foods, such as pork sausage and butter beans and navarin of lamb, are served in ample portions for around £2, and salads are available, too. There is a good variety of wines, of course, with the house wine very reasonably priced. Large bags hanging from brass rods provide comfortable backrests to the bench seating. A welcome change is the background of classical music – piped, certainly, but nevertheless a soothing change from the roar of London's traffic.

Caravela, 11 Beauchamp Place, Chelsea
(01-581 2366)
Open: Tue–Sat 12noon–2.30pm,
Tue–Sun 7pm–1am

[C][F][P][S][&]

Delicious squid is served at this simple, semi-basement Portuguese restaurant, so if you're adventurous – or Portuguese – you'll enjoy such novel dishes as grilled squid or highly spiced pork chops, each for about £3.50. But there are less exotic dishes to choose from in a warm cosy atmosphere, with varnished wood slats cladding the ceiling, walls and arched alcoves. A fine model galleon on the bar, and pictures, continue the theme of ships and the sea. Victorian gentlemen would have loved the continually-changing view through the window, which is at ankle-level to the street. Watch the prices, too – vegetables are sometimes charged extra and there's a cover charge of 65p – but it's not expensive for this part of London and it may be useful to know somewhere which is open until 1am every day of the week.

Cheyne Walk Wine Bar, Pier House, 31 Cheyne Walk
(01-352 4989)
Open: Mon–Sat 11.30am–3pm,
6.30–11pm

[C][F]

Inner London SW6–SW15

Behind the graceful statue of David Wynn's 'Boy on a Dolphin' is a wine bar where you can eat until late evening (and drink until midnight) to the accompaniment of live piano music. The Victorian-style interior in shades of brown and hung with carriage lamps and old prints overlooks a splendidly romantic night view of the illuminated Albert Bridge. The chef provides tantalising starters, main courses such as hot Sussex smokie (smoked haddock in white wine sauce with cheese), or Russian lamb casserole for about £3, a range of salads and cold meats, and at the higher end of the price scale, fresh lemon sole for £3.75.

SW6

Crocodile Tears, 660 Fulham Road (01-731 1537)
Open: Mon–Sun 11.30am–2.30pm, 2pm Sun, 6.30–10.30pm

C S

This is no run-of-the-mill wine bar; the décor is original – with a stuffed crocodile dangling from the ceiling – and the food likewise. For an adventurous meal try the carrot and orange soup or gazpacho, both around £1, seafood kebab at about £3 and finish with ice cream gâteau or hot treacle tart with cream – a sweet sensation for around £1.50. All this will be served by pleasant waitresses who will bring you a freshly-ground coffee at 50p or so per cup. If you come here for the wine you won't be disappointed – there are 15 varieties served by the glass.

SW7

Daquise, 20 Thurloe Street, South Kensington
(01-589 6117)
Open: Mon–Sun 10am–12mdnt

S

Full meals can be obtained here at any time between midday and midnight, so if you fancy goulash for tea you can have it. You can buy a selection of other dishes at this Polish restaurant, from meat Pierozki – a savoury pasty – at about £2.20, to Wienerschnitzel at £3.20, as well as straightforward salads and omelettes costing around £1.60. Vegetables will add another 50p or so, and soup will cost about 65p. Ice cream and pastries are available if you want a sweet to finish the meal. From noon until 3pm, set-price two-course lunches are served. Soup, followed by meat Pierozki or stuffed aubergine, for instance, costs around £1.80. Desserts are mainly gâteaux (from 60p–£1). Downstairs there is a small licensed restaurant where the atmosphere is cosily intimate.

SW8

Atuchaclass, 24 Queenstown Road
Open: Mon–Sat 6.30–11.30pm

P S

An offshoot to the up-market 'Alonso's' (next-door-but-one), this intimate bistro certainly has a touch of class, from its quarry-tiled floor and a subdued lighting to its imaginative international cuisine and the excellence of its fresh vegetables. The prices are just about within our limit, which for this type of establishment is surprising in itself. How about this for a meal: chicken liver pâté with herbs, spinach and chutney; Indonesian lamb in pastry (pieces of lamb, prawns, rice, raisins, mushrooms, chutney, light curry sauce) served with a selection of fresh vegetables; raspberry sorbet and coffee.

SW11

Just Williams, 6a Battersea Rise
(01-223 6890)
Open: Mon–Sat 12noon–3pm, 5.30–11pm, Sun 12noon–2pm, 7–10.30pm

C P S

This intimate wine bar, with its pine display counter, colourful check tablecloths and rear garden for the summer months is enthusiastically managed by ex wine merchant Michael Walker. The blackboard menu lists interesting starters such as taramasalata, served with pitta bread for about £1. Hot dishes of the day include goulash and boeuf bourguignon at around £2.50. Desserts include cheesecakes and gâteaux such as passioncake – a delicious fantasy of walnuts, apples and cream – about 75p.

Le Grand Café, 25 Battersea Rise
(01-228 7984)
Open: Mon–Sat 12noon–3pm, 6pm–12mdnt, Sun 12noon–3pm, 6–11.30pm

C P

You can't miss this modern burger restaurant near Clapham Common: just look for the flashing lights at the entrance which reflect on the silver awning. There are three split-level dining areas and the décor is bright and modern. Starters range from soup at 90p to deep-fried clam strips at £1.60, there are also daily specials. The burgers are generally under £3 and there is a range of other dishes under £5. (Try the chicken Kiev at £3.50). For dessert try meringue delight at £1.45. Coffee is 35p and a glass of wine 85p.
See advert on page 90

SW15

La Forchetta, 3 Putney Hill
(01-785 6749)
Open: Mon–Thu 12noon–2.45pm, 6.30–11.15pm, Fri–Sat 6.30–11.30pm

C P

You'll find this bright little Italian restaurant at the bottom of Putney Hill. You can buy a cheap pasta dish here for around £1.60. A more elaborate meal could exceed budget but won't if you take care. Starters range from soup at about 90p to Parma ham and melon at around £2.60. Similarly, you could choose scampi alla provinciale at about £4 or piccatina al Marsala (veal escalope in Marsala) at about £3, or steak dishes at £4 or so. Vegetables add about 60p, and you can choose a sweet from the trolley or try zabaglione al Marsala – good value at around £1. There is a cover charge of 50p. A good place for a tête-à-tête dinner.

CHEYNE WALK WINE BAR
by the Albert Bridge

Balls Brothers Chelsea Wine Bar, where you can enjoy fine, quality wines and an imaginative selection of freshly prepared dishes in comfortable and stylish surroundings. Speciality traditional Sunday lunch.

OPEN SEVEN DAYS A WEEK   PRIVATE PARTIES CATERED FOR

31 Cheyne Walk, London SW3. (Tel: 01-352 4989)

Inner London SW16–SW19

Mr Micawber's, 147 Upper Richmond Road, Putney
(01-788 2429)
Open: Mon–Fri 12noon–3pm, 5.30–11pm, Sat 12noon–3pm, Sun 7–10.30pm

[♩][S]

There's sometimes a queue for food, but you won't have to wait too long for something to turn up in Mr Micawber's wine bar. You should be able to heed Mr Micawber's maxim about annual expenditure too, for food is very reasonably priced. Choice is limited; but there are hot casseroles, chili con carne and quiches as well as cold meats, pies and salads.

SW16

Mr Bunbury's Bistro, 1154 London Road, Norbury
(01-764 3939)
Open: Mon–Fri 12noon–2.30pm, 7–11pm, Sat 7–11pm, closed Sun

[C][♩][S]

A small bistro with Victorian décor and a cosy atmosphere enhanced by the oil lamps and old photographs and prints. Owner Kenneth Williams keeps busy in the kitchen preparing such delights as Bunbury pie (a large individual pie filled with lean chunks of beef, mushrooms, onions, and carrots topped with flaky puff pastry). The set lunch at around £5 is excellent value. Vegetables are plentiful and served in separate earthenware dishes; the puddings (always generous helpings) are home-made.

Rino's Restaurant, 82/84 Streatham High Road, Streatham
(01-769 7916 or 6033)
Open: Mon–Sun 12noon–3pm, 6pm–2am (dinner and dance)

[C][S]

A large regular clientele haunts this very busy Italian trattoria – and not just because Salvatore Polumba, one of the proprietors, otherwise known as Rino, is always chatting with the diners. The menu is very extensive – 14 starters and five soups offer an interesting choice including snails, tunny fish and Italian hors d'oeuvres. Pastas, pizzas and omelettes are around £1.85 and Rino's specialities, served with two vegetables of the day, include pollo principessa (chicken with white wine, cream and asparagus tips) or piccatina al Marsala (veal escalopes cooked in butter and Marsala wine) priced from around £3.30. Sweets such as zabaglione al Marsala (about £1), crêpes Suzette (around £2) or lemon sorbet (about £1), complete a very substantial meal. This restaurant does a roaring late-night trade.

SW19

The Crooked Billet, 15 Crooked Billet, Wimbledon Common
(01-946 4942)
Open: Mon–Fri, Sun 12noon–2.30pm, Fri–Sat 12noon–2.30pm, 7.30–10.30pm. Evening parties catered for

[C][♩]

A building which started life as a barn way back in the 15th century, is now an olde worlde restaurant, retaining some of the bygone features such as timbered beams and pillars. Fare is varied and at sensible prices. Starters range from 50p–£1.20, featuring egg mayonnaise and prawn cocktail. Of the main dishes, beef curry or steak pie with two veg are both good value at around £1.95, whilst huge egg or cheese salads are a snip at around £2.50. Home-made apple pie and Black Forest gâteau make delicious desserts from 90p.

Downs Wine Bar
40 Wimbledon Hill Road
(01-946 3246)
Open: Mon–Sat 12noon–3pm, Mon–Fri 5.30pm–2am, Sat 7pm–2am

[C][♩][S]

Unobtrusive décor gives an atmosphere of intimacy and informality, both in the cosy cellar bar, with its alcoves and dance floor, and in the ground floor bar, where one can take a quieter meal. A relaxed, friendly atmosphere, restful decor — and, if you want it, disco dancing, below decks. You'll love the food and excellent wines . . . and the very moderate prices. Discover Downs and you'll come back again and again. Open Mon.-Sat., until 2 a.m.

LE GRAND CAFÉ
25 BATTERSEA RISE LONDON SW11
TELEPHONE 01-228-7984

Open 7 days a week for lunch and dinner. Garden Terrace.
Business Lunches. Birthday Parties. Wedding Receptions.
Promotion Parties. Children Welcome.
"Probably the best cafe in the world"

'INNER LONDON' — BUT OUT OF TOWN . . .

. . . right next to Wimbledon's main shopping centre, but officially designated 'Inner London'. Who? What? Why, Downs famous Wine Bar and Restaurant where you can eat like a King without paying a King's ransom. At least 18 starters and 16 main dishes.

Downs

WINE BAR & RESTAURANT
40 Wimbledon Hill Road, SW19
(easy parking) **01-946 3246**

popular new addition is the flower garden restaurant bar for the long summer evenings. The menu is changed daily, but there's always a good selection of both hot and cold dishes. Pâté maison comes at around £1.15 while a variety of quiches and deep fried camembert cost slightly more. Hot dishes, such as chicken Kiev, scampi provençale and lamb kebab are around £3.50 but extremely tasty. House special is chicken caribbean which is stuffed with exotic fruit and served with rice at around £3.

W1

L'Artiste Musclé, 1 Shepherd Market
(01-493 6150)
Open: Mon–Sat 12noon–3pm, 5.30pm–12mdnt, Sun 7–11pm

[F][S]

In the heart of the Shepherd Market lies L'Artiste Musclé, a French wine-bar-cum-bistro in a 19th-century building which at first sight appears to be a well-populated junk shop. Closer inspection discloses that people are actually eating and drinking inside, though with a minimum of ceremony as they rub shoulders with anything from old chests to chamber-pots while doing so. The menu is short, but has a real French-peasantish flavour, with items such as jambon and quiche. Typical prices are about £2.95 for côte de porc or ragout d'agneau.

The Chicago Pizza Pie Factory
17 Hanover Square
(01-629 2669)
Open: Mon–Sat 11.45am–11.30pm

[F][S][♦]

This popular pizza restaurant has a very informal atmosphere, the walls lavishly decorated with Chicago memorabilia. The deep-dish Chicago-style pizza originated here: it has a thick crust and rich filling based on mozzarella cheese. Don't go alone however, as the smallest serves two – and is priced accordingly (around £4.50). If you think you can tackle more than a pizza, start with savoury stuffed mushrooms with sherry and garlic and finish with a delicious cheesecake. Owner Bob Payton's great passion, second after pizzas, is music and a sophisticated stereo system keeps his customers entertained while they wait the customary 30 minutes for their culinary masterpiece to appear from the kitchen.

Downs Wine Bar, 5 Down Street
(01-491 3810)
Open: Mon–Sat 12noon–3pm, 5.30pm–12mdnt, Sun 12noon–3pm, 7–11.30pm

[C][F][P][S][♦]

A wine bar situated in an 18th-century backwater of Mayfair might be expected to price itself into the millionaires-only class, so it is a pleasant surprise to find that a dinner for £5 is eminently possible at Down's. True, one could choose a more expensive meal, but with a starter of smoked mackerel at about £1 or rough country pâté at £1.75, a daily special

Inner London
W1

(barbecued spare ribs for instance) or trout costing about £3 with vegetables and a sweet such as cheesecake averaging £1.20, even the addition of the 10% service charge does not take us over the top. There is also a well-stocked 'downstairs' cold table.

Granary, 39 Albemarle Street
(01-493 2978)
Open: Mon–Fri 11am–9pm, Sat 11am–2.30pm

[S]

Baskets of ferns and air-conditioning create a fresh, cool atmosphere in which to enjoy your meal in this delightful restaurant. Choose what you fancy from the tempting array of food on display, and one of the attentive waiters will carry it to your table. The menu is chalked up and is sure to include a choice of nine main dishes, all at around £2–£2.55. Prawn provençale, beef Stroganoff and steak and kidney pie are likely choices. Salads are less than £1, and there is a delicious array of sweets priced at about 95p.

Ikaros, 36 Baker Street
(01-935 7821)
Open: Mon–Sat 12noon–3pm, 6pm–12mdnt

[C][F][S][♦]

This small Greek restaurant has an authentic air. The charcoal grill wafts the most delicious smells to the diner and gives a flavour to the food not found in normal cooking. An interesting Greek starter such as taramasalata or longaniko sausage costs around 85p, and main dishes include doner kebab at around £3 and moussaka at £2.95. Vegetables cost about 60p a portion and sweets come from 75p. This is another restaurant where it would be all too easy to exceed the limit, but for central London the prices are not unreasonable.

Lord Byron Taverna, 41 Beak Street
(01-734 0316)
Open: Mon–Sat 12noon–3pm, 6pm–3.30am, closed Sat lunch

[C][F][S]

'You have to kiss a helluva lot of frogs before you find Prince Charming'. This is just one of the thousands of comments that decorate the walls and ceiling of this Greek taverna. Hardly Byronic, but most of the graffiti are quite amusing, and if you can think up something better you are welcome to add your piece. The restaurant premises were once lived in by Canelotto, the Venetian painter, and there is a blue plaque to commemorate this above the entrance. Food is almost entirely Greek, starters including a special variety of taramasalata and avgolemono (chicken soup with egg, lemon juice and rice), either costing about 70p. Most of the main course dishes are priced around £2 but salad and other vegetables are charged extra.

There is a wine bar in the cellars serving Greek wines, moussaka and kebabs are at around £1.

Rasa Sayang, 10 Frith Street
(01-734 8720)
Open: Mon–Sat 12noon–3pm, 6pm–12mdnt

[C][F][S]

Attentive waiters at this cool, airy South East Asian restaurant, with its tasteful wood and wicker décor, will help you to select dishes from the intriguing menu. Starters include a variety of soups and a host of main courses is offered – seafood, chicken, beef, pork and vegetarian dishes. Speciality of the house is 'satay' – tender skewers of chicken and beef marinated in Malaysian spices, gently grilled and served with fresh cucumber, rice cakes and a rich savoury peanut-based sauce – all this for not much more than £2. Desserts costing around £1 include kolak pisang – banana slices in coconut milk sweetened with brown sugar or seasonal fresh fruits. Side dishes are extra, so you will have to select with care to remain within the budget.

Ristorante Alpino, 42 Marylebone High Street
(01-935 4640)
Open: Mon–Sat 12noon–11.30pm

[C][F][S][♦]

A typical Alpino this, with décor in the chalet style; skis on the wall, and the standard Alpino menu including scampi and escalopes of veal cooked in Marsala, both at just over £3. A three-course meal can cost under £6. A very friendly little restaurant, managed with Italian flair and Italian charm. An accordionist plays light music to aid the digestion of the supper trade. Madame Tussaud's is close by.

Ristorante Alpino, 102 Wigmore Street
(01-935 4181)
Open: Mon–Sat 12noon–11.30pm, Sun 7–11.30pm

[C][F][P][S][♦]

This is the Alpino for Oxford Street shoppers, with a small front section for afternoon teas, a main restaurant of about 60 covers and a side rear room with 50 more. The gâteaux for all the Alpinos are made in the patisserie beneath this particular restaurant and very good they are. 'My Black Forest gâteau is the best in London' the pastry cook has been known to boast, and no one – but no one – argues with a Sicilian pastry cook.

The Rose Restaurant, Dickins and Jones, Regent Street
(01-734 7070)
Open: Mon–Sat 11.30am–3pm, 3.15–5.15pm

[C][S][♦]

Judging by the starched linen tablecloths, heavy cutlery, thick carpets and cool, green plants hanging in baskets from the elegant supporting pillars, Dickins and Jones work hard to maintain the old traditions. There is both a

Inner London W2–W9

cold carvers table at around £5.75 (including sweet), and a hot carvers table for £6.50 (including sweet). Ask your waitress for a voucher, and choose what you fancy from roast rib of beef or roast lamb and veg, fish and salads. In addition, there are the hot dishes of the day such as chicken kebab £3.60, or fillet of plaice with French fried potatoes for around £3.70, or a choice of grills such as Scotch entrecôte or lamb cutlets, with a mouth-watering selection of freshly-made gâteaux, trifles and pastries on the buffet, and a good range of ice cream-based sweets – none more than £1.

Swiss Centre Restaurants
Leicester Square
(01-734 1291)
Open: Mon–Sun 11.30am–12mdnt
Imbiss Snack Bar (entrance in Wardour St)
Open: Mon–Sun 8.30am–11.30pm

C F P S &

There are three separate restaurants at the Swiss Centre, each with its own décor and menu. Of these only the Chesa prices itself out of this book. The other two are predominantly Swiss in style and offer regional specialities, most of which are within our price range. Of special interest are the hors-d'oeuvres (which may be ordered either as an appetiser or as a main dish), herrings cooked in a number of intriguing ways, and a range of sausage meats, bread, ice cream gateaux and chocolates, all freshly-made on the premises. The Taverne specialises in Fondue, whilst the Rendez-Vous offers a range of Toggeburger (beefburgers), try the Appenzeller (with pineapple and Appenzeller cheese) at £3.30. The Imbiss Snack Bar offers sandwiches, salads and flans from £1.60.

W2

The Gyngleboy, 27 Spring Street
(01-723 3351)
Open: Mon–Fri 11am–3pm, 5.30–9pm

C S

The 'Gyngleboy' was a leather bottle, or black jack, lined with silver and ornamented with little silver bells 'to ring peales of drunkeness'. So now you know. Conveniently close to Paddington Station, this is a very superior wine bar offering a substantial choice of cold dishes – game pie, smoked chicken and smoked salmon specials, are among the choices. But start with the soup – that's piping hot. The cellar is extensive and there's a sophisticated range of château bottled vintages.

Oodles, 128 Edgware Road, Marble Arch
(01-723 7548)
Open: Mon–Sat 11am–9pm,
Sun 12noon–8pm

S &

You've got to hand it to Oodles Ltd. The name over its restaurants conjures up visions of plenty. And that's just what it offers – large helpings of nourishing country-style dishes, just like Mother used to make them. Casseroles, beef stew, chicken curries, steak pie, are all around £2, which with a modestly priced wholesome sweet and starter selection will keep the bill to about £5. This Oodles is the most recently opened of the five branches in London, and each has the same simple décor – rough wooden tables, bench seats, white stucco walls hung with wooden advertising plates such as used to be seen on horse-drawn delivery carts. See listing under EC4 and WC1 for other branches.

W3

North China, 305 Uxbridge Road, Acton
(01-992 9183)
Open: Mon–Thu, Sun 12noon–2pm, 5.30–11.30pm, Fri–Sat 12noon–2pm, 5.30–12mdnt

Proprietor Lawrence Lou specialises in Peking cuisine – particularly in Peking Crispy Aromatic Duck – a rare delight which can be enjoyed whole (around £11) or in portions (the smallest is about £3). Special dinners are on offer for two people at around £5.75 each – mixed hors d'oeuvres, spare ribs, Peking duck, prawns in chili sauce or sweet and sour pork, shredded beef, diced chicken with cashew nuts in yellow bean sauce and Chinese-style toffee apple or banana is one example. The usual baffling à la carte menu with hundreds of dishes is also astonishingly reasonable.

W4

Fouberts Wine Bar, 162 Chiswick High Road
(01-994 5202)
Open: Mon–Sat 12noon–3pm, 7–11pm

F S &

This is a small basement wine bar which uses both wooden and cast-iron furniture to give a slightly Bohemian air. Italian dishes such as lasagne (about £1.80) are good here, or if you prefer English no-frills food you can get steak and chips for around £3.50. Soup with roll and butter costs 50p or so. A large selection of wines includes several which can be bought by the glass for around 60p. Italian, German, French and Portuguese varieties prove popular with cosmopolitan visitors.

W5

Crispins Too Wine Bar, 46–47 The Mall, Ealing
(01-567 8966)
Open: 12noon–2.30pm, 6–8pm and normal licensing hours

S

The unusual exterior is reminiscent of an old railway station, with its cast-iron-and-glass portico forming a protected area where ironwork tables and chairs are available for patrons. There is a similarly-equipped garden at the back for rain-free days. The bar itself is reputed to be the largest in London, stretching almost the full depth of the premises, with cast iron tables and chairs arranged along one side. In spite of its size it gets very crowded on Friday and Saturday evenings. The interior is French bistro-style, the décor somewhat barn-like with natural wood beams and panels and a quarry-tiled floor. Food is cheap and good. At lunchtime around £2 buys a hot dish such as moussaka, curry or hotpot with accompanying vegetables, and cold food such as quiche with salad is available at lunchtime or in the evening at similar prices. Desserts are about 50p a portion. There is another Crispins at 14 The Green, Ealing.

Crusts Gaff, 17 The Green, Ealing
(01-579 2788)
Open: Mon–Thu 12noon–11.30pm,
Fri–Sat 12noon–12mdnt,
Sun 12noon–11.30pm

C F P S

An abundance of natural wood comes in handy for hanging numerous knick-knacks including a spinning wheel, steel helmets and statues. Walls covered with old prints and mirrors complete the individual décor of this popular bistro. Emphasis is on good, wholesome food. Starters include soup at around 75p or pâté at about £1. Main dish specialities such as lasagne are on offer at around £2.65, spare ribs at about £3.25. Meat and cheeseburgers are rock bottom budget items and there is a selection of competitively-priced salads. Sweets include apple pie and crème caramel for around 95p–£1.25.

W8

The Ark Restaurant, 122 Palace Gardens Terrace
(01-229 4024)
Open: Mon–Sat 12noon–3pm,
6.30–11.30pm, Sun 6.30–11.30pm

C S

You won't need to walk into The Ark two by two, but it is advisable not to arrive with a large family party unannounced. The Ark is a small, intimate bistro in the true French tradition. It has plain tables and a warm, friendly staff. The plat du jour, though not entirely French, ranges from crevettes roses (a shrimp concoction at around £1.50), to moules marinières at about £1.75 for starters. For the main course, coq au vin (only around £3.50) or foie de veau à l'ail (calf's liver with garlic) linger in the memory – and on the palate. Follow on with profiteroles, or a gigantic portion of sorbet.

W9

Elgin Lokanta, 239 Elgin Avenue
(01-328 6400)
Open: Mon–Sun 12noon–12mdnt

C S

The grill-kitchen of this Turkish restaurant

Inner London W11–WC2

is at the front and takeaway kebabs are a favourite of the locals. Mezeler (starters) include deliciously flavoured calves' livers at about 90p and there are over 20 more starters on the menu. Main courses are from around £2.25–£3.75 and are all served with pilaf rice. Try one of the lamb specialities such as sis saslik (skewered lamb with mushrooms and onion slices). Honey and walnut baklava (75p) is a tempting dessert from the trolley with which to complete your meal. There is a nominal cover charge for which you receive butter, hot pitta and black olives.

W11

Finch's Wine Bar
120 Kensington Park Road
(01-229 9545)
Open: Mon–Sat 11am–3pm, 6–11pm
[C][P][S]

Only a stone's throw from the Portobello Road antique market is this neat little basement premises, with its plain white walls and pillars forming intimate alcoves. Hot dishes include a quiche or pie from £1.75 or lasagne or moussaka from £1.55. The cold collation offers such tempting delicacies as fresh prawns for around £1.50, pâté (about £1.20) and porc en croute

Tootsies, 120 Holland Park Avenue
(01-229 8567)
Open: Mon–Sun 8am–12mdnt,
Sun 11.30pm
[F][S][♦]

The menu at Tootsies offers 'Eye Openers': orange juice with raw egg 'for those who did and wish they hadn't' and a full English breakfast 'for those who didn't and wish they had'. This is primarily a hamburger house – a dozen varieties are listed costing from about £1.55 to about £2.05, all prices including chips (except in the case of the 'calorie counter' version, where bun and chips are replaced by pineapple and cottage cheese) and a selection of relishes. You can get a number of other dishes here – steak, salads, quiches, for example, at very reasonable prices, and there are delectable cakes and ice-cream specialities.

W12

Shireen Tandoori ✕
270 Uxbridge Road
(01-749 5927)
Open: Mon–Sat 12noon–3pm,
6–11.30pm
[C][F][P][S][♦]

You can drink an aperitif and nibble spicy Indian nuts at the bar and seating area at the far end of this smart little restaurant, just 10 minutes' walk from Shepherds Bush roundabout. Attractive Indian prints are displayed against matt black walls, and the natural wood of the ceiling is echoed in the herringbone-patterned latticework which screens diners from the main road. Main course prices range from about £2.50 (for Tandoori chicken)

to around £4.75 (for Jhinga tandoori, a prawn speciality). The addition of vegetables (about £1.30), coffee (around 55p) and wine (bottles only) could bring the total over £5 even without a sweet. But if you appreciate the art of Tandoori cooking you will enjoy your meal.

WC1

Oodles, 113 High Holborn
(01-405 3838)
Open: Mon–Fri 11.30am–9pm,
Sat 11.30am–2.30pm
[S]

Apart from staying open more hours in the week than the others, this branch of Oodles is no different from any other, but catch the flavour of its menus by reading the description in the entry under W2.

Oodles, 42 New Oxford Street
(01-580 9521)
Open: Mon–Fri 11am–9pm,
Sat 11am–8pm, Sun 12noon–7pm
[S]

The frontage may be reminiscent of 'Ye Olde Tea Shoppe', but inside this eating house is unmistakably Oodles. No time to linger over evening meals, but a glass of wine can be had here. See under W2.

WC2

Corts, 84–86 Chancery Lane
(01-405 3349)
Open: Mon–Fri 11am–3pm, 5.30–8pm
[C][F][S]

You are less likely to meet criminals here than in the Old Bailey Corts, but lawyers abound as the wine bar is handy for the Strand Law Courts and is not far from the various Inns of Court. Here you will find an air-conditioned basement self-service bar and a ground-floor restaurant in which olive green and red blend with polished wood to create a warm ambience which is matched by the pleasant and helpful waitresses. Food is on the same lines as the original Corts (see under EC4) and starters include items such as smoked mackerel or avocado pear vinaigrette at around £1.30, or potted shrimps. Followed by a main course of duck and walnut pie (£2) and a sweet or fruit and cheese (about £1.50), a three-course meal should cost about £5.

Hobson's Wine Bar
20 Upper St Martin's Lane
(01-836 5849)
Open: Mon–Fri 11am–3pm, 5.30–11pm,
Sat 5.30–11pm, Sun 7–10.30pm
[C][P]

This wine bar, close to Covent Garden, is located below ground and is on the whole candlelit with the occasional modern discreet light. There's bags of cosy atmosphere here with wood-panelled walls, a 'Horse-Box' window and even sawdust. Of the various

starters, spicy chicken and wine pâté (£1.40) is highly recommended. Main course options are fish-biased and include smoked trout (£3) and potted prawns. If you fancy spoiling yourself with some wine, on this occasion you'll find Hobson's choice from the wine cellars immense.

Plummer's Restaurant, 33 King Street, Covent Garden
(01-240 2534)
Open: Mon–Sat 12noon–3pm,
5.30pm–12mdnt
[S]

Victoriana epitomised by old photographs, prints and large mirrors, characterises this eating house, one of the original of the 'new wave' of restaurants in Covent Garden. Dishes include home-made steak and kidney pie, Californian chili served with Chef's salad (both around £4) and Plummer's Superburgers (8oz 100% pure Scottish beefburgers topped with bacon, egg and melted cheese).

Solange's Wine Bar, 11 St Martin's Court
(01-240 0245)
Open: Mon–Sat 11am–3pm,
5.30–11pm
[C][F]

A great attraction of this large, unpretentious wine bar is the excellent food, which is prepared in the famed neighbouring two knife and fork restaurant, Chez Solange. The four rooms can accommodate 200 people and more on the white-painted garden furniture outside. The menu changes daily, and is written on a blackboard. As an appetiser you could sample one of about a dozen cold dishes – champignons à la Grecque at 85p, pâté maison or ratatouille at £1.45 are tasty examples. Hot dishes of the day cost less than £2.55 and might include coq au vin, veal or spare ribs – delicious with a serving of cauliflower cheese at 45p. Desserts such as fruit salad or cheesecake are in the 65p–80p range.

Tuttons, 11–12 Russell Street
(01-836 1167)
Open: Mon–Sat 9am–11.30pm,
Sun 12noon–10.30pm
[C][S][♦]

This cream-decorated brasserie with plain pine furniture offers a good range of snacks and salads, and some unusual main dishes such as vegetables and spices wrapped in pastry and baked at around £2.90 or smoked chicken and avocado salad at about £3.80. A three-course meal can cost around £6. You are welcome to drop in for a late breakfast, or perhaps just a coffee.

Vecchia Parma, 149 Strand
(01-836 3730)
Open: Mon–Sat 12noon–3pm,
5.30–11pm
[C][F][P][S][♦]

In the best traditions of Italian restaurateurs, the Ronchetti family do a grand job in running this restaurant close to London's theatreland – Signor Ronchetti is the barman and his wife is also behind the bar. Of their two sons, Sergio cooks and Silvano produces the 'service with a smile' of which they are so proud. Apart from the usual pasta and pizza dishes, mostly around £1.45, there are several tasty grills, omelettes, fish and salad choices, many of them costing not much more than £3.50 and served with potatoes and vegetables.

OUTER LONDON

BARKING

The Spotted Dog, 15 Longbridge Road
(01-594 0288)
Open: Mon–Sun normal licensing hours
[C][S]

Genuine East London atmosphere abounds in The Spotted Dog, one of Davy & Co's original enterprises (near Barking tube). The ground floor 'doghouse' offers good old steak and kidney pie with vegetables and potatoes for under £3, but a steak or a mixed grill will be more pricey (around £4.50 with vegetables). Bar snacks such as sandwiches, filled rolls and toasted fingers are also available. An enormous antique fireplace dominates the room. Downstairs, you find yourself in the 'clink' – a dungeon-like place complete with all ill-looking

Outer London
Barking–Bromley

skeleton. No bread and water here, but plaice or scampi and chips can be had at around £3.50.

BARNET

Franco and Gianni, 45 High Street
(01-449 8300)
Open: Tue–Sat 12noon–3pm
[C][S]

This attractive little Italian restaurant is somewhat out of our league in the evenings but at lunchtimes a typically Italian table d'hôte menu prevails, offering such dishes as cannelloni or lasagne for starters, medaglioni di manzo (thin fillet steak in red wine and mushroom sauce) with cauliflower and potato to follow, gâteau of the day plus coffee – all for around £5.50.

The Two Brewers, 64 Hadley Highstone
(01-449 3558)
Open: Mon–Thu 10.30am–2.30pm,
Fri–Sat 10.30am–2.30pm, 5.30–11pm,
Sun 12noon–2pm, 7–10.30pm
[P]

A one-time 'Pub of the Year', this superb Tudor-style building is well-known to the locals, and they take full advantage of the high standard of cooking. Meals are eaten in the restaurant which echoes the Tudor theme, with warm red curtains and

carpet. A daily-changing menu offers traditional Old English dishes such as grilled gammon and pineapple, cod and chips or home-made steak, kidney and mushroom pie all around £4.

BROMLEY

Hollywood Bowl
5 Market Parade, East Street
(01-460 2346)
Open: Mon–Thu 11.30am–2.45pm,
6–11.15pm, Fri–Sat 6–11.45pm,
Sun 6–11pm
[F][P][S][◊]

Old enamelled bill posters and hanging plants decorate this popular hamburger restaurant. There are nine burgers to choose from, all with interesting names; for example, the 'hen house' has a fried egg topping and the 'Bronx boiger' is 'overflowing with spicy baked beans'. The star of this show is 'Hollywood Bowl's de-luxe cheeseburger' – a hunky half-pounder with a generous topping of melted cheese, lettuce, tomato and pickles smothered in thick mayonnaise. All of them are served in a toasted sesame bun with French fries. A rump steak at around £3.95 with a choice of three salads around £2.30 each are alternative main courses. Fresh home-made apple pie is a tasty dessert at around 70p.

---

45 HIGH STREET, BARNET
Telephone 01-449 8300

FRANCO & GIANNI

CHEF'S SPECIALITIES

Insalata Mafiosa   Avocado Gratinato   Crespelle alla Pescatore

Tortelli Mantovani   Penne Amatriciana   Pasta e Piselli

Lobster Thermador   Branzino   Venison

The Two Brewers

Telephone: Barnet 3558

Fully Licensed

A WATNEY HOUSE
Cold Buffet always available.
Hot luncheons 12 to 2pm.
Monday to Friday.
Car Park. Garden

MRS G TRIM
Hadley Highstone, Barnet

Outer London
Croydon–Ilford

CROYDON

Fusto D'Oro Pizzeria, Leon House,
237–239 High Street
(01-688 4869)
Open: Mon–Sat 11am–3pm,
6pm–12mdnt

C 🍴 P S

If pizza's your dish you'll be quite spoiled for choice at this popular Italian pizzeria in the heart of Croydon. There are 22 varieties. For the quickie meal, eat your pizza in the busier section of the restaurant where the décor is simple, with formica-topped tables. When you want to linger and enjoy a more romantic atmosphere, dine by candlelight in the other section. Wherever you eat the food is the same, with pizzas from the basic Margherita to an elaborate Mediterraneo with seafood and tomatoes, pasta dishes, salads and steaks. For dessert there's a choice of either 'dolci', including such tempters as rum baba, zabaglione or cheesecake.

The Wine Vaults, 122–126 North End
(01-680 2419)
Open: Mon–Sat 11am–2.30pm,
Mon–Thu 5.30–10.30pm,
Fri 5.30–11pm, Sat 7–11pm

C P S 🍴

Another Davy & Co outlet this, with solidly Victorian décor and sawdust on the floor in true Davy fashion, in basement premises on Croydon's busy High Street close to the railway station and next door to Marks & Spencer. Toasted fingers cost about 25p each here, or £1.35 a plate of six, but otherwise the menu and prices are fairly typical of the company. A popular meal is charcoal grilled ribs of prime beef with a tossed mixed salad, but this will cost about £5.50 without any other courses.

ENFIELD

Divers Wine and Cocktail Bar
29 Silver Street
(01-367 2549)
Open: Tue–Fri 12noon–2.30pm,
Mon–Sun 7.30–10.30pm, 11pm Fri & Sat

🍴 P S

This rather smart little wine bar is a distinctive feature of the tree-lined street. The blackboard menu offers daily specialities such as chili con carne, goulash or roast chicken. Pizzas, quiches and ploughman's are always available for around £1.50 and desserts include a delicious chocolate cherry gâteau for around 90p. A dazzling selection of wines and good background music make this a popular mealtime haunt. Summer visitors may like to eat in the sheltered, paved garden to the rear of the restaurant.

HAMPTON COURT

Cardinal Wolsey, The Green
(01-979 1458)
Open: Mon–Sun 12.30–3pm,
7–10.30pm

C P 🍴

This charming inn, pleasantly sited close to Hampton Court, offers sound home-made English fare for the footsore and famished foreign tourist's enjoyment – and British visitors are equally welcome. A three-course table d'hôte meal, changed daily, but always providing interesting choices, costs around £6. Portions are very generous and old favourites frequently featured include Chef's stock pot soup, home-made pâté, roast beef and Yorkshire pud, steak and kidney pud, apple pie and peach Melba – a taste of old England at its best.

HARROW

Plato's, 294 Preston Road
(01-904 8326)
Open: Mon–Sat 12noon–3pm, 6–11pm

C P S

This Greek restaurant is furnished in the modern style and specialises in French and English as well as Greek cuisine. The manager is always on hand to ensure your enjoyment of his food. The à la carte menu offers a dazzling choice of over 20 starters, more than 30 main courses and about 20 sweets. You could break the bank by going for all the most expensive items, but there is still a wide choice awaiting you. An all-Greek meal could include zsatsiki as an appetiser at around 80p, with dolmades or kleftiko as your main dish for about £3.35 and baklava or kateifi as delicious desserts at around 90p. Vegetables are extra and there is a cover charge for bread and butter.

HOUNSLOW

The Travellers Friend, 480 Bath Road
(01-897 8847)
Open: Mon–Fri 12noon–2.30pm,
Fri–Sat 7–9.30pm

C P

Tudor architecture is reflected in the oak beams, pillars, plain brick and stone walls and olde worlde furnishings of the charming restaurant in this hostelry. Cuisine is basically English with the odd French dish to vary the pace. Starters include soup at around 60p, pâté maison at about £1.20 and prawn cocktail for around £1. Main courses include fish (from £2.50–£5.50), grills (from £2.20 for lamb cutlets to £4.50 for fillet or T-bone steak) and entrées such as escalope of veal cordon bleu. Vegetables are 50p extra. Various gâteaux cost around 60p.

ILFORD

Harts, 545 Cranbrook Road, Gants Hill
(01-554 5000)
Open: Mon–Thu 12noon–3pm,
6–10.30pm, Fri–Sat 12noon–3pm,
6–11pm, Sun 7–10.30pm

C 🍴

Leonard and Alan Hart's wine bar specialises in good home-made cooking ideal for business people and travellers alike. Start with home-made cabbage soup (about 70p) or crab cocktail at £1.35, then sample lasagne (about £1.80). Freshly caught trout from Hanningford or Australian Pacific prawns cooked with garlic may stretch the budget but are good value. Hard-to-resist desserts include hot black cherries with port and ice cream (about £1). In fine weather you can enjoy your meal on the tree-lined terrace to the rear.

AA SELF CATERING IN BRITAIN

15000 AA-inspected self-catering holiday houses, chalets and cottages on which you can rely for a comfortable holiday.

Written description of each entry plus symbols and abbreviations for a wide range of facilities.

Hints for Self-Caterers

Maps to help you locate the holiday home of your choice.

On sale at AA shops and major booksellers

KEW

Le Provence, 14 Station Parade, Kew Gardens
(01-940 6777)
Open: Tue – Sat 6 – 9.15pm, Sat 12noon – 3pm

P

This traditional French restaurant, tucked away under the oak tree-lined parade at Kew Gardens, offers honest French cooking at no-nonsense prices. Daily specials are excellent value – fresh artichoke vinaigrette is around £1.40, risotto du chef around £1.40 and foie saute à la Venitienne (sliced liver cooked in butter with sherry and sliced onions, served with a selection of vegetables) at about £3.70 are typical examples. Main courses, all served with vegetables, range in price from around £2.20 – £3.70. The desserts are a delight – real fruit sorbet (usually raspberry) or meringue glacé Chantilly (around 90p) are both superb. Booking is essential.

Maids of Honour, 288 Kew Road
(01-940-2752)
Open: Monday for coffee only, no lunches. Tue – Fri 10am – 5.30pm, Sat 9am – 5.30pm

P &

The Maids of Honour has a pretty, double bow window frontage and the tiny cottage restaurant, decorated with Staffordshire pottery, is very popular, so you will probably have to queue and share a table, but it is well worth it. The restaurant is open for morning coffee, lunch and afternoon tea. For lunch, traditional English food is served, usually a choice of two roasts and steak pie, plus delicious pastries and cakes for £3.10. Home-made soup to start your meal is 55p. Children's portions of main course and sweet cost £2.60. Maids of Honour offers excellent value for money and presents English food at its very best.

KINGSTON-UPON-THAMES

Blueys, 2 Station Buildings, Fife Road
(01-546 6614)
Open: Mon – Thu 12noon – 11.15pm, Fri & Sat 12noon – 11.30pm

C F P &

Outer London
Kew – Richmond

This small, two-storey restaurant has polished table tops and simple décor. A three-course meal of soup, chili con carne, cheesecake and coffee costs about £4.50. There is also a good range of snacks, including baked potatoes served with salad, and burgers served with chips or baked potato, and salad, mainly priced at under £3.

Clouds, 6 – 8 Kingston Hill
(01-546 0559)
Open: Mon – Sun 11am – 11pm

P S &

This busy, friendly restaurant operates on two floors, the first floor is a cocktail bar. The ground floor menu offers stuffed mushrooms among other appetisers, quiches, spaghettis, hamburgers, spare ribs, salads, steaks and chicken as main course (from £1.95 – £4) and cheesecakes or fantastic ice creams for dessert. Children's portions come at £1.

The Farmhouse Kitchen, 3/5 Thames Street (rear of Millets)
Open: Mon – Sat 9am – 5.30pm

P &

This self-service style cafeteria, with padded bench seating, offers a range of good, hot, tasty dishes. Cheese and savoury potatoes are 70p, chicken breast in wine sauce, with mushrooms, tomatoes and parsley £1.80, and apple pie and cream 60p. Coffee is 33p and a glass of wine 70p. There is also a special area for non-smokers. If you just want a snack try the French stick sandwiches or one of the cakes or pastries.

Flames, 14 Kingston Hill
(01-549 5984)
Open: Mon – Sun 12.30 – 2.30pm, 7 – 11pm

C F P &

There is a continental air about the rustic wood-and-house-plant décor of this restaurant. Its windows overlook the wide tree-lined pavement of Kingston Hill, on the outskirts of an old market town which is now almost part of London. Food is imaginative and not overpriced though one could exceed the limit when choosing from the à la carte menu. Mushroom Dijonaise followed by chicken farci and Grand Marnier pancakes comes to around £5.75 and there is a 60p cover charge. A traditional three-course Sunday roast costs around £5 a head.

PINNER

The Old Oak, 11 High Street
(01-866 0286)
Open: Mon – Fri 12noon – 2pm, 7 – 10.30pm, Sat 12noon – 2pm, 7 – 11pm, Sun 12.30 – 2.30pm, 7.30 – 10pm

C

The set price for a three-course lunch is only about £3 here, including service charge. Business person's lunch starters include delicacies such as avocado and grapefruit salad, Waldorf salad (apple, celery and walnuts in sour cream) or crevettes aioli (peel-yourself prawns and garlic mayonnaise). There is a wide choice of main dishes: meat which could be pork in an apple, sage, cider and cream sauce, or a spicy dish such as chili con carne or curry de volaille aux bananes. To finish a satisfying repast, sweets include rum and coffee mousse and Old English flummery, or you might prefer Brie or Camembert to keep the meal memorably continental.

RICHMOND-UPON-THAMES

Mrs Beeton's, 58 Hill Rise
(01-948 2787)
Open: Mon – Sun 10am – 5.30pm, Wed – Sat 6.30pm – 12mdnt

S &

This village-style restaurant has a craft shop in the basement selling local crafts and kitchen items. The informal restaurant is run by a co-operative of women who are each allocated a day to prepare and serve the food, which is home-made and excellent value for money. Starters include minted cucumber soup or liver pâté with toast for around 60p. Cheese and courgette quiche is about £1.60 with a salad,

---

Blueys Restaurant

2 Station Buildings, Fife Road, Kingston-upon-Thames, Surrey.
Telephone: 01-546 6614

Open from mid-day till late every day including Sundays.
Blueys is ideal for a quick lunch or a leisurely dinner.
Come and sample our excellent food, inventive cocktails and
warm and humerous service —
all at prices guaranteed to keep you smiling.

See you soon at Blueys.

Outer London
Stanmore – Wembley

fricassée of chicken and mushrooms with rice or lasagne are both around £1.85. A huge choice of desserts includes a very light chocolate layer cake – a very large portion costs about 75p.

STANMORE

Peking Duck, 35 The Broadway
(01-954 4050)
Open: Mon–Sat 12noon–2.30pm,
6pm–12mdnt, Sun 6pm–12mdnt

C S

For those who understand the language, the extensive Peking Duck menu is in Chinese as well as English. The westernised Chinese dishes, familiarised by a thousand take-aways are there, but supplemented by more convincingly eastern-sounding dishes such as Gota fish with garlic and ginger (£2.10), or crab meat with straw mushroom (£1.55). A lunchtime special menu, with six choices of main courses costs under £2, and the restaurant specialises in meals consisting of six to eight dishes ranging from £3.80–£7.35 per person. The décor of the first-floor restaurant is pleasantly muted, coloured in shades of cream and brown, with modern Chinese prints on the walls and wicker-shaded lights hanging low over the tables.

SUDBURY

Terry's Restaurant and Banqueting Suite, 763–765 Harrow Road
(01-904 4409)
Open: Mon–Fri 12noon–2pm

P &

The main operation here is catering for large parties, but on weekday lunchtimes the reception area is utilised for serving what could be one of the cheapest three-course lunches in London. For around £1.65 you get a choice of starters which include items such as melon cocktail and egg mayonnaise, a choice of four main dishes such as roast or meat pie with a good selection of the appropriate, well-cooked vegetables, tasty omelette, or cold meat salad, and a choice of four mouth-watering sweets or cheese and biscuits with which to round off the meal.

SURBITON

Cars Café, 7 Brighton Road
(01-940 4607)
Open: Mon–Fri 6–11.30pm, Sat & Sun 12noon–11.30pm

C F P &

As the name may indicate motor cars and traffic lights are the focal points of this buttery. The plain brick walls are decorated with prints of motor cars, spot lights and the occasional potted plant. The menu includes a good range of starters, hamburgers, grilled steaks, spaghetti dishes, quiches, chef's specials, salads and desserts. A three-course meal of soup, steak and kidney pie and meringue glacé will cost £4.55.

The Good Life, 3 Central Parade
(between Ewell and Brighton Roads)
(01-399 8450)
Open: Mon–Sun 12noon–2.30pm,
6.30–11pm

♫ &

Open-plan, wood-panelled rooms with wall prints lend an authentic air to this popular bistro. Starters include pâté at 90p and sauté mushrooms at £1.15. Steaks are £3.55 (served with French fries or jacket potatoes), boeuf bourguignon is £2.75 and lasagne, spaghetti bolognese and chili con carne are all at around £2. Desserts include apple pie and cream at 80p. A cup of coffee is 35p and a glass of wine 75p.

UPMINSTER

The Mill, Roomes Department Store, Station Road
(Upminster 50080)
Open: Tue–Thu 9am–5pm,
Fri–Sat 5.30pm

S &

Recently modernised, this pleasant restaurant, with its attractive wall mural and soft lighting is on the second floor of Roomes department store. Service is personal and friendly and good, no-nonsense food is excellent value for money. The menu changes every day, but particularly recommended is the home-made steak pie, bursting with meat and served with two veg. With a starter and sweet, the meal is likely to cost about £2.50. Children's portions cost about 50p–£1.

WEMBLEY

Peking Castle Restaurant, 379 High Road
(01-902 3605)
Open: Mon–Sun 12noon–2.30pm,
6–11.30pm

S

Apart from the à la carte menu, this quiet haven from the rush of the High Road traffic, where hanging Chinese lanterns and a dragon motif evoke the East, offers special dinners for two or more people at about £4.50 a head for seven items or around £5.50 a head for nine items. If you fancy a meal composed of soup, crispy duck, chicken in yellow-bean sauce, prawns in chili sauce, vegetables, fried rice and toffee apple, £4.50 is not overmuch to pay for it. The main menu includes the usual array of fish, poultry and meat dishes, the cuisine is the upper-class Peking style. Economy-minded diners would be well advised to skip wine with their meal, instead drinking china tea, which will be served ad infinitum.

TELEPHONE NUMBERS

In some areas telephone numbers are likely to be changed by British Telecom during the currency of this publication. If any difficulty is experienced when making a reservation it is advisable to check with the operator.

JUST READING THE MENU COULD MAKE YOU HUNGRY

Charcoal-grilled steaks, Chicken-Kiev, Poached Salmon, Scampi Provençale — at least 18 starters and 16 main courses, superbly cooked by a master chef. Wines that don't cost the earth . . . and a friendly, informal atmosphere you'll love.

There's even disco-dancing (below decks) and we're open Mon. to Sat. until 2 a.m. Downs is the 'in' place for people who enjoy a night out. They come back again and again. So will you if you enjoy superb food at unusually moderate prices.

— *See page 90 for editorial*

Downs WINE BAR & RESTAURANT
40 Wimbledon Hill Road, SW19
(easy parking) **01-946 3246**

EAST ANGLIA

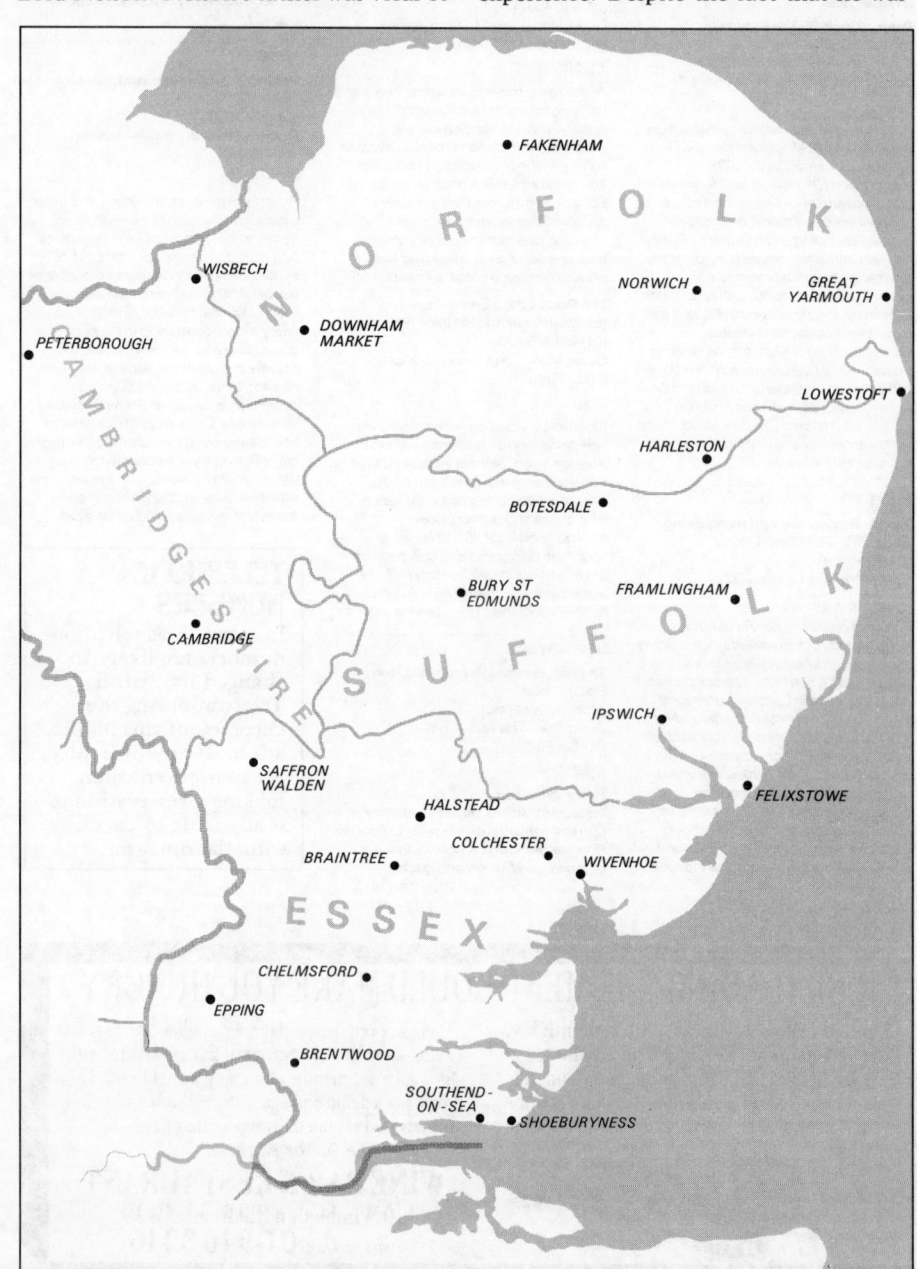

Among other things, East Anglia has huge skies, an irascible sea, flint churches, and Lord Nelson. Nelson's father was vicar of Burnham Thorpe in Norfolk. During a spell of unemployment between the wars with France, Nelson cultivated the rectory garden. He did not enjoy the experience. Despite the fact that he was often seasick and obviously accident prone (anyone who loses the sight of an eye and one arm *must* be), he longed for another war and another ship.

For less intrepid navigators, there are, of course, the Norfolk Broads – and for anyone who actually hates the sea, the western parts of Norfolk, Suffolk and Essex are rewarding. The villages recall the counties' onetime importance in the wool trade. They also offer some very fine examples of Tudor buildings. Cambridgeshire has Cambridge, the cathedral town of Ely, and some very flat fens.

The small resort of Aldeburgh in Suffolk is famous for Benjamin Britten – who founded the annual music festival and was also responsible, if indirectly, for that uncommon concert hall at the Snape Maltings not far away.

The coast of East Anglia is under continuous threat from the sea. The Suffolk village of Dunwich – sometimes known as 'the lost city' – had forfeited at least nine churches to the encroachment of the eroding tides. They say you can hear the bells ringing during a storm. We have listened – and heard no bells.

Slaughden, less than a mile south of Aldeburgh, used to be a prosperous port and shipbuilding centre. Within almost living memory, there was a pub named The Mariners' Arms. Now, there are two tin sheds, a lot of shingle, and the largest Martello tower in the country.

The best local dish, in the opinion of some people, is cod – not the stuff you buy in fish shops. You need to go down to the beach when the inshore fishermen return and buy it when it comes off the boats. Fresh cod is almost another species: a very prince of fish.

Cromer supplies some excellent locally caught crabs: Orford in Suffolk and Colchester in Essex are the places to visit, if you enjoy oysters. Most of the latter's harvest comes from Pyefleet Creek. Richard I gave the town the exclusive rights to fish in these narrow waters.

Bloaters are another speciality of the region. For those who are never quite sure what a bloater is, they are herrings that have been caught close inshore – and, consequently, have not needed to be preserved for days on end by salting aboard the boats. Yarmouth is the best place in which to find them.

You may have noticed on menus that there are turkeys and *Norfolk* turkeys. The latter are smaller, plumper and, perhaps, more succulent. In some eating places, you may find samphire on the bill of fare. This is a curious plant grown on the marshes near the coast of North Norfolk. It has a delicate flavour, not unlike asparagus when eaten hot, with butter, and a bit like a gherkin when pickled in vinegar. If you are lucky, you may find delicious home-made Suffolk or Norfolk dumplings on the menu. Pig's fry is another homely dish that East Anglians pine for.

Superstitious villagers used, once upon a time, to put out at night a concoction called thruminty (sometimes 'fermenty', see p. 43) The ingredients included wheat, currants, suet and apple. It was intended for the fairies.

At Dunmow in Essex, a flitch (meaning a side of bacon) is awarded every Whit-Monday to the couple who can claim, in all honesty, that they have never quarelled, never once wished they had remained single since their wedding day.

Buns named 'Brotherly Love' are another regional eccentricity – and rarity. Suffolk cheese has less to commend it: too hard. One local saying has it that 'Hunger will break stone walls, and anything except a Suffolk cheese'.

Botesdale — Cambridge

BOTESDALE

Hamblyn House, Rickinghall
(Botesdale 292)
Open: Tue–Sat 12noon–2pm, 7–10pm,
Sun 12noon–2pm

C P &

This delightful beamed restaurant forms part of a fine 16th century property. Imaginative meals, from bar snacks, through to the elaborate à la carte, are enhanced by fresh vegetables grown in the garden and prepared by chef Steve. A typical bar snack would be small Dover soles with chips and salad at £2.50 or for slightly less, steak and kidney pie with potatoes and two veg. A three-course table d'hôte menu is available at £4.95 and there are children's meals. The à la carte menu offers a good choice but the prices are over our limit.

BRAINTREE

Tudor Rose, Little Square
(Braintree 45349)
Open: Mon–Sun 12noon–2.30pm, 7pm onwards, last orders 10pm

S

This attractive 17th-century restaurant is situated in the oldest part of town, in a particularly historic area with 'Cromwell's Court' nearby. Original beams, inglenook fireplace and wooden wheelback chairs give the room an atmosphere of history. A full à la carte menu is available, but for the budget-conscious the set three-course lunch offers an excellent choice of dishes at around £3.50 each. The business person's lunch at £4.50 might consist of grapefruit, steak and kidney pie, sweet and coffee, and a three-course meal including lasagne or other 'special' pasta dishes will be about £6, including coffee. A three-course traditional roast lunch is about £5, including coffee. It is advisable to book.

BRENTWOOD

The Eagle and Child, 13 Chelmsford Road, Shenfield
(Brentwood 210155)
Open: bar snacks:
Mon–Sat 11.30am–2pm

Carvery: Tue–Sat 7–10.30pm,
Sun 12noon–2pm

F P

This popular Tudor-style pub houses a carvery restaurant which has wood-panelled décor reminiscent of a private club. Value for money is self-evident with modestly priced starters such as pâté at about 80p, followed by a choice of meats carved to your liking. Fresh roast pork, topside of beef and whole turkeys are on display and James or Keith, the waiters, will only stop filling up your plate when you say so. All this plus generous portions of vegetables for about £4.50. Alternative main courses include home-made steak pie or salad selection for £2. A choice of sweets is also included in the price. There is an attractive garden and if you're lucky you may see a display of Morris dancing.

BURY ST EDMUNDS

The Beefeater Restaurant
27 Angel Hill
(Bury St Edmunds 4224)
Open: Tue–Sat 12noon–2pm,
6–12mdnt, Sun 12noon–3pm, 6–11pm

C F P S &

Don't let the name mislead you, this is a Greek restaurant typical of any to be found on the Greek islands – the weather being the only difference! However, you'll hardly miss the sun as you sit amidst the fishing nets and Greek bric-à-brac enjoying the traditional moussaka, kleftiko or dolmadakia. The cost of a three-course meal is a bit over the budget at £6.25, but qualifies, as a glass of wine is included. Go for a Greek dish such as fresh squid with rice and salad, rounding off with traditional Greek coffee. The less adventurous may have to pay more for the conventional English dishes (about £6.70); the charcoal-grilled steaks are a credit to proprietor Andreas Paraskeva and his family.

Peggotty's Carving Room
30 Guildhall Street
(Bury St Edmunds 5444)

Open: Tue–Fri 12noon–2pm,
6.45–10pm, Sat 12noon–2pm,
6.30–10.30pm, Sun 12noon–2.30pm

C S &

Notice the Dickensian-type exterior with eye-catching red canopies over the windows. Inside, the heavy wooden tables, tapestry-upholstered chairs, brick pillars and sand-coloured walls lined with prints create a cottage-like atmosphere. Starters are served to your table, then, in the carvery style, you take your pick from an array of hot or cold roasts, carved for you by the chef, or proprietor Luigi, and add to this your own selection of vegetables or salad. Roll and butter and sweet are included in the price of the main course with starters and coffee additional, totalling under £5. After a good lunch at Peggotty's why not take time to explore Bury Cathedral or the Athenaeum, where Dickens gave two readings.

CAMBRIDGE

Eros, 25 Petty Cury
(Cambridge 63420)
Open: Mon–Fri 12noon–3pm,
5.30–11pm, Sat–Sun 12noon–11pm

C F S &

Eros has the atmosphere of a taverna, complete with Greek music, despite very English décor with college arms on panelled walls. The menu is enormous, with fish, omelettes, roasts, grills, salads and a formidable variety of steaks, not to mention Greek, Cypriot and Italian dishes by the dozen. For a satisfying three-course Greek meal, start with taramasalata, followed by sousoukakia and round it off with Grecian-style gâteau – all this for around £5 or so.

The Roof Garden, and **The Pentagon,**
The Arts Theatre, 6 St Edwards Passage
(Cambridge 355246)
Open: Roof Garden: Mon–Sat
9.30am–8pm Pentagon: Mon–Sat
12noon–2pm, 6pm–11.30pm

C S

These self-service restaurants over the Arts Theatre comprise one of the busiest rendezvous in the city. The main dining area of the Roof Garden is light and airy but in fine weather many customers

Hamblyn House
16th CENTURY INN

Rickinghall, Diss, Norfolk
(Between Diss and Bury St Edmunds on A143)

A fully licensed freehouse with an intimate à la carte restaurant, hot and cold home made bar snacks and comfortable accommodation.
Adnams, Greene King and Tolly Cobbold traditional ales.
Extensive wine list.
Outside catering service.
Access & Visa.

Tel: Botesdale (0379 898) 292

prefer to sit outside on the roof. You can eat here from early morning when a full English breakfast is served, through to the 'theatre supper' of hefty ploughman's, cottage pie, fried chicken in a basket and the like. At the Pentagon a selection of cold buffet dishes are available, with at least three hot dishes will cost around £3.50. A special item is a two-course lunch for about £1.50.

University Arms Hotel ★★★★
Regent Street
(Cambridge 51241, 351241 after May 1983)
Open: Mon–Sun 12.30–2pm, 7–9pm

|C|♬|P|S|♿|

The large ground-floor restaurant of this imposing hotel overlooks the park through windows which depict the arms of the colleges in stained glass. Only by sticking to the three-course table d'hôte menu will you be safe on the budget as an à la carte meal plus wine would be over £6. For about £5.90 you can choose from a menu of traditional dishes such as fried lemon sole, roast leg of pork with apple sauce, or cold ham salad plus a sweet. A simpler lunch may be chosen from the buffet set up in Parker's Lounge, where sandwiches and simple salads cost as little as 80p, and a selection of cold meats, savouries and salads will set you back about £3.

Varsity Restaurant, 35 St Andrew's Street
(Cambridge 56060)
Open: Mon–Sun 12noon–3pm, 5.30–11pm

|S|

This two-storey Greek restaurant is housed in one of Cambridge's many listed buildings in one of the city centre's not-so-busy streets. The atmosphere is very authentic, with Greek pictures scattered on white-washed walls, an effect which is emphasised by black wooden beams and doors. A good three-course meal, including wine and coffee,

Chelmsford — Colchester

can be enjoyed for around £5–£6. Food is basically Greek with some French and English dishes. Kebab of the house – two skewers of tenderloin, served with Greek salad and fetta cheese, is one of four speciality dishes. Service is quick and friendly despite the fact that the restaurant seats 105.

Wilson's Restaurants, 14 Trinity Street
(Cambridge 356845)
Open: The Restaurants: Mon–Thu 12noon–3pm, 6–11pm,
Fri–Sat 12noon–3pm, 6pm–12mdnt
The Granary: Mon–Sat 10.30am–10.30pm, Sun 10.30am–6pm

|P|S|

Wilson's is a fine black and white, 16th century building housing three restaurants. The two Restaurants, on the top floors, retain the Tudor style. There is a good choice of starters, desserts and main courses served by waitresses. Light snacks are available from 90p. There is a carvery where the chef will carve beef and pork for Sunday lunch. Three courses cost around £5. For a quicker, less expensive meal, try The Granary. A separate entrance takes you into the original cellars and here up to 10 hot dishes are on display. Beef casserole, curried chicken and sweet and sour pork are all about £1.80, while a selection of hot quiches are on offer for around £1. Fresh cream desserts are available for about 80p.

CHELMSFORD

Corks, 34a Moulsham Street
(Chelmsford 58733)
Open: Mon–Sat 12noon–2.30pm, 6–11pm, Sun 7–10.30pm

|C|♬|P|S|

Situated opposite the AA office, this trendy wine bar is a popular place for a good meal or informal drink and chat. A brown-painted window front and the Tudor beams beyond entice you over the threshold, where a tempting menu chalked on the ubiquitous plât du jour blackboard announces moussaka and salad, at around £1.75, or turkey pie and pâté (about £1). The competent staff is led by Michael Dunbar who is always on hand to extend a friendly welcome to his guests.

Pizza Pasta Rendezvous
44 Moulsham Road
(Chelmsford 352245)
Open: Mon–Sat 12noon–2.30pm, 6–10.30pm

|C|P|S|♿|

A decorative brown awning and Venetian blinds adorn this highly original-looking Italian restaurant and garden terrace. The simple but appetising menu specialises in the pizzas and pastas anticipated. Starters include Spanish gazpacho and minestrone soup at about 95p. An imaginative pizza is napoletana, with mozzarella cheese, tomatoes, capers, anchovies and olives for around £2. Pastas include delicious fetuccine mastriciana (noodles with tomato, onion and bacon) at about £2. Selection of sweets is good with home-made cheesecake and strudel at around £1. A 'Happy Family Menu' is available Mon–Fri for lunch, and dinner (6–8.30pm) at £4.50 for three courses (£2.50 for children under 10).

COLCHESTER

Bistro 9, 9 North Hill
(Colchester 76466)
Open: Tue–Sat 12noon–1.45pm, 7–10.45pm

|C|S|♿|

This small bistro has a short menu of home-made dishes served with fresh vegetables and home-made bread. It will be easier to keep within the £5 limit in the basement, where substantial 'snacks' are served. Home-made soup and bread, the hot dish of the day (such as moussaka or chilli con carne), and a pudding from the à la carte menu – will cost about £3.50. With quiche and salad as a main course, you'll spend less than £3. The Bistro always offers a vegetarian dish of the day at under £3 and on Saturdays a set lunch of two courses and coffee for £3.95. The service by friendly waitresses is guaranteed to please, as is the pleasantly

---

THE PENTAGON
6 SAINT EDWARDS PASSAGE CAMBRIDGE

AT THE ARTS THEATRE
LUNCH: 12-2pm
SUPPER: 6-11.30pm
MONDAY TO SATURDAY

Cold Buffet our speciality — also home-made pâtés, soups and delicious desserts.
4 hot dishes each day.
Good Wine list. Fully licensed. Small private room for 10 persons.
Wedding receptions, Theatre/Dinner parties undertaken.
Details from our Catering Manager. (Tel: Cambridge 355246).

informal atmosphere, the large refectory tables (you may have to share), and pretty country décor.

Wm Scragg's ××
2 North Hill
(Colchester 41111)
Open: Mon–Sat 12noon–2.15pm, 7–10.30pm

C

This elegant seafood restaurant bears the name of the journeyman bricklayer who bought the premises in 1832, and lived there peacefully until the ripe old age of 78. Many of the appetising dishes come dangerously near to our limit, a couple of the cheaper ones being Hungarian turbot and halibut steak, both under £4.50. However, a fine selection of bar snacks is available; fish pâté at £1.40, crab mousse with salad or smoked mackerel at around £2.25, and a good choice of inexpensive sandwiches such as prawn and lettuce or fish pâté and cucumber. A sweet may be chosen for about £1.30.

DOWNHAM MARKET
Crown Stables, Crown Hotel
(Downham Market 382322)
Open: Mon–Sun 10am–10pm

C P ♿

This 300-year-old coaching inn has always been a popular haunt of locals in the quiet town of Downham Market.

Downham Market
—
Fakenham

However, since the spring of 1980, the old stables have been converted into a slick grill room and buttery with natural wood tables, tiled floor, brick walls and horsey bric-à-brac creating a clean and simple atmosphere. Here, a very reasonably-priced cold buffet comprises home-cooked cold meats and hand-raised pies, quiches, pâtés and flans with a selection of salads at under £2.75. Charcoal grill steaks or kebabs will push up the price, but ploughman's platter, pizza or a steak sandwich are tasty alternatives at the other end of the price-scale. Home-made gâteaux and flans are around 80p.

EPPING
Beaton's Wine Bar, 319 High Street
(Epping 72096)
Open: Mon–Sat 12noon–2.30pm, Mon–Sun 6–10.30pm

P ♿

This small wine bar is very popular with the locals. Have a look at the blackboard menu and choose from lasagne verdi (£2.45), trout riesling (£2.95) or try one of the Beatons 'specials' such as carbonnade of beef at £3.45. There is simple wooden pew seating and a pleasant candle-lit atmosphere. A small selection of wines is available.

FAKENHAM
The Crown Hotel, Market Place
(Fakenham 2010)
Open: bars: Mon–Wed, Fri–Sun, licensing hours, Thu 10.30am–4.30pm, 5.30–11pm
restaurant: Mon–Sat 12.15–2pm, 7.15–9.15pm, Sun 12.15–2pm

C ♫ P S

In the restaurant, dark oak beams and panelling are offset by gold tablecloths and napkins, a red carpet and red-globed oil table lamps. A three course table d'hôte lunch is only around £3.50 and offers a good choice for all courses. Sardine and tomato salad, Florida cocktail or ravioli are examples of starters, a selection of roasts make up the main course and sweets from the trolley include cheesecake, fruit and cream or éclairs. A slightly extended menu operates for a three-course dinner at about £4.50. A three-course Sunday lunch for around £3.95 is good value. The à la carte menu offers more exotic dishes – still reasonably priced at between £6–£8 including fresh vegetables.

The Limes Hotel, Bridge Street
(Fakenham 2726)
Open: Mon–Fri 12noon–1.30pm, 7–9.30pm, Sat 12noon–1.30pm, 7.30–10pm, Sun 12noon–1.30pm

P S

THE CROWN HOTEL
Market Place, Fakenham.
Telephone: Fakenham 2010

The restaurant, with it's oak beams and panelling, offers a good choice for all courses on the table d'hôte menu. À la Carte menu available.

Restaurant Open:
Monday - Saturday 12.15 - 2pm, 7.15 - 9.15pm. Sunday 12.15 - 2pm.

Bars Open:
Monday - Wednesday, Friday - Sunday, Licensing hours. Thursday 10.30am - 4.30pm

---

THE LIMES HOTEL AND RESTAURANT
FAKENHAM, NORFOLK

We specialise in Home Cooked Dishes reflecting the tastes of several different countries; England, France, Italy, Southern States, Hungary, Australia.
Of particular interest is our selection of steaks served with various sauces, e.g. Beef Steak with Creamed Stilton, and our range of Casseroles e.g. Beef Creole, beef flamed with dark rum and cooked in Louisiana Sauce.
Additionally, varied Home Cooked bar snacks are available every day in our Lounge Bar, from around £1.00.
A traditional Lunch is served in the Restaurant from 12 o'clock every Sunday.

Telephone: Fakenham (0328) 2726

Felixstowe — Lowestoft

This friendly free house was only created in 1975, but already it has an excellent reputation for fresh, home-cooked food. The 'Summer Special' three-course lunch costs £3.75 and the choice is good for each course. The 'Winter Special' offers warming starters and sweets. A cold lunch buffet is on offer in the conservatory – and all the meats are home-cooked. À la carte dinner by candlelight offers a very wide selection.

FELIXSTOWE

Butter Bar, Orwell Moat House ★★★★
Hamilton Road
(Felixstowe 5511)
Open: Mon – Sat 12noon – 2pm, 6 – 9.15pm, Sun 12noon – 2pm summer only

C P &

This elegant buttery with its dark oak panels and richly-ornamented ceiling offers you all the comfort and luxury of a four-star hotel without the prices. Home-made soup of the day could be followed by smoked Scotch salmon, Norfolk turkey, ox tongue or other cold meats all served with salads, pickles, and a roll and butter. Finish with home-made fruit pie and you'll still be within the budget. In the restaurant, table d'hôte lunch and dinner are both around £5.75.

FRAMLINGHAM

Market Place Restaurant, 18 Market Hill
(Framlingham 723866)
Open: Tue – Sat 12noon – 2pm, 7 – 9.30pm

P

This tiny cottage restaurant on the corner of the market place has shuttered windows and a light, modern interior. A range of light snacks and elaborate meals is available suitable for both families and the discerning diner. Paul Stracey, the manager and head chef, also offers a series of light-hearted but interesting cookery lessons at the restaurant. The lunch menu offers starters from 70p – £2.50. Main courses include open sandwiches, burgers and omelettes all at under £2, beef salad (£2.95) and tagliatelle (£3). Vegetables are extra. There is a range of sweets at 85p. Take care with your choice as some of the dishes will take you over the limit. The extensive dinner menu is, alas, too expensive for this guide.

GREAT YARMOUTH

Moments, 149 King Street
(Great Yarmouth 2967)

Originally two merchants' houses, Moments is an American-style restaurant, serving a range of hamburgers, spare ribs, club sandwiches, pizzas and pancakes. Starters: clam chowder, Caribbean melon, prawn and tuna cocktail cost from 60p – £1.10, and hamburgers, served with French fries or baked potatoes, start at about £2. Desserts are around £1, and coffee is 35p.

HALSTEAD

Halstead Wine Bar (Pendle's), 70a High Street
(Halstead 477736)
Open: Mon – Sat 10am – 2.30pm, Sun 12noon – 3pm, Thu – Sat 8 – 11pm

S P &

Home cooking at its best is provided by the proprietors Hazel and Roy Boyle along with cordial and efficient attention. The simple wooden tables and seating are complemented by the authentic exposed old beams in this 16th century wine bar. The many home-made dishes are listed on the 'blackboard' menu and you might choose lasagne or chicken with almonds at £3.25 or coq au vin at just £2.25. The dinner menu also provides a wide variety of dishes. There is a good selection of fine wines to enjoy with your meal.

HARLESTON

The Dove, Wortwell
(Homersfield 315)
Open: Tue – Sat 11am – 2.30pm, 7 – 9.30pm, Sun 12noon – 3pm

P &

Freshly-prepared food and friendly service are the watchwords at John and Pat Oberhoffer's tiny restaurant. Once a pub and smithy, it is conveniently placed at the junction of the A143 and B1062 for travellers in need of refreshment on their way to and from the coast. The limited lunch menu offers a three-course meal for between £3 – £4, but the more extensive dinner menu costs considerably more and is outside the scope of this guide. Cream teas and light grills are available between 3.30 and 6pm.

IPSWICH

Great White Horse ★★
Tavern Street
(Ipswich 56558)
Open: Coffee Shop: Mon – Sun 11am – 9.30pm
Courtyard Lounge for snacks: 12noon – 2pm

C S &

A leading inn in Ipswich since the 16th century, the Great White Horse was once the haunt of Charles Dickens when the author was employed as a reporter on the Ipswich Chronicle and it was to receive a mention in his Pickwick Papers. The newly-decorated Coffee Shop offers a wide range of food from cream teas at £1.10 to omelettes and grills (£3 – £6) served all day. There is a special menu for the under 14's, and a good selection of fine wines. Lunches served from the Courtyard Table Buffet include hot and cold dishes from 95p – £2.95, from a bowl of soup with granary bread to ploughman's lunches and home-made sweets.

Henekey's Hotel ★★
Westgate Street
(Ipswich 58506)
Open: Mon – Sun 12noon – 2.30pm, 6 – 10.30pm, Fri – Sat 11pm

C ♫ P S &

Behind an ornate gothic, stone façade, this Trusthouse Forte concern has been completely modernised and refurbished. There are two comfortable restaurants, the Grill and the Sherry Restaurant, the latter being slightly more expensive. Although described as 'Henekey's Steak Bars', plaice (about £3.50), Barnsley chop (about £4) and chicken cordon bleu (£4.20) are also available and the prices include sweet or cheese. Appetisers are around the £1 mark, and include whitebait and smoked mackerel.

Marno's, 14 St Nicholas Street
(Ipswich 53106)
Open: Summer Mon – Wed 10am – 2pm, Thu – Sat 10am – 2pm, 7.30 – 10pm, Winter closed Wed pm

♫

A vegetarian restaurant with dishes imaginative enough to tempt the most confirmed meat-eater. The lunch menu includes savoury flans, bean hotpot, nut rissoles, freshly-made salads and fruits for about £3.70. The much more extensive evening menu averages around £6.25 for three courses such as mushroom pâté, Cheshire cheese and herb pie, pashka (a Russian mixture of curd cheese, butter, cream, raisins and brown sugar), followed by herbal tea. Live music is provided by local folk musicians at weekends.

Noble Romans, 9 Buttermarket
(Ipswich 219376)
Open: Mon – Sat 10am – 11pm, Sun 5.30 – 10.30pm

♫ S &

Claudius and Tiberius are among the 13 noble Romans whose names are taken in vain for the pizzas in this trendy Italian restaurant. A 'Claudius' has mozzarella cheese with tomato and costs about £1.35 while a 'Tiberius', at the top of the range, has tuna, sardine, anchovy, onion, lemon, olives, capers, mozzarella and tomato for around £2. A full three-course meal here need only cost about £3.50, with appetisers such as melon for around 90p and most desserts costing around £1 – try chocolate fudge cake or morello cherry and fresh cream waffle. All this and décor in oatmeal, fawn and brown with basket-weave chairs has attracted a regular clientèle.

LOWESTOFT

Victoria Bar Buttery, Victoria Hotel ★★★
Kirkley Cliff
(Lowestoft 4433)
Open: Mon – Sat 12noon – 2pm

C P &

A well-stocked cold buffet table holds roast Norfolk turkey, ox tongue, beef, ham and prawns in cocktail sauce, which with a serve-yourself salad average at about £2.50 a head. Hot meals include grilled minute steak, breaded scampi or fillets of Lowestoft plaice, but the Chef's special (changed daily) is warmly recommended. At the cheap end of the scale are sandwiches, a ploughman's lunch or hamburgers with salad garnish. Sweet and a starter add around 50p.

NORWICH

Le Bistro, 2a Exchange Street
(Norwich 24452)
Open: Mon 11.30am–2pm,
Tue–Fri 11.30am–10pm,
Sat 11.30am–2.30pm, 5–10pm

C F P S ☼

Table d'hôte at Le Bistro is very good value, an English lunch costing around £2.50 and dinner – with some French dishes – about £4.80. You could choose a good meal from the à la carte menu for less than £6, too. Veal Lyonnaise is a popular choice; other favourites include sole Normandy and duck with orange sauce. The first and second floor restaurants are pleasant and comfortable (once the stairs are negotiated), with fresh flower arrangements set against brocade-patterned wallpaper and oak tables.

Norwich

Mano, 72 Prince of Wales Road
(Norwich 613143)
Open: Mon–Sat 7–11.30pm

S

The bright orange and white exterior of this bistro proclaims its presence on the corner of Prince of Wales Road and Cathedral Street. As a striking contrast the interior is a faithful reproduction of a Parisian café with dark red paintwork, red velvet café curtains on brass rails and French posters. Green and white tablecloths cover the 10 cast-iron tables which provide seating capacity for 34 people. Contrary to appearance, owner Mano is in fact Turkish and his restaurant boasts a truly international menu. A meal of whitebait, followed by duck pilaff plus pears in burgundy wine and coffee will cost around £5.

Rembrandt Restaurant, Easton
(Norwich 880241)
Open: Tue–Sat 12noon–2.15pm,
7–10.15pm, Sun 12noon–2.15pm

C F P ☼

Proprietors Bruno (who is also the chef) and Trudie Riccobena extend a warm welcome to all, and have a wide range of menu styles to suit all tastes, including one for children. The restaurant also has facilities for invalids. Without careful

selection, the à la carte can easily exceed our limited budget, but the special 'Business Lunch' and 'Holidaymaker's Lunch' at around £3.75–£4 are very good value. Main course might be gammon, calves' liver, minute steak, omelette or salad. Under the Rembrandt chef's 'Taste of England' series, steak, kidney and mushroom pies, in particular, are selling like hot cakes! A traditional Sunday lunch will cost around £5.

Savoy Restaurant ✕✕✕
50 Prince of Wales Road
(Norwich 20732)
Open: Mon–Sun 12noon–2.30pm,
6pm–1.30am

C F P

The Athenian Room on the ground floor is elegantly green with chandeliers, Greek pictures and small booths. The windows overlook an enclosed patio with vines and plants galore. Downstairs is the Cellar Taverna, seating over 100 on two levels, complete with a small dance floor and nightly live music. Three-course table d'hôte lunch in the Athenian Room is about £3 on weekdays and £4 on Sundays. Main course choices are particularly good – roast beef or chicken, moussaka, kebabs, plaice or ham salad. The à la carte menu is very extensive, with Greek, English, Italian and French cuisine, but you will have to select a three-course meal carefully to stay around the limit.

VICTORIA BAR BUTTERY

Superb food & quick service for busy people.
Open 12-2pm Monday to Saturday

**Victoria Hotel, Kirkley Cliff,
Lowestoft, Suffolk.
Telephone: (0502) 4433**

For soup, omelettes, fish, hamburgers,
steaks, gammon,
cold buffet, sweets & cheeses,
coffee & wine.
Each day the Chef prepares a
Hot Main Course Dish.
Bar snacks available.
Morning coffee 10.30 - 12.00.

COSTERS

Restaurant and Bar
Open All Day
For Snacks and Light Meals

Help yourself buffet
for well under a fiver

Free parking,
convenient for city centre

**Station Road, Peterborough
Tel. (0733) 52331**

Tatlers, 21 Tombland
(Norwich 21822)
Open: Mon–Sat 6–11.30pm,
Sun 12.30–2.30pm, 7–11pm

You'll find Tatlers amongst the beautiful buildings of Tombland. A group of young people have converted an old house into this attractive restaurant, with a bar upstairs, and have succeeded in creating an air of Victorian opulence by the use of floral wallpaper, red curtains, Victoriana lamps, and mirrors. High-backed settles arranged around plain wooden tables provide a degree of privacy and seclusion. All food is prepared on the premises, the accent being on traditional Norfolk dishes prepared from local produce. Starters include pâté or mussels in white wine and main course dishes range in price from £2.50 to about £5. More unusual dishes include rabbit in mustard and rosemary or pigeon, duck and orange pie for around £3. Vegetables are likely to add about 70p to these prices. Sweets (the list includes syllabub and chocolate fudge cake) cost around £1.

PETERBOROUGH

Costers, Great Northern Hotel
Station Road
(Peterborough 52331)
Open: Mon–Sun 10am–10pm

Peterborough
Shoeburyness

The 'barrow boy' theme of this restaurant is emphasised by an original costermonger's barrow which is piled high with a 'help yourself' selection of freshly-made salads, cheeses, pâtés and fruit for £3.25. A three-course meal will cost below £5, whether you choose from the small à la carte menu or the daily table d'hôte menu. If you want something lighter, then try one of the snacks (pizza, pasty, quiche, scrambled eggs served on muffins and pancake rolls) all at around £1. The hotel car-park fee can be recovered when buying your meal.

SAFFRON WALDEN

Eight Bells, Bridge Street
(Saffron Walden 22790/22764)
Open: Restaurant Tue–Sun 12.30–2pm,
Mon–Thu 7.30–9.30pm,
Fri–Sat 7–10pm and normal licensing hours

Situated in a comfortable spot on the edge of town, like the noble old sentinel it is, this 400-year-old inn retains its original pub sign and a good deal of olde worlde charm. The table d'hôte lunch menu at £6.50 is of an extremely high standard and includes a main course of roast ribs of beef carved from a silver trolley. The price is inclusive of three courses and coffee. There is also a selection of hot and cold meals available in the bar around £2–£3.25 (steak and oyster pie is £3.25, farmhouse grill £3.25, hot devilled crab with garlic bread and salad £2.85). The à la carte menu is beyond the scope of this guide.

SHOEBURYNESS

Shore House Restaurant, Ness Road
(Shoeburyness 3408)
Open: Tue–Fri & Sun 12noon–3pm, last orders for food 1.45pm,
Tue–Sat 7.30pm–12.30am, last orders for food 10.30pm

If the fresh air gives you an appetite you'll find this sea-front eating place a very tempting proposition. However, the plush restaurant with its warm red décor is likely to just tip our limit in the evenings. Three courses from the interesting à la carte lunch menu can cost from £5.30 although a set three-course lunch with excellent choice of dishes is £3.90. The buttery is open at lunch-time for bar snacks and salads from 55p–£1.70.

Rembrandt

EASTON · NORWICH
Telephone Norwich 880241

TRADITIONAL SUNDAY LUNCHEONS
LUNCHEONS · DINNERS · CHILDREN'S MENU

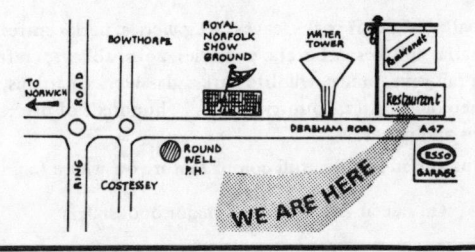

SOUTHEND-ON-SEA

Chinatown, 28 York Street
(Southend-on-Sea 64888)
Open: Mon–Thu 12noon–2.30pm,
5pm–12mdnt, Fri–Sat 12noon–2.30pm,
5pm–1am, Sun 12noon–12mdnt

P S

This cosy Chinese restaurant close to the town centre offers an enormous choice of traditional Chinese and English dishes at budget prices. Well-cooked and pleasantly served by Ken, the owner's son. Wan Tun soup is extremely tasty and roast duck Hong Kong style, decorated with Chinese mushrooms and peppers and costing about £2.50 is highly recommended. Chop suey and chow mein dishes are excellent value for money. A special set dinner for one person, which includes coffee, costs around £2.50 and is excellent value for money when you consider the amount of time spent in preparing the dishes.

Cotgroves Restaurant, 11 High Street
(Southend-on-Sea 338155)
Open: Mon–Thu 11.45am–9.15pm,
Fri–Sat 11.45am–9.45pm,
Sun 11.45am–9.15pm

C F P S ♦

David and John Cotgrove now run the successor to their grandfather Arthur's original High Street restaurant opened in 1896 – a modern, 185-seater imaginatively adapted from a former supermarket building. The décor carries forward a family tradition of 'fish and ships' including a colourful tiled entrance lobby – the work of a local sculptor – and several drawings and oil-paintings executed by John himself. Almost everything you could wish for is on the menu, from a T-bone steak or fresh crab salad down to steak, kidney and mushroom pie or a three-course 'special' at lunchtime for about £2.50. A wide range of good quality fried or grilled fish is featured, and the sweets vary from a simple ice-cream to a 'banana special' complete with ice-cream, chocolate sauce and whipped cream.

The Pipe of Port, 84 High Street
(Southend-on-Sea 614606)
Open: Mon–Thu 11am–2.30pm,
6–10.30pm, Fri–Sat 11am–2.30pm,
6–11pm, Sun 12noon–2pm

C P S

This wine bar is situated just off the High Street in a basement premises underneath Greenfields. There is a good, and recently-expanded menu with some interesting starters, such as the toasted fingers topped with anchovy, sardine or Stilton at around £1.30 for six. A three-course meal of soup, smoked mackerel (two fillets) with salad and fresh fruit salad can be had for around £4.95 – a very satisfying and nutritious repast.

Spencer's, 20 High Street, Hadleigh
(Southend-on-Sea 558166)
Open: Mon–Sat 10am–2.30pm,
6–11pm, Sun 12noon–2pm, 7–10.30pm

C F P S

This wine bar is easily spotted by the attractive pavement patio. Comfortable banquette seating and French cane-back chairs enable you to take your ease while absorbing the interesting reading on the walls. Chalkboards display the menu, offering plenty of choice. Pâté is about 90p, lasagne around £1.50 and hot salt beef on rye £1.50. The poppy seed French bread is very good as is the help-yourself salad selection from around £1.50 and the chili con carne at about £1.20. There is a selection of toasted sandwiches at 70p. Brian Spencer selects all his own wines and a glass of excellent French house wine costs around 65p in the restaurant.

Southend-on-Sea — Wivenhoe

WISBECH

Dickens Tavern, 17 Hill Street
(Wisbech 583476)
Open: Tue–Sat 12noon–2.30pm,
7.30pm–12mdnt

C F P S ♦

Built in the early 18th century, this former private residence was recently converted into the Dickens Tavern – a restaurant and wine bar. The Tavern is on two levels with the wine bar on the ground floor and the main restaurant on the first floor. The tastefully decorated Georgian Room on the ground floor is used by restaurant diners and private parties. Of the two menus on offer, only the Tavern Fare Menu is suitable for this guide. Listed on this menu are omelettes, salads, spaghetti bolognese, lasagne, moussaka and chicken and chips. Weekly 'specials' could include gammon, steak, seafood platter and steak and kidney pie. Prices range from 80p–£3. Sweets from the trolley are £1, coffee is 45p and a glass of wine 60p.

WIVENHOE

Maria's Ristorante, 30 The Avenue
(Wivenhoe 2221)
Open: Tue–Fri 12noon–2pm,
Tue–Sat 7–10pm

C P ♦

An interesting, short, but imaginative menu contains authentic Italian dishes which are all freshly cooked and skilfully presented. Try the home-made canneloni at £1.60 as a starter or £2.75 as a main dish when served with mixed salad or vegetables. Stuffed pork fillets at £4.80 are also popular. Select your dessert from the trolley at £1. A good range of Italian wines is available.

AA STATELY HOMES, MUSEUMS, CASTLES AND GARDENS IN BRITAIN

Stately homes, model villages, safari parks, caves, art galleries, park centres, museums, forest centres, dolphinaria, colleges, arboreta, potteries, zoos, abbeys, craft centres, castles, bird collections, steam railways, mines, wildlife parks, glassworks, gardens, nature reserves, distilleries, mills, archaeological sites, country parks ... hundreds of places to go, with full details of opening times and prices.

ALSO ... location maps and index plus full colour feature on where to go with all the family

On sale at AA shops and major booksellers

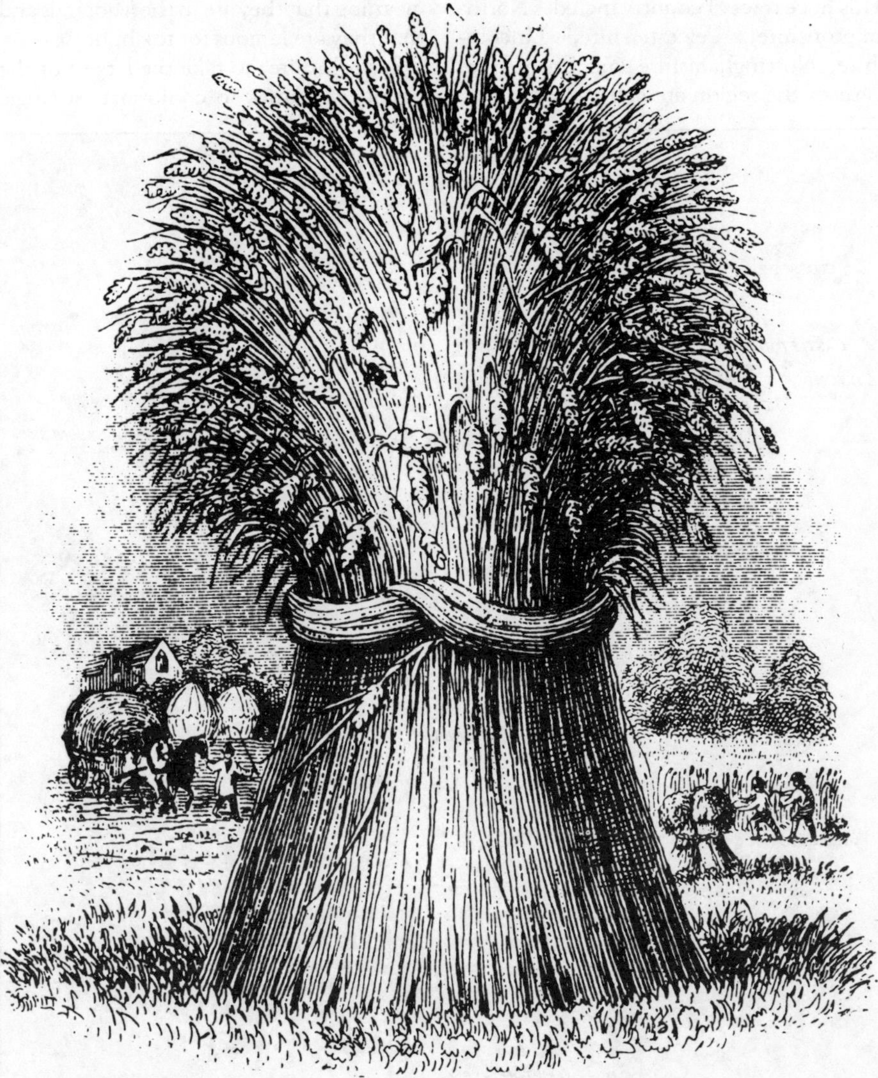

EAST MIDLANDS AND PEAK DISTRICT

This huge tract of country includes Northamptonshire, Leicestershire, Lincolnshire, Nottinghamshire and Derbyshire. Parts of the region are called the 'Shires', meaning that they are in the Midlands and that they are famous for fox hunting.

Lincolnshire, to take the largest of the counties, refuses to conform to a single pattern. It does, admittedly, tend to be flat – with the city of Lincoln and its superb cathedral standing high above the landscape, as if on an island.

Gainsborough, Scunthorpe and Corby are darkly industrial. Spalding, on the other hand, is surrounded by tulip fields. Boston, which was once second only to London as a port, has its Stump. In fact, it is the tower of St Botolph's church, and the word 'stump' is a fine example of English understatement. With a height of 272½ft, it is the country's second tallest church tower. The idea was inspired by a similar construction at Bruges in Belgium – brought home, no doubt, by the wool merchants who used to do a considerable trade with Flanders.

Leicestershire is famous for fox hunting, and no hunt is more illustrious than the Quorn (unless you belong to that other Leicestershire institution, the Pytchley).

Oscar Wilde described fox hunting as 'the unspeakable in full pursuit of the uneatable'. Dispute it if you like, but the pig, and certainly not the fox, is the preferred meat of the Shires. Melton Mowbray Pie contains diced pork; Quorn bacon roll is exactly what its name suggests; and boiled beans and bacon are popular in some circles.

Despite the fact that the village of Stilton is in Huntingdonshire, the making of good Stilton cheese originated in Leicestershire, where most of it is now produced. Accompanied by a glass of port, it goes down very nicely after a hard day in the saddle.

Richard III lost his life and his crown at the battle of Bosworth in Leicestershire (22 August, 1485). His personal chef fared better: he lost only his recipe book.

Somebody later found it and was attracted by the formula for a biscuit named Jumbly. The dead sovereign had been very partial to it. Now, his Leicestershire subjects were able to inherit his enjoyment.

To the north, at Nottingham, they used to make lace, and in the autumn, held a large and important Goose Fair, in the days when a Christmas goose, not a turkey, was the traditional dish. The fair is still held under the same name, but the geese have long since gone.

Derbyshire is notable for Rolls-Royce, the Peak District and Buxton. Rolls-Royce needs no introduction from us. The peaks of the district are not quite mountains, but wonderful hills with dry stone walls, lonely white cottages with slate roofs, and a few wooded valleys, and a lot of very fresh air.

Buxton, at 1,000 feet above the sea, is the highest town in England. Its healing waters were particularly appreciated by followers of Queen Elizabeth I, who went there to recuperate from the rigours of court life. Among their merits is that, unlike those of many other spas, they neither taste nor smell unpleasant.

Not far away, at Bakewell, they make Bakewell Tart, which is delicious. So is stuffed chine – if you can find it. It's a neck of bacon that has been soaked for twelve hours, and cooked with raspberry and blackcurrant leaves. Another rarity is potato whisky – the Midlands' reply to the Irish poteen. Making it needs patience. It should be left for at least a year before drinking.

Derbyshire cheese is very good indeed, especially when flavoured with sage leaves. These are either put in in one thick layer, or chopped finely and mixed throughout.

ASHBOURNE

The Ashburnian, Compton
(Ashbourne 42798)
Open: Mon–Sat 12noon–2pm, 6–10pm,
Sun 12noon–6pm

[C][S]

The restaurant with its white rough-plaster walls and dark beams with reproduction brass lanterns, has a pleasantly olde worlde atmosphere. A comfortable cocktail bar adjoining has hessian-clad walls and copper-topped tables. The menu is very reasonably priced, with starters ranging from around 50p–£1.15–including prawn cocktail and a choice of 10 main courses, all served with vegetables and including a sweet (such as apple tart with cream) in the listed price of from £3.80–£5.25. Half a roast chicken is around £3.

Cary's, Workhouse Yard, Dig Street
(Ashbourne 42811)
Open: Mon–Sat 10am–3pm, 7–11pm,
Sun 12noon–2pm, 7–10.30pm

[C][♫][&]

Named after John Cary, the famous 18th century cartographer, Cary's is a pleasant, rather trendy place, situated near the centre of this old market town in premises that date back some 300 years. Recently opened as a wine bar, it is run by the Blunstone family and some young female assistants in a friendly and informal manner. Décor is clean and fresh with exposed brickwork and ceiling beams and stripped pine furniture. Diners are entertained by piped music. A typical meal might include mushrooms à la grecque (95p), lasagne and side salad (£2.45) and crêpes with fruit filling and fresh cream (85p).

Ashbourne
##
Boston

BAKEWELL

Fischer's, Bath Street
(Bakewell 2687)
Open: Mon–Sat 12noon–3pm, dinner 7.30pm onwards, closed Thu and Sun evenings

[P][&]

This olde-worlde restaurant, originally a barn, features white painted stone walls and cottage furniture. Set lunches consist of traditional, home-cooked dishes, with choices such as home-made soup followed by steak and kidney pie or braised beef in brown ale followed by a good English pudding or ice cream at around £3.50. The evening meal is just beyond our limit.

Milford House ★
Mill Street
(Bakewell 2130)
Open: Mon–Sun 7-7.30pm, Sat & Sun 1–1.30pm

[P]

Situated on the ground floor of the Milford House Hotel, this pleasant 10-table dining room offers quality meals at sensible prices. The whole operation has been personally run by the Hunt family for many years and service is their keynote. Set lunches, at weekends only for non-residents, are £5.75 and feature roast chicken and roast beef. Five-course evening meals are only slightly dearer (£6), with roast stuffed loin topping the bill. After tasting dessert specialities such as strawberry pie with cream and orange trifle, you'll surely agree that Bakewell is an apt location for the restaurant. Coffee is included in the price. A word of warning – the short opening hours mean that advance booking is a must.

BOSTON

The Carving Room, New England Hotel ★★
Wide Bargate
(Boston 65255)
Open: Mon–Thu 12noon–2pm, 7–10pm,
Fri–Sun 12noon–2pm, 7–10.30pm

[C][P][&]

At the rear of the imposing New England Hotel is the elegant, Regency-style Carving Room, with white pillars, rich red-patterned carpet and green wallpaper, leather upholstery and tablecloths. Here you may eat a superb roast lunch or dinner. The carving table is bedecked with large roast joints, fresh vegetables and salads – you help yourself to as much

---

FALSTAFF TAVERNS

FINE FOOD AND A WARM WELCOME

Green Dragon	Waterside North, Lincoln	Tel. Lincoln 24950
Centurion	Newark Road, North Hykeham, Lincoln	Tel. Lincoln 680222
Fox & Goose	London Road, Coalville	Tel. Coalville 32342
Tom Lock	Lincoln Road, Peterborough	Tel. Peterborough 67558
Queen's Head	Market Place, Newark	Tel. Newark 702327

IN THIS REGION
YOU'RE NEVER FAR FROM
A
FALSTAFF TAVERN

Bourne — Derby

BOURNE

The Wishing Well Inn, Main Street, Dyke, 1¾m N of Bourne off the A15
Open: Mon–Sun 12noon–2pm, Mon–Sat 7.30–10.30pm, Sun 7.30–10pm

P &

as you want. This, together with the choice of a sweet from the trolley, will set you back £5.35. Appetisers are extra, but hardly necessary! Potted shrimps or avocado pear with prawns are the most expensive at around £1.50, but soup is only 70p. Children can help themselves and are charged the special reduced price of £3.

This pleasant, old inn has a small restaurant with exposed beams and stonework. Grills are the speciality, but the menu also features poultry dishes and pork and lamb chops. The starters and desserts are all under £1, though some of the choices for a three-course meal would take you over our price limit. Bar snacks are also available. There is a self-service carvery (though available only two lunch-times a week, including Wednesday; and Saturday evening) when you can help yourself to as much as you want for under £3.

BUXTON

Barbecue, 25 Spring Gardens
(Buxton 4312)
Open: Mon, Tue, Thu–Sun 10am–8pm

C &

This busy restaurant, situated in the centre of town, provides meals all day long. It is pleasantly furnished with local prints on the part-wood-panelled walls. Morning coffee and afternoon tea with cakes and pastries are available and there is a special late breakfast. The set three-course lunch offers a choice of three main dishes and is good value at £3. There is a separate à la carte menu and a children's menu.

CASTLETON

The Castle Hotel and Restaurant
(Hope Valley 20578)
Open: Mon–Thu, Sun 12noon–2pm, 7–10pm, Fri–Sat 12noon–2pm, 7–10.30pm

C P

Within the Peak District National Park and in the village centre, is this stone-built 17th century coaching inn, its interior a wealth of exposed stonework and beams. Excellent table d'hôte menus operate for lunch and dinner – you are spoiled for choice. Lunch costs £4.85, with 20 starters including avocado viniagrette, pâté-filled mushrooms in batter and smoked mackerel. Four roasts head the long list of main dishes. The roast beef with vegetables, ratatouille, horseradish sauce and Yorkshire pudding is particularly recommended. Fillet of pork à la crème, chicken chasseur and cider-baked ham with cinnamon peaches are other possibilities. A selection of sweets on the trolley are all served with fresh cream. Dinner is £5.35 and offers even more choices.

DERBY

Ben Bowers, 13–15 Chapel Street
(Derby 367688/365988)
Open: Mon–Fri 12noon–2pm, 7–11pm, Sat 7–11pm, Sun 12noon–2pm

C ♬ P S &

Located above the Blessington Carriage public house is this charming 'olde worlde' restaurant with seating for about 60. A three-course lunch of (for instance) home-made soup of the day, chicken chasseur, new potatoes, salad and a sweet costs about £4.35, children's portions are half price. The dinner menu features à la carte or a table d'hôte menu, £5.95 for four courses. The à la carte menu includes dishes from France, Italy, Greece, Hungary and, of course, Britain. Downstairs in Betty's Buffet Bar, excellent pub meals are served.

The Cathedral Restaurant Ltd ××
22 Iron Gate
(Derby 368732)
Open: Mon–Wed, Fri 12noon–2pm, 7–10pm, Thu 12noon–2pm

C ♬ P S &

In the shadow of Derby Cathedral, this elegant little restaurant with its low ceiling, exposed central beam and sparkling table tops, glassware and cutlery, is housed in a building dating back to 1530. Then a nunnery, it has since been a Ladies' club and a chartered accountants' office. At lunchtime a three-course table d'hôte menu is available at £3.50. Choice is good and dishes include salads, omelettes, roasts and steak, kidney and mushroom pie while shish kebab, grilled trout, chicken cathedral, sirloin steak and jumbo scampi are examples of the more pricey fare. In the evening there is a similar, though slightly dearer table d'hôte dinner at £6.45 and the à la carte menu, though tempting, is expensive.

The Lettuce Leaf, 21 Friar Gate
(Derby 40307)
Open: Mon–Sat 10am–7.30pm

P S

Beyond the little craft shop selling handthrown pottery, woodcrafts and books on yoga and health food is this white-walled restaurant with its bright curtains, basket-work lamp shades, wooden tables and tasty vegetarian menu. Vegetable soup or fruit juice are inexpensive starters at around 35p. Omelettes, salads, savouries and snacks supplement a daily speciality such as marrow provençale, lasagne, gratin Dauphinois, pizza or celery hotpot. Most main dishes cost under or around £1.35 with sweets such as fresh fruit salad, yoghurt with honey or lettuce leaf muesli under 65p. Finish with a dandelion coffee – full of flavour.

The Lettuce Leaf

Licensed Vegetarian Restaurant
Meet your friends for wholesome fresh baked food in a quiet, relaxed setting.
Open 10 am to 7.30 pm Monday to Saturday
Morning coffee ● Lunches ● Snacks ● Cream teas
Homemade cakes, Free range eggs, Craft shop
Luncheon Vouchers Tel: 40307

Swiss Cottage, 23–4 Audley Centre
(Derby 32593)
Open: Mon–Sat 9.30am–7pm

P S

One of a chain of similar establishments in Nottingham and Leicester, the Swiss Cottage is situated in modern premises in a shopping precinct in the city centre. It is very popular with shoppers who enjoy morning coffee and afternoon tea as well as satisfying three-course meals which are available for around £4.50 and under. There is a good range of starters, omelettes, fish dishes, salads, snack meals, grills and desserts. The Forge Salad and Wine Bar is situated on the first floor.

FOLKINGHAM

Quaintways, 17 Market Place
(Folkingham 496)
Open: Mon–Sun 11.30am–2.30pm,
Thu–Sat 7–10.30pm

F P

The Dutch-barn-style brick building with a bow window stands in the centre of this lovely village. Andrew and Robert Scott opened the restaurant and tea room in June 1982, and hospitality combined with value for money is the simple secret of their success. Robert entertains the diners in the evening by playing the organ. The lunch menu is excellent value at £2.95 though there is a rather limited choice, this also applies to 'Tonight's Supper Menu' at £2.25 with an extra charge for sweet. The 'Chef's Specialities' menu offers some very tempting meals but they are beyond the price range of this guide.

GLOSSOP

Crowton's, 14 High Street East
(Glossop 63409)
Open: Tue–Sat 12noon–2pm, 7–9pm

P S

If Victoriana is your scene you'll love this restaurant. For behind its brown and cream exterior lies an eating place furnished in the style of great-grandmama's front room – complete with black lead grate! The food however is right up to date, with steaks, poached

Folkingham
—
Leicester

salmon and scampi featuring on the menu for around £4–£5. There's the usual array of starters, and to finish with you might fancy a chocolate nut sundae or fresh pineapple with cream for less than £1. Coffee and mints are served for around 30p in an atmosphere of bygone days. It comes as quite a surprise to learn that Crowton's was established in 1979. The restaurant is also open for morning coffee and afternoon tea.

GRANTHAM

Catlin's, 11 High Street
(Grantham 5428/9)
Open: Mon–Tue 9am–6pm,
Wed 9am–2pm, Thu–Sat 9am–6pm

P S

Steeped in history, the olde worlde grocery and confectionery shop of Catlin Bros Ltd, boasts a restaurant with wood-panelled walls, oak beams, pottery and bric-à-brac on the first floor. The property dates back to 1560 and its claims to fame include the 'discovery' of Grantham gingerbread and the ghost of one Captain Hamilton, a Royalist officer during the Civil War. Snacks are served throughout the day and a typical meal from the à la carte menu might be home-made soup, pepper and salami pizza with salad and fresh fruit pancake with cream, and the bill will be well within budget. French house wine is very reasonable and, in fact for the buff there is an interesting range of wines from non-fashionable countries. Service is efficient and courteous.

HATHERSAGE

Bradgate Buttery, Main Road
(Hope Valley 50665)
Open: Tue–Sun 10am–10pm

F P S

English cuisine is the order of the day at this attractive Tudor-style restaurant with its Minstrel's Gallery where 50 evening diners can enjoy a meal with a view. Entrées include lamb chops with mint sauce, mixed grill and chicken and range

in price from £2.50–£4.60. Together with farmhouse soup, roll and butter, home-made gâteau, coffee with cream the average meal costs £5.

KIRK LANGLEY

Meynell Arms Hotel ★★
Ashbourne Road
(Kirk Langley 515/6)
Open: Bar meals
Mon–Sat 12noon–2.30pm,
6.30–9.30pm, Sat 8.15pm,
Sun 12noon–2pm, 7–8.30pm
Restaurant: Mon–Sat 6.30–8.30pm

C P

An excellent stopping place en route for the Peak District, the lounge bar serves a range of wholesome dishes at lunchtime and in the evening. Three courses can be easily enjoyed for less than £3.25 – soup of the day, followed by chicken and chips or home-made steak and kidney pie and a sweet from the trolley is a typical example. A three-course table d'hôte dinner offers a good choice for around £6.50. Main courses include roasts, lemon sole and Heynell mixed grill.

LEICESTER

Du Cann's Wine Bar, 29 Market Street
(Leicester 556877)
Open: Mon–Fri 11.30am–2.30pm,
Sat 11.30am–3pm,
Wed–Sat 5.30–10.30pm

F P S

In one of the city's many little side streets is this popular split-level wine bar. The attractive ground-floor room offers self-service selection of a variety of cold carvery items (turkey, ham, beef etc and some speciality seafood dishes) against a background of plain green walls, livened up by old prints, shelves of crock casks and old wine bottles. A varied three-course meal can be had for about £4.50. Below it is the white-walled cellar with its glimpses of original brick, where a full waitress service operates. In the evenings a number of home-made dishes, including Turpins Pie and chili con carne, are available from £1.95, supplement the cold selection.

Morning coffee, Lunches
Afternoon teas, Dinners
Licensed
Est. 1979

CROWTON'S
HOTEL & RESTAURANT
**14, High Street East, Glossop, Derbyshire
Tel. Glossop 63409**

Leicester

The Good Earth, 19 Free Lane
(Leicester 26260)
Open: Mon–Thu 12noon–3pm,
Fri 12noon–3pm, 7–11pm,
Sat 12noon–6pm

[P][S]

Tucked away in narrow Free Lane is this inviting first-floor wholefood restaurant. Inside all is natural wood, with displays of farming implements, hanging brass lanterns and a large farmhouse dresser with old plates and storage jars of preserved fruits, vegetables and grains. Help yourself to hot or cold dishes from the buffet display. A full meal will cost around £3.50, for which you choose from a selection of soups, hot savoury dishes or roasts, savoury rissoles, a variety of nourishing salads, home-made cakes, fresh fruit and natural goat's milk yoghurt. Parties of 20 or more can arrange to eat an evening meal on nights other than Friday.

The Hayloft, Holiday Inn ☆☆☆
St Nicholas Circle
(Leicester 531161)
Open: Mon–Sun 11am–10.30pm

[C][♫][P][♿]

In striking contrast to the modern hotel accommodation, the Hayloft restaurant has an old tithe barn atmosphere, with suitable décor of a hay cart, horse and oxen trappings, and enough room for 120 people. A satisfying three-course meal can be had here for around £6.45. Try the farmhouse soup (fresh made from the cauldron) followed by a 'good and wholesome salad' or baked mackerel with capers 'just like mother used to make', and parsley potatoes. To finish you may choose crème caramel or pie or gâteau from the pastry shop plus a cup of coffee (served from a bottomless pot for one charge). A special attraction on Sundays is the 'splosh and nosh' menu; for just over £6 (half-price for children) per person you can enjoy a sauna and swim in the hotel pool, followed by a three-course meal with coffee. If you find swimming a little too energetic, the regular weekend dinner dances might be just your thing.

The Post House Hotel ☆☆☆
Branstone Lane East
(Leicester 896688)
Open: Barge Buttery: Mon–Sun
7am–10.30pm

[C][P][♿]

Longboat owners will feel very much at home in this bright and original coffee shop, where the ceiling is curved to resemble an abstract version of an upturned boat, and the walls sport a colourful mural of a bargee family and their craft. Cream paintwork and a scattering of pictures depicting canal scenes complete the atmosphere. The imaginative menu gives excellent scope for a satisfying three-course meal for upwards of £4. Tasty starters and grills supplement the quick-and-easy hamburgers, salads and omelettes, most of which are around £2.75. A children's menu is available on request, children under five eat free, those under 14 may choose full adult portions at half price. Place mats and lollipops with the famous 'munch bunch' cartoon characters make this a very popular place for all young guests.

A Spanish Place, 38a Belvoir Street
(Leicester 542830)
Open: Mon–Sat 9am–6pm

[S]

An orange awning and pot plants gives this small modern restaurant a continental flavour. Inside, the emphasis is on home-made cuisine and a friendly, hospitable atmosphere, heightened by the fresh posy of flowers on each table. Snack foods and main meals are available throughout the day. Sandwiches and toasted snacks are made from freshly baked bread and cost between 85p–£1.20. A tasty three-course meal could include a Spanish omelette as an appetiser (around 80p), fried chicken, peas and jacket potato (about £2.20) and home-made fruit pie with fresh cream for around 65p. Business lunch boxes are made up by Susan and Josef Arroyo, the proprietors, to suit individual customers' requirements. Unfortunately, A Spanish Place is unlicensed.

Swiss Cottage Restaurant,
52–54 Charles Street
(Leicester 56577)
Open: Mon–Sat 9.30am–7pm

[P][S]

Opened about 18 years ago, this smart restaurant with attractive exposed brickwork, dark wood-effect tables, copper light shades and waitresses dressed as Swiss maids, was the first of six similar restaurants which have sprung up in Leicester. Each site has been chosen for its ease of access for shoppers and business people in the city centre. At lunch-time, chops, steaks, home-made steak and kidney pie, chicken and gammon steak are served at prices ranging from around £2–£4.05. Soup is around 40p and there is an excellent choice of home-made pies served with fresh cream for around 60p. Sister establishments are located in Churchgate, Lee Circle, Odeon Arcade and the Haymarket. The Swiss Cottage Garden, one of two places at the Haymarket, is the only licensed premises.

Tower Restaurant, Lewis's,
Humberstone Gate
(Leicester 23241)
Open: Mon–Sat 11.30am–3pm

[C][P][S][♿]

The sleek, 137-foot tower of Lewis's store, topped with coloured lighting was the talk of Leicester and district in 1936, when it was built. The fourth floor restaurant takes its name from this and its interior décor is based on one of the Queen's ships of the Thirties – all turquoise and gold with a rich, red patterned carpet. A special shopper's lunch costs just £2.50. The table d'hôte three-course lunch is also excellent value at just under £3.50. There is a choice for each course and a typical meal would be soup, followed by grilled ham and pineapple with sweet of the day to finish. The à la carte menu is extremely reasonable, with most main courses such as roasts around £4 and sweets from the trolley from 50p–70p. There is a special children's menu for under 11s. There is no service charge and VAT is included.

Swiss Cottage restaurants

18 CHAPEL BAR, NOTTINGHAM
Telephone 411050
ODEON ARCADE, MARKET PLACE
Telephone 59756
46-48 CHURCHGATE, LEICESTER
Telephone 27752
52-54 CHARLES STREET, LEICESTER
Telephone 56577
LEE CIRCLE, LEICESTER
Telephone 24190
HAYMARKET, LEICESTER
Telephone 24489
AUDLEY CENTRE, DERBY
Telephone 32593

Lincoln — Nottingham

LINCOLN

Crusts Restaurant, 46 Broadgate
(Lincoln 40322)
Open: Mon–Sat 11.30am–2.30pm,
7pm–12mdnt

[C][F][P][&]

Only the name 'Crusts', printed in bold lettering on the window distinguishes this restaurant from the quaint little shops on either side of it. This is a comfortable place in which to enjoy the good food and hospitality of proprietors Clive and Rita Barkes. Business lunch is a must for the budget-conscious as you can have three courses at a very reasonable price.

The Duke William, 44 Bailgate
(Lincoln 30157)
Open: Mon–Thu 11.30am–3pm,
6.45–10.30pm, Fri–Sat 11.30am–3pm,
6.45–11pm, Sun 12noon–2pm,
7–10.30pm

[C][P][&]

This charming 18th century pub stands in the oldest part of the city, close to the famous cathedral. Lunch here is a homely affair with dishes such as home-made steak and kidney pie, grilled plaice or ham salad, and the price of a three-course meal is around £3. For around £6.50, a fairly extensive dinner menu offers such dishes as fried whitebait or grilled trout with almonds.

Harvey's Cathedral Restaurant
1 Exchequer Gate, Castle Square
(Lincoln 21886)
Open: Mon–Sat 12noon–2pm,
7pm–12mdnt, Sun 12noon–2pm

[C][P][S][&]

In the shadows of Lincoln Cathedral and Lincoln Castle is Bob and Adrianne Harvey's bright, split-level restaurant. Lunch here any day and you will receive excellent value for money and a good choice of well-prepared food. On Sundays the three-course lunch always includes massive ribs of roast beef and costs £6.50, £2.50 for children. A weekday lunch for Senior Citizens costs around £2.50.

Zorba's Restaurant, 292–3 High Street
(Lincoln 29360)
Open: Mon–Fri 11.45am–2.30pm,
6.30–11.30pm, Sat 11.45am–11.30pm

[C][P][S][&]

Modern décor with banquette seating and contemporary refectory tables recommends this city-centre first-floor restaurant where good wholesome English and Greek cuisine is served with speed and efficiency. A small adjoining bar with Mediterranean bric-à-brac completes the scene. Lunch time you can enjoy a three-course special lunch from £3, with plenty of choice of English fare such as roast beef and Yorkshire, haddock and chips or farmhouse grill. The à la carte menu includes hors d'oeuvres from around 75p for spaghetti bolognese to about £1.25 for prawn cocktail. Roasts and grills vary from around £3–£5. A dozen continental dishes are on offer as are some Greek specialities such as Cyprians meze – a selection of hot and cold Greek dishes for about £5.

MATLOCK

The Elizabethan Restaurant
Crown Square
(Matlock 3533)
Open: Mon–Thu & Sun 11am–6pm, Fri & Sat 11am–9pm

[S][&]

The Gilding family's pleasant dining-house stands near the town centre on the main A6 through-road. Two adjoining rooms are cleanly decorated with white-painted, half timbered walls and there are refectory-style tables with Windsor chairs in simple surroundings. Smart and friendly waitresses have been serving good, wholesome food here since 1978. Starters range from 45p – £1 and examples are pâté de maison and egg mayonnaise. Main dishes are very good value (how about gammon at £2.65 or grilled rump steak at £4.20?) and include potatoes and vegetables of the day. All desserts are under £1, so why not go mad and finish with a knickerbocker glory? On Friday and Saturday evenings (until 9pm) a three-course menu is available at £6.20 and includes specialities and steaks.

MELTON MOWBRAY

Cervino Ristorante Italiano
1–3 Leicester Street
(Melton Mowbray 69828)
Open: Mon–Sat 12noon–2pm,
6.30–11pm, 11.30pm Sat

[C][&]

Unmistakably Italian, this pleasant restaurant is rich in memorabilia from the empty Chianti bottles that hang from the ceiling to the many picture postcards and posters of the home country which adorn the walls. An all-Italian menu offers such specialities as home-made pâté for £1.50, breast of chicken stuffed with cheese for £4 and apple tart and cream for 90p. Coffee with cream is 35p.

NORTHAMPTON

The Vineyard ×
7 Derngate
(Northampton 33978)
Open: Mon–Fri 12noon–2pm,
Tue–Sat 7.30–10.30pm

[C][F][S]

A gaily striped canopy and half-curtained window give a continental-café look to this modern restaurant in Northampton's busy centre. Inside, the décor is simple and effective, one wall being clad in pine with illuminated niches displaying a variety of antiques and bric-à-brac. The short but imaginative menu is changed fortnightly and offers dishes of British, European and Middle Eastern origin. For a truly international meal you might choose Mrs Cromwell's Grand Sallet (a 17th-century English dish with chicken or prawns) as an appetiser followed by jambonneau aux lentilles, with dondurma kaymakli (an Egyptian ice-cream flavoured with mastic) for dessert.

NOTTINGHAM

Ben Bowers, 128 Derby Road
(Nottingham 413388)
Open: Mon–Fri 12noon–2pm

[C]

Crusts Restaurant

46 Broadgate, Lincoln. Telephone 40322 & 790436

A lifetime's ambition was realised when Master Chef, Mr Victor Vella recently acquired Crusts Restaurant. In the warm and olde worlde charm of the restaurant, the customers can relax and enjoy the fruits of his 27 years experience and love of haute cuisine. The lunchtime diner can "Discover a Taste of England", for as little as £2.00 from a wide choice of traditional English dishes. Main courses also include grills, fish dishes, poultry, gammon and pork and there are 17 starters to choose from. House specialities have a French bias and when in season, smoked salmon and other delicacies can be savoured.

As well as the main restaurant upstairs, there is a small front coffee lounge and the quaint cocktail bar behind offers a full range of spirits, liqueurs and aperetifs and beers.

On display is an interesting selection of bills dated 1839 found in the attic during recent renovations. Mr Vella, a Maltese by birth, is no stranger to Lincoln having lived here for 18 years.

Nottingham

A sister to its namesake in Derby, this restaurant offers a good value three-course meal (main courses include chili con carne, minute steak au poivre and Almond Malakof) plus coffee for under £5. Below in the basement, Betty's Buffet Bar has a wide range of snacks (50p – £1.65) and cold meat and salad 'help yourself' buffet for £1.65. Next door in the basement is Palms 'Freehouse' bar and restaurant serving home-made snacks and bar meals, and a three-course meal for under £6.

Eviva Taverna and Kebab House
25 Victoria Street
(Nottingham 50243)
Open: Taverna: Mon – Sat 7pm – 2am
Kebab House: Mon – Sat 10.30am – 12mdnt
C ♫ P S

If you want to let off steam you can buy plates for smashing here. First, though, enjoy your meal in this basement restaurant transformed by white walls, vines, bunches of grapes and olive branches to a little bit of Greece in the heart of England. There are a few grills and roasts on the menu, but the chef's specialities – stifado (a rather special beef stew), kleftiko (lamb cooked with herbs) and dolmas (stuffed vine leaves) are particularly good and won't break the bank. Starters are priced from around 60p and most of the sweets (including paklava) cost in the 80p range. For two people dining together a half bottle of wine is provided free of charge, or you may choose from the list and have £1 knocked off the wine bill, which really is a worthwhile concession. Having enjoyed all this, listened to Greek music and watched Greek dancers in an adjoining room, you may feel like showing your appreciation by a bit of plate-smashing. Above the taverna is a kebab house run by the same proprietor, Mr Kozakis. This is a pleasant place to stop for a snack or for lunch, and the doner kebab, is specially recommended.

Food for Thought, 6 Hurts Yard, Upper Parliament Street
(Nottingham 46888)
Open: Mon – Sat 12noon – 2.30pm
C ♫ S ❀

Simple, good taste is the hallmark of this lunch-time restaurant, tucked away in a narrow alley dating back to Georgian times. Habitat furniture, posters, pictures and plants create a 'trendy' air. Food is cheap, home-made and varied. Starters include chili con carne (around £1), soup of the day and deep fried mushrooms (both at £1.10). FFT specials such as chickebab (chicken pieces with herbs on a skewer, served with French fries) pizza or lasagne are all around £2.15. A 'help yourself' buffet is fantastic value at £1.75. Salads and burgers are also available along with chef's specials which change daily. Super desserts such as South Sea Bombe or Bananarama will ruin any diet.

Grange Farm Restaurant, Toton
(Long Eaton 69426)
Open: Mon – Sat 12noon – 1.45pm, 7 – 9pm
P

A much extended brick-built farmhouse dating back to 1691 is quite a find just two miles off the M1 (exit 25), especially if it offers generous portions of wholesome English fare attractively presented, as this restaurant does. The dining room itself is in one of the oldest parts of the building, where oak beams and white brick abound, and there you can sample a quite superb table d'hôte lunch for around £4.85. A seemingly limitless choice of dishes is available – there are around 19 starters including whitebait, lasagne, melon and pâté, 12 main dishes such as rainbow trout, rabbit pie or supreme of chicken Marengo, all served with two vegetables and both creamed and roast potatoes, and almost 20 different sweets, some rather unusual.

La Grenouille Restaurant ✕
32 Lenton Boulevard
(Nottingham 411088)
Open: Mon – Fri 12.30 – 1.30pm, 7.30 – 9.30pm, Sat 7.30 – 9.30pm
♫ P ❀

Imagine white-painted tables (only seven

THE VINEYARD

LICENSED RESTAURANT

Northampton's most individual restaurant.

Marvellous food, always fresh, with a small frequently changed menu, giving tremendous variety and incredible value for money.

Excellent wine-list   *   Superlative cheeseboard

Luncheon: Fixed price and à la carte
Monday to Friday 12.00 - 2.00 pm

Dinner: à la carte only
Tuesday to Saturday 7.30 - 10.30 pm

7 DERNGATE NORTHAMPTON NN1 1TU

For reservations please telephone Northampton (0604) 33978

GRANGE FARM Restaurant

Toton, Nottingham.
Tel: Long Eaton 69426

M1 exit 25, 2 miles. 1691 Farmhouse with charm and atmosphere.
Midlands International Restaurant.
Traditional English Fayre served.
Finest collection of porcelain.
Lunch served from 12.00 - 1.45pm.
Dinner served from 7.00 - 9.00pm.
Saturday evening Dinner/Dance.

Proprietor: R H Skinner

Nottingham — Oundle

of them), white chairs with black cord upholstery, placed on black and white vinyl flooring against brick-red hessian walls highlighted with French posters; then add red tablecloths and matching table napkins. There you have La Grenouille – a little corner of France on the corner of a terrace of large Victorian houses. Young owner Yves Bouanchaud provides superb French food using mainly fresh products. Don't chance the à la carte menu if you're really hard up but it's worth going a bit over the £5 to enjoy a meal here if you can afford it. The table d'hôte menu offers a starter of home-made soup or terrine, a main dish such as boeuf bourguignon with vegetables and salad (this changes daily) and a sweet such as fruit salad or chocolate gâteau with cheese as an alternative, at around £5.45. Coffee is extra.

The Kingfisher, 127 Mansfield Road (Nottingham 45449)
Open: Tue–Sat 12noon–2pm, 7–11.30pm

P S

Salmon steak, shark, swordfish, halibut and haddock are amongst the 20 main dishes available in this licensed fish restaurant on a busy road from the town centre. The rear of the premises houses a functional dining room with plain wooden tables and curtain-divided booths in which to take your meal in comfort. Eight starters and sweets such as rum baba, gâteau and apple pie with cream are available, all at around 60p a fattening portion.

Moulin Rouge ✕
5 Trinity Square (Nottingham 42845)
Open: Mon–Sun 12noon–2pm, 6–10.30pm

C P S

Not strictly a French restaurant but very much a Continental haunt, the Moulin Rouge is close to the Victoria shopping centre and the Theatre Royal. The sparkling restaurant has predominantly red décor, with crisp white table linen and banquettes. The à la carte menu includes appetisers, soups, fish, omelettes, entrées, poultry, curries, grills, salads and desserts, with a wide range of prices. A daily main course 'Special' costs £1.95, but three-courses must be selected with care if you are to avoid going too much over £5. If you canot find the meal you crave 'the menu is only a suggestion, our chef is at your command'.

The Paraquito Restaurant
473 Mansfield Road (Nottingham 609447)
Open: Tue–Sat 12noon–1.45pm, 7–10pm

Since taking over the Paraquito Philip and Jean Glanfield have offered fine service and a good quality menu. Their three-course lunch embraces choices of starter, one of four main dishes such as roast pork, chicken chasseur or braised lambs liver, plus vegetables of the day and a choice of sweet or cheese. Alternatively, try the steak platter, which includes prawn cocktail, sirloin steak, a side salad, chips and all the trimmings with a dessert or cheese for under £6. In the evening, a four-course dinner is available, under £6, with main dish choices of trout, chicken, lamb cutlets and many more. There's a 10% service charge in the evening only, when the restaurant becomes crowded with the famished folk of Nottingham.

The Savoy Hotel ★★★
Mansfield Road (Nottingham 602621)
Open: Colonial Restaurant: Mon–Sat 12noon–2.15pm, 7–9.30pm, Sun 12noon–2.15pm
Steak Bars: Mon–Thu 12noon–2.15pm, 6–11pm, Fri–Sat 12noon–2.15pm, 6–11.30pm, Sun 12noon–2.15pm, 7–10.30pm
Salad Bar: Mon–Fri 12noon–2pm

P

One of the most popular eating places in Nottingham, this large, luxurious hotel has a sumptuous restaurant and richly decorated steak bar on the ground floor. The lower ground floor houses a second steak bar with exposed stonework and a salad bar with exposed wall and ceiling timbers. Food is excellent value for money. The restaurant offers a three-course lunch with a vast choice for all three courses, from around £4.50. A five-course dinner with even more choice is about £6, some choices such as poached salmon steak with prawn sauce adding around 60p to the bill. The steak bars provide, efficiently and quickly, a wide range of inexpensive quality meals. The 'all in' price includes a starter, main course and sweet. T-bone steak with all trimmings is only £5. A children's menu is available as well as half portions on certain dishes.

Swiss Cottage, 18 Chapel Bar (Nottingham 411050)
Open: Mon–Sat 9.30am–7pm

F P S

Peter and Bernard Morritt have made this modern, canopied premises in a cul-de-sac the seventh of their family chain of restaurants. Amidst the exposed brickwork and copper lighting it is possible to sample anything from the most simple sandwich (around 25p) to the tastiest rib steak (about £4.05, with all the trimmings, chips and vegetables) preceded by a choice of soups at around 35p. Finish with a delicious strawberry pancake topped with fresh whipped cream (at around 80p), home-made cherry pie or cheese and biscuits. The restaurant is unlicensed so you will have to forego a glass of house wine.

The Waterfall, 7–8 Hurt's Yard, Upper Parliament Street (Nottingham 42235)
Open: Mon–Fri 12noon–2.30pm, 7–11pm, Sat 10am–5pm, 7–11.30pm

C F S

It's well worth the search for this interesting little restaurant nestling in the Georgian shopping centre, reached by means of a narrow flagstoned alleyway by the side of the Fox Inn. A wide bow window fronts the restaurant which seats about 60 within its three sections, each with a distinctive olde worlde atmosphere. The waterfall forms part of a cool and splashing grotto which provides an attractive focal point. The dark-wood tables take on a more sophisticated look in the evenings with the addition of Nottingham lace tablecloths and flickering candles. An interesting and reasonably-priced à la carte menu offers a traditional selection of dishes including minute steak at around £2.50. For the same price, a three-course business lunch offers such dishes as home-made soup, roast lamb or pork cutlet chasseur, sweet plus coffee. If your taste is for the more exotic, you may choose veal cordon bleu or fillet of sole Monte Carlo from the speciality à la carte menu – but beware, prices are higher and you'll have to be selective.

OLLERTON

Rose Cottage, Rufford (Mansfield 822363)
Open: Mon–Sun 12noon–10pm

F P

Two miles south of Ollerton on the A614 and almost opposite the entrance to Rufford Abbey is this quaint brick cottage with small leaded windows, surrounded by an immaculate garden. Inside is all wood panels and beams, with three separate areas for dining. A wide range of fare is available from midday throughout the week. A three-course table d'hôte lunch could include minestrone soup, braised lamb chops and vegetables and ice cream gâteau. A more sophisticated menu is used in the evening, when care will be needed to avoid exceeding the budget.

OUNDLE

The Falcon Inn, Fotheringhay (4½m N of Oundle off the A605) (Cotterstock 254)
Open: Mon–Sun 12.30–2pm, Tue–Sun 6.45–9.30pm

P

The Falcon Inn, built in 1820, is situated in the middle of a picturesque and historic village. The popular village pub restaurant has an excellent reputation for good food at very reasonable prices – so be warned, table reservations are required for all meals, with some evenings booked solid for three months.

Skegness — Uppingham

The menus vary daily, hot food is not served Monday and Saturday lunch-time – but an appetising cold buffet is available. A three-course meal could include iced gazpacho, roast duckling with orange and almonds, and fresh peach melba, with coffee and a glass of wine the bill will still come to under £6.

SKEGNESS
The Copper Kettle, Lumley Road
(Skegness 67298)
Open: Summer Mon–Sun 9.30am–10pm, Winter Mon–Sat 10am–5.30pm, closed Jan–Feb

[F][P][S][♿]

Set amongst the shops in one of the town's busiest streets, you could easily dismiss this brown, bow-windowed restaurant as yet another gift shop. However, once inside, you can forget the hurly-burly world of amusement arcades and trumpery, and relax in the peaceful atmosphere created by rich green carpeting with subtly contrasting white plaster and plain brick walls. Modern lights, masquerading as old-style oil lamps, hang from the ceiling at strategic points between the pine tables. The fare is limited, but will prove very good value for money. Starters include pâté and prawn pil pil and cost between 85p and £1.50, with main courses such as Somerset Pork at £4.25. Home-made desserts are about 80p.

SLEAFORD
Carre Arms Hotel ★
(Sleaford 303156)
Open: 12noon–2pm, 6.30–8pm

[C][P][S][♿]

The red-brick public house built in 1906 is on the edge of the town centre near a level crossing. The bright, well-maintained dining room offers a good selection of mainly grill and roast dishes at reasonable prices. Even if you do splash out on a steak, surrounded by a simple starter and sweet, you are unlikely to go far beyond £6.

STAMFORD
The Bay Tree Coffee Shop, 10 St Pauls Street
(Stamford 51219)
Open: Tue, Wed & Fri 9.30am–5.30pm, Sat 9.30am–5pm, Sun 1–5pm

[S][♿]

This quaint, bow-windowed little coffee shop is located in one of Stamford's quieter streets close to the main shopping area. Horse brasses displayed on dark beams and prints on the cream walls create a pleasant period atmosphere. Emphasis is on home-made fare and prices are astonishingly reasonable. A three-course meal of soup and roll, home-made steak and kidney pie, fruit pie and cream, coffee and a glass of wine costs under £3.

Ye Olde Barn Restaurant, St Mary's Street
(Stamford 3194)
Open: Mon–Sun 12noon–2pm, 6–10pm, closed Mon evening & Sun all day in winter

[P][S]

Step into the alleyway at the rear of Ye Olde Barn coffee shop and you will find this two-storey restaurant, crowded with fine antiques and gleaming with well-polished copper and brass. The upper floor seats 60 below the rafters of the fine timbered roof, where a small cocktail lounge is also to be found. Downstairs is a slightly smaller restaurant boasting the same low prices and excellent value for money. Gammon steak, pork chop, steak and mixed grills are served with vegetables and cost anything from £1 upwards, with warming dishes such as home-made steak and kidney pie served with jacket and creamed potatoes and a selection of vegetables at around £2.15. Cold meat salads are under £2.50. A sweet such as profiteroles with chocolate sauce rounds things off nicely.

STRETTON
The Shires, on southbound carriageway of the A1 close to its junction with the B668, approx 8m N of Stamford
(Castle Bytham 316 and 332)
Open: Tue–Sat 10.30am–2.30pm, 7–11pm, Sun 12noon–2pm, 7–10.30pm

[P][♿]

The Shires is accessible to both north and southbound travellers and there is plenty of space in the grounds for customers with touring caravans. The stone building was originally a rectory and the farmhouse tables in the large, open-plan, ground-floor room can each seat up to 10 diners. Starters at under £1 include mussels in a cream and wine sauce and the main courses include gammon steak with spiced peaches. Most dishes are under £4, except for the steaks. There is a choice of sweets at 75p.

SUTTON-ON-SEA
Anchor, 12 High Street
(Sutton-on-Sea 41548)
Summer Mon–Sun 10am–5.30pm, 7–10pm, Winter Fri–Sat 10am–2.30pm, 7–10pm, Mon–Wed, Sun 10am–2.30pm

[C][P][♿]

A canopied doorway and bow windows pick out this country-style restaurant, converted from an old house reported to be a home to Alfred Lord Tennyson. Food to suit the pocket and palate of any poet is served here. For around £3.85 a three-course lunch including minute steak garni is yours, and for £5.50 a three-course dinner plus coffee could include melon, steak chasseur and a sweet from the trolley. The à la carte menu is also very reasonable, with a good choice of starters, roasts, fish dishes, salads, grills and desserts well within our budget. Half portions are available for children.

THRAPSTON
The Court House, Huntingdon Road
(Thrapston 3618)
Open: Mon–Sun 12noon–2pm, 6.45–10pm, 10.30pm Fri & Sat

[C][P][♿]

This restaurant is contained in the old Thrapston court and police station, but grim-faced magistrates handing out fines and sentences have been replaced by smiling waitresses with plates of food. Relics of the former function decorate the dining room, in the shape of police memorabilia, helmets, badges, truncheons and handcuffs. The old cells were demolished to make room for modern bedrooms, so even the worst-behaved guests need have no fear of being locked up for the night! A wide range of food is offered at The Court House; from sandwiches, ploughman's and beefburgers, through to more substantial dishes of steak, fish, gammon etc – all fitting easily into our budget. In the evening try the chef's special which could be carbonnade of beef, chicken supreme or even Bobby's Buster (no it's not a truncheon but a huge steak, kidney and mushroom pie).

TIDESWELL
Madeira House, 5 Commercial Road
(Tideswell 871176)
Open: Tue–Sun 12noon–2pm

[S][♿]

Portuguese proprietor Mr Abreu is proud that his restaurant dates from before the discovery of the New World by his fellow countryman Christopher Columbus. So be prepared for the low ceilings, supported by sturdy oak beams. Although open in the evening when an international cuisine is served, it is for the more simply-priced and prepared lunch and bar meals that Madeira House is noted in this guide. A home-made soup of the day (60p), can be followed by a choice of main dishes (such as fish, pizza, or minute steak) all served with salad and chips, and none costing more than £2. Sweets are around 75p.

UPPINGHAM
The White Hart Inn, High Street West
(Uppingham 2229)
Open: Mon–Sun 12noon–2pm, Mon–Sat 6–9.45pm, Sun 7–9.45pm

[P][♿]

This pleasant, old inn provides good portions of simple fare at reasonable prices either in the lounge bar or the restaurant. The starters priced from 45p, can be followed by salads (from £1.95) or a range of hot meals priced between £1.65 and £2.50. Steaks are more expensive. The 'special' is about £1.50, plus a sweet at 60p.

THE HEART OF ENGLAND

The Heart of England, as defined by the map, is Staffordshire, Shropshire, West Midlands, Warwickshire, Hereford and Worcester. When the originators of that rustic soap opera, *The Archers*, decided to site Ambridge in this area they knew what they were doing: you really can find villages quite like the one in the story – the quintessential English village.

Warwickshire has given us Stratford-upon-Avon and Shakespeare; Staffordshire, porcelain and part of the Peak District; the West Midlands were the cradle of the Industrial Revolution, and Worcestershire has given us the famous sauce. In the Vale of Evesham there is another garden of England, almost as rich in hops and apples as Kent, but more compact.

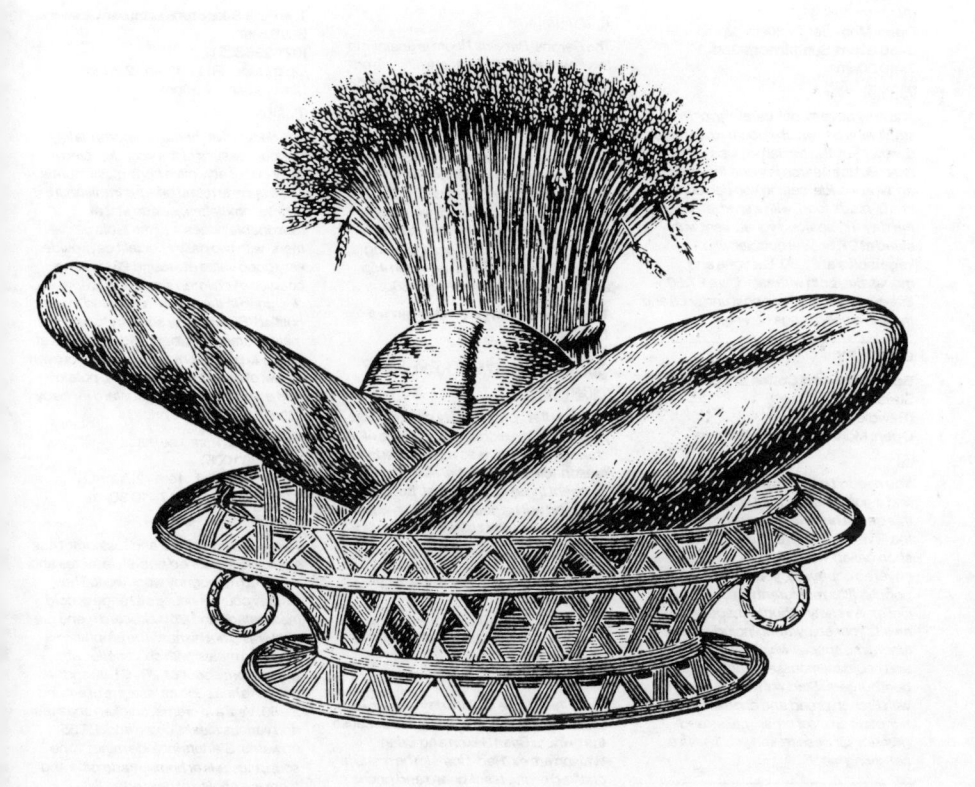

Hops abound in Herefordshire, and there is some good beer too.

At Coleshill in Warwickshire, or so the story goes, the vicar used to set the young men an Easter Monday task: they had to catch a hare and bring it to the rectory before 10am. If they succeeded they were rewarded with a huge breakfast, the menu included a calf's head and 100 eggs. Each lad was also presented with a groat (a small silver coin worth about 4p).

In Herefordshire, they used to be fond of a dish called 'Love in Disguise'. Among the ingredients were vermicelli, the pipes from a calf's heart and bacon, but nobody seems to know the origin of the name.

Shrewsbury has given its name to a kind of currant biscuit, and Shropshire herb roll is a delicious variant of suet pudding. The crust is filled with a mixture of fresh herbs, onions and minced rabbit and bacon. Faggots, a sort of rissole of liver and other offal, baked in the oven and served with thick gravy, are well liked in the Black Country and in the Midlands generally. In Staffordshire, oat-cakes, quite different from the Scottish biscuit of that name, are still made by local bakeries: they are a type of oatmeal pancake, served hot with bacon and eggs or toasted cheese. They can also be spread with butter and syrup.

ALCESTER

The Three Tuns Wine Bar, 34 High Street
(Alcester 764042)
Open: Mon–Sat 11.30am–2pm, 6–10.30pm, Sun 12noon–2pm, 7–10.30pm

[F][P][&]

You may have to look carefully for this small wine bar which is located, or rather dwarfed, by the two large pubs either side. But the search is worth the effort. In an 'olde worlde' setting you can enjoy home-made food, with a special dish of the day. Try seafood vol-au-vent with salad at £1, or beef cobbler with vegetables at £1.80. Lasagne and moussaka, both with salad, are £1.60. A three-course meal can cost under £3 and there is a good range of wines.

BEWDLEY

Back of Beyond Coffee Shop, 55 Load Street
(Bewdley 403114)
Open: Mon–Sat 10am–4.45pm

[S]

You needn't go to the back of beyond to find a good meal or light snack – just visit this quaint historic town on the banks of the River Severn. Here, at the rear of a shop called 'Room Interiors' and across a covered courtyard, you will find the popular little restaurant run by Angela Collip. A variety of home-made goodies awaits your enjoyment, including the lunchtime special which changes daily and could be moussaka, cottage pie or beefburgers. Start with home-made soup with French bread and choose from a tempting array of cream cakes and gâteaux for dessert and you'll have a satisfying meal.

BIRMINGHAM

Black Horse Hotel, Northfield
(021-475 1005)
Open: Mon–Fri 12noon–2pm, 7–10pm, Sat 7–10pm

Alcester — Birmingham

[C][F][P][&]

The Barons' Bar Grill Room is upstairs in this impressive 'black and white' inn on the Bristol road. Overhead is the original raftered roof, but the barn-like aspect is counteracted by hessian-covered walls and the solidity of oak furniture. The menu is standard for Davenport inns, and the main dishes are those found in most grill rooms, the accent being on steaks for between £4.50 and £5.75, with other dishes including plaice and gammon (both around £3), all prices including vegetables. Starters fall between 45p and £1, desserts from around 80p.

The Conservatory, Holiday Inn ☆☆☆☆
Holliday Street
(021-643 2766)
Open: Mon–Sun 7am–10.30pm

[C][F][P][&]

Meals at the conservatory can be a little pricey, with an extravagant choice of starters. Main courses and desserts are reasonable. You can therefore eat a pleasant three-course meal, but careful selection will be needed to keep within our limit. A novelty children's menu is available.

Dingos, 6 Great Cornbow, Halesowen
(021-503 0480)
Open: Mon–Sat 10.30am–2.30pm, 7–10.30pm, Sun 12noon–2pm, 7.30–10.30pm

[P][S][&]

If you think there is a holiday atmosphere in this wine bar and bistro, that's because the owners Brian Saxon and Brian Watson are ex 'Red-Coats'. The menu is chalked on the blackboard and prices range from 60p–£3.30. At lunch-time home-made pizzas, lasagne and moussaka are available, and there is a 'self-service' cold table for £1.50. Coffee is always available, but why not try one of the special wine cocktails at 75p.

The Four Seasons Restaurant, Lewis's, Bull Street
(021-236 8251)
Open: Mon–Fri 11.45am–2.30pm, Sat 11.45am–2.30pm

[C][S]

The decorative theme is, appropriately, the four seasons of the year depicted in relief in four attractive fibre-glass murals. The à la carte menu offers a traditional list of grills, omelettes, salads etc, at reasonable prices and the table d'hôte menu with two daily specialities provides very good value at around £3 for three courses. A children's menu, cleverly designed in the form of a 'Wanted' poster entitled 'Big shots for small fry' offers a main course, ice cream and cold drink at prices to please any parent. There is even a bowl of assorted vegetables, potato and gravy plus a dish of custard for baby at half the children's price.

La Galleria, Paradise Place
(021-236 1006)
Open: Mon–Sat 11am–2.30pm, 5.30–10.30pm, Sun 7–10.30pm

[C][F][P][S][&]

This modern wine bar and restaurant has small, old fashioned pub-style tables and deep red mahogany woodwork. The display counter houses a range of cold meat salads and a blackboard menu above lists hot dishes. The emphasis is on Italian meals, with six varieties of pizzas from about £1.20–£1.80 and pasta dishes such as lasagne at around £1.80. Veal à la crème, chicken chasseur and various steaks come from £2.55 upwards. Starters include minestrone soup, mussels or home-made pâté and there is a choice of desserts.

Gaylord ×× 61 New Street
(021-632 4500)
Open: Mon–Sun 12noon–3pm, 6–11.30pm

[C][S]

THE BLACKHORSE HOTEL STEAK BAR
919 BRISTOL ROAD SOUTH, NORTHFIELD, BIRMINGHAM B31 2QT.
Telephone: 021-475 1005

Built 1929 — Architecturally interesting interior, sculptured fireplaces, baronial atmosphere.
Steak Bar — 1st Floor.
Adjacent bar for sole use of diners.
Seating 100. Intimate alcoves.
Georgian Suite — separate private room for parties, seating 40.
Ample parking.
Wide range of grills, good choice of wines; weddings, private parties catered for. On the A38.

Birmingham

The mirror-lined hallway decorated with pot plants is a foretaste of the authentic Indian atmosphere in the spacious green restaurant above, where Tandoori cooking can be viewed through glass windows while you wait. The menu offers a wide range of dishes with a lunchtime 'eat as much as you like' menu for around £5. A special vegetarian meal is offered for around £4.95. Dishes on the à la carte menu are reasonably priced at lunchtime and chicken, lamb or fish delicacies flavoured with oriental spices abound within our price range.

Ginger's Vegetarian Eating House,
7 High Street, Kings Heath
(021-444 0906)
Open: Mon–Sat 12noon–2pm, 7–10pm
🎵 P ♿

You should have very little difficulty in locating this delightful little restaurant, as the restaurant name is emblazoned in large, colourful letters on the large window. The blackboard menu, which stands in one corner, offers such delights as carrot and rosemary soup at 75p, butterbean hot pot at £1.85 and creamed cottage cheese and parsnip bake at £2. All main-course prices include a choice of two salads. The home-made sweets cost around 75p each.

Gino's Belvedere Restaurant, East Mall Shopping Centre
(021-643 1957)
Open: Mon–Wed 12noon–11pm,
Thu–Fri 12noon–11.15pm,
Sat 12noon–11.30pm, Sun 12noon–10.30pm
C 🎵 P S ♿

THE CONSERVATORY

Dine in the splendour and opulence of our Victorian Conservatory. Let us introduce you to traditional dishes such as the 'Returned Hunter's Omelette' or 'Mrs Glass's Salamongundy' featured in our extensive a la carte menu. This menu is available at lunchtimes and evenings in addition to our daily lunchtime buffet.

For table reservations phone 021-643 2766
or write to:

Holiday Inn®
Holliday Street, Birmingham B1 1HH.

GINGER'S
VEGETARIAN EATING HOUSE

7 High Street, Kings Heath, Birmingham.
Telephone: 021-444 0906

> Sample such delights as
> Carrot and Rosemary Soup, Butterbean Hot Pot,
> Creamed Cottage Cheese and Parsnip Bake, Choice of Salads
> Home Made Sweets
>
> *Open: Monday - Saturday 12 noon - 2pm, 7pm - 10pm*

Birmingham

Walls decorated with enlarged engravings of old Venice give an immediate Latin flavour to this popular, centrally-situated Italian restaurant. You can make do with just a pizza or omelette, or choose from the extensive à la carte menu at around £4.60 for three courses and coffee. A special three-course lunch is available at an all-inclusive price of £2.50 and a glass of wine for about 60p. There is a speciality menu offering a selection of more sophisticated items which are a little more expensive.

The Grape Vine, Units 2 and 3, Edgbaston Shopping Centre, Hagley Road, Five Ways
(021-454 0672)
Open: Mon–Sat 12noon–2.30pm, Mon–Wed 5–9pm, Thu–Sat 5–10pm
C F P S

Proprietor Peter Gully is a man with a mission. His aim is to lead people away from using processed foods – artificially flavoured, bleached or dyed, and preserved with chemicals; he is opposed to 'battery' farming too, and believes a sensible vegetarian diet can improve health as well as making inhumane production of animal proteins unnecessary. There are always home-made soups, hot flans and nut roasts, and main dishes use peas, beans, nuts, rice, free-range eggs and rennet-free cheeses to provide the necessary protein element. A representative three courses such as soup (85p), cashew nut roast (£2.95) and trifle (£1) gives some idea of what to expect.

Happy Gathering, 54–56 Pershore Street
(021-622 2324/3092)
Open: Mon–Sun 12noon–12mdnt
C F P

This successful Cantonese restaurant is situated on the outskirts of the main city centre. The interior is very clean and typically Chinese with red embossed wallpaper, wood panelling and brightly-painted oriental pictures. Food is authentic Cantonese and proprietor Mr Lai is particularly proud of the baked crab in black bean sauce and the duck in plum sauce. Because of the nature of Chinese eating, a choice from the à la carte menu can be as cheap or expensive as you like depending on the variety of dishes chosen. Chicken with lemon sauce is £2.60. There is a more formal set dinner at around £4.

Hawkins Cafe-Bar, King Edward Buildings, 205–219 Corporation Street
(021-236 2001)
Open: Mon–Fri 8.30am–10.30pm, Sat 10am–10.30pm, Sun 5–10.30pm
C F P S

Situated close to the law courts and Aston University is this new concept in food and drink. The strong art nouveau décor proves an interesting blackcloth to the half-hour lighting extravaganzas on Friday and Saturday and occasional appearances of guests artists such as George Melly or Georgie Fame. On to the food – prices range from about 90p for home-made soup to around £2.90 for roast rib of beef with fresh salad. A dish of the day, filled baked potatoes and pizzas are also available – all freshly-made on the premises.

Heaven Bridge ××
308 Bull Ring Centre, Smallbrook Ringway
(021-643 0033)
Open: Mon–Fri 12noon–11.30pm, Sat 12noon–12mdnt, Sun 12noon–11.30pm
C F P S

The à la carte menu, in Cantonese and English, lists nearly 200 dishes. Hors d'oeuvres, from around 80p–£1 include rice rolls, dumplings, croquettes and water-chestnut pâté and in addition 24 choices of soup are offered. Main

---

Gino's Restaurant

Belvedere (Birmingham Shopping Centre)
Telephone: 021-643 1957
Set in the heart of the Birmingham Shopping Centre (above New Street Station).

The rendezvous of the shopper commuter.

Serving from a varied Menu of Italian, Continental and English specialities.

Open from 12 noon every day.

To serve is our duty …
… To serve well is our pleasure

HAPPY GATHERING

慶相逢酒樓

Authentic Cantonese Cuisine served in the cosy, friendly and unhurried atmosphere of the

HAPPY GATHERING
Bring Your Own Wine!!
PERSHORE STREET, BIRMINGHAM 5
The Original Cantonese Restaurant established 10 years.
Open 12 noon till Midnight - 7 days per week!!
Telephone: 021-622 3092
For a dining out experience!

Birmingham

courses, varying in price from about £3–£5 include an exciting array of dishes – seafoods such as cuttle-fish, crab, oysters and lobster and game and poultry in main guises. A large glass of che foo (Chinese sweet wine) costs around 80p.

Horts Wine Bar and Bistro, Harborne Road, Edgbaston
(021-454 4672)
Open: Mon–Sat 12noon–2.30pm, Sun 12noon–2pm,
Mon–Fri 5.30–10.30pm, Sat & Sun 7–10.30pm

[P][S]

Easily recognised in fine weather by the 'overspill' of tables and chairs onto the wide pavement outside and the distinct French flavour in the simple brown-and-beige décor, this is a popular haunt of local business people. An assortment of nourishing English and Continental food is available, including a dish of the day such as risotto, pâté and various salads at around £2. Home-made soup is 55p, whilst desserts such as gâteau or American cheesecake are about 85p, leaving you plenty of change from £5. There's a small raised area at the rear, for the more intimate and quiet meal.

The Loft, 8 Churchill Precinct, Dudley
(Dudley 57801)
Open: Tue–Fri 11.30am–3pm,
Sat 11.30am–4pm, Sun 12noon–2pm,
Wed–Sat 7–10pm

[P][S][♦]

This restaurant sits proudly over a butcher's shop, so take care not to miss the entrance which is a doorway between two shops. After climbing the stairs you will find yourself in a large, white-walled room with black-beamed ceiling and alcoves along one wall. There is a good range of dishes on the lunch menu including steak and kidney pie and a mixed grill. Starters are under £1, main courses under £3.75, lunch-time specialities around £2 and sweets around 50p. The evening menu has a range of three-course meals for under £6 and one of the main features of the restaurant is the 'Recession Special' menu available Thursday to Saturday.

Madisons, 40 Cannon Street
(021-643 3650)
Open: Mon–Thu, Sun 12noon–12mdnt,
Fri–Sat 12noon–1am

[S]

A quiet side street, close to one of the city's main shopping areas, is the setting for this American-style restaurant. Food is cooked in the open kitchen area and consists mainly of a variety of grills and more exotic Continental cuisine. Madison's cocktails are an experience in themselves, and during 'Happy Hour'

they are even better value than usual. Tuesdays to Thursdays, diners can enjoy live blues and jazz.
See advert on p. 124

Maxwell's Plum Wine Bar & Bistro, 163 Broad Street, Fiveways
(021-643 0274)
Open: Mon–Sat 12noon–2.30pm,
Mon–Fri 5.30–10.30pm,
Sat–Sun 7–10.30pm

[♬][P][S]

Plate glass windows and a gay striped awning distinguish this wine bar from its neighbours in the shopping area. A speciality worthy of note is the spicy Welsh sausage, served with fried potato, tomato and onions, but a good selection of quiches, flans and home-made sweets are available on the buffet. Daily hot dishes include prawn provençale, lamb curry, pork chop Milanese and cod Mornay.

HORTS WINE BAR AND BISTRO
HARBORNE ROAD, EDGBASTON, BIRMINGHAM
Telephone: 021-454 4672

OPEN: Mon-Fri 12noon-2.30pm, 5.30-10.30pm
Saturday 12 noon-2.30pm, 7-10.30pm
Sunday 12noon-2.00pm, 7.00-10.30pm

Named after an infamous local character, Horts offers a full range of wines and imaginative English and continental foods all at sensible prices. Horts now boasts a champagne bar where bubbly is served by glass as well as magnum.
For under £5 you can enjoy a four course meal of prawn cocktail, smoked ham salad and a sweet followed by cheese and biscuits, accompanied by a glass of house wine for 45p. Main course prices, including a four salad choice range from quiche lorraine at £1.40 to fresh salmon at £1.90.
Recently extended with new and sumptuous surroundings makes Horts just about the most luxurious wine bar and bistro in Birmingham.

Madisons

40 CANNON STREET, BIRMINGHAM 021-643 3650
Open 10 a.m. - 12 p.m. 7 Days

LICENSED RESTAURANT & COFFEE LOUNGE

- ★ Cocktails & Happy Hour
- ★ Live Blues & Jazz
  Tuesday, Wednesday and Thursday 6-8
- ★ Discount For Party Bookings
  (Complimentary House Wine)
- ★ American & Continental Cuisine
- ★ Afternoon Menu
- ★ Fancy Dress Parties
- ★ Student Discount

IT'S NOT AN EXPERIENCE . . . IT'S AN EDUCATION

New Happy Gathering Chinese Restaurant

新慶相逢酒樓

Licensed

43-45 Station Street, Birmingham

Enjoy Authentic Cantonese Cuisine at its very best, in the Sophisticated Atmosphere of Birmingham's most Luxurious Restaurant.
A high standard of service and Gourmet dishes all at very moderate prices.

Telephone: 021-643 5247
Open 12 noon to Midnight
(Between Classic Cinema and Market Hotel)
Facilities for Conference and Banqueting in private

Plaka

Greek Restaurant & Take Away
63 New Street, Birmingham B2 4DU
Telephone: 021 643 6694

Greek Take Away
35 Pinfold Street, Birmingham B2 4DG
Telephone: 021 643 6601

Open 7 days a week 12.00 - 2.30 and 5.00 - 12.00

Yes it is all Greek at the Plaka, but it is also high quality food and service at low prices. Offered to you by TONY PITSILLIDES who introduced most of the Birmingham people to Greek food.
Live Music
Credit cards accepted
English, Greek, French, Italian, Spanish, Turkish and Iranian spoken.

Birmingham

Michelle ✕
182–184 High Street, Harborne
(021-426 4133)
Open: Mon–Sat 12noon–2pm, 7–10pm
[S] [&]

Step into Michelle's French restaurant and you move back in time – to the heyday of the small-time grocer's shop. Dark mahogany shelving, a tiled bacon area and large mirrors belonging to the original Co-op grocers shop it once was, form the basis of a most unusual décor. Of the typically French cuisine, the coq au vin and boeuf bourguignon are among the best French dishes to be had this side of the Channel. Even the à la carte dinner menu allows you to eat well for around £7 but, the one-choice-only table d'hôte at lunchtime is excellent value at only £2.65.

New Happy Gathering ✕✕
43–45 Station Street
(021-643 5247)
Open: Mon–Sun 12noon–12mdnt
[C]

Mr Eric Ming Fat Chan offers traditional Cantonese cuisine at this gracious and comfortable restaurant. A staggering menu boasts more than 100 dishes, the majority in the £3–£5 range. Portions are generous and you can choose from a variety of not-so-familiar dishes such as a steamed duck with plum sauce, waterchestnut pudding or braised duck's web in oyster sauce. Sweets include various fritters in syrup for around 80p and Chinese pastries cost about 35p. Set meals offer a good variety of savoury dishes from around £6.

Pinocchio's ✕
Chad Square, Hawthorne Road, Harborne
(021-454 8672)
Open: Mon–Sat 12.15–2pm, 6.30–10.30pm
[P] [S] [&]

Tucked between a hairdresser's shop and a newsagent, in a tiny, modern shopping centre, close to the village of Harborne, this converted shop also acts as a sort of unofficial art gallery, for the restaurant exhibits and sells pictures by local artists. The menu is wide-ranging and tempts extravagance, but if you stick to the three-course table d'hôte lunch menu you'll be surprised how reasonable it is.

Plaka Taverna, 63 New Street
(021-643 6694)
Open: Mon–Fri 12noon–2.30pm, 5pm–12mdnt, Sat 12noon–12mdnt, Sun 5pm–12mdnt
[C] [♫] [S] [&]

Of the many Greek specialities served here, Kleftiko – lamb cooked in the oven, served with a Greek salad and pitta – is worth a special mention as it is very tasty, filling, and good value at around £4.50. With main courses like this you don't really need a starter but one of the 'dips' at about 95p may tempt you, or there are stuffed vine leaves costing a little more. If you've fallen for an hors d'oeuvre you'll need to look for a less-filling (and less-expensive) main course. There are a number to choose from with prices under £4 – kebab lamb or pork, two different sausage dishes, and fillet of sole served with chips and salad, are examples. A dessert will not add much more than 95p. The lunch menu is much cheaper. Step out of busy New Street into the discreetly-illuminated interior of this restaurant and you can imagine yourself in Greece. Paintings from the Mediterranean create an exotic atmosphere. It comes as a surprise when the oracle speaks with a Midlands accent.

Rajdoot ✕✕
12–22 Albert Road
(021-643 8805)
Open: Mon–Sat 12noon–2.30pm, 6.30pm–12mdnt, Sun 6.30pm–12mdnt
[C] [♫] [P] [S]

Ornate brass, red silk and hessian walls and burning joss sticks complete the transition from West to East, in this authentic Indian restaurant offering Punjab and Tandoori cuisine. Excellent set lunches are available from Monday to Saturday and dinners are à la carte, with an average meal coming just outside our budget. Tandoori specialities (charcoal clay oven barbecues) include delicious rashmi kebab – chicken minced with onion, chillies, fresh mint, coriander and herbs and spices.

Rock Candy Mountain, High Street, Harborne
(021-427 2481)
Open: Mon–Sat 12noon–2.30pm, 5.30–10.30pm, Sun 12noon–2pm, 7–11.30pm
[C] [♫] [S] [&]

Bright, gaudy, garish but immaculate is the only way to describe this 'latest concept in wine bars – music – restaurants – meeting places and astral food'. Set in the centre of Harborne, it hums with activity and welcomes everyone. 'Kiddies' have their own special spaghetti-hamburger-ice-cream menu. The comic-strip menu offers pizzas, salads, hamburgers, BBQ ribs, chicken Kiev, chili con carne and steaks. Prices start at £2. Kick off with corn on the cob (95p) and finish with chocolate fudge cake with ice cream (85p) – one of a selection of way-out desserts.

The Salad Bowl, The Old Mill Inn, Windmill Street, Upper Gornal (just off the A459 Dudley–Wolverhampton Road) (Sedgley 3000)
Open: Wed–Sat 12noon–2pm, 7–10.30pm
[♫] [P] [&]

It is worth leaving the main road to find this white-painted inn. The restaurant is above the inn and seats 40 people comfortably in traditional style. Old farming and riding equipment add to the cosy, rural atmosphere. In keeping with the name, the main meals are salads on a 'help yourself' basis and they range in price from £2.75–£3.50. Scampi, rump and fillet steaks are also available, although steak with a starter and sweet would take you over our limit. One of the original Black Country ales is served at the inn.

Sandonia, 509 Hagley Road, Bearwood
(021-429 2622)
Open: Tue–Sat 11.45am–3pm, 6–11.30pm
[C] [S] [&]

Owner Mr Constantinou (known to his regulars as Mr Conn) comes from Cyprus and opened this restaurant over 17 years ago. 'Regulars' include a couple who have dined at the same table every Thursday night for 15 years – there's faithfulness for you! The table d'hôte lunch at around £1.65 consists of soup or fruit juice, a choice of items such as roast or braised steak with vegetables, and ice cream or fruit pie with custard. A three-course lunch à la carte is likely to cost about £4: for this one might have soup; a main course of a roast or a 'fry-up' such as egg, sausages, chips and peas, an omelette or a fish dish. A sweet chosen from a long list if likely to cost around 45p. The dinner menu is more expensive but one could still make a choice within the limit. Grilled halibut or curried prawns, roast Norfolk turkey, a number of grills and kebab or chicken pilaf all under £3 are examples, these prices including potatoes and two green vegetables. There is a good selection of starters at about 80p and sweets are priced from around 65p.

Valentino's ✕
High Street, Harborne
(021-427 2560)
Open: Mon–Sat 12.30–2pm, 7–10.30pm, Sun 12.30–2pm
[C] [♫] [P] [S] [&]

A smart little Italian place, converted from one of the main street shops in which decoration is kept simple enough to have a relaxing effect. A table d'hôte lunch of egg mayonnaise, grilled sirloin steak and a piece of gâteau costs about £3.85 with coffee and wine extra, though the à la carte menu could tempt you over the limit if you have extravagant tastes. Coffee and cream is around 60p.
See advert on page 126

White Swan, Harborne Road, Edgbaston
(021-454 2359)
Open: Mon–Fri 12.30–2.30pm, Mon–Sat 7.15–10pm
[C] [P]

When Ron and Norma Phillips took over this old established inn they were told that a ghost prowled around the upstairs area; so far they have no trace of the uninvited guests, but keep your eyes open just in case! Ghost or no ghost, the White Swan is a popular eating place, so booking is advisable. Steaks and grills are served in the restaurant at prices from around £3–£5. Appetisers range from about 50p–£1, sweets from 60p–80p. At lunchtime a cold buffet is available in the skittle alley and includes an extensive range of home-made salads.

Wild Oats, 5 Raddlebarn Road, Selly Oak
(021-471 2459)
Open: Tue–Sat 12noon–2pm, 6–9pm, closed Sun, Mon, Bank Hol wkend & two weeks Xmas and New Year
P &

Not far from the Birmingham University complex, Roy Nutt's small vegetarian restaurant seats 26 at well-scrubbed kitchen tables; the brown and cream décor gives it a warm, earthy appearance. The daily menu consists of three or four starters and main courses which can be accompanied by salad or potato dishes. Our inspector had Maltese soup (a delicious blend of orange and tomato) followed by casserole of Chinese vegetables and pasta, with a fresh green salad. The restaurant is not licensed and there is a corkage charge (20p per person) if customers wish to bring their own wine. There is also an extensive menu of 'take-away' and 'freezer' dishes which is proving very popular.

Bridgnorth
—
Broadway

BRIDGNORTH
Baileys Wine Bar and Bistro, 78 High Street
(Bridgnorth 3445)
Open: Mon–Sat 11am–2.30pm, 6–10.30pm, 11pm Fri–Sat, Sun 12noon–2pm, 7–10.30pm
S

John Porter opened Baileys in September 1980, after he and his wife had completely gutted the original premises and removed a remarkable 300 tons of rubble. The exposed beams, stained wood floors and occasional rugs create a pleasing atmosphere, and diners should scan the walls for details of special offers of the day. Popular dishes such as beef provençale (£2.25), Bailey's potato and meat pie (85p), and turkey vol au vent take a lot of beating, but salads and open sandwiches are warm-weather winners. Sweets and starters are excellent value for under £1.

BROADWAY
The Coffee Pot, 76 High Street
(Broadway 858323)
Open: Mar–Oct
Mon–Sat 10am–5.30pm,
Sun 11am–5.30pm, Nov–Feb

Fri–Sat 10am–5.30pm,
Sun 11am–5.30pm
P &

This charming converted house lies on the edge of the village. In winter log fires blaze in the huge, open, stone fireplace in the restaurant, where an impressive embroidered silk hanging decorates the wall. Tea, coffee and home-made soup and cakes are available throughout the day. The three-course lunch, with a choice of three main dishes, is £3.25 (the price includes a cup of coffee), and there is a small but selective wine list.

Cotswold Cafe and Restaurant, The Green
(Broadway 853395)
Open: Summer Mon–Fri 10am–6pm, Sat–Sun 10am–8pm, Winter Mon–Sat 10am–5.30pm, Sun 10am–6pm
&

The Cotswold Cafe and Restaurant has counted amongst its customers John Wayne and the pop group Genesis. Delicious home-made ice creams are for sale, a speciality of Mrs Susan Webb's family since 1945. The restaurant serves snacks and three-course à la carte meals throughout the day, with prices varying from about £2.50 for roast chicken, fresh vegetables and two kinds of potato to around £4.75 for sirloin steak. There is a range of home-made sweets.
See advert on page 78

Valentinos Restaurant

WE CATER FOR PRIVATE PARTIES

FINEST CONTINENTAL CUISINE

Telephone: 021-427 2560
73 High Street, Harborne, Birmingham.

WILD OATS

VEGETARIAN RESTAURANT
5, Raddlebarn Road, Birmingham B29 6HJ.
Tel: 021-471 2459

We specialize in home-cooked vegetarian and vegan food and offer an interesting range of salads. Our menu changes daily. Private functions catered for.
Our take-away and freezer food services enable customers to order food of their own preference at advantageous prices.
Bookings not necessary but please advise of parties of eight or more.
Customers may bring their own wine.
OPENING TIMES: 12 - 2pm (last orders). 6 - 9pm (last orders).
Closed Sundays, Mondays, Bank Holiday weekends, Christmas and New Year.

The Gallery Restaurant, North Street
(Broadway 853555)
Open: Tue–Sun 11am–9pm. Closed Jan

[P][♿]

A former 16th-century coach house, this restaurant's white-painted interior has a wealth of black timbers supporting the barn-type ceiling and a minstrel's gallery at the far end. A special three-course lunch includes fresh orange juice, roast beef and Yorkshire pudding and a choice of desserts such as lemon meringue pie, sherry trifle or gâteau for around £3. Lunchtime specials offered include home-made steak and kidney pie, fried chicken or cod – all for around £1.50.
See advert on page 139

Goblets Wine Bar, High Street
(Broadway 852255)
Open: Mon–Sun 12noon–5pm,
6–9.30pm

[C][♪][P][S]

Dating back to 1631, this stone-built one-time inn is now a thriving wine bar. A stone-flagged floor with scatter rugs, and black and white half-timbered walls adorned by tapestry panels make an ideal setting for the numerous antiques. Imaginative home cooking and a warm welcome have made Goblets very popular with the locals. Appetisers include home-made mackerel pâté at around £1 and Andalusian gazpacho (chilled tomato soup with garlic, onions and peppers). Chicken à la Indienne (strips of chicken in mild curry and peach sauce) is about £3, with honeyed pork or beef and prune casserole in the same price bracket. Desserts include Goblets gâteau and home-made coffee and walnut ice cream.

BROMSGROVE

Andrés, 7 High Street
(Bromsgrove 73163)
Open: Mon, Thu 11am–3pm,
Wed 11am–7pm, Tue, Fri 9.30am–7pm,
Sat 8.30am–6.30pm

[♪][♿]

Gay brown and gold awnings tell you that you've arrived at Andrés, a modern restaurant, tastefully decorated in pine with pottery lampshades and tiled floors.

Bromsgrove
—
Clent

A daytime menu provides quick grills, salads and omelettes for shoppers and business people at less than £4 for three courses. There is an extensive selection of traditional English fare such as sirloin steak with trimmings and scampi.

BROMYARD

The Old Penny ✕
48 High Street
(Bromyard 83227)
Open: Mon, Wed–Sat 12.15–1.30pm,
7–9pm, Sun 12.15–2pm

[C][S][♿]

This simple, 17th-century restaurant has exposed beams and white walls. The dining room is divided by an attractive archway. Proprietors Norman and June Williams are known locally for using only best-quality meat and fresh vegetables in their wholesome English meals. Speciality of the house is roast duckling with orange sauce. The budget conscious are advised to stick to the table d'hôte lunch at £3.50 and dinner at £6.40. A typical meal from these low price menus would consist of mushrooms in garlic butter followed by sirloin of beef and Yorkshire pudding and chocolate nut sundae with fresh whipped cream.

CANNOCK

Roman Way Hotel, Watling Street, Hatherton, 1m SW of Cannock on the A5
(Cannock 72121)
Open: Restaurant: Mon–Fri 12.30–2pm,
7.30–10pm, Sat 7.30–10pm,
Sun 12.30–2pm, 7.30–9.30pm
Lounge carvery:
Mon–Fri 12.15–2.15pm, 6–8.30pm,
Sat 12.15–2.15pm

[C][♪][P][♿]

This modern hotel complex offers diners a choice of menus in the restaurant and the lounge carvery. In the restaurant a three-course table d'hôte menu at around £5 could offer melon and orange cocktail, veal Milanaise and gâteau. If you prefer a simpler meal, then try the lounge carvery, which offers pizzas, pies, fish and chicken dishes and salads. Here a three-course meal with coffee costs around £3.50.

CHURCH STRETTON

The Studio, 59 High Street
(Church Stretton 722672)
Open: Summer Mon–Sat 12noon–2pm,
7.30–10pm, Winter Mon 7.30–10pm,
Tue–Sat 12noon–2pm, 7.30–10pm

[C][♪][P][S][♿]

After housing a potter's studio earlier this century, part of this row of 300-year-old white-painted cottages has reverted to its former business of hospitality. For in the days when there were reputedly more pubs than houses in Church Stretton, the 'studio' was an inn. Inside is a small, cosy bar and a dining room with an atmosphere of clean simplicity. The standard lunch menu can easily keep within £3.50 for three courses, and features home-made steak and kidney pie. The more exciting dinner à la carte has tempting specialities together with more conventional dishes, but is likely to break the budget.

CLENT

Four Stones, Adams Hill
(Hagley 883260)
Open: Tue–Sat 12.30–2.30pm,
7–11.30pm, Sun 12.30–2.30pm

[♪][P][♿]

In the heart of the scenic Clent Hills, just south of the A456 'twixt Kidderminster and Halesowen, is this quaint little bow-window fronted cottage which has been converted into a country-style restaurant. Dark wooden beams, posts and horsebrasses complete the rural atmosphere. Here you may enjoy a set three-course lunch which could include soup of the day, a choice of roasts and a home-made dessert for less than £3.50. The à la carte menu is much more extensive, and provided you avoid the Chef's Specials, you should be able to have a feast within our budget.

Four Stones Restaurant

Enjoy the scent of country air and home cooking in the delightful period restaurant set in the heart of the Clent Hills.

★ Set 3 course lunch ★ Extensive à la carte menu including Chef's specials
★ Fully licensed ★ Friendly relaxing atmosphere
★ Small weddings and parties catered for

Table reservations phone Hagley 883260

Coventry — Evesham

COVENTRY

Corks Wine Bar, Whitefriars Street
(Coventry 23628)
Open: Mon–Fri 11am–2.30pm,
6–10.30pm, Sat 6–11pm,
Sun 7–10.30pm

🎵 P ♿

Dark green walls, a raftered ceiling, tiled floor and old tulip-shaded wall lights create a yester-year effect enhanced by cast-iron and refectory tables, old French street name plates, prints and mirrors. Two plat du jour blackboards list the range of cold and hot dishes available, these changing every day. Prices range from around 50p–£3. Soup of the day is about 45p, gâteau 80p, pizzas about £1, meals of the day such as spaghetti or boeuf bourguignon just over £1.25, meat salads £1.80 and steak at around £3.80. If you're feeling adventurous, escargots at £1.80 are an interesting alternative.

Nello Pizzeria, 8 City Arcade
(Coventry 23551)
Open: Mon–Thu 9.30am–11.30pm,
Fri–Sat 9.30am–1am

C P S

An informal atmosphere and freshly-baked food have established the Nello as a popular eating place – ideal for weary shoppers and tourists alike. Pastas are listed as starters on the menu, though a plate of home-made lasagne or cannelloni is a tasty meal in itself. Pizzas include the Special Pizza Nello – a banquet of cheese, tomato, tuna, prawns, mushrooms, anchovies, egg, ham and olives – all this for around £2.25. Grills and roasts are also available, ranging in price from £2–£5.

DROITWICH

The Spinning Wheel Restaurant, 13 St Andrews Street
(Droitwich 770031)
Open: Mon–Sat 10am–5.30pm,
Tue–Sat 7.30–10pm,
Sun 12noon–2.30pm

🎵 P S ♿

Popular with shoppers, tourists and local business people, the Spinning Wheel enjoys a prime position in Droitwich's new shopping centre. Access to this attractive cottage-style restaurant is across a paved patio area complete with fish pond and garden furniture. Friendly waitresses will serve you from a comprehensive menu ranging from light snacks to more substantial grills, omelettes etc. A table d'hôte three-course meal consisting of soup of the day, roast pork and apple sauce with vegetables, plus sweet costs £2.25. Main dishes from the à la carte are also reasonably priced with pizza or steak and kidney pie at around £1.65 to grilled gammon with pineapple at £3.45. With starter, a fresh cream sherry trifle at 60p and coffee, the whole need cost no more than £3.

ELLESMERE

The Black Lion, Scotland Street
(Ellesmere 2418)
Open: Restaurant Mon–Fri 6.30–9.30pm
Bar: Mon–Sat 11.30am–2pm,
6.30–9.30pm, Sun 12noon–1.30pm,
6.30–9.30pm

C P S ♿

This early 16th-century inn stands in the centre of Ellesmere. In the dining room, with its exposed beams and simple décor, steak, chicken and scampi are supplemented by sole in prawn and mushroom sauce (one of the most expensive dishes), and lasagne. There's a wide range of standard bar meals. The special Black Lion Ploughman's for around £1.50 is guaranteed to satisfy the most ravenous ploughman, with its red and white Cheshire and Stilton cheeses, bread and salad.

ENVILLE

Granary Wine Bar, The Cat Inn
(Kinver 2209)
Open: Mon–Sat 12noon–2pm,
7.30–10.30pm

P ♿

The wine bar is located on the first floor of this original coaching inn. It is furnished with country-style tables and chairs and the countryside theme is completed with a display of farming implements. Salads are served during the summer, except for Friday evenings when a large roast is available at £3.50, and hot dishes are served during the winter. Fresh salmon is on the menu, as is lobster (when in season), but with a starter, sweet and wine (60p a glass) these dishes could be over our limit.

EVESHAM

Brookes, Trumpet Yard, Merstow Green
(Evesham 45312)
Open: Mon–Sun 12noon–2.30pm,
Mon–Fri 7–11.30pm, Sat 7–11pm

C P ♿

Set in a quiet corner of Evesham, this beautiful black-and-white timbered restaurant offers a filling meal in peaceful surroundings. There is a lounge bar on the ground floor and the restaurant is situated on the first floor. The lunch menu offers a three-course meal at around £4.50 with coffee. A typical meal could be fried mushrooms with a garlic and mayonnaise dip, chicken portugaise, and a sweet. Coffee is served with fresh cream and home-made fudge. There is a similar table d'hôte menu in the evening at an inclusive price of £5.45. The à la carte menu is outside our budget. A traditional Sunday lunch with coffee is around £5.50 and there is a special menu for children.

The Vine Wine Bar, 16 Vine Street
(Evesham 6799)
Open: Mon–Sat 11.30am–2.30pm,
Mon–Thu 6.30–10.30pm, Fri &
Sat 6.30–11pm

P ♿

This small, intimate wine bar is situated opposite the old stocks in Evesham. Inside the tables are decorated with fresh posies, and church pews are used for seating. Meals are ordered at the servery and are accompanied by one of the 20 salads which are available. The average price of lunch is £2–£3. There is a more extensive menu in the evening which features fish, cutlets, steak and poultry dishes from around £3 to just over £5.

THE BLACK LION HOTEL

Ellesmere, Shropshire.
Telephone: Ellesmere 2418

FULLY RESIDENTIAL
- Open to non-residents for Morning Coffee
- Hot & Cold bar snacks • Main meals
- Private parties & functions etc by arrangement

Ann and Colin Croft

Foxt — Ironbridge

The extensive wine list includes wines from America and Australia as well as Europe.

FOXT

The Fox and Goose, Foxt, off the A52 (Ipstones 415)
Open: Mon 7–10pm,
Tue–Sat 12noon–2pm, 7–10pm,
Sun 12noon–1.30pm, 7–10pm

P

This charming 17th-century inn is situated in the rather remote village of Foxt on the Staffordshire moors. It is popular with both locals and tourists and the proprietors, Ken and Eve Tudor, extend a warm and friendly welcome to all. A three-course meal in the small dining room will cost around £4 and could be soup, gammon with pineapple and Black Forest gâteau. If you prefer something lighter then try one of the bar snacks which are all under 75p.

GOLDSTONE

The Wharf Tavern, Goldstone Wharf (off A529 S of Market Drayton) (Cheswardine 226)
Open: Mon–Sun 12noon–2pm,
Mon–Fri 7–9pm, Sat & Sun 7–9.30pm

P

This small canal-side inn was once a bargees' alehouse and stables, looking after the needs of up to 100 bargees, their families and horses. It now caters for the new generation of Shropshire canal users who can tie up at the moorings. The chef has been here for over 20 years and is so organised he can be found serving and clearing the tables as well as cooking the huge succulent steaks. The evening menu, offers a variety of grills and most of the dishes are priced at £5.95, so with a glass of wine these are over the limit of this guide, but if you want to splash out a bit you will have a thoroughly enjoyable meal. Lunch-time bar snacks and basket meals are also available.

HENLEY-IN-ARDEN

The Little French Cafe, 28 High Street (Henley-in-Arden 4322)
Open: Tue–Sat 10am–6pm,
Sun 2.30–6pm

Stop at this pretty creeper-clad cottage with its heart-shaped sign in picturesque Henley-in-Arden for a snack or a well-prepared, home-cooked light lunch. Mike and Linda Parker have recently re-opened the café which is now convincingly Olde Worlde in style – whitewashed walls, exposed beams, stone-flagged floor, chintzy curtains and all. Start with home-made pâté, then decide between a selection of cold savoury flans with salad at around £2 or Hot Dish of the Day – such as kedgeree served with a selection of side salads at around £2.20. A delicious home-made dessert costs about 60p. An assortment of drinks is available – none of which is alcoholic as the café is unlicensed.

HEREFORD

Cathedral Restaurant, Church Street (Hereford 265233)
Open: Mon–Sat 10.30am–2.30pm, 7–10.30pm

C

As its name would suggest, this small restaurant is set close to the cathedral in a quiet street. The black beams and white walls typify the tourist's idea of Hereford. John Browne, who for eight years worked in Florida and Bermuda, recently bought this restaurant and opened a cellar extension. Special meals of the day are listed on a blackboard, and usually include fresh local produce. A four-course dinner including pâté, chicken romana, fruit pie, coffee and wine can be had for the all-inclusive price of £6.

The City Walls, 67 St Owen Street (Hereford 67720/69134)
Open: Wed–Fri 12noon–2pm,
Tue–Sun 7–11pm

P S

This restaurant is built on part of the original city wall – at a point where taxes were collected in bygone days. Included in the price of the main dish (half roast duckling or chicken, for instance) is the vegetable of the day, French fries, home-made apple pie with cream or ice cream. With a starter and coffee the budget may just be exceeded.
See advert on page 130

Tudor Restaurant, 48 Broad Street (Hereford 277374)
Open: Mon–Sat 9.30am–5.30pm, Sun (Jun–Oct) 10.30am–5pm

S

This 17th-century building in one of the busiest streets of Hereford is situated near the cathedral. A variety of appetising salads such as continental salad with salami and olives, the Tudor Danwich (brown bread with lettuce, cheese, egg and tomato) and many others, supplement the usual list of grills and pies. Children are given a particularly warm welcome in this homely restaurant.
See advert on page 130

IRONBRIDGE

Old Vaults, 29 High Street (Ironbridge 2295)
Open: Mon–Sat 11.30am–3pm, Sun 12noon–2pm,
Mon–Thu 6.30–10.30pm, Fri & Sat 6.30–11pm

P

Situated in the centre of Ironbridge, close to Thomas Telford's famous 18th-century bridge, this compact wine bar offers visitors and locals alike good, basic dishes, with wine, well within our financial limits. Pâté and other first courses cost less than £1; pasty, quiche and salad are around £1.50, chicken in wine, beef in red wine and moussaka are around £2.50 and sweets are around 75p. The interior has been imaginatively renovated on two levels. There is a dining area at street level, and the wine bar, also with dining area at cellar level has a glass roof leading out to the terrace which gives it an airy spacious feel. The terrace overlooks the river Severn and accomodates 24 diners. Real ale is served in the wine bar and the selection is changed regularly.

Brookes Restaurant

Trumpet Yard, Merstow Green, Evesham
Telephone: Evesham 45312

Licensed restaurant.
Speciality a la carte menu.
Business lunches.
Wedding and all special functions catered for.

Proprietors: W A Huson. J M Huson, C A Huson. S J Osborne

KENILWORTH

Ana's Bistro, 121 Warwick Road (Kenilworth 53763)
Open: Mon–Sat 6.30–10.30pm

P &

This cosy cellar bistro is part of Diments restaurant in the small town of Kenilworth. The bill of fayre is recorded each day on a blackboard and includes a choice of four or five hot dishes of the day with such exotic items as chicken in courgette and mint sauce or dressed crab. Soups are home-made and the average three-course meal costs around £5. Although the main menu in the upstairs restaurant is above our limit there is a good table d'hôte menu on offer for around £4.20.

Kenilworth — Kingswinford

With a stock of over 80 wines you'll be spoilt for choice for an accompaniment to your meal.

KINGSWINFORD

Bickley's Bistro, 11 Townsend Place (Kingswinford 287148)
Open: Tue–Fri 12noon–2.15pm, Tue–Sat 7–10pm

C P S &

Tucked away in a small shopping area off the busy A491 is this charming little bistro. Originally the local post office, it has been transformed into a cosy eating place of mainly black-and-white brickwork decorated with antique cooking utensils and pot plants. The tempting menu offers excellent variety, but care is needed to stay within our budget. A typical meal could comprise a tomato/herb salad starter at around 85p, brown trout in rosemary with seasonal vegetables at around £3.90, and a lemon water ice dessert at 95p; with fresh coffee and cream for about 35p, you have a meal to remember. The plat du jour changes daily and is good value at around £1.90, and for a really special finale how about café calvados: a fine Viennese coffee, blended with calvados

---

The City Walls
Licenced Restaurant

67 St. Owens Street, Hereford.
Telephone: Hereford 67720 & 69134

Try our small but select à la carte menu in the intimate surrounds of the old City walls.
Good steaks at reasonable prices are our speciality combined with friendly and efficient service.

Traditional Sunday Lunches
Bar Snacks available lunchtime
Dinner Tuesday to Sunday 7pm - 9pm

RESTAURANT OPEN TO NON-RESIDENTS

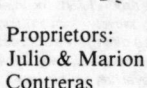

Proprietors:
Julio & Marion Contreras

Orles Barn Hotel & Restaurant

Ross-on-Wye, Herefordshire.
Telephone: Ross-on-Wye (0989) 62155

Tudor Restaurant

48 BROAD STREET, HEREFORD
(next door to Green Dragon Hotel)
Telephone: 277374

Eat, drink and relax in our charming XVIIth Century dining rooms.
Open 9.30 to 5.00 (also Sundays May to September).

MORNING COFFEES — LUNCHEONS — AFTERNOON TEAS
Table licence for wines, beers, spirits. Party bookings considered.

brandy and toppped with whipped cream and cinammon.

KINVER

Magpie Restaurant, 116 High Street (Kinver 2621)
Open: Mon–Sun 12noon–2pm, 7–10pm, (closed Sun eve)

[P][&]

Known locally as a beauty spot for its sandstone caves and breathtaking views, the village of Kinver now boasts a stylish new main street restaurant. Parts of the black-and-white beamed premises date from the 13th century, and the several small dining rooms ooze olde-worlde charm. Home-made soup, steak and kidney pie and lamb cutlets often feature on the menu, and three courses should cost from £5–£6. Home-made bar meals are also available.

KNOWLE

Ye Olde Bakehouse, Warwick Road, Chadwick End
(Lapworth 2928)
On the main A41 Birmingham/Warwick road
Open: Tue–Sun 12.30–1.30pm, Mon–Sat 7.30–9.45pm

[C][P][&]

Inside this black-and-white shuttered cottage with its bright flower tubs, diners receive a warm welcome from mother-and-son team Nick and Iris Worrall. Bits and bobs of bric-à-brac and open fires add to the homely atmosphere. A table d'hôte lunch, with the choice of four starters and five main courses, comprises fresh vegetables such as new potatoes, French beans, peas, broad beans, carrots and stuffed marrow and the price includes a home-made sweet and coffee. In the evening the à la carte menu lists specialities such as Bakehouse breast of chicken at £3.65.

LEAMINGTON SPA

Parkes, 19 Park Strett
(Leamington Spa 23741)
Open: Mon–Sat 12noon–2pm, 7–11pm

A décor of pink, green and white, with lots of plants and mirrors, sets the scene for this bright, lively restaurant. Open your meal with Parkes' special mushrooms, or a bowl of chili, or crudités with a selection of dips at about £1.40. Main courses, all served with Parkes' own special sauces, cost about £4, and a plate of lasagne and side salad offers good value at about £2.85. Fresh fish from the local trout farm is about £3.95. For dessert, there are home-made ice creams and should diners feel the need for exercise, there is a small dance floor.

The Regent Hotel ★★★
Regent Street
(Leamington Spa 27231)
Open: The Vaults Restaurant: Mon–Sat 12.30–7.30, 7.30–11pm
Chandos Restaurant: Mon–Sat 12.30–2pm, 6.45–8.45pm, Sun 12.30–2pm, 7–8.30pm
Fast Food Bar: normal licensing hours

[C][♫][P][&]

The imposing Regent Hotel in the centre of this famous spa was the largest hotel in Europe when it was built in 1819 and renowned for its VIP visitors, including Queen Victoria and Napoleon. Today it boasts three excellent eating places. The Vaults, a transformed basement wine cellar serves an excellent table d'hôte lunch. A choice of seven starters, four main courses including sweetbread à la crème and coffee costs just under £6. The elegant Chandos Restaurant offers a table d'hôte lunch with far greater choice but is likely to go beyond our budget. Fish and salad, roast beef and Yorkshire pudding and a sweet from the trolley makes a satisfying meal. If you only want a quick snack, try the Cork and Fork Bar, where you can choose one of 12 very reasonably priced hot dishes and get a starter and sweet thrown in.

LEDBURY

Applejack, 44 The Homend
(Ledbury 4181)
Open: Mon–Sat 12noon–2.30pm, 7.30–10.30pm

Kinver — Leek

[C][S][&]

The cosy 'old inn' atmosphere is retained here at Applejack where owners Anna and Bob Evans have converted this 17th-century inn into a snug two-storey bistro and antique shop. A racing driver, Bob started the bistro as a hobby while his wife Anna concentrates on the antique business. At lunchtime the menu is chalked on a large blackboard where a limited selection of interesting dishes is offered. A sample meal could be home-made pea soup, guinea fowl casserole with trimmings and a generous helping of rhubarb crumble followed by as much freshly ground coffee as you can drink – all for under £5. The printed dinner menu is more extensive with dishes such as Hoi-sin pork (charcoal-grilled chops with barbecue sauce) at £3.95 or asparagus chicken (marinated in cider with fresh asparagus and cream) at £3.95 to tempt your palate. Vegetables are included in the evening and with reasonable care the bill need not exceed £6.50. Situated in the main shopping street of Ledbury, this black and white inn is convenient for shoppers and business people.

LEEK

The Jester At Leek, 81 Mill Street
(Leek 383997)
Open: Mon–Sun 12noon–2pm, 7–10pm

[P][&]

This beige, pebble-dash restaurant has an inviting, cottagey interior. A good variety of wholesome basic English fare is available and a three-course Sunday lunch with a choice of seven starters, eight main courses and sweets from the trolley comes at around £4. The à la carte menu, with starters, grills and roasts at reasonable prices, includes a lot of fish and seafood. Try fresh salmon at around £3.90, or golden seafood platter at about £3.75. Budget meals at lunchtime cost about £1.85 and include home-made steak and kidney pie, breaded plaice and a dish of the day.

Ye Olde Bakehouse

Warwick Road, Chadwick End, Knowle.
Telephone: Lapworth 2928

Situated on the main A41 Birmingham/Warwick road, the black-and-white shuttered cottage with it's bright flower tubs, offers a warm welcome, with the open fires and bric-à-brac adding the homely touch.

Open:
Tuesday - Sunday 12.30 - 1.30pm
Monday - Saturday 7.30 - 9.45pm

Ludlow — Pershore

LUDLOW

Eagle House, Corve Street
(Ludlow 2325)
Open: Oak Room: Mon–Sun
12noon–2.30pm, 7–10pm
Pine Room: 9am–7pm

[P] [S] [&]

Known as 'The Eagle and Child' when it was first built in the 17th century as a coaching inn, this half-timbered building still retains evidence of a cobblestoned blacksmith's yard. In the entrance, traces of wattle and daub plastering have been exposed to show the original construction. Extremely fine oak panelling in the Oak Room restaurant came from nearby Acton Scott Hall and Bitterley Court and is an outstanding feature. The three-course lunch is remarkable value at £3.50 – you could start with grapefruit and orange cocktail, then savour roast lamb and finish with Queen of Puddings – though there are several other choices for each course. Table d'hôte dinner costs £5.50 and offers a wide selection including roast duckling and chicken à l'espagnole. With careful choice, the à la carte menu could be within our budget. If you are after a quick snack, then climb the stairs to the Pine Room, where anything from a pot of tea to steak and chips is available.

Penny Anthony ✕
5 Church Street
(Ludlow 3282)
Open: Mon–Sat 10.30am–2pm,
7–10pm

[C] [P] [S] [&]

Close to the castle entrance, a charming Georgian-style building houses this popular little restaurant. A bar menu is available lunch-time and evenings (not Saturday) and dishes range from pâté at £1.50 to entrecôte steak at £3.95. There are three set menus (two of these come within the scope of this guide) available for lunch and dinner. The £3.95 menu (not available on Saturday) includes soup, chicken casserole and dessert; on the £5.95 menu you could choose celery and walnut soup, pork kebabs and dessert.

NESSCLIFFE

The Old Three Pigeons
(Nesscliffe 279)
Open: Mon–Sat 10.30am–2.30pm,
6.30–10.30pm, Sun 12noon–2pm,
6.30–10pm

[P] [&]

You'll find more than just good food and ale at this 15th-century roadside inn. For pre-dinner entertainment you can enjoy tales of philanthropic highwayman Humphrey Kynnaston who supped many a jar at The Old Three Pigeons, his favourite retreat. The country-style décor features a grandfather clock and large Welsh Dresser. Home cooking is the order of the day.

PERSHORE

Sugar and Spice, High Street
(Pershore 553654)
Open: Mon–Sat 9.30am–5.30pm

[&]

Painted pink, this eatery stands out from its more sober-fronted high street neighbours. In true tea shop tradition, you'll find the cheerful restaurant by walking through a patisserie and extensive gift shop. At the rear there is an attractive patio setting for when the weather's fine. Soup here with roll and butter costs 60p and pizza 75p, whilst cottage pie with potatoes and peas (£1.85) and ploughman's lunch (£1.20) are examples of the no-nonsense main dishes available. For dessert, there's a large counter of mouth-watering confectionery to delight the most discerning gâteau gourmet. Whatever your choice, the meal (including coffee) will cost much less than £5 per head.

Eagle House Restaurant

Corve Street, Ludlow, Shropshire.
Telephone: (0584) 2325

Open 9 am - 10 pm including Sundays
Licensed. Car and Coach Park.

OAK ROOM — seating 50
Luncheons, Grills, Evening Dinner. Local meat, poultry and game.
Fresh vegetables. Home made sweets, puddings and pies.
Traditional English and Spanish Dishes.

PINE ROOM — seating 100
Breakfast, Coffee, Snacks, Afternoon and High Teas, Grills.
Wine and Food Bar.

Coaches and Private parties welcomed.

---

penny anthony restaurant

there's nowhere else

5 church street   ludlow   phone 3282

ROSS-ON-WYE

The Old Pheasant, 52 Edde Cross Street
(Ross-on-Wye 65751)
Open: Easter–Sept: Mon–Tue, Thu–Sat 10.30am–5pm, Sun 2–5.30pm

[P][&]

Step into this brightly painted cottage-style restaurant and enjoy a snack or lunch, personally prepared by Meryl Taylor. Many of her recipes have been gleaned from her Welsh forebears, for example chocolate orange drizzle cake and rice cake. At lunch-time there is a small choice of home-made hot meals, including steak pie, chicken, mushroom and ham pie, served with new potatoes and two fresh vegetables all for under £2; salads are also under £2.

RUGBY

The Carlton Hotel, Railway Terrace
(Rugby 3076)
Open: Mon–Fri & Sun 12noon–2pm, Mon–Sat 7–10pm

[P][&]

This brightly painted hotel, close to the railway station and the town centre, has a small licensed restaurant which offers a three-course luncheon for £4.25. There is a choice of six starters including smoked mackerel and asparagus omelette. Main courses include a roast, steak, kidney and mushroom pie and a Punjab dish prepared by Mrs Singh who runs the hotel with her husband. The evening meal is £5.45, and there is also an à la carte menu.

SHREWSBURY

Bristol Frigate, Frankwell Quay
(Shrewsbury 4225)
Open: Mon–Sat 7pm–12mdnt, Sun 12noon–2pm

[C][P][&]

It's the fact that it floats that will probably attract you to the Bristol Frigate initially. The bright blue and white painted 'vessel' stands out against the duller colours of the River Severn near the Welsh Bridge. Though purpose-built as a restaurant, brave attempts have been made to create a nostalgically salty atmosphere, the focal point being the original wheel

Ross-on-Wye — Shrewsbury

from an old clipper, together with admirals' swords, bells and ropes. The soft lighting and carpeting are definitely geared to modern comfort – and you certainly won't get scurvy! There are a good range of home-made dishes available with roast duckling as the house speciality. An interesting selection of mouthwatering home-made desserts and a reasonably priced wine list promises a meal to remember.

Cornhouse Restaurant and Wine Bar, 59A Wyle Cop
(Shrewsbury 241991)
Open: Mon–Sat 11.30am–2.30pm, Mon–Thu 6.30–10.30pm, Fri–Sat 6.30–11pm, Sun 7–10.30pm

[C][♬][&]

This restaurant occupies the ground and first floors of a warehouse built in the mid 1800s, a few minutes walk from the town centre. The present proprietor has carried out considerable improvements to the premises, including the installation of a beautiful wrought-iron spiral staircase. Stripped pine furniture, exposed brickwork and beams, polished floorboards, potted plants and spotlights complete the pleasing effect. Customers may choose to eat a light meal or snack in the ground floor wine bar, or go upstairs to the restaurant for a more substantial meal. There is live music on Sunday evenings.

Delany's, St Julians Craft Centre for Shropshire, off Fish Street
(Shrewsbury 60602)
Open: Mon–Sat 10am–5pm (evenings for party bookings)

[♬][S][&]

A more unlikely place for a restaurant than the vestry of a church is hard to imagine, but Delany's – a vegetarian's delight – looks quite at home among the original wood panels and highly-polished boards and beams. Soups instead of sermons are the order of the day now the old church has become a restaurant and craft centre. Tasty and original dishes such as Syrian aubergine and lentil

casserole (95p) and cauliflower and peanut crumble (£1.05) are served on the cheerful green-and-white clothed tables, each equipped with flowers, a pot of fresh ground rock salt, dishes of soft brown sugar and unsalted butter. The menu is not extensive but all the dishes are inexpensive.

The Dickens Restaurant, Lion Hotel
★★★
Wyle Cop
(Shrewsbury 53107)
Open: Mon–Sat 12.30–2pm, 7–10pm, Sun 12.30–2pm, 7–9pm

[C][P][S][&]

The popular, elegant 18th-century Lion Hotel stands in the centre of Shrewsbury. Distinguished visitors have included Disraeli, Paganini and, of course, Dickens. Roast of the day, carved at the table, and including coffee, costs around £3.95. The four-course table d'hôte meal, including coffee, costs around £7.95.

Dun Cow, Abbey Foregate
(Shrewsbury 56408)
Open: Mon–Sun 12noon–2pm, 6.30–10.30pm

[C][♬][P][&]

You're not likely to find a more historic eating house than the Dun Cow, reputed to be one of the oldest pubs in England, dating from circa 1085. Thanks to the research efforts of the owners, you can read about its amazing history including the sightings of a ghost in the dress of a Dutch cavalry officer, from the special leaflet they have produced. The dining room is more modern than the rest of the premises but an effort has been made to capture the 'olde worlde' atmosphere with exposed beams, rough plaster walls and some exposed stonework. Dishes on the interesting à la carte need careful selection as some prices will exceed our limit. Trout Sabrina – two trout dressed with almonds and lemon, and lamb Shrewsbury – cutlets of lamb with port wine and honey, are two of the more unusual and less expensive main courses.

Just Williams, 62–63 Mardol
(Shrewsbury 57061)
Open: Mon–Sat 11am–11pm

Carlton Hotel and LICENSED RESTAURANT

Enjoy superb food and wine in one of the finest restaurants in Rugby. Excellent service, varied choice and reasonably priced menu. Small wedding receptions, parties etc. Individually styled bedrooms, all with colour TV, tea and coffee making facilities and central heating.

**For reservations telephone: Rugby (0788) 3076
Railway Terrace, Rugby.**

Solihull — Stoke-on-Trent

⌐C⌐♫⌐P⌐S⌐☕

Not far from Shrewsbury's main street is this pretty little wine bar, where a small bow window gives glimpses of a black and white, flower-decked interior. Renoirs and other French prints adorn the walls and old converted gas lamps add atmosphere. The food includes home-made soup (around 55p), meat salads (ranging from about £2.25 to £2.95) and the hot dishes such as pork casserole with peppers (at around £2.50) or local steaks from £4.25 are advertised on a blackboard. With desserts at around 75p, the average cost of a three-course meal and coffee is still under £4.50. Wine is 70p a glass and real ale and farmhouse cider are available.

The Olde Tudor Steak House, Butcher Row
(Shrewsbury 53117)
Open: Tue–Sun 12noon–2.15pm,
Tue–Fri 7–10.30pm, Sat 7–11.30pm

⌐C⌐P⌐S⌐☕

The Steak House restaurant occupies the second floor of fine 16th-century black and white timbered premises. Refectory tables, paintings and bric-à-brac help to create a Tudor atmosphere. Table d'hôte lunch is very good value at around £2.50 on weekdays, £3.20 on Sundays. Three courses include soup of the day, a choice of seven main courses such as chicken in red wine and a sweet of the day which could be a delicious chocolate mousse. The à la carte menu is predominantly grills and though more expensive, with care three courses can be enjoyed for around £5.

Steak and Pizza Bar, 50 Mardol
(Shrewsbury 4834)
Open: Mon–Sat 11.30am–2.30pm,
Mon–Sun 6–11pm

⌐C⌐☕

A large bay window and a vivid sign announce these charming little premises, ideally situated for cinemagoers, shoppers and riverbank walkers. The walls are dotted with posters of Italian landmarks and bright red and white gingham cloths cover the tables. All beefburgers and pizzas are freshly made on the premises, and represent excellent value for money.

SOLIHULL

Bobby Brown's, 183 High Street
(021-704 9136)
Open: Mon–Sat 12noon–2.30pm,
7–11pm

⌐♫⌐S

Chris, Caroline and Annie are three young friends who met while working in someone else's wine bar. They decided to stay together as a team and open their own restaurant. The result of their labours is this cosy, informal place with a courtyard where spontaneous barbecues are often held. A blackboard lists specialities of the day such as cold celery and apple soup (80p), spicy chicken with rice (£3.25) and many more. Choices from the cold table include cheddar cheese and pineapple, home-made chicken liver pâté and honey baked ham served with three kinds of salad. Sweets cost around £1.

STAFFORD

Anemos, 22 Crabbery Street
(Stafford 48940)
Open: Mon–Wed 9am–5pm,
Thu–Sat 9am–5pm, 7.30–11pm

⌐S⌐☕

The small upstairs dining room of this shop-fronted Greek restaurant serves a cosmopolitan range of light lunches – omelettes, salads, pizzas, pasta dishes and moussaka are all between £1–£2. A more substantial lunch can be enjoyed from a choice of 14 starters – including soup of the day at 40p or dolmades at £1.20. Main course could be sofrito (a Corfu speciality of beef in wine sauce served with a side salad – costing about £4.50), beef Stroganoff (£3) or prawn kebab with salad and rice at £5. Desserts include gâteaux at about 65p. The evening menu is basically Greek and more expensive, but three courses could be savoured for around £5.

STOKE-ON-TRENT

Capri Ristorante Italiano, 13 Glebe Street
(Stoke-on-Trent 411889)
Open: Mon–Sat 12noon–2.15pm,
6–11pm

⌐C⌐P

Entering the rear of this little Italian restaurant from the car park has been compared with walking into the famous Blue Grotto of Capri. Blue and green lighting creates the illusion, which is enhanced by scenes of Italy painted on the white stucco walls by proprietor Vittorio Cirillo. Good, home-cooked Italian fare is highly recommended, with minestrone or salami to start at around £1, lasagne, spaghetti, penne alla arrabiata or penne al ragu as the main course, all about £1.90 and delicious desserts such as profiteroles (95p) or orange slices with liqueur (80p). You will be left with plenty of change from £5 for a cup of espresso or cappucino coffee.

The Poachers Cottage ××
Stone Road, Trentham
(Stoke-on-Trent 657115)
Open: Mon–Sun 12noon–2pm,
Tue–Sat 7–9.30pm

⌐P⌐☕

This black and white cottage is easily located on the A34, close to Trentham Gardens. The cottage atmosphere has been retained inside, with black beams, natural stone and tapestry upholstered chairs. White linen tablecloths and colourful carpets add a touch of luxury. The lunchtime menu has excellent value roasts and grills. Rollmop herring hors d'oeuvres, roast chicken with trimmings, a sweet and coffee will just top £5.

Rib of Beef, Grand Hotel ★★★
66 Trinity Street, Hanley
(Stoke-on-Trent 22361)
Open: Mon–Sun 12.30–2.30pm,
7–10pm

⌐C⌐P⌐S⌐☕

Situated on the lower ground floor of the impressive Stakis-run hotel close to Hanley city centre, the Rib of Beef restaurant boasts some tasty local favourites. Try the excellent table d'hôte menu. For only about £4.50 at lunchtime you can choose home-made broth – one of three starters – then take your choice of roast ribs of beef, fish, grilled lamb chops – it's different every day! Try the delicious vegetables and sauces, if you have room for it, the sweet trolley offers a host of gooey goodies. A two-course supper and coffee costs £5.25.

Riverside Restaurant, Trentham Gardens
(Stoke-on-Trent 657341)
Open: Mon–Sun 6–11pm

⌐C⌐♫⌐P⌐☕

This unique restaurant is within the grounds of the well-known pleasure complex on the A34. There is a charge for admission to the gardens (currently £1.50) but by entering after 5.30pm you can obtain a voucher from the gate and this charge can be redeemed against the price of a meal in the restaurant. A selection of cold appetisers, dips and relishes is served, followed by freshly-made soup. There is a choice of about eight main dishes including barbecued pork, Nasi Goring (an Indonesian fried rice dish) Blind Sparrow (beef roulade in wine) and poultry Phoenecia (turkey breast stuffed with melon). A simple choice of sweet will end the meal, and the price? just £5. A walk by the illuminated fountains and Italian gardens will complete a romantic evening.

Roosevelt's Restaurant, 24 Snow Hill
(Stoke-on-Trent 269544)
Open: Mon–Sun 12noon–12mdnt

⌐C⌐♫⌐☕

As the name implies, an American-style fast service operates here, the result of owner Philip Crowe's long observations in the States. Judging by the hordes of people that frequent the restaurant, the system is a great success. Brown hessian walls, a quarry-tiled floor and Liberty-print tablecloths create a warm, welcoming effect and the many photographs and posters continue the Americana theme. Having started with, perhaps, corn on the cob (75p), you can choose from several hamburger specials, all with French fries and trimmings, costing around £1.80 or £2.60, depending on burger size. At these prices you can afford to splash out on a knickerbocker glory, enjoy a cup of coffee and still get change from a fiver.

STOURBRIDGE

The Gallery Restaurant ✕
121 Bridgnorth Road, Wollaston
(Stourbridge 2788)
Open: Tue–Sat 7.30–9.30pm

[C] [S]

Just mention the 'restaurant above the butcher's' to anyone in this area and you will be directed to Bill and Janet Harris's popular 'Gallery'. Bill runs the butcher's shop on this main shopping street and Janet is in charge of the successful little eating house above. Lamb chops, sole and scampi feature on the à la carte menu, all at around £4.50. With soup at 70p and trolley desserts around £1 you may have to break the bank to sample coffee.

The Gypsy's Tent, Birmingham Road, Hagley
(Hagley 883120)
Open: Mon–Sat 12.30–2.30pm, 7–10.30pm, Sun 12.30–2pm

[C] [P] [♿]

This is a well-known restaurant in the Black Country and it has gained a reputation of giving good value for money. The 'roast of the day' at £5.50 offers a choice of any sweet and starter from the main à la carte menu. Other dishes such as chili con carne (£2.90), paella (£2.90) or whole baby chicken (£3.80) are always available. Snacks are served in the lounge bar, cottage pie is £1.50 and ploughman's £1.15.

Penny Farthing Restaurant, Pedmore House, Ham Lane
(Stourbridge 3132)
Open: Tue–Fri 12.30–2.30pm, Tue–Sat 7–10.30pm

[C] [P] [♿]

Pedmore House, situated on a busy roundabout, has gained a worthy reputation over the years, and has three restaurants to choose from: The Highlander Restaurant and Grill offers an extensive à la carte menu which is outside the range of this guide; The Regency Bar provides substantial bar meals from 90p–£1.40, but if you want a three-course meal at a reasonable price, then try the Penny Farthing basement restaurant. Here a roast of the day, with starter and sweet is £5.25. Fish, pasta, steak, chops and steak and kidney pie are among the other dishes on the menu.

Talbot Hotel ★★
High Street
(Stourbridge 4350)
Open: Mon–Sun 12noon–2pm, 7–9.30pm

[C] [F] [P] [S] [♿]

This town centre hotel has been popular for many years. The ground floor dining room seats about 70 in comfortable alcoves screened by velvet half-curtains hung from brass rails, and it is here that lunch on weekdays, Saturdays and Sundays is chosen from a buffet with hot and cold dishes. A Chef's Special is also provided. The Sunday lunch menu offers traditional roasts. There is a full à la carte menu in the evening. Prices are very reasonable for both table d'hôte and à la carte.

STRATFORD-UPON-AVON

The Dirty Duck, Waterside
(Stratford-upon-Avon 297312)
Open: Mon–Sat 12noon–3pm, 6–12mdnt

[C] [S] [♿]

This typically English pub-restaurant is a favourite haunt of the theatre world, due to its olde worlde charm, and its nearness to the Shakespeare Theatre. Apart from serving meals before and after performances, they also offer a good lunch here. Main dishes range in price from £3–£6.50 with plaice fillet and braised kidneys are representative examples. There are 10 or so starters with prices up to £1 and a sweet or cheese costs about 60p.
See advert on page 136

Hathaway Tea Rooms and Bakery,
19 High Street
(Stratford-upon-Avon 292404)
Open: Mon–Sat 9am–5.30pm, Sun 11.45am–5.30pm (later by arrangement)

[S]

Although the name suggests otherwise, this impressive building, with its olde worlde atmosphere goes a good deal further back than Shakespeare's era – the original site dates back to 1315. The tea rooms are reached by passing through the shop up the Jacobean staircase to the tiny landing, which houses a superb grandfather clock. Once inside, you will find everything you expected – dark oak beams, white walls, an open fireplace and antique dressers and tables. A good old-fashioned lunch menu offers traditional dishes such as roast beef and Yorkshire pudding or steak and kidney pie, each for about £2.50, spotted Dick, apple and raspberry tart and banana split at around 65p.
See advert on page 136

Horseshoe Buttery and Restaurant,
33–34 Greenhill Street
(Stratford-upon-Avon 292246)
Open: Mon–Sun 9am–10pm

[P] [♿]

Handy for pre-film and theatre snacks, this bay-windowed, period-style restaurant with its charming mock-Tudor façade lies opposite the cinema and just 50 yards from the famous clock tower. An exceptionally good value table d'hôte lunch still costs less than £2.50 for three courses (e.g. soup, steak and kidney pie, home-made fruit pie), and coffee. A special two-course meal costs under £2. Both are served in a warm, friendly atmosphere.

The Opposition Restaurant, 13 Sheep Street
(Stratford-upon-Avon 69980)
Open: Tue–Sat 12noon–2.30pm, Mon–Sat 6–11.30pm

[F] [S] [♿]

No need to feel bloodthirsty to enjoy the steakburger – Macbeth style. It's innocent enough to look at with its topping of melted cheese. Other varieties (including Texan and American styles) are well worth trying, as they are made to the proprietor's own recipe by a local butcher. Pizzas (all around £2), spaghetti and pastas are also available, and there's a small list of 'specials' including sirloin, fillet or rump steak, and chicken Kiev, tagliatelle with prawn and wine sauce.
See advert on page 136

Roosevelt's RESTAURANT

24 SNOW HILL, SHELTON, STOKE-ON-TRENT
Telephone 0782-269544

Licensed American Restaurant
Famous for its Chargrilled Steaks and American Burgers
Fast Friendly Service — Children Welcome
Open 12 noon to midnight - 7 days a week

WORLD FAMOUS ENGLISH PUB

RESTAURANT OPEN
12 noon - 3pm
6pm - midnight

Telephone Stratford-on-Avon 297312

THE DIRTY DUCK
STRATFORD UPON AVON

HATHAWAY
TEA ROOMS & BAKERY
19 High Street, Stratford-upon-Avon
Telephone: 292404

MORNING COFFEE ● LUNCHEON ● AFTERNOON TEA ●
Home-made cakes a speciality.
Licensed.
OPEN 7 DAYS A WEEK

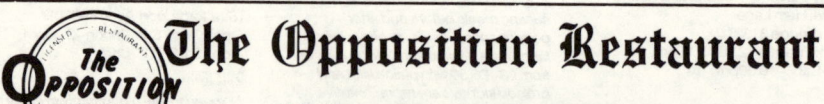

The Opposition Restaurant

The Opposition
Restaurant
13 Sheep Street
Stratford-upon-Avon
Tel: 69980
& Bistro

13 Sheep Street, Stratford-upon-Avon
Telephone 0789 69980

Dine with the theatricals at Stratford's extremely popular intimate restaurant. Situated just two minutes from the theatre, we serve appetising French, Italian, American and English foods (mostly home-made) followed by a delicious selection of sweets.
We are open for lunch 12 noon-2.30pm and for dinner 6pm-11.30pm.
Catering for both pre and after theatre diners.
The first restaurant in Stratford to win the British Routiers Award.

The world is your oyster when you eat at the
PIMPERNELL

We can offer dishes from many countries in tasteful surroundings at inexpensive prices.

Open Tuesday - Saturday 12 noon - 2.30pm. 6 - 10.30pm.

59/61 Birmingham Road, Sutton Coldfield.
Telephone: 021-354 9808

The Thatch Restaurant, Cottage Lane, Shottery
(Stratford-upon-Avon 293122)
Open: Mon–Sun 9am–6pm

P

Next to the famous Anne Hathaway's Cottage you will find this delightful thatched restaurant with its olde worlde dining room and rustic canopied terrace. Here you can enjoy a fine traditional English lunch with three courses, including roast beef and Yorkshire pudding followed by a slice of home-made apple or lemon meringue pie for about £5. Cream teas are good value at around £1.20.

SUTTON COLDFIELD

Pimpernell, 59–61 Birmingham Road
(021-354 9808)
Open: Tue–Sat 12noon–2.30pm, 6–10.30pm

C

Just the place to eat before or after a film at the nearby cinema. Green and red tasteful décor complements the excellent and inexpensive cuisine. The à la carte menu offers dishes from many countries and is well within our budget. Particularly good value fare may be sampled from the Daily Special lunchtime menu.

Sutton Coldfield
—
Upton-upon-Severn

TENBURY WELLS

The Peacock Inn, Worcester Road
(Tenbury Wells 81-0506)
1m E of Tenbury Wells on the A456
Open: Mon–Sat 10.30am–2.30pm, 6–10.30pm, 11pm Fri–Sat,
Sun 12noon–2pm, 7–10.30pm

P

Amid the famous hop fields and orchards of the beautiful Teme Valley is this half-timbered, 14th-century inn, run by partners Alastair Hendry and Bernard Bond, who returned to England two years ago after spending almost 30 years in Malaysia. It follows that one of the house specialities should be Malaysian curry (£2.50), but where they learned to make such marvellous lasagne (£2.10) is quite a mystery. A starter such as smoked salmon mousse will cost around £1 and a sweet (could be rum and walnut gâteau) only 75p.

TRUMPET

The Bistro, The Verzons Hotel
(Trumpet 381)
Open: Mon–Sun 10.30am–2pm, 6.30–10pm

C P

Nestling in the peace of the Herefordshire countryside is the busy and popular Verzons Hotel. Originally a Georgian farmhouse, it stands in a lush four acres. In winter bistro diners can wallow in the warmth of an open log fire while supping a plateful of home-made soup followed by a generous portion of lasagne verdi, all for approximately £3. Summer sees guests outside in the wooded beer garden enjoying views of the recently-excavated Victorian sunken garden while their meal is served. A speciality of the bistro is the home-made desserts which include the mouth-watering crunch cake laced with brandy. A fine range of traditional ales and real local cider adds to the convivial atmosphere created here by owners John and Angela Rose.

UPTON-UPON-SEVERN

Cromwells, 16–18 Church Street
(Upton-upon-Severn 2447)
Open: Mon–Sat 10am–2pm, 7.15–9.30pm

C

Oliver Cromwell is reputed to have waved to a pretty lady at an upstairs window of this charming black-and-white half-timbered cottage. The bistro with exposed brick walls and beams leads on to a walled garden where children may let off steam. Upstairs is 'Oliver's Bar' where diners may sip an aperitif and study the

---

The Verzons

Country Hotel & Restaurant
Trumpet, Near Ledbury
Tel: Trumpet (053 183) 381

This large Georgian house overlooking the Malvern Hills offers comfort and elegance for your 'Breakaway'. Full central heating, large bedrooms all with colour TV, some with fourposter beds and bathrooms en suite. Candlelit à la carte restaurant or bar snacks in our 'Character' Bistro Bar with log fire and gleaming horse brasses give guests a choice of menu. Telephone John or Angela Rose for reservation.

Telephone: Upton-upon-Severn (06846) 2447

Cromwells Bistro & Coffee Shop

16 Church Street
(Opposite the "Pepperpot")

Licensed Bistro serving fresh home cooked food in a relaxing atmosphere.

Open Mon.–Sat. for Coffee (10am–12noon)
& Lunch (12 noon–2pm)
Open Tues.–Sat. for Evening Meals
(7.15–9.30 Last Orders)

Warwick — Whitchurch

blackboard menu. A typical lunch menu could be home-made vegetable soup at around £1, prawn and cheese vol-au-vents with a tossed salad (totalling £2.85) and lemon syllabub at around £1.10. The dinner menu offers more choice – 10 possibles for each course including frog's legs as a starter! Stilton and onion soup costs around £1, scrumpy chicken £4.20 and Cromwell gâteau or lemon syllabub around £1.10.

WARWICK

Cindy's, 48 Brook Street
(Warwick 493504)
Open: Mon–Sat 9.30am–5pm

[C] [S]

Only about 20 people can be seated in this country kitchen style restaurant found above a tempting delicatessen, so booking in advance is advised. Dominated by pine furniture, Lowrie prints and paintings for sale by a local artist, it offers freshly prepared dishes attractively displayed on the large pine dresser. During summer, a hot dish of the day, home-made quiches and pies accompanied by a selection of salads and gâteaux are the bill of fare. In the winter months, delicious soup and hot main dishes are available.

Nicolini's Bistro, 18 Jury Street
(Warwick 495817)
Open: Tue–Sun 9.30am–10.30pm

[C] [P] [S] [♿]

Located on one of the main thoroughfares of the city is this delightful little restaurant with its stripped pine chairs, potted plants and effective spot lighting. A well-stocked glass counter displaying fresh salads and tempting sweets (including ice-cream specialities from 75p–£2) immediately attracts the eye, and other dishes are available, such as tasty home-made pizzas. A three-course meal will, on average, be from £4–£5.

The Waterman, Hatton
(Warwick 492427)
Open: Mon–Sun 12noon–2pm,
Mon–Thu 6.30–10pm, Fri,
Sat 6.30–10.30pm, Sun 7–10pm

[C] [P] [♿]

This imposing brick inn was built by the famous Arkwright family in 1842. The main bar offers panoramic views of the daunting 21 Hatton locks of the Grand Union Canal. Bar snacks are about £2 and they can be enjoyed in the garden when the weather permits. In the restaurant the starters are priced at around £1 and for your main course there is a choice of fish, steaks, salads, chicken and duck (£3.25–£5.45). The price of the main course includes a sweet of ice cream or cheese and biscuits. The three-course Sunday lunch is £3.95 and all children's portions in the restaurant are half price.

WATERHOUSES

The Olde Beams
(Waterhouses 254)
Open: Tue–Sat 12noon–2pm,
6.30–10pm, Sun 12noon–2pm

[P] [♿]

In the centre of the village is this charming white stone and brick-built house with shuttered windows. Originally an inn, it was built in 1746, and the restaurant has exposed ceiling beams, refectory tables and Windsor chairs. All the food is home-made, including a selection of delicious sweets on the trolley, the soup of the day, and delicious bread rolls. The à la carte menu offers imaginative fare, some of which is within our budget.

WHITCHURCH

Gallery Restaurant, Wayside
(Symonds Yat 890408)
Open: Mon, Wed–Sun 12.30–2pm,
7.30–10pm

[C] [P] [♿]

Travellers on the A40 often drive straight past Whitchurch, but at mealtimes,

The Waterman

Birmingham Road, Hatton, Warwick.
Telephone: 0926 492427

Much more than just a superb restaurant, 'The Waterman' still retains the hospitality associated with a traditional local pub. From the main bar there is a panoramic view over the Grand Union Canal. In summer you can relax on the patio or among the trees and watch the narrowboats navigate the daunting Hatton locks.
Traditional food is served in the main bar both lunchtimes and evenings, the choice is wide and the standard high. Children are welcome, small portions can be served both lunchtimes and evenings.

Come and Wine and Dine in the Idyllic setting of

The Gallery Restaurant

Whitchurch, Herefordshire
Telephone: Symonds Yat 890408

Traditional English & French Cuisine
Extensive à la Carte Menu
Traditional Sunday Lunches
Bar Meals Available

So 'phone us now and make your meal a memorable one

(CLOSED ALL DAY TUESDAY)

particularly at lunch-time, a detour to the Gallery Restaurant is well worth while. This comfortable and elegant little restaurant provides an excellent table d'hôte lunch menu at £4.95. The menu varies but there is always a choice of at least three starters and main courses. A typical meal could be cream of mushroom soup, roast rib of beef and a choice of sweet from the trolley. Coffee is 55p extra and a glass of wine 65p. The à la carte menu available in the evening at around £10 per person is outside our budget but worth saving for.

WHITTINGTON

Whittington Inn Wine Bar
(Kinver 2110)
Open: Mon – Sat 12noon – 2.30pm, 6.30 – 10.30pm, Sun 12noon – 2pm, 7 – 10.30pm
On the A449

P &

If you want to know the real story of Dick Whittington the legendary Lord Mayor, you could do no better than to eat a meal in the attractive attic wine bar in his ancestral home. A potted history of the Whittington family dating from 1307, is available for any interested diner to read. The interior of the wine bar is mainly white-painted brick, effectively decorated with old prints and posters, antique bed warmers and armoury and with the original black oak beams and rafters a prominent feature. A selection of food is made either from the mouthwatering array of salads, pies, sweets and cheeses displayed behind a glass counter, or from a blackboard which lists hot or cold specialities such as lasagne or chili con carne.

Whittington — Worcester

WOLVERHAMPTON

Le Bistro Steakhouse, 6 School Street (Wolverhampton 24638)
Open: Mon – Sat 12noon – 2.30pm, 6 – 11.30pm

♬ S &

A variety of bottles hanging against white walls, black wrought-iron partitions, and red-patterned carpet create a welcoming atmosphere in this first-floor restaurant. The kitchen is supervised by owner 'Steve' Kyriakou who makes sure that Greek specialities such as moussaka and afelia (around £3.25) are cooked to perfection. Lunchtime table d'hôte menus offer a choice of Greek or English food for around £2 with a sweet about 55p.

Pepito's, 5 School Street (Wolverhampton 23403)
Open: Mon – Sat 12noon – 2.30pm, 6 – 11pm, closed 3 weeks in Aug

♬ P S &

For those who like Italian food, Pepito's offers the real thing in a pleasant modern restaurant with glass partitioning providing a degree of privacy. Owner Mr Catellani supervises the cooking while his wife, helped by two young ladies, looks after the customers. The two-course table d'hôte lunch is good value at around £1.50, with a choice of four starters and a main course pasta dish or, perhaps, goulash or a roast – there are seven or eight items to choose from. A three-course meal could cost from £3.35 – £6.40.

WORCESTER

The Bear and Ragged Staff, Bransford
(4m SW of Worcester off A4103)
(Leigh Sinton 32407)
Open: bar meals: Mon – Sun 12.15 – 2pm, 7 – 9.30pm
Restaurant: Tue – Sat 12.30 – 2pm, 7.30 – 10pm, Sun 12.30 – 2pm

P &

This restaurant is in a large building in the centre of the peaceful village of Bransford which lies at the foot of the Malvern Hills. Inside you can expect a warm welcome from Ian and Jaqueline Stanton who pride themselves on running a good restaurant. An à la carte menu is available in the restaurant, and bar meals are served by waitresses in a separate room (or the pleasant gardens, weather permitting). On the bar-menu soup is 50p and the main courses, ranging from roast chicken to pizza are £1.55 – £2.15. Sweets are 75p. The popular Sunday lunch is £4.75.

Natural Break, 17 Mealcheapen Street (Worcester 29979)
Open: Mon – Sun 10am – 4.30pm

S &

Brown-tiled tables and natural pine create an informal, cottagey atmosphere in this popular rendezvous, where proprietors Sandra and Nigel Wolfenden pin notices of local societies' meetings on the wall alongside paintings by local artists which are offered for sale. The board menu lists a choice of eight interesting salads at around 30p – potato, carrot and cheese, mushroom, apple, celery and walnut – ideal to accompany the home-made savoury flans and quiches which only cost about 70p. Desserts include home-baked apple pie, meringues and pastries – freshly prepared every day.

The Gallery Restaurant
Broadway, Worcs.

Lunches and dinners served in unique 16th century coach house surroundings.

Children's menu for lunch/dinner.

Licensed bar, seating for 60.

Parties catered for.

Telephone: Broadway 853555

139

THE NORTH WEST

Here, in the north-west, we have Cheshire, Lancashire and the new creations of Merseyside and Greater Manchester.

The two big cities of Liverpool and Manchester have been stolen from Lancashire and form the nuclei of Merseyside and Greater Manchester respectively. Both have fallen on hard times, but both are cities of enormous character. Walking through the centre of Liverpool it is easy to imagine the ghost of wealthy shipowners going about their business, sometimes pausing to chat to one another about freight charges, tides, bills of lading. As recently as twenty years ago, Prince's Landing Stage used to be thronged with their liners – whilst, on the far side of the river at Birkenhead, new vessels were under construction. Nowadays, the only passenger ships you are likely to see are the Isle of Man boats and the ferries that ply briskly from bank to bank.

Mancunians sometimes proudly say that 'what Manchester thinks today, London thinks tomorrow'. It is not entirely untrue. The city's grammar school invariably tops the league for university scholarships. Manchester University had already produced a frighteningly sophisticated computer in 1950 (newspapers called it 'the electronic brain') and it is the home of *The Guardian*. The Hallé Orchestra is a Manchester orchestra, and the public library is one of the very few such establishments to have a theatre – the home of a progressive company that stages extremely good plays.

Gastronomically, Lancashire is mostly famous for its hotpot, mutton, or these days lamb, onions and potatoes, sliced and arranged in layers, the whole dish cooked slowly in the oven. In more up-market versions, cooks are said to add oysters, and Liverpool has its own version which the cognoscenti call 'scouse' (hence 'scouser' for a Liverpudlian and 'scouse' for the local dialect). They must eat a lot of it for the name to have achieved such usage. Somewhere close to the social summit, gourmets enjoy Lancashire boar's head – having first carefully removed the snout. According to one tale, King James I impetuously knighted a particularly good sirloin of beef ('Arise, Sir Loin') when staying at Hoghton Towers in Lancashire. But, since the story is told about several sovereigns in several places honouring several loins of beef, it should not be taken too seriously.

Lancashire cheese comes in two versions – 'tasty' and mild. 'Tasty' can sometimes blister the tongue, but it is an excellent cheese for toasting. The Manchester area, especially Bury, is famed for its black puddings, and what better to follow them than an Eccles cake, from the town of that name east of Manchester, or the more substantial version, a Chorley cake – delicious buttered. Cheshire is, of course, well-known for cats and cheese, which comes in three patriotic kinds: red, white and blue.

ALDERLEY EDGE

No. 15 Wine Bar, 15 London Road
(Alderley Edge 585548)
Open: Mon–Sat 12noon–2pm,
7–10.30pm, Fri–Sat 7–11pm

🎵 P S

The blackboard menu offers starters including pâté and prawn cocktail at around £1.25 and hot main dishes such as moussaka, lasagne, chili con carne and tagliatelli, all for around £2.55. Prawn or trout salads are slightly dearer. Desserts at around 90p include Jamaican fudge cake. A good selection of wines is available by the glass at about 65p. In summer you can eat in the walled and well-tended garden.

ALTRINCHAM

The Cresta Court Hotel ☆☆☆
Church Street
(061-928 8017)
Open: Lodge: Mon–Sat 12noon–2pm,
6–10.30pm, Sun 12noon–2pm
Quarterdeck: Mon–Sun
12noon–2.30pm, 6.30–11pm,
Sun 6.30–10.30pm

C 🎵 P ⌘

This bright, new hotel has two steak bar restaurants. The Tavern Lodge offers the usual combination of steak, chicken, scampi and fish costing from £2.25 to about £4.45 all served with vegetables. The Quarterdeck is a little more

Alderley Edge — Blackburn

sophisticated, with main dishes from over £2.95–£5.25 and a good selection of vegetables in addition to those included in the price of the meal.

Ganders, 2 Goose Green
(061-941 3954)
Open: Mon–Thu 12noon–3pm,
7–10.30pm, Fri 12noon–3pm, 7–11pm,
Sat 12noon–4pm, Sat–Sun 7–10.30pm,
morning coffee: Mon–Sat 10–11.45am,
afternoon coffee: Sat 3–4pm

C S

Surprisingly, goose is not on the very varied menu of this pleasant wine bar and bistro, housed in a 300-year-old cottage in a quiet alley close to the town centre. A dozen appetisers range in price from 50p for home-made soup to £1.60 for avocado with crab. Tuna fish pâté, ham and prawn cornets, rollmop herring or 'Cranks' vegetarian salad are other tasty choices. Lancashire hot pot is a good, traditional main course for £1.85, but why not go overboard and try fondue bourguignon — a bargain at around £3.75 per person? You will need to have three other people with you to sample this delicacy. Desserts are in the 60p–70p bracket and include such delights as passioncake, fresh strawberries and cream and 'real' sherry trifle.

ASHTON-UNDER-LYNE

Corniche Grill, Oldham Road
(061-339 5469)
Open: Mon–Sun 12noon–2.30pm,
6–10.30pm, Sun 7–10.30pm

C P S ⌘

Car dealers, Wm Monk claim that this gallery restaurant overlooking the car showroom is a new idea 'direct from Paris', and the first of its kind in this country. Grills are the main feature on the menu with rump steak for £4.86 or so, and all dishes include French fries or jacket potato and a roll and butter. Sweets or cheese and biscuits are also included in the price of the main course. For about 90p you can choose a connoisseur coffee such as a Monte Carlo (with Cointreau) or a Brands Hatch (with whisky), or have a 'customised' coffee to suit your taste.

BLACKBURN

Kenyon's Studio Buttery, 31 Penny Street
(Blackburn 60347)
Open: Mon–Wed 9am–4.30pm,
Thu 10am–1.30pm, Fri 9am–5pm,
Sat 9am–4.30pm

P S

This sparkling, modern coffee chop in the centre of town is a self-serve style operation offering good food at remarkably low prices. A three-course meal starting with soup of the day at

William Monk Ltd.

Corniche Grill
RESTAURANT

... is the perfect setting for your Wedding Reception; celebrating that special occasion; or having a splendid meal just for the pleasure of it.

The menu is complemented by our extensive wine cellar of vintage, non-vintage and superb house wines.

Lunchtime, evening (a two-course meal for less than £5), or for a Sunday family lunch (three courses £3 — children's special half-price menu), come and enjoy the Corniche; we'll really take care of you

Telephone Tom Burgess now with your booking — or just call in.

Oldham Road, Ashton-u-Lyne. Tel: 061-339 5469.

about 25p, followed by lasagne or steak and kidney (both less than £1 but the most expensive savoury dishes on the menu) and completed with Black Forest gâteau at around 45p is excellent value.

BLACKPOOL

The Danish Kitchen, Vernon Humpage, Church Street
(Blackpool 24291)
Open: Mon–Sat 9am–5.30pm

⑤

Pine tables and pine beams with mock oil lamps adorn this bright, clean, split-level serve-yourself operation in the centre of town. Freshly made soup is about 40p and there is a tempting array of Danish open sandwiches (crab, prawn, beef, smoked salmon etc) from around 60p, salads from 79p, omelettes from 79p and pizzas from £1.10. The Danish pastries from 34p, are excellent.

BOLTON

The Drop Inn and Mr Bumbles, The Last Drop ★★★
Bromley Cross
(Bolton 591131)
Open: Inn: Mon–Sun 12noon–2pm, Mr Bumbles: Mon–Thu 7–10.30pm, Fri–Sat 7–11pm, Sun 3.30–9.30pm

ⒸⒿⓅ

A collection of derelict 18th-century farm buildings has been imaginatively converted to create a modern hotel complex with traditional village atmosphere. The Drop Inn pub even sports a honky-tonk piano to accompany evening sing-songs, as well as oak beams and a blazing log fire. Bar snacks are served in the evening, but it's at lunchtime that the food scene is best, with an excellent, self-service lunch for around £3. The stone-floored Mr Bumbles with its low-arched ceiling, wood and brick surfaces and candlelight, offers dishes from £1.50. The menu is changed monthly and includes fish, salad, burger and one or two more unusual dishes.

The Lamplighter, 26 Knowsley Street
(Bolton 35175)
Open: Mon–Fri 12noon–2pm, 5.45–10.30pm, Fri 12noon–2pm,

Blackpool — Chester

5.45–11pm, Sat 12noon–11pm, Sun 3–6pm

Pictures, prints and posters of the Victorian era cover the walls, and gas lamps and stuffed animals' heads add to the overwhelming 19th-century atmosphere. Every dish is given the name of a Victorian cigarette card character; the Pawnbroker's Treat, for instance, is hot poached salmon dripping in best butter, and the Knocker's-Up Nosh – a juicy rump steak with garden peas and a garnish of cress, tomato and potatoes. Fresh fruit, ice cream or cheese is included in the main course price, so nothing tops our limit

BOLTON-LE-SANDS

Willow Tree, By Pass Road
(Hest Bank 823316)
Open: Tue–Fri 9.30am–1.45pm, 4.30–8.30pm, Sat 4.30–9pm, Sun 11.30am–9pm

Ⓟ

This single-storey building with its neatly tiled roof and white stucco walls is just the place to feed the family. Service is prompt and efficient in the two well-appointed, wood-panelled dining rooms, where a lunch of soup or fruit juice, minute steak, lamb chops or grilled plaice, served with potatoes or chips and peas, a sweet and coffee, is likely to cost around £3.50. Light lunches run from 85p–£1.75. The reasonably-priced evening menu offers more choice.

BROUGHTON

The Orchard, Whittingham Lane
(Broughton 862208)
Open: Tue–Sat 12noon–2pm, 7.30–9.30pm, Sun 12noon–2pm

ⒸⒿⓅ

The cluster of buildings which forms 'The Orchard' includes a barn now used for functions. Natural stone walls and beams are a foil for brass, copper, china and pictures, the general effect being neat, bright and cheerful. The set lunches are excellent value, three courses costing

from £3 on weekdays and from about £3.15 on Sunday, the main course giving several choices including traditional roasts. The à la carte menu offers a wide range of speciality dishes and costs from £5.50 upwards.

BURNLEY

Smackwater Jacks, Ormerod Street
(Burnley 21290)
Open: Mon–Sun 11.30am–3pm, 7–11pm

ⒿⓅⓈ

A town centre steak and hamburger joint set in a stone and brick-built cellar. The lighthearted menu is written in brash Americanese – start with fruit juice ('we got orange an' we got tomato') and move on to stuffed baked potatoes or a 'hillbilly chili' – ('the way Pa likes it') – at about £1.45. For dessert there's cheesecake 'frigate', fruit salad and various sundaes, all under or around £1.

CHESTER

The Carriage Restaurant, Mercia Square, Frodsham Street
(Chester 23469)
Open: Mon–Sat 12noon–2.30pm, 5.30–10.30pm, Sat 5–11pm, Sun 5–9pm, Summer only

ⒸⓅⓈ

This modern glass-fronted restaurant, with its separate wine bar, is to be found in a shopping precinct close to the city walls. The interior is of unusual design with iron and wood arches forming banquettes at one end of the room and an open-plan area with mock-Gothic ceiling at the other. The restaurant also boasts two refurbished carriages. An extensive menu offers a three-course meal, with coffee for around £4.50. To be on the safe side however, choose from the excellent selection on the more modestly priced set menu: there are only four starters but chicken provençale, Cumberland grill and deep-fried fillet of plaice served with lemon wedge, home-made tartare sauce and fried croquette potatoes are among the main dishes. Puddings such as the giant éclair filled with ice cream and topped with chocolate sauce and the

---

KENYONS STUDIO BUTTERY
31 Penny St., Blackburn.
OUR SPECIALITIES:-
✻ COFFEE & FRESH CREAM GATEAUX
✻ LIGHT MEALS THROUGHOUT EACH DAY
And pop into our butteries in other Lancashire towns

Chester

Claverton's Wine Bar, Lower Bridge Street
(Chester 319760)
Open: Mon–Sat 12noon–2.30pm,
5.30–10.30pm, Sun 12noon–1.45pm,
7–10.30pm

🍴

Come early to this popular basement wine bar, as it's sure to be busy, especially in the evenings. The white rough-cast walls, stone floors and polished tables with white cloths give a bright, clean appearance, enhanced by the tempting array of food. A selection from the cold table costs around £2, and for a little less you might choose avocado poisson or pâté with bread. Home-made soup costs around 60p, as does the cheesecake or gâteaux for dessert. On a fine day you can sip your wine on the patio and watch the world go by.

The Courtyard ××
13 St Werburgh Street
(Chester 21447)
Open: Mon–Sat 10.30am–2.30pm,
7–10pm

C ♫ 🍴

This popular gourmet restaurant is set around a pretty courtyard, within the city walls and the sound of the Cathedral bells. Upstairs at lunchtime a 'help yourself' smørgasbrød operates. À la carte lunch includes sirloin steak at around £4.50, gammon at about £3.20, and a selection of starters and sweets. Dinner is more adventurous with such delights as lambs' sweetbreads braised in Madeira, but it is more expensive. There is also an evening bistro offering a very reasonable fixed price buffet at £6.95.

The Farmhouse, 9–13 Northgate Street
(Chester 311332)
Open: Mon–Sat 9am–6pm

P 🍴

This friendly mid-city eaterie, situated above Millett's camping stores, has a pine-equipped interior interspersed with oodles of pot plants. The daily-changing choice of dishes is chalked up on a blackboard, but there's always a very good salad selection and, with prices ranging from £1.50–£2, you should find this farmhouse-style kitchen an economical haven.

The Gallery, 24 Paddock Row
(Chester 47202)
Open: Mon–Sat 12noon–2.15pm,
Tue–Sat 6.30–9.30pm

♫ P S 🍴

Owner Edward Jones has created a refreshingly-different eating place along the lines of a conservatory with earthy brown carpets and tree-green walls. A beautiful array of pot plants add to the atmosphere. Meals too are a little out of the ordinary. Soup of the day is laced with sherry and cream and main dishes include asparagus and cheese-filled crêpes and rainbow trout – pan fried with almonds and cream. Situated at one end of one of Chester's Rows in the centre of town it is also the ideal rendezvous for shoppers. Price is right here too – three-course lunch with coffee and wine will cost around £4.50.

Maison Romano, 51 Lower Bridge Street
(Chester 20841)
Open: Mon–Sat 11.30am–2.30pm,
5.30–11.30pm, Sun 12noon–2pm,
7–11pm

C ♫ P 🍴

The lower-ground-floor restaurant is part of a city-centre hotel and caters for English, French, Italian and Spanish tastes. The three-course lunch at £2.50 represents excellent value for money. Our inspector had the lasagne (£2.70 at lunch-time) and was suitably impressed. The à la carte menu has an extensive list of dishes, but many will take you over our limit. Coffee is from 60p and a glass of wine 65p.

Pierre Griffe Wine Bar, 4–6 Mercia Square
(Chester 312635)
Open: Mon–Fri 11.30am–3pm,
5.30–11pm, Sat 11am–3pm,
5.30–11pm, Sun 12noon–2pm,
7–11pm, Sun in summer only

P S

Close to the Cathedral, this very popular wine bar has brown walls and carpeting which give emphasis to the attractive pine furniture. A long bar counter has a good display of salads and meats. The menu is displayed on a blackboard and three courses can easily be savoured for around £3. Start with French onion soup at 65p, then try pork goulash with rice, Malayan chicken salad or minced beef curry – all at around £1.65. Cheesecake and gâteau both cost 60p.

Sir Edward's Wine Bar, 30 Bridge Street
(Chester 24921)
Open: Mon–Sat 12noon–2.30pm,
6.30–10.30pm, 11pm Fri & Sat

C ♫ P S

This cosy little wine bar enjoys an attractive situation on street level beneath one of Chester's famous 'Rows'. Inside, walls of open brick-work, 200-year-old wood panelling and dark paintwork are adorned with old books, posters and pots. Green gingham tablecloths and flickering candles contribute to the intimate atmosphere and enhance the simple décor. A good selection of starters include avocado, pâté and home-made soup (with fresh ingredients). If you choose the top-priced main course of prime beef steak at about £3.50 with French fried potatoes and a side salad (priced separately) the total, with dessert and freshly percolated coffee (with cream) would well exceed the budget. However a meal of corn-on-the-cob (hors d'oeuvres), gammon steak with peaches and side salad, gâteau and coffee would total only around £4. Service is at the customer's discretion. As one would expect from a wine bar, there is a comprehensive range of wines available with red, white or rosé house wine.

MAISON ROMANO

**51 Lower Bridge Street, Chester.
Telephone: Chester 20841.**

ENGLISH - FRENCH - ITALIAN - SPANISH CUISINE
Extensive à la carte menu

Open:
Monday - Saturday 11.30am - 2.30pm, 5.30pm - 11.30pm.
Sunday 12 noon - 2pm, 7pm -11pm

CLEVELEYS

Savoy Grill, 6 Bispham Road
(Cleveleys 85 3864)
Open: Summer Sun–Mon
11.30am–7pm, Tue 11.30am–8.30pm,
Wed–Sat 11.30am–10pm, Winter
Tue–Fri 11.30am–7pm, Sat–
Sun 11.30am–9pm

[P][S][&]

A popular, corner-house restaurant near the seafront, the Savoy Grill is well-known for its friendly atmosphere and unpretentious food. Soups and pies are all home-made by proprietor Mrs Dorothy Richardson, and a set three-course meal including soup, steak and mushroom pie and ice cream can be had for the extremely modest price of £1.95, and a three-course meal with roast – beef, lamb, pork, chicken or turkey – for around £2.85. A special children's menu lists old favourites such as fish fingers, beefburgers or roast beef and ranges in price from 75p–£1, though apart from these budget meals, a full à la carte also operates.

CONGLETON

The Gingerbread Coffee Shop, 3 Duke Street
(Congleton 71627)
Open: Mon–Tue 9.30am–4.30pm,

Cleveleys
—
Freckleton

Wed 9.30am–1.30pm,
Thu–Sat 9.30am–4.30pm

[P][S][&]

This is a quaint cream-and-brown painted restaurant where many of the dishes, such as chicken casserole, savoury flan, or pizza are available for just over £1 and all are served with vegetables or salad. Starters, at around 40p include grapefruit segments and soup of the day. A sweet such as home-made fruit pie with fresh cream or meringue glacé costs about 50p.

CREWE

Cheshire Casserole, Earle Street
(Crewe 585479)
Open: Tue–Fri 12noon–2pm,
8–10.15pm, Sat 8–10.15pm

[P][&]

As the name implies, this bistro is famed for its excellent casseroles. Owned and run by Brian and Joan Shannon for the past five years it is well worth a visit. The lunch menu offers the best value, just £1.60 for the casserole of the day, and a three-course meal at under £3. The evening menu is more extensive and comes outside the scope of this guide.

DISLEY

The Ginnel, 3 Buxton Old Road
(Disley 4494)
Open: Tue–Fri 7.30–10.15pm,
Sat 7.15–10.30pm, Sun 12.30–2.15pm

[C][&]

Entry to this cosy wine bar is by means of a narrow passageway, hence the name Ginnel – a local word for passage. Old silk embroideries and open brickwork add character to the delightfully furnished interior, where a tempting menu awaits your attention. Imaginative soups and starters include the ever popular home-made pâté and prawn cocktail at £1.25 each. Tasty casserole dishes to tempt all palates are from £2.45, and with speciality desserts at 90p you can be sure of a memorable meal for under £6. Traditional Sunday lunch is also reasonably priced at around £3.95, with children's portions for just £2.

FRECKLETON

The Ship Inn
(Freckleton 632393)
Open: Quarter Deck Restaurant:
Mon–Sun 12noon–2.30pm, 7–9.45pm
The Gallery: Mon–Sun 12noon–2.30pm,
Sat 7.30–10.15pm

[C][♫][P][S][&]

The Ship was built about 10 years ago on

Cheshire Casserole
and Steak House

EARLE STREET, CREWE

Proprietors: Brian & Joan Shannon

FULLY LICENSED WITH SEPARATE BAR

ALL FOOD COOKED AND PREPARED BY PROPRIETRESS

Ideally situated for after Theatre Suppers

CREWE'S OWN COUNTRY-STYLE RESTAURANT

Open Daily 12-2 p.m. Tuesday to Friday and Nightly 8-10 p.m. Tuesday to Sunday
Closed all day Monday

Ring 585479 for Reservations

the site of a hostelry of the same name which dated back to 1630. The interior is designed along the lines of a ship, with a 'Sharp End' bar and another called the Galley. In the latter you can get a help-yourself repast called 'Scandhovee' for about £3.25 at lunchtime (£2.85 evenings), which is very popular locally. You can take an à la carte meal in the Quarter Deck Restaurant but it would be all too easy to top the £5 mark. The speciality is fish with even the salads weighted on the side of seafoods. The table d'hôte lunch is well within limits, three courses costing around £3.50 – melon, grilled pork chop and apple sauce with vegetables, followed by sherry trifle, is an example of what to expect.

GISBURN

Cottage Restaurant, Main Street (Gisburn 441)
Open: Mon 12noon–2pm, Tue–Sun 11.30am–6pm, closed Wed

🍴 P 🍷

With its low-beamed ceilings and warmth of welcome from proprietors Mr and Mrs Farnworth, the Cottage Restaurant lives up to the traditional charm suggested by its name. Home cooking – the steak and kidney pie and home-cooked ham are particularly good – is accompanied by chips and peas, salad or jacket potato. A meal will cost under £5 for three courses.

HALE

Hale Wine Bar, 106–108 Ashley Road (061-928 2343)
Open: Mon–Thu 12noon–2pm, 7–10pm, Fri–Sat 12noon–2pm, 7–11pm

P S

Two dress shops were transformed into this fashionable wine bar by enterprising owners, Nick Elliot and Tim Eaton. Victoriana is the theme of the two rooms which are on different levels. An excellent menu offers starters such as cheese and tuna pâté or quiche Lorraine for around £1, main courses for about £2.25 include lasagne, moussaka, tagliatelli and prawn salad. Puddings cost around 85p and Jamaican fudge cake, lemon soufflé

Gisburn
—
Liverpool

cake or chocolate mousse are some of the choices. Lunch here is a treat for the weary shopper or jaded office worker.

KNUTSFORD

Sir Frederick's Wine Bar, 44 King Street (Knutsford 53209)
Open: Tue–Sat 12noon–2.15pm, 7–10.15pm

C 🍷 P S

You'll enjoy the relaxed and friendly atmosphere at this pleasant town centre wine bar. Décor is simple with rough cast walls and arches decorated with posters and block board prints. A limited à la carte menu is accompanied by an ample wine list. A three-course meal here will cost around £5 with a choice of cold table and Continental salads. Hot dishes such as gammon steak with peaches cost around £2.50.

LANCASTER

Old Brussels, 53 Market Street (Lancaster 69177)
Open: Mon–Sat 8am–6pm

C 🍷 P S 🍷

Old Brussels is a family-owned and run restaurant serving freshly-cooked foods, reasonably priced and nicely presented. Home-baked pizzas, burgers, steak pittas, farmhouse grill and meat and potato pies are hot favourites. Morning coffee, fruit scones and lemon and meringue pie are also specialities. A three-course meal with a glass of wine will not exceed £6.

The Country Pantry, Co-operative Department Store, Church Street (Lancaster 64355 ext 38)
Open: Mon–Sat 9am–5pm

P 🍷

Situated on the first floor of the Co-op in the city centre, this bright, self-service pantry is furnished in pine with country-kitchen collages decorating the walls. Pot plants (the genuine thing) act as divides between tables. There is a good selection of hot dishes and salads almost all at

under £1. A typical meal of soup, quiche with either jacket potatoes or chips, followed by a cake or pastry would cost just over £2. Sorry, no dividend stamps though.

Squirrels, 92 Penny Street (Lancaster 62307)
Open: Mon–Sat 11.30am–2pm, 6.30–10pm, Sun 7–10pm

C 🍷 P S 🍷

The smart brown-and-cream exterior of this city-centre wine bar attracts hungry shoppers and wine buffs alike. Inside, the cavernous, cellar-like atmosphere has a pleasing effect and complements the good range of food. Main courses include beef steak and oyster pie at £3.95, with filled baked potatoes, pâté and salads as possible (and cheaper) alternatives. With home-made soup as your starter, and a slice of full-cream gâteau for sweet, you have a tasty and wholesome three course meal at under or around £6.

LIVERPOOL

Casa Italia, Temple Court, 40 Stanley Street
(051-227 5774)
Open: Mon–Sat 12noon–10pm

🍷 P S

This bright, bustling pizzeria, surrounded by more sombre city buildings, instantly commands attention. The menu lists a dazzling selection of pizzas and pastas, averaging around £2. If the Italian hors d'oeuvres are sampled (around £2.30), plus one of the delicious sweets from the trolley and espresso coffee, the meal could still cost less than £6.

D'Anna, Armour House, Lord Street (051-709 7946)
Open: Mon–Sat 11.30am–10.30pm, Sun 12noon–2.30pm

C 🍷 P S 🍷

In the heart of 'Scouseland', close to the Mersey, you will find this small, unpretentious restaurant decorated in restful green with alcoves and dark oak tables. The bill of fare covers a broad spectrum, from omelettes and veal dishes at around £2 to fish dishes

---

Cottage Restaurant

**Main Street, Gisburn,
Nr Clitheroe
Telephone: Gisburn 441**

One hours drive from Blackpool, Morecambe or the Lake District you will find a warm welcome waiting for you at the Cottage Restaurant. With its low-beamed ceilings, bamboo walls and hand carved birds it lives up to the traditional charm suggested by its name. Home cooking—specialities steak & kidney pie and roast ham & salad, home made jam and fresh cream gateaux. Situated in a beautiful village setting on the A59, 15 minutes drive to Skipton the gateway to the Yorkshire Dales.

Lymm — Lytham

ranging from £2 for plaice to around £4.50 for Dover sole. Grills are similarly priced and cold buffets, including prawn salad, are around £2.50. Children can order beefburgers and chips at a mere 95p.

Everyman Bistro, Hope Street
(051-708 9545)
Open: Mon–Fri 12noon–11.30pm,
Sat 11am–11.30pm

S &

This interesting bistro is situated in the basement of the Everyman Theatre in the centre of town. Blackboards display a menu based on fresh produce and it is easy to eat three courses here for around £3. Home-made soup or quiche Lorraine are two of the starters (70p–90p) with dishes such as spicy Caribbean pork, broccoli cheese, salads and casseroles as main courses (£1.80–£3). There is a selection of home-made sweets, various cheeses and live yoghurts to finish with (60p–90p).

La Grande Bouffe, 48a Castle Street
(051-236 3375)
Open: Mon 10am–3pm,
Tue–Fri 10am–11pm, Sat 11am–3pm,
7–11pm

C ♫ P S

La Grande Bouffe is a typical French-style basement café. French pictures adorn the walls. The menu is on a blackboard and dishes include home-made soup such as potato and watercress at about 60p, quiches for around 75p, beef sausage-meat and spinach pie for around £1.20 and Armenian lamb or rare roast beef for about £2. Cold dishes include fresh mackerel with salad at about £1.50. Desserts (65p–85p) are also home-made. It is a self-service operation – ideal for a quick, tasty meal. The à la carte evening meal is likely to be beyond our limit.

St George's Hotel ★★★★
St John's Precinct, Lime Street
(051-709 7090)
Open: Buttery: Mon–Sat 10am–10pm

C P S

The stylish modern coffee shop of this sumptuous hotel serves a comprehensive range of food. For a quick snack, toasted sandwiches, hamburgers of all varieties, authentic curried chicken and egg dishes are on the huge menu for around £1.50–£3.50. There is also plenty of scope for a three-course meal within our budget. A choice of six starters includes minestrone with Parmesan at 65p. A good selection of fish and grills from about £2.25–£6.50 make a substantial main course. Sweets range in price from around 75p–£1.25. Afternoon cream teas are £1.25.

LYMM

The Bollin Restaurant, Heatley, 2m NE of Lymm on A6144
(Lymm 3657)
Open: Mon–Fri 12noon–2pm,
7–9.30pm, Sat 7–9.30pm,
Sun 12noon–2pm

C ♫ P &

Mrs Jean Barker runs this enterprising restaurant and catering business as well as the village Post Office and you can be assured of a warm welcome from Jean or her General Manager Peter Davies. The fixed price menu, lunch at £4.50, dinner £6.50, provides extremely good value for money and is available from Monday to Friday. Dishes are varied and interesting and include chicken pancake and Bury black pudding for starters; casserole of rabbit and pork loin with cider and apple sauce are just two of the main courses. End your meal with a choice of sweets from the trolley and a cup of coffee. A slightly more expensive à la carte menu is also available. There is a special family lunch on Sunday, and bar snacks are available Monday to Friday.

LYTHAM

Lidun Cottage Barbecue, 5 Church Road
(Lytham 736936)
Open: Mon–Sun 11.30am–2.30pm,
5–12mdnt

C P &

LIDUN COTTAGE BARBECUE

Licensed Restaurant and Take Home Meals

Delicious "Spit Roasted Chickens".
Barbecued "Loin of Pork"
Succulent Chargrilled 100% pure Beefburger with Relishes.
French Fries. Side Salad.
Choice of Sweets.
Cona Coffee with Cream

*Open 11.30am to 2.30pm. 5.00pm till midnight
Seven days a week*

5 Church Road, Lytham. Tel: 736936

---

the COUNTRY PANTRY

MEALS WITH A COUNTRY FLAVOUR
from our salad bar or hot plate
with fresh cream gateaux
from our Kenyons Bakery

GLC CHURCH STREET   LANCASTER   Telephone 0524 64355

Macclesfield — Manchester

This pleasant restaurant, with attractive bow windows, offers mainly spit-roasted dishes (half a chicken at £2.25, barbecued loin of pork at £2.95). There are also 100% beefburgers at around £1. At present there are no starters, but try 'hot from the oven' Lidun Cottage apple pie for dessert at 50p.

MACCLESFIELD

Da Topo Giglo, 15 Church Street
(Macclesfield 22231)
Open: Tue–Sat 12noon–2pm,
7–10.30pm

P S

Half-way down the quaint, cobbled street of this old silk-manufacturing town is this informal restaurant, named after the famous Italian mouse. Fresh produce is put to good use in the thick minestrone soup – only 75p but almost a meal in itself – chicken carbonara or salmon cooked to choice, both under £3. Home-made sweets start at 95p, so a three-course lunch can cost as little as £4.25 here.

MANCHESTER

The Cafe, 3–5 Princess Street, Albert Square
(061-834 2076)
Open: Mon–Sun 11.30am–4am

♫ P S

Just the place for the late-nighter, this modern-fronted steak and burger restaurant is in the city centre. As well as the char-grilled steaks and pure beefburgers there is a good selection of 'Café Extras' such as poussin Continental – a baby chicken cooked in a rich wine sauce with a hint of garlic for around £3. For the vegetarian there is the veg-burger and the Café-casserole, both under £2. Sweets, including fresh cream Black Forest gâteau, rum baba, sorbets and cheesecakes range from 75p–85p.

Danish Food Centre, Royal Exchange Buildings, Cross Street
(061-832 9924)
Open: Copenhagen Restaurant
Mon–Sat 12noon–3pm, 6–12mdnt
Danmark Inn Mon–Sat 8am–6pm

S

This popular Danish eatery is situated in the city centre, within the Royal Exchange Buildings. A beautifully-decorated three-tier cold table provides the centrepiece of the main restaurant, though a help-yourself choice to as much as you like from the appetising array of dishes offered here will pass the limit a little. Of course, you can always plump for the nourishing open sandwich known as smørbrød. Schapps and a good wine list are available, although the Danish lagers are enthusiastically recommended!

Farmhouse Kitchen, Fountain Street (behind Lewis's)
(061-236 5532)
Open: Mon–Sat 9am–7pm

S

A sister to the restaurant of the same name across the city, but somewhat smaller. Pine tables and partitioning make for a fresh, bright atmosphere. Food is listed on a daily-changing blackboard list. There's always a big variety of goodies and you'll have a job to spend more than £3 per head.

Farmhouse Kitchen, 42 Blackfriars Street (near Deansgate)
(061-832 7001)
Open: Mon–Sat 9am–7pm

P S

This Farmhouse serve-yourself Kitchen attracts shoppers and business people to its convenient location in the city centre. Hot and cold dishes are available at very reasonable prices and the excellent salad selection has proved particularly popular. Of the hot meals, the chicken in wine sauce at £1.80 is worth trying as are the fried haddock and cheese and potato savoury or quiche, all around £1.25. An extremely nourishing three-course meal can be had for around £3.

THE CAFÉ
Manchester

Manchester's very own fast food steak and burger restaurant.

**OPEN 11.30am — 4am
7 DAYS A WEEK**

3-5 Princess Street, Albert Square,
Manchester 2.
Telephone 061-834 2076

Manchester

Harper's, 2 Ridgefield
(061-833 9019)
Open: Mon, Tue, Thu, Fri 10am–7pm,
Wed & Sat 10am–11pm

C P

This newly-opened coffee shop/restaurant lies in a small back street close to St Annes Square. Mr Shapiro, the owner, is rightly proud of his new venture which is as refreshing in style as the bright green and white décor. The buffet menu changes daily and includes soup (75p) open sandwiches (around £2) salads and hot dishes (around £3). There is a delicious choice of puds to end your meal. Harper's is licensed.

The Lancashire Fold, Kirkway,
Alkrington, Middleton
(061-643 4198)
At the junction of Mount Road and Kirkway and near M62 junction 20
Open: during normal licensing hours
Restaurant Tue–Fri, Sun 12noon–2pm, 7–10pm, Sat 7–10pm

C ♫ P S ⌂

For those who prefer to get away from the city centre, The Lancashire Fold may provide the answer. This modern extension to a pub has a brick-and-timber décor and comfortable furnishings. Although the à la carte menu is not cheap, it is possible to choose a three-course meal within the limit. Choose chilled melon at around £1, suprême de poulet Maryland with additional vegetables at around £3.45, a sweet from the trolley or cheese at around 80p and you are left with just enough for a glass of wine. At lunchtime you can get a good table d'hôte meal for about £3.

Market Restaurant, 30 Edge Street
(061-834 3743)
Open: Tue–Sat 6.30–10.30pm

Energetic owners Su-Su Edgecombe and Elizabeth Price have breathed new life into an almost-dead part of the city with their delightful new restaurant. Pale primrose walls offset with dark green woodwork and simple stone flooring create a plain but pleasing effect, with a smattering of pictures, prints and bric-à-brac to add interest. Candles on the tables and lace curtains are the finishing touches. A starter such as chilled Lebanese cucumber soup made with yoghurt, cream and fresh mint costs around £1.05, and could be followed by spinach and mushroom pancakes au gratin (£2.20). Finish with a sweet, such as French gooseberry tart at around £1.20 and you are well within the budget.

Oscars, 11 Cooper Street
(061-236 6752)
Open: Mon–Fri 10.30am–3pm, closed Sat, Mon–Sun 5.30–10.30pm. Late opening Wed–Sat, until 2am

C

This city-centre, self-service restaurant has a popular pub-type atmosphere, particularly at lunchtime. Mock beams and rough-cast walls give a friendly 'local' feel – as does the regular clientele. At lunchtime choose from a blackboard menu such dishes as traditional roast for just under £2.50, kidney turbigo at around £1.95 or chicken and mushroom pie for about £1.85. There is a self-serve salad selection for around £2 and a choice of sweets at around 80p. In the evening you can have a sirloin steak chasseur for £4.75 or, further down the scale there's Spanish omelette for around £1.80. Coffee with cream is about 35p.

Pizzeria Bella Napoli, 1 Kennedy Street
(061-236 1537)
Open: Mon–Sat 12noon–11.30pm,
Sun 6.30–11.30pm

P S

This friendly basement eating house has typical Italian-style décor, stuccoed walls and tiled floors. Being much smaller than the Pizzeria Italia, its sister restaurant across the city, tables can be hard to come by at peak periods. The slick young staff serve a variety of pastas and pizzas, such as cannelloni ripieni (pancakes filled with beef, eggs and spinach – about £2.20) or pizza marinara (mozzarella cheese, anchovy, olives, tuna and

---

Harper's
COFFEE SHOP • RESTAURANT

Visit Manchester's newest AA Recommended Coffee Shop and Licensed Restaurant, serving a wide selection of coffees, homemade ice cream, extra filled sandwiches, fresh cream pastries and baked jacket potatoes with choice of fillings.
Our fresh salads are available all day.
Morning coffee and Afternoon Tea our speciality.
We can meet your needs for that pre-theatre bite — mid evening supper —
after cinema coffee & gateau

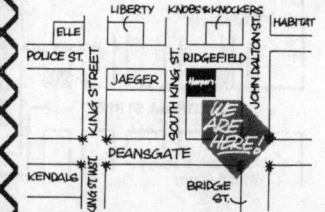

2 RIDGEFIELD, MANCHESTER
(Corner of South King St. opposite Jaeger)

Mon, Tues, Thurs, Fri, 10am-7pm
Wed, and Sat, 10am - 11pm
(last orders 11pm)

Telephone 061-833-9019

prawns in tomato sauce – £2.20). Sweets run from £1.

Pizzeria Capri, 34 Deansgate
(061-834 4423)
Open: Mon–Thu 12noon–12mdnt, Fri–Sat 12noon–2am, Sun 6pm–12mdnt
[C][P][S][♦]

This small, attractive restaurant in the centre of Manchester is run by partners Mano from Brazil and Mario from Italy. The décor is reminiscent of South America, with its tiled floor, rough-cast walls and cane ceiling. There's plenty on the interesting menu that will break the bank, but a selection such as prawn cocktail, fresh trout Brazilia and hot cherries and ice cream will keep you well within the budget.

Pizzeria Italia, 40–42 Deansgate
(061-834 1541)
Open: Mon–Sat 12noon–11.30pm, Sun 6.30–11.30pm
[P][S]

A corner-sited pizza house on two floor-levels, Pizzeria Italia is decorated in the true Italian style with tiled floors and lusty pot plants. Low-priced dishes including soups, fish and chicken supplement the enormous and varied plate-sized pizzas, excellent value at under £2. Service is snappy, operated by well turned-out and efficient all-Italian staff.

Rajdoot Restaurant ××
St James House, South King Street
(061-834 2176/7092)
Open: Mon–Sat 12noon–2.30pm, 6.30–12mdnt, Sun 6.30–12mdnt
[C][♬][S][♦]

One step inside the door of the Rajdoot Indian restaurant is a step into a different world. Waiters in their national costumes wait to greet you – the atmosphere is sultry and authentic. An extremely wide and varied menu is available and the specialities of the house are the Tandoori murghi £4.20, Tandoori fish and Makhan chicken at around £2.95 or lamb pasanda at a little less. A set meal of Tandoori murghi, shish kebab, nan,

---

Marple — Morecambe

rogan josh, prawn masalla, rice, dessert and coffee is excellent value at around £6.50, though three courses need cost no more than £5.

Sam's Chop House ×
Back Pool Fold, Chapel Walks
(061-834 8717)
Open: Mon–Fri 12noon–3pm
[♦]

If you enjoy a lunch in a place which oozes in friendly charm, Sam's Chop House is a must for you. Set in a back alley, below street level, the décor is plain and simple. Stone walls are adorned by large prints and hanging mock oil lamps enhance the cosy atmosphere. Friendly waitresses serve you with good standard English fare: various steaks from between £4–£5, lamb cutlets and roast chicken garni at around £3–£4 are examples. Extra large portions of scampi or plaice are served for gluttons.

Wild Oats, 88 Oldham Street
(061-236 6662)
Open: Wed–Sat 5–11pm
[♬][P][♦]

Our inspector was very enthusiastic about this small wholefood restaurant just a short distance from Piccadilly Gardens. It is furnished with a varied collection of tables and chairs, old mirrors and posters (proclaiming 'Look After Yourself'). The menu concentrates on wholefood and vegetarian dishes but there are also a couple of meat dishes on the menu. All main dishes included baked potato and salad. Aubergine and tomato lasagne costs less than £4 and chicken Dijonnaise just under £5. Starters are around 60p and sweets around 90p. (Home-made ice-cream is strongly recommended.) Fruit wines such as gooseberry and elderberry are 80p a glass and ordinary red or white 85p. It is advisable to book in advance.

MARPLE

Woodheys Farm, Glossop Road
(Glossop 2704)
Open: Tue–Sat 11.45am–2pm, 7–10pm, Sun 11.45am–2.30pm
On A626 between Glossop and Marple
[C][P][♦]

The impressive stone-built Woodheys Farm occupies an idyllic setting overlooking the beautiful Etherow Valley, and once you've feasted on the views outside, an equally impressive culinary triumph awaits you indoors. Unfortunately, a set dinner price of around £8 – although excellent in its class, precludes the evening meal from our readers, but a similar repast can be sampled at lunchtime for a set price of around £4.50. Appetites large and small are catered for here as all food is displayed in a central cabinet where diners can help themselves to as much or as little as they want (second helpings are not frowned upon!). Appetisers include shell fish, melon and pâté on the cold table, or there's farmhouse soup, whitebait or deep-fried mushrooms served hot. The Carvery offers an unrestricted choice of traditional English roast joints, braised game, casseroles and pies with vegetables, potatoes and salad. Remember to leave room for one of the scrumptious desserts such as fresh cream gâteaux, fresh fruits in season or the speciality – brown bread and brandy ice cream. Coffee is served with mints and home-made sweetmeats.

MORECAMBE

Coffee Shoppe, 35 Princes' Crescent, Bare
(no telephone)
Open: Summer Mon–Sat 9.30am–5.30pm, Sun 10.30am–5.30pm, Winter Mon–Sat 9.30am–4.45pm
[P][♦]

This typical, pleasant little tea shop is set in a row of shops, just off the sea front. Salads, home-cooked meat pies, cakes, pastries and sandwiches are available

Wild Oats
Manchester's wholefood Restaurant

"Wild Oats" — Woolworth — City Centre Piccadilly Gardens
OLDHAM STREET ←
Just park outside from 6.00pm

For delicious home-made food, real ales, ciders, fruit wines . . .

and very reasonable and tasty three-course meals can be had for around £2. Try home-made soup, followed by cottage cheese and peach salad then finish with one of Heather Millen's luscious creamy cakes.

OLDHAM

Mother Hubbard's, 270 Manchester Street
(061-652 0873)
Open: Mon–Sun 11.30am–11.30pm
C P

The cupboard is far from bare at this modern, detached fish restaurant. A variety of fresh fish, delivered daily from Grimsby, ensures that you're in for a piscine treat. A smart interior features spindled wooden divisions (to allow that little bit of privacy at tables) and a Georgian-style bar. The friendly waitresses serve a simple starter, plus main fish dish (scampi, halibut, haddock or plaice with all the trimmings, and a coffee) with ice-cream to finish at a cost of £2.50–£4, depending on your choice of fish.

ORMSKIRK

Tower and Steeple, 15 Church Street
(Ormskirk 72017)
Open: Mon–Fri 10am–2.30pm,
7–10.30pm, Thu 10am–4pm,
7–10.30pm, Sat 10am–4pm, 7–11pm,
Sun 12noon–2.30pm
P S

Lunches are particularly tempting here, with lasagne and other Italian dishes for around £2. A three-course Sunday lunch offering a variety of roasts and desserts from the trolley can be had for just over £4. The dinner menu includes a host of seafood starters and a variety of steaks and grills. Special 'family' dinners are available at around £3.50.

POYNTON

Herbs, 43 Park Lane
(Poynton 876666)
Open: Mon–Sat 12noon–3pm (last orders 2pm), 7pm onwards (last orders 10pm)
C P

Oldham
Preston

Outside this small, elegant restaurant Mr Frank Thornley, the proprietor, has created an attractive paved garden with raised beds containing small plants. The entrance door is especially wide, and with no steps to negotiate there is easy access for the disabled (there is also a unisex toilet suitable for the disabled in the restaurant). The lunch menu at £5.50 offers a good choice of dishes and is changed daily. The à la carte menu is more expensive. Real ale is available at the bar.

PRESTBURY

Prestbury Place, New Road
(Prestbury 828423 and 828156)
Open: Tue–Sat 7.30–10pm
P

Built at the end of a row of 17th-century cottages, this 'home from home' is friendly, relaxed and informal with a simple green décor. The menu, chalked up on a blackboard, includes smoked trout and salad at £2.95, game pie, salad and jacket potato at £2.75, Alabama chili or chicken on rice all around £2.75 and an excellent hot chocolate fudge cake at about 85p. Early evening reservations are taken.

PRESTON

Alexanders, Winckley Street
(Preston 54302)
Open: Mon–Fri 12noon–2.30pm,
7–10pm
C P S

Originally a 19th-century coach house and stable, this elegant building is set in a courtyard in the centre of town. A sumptuous atmosphere is created inside with fawn and burgundy suede-look wall covering, dark-wood panels and 'picture' mirrors, and the whole effect is enhanced by subtle lighting from mock-Victorian wall lamps. A very good table d'hôte menu is available at prices around £3.50. Changed twice weekly, it offers superior main courses such as chicken,

Americaine and grilled gammon with mushrooms. An ambitious selection of dishes appear on the à la carte menu which is rather more expensive – but very tempting, soup, sirloin steak and sherry trifle comes within our budget.

La Bodega, 21 Cannon Street
(Preston 52159)
Open: Mon–Sat 11am–2pm,
Tue–Fri 7–10.30pm, Sat 7–11.30pm
P S

Upturned barrels as tables, wine posters and gingham tablecloths exude a Continental air echoed in the names of dishes such as paella and chicken Basque style. Steak forms the basis of most dishes on the menu, try the Drunken Bull – sozzled in red wine and brandy for under £4. Lunchtimes are self-service.

The Danish Kitchen and The Barbecue, 10 Lune Street
(Preston 22086)
Open: Mon–Sat 9.15am–5.15pm
The Barbecue Mon–Fri 12noon–2pm,
from 5.30pm onwards,
Sat 11.30am–2.30pm, 6–11pm
P S

Bright and refreshing, this town centre Danish Kitchen is gaining in popularity with business people and shoppers, with its choice of eating styles. Upstairs is the budget self-service operation where Danish open sandwiches, salads, omelettes and pizzas are available, together with delicious pastries and gâteaux. Downstairs is the new Barbecue, where you choose your own steak from a refrigerated display, then see it cooked over charcoal while waitresses serve you with a starter. Chops, burgers, chicken, kebabs and trout are also on the menu, and a three-course meal is available within our budget. Pine tables and beams accentuate the fresh, Continental atmosphere.

French Bistro ✕
Miller Arcade, Church Street
(Preston 53882)
Open: Mon–Sat 12noon–2.15pm,
7pm–12.15am, Sun 7pm–12.15am
C P S

See advert on p. 152

Try Our Traditional Sunday Lunches

𝕿𝖔𝖜𝖊𝖗 & 𝕾𝖙𝖊𝖊𝖕𝖑𝖊

LICENSED RESTAURANT
15 Church Street, Ormskirk
Telephone Ormskirk 72017

Proprietors: Dorothy & John Fisher

This small intimate Bistro has two bars. At lunch-time chili con carne, beef bordelaise and various salads range from £1–£2.85. In the evening prices range from £3–£7 and the table d'hôte menus are £4.50 and £5.85.

The Patio, Trafalgar Hotel ☆☆☆
Preston New Road, Samlesbury
(Samlesbury 351)
On A59 E of Preston at junction with Blackburn road
Open: Mon–Sun 7am–11.30pm

C P

The nostalgic French design of the menu, the costumed waitresses, and the opportunity to eat all day long sets the scene. Tiled floors and glass-topped tables, potted plants and a fountain makes a refreshing environment. Variety is the order of the day: the French connection is continued with a small selection of sweet and savoury pancakes (for around £2.70), over the borders to Italy for a choice of pizzas, and further afield for chicken Kashmir shish kebab or American burgers. The home front is not forgotten, with Lancashire hot pot or fisherman's pie (at about £3.30) and grills. An added bonus is the invitation to help yourself to the free salad while you wait. At lunchtime the carvery choice features roasts and salads.

The Tickled Trout ☆☆☆
(Samlesbury 671)
Open: Kingfisher Restaurant Mon–Sun

Rochdale
—
St Michaels-on-Wyre

12noon–2.15pm, 7–10.15pm

C P

The oak-beamed Kingfisher Restaurant with its alcoves, antiques and views of the River Ribble offers a table d'hôte, three-course lunch for around £4.50, or a hot or cold buffet from £2.50. The à la carte menu is beyond our means.

ROCHDALE
Alpine Gasthof Pub and Restaurant,
Whitworth Road
(Rochdale 48953)
Open: Mon–Fri & Sun 12noon–2pm, 7–10pm, Sat 7–10pm

C P

The outside of the restaurant has been modelled on its popular namesake at the foot of the Bavarian Alps. Inside, the warm glow of pine weaves a subtle spell, conducive to good eating. The restaurant has been converted into a carvery featuring a selection of eight starters followed by your choice of roast joints or the chef's dish of the day accompanied by fresh vegetables, jacket potatoes or salad. Luncheon during the week is £4.95 and dinner £5.95. Home-made sweets from the trolley are specially recommended.

Mario's Pizzeria, 115 Yorkshire Street
(Rochdale 46286)
Open: Mon–Sat 12noon–2.30pm, 6–11.30pm

Mario Andreotti and his English wife make their cellar pizzeria a warm, welcoming haven for the hungry. Gingham tablecloths, padded benches and plain white rough-cast walls help to give the place a simple charm which compensates for the fairly predictable menu of pizzas and pastas. Even the most expensive dish – a sirloin steak cooked in Chianti – is still likely to be around £4.65. A whole three-course meal will cost little more if you stick to the modest Italian fare.

ST MICHAELS-ON-WYRE
The Cherry Tree Grill, Garstang Road
(St Michaels 661)
Open: Mon–Thu 12noon–8pm (last orders), Sat 12noon–9pm (last orders), Sun 12noon–6pm (last orders)

P

This stone-built end-of-terrace house was once the village smithy and is now a small but pleasant grill restaurant. The three-course lunch is all-inclusive for the price of the main course, varying between £3.50–£5. A more extensive à la carte menu is available for high tea with sirloin steak or scampi at around £5.75. To finish there is a tempting array of desserts – how about raspberry Pavlova or coupe Jamaica?

french bistro

A very easy going Bistro decorated to a French style, giving a typical relaxed atmosphere.

We offer a unique parade of 36 unusual starters, including King Prawns in Chilli Sauce, Creole pan fried, Clam Chowder and Octopus.

Main courses start at around £3.00 and include Bistro Shellfish Parade, Creole Pepper Pot and Flambé Peppered Steak.

The bar offers over 1000 different spirits and liquers and is one of the largest collections in Europe.

A Bistro for unusual food, atmosphere and living.

MILLER ARCADE, PRESTON
Telephone 53882

Southport — Wilmslow

SOUTHPORT

Pizzeria-Ristorante Paradiso, 120 Lord Street
(Southport 40259)
Open: Mon–Sat 12noon–3pm, 5.30–11pm, Sun 12noon–2.30pm, 5.30–11pm
S ♦

With main courses ranging from pizza margherita at about £1.50 and spaghetti bolognese at around £2 to beef Stroganoff at around £5.25 you can be sure of a good meal within our price range. There are seven starters priced between 80p and £2.25 and a sweet from the trolley costs about 80p.

Vesuvio, 329 Lord Street
(Southport 42275)
Open: Tue–Sun 12noon–3pm, 6.30–11pm
C ♫ P S

Set in a small alleyway leading off Lord Street, this diminutive, attractive restaurant offers a whole range of dishes, from pizzas and pastas to scampi provençale. Venetian pictures and bric-à-brac are complemented by cream and brown walls and Chianti bottles. Particularly tempting is a three-course menu, available at lunchtime and in the evening, for only £2.90. A choice of four starters includes minestrone soup. Main dishes offer a choice of English or Italian – plaice or chicken for patriots or lasagne, spaghetti bolognese or cannelloni for those with a more exotic palate. Desserts are apple pie, crème caramel or ice cream.

STOCKPORT

Georgian House, 59–61 Buxton Road
(061-480 5982)
Open: Mon–Sat 12noon–2.30pm, 6–11pm, Sun 5–11pm
P ♦

The bow-windowed Georgian House restaurant on the A6 doesn't go in for frills but you can get good, reasonably-priced meals there, with half-price portions of certain dishes for children. The special two-course lunch is particularly good value. A half roast chicken, garnished, served with vegetables, roll and butter and a choice of sweet costs about £2; replace the chicken by a 5oz rump steak and the price goes up to a moderate £2.30. The à la carte menu, too is modestly priced, starters costing between 35p for soup and £1.40 for smoked trout. The price quoted for main course includes vegetables, roll and butter and a sweet or cheese and biscuits. Only lobster salad at around £6 is beyond reach and the Georgian specialities are all near the £5 mark.

The Wishing Well, 26a Bramhall Lane South, Bramhall
(061-440 8970)
Open: Tue–Thu 12noon–2pm, 6.30–10pm, Fri–Sun 12noon–2pm, 7–10.45pm
C P S

This rather special Yugoslavian restaurant is in an unlikely location above a greengrocery in one of Manchester's desirable residential suburbs. Vlado Barulovic, the proprietor, features some of his country's mouth-watering dishes in the superb value set lunch which will only set you back around £3 – and coffee's included. Try a Podverak ad Curetine (sauerkraut and onions with roast turkey) or Bosanki Lonac (beef and pork with vegetables in wine). The evening à la carte will call upon a strong will if you are going to spend under £6, and has more emphasis on international meat and fish dishes. Mr Barulovic, will, however, prepare a Yugoslavian speciality to order.

WEST KIRKBY

What's Cooking?, 34 Banks Road
(051-625 7579)
Open: Mon–Sat 12noon–11.30pm, Sun 1–11.30pm
C ♫ S

The bright cream and green exterior of this first-floor restaurant is just as inviting as its name. Ideal for shoppers and families, What's Cooking? is located close to the town centre and specialises in American and Continental-style cuisine. Menu selections include beefburgers with a choice of toppings plus home-made dressing, pizzas, steaks and chicken or 'mouth-watering, mammoth salads'. Chili con carne (just under £2.60) or spare ribs (around £2.95) are interesting alternatives. A full three-course meal will cost about £6.50.

WIGAN

Roberto's, Rowbottom Square
(Wigan 42385)
Open: Restaurant
Mon–Sat 11.30am–2pm, 7–10pm, Fri 10.30pm
Pizza Bar Mon–Sat 11.30am–2pm
C ♫ ♦

Nestling in what were once the cellars of the local newspaper, this pine-tabled restaurant, with its pot plants and pictures, offers pastas, pizzas and inexpensive 'English' meals of the chicken or plaice and chips variety in a pizza bar next door, and an excellent table d'hôte menu in the restaurant. A three-course lunch, which could consist of egg mayonnaise, cannelloni and sherry trifle works out at only £2.55 per head.

WILMSLOW

Greyhound Steakhouse, Wilmslow Road, Handforth
(Wilmslow 523193)
Open: Mon–Sat 12noon–2.30pm, 6–1.30pm, Sun 12noon–2.30pm, 7–10.30pm
C ♫ P S ♦

This Schooner Inn steakhouse, about 10 miles south of Manchester, features natural stone combined with timbers from Fleetwood pier. Begin with soup (about 50p) or prawn cocktail (around £1.10). Main courses (the price includes an ice cream sweet or cheese) vary from fillet of plaice with lemon, tartare sauce, peas and jacket potato or chips at the £3.80 mark to a mixed grill (steak, gammon, lamb, sausage and kidney with tomato, peas, jacket potato or chips) at about £6. Lunchtime snacks such as shepherd's pie or filled rolls are available at the bar.

MARIO'S PIZZERIA & RESTAURANT

Is where you'll find the Finest Italian Food in Town

**115 Yorkshire Street, Rochdale, Lancashire.
Telephone 46286**

YORKSHIRE AND HUMBERSIDE

North Yorkshire, Humberside, West Yorkshire and South Yorkshire are a recent invention. Before they re-drew the county boundaries, the area was Yorkshire with a thin slice of Lincolnshire on the far side of the Humber. In the old days (which were not very long ago), the divisions were known as 'Ridings' – very nearly an anagram of the Danish word *treding*, meaning 'a third part'. There was a North, West and East Riding.

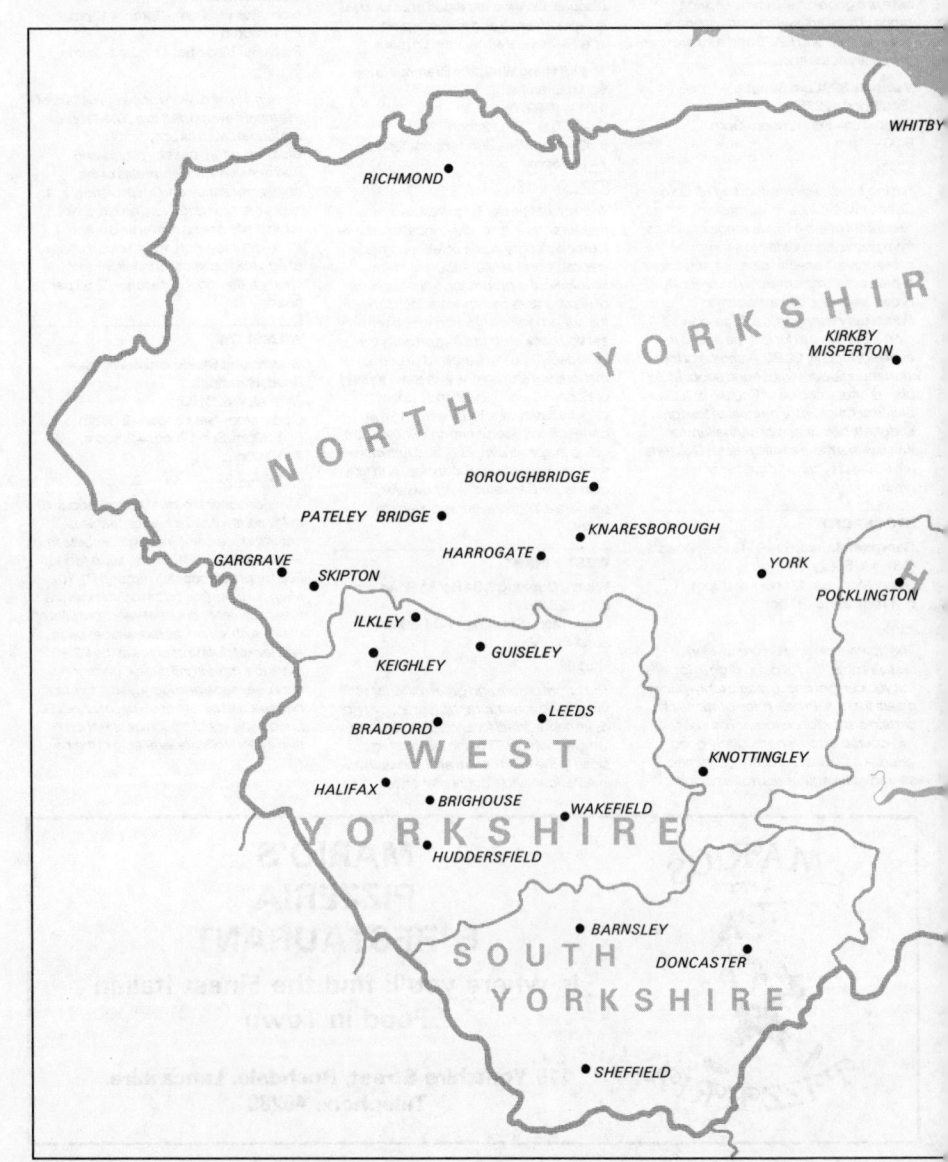

Basically, Yorkshire has two industries: steel, which is centred on Sheffield, and wool which is associated with Bradford and Leeds. A third industry has grown up of recent years: tourism, centred on the Dales.

There are three main Yorkshire dales: Wharfedale, which follows the line of the River Wharfe; Swaledale, which is the River Swale's valley; and Wensleydale, which follows the River Ure (there isn't a River Wensley). Wensleydale is, of course, famous for its cheeses. There are two kinds: one is a double cream not unlike a small Stilton; the other is flat in shape and white in colour. Either is a very good accompaniment to a jar of Old Peculiar, an unusually strong beer that originated in the village of Masham – also on the Ure, but after the river has emerged from the dale.

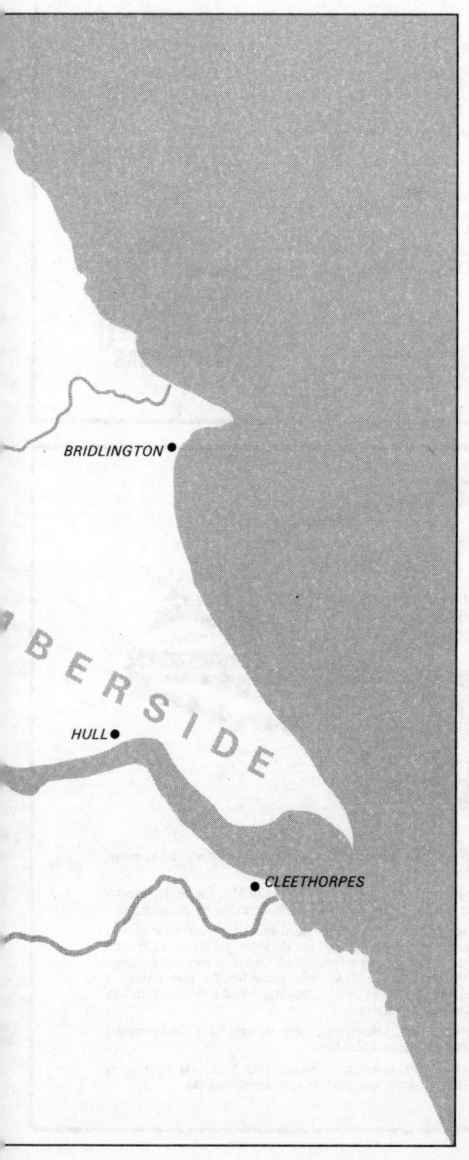

Yorkshire, like most other places, has certain traditions: such as eating simnel cake (a rich, ornamental fruitcake with almond paste inside and out) on Mothering Sunday, and from mid-Lent until Easter. Another takes place after a marriage. You throw a piece of wedding cake from an upstairs window. If it falls to pieces on hitting the ground it means that the bride will have a happy life ahead of her. If it does not... but, thankfully, it usually shatters.

Parkin (a treacle-based cake traditionally eaten on Guy Fawkes night), Yorkshire pudding, Pontefract cakes (from the liquorice fields of Pontefract), Wensleydale cheese, and even Old Peculiar, are all Yorkshire specialities that have become available to the rest of the country. A dish named Solomon Grundy seems less likely to achieve nationwide popularity. Without going into too many details, you take six herrings: remove the bones without breaking them and retain the heads and tails. You boil the rest, and garnish it with anchovies, capers, diced mushrooms and oysters – to mention just a few of the ingredients. Then you carefully arrange the concoction back over the bones so that it looks like a real herring.

If you are not a keen cook, it may be better to confine yourself to Snapdragon, which is easy. You simply heat 1lb of raisins, pour 1½ glasses of whisky over them, and set fire to the lot. Highly recommended for bachelors.

FALSTAFF TAVERNS

FINE FOOD AND A WARM WELCOME

Waggon & Horses	Abbeydale Road South, Millhouses, Sheffield	Tel. Sheffield 361451
Full House	Rotherham Road, Monk Bretton, Barnsley	Tel. Barnsley 84503
Punch Bowl	Blossom Street, York	Tel. York 22619
Jester	Harrogate Road, Alwoodley, Leeds	Tel. Leeds 682738
New Inn	Wetherby Road, Scarcroft, Leeds	Tel. Leeds 892029
Empress	Church Square, Harrogate	Tel. Harrogate 67629

IN THIS REGION
YOU'RE NEVER FAR FROM
A
FALSTAFF TAVERN

Brooklands Restaurant Limited
Barnsley Road, Dodworth,
Barnsley, South Yorkshire
Tel: 0226-84238 & 6364

Brooklands is more than just a restaurant, Brooklands offers the discerning traveller all the comforts of home in a relaxed atmosphere and pleasant surroundings.

Although the Motel is conveniently located a few hundred yards west of junction 37 of the M1, the chalet rooms are quietly situated away from the main road and offer ample car parking adjacent or close by each room.

Each room forms a self contained unit with bathroom, telephone, colour television, mini bar/refrigerator and tea and coffee making facilities, and four of the rooms are especially equipped for disabled persons. All rooms have a direct telephone link to the Administration office and staff are in attendance 24 hours a day. The rooms are double or family sized, and the current single inclusive tariff of £25.00 includes breakfast for one, two or a family of up to four persons using the room. Other meals are available in the restaurant and lunch and dinner menus can be supplied upon request.

The Restaurant and Motel are privately owned, and the proprietors, who live on the premises, have maintained a policy of expansion and improvement since 1967.

Extensive advertising has not been the company policy as the constantly maintained high standards and widespread reputation of the Motel and Restaurant have ensured its continued success.

Barnsley — Doncaster

BARNSLEY

Brooklands Restaurant
Barnsley Road, Dodworth
(Barnsley 84238/6364)
Open: Mon–Sun 12noon–2.30pm,
6.30–9.30pm

C P

Within 500 yards of the M1 is this single storey building housing three dining rooms, each featuring splendid displays of fresh fruit and wines. Meals are exceptionally good value, a three-course lunch costing under £5. The choice is excellent and imaginative (try chicken poche á la crème – chopped, poached chicken with mushrooms in a cream sauce). Chef's special dishes are also included, such as moussaka or roast pork. You are also invited to ask for more – 'and it shall be freely given'!

Queen's Hotel ★★
Regent Street
(Barnsley 84192)
Open: Mon–Sat 12.30–2.30pm,
6.30–10pm, Sun 12.30–2.30pm, 7–9pm

C S

An imposing Victorian three-storey building, conveniently close to the railway station and town centre, houses this cheerful split-level restaurant where décor is in the best tradition of Victorian design. A three-course lunch is from £2.50 and a four-course dinner from £5.50. The recently modernised 'Old Vic' bar provides a delicious hot and cold buffet each lunch-time from £1.

BOROUGHBRIDGE

Three Arrows ★★★
Horsefair
(Boroughbridge 2245)
Open: Mon–Sun 12.30–2pm,
7.30–9.30pm

C P

This restaurant has a long, tree-lined entrance through lawns and gardens. Elegant though it is, the place is not ruinously expensive. Table d'hôte lunch and dinner are both within our price range and they offer three courses of honest-to-goodness English fare, with a selection of vegetables, though the à la carte can work out too dear unless you drop one course. Beef Strogonoff and duckling with cherry sauce are cheap choices.

BRADFORD

The Last Pizza Show
50 Great Horton Road
(Bradford 28173)
Open: Mon–Sat 12noon–2pm,
6–11.30pm (12mdnt Fri & Sat)
Sun 6–11.30pm

C P

A very Italian pizza-restaurant this – complete with marble-topped cast-iron tables, hanging baskets and helpful Italian waiters. If you stray away from the pizza and pasta main courses you could find the steak takes you above our limit, but with a choice of 12 pizzas, including the chef's special at under £2, there should be no need. With corn on the cob as a starter, and a sweet of home-made ice cream, the bill with coffee will total less than £4.50. A set meal with a choice of three starters, main courses such as Pollo Boscaiola or cutlet of pork in white wine followed by dessert, is offered at around £5.65.

BRIDLINGTON

Barn Restaurant, Prince Street
(Bridlington 75661)
Open: Summer Mon–Sun
12noon–11pm, Winter
Mon–Wed 12noon–3pm,
Fri–Sat 12noon–11pm,
Sun 12noon–6pm

P S

This bright and attractive restaurant, with a décor predominantly red, prides itself on being able to suit all tastes by serving salads and burgers plus a variety of home-made 'specials' such as lasagne, moussaka, and chili con carne alongside a more formal à la carte selection. Traditional dishes such as home-made steak and kidney pie are on hand for the less adventurous, children are catered for with sausages, beefburgers or fish-fingers and chips, while other dishes are aimed modestly at the 'gourmet' (try the chef's own charcoal grilled steaks or gammon and roast duckling). A delicious selection of home-made sweets and ices is available, with liqueur coffee to follow.

The Old Forge, Main Street, Sewerby
(Bridlington 74535)
Open: Mon–Sat 10.30am–5.30pm,
7.30–10pm (Fri Jul & Aug only)
Sun 10.30am–6.30pm (evening by appointment)

P

One of a double row of stone-built fishermen's cottages of some age and interest, modernised and converted from its more recent use as a blacksmith's forge, the Old Forge is a convenient eating place for visitors to Sewerby Hall with its gardens, museum and zoo. With children's portions at about half the price of the regular meal, this is a particularly attractive restaurant for the whole family. Service is efficient and a good selection of English fare is offered, locally-caught fish being a speciality with fried haddock around £2.30.

BRIGHOUSE

Black Bull Hotel, Thornton Square
(Brighouse 714816)
Open: Mon–Sat 12noon–2pm

P S

The homely restaurant of the Black Bull Hotel with its rose-patterned wallpaper is an ideal place for shoppers and motorists who enjoy a traditional English lunch. With a choice of starters and good basic sweets, a 'roast beef and Yorkshire' meal complete with coffee will cost about £3.50. Grills are more expensive, but fillet steak garni, accompanied by a starter and a sweet will still be within budget. Established in 1740, this hotel is the oldest in Brighouse and a faithful band of locals make up the best part of its clientele, although dinner is served to residents only.

CLEETHORPES

Commodore Restaurant, The Lifeboat Hotel ★★
Promenade Kingsway
(Cleethorpes 697272)
Open: Mon–Fri 12noon–2pm,
6.30–10.15pm, Sat–Sun 6.30–10.15pm

C P S

The Lifeboat Hotel overlooks the North Sea, so the lounge bar, where you can sip an aperitif and have a quick meal, such as lamb cutlets and vegetables for about £1.65, or just a snack for under £1, has a nautical theme. The restaurant, with contrasting white chipboard décor and dark wooden cubicles under a beamed ceiling, also has nautical pictures and fittings. A special table d'hôte menu operates from Mondays to Fridays – you can enjoy soup, pork casserole or gammon steak, for example, followed by a sweet from the trolley for £5.50. There is also an à la carte menu, but it is beyond our price range.

DONCASTER

Bacchus, 44 Hallgate
(Doncaster 20232)
Open: Mon–Sat 12noon–3pm,
6pm–12mdnt, Sun 7.30–12mdnt

C S

It's tempting to believe that Bacchus, the god of wine, also knew a thing or two about the importance of good quality food – his disciples certainly believed they inherited the powers inherent in what they ate. If you're feeling adventurous you might like to try some stuffed shrimps for a starter and spicy kebabs with pitta bread, yoghurt and fresh green salad sounds like a mouth-watering main course. Evenings are table service only, when the bill can nudge the £5 limit if you're not careful, but you queue at a self-service counter for lunch, choosing from a menu chalked on a blackboard offering a stew of the day for about £1.95, and other English dishes ranging from £1.85–£2.25. The wine list is extensive and reasonably priced – and there's even live music for good measure. From Monday to Saturday, drinks are cheaper during 'Happy Hour' – 6–7pm

Ferrari's Restaurant
36–38 East Laithgate
(Doncaster 63712/63801)
Open: Mon–Sat 11.30am–2.15pm,
6–11.30pm

C P S

If you're doing a day's shopping in the town, where better to break for lunch than this centrally situated (near the famous market) Italian restaurant. You'll recognise it by the prancing horse emblem and the glimmering Ferrari sign. Chrome and black wood furniture and colour pictures of gleaming sports cars form the basis of the interior decoration. Specialities of the day can include grilled trout (around £4.25) and a 308GT pizza at around £2.25. The menu lists several pasta dishes – lasagne, cannelloni and spaghetti. Sweets are priced from about 65p – £1.25 and include a 'dusky maiden' made from soft Italian ice cream, chocolate sauce, fresh cream and a chocolate flake.

Pizzeria San Remo, 8 Netherhall Road
(Doncaster 60501)
Open: Mon – Sat 12noon – 2.30pm,
Mon – Thu 5.30 – 11.30pm, Fri &
Sat 5.30 – 12pm

🎵 P ♿

This small Italian restaurant is situated in a modern terrace of shops close to the town-centre market. It serves entirely Italian food. Choose from the tempting variety of pasta and pizza dishes, or try the fish, chicken, veal or steak meals which are also on the menu. Pizza and pasta dishes cost around £2, and with soup at 90p and a traditional Italian ice cream also at 90p you can still enjoy a glass of wine and a cup of coffee and come away with some change from £6.

Regent Hotel Restaurant ★★
Regent Square
(Doncaster 64336)
Open: Mon – Sat 12noon – 2pm, 6 – 10pm,
Sun 12noon – 2.30pm, 7 – 9.30pm

P S ♿

At the edge of Doncaster's main shopping area, this restaurant serves, in the words of our inspector, 'good substantial, no-nonsense' meals matched by low prices. Sunday lunch (roasts or trout) table d'hôte is about £4, the weekday three-course business lunch (various home-made pies, chicken or plaice), about £2. In the evenings, an à la carte menu only is available, with three courses priced by the main dish. Apart from fillet steak, all these are within our budget – from plaice and tartare sauce at £3.50 to sirloin steak at £5.75. Starters include home-made pâté or ravioli and a choice of various ice creams or Chef's Special sweet of the day concludes the meal which will not burn a hole in anybody's pocket.

Ristorante Il Fiore in Legards
50 – 51 High Street
(Doncaster 23187)
Open: Mon – Sat 9.30am – 5pm

C S

Situated above a smart ladies' boutique, this elaborately-named ristorante has a fresh green décor and overlooks the busy shopping street below from original Georgian bow windows. The menu offers

Guiseley
—
Harrogate

a wide selection of sandwiches, gâteaux and toasted snacks, served all day. There is a three-course lunch available at £2.95 with a choice of dishes. A typical meal could be soup, home-made steak and kidney pie and apple pie and cream. Coffee is 35p.

Ronnies Wine Bar, High Street, Bawtry
(Doncaster 711057)
Open: Mon – Sat 11am – 3pm,
6 – 11.30pm, Sun 6 – 11.30pm

🎵 P S ♿

This two-storey wine bar overlooks the old market place, and has murals of racing and showjumping scenes on its walls. On the ground floor the main room serves bar meals for lunch-time and evening. Home-made minestrone soup is hot favourite here and, along with lasagne, spaghetti or quiche at around £2.25 per portion, appears chalked on a blackboard menu behind the bar. The first-floor restaurant is open evenings only with waitress service, offering a more varied menu, also with an Italian bias. A typical meal might be melon (£1.40), spaghetti bolognese (£2.25) and a scrumptious gâteau from the trolley. House wine is Italian too, and costs 65p per glass.

Vintage Steak Bar, Cleveland Street
(Doncaster 64786)
Open: Mon – Sun 11.30am – 2.30pm,
5.30 – 11.30pm

C 🎵 P S ♿

A Victorian flavour here, with red furnishings and mellow wooden chairs and tables. The varied menu offers 14 starters from about 50p, including smoked trout, iced melon and fried scampi, with a selection of fish, omelettes, grills and salads to follow. Each main course dish, such as steak, duck, chicken, lamb and pork, is served with French fried potatoes, tomato and garden peas and costs from £3.50 for lamb to £5 for steak. A sweet or cheese and biscuits may be chased down by a potent liqueur coffee in the restaurant or bar-lounge, and there's a separate room available for private parties and receptions. The central position of the Vintage Steak Bar is another plus.

GUISELEY

Harry Ramsden's, White Cross
(Guiseley 74641)
Open: Mon – Sun 11.30am – 11.30pm

P ♿

Claiming to be 'the most famous fish and chip restaurant in the world', this biggish restaurant has changed hands many times since one Harry Ramsden first opened up over 60 years ago. Outside the mainly brick building, several benches are interspersed along a

verandah for 'eating out'. Inside, the smartly-dressed waitresses scurry between the many pot plants with high efficiency. After a soup or fruit juice starter, you can choose from any one of the nine main fish dishes, all at under £4 and including chips, bread and butter and a drink (children's portions are about £1.40). If you're not already full up, a strawberry sundae or choc'n'nut dessert will soon put that right!

HALIFAX

Da Camillo, Southgate
(Halifax 54573)
Open: Mon – Sat 12noon – 2pm, 7 – 11pm,
Sun 11.30am – 3pm

S

Conveniently sited over a central pedestrian precinct in a busy shopping area is this second-floor pizzeria. The simple décor is predominantly deep brown with cork and plaster walls. Red linen tablecloths add a splash of colour. Business lunch and the fixed evening menu consist of tasty Italian dishes – cannelloni, lasagne, spaghetti bolognese, plus a selection of salads all in the £2 range – including a starter. Coffee is extra and a sweet can be had for around 30p, bringing the total to around £3. Sirloin or fillet steak served with mushrooms, peas and jacket potato or salad are also available but will add another £2 to your bill.

HARROGATE

Apollo Restaurant, 34 Oxford Street
(Harrogate 504475)
Open: Tue – Sat 12noon – 2.30pm,
6 – 11pm

🎵 P S

Apollo is a first-floor city centre restaurant, situated close to the multi-storey car park. The classical décor of Ionic pillars is reminiscent of the Parthenon and the atmosphere is enhanced by the Greek music in the background. Dishes offered are international, with a Greek bias, but most of those appearing on the à la carte menu are too expensive for a meal around £5. However, a three-course lunch with home-made soup of the day, a main course of fish, grill, chicken, a Greek special or salad, and home-made fruit pie or Greek sweet, coffee and wine can be had for around £4. Seating is mostly in curtained cubicles just right for an intimate dinner.

Betty's, 1 Parliament Street
(Harrogate 64659)
Open: Mon – Sat 9am – 5.30pm

🎵 P S ♿

This popular tea-room offers tea and cakes, snacks and salads all day long. Daily specials such as home-made soups, pâté, pies and cauliflower cheese are available at lunch-time. An excellent three-course lunch of home-made celery soup, chicken pie and chocolate

158

WELCOME TO

Harry Ramsden's

The worlds largest fish and chip shop.

Enjoy traditional Yorkshire fish and chips in this famous restaurant with its chandeliers, plush decor and waitress service. A choice of prime fish, chips, bread and butter, with tea, coffee or mineral all for around £2.30 per head.

Restaurant and take-away open every day
11.30 am-11.30 pm

Situated at Guiseley on the A65 between
Leeds and Ilkley Moor.

**White Cross, Guiseley, nr Leeds, West Yorkshire
Telephone: (0943) 74641.**

supreme will cost under £4.
Tasty home-made cakes and pastries are also sold in the confectionery department at the entrance. Betty's enjoys a fine view across the Montpelier Gardens.

The Empress, Church Square (Harrogate 67629)
Open: Mon-Fri 12noon–2pm, 7–10pm, Sat 7–10.30pm, Sun 12noon–1.45pm

[C] [P] [♿]

In a stone building on the edge of town, with rich gold, turquoise and purple Regency décor and tasteful fittings, the restaurant is on the first floor, above the ground-floor lounge bar. A three-course business person's lunch including a choice of varying hot dishes or cold meat salad, served with potatoes and two veg is particularly good value at around £3.50 and even an extensive à la carte comes easily within our limit except in the case of a few speciality dishes. An extensive buffet table laden with flans, cold meats and salads is available at lunch-time. Children are also well catered for with a specially-designed menu complete with children's puzzles which they can take away as a souvenir.

Mae's Dining Car, Station Road, Pannal (Harrogate 870982)
Open: Tue-Sun 12noon–2pm, Tue-Thu 7–11pm, Fri & Sat 7–11.30pm

[C] [P]

This smart Pullman railway coach is drawn up outside the village railway halt and offers a daily fixed-price menu, which may include roasts, casseroles, or steak and kidney pie, with a choice of first course and sweet, for £4.95. Coffee is 50p and a glass of wine 80p. There is also an à la carte menu, but it is beyond our budget.

Open Arms, 3 Royal Parade (Harrogate 503034)
Open: Tue-Sun 12noon–2pm, Tue-Sat 6–10pm

[C] [S] [♿]

Now with the extra title of 'Taste of Yorkshire' this town-centre licensed restaurant offers a warm welcome with a

Huddersfield
Ilkley

glowing red décor, oak-clad walls and a menu designed to tempt the family. The famous Yorkshire pudding is available for lunch or dinner as a starter, main course or even as a sweet. A large golden Yorkshire pud with a stewed meat and veg filling costs around £2. Traditional English roasts, home-baked pies, grilled meats and fried fish dishes are always on the menu. Children's portions of Yorkshire pork sausages, filled Yorkshire pud or fish cost around £1.15.

Pinocchio's, Cheltenham Parade (Harrogate 60611)
Open: Mon–Sat 11.30am–2.30pm, 5.30–12mdnt, Sun 5.30–11.30pm

[C] [♪] [♿]

Immediately you walk inside this pizzeria, with its gay posters and pictures of the Italian homeland, unashamedly deep pink and brown walls plus foot-tapping Latin music, you could easily imagine yourself on an Adriatic holiday. Once seated at one of the marble-topped tables, you'll find that the menu continues the dominant theme with a mouth-watering variety of pastas and pizzas ranging from £1.65–£2.10. Calamari Fritti (deep-fried squid with oodles of lemon) is specially recommended. Apart from Italian dishes there's chicken Kiev, chili con carne or barbecue spare ribs. Soup costs 75p and desserts (including Black Forest gâteau and profiteroles) are around £1.

HUDDERSFIELD

Pizzeria Sole Mio, Units 3 and 4, Imperial Arcade, Market Street (Huddersfield 42828)
Open: Mon–Fri 12noon–2.30pm, 5–11.30pm, Sat 12noon–11.30pm, Sun 5.30–11pm

[S]

Here you will discover Italy in the heart of Huddersfield, in a shopping arcade. Outside it has a terrazza and canopy blinds, inside roughcast walls, open brickwork, ceramic tile-topped tables

and high-backed ladder chairs emphasise the Italian atmosphere. There is an extensive menu of home-made pastas including lasagne and cannelloni at around £2. The formidable list of pizzas range in price from under £1.55 to £2.30. Imaginative starters, including snails, are available.

HULL

Pecan Pizzeria. 32 Silver Street (Hull 20835)
Open: Mon–Thu 12noon–2.30pm, 6–11pm, Fri,–Sat 12noon–2.30pm, 6–11.30pm, Sun 6–11pm

As part of an imposing stone Victorian building in the heart of Hull's commercial district, the Pecan could be taken for another finance house. Even inside, there are strong overtones of the Stock Exchange, with lofty ceilings, classical pillars and arches and Victorian décor. But enthusiastic Italian waiters in red-check shirts, contemporary music and an extensive, mainly Italian menu dispel any stodgy banking atmosphere. The menu is almost a meal in itself with its mouth-watering descriptions, but tread carefully as far as the specialities are concerned. If you stick to the interesting starters, pizza or pasta dish and a sweet you should spend around £5.

ILKLEY

Betty's Café Tea Rooms
32–34 The Grove (Ilkley 608029)
Open: Mon–Sat 9am–5.30pm, Sun 2–5.30pm

[P] [S] [♿]

In Ilkley's main shopping street, Betty's modern restaurant serves snacks all day with a limited selection of hot dishes and a mouth-watering variety of cakes, sandwiches and savouries. A satisfying meal could consist of home-made soup, Welsh rarebit (made with farmhouse cheddar and Yorkshire ale) served with apple or tomato chutney or ham and pineapple salad, followed by Yorkshire curd tart and coffee – for less than £5. A wide selection of speciality coffees and teas can be chosen from separate descriptive menus. Alsatian wine is from 70p a glass.

MAE'S — The Exciting New Dining Out Experience

Pullman Car · Platform · Cocktail Bar
A la Carte and Table d'hote Menus with a superb selection of fine Wines

STATION HOUSE, STATION ROAD PANNAL · Harrogate 870982
(5 mins from Harrogate Centre)

MAE'S RESTAURANT adjoins PLATFORM 1.
Yorkshires Famous 'Railwayana' Real Ale Pub

ACCESS & BARCLAYCARD

Cafe Konditorei, Spa Flats, The Grove
(Ilkley 601578)
Open: Mon–Sat 10am–5.30pm,
Sun 12noon–5.30pm
P S &

Converted from one of the old spa hotels, all the produce served in this café is home-made. Lunches start at noon and high teas after 4pm, when children's portions are available. Cork walls and classical pillars create an elegant, restful atmosphere. Soups are home-made and are delicious eaten with hot herb or garlic bread (about 70p for the two). Special dishes of the day include seafood vol-au-vents with chips and salad for around £2.75. Danish open sandwiches – try chicken with peach and Waldorf salad at £1.80, omelettes and salads are also served. Desserts range from 40p–80p and examples are fruit-filled pancake, and continental gâteaux.

KEIGHLEY

The Vaults, 61 North Street
(Keighley 681550)
Open: Mon–Sat 12noon–2pm,
6.30–10.30pm
C ♬ P &

This pleasantly decorated wine bar was once a branch of Barclays Bank, and is now furnished with circular tables and barber's-shop chairs. The food is advertised on the blackboard and the menu changes daily. Our inspector chose a lasagne, at £1.95, that would have graced the best of Italian restaurants. Also available were sandwiches made with wholemeal bread at around £1, a variety of crêpes at £1.95, grilled gammon at £3.50 and a choice of sweets. The dinner menu is more extensive but with careful selection you can still enjoy a meal within our budget.

KIRBY MISPERTON

Bean Sheaf Restaurant ××
(Kirby Misperton 614)
Open: Tue–Sun 12noon–2pm
♬ P &

This single-storey wayside cottage, converted and extended, offers a

Keighley
Leeds

comfortable respite to the motorist, and to visitors to Flamingo Land Zoo. On entry, a comfortable lounge bar decorated in quiet fawns and browns leads through to a large, colourful dining room divided in two by an arch with classical pillars. Evening meals are rather above our limit but three-course lunches, weekdays and Sundays are very good value at under £4. All dishes are prepared personally by the proprietor and include such main meals as steak and kidney pie, whole grilled sole and jugged hare. An extensive wine list offers a choice of over 100 reasonably-priced wines.

KNARESBOROUGH
High Bridge Restaurant
Harrogate Road
(Harrogate 862521)
open: Summer Mon–Sun 10.30am–7pm, Winter Sat–Mon, Wed & Thu 12noon–7pm (party bookings by telephone in evenings)
&

This pleasant licensed restaurant is delightfully situated on the main A59 overlooking the River Nidd, beside the famous Dropping Well. Nearby there are amusements, boating and the small Knaresborough Zoo. Inside, two separate rooms are carpeted in blue and there's plain chipboard on the walls interspersed with pictures. A choice of five standard starters range from 38p–£1.10. Main courses are very reasonably priced – roast chicken with stuffing, chips and vegetables costs £2.65 (and just £1.65 for children). The dearest sweet is fresh cream gâteau at 75p, so you'll be well within the budget. In addition, late afternoon salads are popular here and a traditional Sunday lunch won't be over £4.50 all in – a real bargain.

KNOTTINGLEY
The Bay Horse, Fairburn, 4m N of Knottingley just off the A1
(Knottingley 85126, 82371)

Open: Mon–Fri 12noon–2pm, 7–10pm,
Sat 7–10pm Sun 12noon–2pm
C ♬ P

This attractive restaurant boasts a large table d'hôte menu priced at £4.95. Coffee is an extra 50p and a glass of wine 65p, so with the 10% service charge this brings the total to just over £6.50. This certainly represents good value for money as it includes 'silver service' by uniformed staff – something the Roman 9th Legion never had as they trudged up the Great North Road to York. The modern traveller could choose Arbroath smoked mackerel or crab Valencia, followed by roast joint of the day or chicken Maryland and a sweet from the trolley to complete the meal. There is also a table d'hôte Sunday Lunch Menu available for £3.95.

LEEDS

The Allerton, Nursery Lane, Alwoodley
(Leeds 686249)
Open: Mon–Fri 12noon–2pm,
7.15–11pm, Sat 7.15–11pm
C P

The tasteful restaurant is dominated by the ceiling, which is buttressed by low, shallow arches. The table d'hôte lunch is excellent value at around £3 and includes a choice of four starters, seven main courses and sweets from the trolley. There is a set three-course special dinner which includes steak or scampi at about £5 and there is also an extensive à la carte menu from which it is possible to keep within the limit of the guide by choosing dishes carefully.

Ken Marlow's Fish Restaurant
62 Street Lane
(Leeds 666353)
Open: Tue–Fri 12noon–2pm, 5–10pm,
Sun 4.30–10pm
S

Fish is the order of the day at this restaurant set in a modern development close to the northern ring road. A small bar with a few seats leads into an open-plan restaurant with bold décor. All main courses feature fish – fried, except when in salad form, and chipped potatoes are

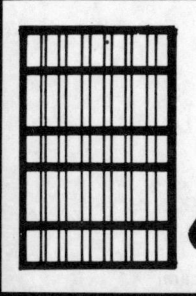

RESTAURANT
and
WINE BAR
61 North St., Keighley

The Vaults

With a menu as varied as Chicken and Chili and Lasagne and Steaks, it won't break the bank to eat at The Vaults.

Open Daily except Sunday for Lunches and Dinner.

included. No fancy fare is offered, but a wholesome three-course meal can be had at around £4 per person with coffee extra.

New Inn, Wetherby Road, Scarcroft (Leeds 892029)
Open: Mon, Wed–Sat 12noon–2.30pm, 7–10.30pm, Sun 12noon–2pm, 7–10pm
C ♫ P ♿

This modern pub and restaurant stands by the roadside and has extensive lawns. The fawns and browns of the pleasant décor blend well with the exposed brickwork and coloured spotlights. Pictures of Falstaffian scenes decorate the walls. Only the set lunch menu at £3.50 qualifies for the limited budget meal as the à la carte menu would need very careful choice to keep to a bill of around £5. For lunch, starters include ravioli au gratin and Florida cocktail, with roast pork or lambs liver with onions for main course.

New Milano ××
621 Roundhay Road (Leeds 659752)
Open: Mon–Fri 12noon–2.30pm, Sat 7–11.30pm
C P S ♿

On the main road into the town stands this smart, ground floor restaurant; an oasis in the desert of shops around it. Food is English and Italian – expensive in the evening but well within our means for lunch. A table d'hôte menu offers a choice of nine starters and eight main-course dishes served with vegetables of the day. A sweet from the trolley or cheese completes a very substantial meal for around £3.50.

The Traveller's Rest, Harewood Road, East Keswick
(Collingham Bridge 72766)
Open: Mon–Sat 12noon–2pm, 7–10.30pm
Sun 12noon–2pm, 7–10.30pm
C ♫ P ♿

This first-floor restaurant enjoys a prime location overlooking the beautiful Wharfe Valley. The small Tudor-style room with its dark wood beams and furniture,

---

Pateley Bridge
—
Sheffield

partitioned cubicles and rich red carpeting provides a cosy, restful eating place for about 50 people. Main courses comprise grills and fries, with a choice of steaks at the top end of the price scale. It is possible to overdo the limit here, but it is also quite easy to stay within £5 with a meal such as soup, followed by lamb cutlets plus a choice from the sweet trolley and coffee.

PATELEY BRIDGE
Bridgeway Restaurant, 1 High Street (Harrogate 711640)
Open: Tue–Fri, Sun 12noon–5pm
P ♿

This first-floor restaurant overlooks the valley of the River Nidd in upper Nidderdale where the road bridge spans the river. Dark oak tables, wheelback chairs, light oak-clad walls and a beamed ceiling complete the rustic feeling. Home-made country fare is a special feature, from lentil soup at 70p to English kidneys braised in red wine sauce (£2.50), home-made beef steak, kidney and mushroom pie, roast topside and Yorkshire pud and roast Nidderdale turkey – both around £2.75. Home-made fruit pies with fresh cream cost 75p.

POCKLINGTON
Bayernstubi, 4–6 Market Place (Pocklington 2643)
Open: Tue–Sun 12noon–10.15pm, (10.45pm Sat)
P S ♿

This converted pantiled cottage in the centre of town is furnished in natural wood to emphasise the Bavarian atmosphere. The popular lunch-time menu is basically English fare with sandwiches, home-made fruit pies and gâteaux at extremely reasonable prices, enabling one to eat a three-course meal for about £1.80. A meal from the main 'Speisekarte', written in German with English subtitles, will probably cost you around £5.50. Start with krabben salat (prawn cocktail), then sample a rich,

---

spicy German dish such as paprika huhn (paprika roasted chicken) and round it off with apfel strüdel and cream.

RICHMOND
The Black Lion Hotel, Finkle Street (Richmond 3121)
Open: Mon–Sun 12noon–2pm, 7–9.30pm
P

Once a coaching inn, this quaint 17th century building has a restaurant on the first floor with a low, beamed ceiling, white décor, wheelback chairs and 19th century prints. Meals are honest-to-goodness English fare, well-prepared, pleasantly served and excellent value, with a table d'hôte three-course lunch at around £4 and a three-course dinner at about £6. Main dishes include roasts, hot pot, curry, steak and kidney pie and pork chops in cider. Home-made desserts include fresh gâteaux.

SHEFFIELD
Ashoka, 307 Eccleshall Road (Sheffield 686177)
Open: Mon–Thu 12noon–2pm, 6–12mdnt, Fri–Sat 12noon–2pm, 6pm–1am, Sun 12noon–2pm, 7–12mdnt

What the Ashoka lacks in ethnic décor and atmosphere it more than compensates for by the range and quality of its Indian cuisine. Main courses, all eastern variations on a theme of chicken, fish or meat, are reasonably priced at around £2.65. Two or more people could dine in style very easily for around £4.50 per head by sharing a selection of dishes. For that special celebration, a party of six can order a lamb massallam – a leg of lamb marinated in a rich sauce with herbs and spices, roasted and then carved at your table. It is served with ghee rice and costs around £30. But you'll have to warn the chef you are coming – he requires two days' notice if he is to prepare this masterpiece to your satisfaction. Authentic starters and sweets can be had for around £1.15.

Black Lion Hotel
Finkle Street, Richmond, Yorkshire

OLD COACHING HOUSE

TRADITIONAL FAYRE
fresh produce prepared by experienced chef.
Enjoy a good wine list and ale by Camerons Brewery
SPECIALITIES
Beef Wellington, Steak Cordon Range,
Whole roast sirloin of Beef, Legs of Pork, Saddle of Lamb
TELEPHONE 3121

Dam House Restaurant
Crookes Valley Park
(Sheffield 661344)
Open: Mon-Fri 12noon-2.30pm,
Tue-Thu 7-11pm, Fri-Sat 7pm-2am

C 🎵 P S

The 18th century Dam House is set in a lush green valley overlooking a boating lake. Food is predominantly English, with the traditional Yorkshire pudding with onions and gravy featuring as a starter. Main dishes on the three-course lunch menu, which costs around £4 include the tried-and-true favourites, beef and kidney hotpot and home-made steak and kidney pie. A glass of house wine, cheese and biscuits and coffee with cream will add another £1.30 or so to your bill. Beware of dinner prices; the extensive à la carte menu in the evening is likely to be rather more than £6.

Nameless, 16-18 Cambridge Street
(Sheffield 29751)
Open: Mon-Sat 11am-12mdnt,
Sun 12noon-11.30pm

🎵 P S 👶

This pizza-biased restaurant is located in the city centre and boasts an authentic Victorian atmosphere. The food, however, is bang up-to-date with a wide variety of burgers, pizzas and other Italian dishes ranging from £1.50-£2.50. Leaving aside sirloin and T-bone steak, you'll soon see that it's difficult to reach the £5 limit – even if you sample a delicious Tia Crêpe dessert (ice cream plus Tia Maria folded into a crêpe, topped off with whipped cream). A special kiddies' meal costs just over £1.50 for a mini pizza, ice cream and a fizzy drink.

Raffles, Charles Street
(Sheffield 24921)
Open: Mon-Sat 12noon-2.30pm

🎵 S 👶

A small entrance between shops in busy, down-town Sheffield leads to this first-floor restaurant. A grotto-like staircase takes you, via goldfish tanks, to a pleasant green-ceilinged room with mood-setting floodlights. Glass-topped bamboo tables are interspersed across a green-striped carpet. Random fishing nets and glass floats set the scene for a predominantly seafood menu. Prawns, oysters, mackerel and crab are all available with side-salad from £1.60-£3. Cold meat salads and curries are alternatives for non-fish lovers. If you choose cheesecake, for example, at 50p and round things off with a coffee (30p), you'll see a fair bit of change from a fiver. In the evenings there's a disco here, but the menu soars out of our range.

Waggon and Horses
Abbeydale Road, Millhouses
(Sheffield 361451)
Open: Mon-Sun 12noon-2.45pm,
7-10.30pm

C P 👶

Skipton
—
Whitby

Part of the Falstaff Taverns group, this two-storey, stone-built inn overlooks a pleasant recreation area. A three-course lunch is served here daily, when for about £6 you can sample a plain but wholesome range of dishes against a charming background of exposed stone walls, oak beams and wrought-iron screens. Typical choices from the menu would be soup, pâté or melon followed by halibut steak, chicken Falstaff or rump steak, plus a sweet from the trolley. Specialities and à la carte dishes are reasonably-priced, and the Sunday lunch menu, offering two roast dishes and other choices is inexpensive.

SKIPTON

Herbs, 10 High Street
(Skipton 60619)
Open: Mon, Wed-Sat 9.30am-5pm

P 👶

This bright, clean, wholefood and vegetarian restaurant can be found above a wholefood shop in the centre of town. Green and white décor with pine tables and chairs give the place a nice fresh feel. The menu offers a good home-made dish of the day at £1.75 and a variety of salads also at £1.75. There are 14 different fruit and vegetable juices available and a range of desserts. Also included on the menu are 19 different herbal teas, so if you have never tried this type of tea before – here's your chance!

WAKEFIELD

Stoneleigh Hotel and Restaurant ★★★
Doncaster Road
(Wakefield 369461)
Open: Mon-Sun 12noon-2pm, 7-10pm

C P 👶

Once a row of elegant Victorian terraced houses, this smart hotel is located close to the town and the open country. 'Quality' is the key word in the sophisticated dining room where full silver service is employed to complement high class international cuisine. Dinner (as may be expected), outstrips the budget, but a good table d'hôte lunch is within our means at around £6. There is a choice of eight starters followed by nine main-course alternatives such as lemon sole mornay, grilled lamb chops with mint sauce or sauté of beef with tomato. Finish with the pick of the sweet trolley, fresh fruit or cheese.

The Venus Restaurant, 51 Westgate
(Wakefield 75378)
Open: Mon-Sat 12noon-2.30pm,
6.30-11.30pm, Sun 7-11pm

C 🎵 P 👶

The menu here is rich in English and Greek cuisine with some Greek speciality dishes such as kebabs and afelia (pork fillet cooked in wine sauce with coriander and cream) both around £4.50 including rice or Greek salad, but the à la carte menu will require careful selection to keep the cost around £5. The three-course table d'hôte lunch is ideal, offering traditional dishes such as fish, roasts or salads, with one Greek special for around £3.50. Though part of the Black Bull Tavern, children are catered for with half portions of selected dishes – at half price.

WHITBY

The Georgian, 25 St Hilda's Terrace
(Whitby 603345)
Open: Summer Mon-Sun
11.45am-6pm, 7-10.30pm, Winter private functions only

🎵 S 👶

Did you know that many of the horrible deeds of Bram Stoker's Count Dracula actually took place in Whitby? Well, you may rest assured that such fiendish goings on will not trouble you in The Georgian restaurant – it used to be the vicarage. Attractively situated, with fine lawns and rose beds, the restaurant is conveniently placed for access to the town centre. Prices are reasonable and a set lunch, with a varied menu, costs £3. Dinner of home-made soup, rump steak and home-made cherry pie is £6.

Khyber Pass Restaurant and Grill
(Whitby 603500)
Open: Summer Mon-Sun
11am-5.30pm, Winter
Sat-Sun 11.45am-5.30pm

🎵 P 👶

The wandering road from the harbour up on to the West Cliff is called the Khyber Pass – the name has been adopted by this single storey café which overlooks the beach and harbour entrance. At lunch-time three courses are priced by the main dish – from sausage at £2.15 to roast beef and Yorkshire pudding at around £3.65. Whitby crab salad is offered at £3.45. Starters include soup of the day and a selection of six desserts offer home-made fruit tart and custard and crème caramel. Junior Choice at £1.30 is served all day – choose from fish fingers, fish, sausage, beans, eggs – any of these with chips, ice cream and a glass of squash. The evening menu is more sophisticated – curries, kebabs, fish and grills all cost over £3, so three-courses can only be enjoyed with the cheaper main dishes.

Magpie Cafe, 14 Pier Road
(Whitby 602058)
Open: Mon-Thu, Sat-Sun
11.30am-2.30pm, 3.30-6.30pm

👶

Proprietors Sheila and Ian McKenzie claim that their menus provide a meal to suit all tastes though a special effort is made to cater for families, with cradles and high chairs provided. A Magpie Special Lunch for about £3.30 offers home-made soup of the day as one starter, home-made steak pie, chips and peas and a choice which includes fresh

York

cream sherry trifle or strawberry flan, Black Forest gâteau or apple pie. The Magpie Special Fish Lunch at £4.25 offers a choice of Whitby crab, prawn cocktail or potted shrimps as appetisers, cod or haddock with chips and a selection of about 26 sweets. With both lunches a pot of tea is included, since The Magpie is unlicensed, but since there is a choice of four liqueur mousses in each case, you won't be totally on the wagon! A special children's meal for around £1.50 offers sausage, beans and chips, jelly and ice cream and a glass of orange.

YORK

Bess's Coffee House, Royal Station Hotel, Station Road
(York 53681)
Open: Mon–Sat 12noon–2.30pm, 6–8.45pm, Sun 12noon–2pm

C P S &

The tables here are set between stage coach doors; a highwayman's pistol and a mural depicting Turpin's ride and ultimate capture, line the walls. The menu offers a good range of well-priced dishes and a typical meal might include Yorkshire broth (made from an ancient local recipe) at around 60p, savoury steak and kidney pie for around £2.25, and cheesecake with whipped cream for about 85p. The set lunch is a satisfying meal for less than £3 and children can have a main meal of chicken leg and chips or fish fingers and chips for around £1.

Betty's Oakroom Restaurant and Tea Room, St Helen's Square
(York 22323)
Open: Mon–Sat 9am–5.30pm

P S &

The main restaurant in this three-storeyed corner house complex is in the basement and takes its name from the all-oak furnishings. A three-course meal here such as Chef's special cauliflower soup, roast beef and Yorkshire pudding and Swiss sherry trifle to finish, is around £5.10. Above, in the cafeteria you can dine on fruit juice, roast beef and Yorkshire pud, plus a gâteau for less than £3.50.

Bibis, 115–119 Micklegate
(York 34765)
Open: Mon–Fri 6–11.30pm, Sat 12noon–2.15pm, 6–11.30pm, Sun 12.15–2.15pm, 6–11pm

P S

Very Italian, this ballroom-sized ground-floor restaurant with its wide selection of pastas and pizzas as well as blackboard-listed specials such as chicken, fish, or steak dishes. Starters include fresh Whitby crab when in season, buttered corn-on-the-cob, and honeydew melon, and there is a selection of home-made desserts and flambé ice creams. A three-course meal is likely to cost around £5 with coffee.

Charlie's Bistro, County Hotel, Tanner Row
(York 25120)
Open: Mon–Thu 12noon–2pm, 6–11pm, (closed Mon evenings) Fri–Sat 12noon–2pm, 6–12mdnt

♫ P S &

This little bistro on the ground floor of the County Hotel is decorated in 1920s style, with pictures of Charlie Chaplin around the walls. The choice of dishes à la carte includes peppered fillet steak with baked potato and salad at about £5 and York gammon with egg and chips at about £3, and there are a number of delicious sweets around 65p. For a really cheap meal you'd find it hard to beat the two-course lunch costing about £1.50.

Dreamville, King's Square
(York 36592)
Open: Mon–Sun 10am–11pm

S &

Dreamville is exactly what it sounds – an American-style food-fantasy, with a colourful gangster theme, and décor reminiscent of the 1920s. The menu lists hamburgers from £1.75, charcoal-grilled sirloin and T-bone steaks from £4.25, pizza, pasta and barbecued spare ribs from £2.25 and freshly caught local fish.

End your meal with an exotic ice cream sundae from 75p. Dreamville is fully licensed.

Punch Bowl Hotel, Micklegate Bar
(York 22619)
Open: Mon–Sat 12noon–2.30pm, 7–10.30pm, Sun 12noon–2pm, 7–10pm

C ♫ P &

You can imagine yourself in an old coaching inn when you take a meal at the 18th century Punch Bowl. In fact this is what it once was, but it has now been refurbished as a hotel and steak house, offering a very reasonable table d'hôte lunch of starter, main dish and dessert. An example is grapefruit cocktail, Sam's original recipe game pie with vegetables and potato, and apple pie and cream at around £3.50

Raffles Tea Rooms, 41 Stonegate
(York 29812)
Open: Summer Mon–Sat 9.30am–8.30pm, Sun 11am–6pm, Winter Mon-Sat 9.30am–5pm

C S

Apart from the mouthwatering selection of sandwiches, cakes and cream teas which are served all day, the lunch and supper menu includes pâté de campagne as a starter for around £1.20, pizza Marina (seafood special) at £2.20 for main course and a dessert for about 85p.

Ristorante Bari, 15 The Shambles
(York 33807)
Open: Mon–Sun 11.30am–2.30pm, 6–11pm

C ♫ P S &

Do you fancy Sophia Loren? A 'scalloppe' of that name, made of veal with cheese, brandy and tomato sauce, costs about £4.85 (including vegetables) in this Italian pizzeria. The range of pasta and pizza includes lasagne or cannelloni at around £2.15, spaghetti bolognese at around £1.95 and the Chef's special pizza at about £2.35. Coffee costs 45p for espresso or cappuccino.

Magpie Cafe

14 Pier Road, Whitby
Telephone: (0947) 602058

Fine food from local produce.
We specialise in home-made, wholesome Yorkshire food.
We welcome families.
1 to 4 courses
Served 11.30-2.30 — 3.30-6.30

Proprietors: Sheila & Ian McKenzie

Dreamville

1920's style Licensed Restaurant, opposite the famous Shambles.

Charcoal grilled steaks and hamburgers · Pizza · Pasta · Exotic ice cream sundaes

PROBABLY THE BEST VALUE FOR MONEY IN YORK!
Open 7 days/nights a week GOOD FOOD – GOOD SERVICE

'AN OFFER YOU CANNOT REFUSE'

KINGS SQUARE, YORK. tel: 36592

BIBIS

115-119 Micklegate, York
Telephone 34765
and at
7/8 Mill Hill, Leeds
Telephone 430905

For the very best in home made Italian cooking specialising in Pizzas and Pasta Dishes.
Specialities also available including Steaks, Chicken and Fish.
Excellent selection of starters and desserts.
Italian wines by the Caraf and bottle at reasonable prices.

Opening times

LEEDS
Tuesday to Sunday
12.00 to 2.15 pm
6.00 pm to 11.30 pm

Closed All Day Monday

Please Note:
Open Bank Holiday Monday
Evenings Only

YORK
Tuesday to Sunday
Evenings 6.00 to 11.30 pm

Saturday & Sunday Lunch
12.00 to 2.15 pm

Closed all Day Monday
Please Note
Open Bank Holiday Monday
Evenings Only

THE NORTH AND THE LAKES

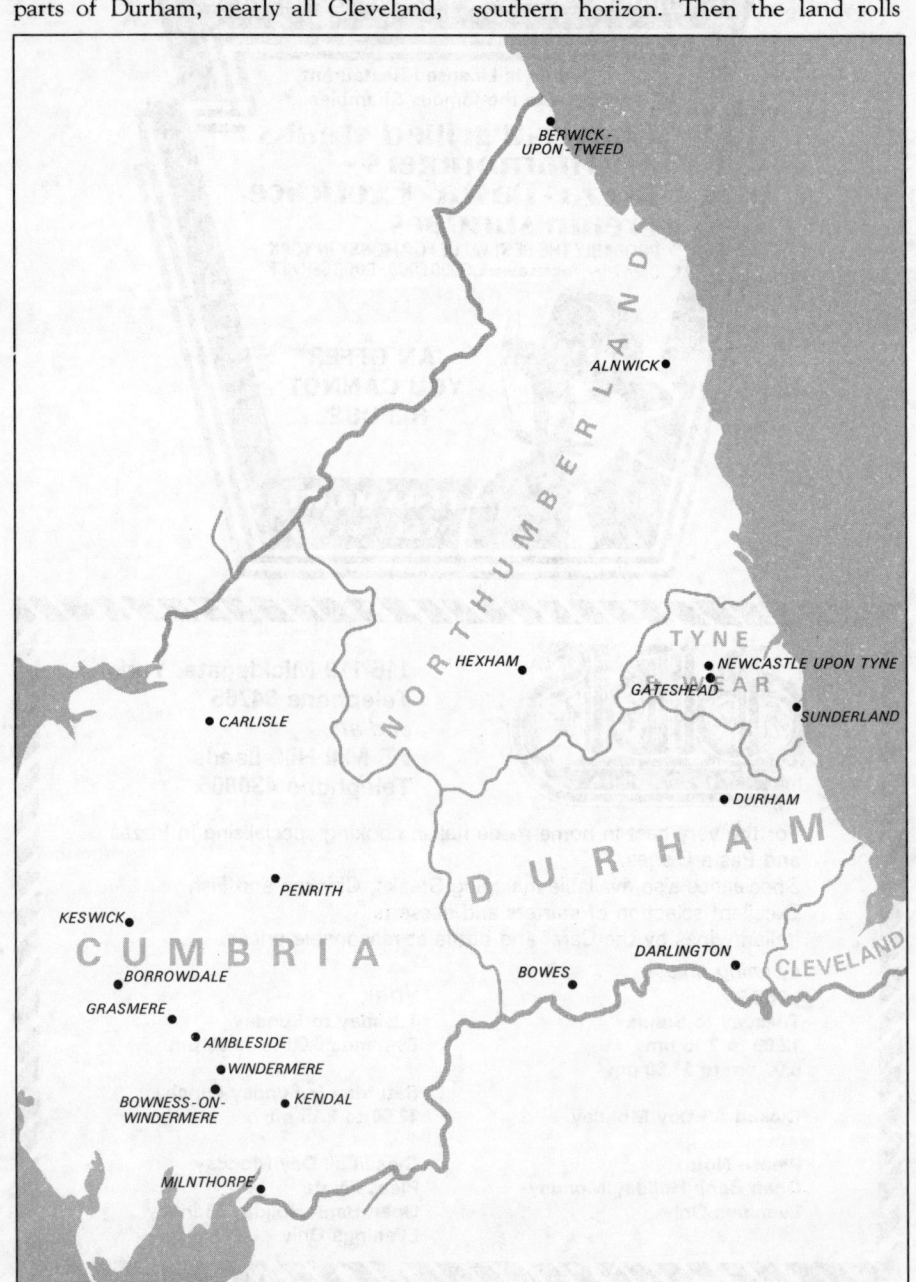

England, as if reluctant to part with its industries, hangs on to them doggedly in parts of Durham, nearly all Cleveland, and in Northumberland until Newcastle upon Tyne has become a speck on the southern horizon. Then the land rolls away in exquisite freedom towards Hadrian's Wall. Over in the west, the transition from urban clutter has already been accomplished. The Lake District is within tolerably easy distance from Liverpool or Manchester. Nevertheless, nobody in his right mind would dream of despoiling it with a factory – any more than the local authority would dream of permitting it.

The Lake District is inevitably associated with Wordsworth and his daffodils. Some see it, however, as a place in which to walk long distances, compete in gruelling mountain races, sheep dog trials, or attempt the Water Speed Record on the larger lakes, sometimes tragically. In 1930, Henry Segrave was killed when trying to be fastest; in 1967, Donald Campbell died when his boat crashed on Coniston. Wordsworth would not have approved; he once remarked that 'action is transitory', and so it is.

Many of the traditional dishes are associated with particular occasions. For instance, Clipping Time Pudding was consumed at Keswick when farmers sheared their sheep. In County Durham, they ate Groaning Cheese when a baby was being born – and Groaning Cake once it had arrived. Appropriately, the doctor was usually invited to make the first incision.

Rum butter is a well-known product of Cumbria, though vendace – a freshwater herring caught in Derwentwater and Lake Bassenthwaite – is probably less widely appreciated. And so, indeed, are flukes and yarb. These are flat fish with longish tails that inhabit the sea off Flookburgh. Kendal mint cake has become the staple food of adventurers. It is a hard, flat cake of mint cream, packed with energy-producing calories, and therefore handy as iron rations in conditions of extreme hardship. Unlike other iron rations it tastes nice. Cumberland sausages are a delicacy much sought after all over the country and Cumberland sauce, made with red-currant jelly and port is delicious with hot gammon. It may, of course, be named for the Duke and not the region.

Panacketty in County Durham should not be confused with Northumberland's Panhaggerty. The one contains meat; the other, cheese, onions and potatoes. As for Cold Water Willies, these are uncommonly tough cakes sometimes called 'pul-lit' (the inference being that you have to pull it to pieces). Newcastle Brown is the beer the locals swear by. But, for sheer gastronomic extravagance, nothing can beat a banquet given by the Bishop of Durham for Richard II in 1387. Among the items on the menu were 50 swans.

Alnwick — Berwick-upon-Tweed

ALNWICK

Hotspur Hotel ★★
(Alnwick 602924)
Open: Billy Bones Buttery: Mon–Sun 12noon–2pm, 6–9pm
Percy Restaurant Summer Mon–Sun 7–9pm, Winter Mon–Sun 7–8pm

F P S &

Billy Bones was piper to the Duchess of Northumberland in 1815, when the Duke leased Hotspur House to him. There he established a hostelry. In 1971, a local businessman turned it into a hotel again and converted the stable into the Billy Bones Buttery, where horse brasses on the walls proclaim the building's former use. Here you can get a super lunch for about £3.75 – soup or fruit juice, a choice of four main dishes likely to include a roast, fish, and cold meat with salad, and an 'English' sweet – perhaps fruit crumble with custard or a sponge pudding. The à la carte menu is also within our budget, with basket meals including pork sausage, tomato, onion and chips at around £1.65 and – at the other end of the scale – deep-fried seafood selection with chips at over £3.25. Steak is the most expensive bar meal, costing £5.25. Starters include soup and fruit juice and sweets are ice cream-based, costing up to £1.15. The Percy Restaurant (Percy is the family name of the Dukes of Northumberland) does a table d'hôte dinner at around £7.

AMBLESIDE

Gemini Restaurant, Lake Road
(Ambleside 2528)
Open: Feb–Dec Mon–Sun 12noon–2pm, 5.30–approx 8.30pm

P S &

A friendly, informal family-run roadside restaurant with large rear car park. Two small open-plan areas and a bar area create a comfortable atmosphere and a good selection of wholesome hot dishes are provided. Starters include grapefruit and mandarin cocktail at around 60p and main courses, predominantly grills, range in price from around £1.65–£4 with specialities such as duckling à l'orange or sole in prawn and mushroom sauce –

both about £5. There is an excellent choice of desserts from around 80p. Special children's dishes are around £1.25. There are a selection of wines available along with draught lager and beer.

BERWICK-UPON-TWEED

King's Arms Hotel ★★
Hide Hill
(Berwick-upon-Tweed 7454)
Open Summer Mon–Sun 8–9.30pm, 12noon–10pm, Winter Mon–Sun 12noon–2pm, 6.30–9pm

C P S &

The King's Arms was once a coaching inn, a regular stop for the London to Edinburgh Highflyer – 18th-century equivalent of the Flying Scotsman. Today a Highflyer menu ranging in price from £3.65–£5.75 is served in its oak-panelled dining room at lunchtime or evenings. The adjoining Brambles Bistro, open all day in summer provides a quick-service meal from £2. You may buy a three-course table d'hôte Sunday lunch for about £4.50. The Hunting Lodge bar does lunches, including farmhouse soup for around 40p and hot meals around £1.50.

Popinjays, 30 Hide Hill
(Berwick-upon-Tweed 7237)
Open: Mon–Sat 9.30am–5pm

P S &

Georgina Home-Robertson is the enthusiastic owner of this farmhouse-style coffee shop which boasts a walled patio at the rear with ruined stables providing a dramatic backcloth. Coffee shop Popinjays may be, but down market it definitely is not. Food here is simple but nicely prepared with salads at around £1 and various hot dishes including basic grills and omelettes at about 75p. All ingredients for a good three-course meal are here except for a glass of wine – Popinjays is unlicensed.

Queen's Head Hotel ★
Sandgate
(Berwick-upon-Tweed 7852)
Open: Mon–Sun 7.30–9.30am, 12noon–2pm, 7–9.30pm

P S &

One of three Berwick hotels owned and run by Mr and Mrs Geoffrey Young and family, the Queen's Head lies at the bottom of Hide Hill, near the river. The pleasant restaurant with its dark oak furniture and flock wallpaper offers three-course table d'hôte lunch at around £4 with coffee extra. There is also an à la carte menu with fish, entrées and roasts at prices ranging from £4–£4.50, the total cost working out between £5 and £6 for three courses.

Ravensholme Hotel ★★
Ravensdowne
(Berwick-upon-Tweed 7170)
Open: Mon–Sun 7.30–10am, 12noon–2pm, 6.30–9.30pm

C P S &

The Youngs own this hotel, too, as well as the Queen's Head. The Ravensholme has two restaurants, a downstairs Wallace Room with Wallace tartan carpet, and an upstairs Gold Room. The Wallace Room offers a good range of dishes including fried fillet of Eyemouth haddock or two lamb chops and various steaks on the à la carte menu, and three courses can cost around £6. An excellent table d'hôte lunch offers three courses for under or around £5. The Gold Room serves bar lunches and suppers in summer. The historic building, formerly a private house adjoins the town's interesting Elizabethan fortifications.

The Rum Puncheon Restaurant,
Golden Square
(Berwick-upon-Tweed 7431)
Open: Mon–Sat 9.30am–9.30pm

C P S &

You can't linger late over dinner here, but this oak-clad 18th-century restaurant is certainly worth a visit. The Stoddart family has been in business selling groceries, wines and spirits there since 1834. In the restaurant you can buy a three-course lunch for something around £4 or the

---

Gemini Restaurant

adjoining Hayes Nurseries, Lake Road, Ambleside.
Tel. Ambleside 2528

Morning Coffee 11–12pm; Luncheon 12–2pm; Dinner 5.30–approx 8.30pm

Open Daily. Licensed.

High Quality Art Gallery

A La Carte Menu. Steaks a Speciality.

Large car park. Coaches welcome by prior appointment.

Proprietors: David & Jill Smith.

Borrowdale — Darlington

main course only for about £2.50 as well as separate à la carte dishes such as scampi, steak or salmon, all at between £2.50–£4. Substantial bar lunches are also served with main courses for just over £1.35 to about £3 and sweets from 55p upwards.

BORROWDALE

The Yew Tree, Seatoller
(Borrowdale 634)
Open: Tue–Fri Sun 12noon–8pm,
Sat 6–9.30pm

[P][&]

Nestling at the foot of the spectacular Honiston Pass, this whitewashed restaurant was originally built as two cottages in 1628. Massive oak beams and a slate floor emphasise the antiquity of the dining room, with its wheelback chairs and wooden tables. Food is simple and wholesome. Try home-made soup with a roll as a starter for 70p. Smoked salmon at £1.75 is one of the more expensive appetisers. Main courses offered are grills, omelettes and salads. Speciality of the house is Borrowdale trout with almonds (£3.50) and ham and egg (£3). Cumberland sausage with salad and mushrooms is £3. A very tempting selection of sweets include pot of chocolate (85p), brandy meringue (90p) or bilberries and cream (90p). Starred items on the menu are available in smaller portions for children at two-thirds of the full price.

BOWES

Ancient Unicorn Hotel ★★
(Teesdale 28321)
Open: Mon–Sun 11.30am–2.30pm,
6–10pm

[C][P][&]

This attractive coaching inn, built around a cobbled courtyard, has been offering accommodation and refreshment to weary travellers since the 16th century. Prices in the restaurant of this two-star hotel are somewhat beyond our limit so we are concentrating on the very reasonable and extensive bar snack menu. A sample of dishes available are sardine and tomato salad for starter at £1, chicken curry with rice and peas at about £2.60 and, to finish with, a sweet chosen from a selection at 90p.

BOWNESS-ON-WINDERMERE

The Quarterdeck, The Glebe Centre,
Glebe Road
(Windermere 5001)
Open: March–Oct, Mon–Sun
8.30am–10.30pm, Barbecue menu
7–10.30pm

[♪][P][&]

This restaurant, with a coffee-shop and lounge is situated on the edge of Lake Windermere and has excellent views over the marina and surrounding hills. It caters all day – starting with breakfast. At lunch-time, roasts are a speciality and there is a barbecue menu in the evening.

There is also a special menu for children. A typical evening meal would be gazpacho at 85p, spiced breast of chicken £3.40, sweets from 95p, and coffee 40p.

CARLISLE

The Central Hotel ★★
Victoria Viaduct
(Carlisle 20256)
Open: Mon–Sun 12noon–2pm, 7–9pm

[C][♪][P][S][&]

A comfortable and popular Greenall Whitley hotel managed with great style by Stanley Cohen. Bar lunch here is excellent with a good ploughman's at about £1.25, a wide range of cold and hot dishes for around £1.60 and specials including scampi at about £2.10. Outstandingly good value, too, is the Central's table d'hôte dinner at about £5.75.

The Citadel Restaurant, 77–79 English Street
(Carlisle 21298)
Open: Mon–Sat 11.30am–10.30pm, Sun normal licensing hours

[C][♪][P][S][&]

Is this the ideal haunt? Certainly the friendly ghosts keep coming back for more. So, it seems, do the patrons who claim to have seen several unearthly apparitions in this 100-year-old citadel, including a wizened old lady and a chap in 18th-century garb. The restaurant is situated above a tangle of ancient passageways which once led to the cathedral and old jail. Now it's handy for the station and shops. Warm and bright, it serves straightforward no-nonsense meals at fairly reasonable prices. Particularly good value are a three-course shopper's lunch at about £2.50 including coffee, and the à la carte seafood dishes, none of which will set you back more than about £4.

The Crown and Mitre ★★★
English Street
(Carlisle 25491)
Open: Restaurant Mon–Fri
12.30–2.30pm, Mon–Sat 6.30–10pm
Coffee House Mon–Sat 9am–10.30pm,
Sun 10am–10pm

[C][♪][P][S][&]

The Restaurant, within the Crown and Mitre Hotel, offers a full à la carte menu and a table d'hôte from £5, with starters such as prawn cocktail followed by delicious meat dishes featuring steaks, lamb cutlets, pork chops or Cumberland sausage. A typical sweet would be gâteau or ice cream. There are two bars, the Peace and Plenty has a substantial bar food menu.

Cumbrian Hotel ★★★
Court Square
(Carlisle 31951)
Open: during normal licensing hours,

Victoria's Restaurant 12noon–2pm,
7–9.30pm
Cumbrian Kitchen, Summer
9.30am–9.30pm, Winter 10am–8pm

[C][P][S][&]

As its name implies, the Cumbrian's well-appointed main restaurant has a Victorian décor. The à la carte menu is very English, but rather expensive, although the table d'hôte lunch at about £3.50 and dinner at around £6.50 are both excellent buys. The Cumbrian Kitchen is a different matter altogether. You can have a snack and a cup of coffee here, with change from £1.50, or a substantial meal for less than £4. Bar snacks, available at lunchtime, include chicken salad at about £1.60, and an Albert's Special (half a French loaf buttered and filled with just about everything) at about 55p.

The Malt Shovel, Rickergate
(Carlisle 34095)
Open: during normal licensing hours,
Brew House Restaurant Mon–Sat
12noon–2pm, 7.30–9.30pm

[C][♪][P][S][&]

The Brew House Restaurant has a most appropriate décor of malt sacks and malt shovels and is very bright and clean, with comfortable chairs and a relaxed, intimate atmosphere. The lunch menu prices start at around 95p for a ploughman's. A T-bone steak garni at about £4.75 apart, none of the main dishes costs much more than £2.50. But the Malt Shovel is at its best in the evening, with 19 starters at prices ranging from around 40p–£1.50, and a superb selection of fish dishes, poultry, roasts, grills and entrées at prices that average out around £4. Incidentally, Scottish bard Robert Burns slept at the Malt Shovel, we are told. It's a pity he missed the food.

DARLINGTON

Taj Mahal Tandoori, 192 Northgate
(Darlington 68920)
Open: Mon–Sun 12noon–2.30pm,
7pm–12mdnt

[C][♪][P]

A small, intimate restaurant situated very close to the town centre, the Taj Mahal offers unbelievable value with its three-course lunch for only £1.60. The lunch menu includes 12 Indian dishes such as chicken and prawn curry and four English dishes including rump or sirloin steak with soup or fruit juice to start and a sweet to follow. A prominent feature of the dining area is a large Eastern-style mural covering one wall, the other three walls are hung with soft drapes, and the Indian atmosphere is enhanced by traditional background music. The à la carte menu offers a large variety of dishes with many tandoori specialities for around £2–£3.

Durham — Kendal

DURHAM

Dennhöfers, 4 Framwellgate Bridge, Milburngate Centre
(Durham 46777)
Open: Mon–Sat 12noon–3pm, 7–10.30pm

C P S

Situated in the shadow of the Gothic cathedral and castle is this olde worlde eating place. The lower of the two wine bars has a limited and inexpensive menu, and the upstairs bar offers a greater variety of dishes, both at lunch-time and in the evening. A three-course meal could easily come to less than £5, and a glass of wine costs about 70p.

The Happy Wanderer, Finchale Road, Framwellgate Moor, 1m N of Durham
(Durham 64580)
Open: Mon–Sat 12noon–2pm, 7–9.30pm, Sun 12noon–1.30pm

P

Midway between Durham City and the ancient monument of Finchale Priory stands this popular pub with its comfortable restaurant. Bar meals represent excellent value, but for a little extra, diners can enjoy the comfort of the restaurant and its very friendly service. Chef's pâté at 65p and 'Wanderer' mixed grill £3.75 would satisfy a large appetite and for those with a sweet tooth why not complete your meal with banana fritters at 50p. Real ale is served at the bar.

Ristorante La Cantina, North Road
(Durham 46050)
Open: Tue–Sat 11.30am–2.30pm, Mon–Sat 6–10.30pm

C F S

Once inside this second-floor restaurant, one could almost be in an eating place in Rome or Florence. Inside, there are no windows and lighting is by coach lamps. Italian music strums gently in the background and Italian posters and Chianti bottles decorate the brick and rough-cast walls. A gallery dining area completes the scene with large wagon wheels and halved barrels set into the walls. An excellent selection of pasta and pizza dishes are offered, all for around £2, so that a three-course meal could easily be had for around £5.

Royal County Hotel ★★★★
Bowes Coffee House, Old Elvet
(Durham 66821)
Open: Mon–Sat 10am–8pm, Sun 10am–5.30pm

C F P S

Youngsters enjoy their meals in this attractive buttery as there is a menu of children's favourites such as bangers and mash at about 75p and sweets (including 'Thunder and Lightning' – ice cream, golden syrup and whipped cream!) at around 45p. À la carte dishes are reasonably priced and you can choose an appetising meal such as soup with roll and butter, fried breast of chicken with banana fritter, chips and peas, a slice of chocolate gâteau and coffee for around £5.60.

The Squire Trelawny, 80 Front Street, Sherburn
(Durham 720613)
Open: Tue–Sat 7.30–12mdnt

C P

Away from the city centre, this tiny, low-ceilinged bar and restaurant has a wealth of heavy old beams, horse brasses, harnesses and stirrups, set off by heavy rough-cast walls. Subtle lighting is by coach lamps. The à la carte menu is pricey, but an excellent-value 'snack' menu is served from Tuesday to Thursday inclusive. A choice of minute steak, scampi, roast chicken or gammon and apricot – all served with chips and peas – costs £2.30. Soup of the day at 75p and a sweet from the trolley at around the same price, complete a satisfying and inexpensive three-course meal.

GATESHEAD

The Griddle, 409 Durham Road, Low Fell
(Gateshead 874530)
Open: Mon–Sat 9am–5.30pm, 7.30–10pm

P

Morning coffee and afternoon tea are served with a range of snacks in this first-floor restaurant. At lunch-time salads and a choice of hot dishes all at around £2 are available. The delicious pastries and pies are home-made. Tempting three-course meals are on the menu in the evenings, all at under £6.50.

GRASMERE

The Singing Birds Restaurant, Town End
(Grasmere 268)
Open: Mar–Nov Mon–Sun 10.30am–3pm, 3.30–6pm, 7–9.30pm

C P

Close to Dove Cottage and the Wordsworth Museum is a quaint white cottage housing an antique shop and restaurant. Inside, rough-cast walls, dark beams and brass and copper bric-à-brac emphasise the rustic atmosphere. All the lunch menus include a host of home-made dishes. 'Light' lunches include soup of the day with granary bread for around 75p, savoury flan or quiche served with an interesting salad for about £2.75 and open sandwiches such as 'shrimps in a crowd' for around £1.75. Three-course à la carte lunches vary in price from £4 upwards and include pâté maison, home-made chicken and mushroom pie or spaghetti bolognese. A three-course Sunday table d'hôte lunch for about £5.50 offers excellent choices – try egg and prawn surprise followed by chicken chasseur or lamb's kidneys turbigo.

HEXHAM

Hadrian's Wall
(Hexham 81232)
Open: Mon–Sun 12noon–2pm, 7–9pm

P

Overshadowed by the Roman wall, this smart ivy-clad inn dating back over 250 years enjoys a well-deserved local reputation for its good and efficient service. A four-course lunch of home-made soup, a fish dish, a main course of steak and kidney pudding, lemon sole, curry or trout plus a sweet and coffee with cream will come to around £5.

KENDAL

Cherry Tree Restaurant, 24 Finkle Street
(Kendal 20547)
Open: Mon–Sun 10am–9.30pm, closed early Thu in winter

S

The entrance to the Cherry Tree lies up an alleyway. The main first-floor restaurant is very bright and clean, with good dark furniture and excellent quality crockery. The décor has white rough-cast walls and beams. You can buy hot and cold snacks here and Danish open sandwiches, as well as a four-course lunch for about £3.50. Dinner costs very little more and offers an excellent choice with salmon, veal, chicken and turkey well within the budget.

Gateway Hotel, Crook Road, Plumgarths (2m NW on B5284)
(Kendal 20605)
Open: Mon–Sat 12noon–2.30pm, 6–10pm, Sun 12noon–1.45pm, 7–9.30pm

C P

There is a varied menu and you can choose to dine either in the bar, lounge or the restaurant. Starters or snacks start at 65p and the popular main meals, including traditional Cumberland sausage at £2.10, are served with baked potato, French fries or salad. The grills, game and fish dishes are more expensive. Desserts are from 50p, and there is a range of children's meals.

The Mash Tun, The Brewery Arts Centre
(Kendal 25133)
Open: Mon–Sat 10am–3pm, lunch 12noon–2pm

F P

The Mash Tun is housed in a converted stone-built brewery. The food is under the personal supervision of Annette Tarver. Popular with local business folk and farmers, the Mash Tun offers a choice of pies and flans at about £2 and all with chips or salad, as well as a great variety of similarly-priced fish or cold meat salads. There is a choice of three sweets for about 50p.

The Woolpack Hotel ★★★
Stricklandgate
(Kendal 23852)
Open: normal licensing hours, Ca Steean Restaurant Mon–Sat 12.30–2pm,

7–10pm
Shepherd's Pie Buttery, Summer
Mon–Sat 10am–9.30pm, Winter
Mon–Sat 10am–6.30pm

C F P S ♫

The Ca Steean Restaurant offers fine food in elegant surroundings. A three-course meal can be had from the à la carte menu for around £6, if you stick to the lower price range, or there is the table d'hôte at around £3.50 for lunch and around £7.50 for dinner with hot grill-style main courses or cold buffet. The Shepherd's Pie Buttery is a more casual eating place with pine-clad walls and lantern-style lighting where a three-course meal costs around £3. Bar snacks include a good ploughman's lunch at around £1.25.

KESWICK

Bay Tree, 1 Wordsworth Street
(Keswick 73313)
Open: Mon–Sun 10am–4.30pm, 7–9pm, Winter evenings only

P S ♫

This attractive terrace restaurant and guesthouse is easy to spot by its brown canopy and corner position. Victoriana is the style for interior décor, with old prints, china, porcelain and highly-polished tables and chairs. The three-course dinner menu (changing daily) is just in our range at £5.95–£6.95.

Keswick
—
Milnthorpe

Derwentwater Hotel ★★★
Portinscale
(Keswick 72538)
Open: Mon–Sun 8.30–9.30am, 12noon–2pm, 4–5pm, 7–8.30pm

C P ♫

A friendly, informal hotel this, in a superb position close to the shores of Derwentwater. An excellent bar lunch, chosen from a variety of salad platters, will set you back a little over £3. There is a half-price menu for children.

The Dog and Gun, 2 Lake Road
(Keswick 73463)
Open: Mon–Sun, during normal licensing hours

P S

This is a genuine old coaching inn, and one of the oldest pubs in Keswick. The intimacy of its low, beamed ceiling and, in winter time, the welcoming open fire, make the Dog and Gun popular with locals and visitors alike. Food is prepared by the proprietress and is available during opening hours. Last orders are at 2.30pm (1.30pm Sundays) and 10pm. There is a wide selection of hot and cold dishes to choose from, all priced at around £3. Hot dishes include Hungarian goulash with dumplings, Roman fried chicken, lamb curry and ham with Cumberland sauce. Cold dishes could be rare roast beef with tossed salad and Cumberland ham with salad, both served with jacket potatoes. Snacks are around £1. Sweets include home-made apple pie and chocolate orange pot served under a float of orange curaçao.

Yan Tyan Tethera, 70 Main Street
(Keswick 72033)
Open Summer Mon–Sun 12noon–3pm, Tue–Sun 6.30–10pm, Winter Mon–Sun 12noon–2.30pm, Thu, Fri, Sat evenings by appointment only

♫ P S ♫

No Chinese chippy this, as you might think, for 'yan, tyan, tethera etc', is how they count sheep in Borrowdale. The day menu includes starters from around 50p–£1.30, hot dishes, including Cumberland sausage, from about 70p–£2.50, and fish from about 80p–£2.50. In the evening, owner Judith Szucs' specialities have a bias towards seafood, but they are popular, so do book. 'No service charge or gratuities please' the menu says. 'Just come back again!' English wines are a speciality here.

MILNTHORPE

Crooklands Hotel Buttery and Jakes
(Crooklands 432)
Two minutes from the M6 (No. 36 interchange) on the A65 going towards

GATEWAY HOTEL

8 miles from M6 — junction 36,
set back from the A591 & B5284.

Our friendly restaurant welcomes the happy holidaymaker or tired traveller with superb food.

From homemade soups, pate's and pies, to succulent sirloins, seafood shanties, lakeland trout and venison.

Something to please every palate and pocket.

Crook Road, Plumgarth, Kendal LA8 8LX.
Telephone Kendal 20605

Dog & Gun

2 Lake Road, Keswick.
Tel: Keswick 73463

An attractive old pub dating from the 17th century offering hospitality, warmth and bar meals throughout the year. Situated in the town and within walking distance of the lake. Everyone is assured of a welcome and food is provided until closing time.

A Matthew Brown House.

Kendal town centre.
Open: Mon–Sun 7.30am–2.30pm,
6.30–10.30pm

C P ✦

The Buttery of the Crooklands Hotel is a small, bright and cheerful restaurant, well worth knowing about. You can get a good lunch here, including home-made soup with roll (about 55p) and the 'pie of the day' (around £2.40 with vegetables). A three-course meal with coffee is an unbeatable £3.50 and includes some traditional choices such as hot pot and liver and onions. Jakes, the American Winer Diner offers three-course evening meals at about £5.50. Steaks, burgers and giant American Spider Crab Claws are on the menu and there are a selection of American beers and wines.

NEWCASTLE UPON TYNE

Cavalier Steak Bar, Denton Hotel, West Road
(Newcastle upon Tyne 742390)
Open: Mon–Sun 12noon–2pm,
7–10.30pm

C ♫ P S ✦

The impressive Denton Hotel's steak bar has a bright cocktail bar and an intimate, beamed restaurant with subdued lighting. Soup is around 45p, and there is a fine choice of steaks, fish and poultry. Gammon steak is about £3 and Cavalier mixed grill is excellent value at around

Newcastle upon Tyne

£4.20 – both are served with potatoes, peas and salad garnish. A sweet from the trolley is about 80p and a glass of house wine costs around 60p. A 'Junior Cavalier Menu' is available for children.

Coffee House, Northumbria Hotel ★★★
Osborne Road
(Newcastle upon Tyne 814961)
Open: Mon–Sun 10am–11.30pm

C P S

The Scandinavian pine décor of this attractive buttery is complemented by a cocktail bar where the works of local artists are displayed. The Coffee House serves Danish pastries, lunchtime snacks such as seafood pancake at about £1.85 and full three-course meals. Home-made soup of the day, a main dish such as asparagus and cheese pancake or fillet of plaice and a generous slice of fresh cream gâteau will leave you plenty of change from £5 to sample a cup of coffee.

Dante and Piero, 8 Douglas House, Neville Street
(Newcastle upon Tyne 324035)
Open: Mon–Fri 11.30am–2.30pm,
5.30–11.30pm, Sat 11.30am–2.30pm,
5.30am–12mdnt, Sun 7–10.30pm, Nov & Dec, Mon–Sat 11am–1am,
Sun 7–10.30pm

C ♫ ✦

There is a nice, intimate atmosphere in this restaurant which is created by soft lights and background music. There is dancing in the evening, but those wanting a quiet corner will not be disappointed in this large restaurant. The Italian menu offers pizzas, pastas and a range of meat dishes. Soup of the day is 40p, pizzas are from £2.20 and there is a selection of home-made desserts.

The Falcon, Prudhoe
(Prudhoe 32324)
Open: Mon–Sat 12noon–2pm,
6.30–10pm, Sun 12noon–1.45pm,
7–10pm

C P ✦

The grill room of this modern pub has picture windows the full length of one wall, giving a view of the surrounding countryside. Clean lines and simple furnishings, with an open grill bar give a feeling of uncluttered elegance. The menu is unpretentious and you can get a good three-course meal very reasonably. Starters, which include smoked mackerel at around £1, range in price from 30p–£1.05. Main dishes include pork chop at £2.95 and mixed grill in the region of £4.50, all served with chipped or croquette potatoes, and there are various salads, all priced at £2.50. Desserts range from about 30p for ice cream-based sweets to 75p if you select from the trolley. For children there is a special 'Mr

DANTE & PIERO

8 DOUGLAS HOUSE, NEVILLE STREET, NEWCASTLE-UPON-TYNE
Telephone (0632) 324035
(Positioned outside Newcastle Central Station)

Italian Restaurant, Pizzeria, Tavola, Calda, Vegetarian Food, Coffee Shop, Continental Cakes, Evening Disco.

Opening Times
Monday to Friday 11.30am–2.30pm, 5.30pm–1.00am
Saturday 11.30am–12 mdnt
Sunday 7.00pm–10.30pm

Gibby's RESTAURANTS
WINDERMERE BOWNESS AND CHESTER

These licensed restaurants are prominently situated in the Central areas, and serve a wide choice of good value dishes and lighter meals.

For that evening with a difference, why not enjoy a candelit Barbeque at our new Quarterdeck Restaurant overlooking Lake Windermere at Bowness Bay.

Enquiries and reservations Telephone: Windermere 5001

Menu' which includes a main meal, an orange, ice cream (and the colourful menu itself!), all for £1 or thereabouts.

The Golden Bengal Restaurant,
39 Groat Market
(Newcastle upon Tyne 320471)
Open: Mon–Sat 12noon–2.30pm,
6–11.30pm, Sun 7–11pm

C 🎵 P S

Soft Indian background music and a décor of Indian murals capture an Oriental atmosphere in this city centre restaurant. Soup or fruit juice are followed by chicken curry, keema pillau with vegetable curry or roast chicken and vegetables, with a sweet or fruit to complete the meal. The à la carte menu contains a wealth of Indian specialities – curries mild and hot, medium hot or very hot – at around £2.35. Biriani dishes served with vegetable curry are in the £3–£4.50 range and Tandoori clay oven-cooked chicken or king prawns are around £2.80–£3.80. Fruit such as guava or mango served with fresh cream is about 75p–£1.10.

Ristorante Roma ✕
22 Collingwood Street
(Newcastle upon Tyne 320612)
Open: Mon–Sat 12noon–2.30pm,
7–11.30pm, Sun 7–11.30pm

C 🎵 P S 🍷

A Spanish guitarist entertains guests every night in this charming restaurant. As a gesture to Italian culture the menu has everything from chariot races to Chianti bottles and offers Sophia Loren (a juicy steak dish) and Gina Lollobrigida –

Penrith — Windermere

the Chef's secret on a plate in the à la carte menu. Who could ask for more? Further temptations are artichoke hearts in a cream sauce and lobster mornay, plus a star-studded list of sweets headed by crêpes suzette and banana, peach or pineapple flambés. Midday budget items include lasagne or cannelloni for around £1.80, sole or chicken for around £2.50 with vegetables and sirloin steak for around £2.65 with vegetables!

PENRITH

Waverley Hotel, Crown Square
(Penrith 63962)
Open: Summer Mon 10am–2pm,
6.30–8.30pm, Tue–Sat 10am–8.30pm,
Sun 12noon–2pm, Winter
Mon–Sat 12noon–2pm, 7–8.30pm
Coffee Shop Summer only

C P S 🍷

On the fringe of the town centre is this very popular hotel dining room with a small, intimate cocktail bar. The attraction is very reasonably-priced home-made food and fresh vegetables. The main menu includes barbecued spare ribs, steak and kidney pie and beef curry, all for around £2.25 and a selection of pizzas for around £1.50. Various dishes of the day cost from £1.30, and there is a newly-opened cold buffet table from £1.25. A choice of home-made sweets cost about 85p.

SUNDERLAND

The Melting Pot, 9 Maritime Terrace
(Sunderland 76909)
Open: Mon–Sat 12noon–2.30pm,
6pm–12mdnt

C P S

Peacock blue drapes covering three walls create a comfortable atmosphere in this intimate Indian restaurant situated in Sunderland's pedestrian precinct. The 'lunchtime special' menu, offering a choice of soup or fruit juice, 10 traditional Indian dishes such as chicken or prawn curry, five English dishes including rump steak, plus sweet, is superb value at £1.50. The extensive à la carte is also well within our budget. Wine is not sold by the glass, but in a minimum of half-bottles at around £2.75 a time, so you would be wise to take a friend or two along.

WINDERMERE

Gibby's, 43 Crescent Road
(Windermere 3267)
Open: week before Easter–end October,
Mon–Sun 11.15am–2.30pm, 4.30–9pm

🎵 P S 🍷

This small, canopied restaurant, in Tudor style, can be found in Windermere town centre. A full meal is available for well under £6 and the daily three-course 'special' for lunch or dinner is just £2.65. 85p will provide the children with a plate of sausage, beefburgers or fish-fingers with chips. There is also a selection of special coffees. This is an unpretentious restaurant, popular with families, holidaymakers and business people alike.

EDINBURGH AND THE BORDER REGIONS

If you motor into Scotland, whether you cross the border at Carter Bar on the A68 or at the conclusion of the M6 further west, you are prepared for the scenery. There are hills and dales, tracts of moorland and trout-thronged rivers. Somewhere in the wild hinterland, the Grey Mare's Tail waterfall pitches from a small loch on the high ground into a river 200 feet below. Elsewhere, the ruins of old abbeys celebrate the sacred history of the border country; those of forts and castles testify to the profane.

This is a land of legends. Some people drove sheep and cattle to market; others 'reaved', which means to say that they stole them. These border raiders were wild men: brave, ruthless, and full of cunning. Sir Walter Scott and the old ballards told their story. More recently, John Buchan set many of his stories here. The countryside has never been better described than in *The Thirty-Nine Steps*.

Sir Walter Scott's home at Abbotsford near Melrose is a huge, imposing building. The library contains 20,000 books: Sir Walter was after all, an author who liked to get his facts right. He produced a prodigious number of words each day and a no less impressive number of novels. His massive memorial in Princes Street, Edinburgh, is hardly less imposing than the Albert Memorial in London. Edinburgh itself is more or less three cities: the Old Town, which is very old indeed; the New Town, which was built about 200 years ago and isn't new at all: and the rest – which is comparatively modern.

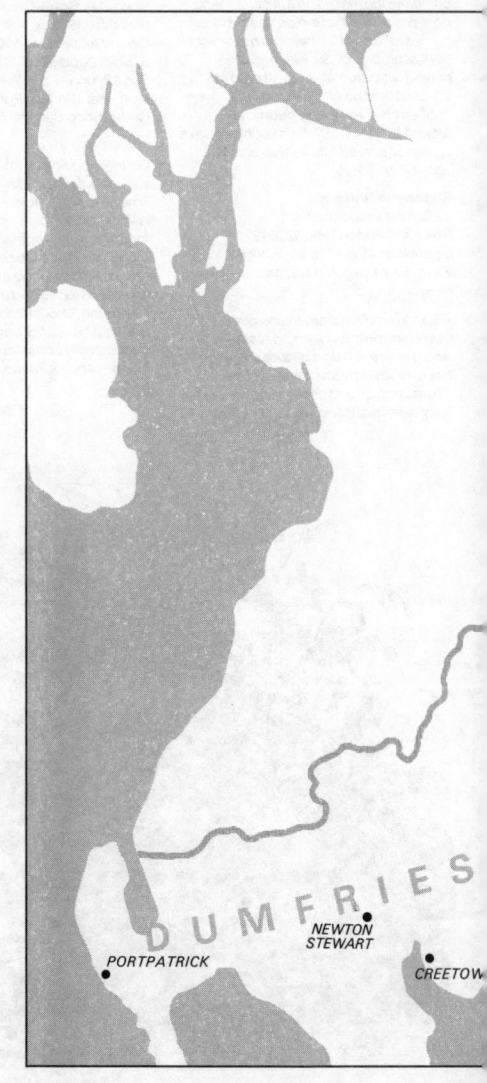

It is very difficult to associate dishes with particular regions in Scotland. Haggis, for example, is by no means the product of one particular place, but because it was praised by Burns and is eaten by Scots the world over on Burns' Night it belongs here, in the region where he was born and died (born in Alloway – died at Dumfries). Its traditional accompaniments – apart from whisky – are boiled potatoes and 'neeps' (swedes). Porridge, admittedly, goes by different names in different places (in Gaelic, for instance, it is called 'brochan'). Oatmeal is, indeed, common to a lot of recipes – notably biscuits known as 'bannocks'. Although they all taste very much alike, some are required eating on special occasions. Matrimonial bannocks are for weddings; Cryin' bannocks for the birth of a child; Teethin' bannocks for when it cuts its first tooth, and so on.

Just as Edinburgh is famous for its festival (on the Fringe, aspiring thespians can taste glory for a week or two, and then disappear without trace), so it is renowned for Edinburgh rock, a sugary, pastel-coloured confection that does not remotely resemble the English seaside product. Its factories also manufacture tons of shortbread. But, wherever you go in Scotland, you'll find shortbread, delicious scones, good fresh bread, and a variety of hot meat pies and pasties.

Creetown — Edinburgh

CREETOWN

Creetown Arms Hotel, St John Street (Creetown 282)
Open: Summer Mon–Sun 12.30–2pm, 7–9pm, Winter Mon–Sun 12.30–2pm, 7–8pm

P &

This small granite inn with its blue shutters dates from 1780 and is situated on the main road (A75), in this attractive village overlooking Wigtown Bay. A good range of Scottish fare is offered here with specialities including venison, Galloway beef and fresh local salmon. Meals are served in the bar or restaurant and prices vary accordingly. A typical bar meal costing around £2.85 might be egg mayonnaise followed by braised steak with vegetables and croquette potatoes and fresh cream trifle for dessert. In the restaurant you could have pâté maison followed by gammon steak and pineapple with meringue glacé and coffee for less than £5. For 50p extra you may choose from a more adventurous à la carte with such main courses as fillet of pork marsala and braised venison in port and red wine sauce.

DALKEITH

Giorgio Pizza & Spaghetti House, 128 High Street
(031-663 4492)
Open: Mon–Sun 12noon–2.30pm, 5pm–1am

C ♫ P S &

Grapes, hanging bottles, wrought-ironwork and lighting by lanterns convey the atmosphere of an Italian bistro, and indeed owner Giorgio Crolla does come from Rome. Pasta dishes are prevalent as may be expected, and £1.70 or so will buy a substantial main course such as lasagne al forno or spaghetti marenara. A three-course business lunch for around £1.85 offers exceptionally good value, and high teas are served from 5pm to 7pm. If you want a special meal, you may prefer to choose escalope Garibaldi or bistecca pizziola, either of which costs about £3.50.

DUMFRIES

Opus, 95 Queensberry Street
(Dumfries 5752)
Open: Mon–Wed, Fri–Sat 9am–5pm, Thu 9am–1pm

P S &

A bright, cosy restaurant decked out with red tables and much wood panelling, but tricky to locate. You'll find it up two flights of stairs above a fabric shop. Snacks are served throughout the day, but at lunchtimes a blackboard menu offers a bewildering variety of goodies. Take your pick from several salad bowls and cold meats for just £1. Or how about the hot dishes? Spicy vegetable pie and aubergine casserole are both £1.10, and lasagne is £1.30. Desserts, calculated to test a weightwatcher's resolve, include cheesecake and fresh cream gâteau.

The restaurant is unlicensed but try the excellent coffee.

Pancake Place, 20 English Street (Dumfries 68523)
Open: Apr–Sept Mon–Sat 9.30am–5.30pm, Sun 11.30pm–5.30pm

S &

This is one of the growing number of Pancake Places to open in Scotland. As the name suggests the menu is devoted to pancake (Scottish style) dishes, except for soup as a starter. Take your pick from savoury or sweet, large or small. The main dishes cost around £1.70 for large size and 90p for the snack size. Try the chicken and pineapple, or the bacon and maple syrup American style – a stack of three pancakes, layered with bacon and served with a jug of maple syrup. Don't despair if you are watching your waistline, there are some delicious cold meat or salad pancakes. For those with a sweet tooth try the 'Pippin' – hot apples and cinnamon folded into a sweet pancake and laced with fresh cream at £1.20. Spoon-sized portions of the sweet pancakes are available at about half the size and price.

EDINBURGH

Bar Italia, 100–104 Lothian Road
(031-228 6379)
Open: Mon–Sun 12noon–4am

P S &

Pizza delle Stagioni, with tomatoes, mozzarella, ham, salami, clams, mushrooms, artichokes and green peppers, costs around £3.10 and you have a choice of 12 other varieties, the cheapest being a pizza margherita for about £1.95. In the same price range you can choose from 15 pasta dishes, and there are also a number of more straightforward dishes such as roast chicken with chips (£3.20) or grilled sirloin with chips at around £4.70. A starter and sweet could add two or three pounds to the bill, but if you're watching the pennies you could choose soup and ice cream (the cheapest choices).

Bar Roma, 39a Queensferry Street
(031-226 2971)
Open: Mon–Sun 11am–2.30am

S &

This bright, spacious restaurant-cum-pizzeria is a sister to the Bar Italia in another part of the city. A very good selection of Italian dishes appear on the menu at fairly keen prices. Risotto con funghi (rice with mushrooms) at £2.30 and penne piccanti (hot chili and tomato sauce) at £2 are examples of the pasta range. There are over a dozen different pizzas, varying in price from £1.95–£3.20. Desserts start at 65p, rising past assorted gâteaux at £1.20 to affocato al cognac at £1.60. If you indulge in some of these fancier desserts

---

(and why not?) you'll probably need to forgo the antipasto (starter). Flavoursome expresso coffee is 45p but for the liqueur variety add £1.

Mr Boni's, 4–6 Lochrin Buildings
(031-229 5319)
Open: Restaurant Mon–Sat 5.30–10pm
Ice-Cream Parlour Mon–Sat 10.30am–10.30pm,
Sun 12noon–9.30pm

C ♫ P S &

Juicy steaks and American burgers feature at Mr Boni's, a restaurant and ice cream parlour famous hereabouts for its ice cream and extremely popular – particularly with King's Theatre folk, both audiences and performers – for its good, but inexpensive, home-cooked food. Italian dishes include various spaghettis at around £2.85 and a juicy steak at around £4.65. McBoni Burgers and ordinary burgers are around the £2 mark.

Café Cappuccino, 15 Salisbury Place
(031-667 4265)
Open: Mon–Sat 9am–8.30pm

P S &

The menu includes a wide variety of omelettes, salads, toasted sandwiches and filled rolls, all very reasonably priced, and if you are looking for a real meal there is an equally wide choice of fish or meat dishes which, with vegetables, mostly cost between £1 and £2.50. There is a good selection of ice-cream confections with prices around 50p. The Café Cappuccino is not licensed but you can take your pick from a range of 20 non-alcoholic beverages of which frothy cappuccino coffee is one choice.

Le Château, Castle Terrace
(031-229 1181)
Open: Mon–Thu 12noon–2.30pm, 5pm–12mdnt, Fri, Sat open all day

C ♫ &

From its impressive frontage you might expect Le Château prices to be well above our limit, but Bill Morgan's restaurant is recommended for good food at reasonable prices, for its bright and comfortable interior, and friendly atmosphere. Starters include a house pâté, prawn cocktail for around £1.35 and piping-hot soup at 60p or so. There is a choice of four or five dishes and of the usual grills at around £4.85. Among the house specialities are lasagne and chicken chasseur.

Crawford's, 31 Frederick Street
(031-225 4579)
Open: Summer Mon–Sat 8am–11pm, 7pm Winter

S &

This is one of the very handy Crawford's chain of restaurants, catering for families and shoppers. The ground-floor restaurant's décor has a country theme with pine wood and terra-cotta ceramic tiles. As with most Crawford's you can get a quick and reasonably-priced meal from the attractively laid out cold counter, or if

When you think of Mr Boni's you think of

Now try thinking of

We think they're the <u>best</u> in town

mr.boni's
ice cream
parlour

LATE LICENCE THUR · FRI · SAT
4-6 LOCHRIN BUILDINGS OPPOSITE KING'S THEATRE Tel: 031-229 5319

Edinburgh

you prefer, there is a tempting range of flans, pies and casseroles. To finish with, the range of gâteaux befits one of Scotland's best known bakeries. Wine and beer is available to accompany your meal.

Danish Kitchen, 124 Princes Street
(031-226 6669)
Open: Mon–Sat 9.30am–4.50pm

[S]

On the mezzanine floor of Austin Reed at the west end of Princes Street, the self-service Danish Kitchen provides very good food at a reasonable price, in most pleasant and comfortable surroundings. You can choose from freshly-made soup, Danish open sandwiches, salads, toasted sandwiches and omelettes. There is a tempting selection of sweets and freshly-based pastries, and beverages include tea, coffee, fruit drinks, and milk shakes. Indeed a satisfying meal here need cost no more than £2.50 including wine.

Desperate Dan's, 231 High Street
(031-225 7992)
17A Frederick Street
(031-225 5697)
Open: Mon–Sun 12noon–12mdnt

[C][S]

Taking their name from the famous comic-strip character, these two diners have the same menus and they specialise in chargrilled dishes. Cheerful young waitresses attired as cowgirls serve Danburgers (beefburgers) with various fillings at around £2 at lunch-time and £2.60 for dinner. Steaks are from £4.55–£6.95 for a massive 20oz rump steak and lamb cutlets range from £3–£4.20. Desperate Dan's Special Cow Pie (minus horns and tail) is available from £3.95 in the evening. All main courses are served with chips and garnish at lunch-time and salad in the evening. Starters are from 40p for soup and there is a good range of sweets including various pancakes and ices.

The Doric Tavern ×
15–16 Market Street
(031-225 1084)
Open: Mon–Sat 12noon–2.30pm, 6–9.30pm

[S]

If local lawyers and journalists gather in a restaurant, it's a sure sign that you'll get value for money. With a set three-course lunch for under £3 and four-course dinner for under £4, prices are hard to beat. Filling British dishes such as boiled silverside and dumplings or haggis and turnips are featured. The extensive à la carte, which includes an excellent mixed grill for about £2.50, is also very good value. Mr McGuffie, proprietor for the last quarter-century, believes in traditional service.

Es Danes, 45 Thistle Street
(031-225 9830)
Open: Mon–Sat 10am–2.15pm, 5.30–10.15pm

[P][S]

If you like smørrebrød – Danish open sandwiches – then this is the place for you. It is a small, compact restaurant and the all-white décor includes the tablecloths, crockery, flowers and ornaments. All the sandwiches come on a base of rye bread and are priced around £1.40–£1.80. Obviously the overall cost will depend on how many you order, two or three should be sufficient for the average appetite. For a full meal, start with soup and finish with gâteau, both at 70p. Because of the size of the restaurant, it is advisable to book in advance.

Fortrose Grill, 71 Rose Street
(031-225 8012)
Open: Summer Mon–Sat 11am–10pm, Sun 12.30–10pm, Winter closed Sun

[S]

Rose Street, with its boutiques and up-market restaurants is the 'in' shopping and eating area of Edinburgh. The Fortrose Grill is small and simple, the welcome and service friendly and informal. There is a good-value business lunch at about £2 and the à la carte menu is quite reasonable, with soup and 'fruity' starters up to 50p. Salads, pastas, and omelettes are in the £2–£3 range and a mixed grill of steak, sausage, bacon, tomato, mushroom and chips is one of the most expensive meals at around £4.40. Sweets are variations on the theme of ice cream, coffee is around 30p. The menu finishes with the words 'Servis non compris' which doesn't mean 'I don't understand how the washing machine works' but suggests discretion when tipping.

The Pancake Place, 130 High Street
(031-225 1972)
Open: Mon–Sat 10am–6pm, 9pm Summer, Sun 11am–9pm

[F][S]

Occupying a prime position in the city's historic Royal Mile, this restaurant, as its name suggests, specialises in pancakes large and small, sweet or savoury. The limited range of starters offers soup of the day or fruit juice at prices around 35p. You then launch into the mind-blowing array of savoury pancakes; hot ones with such fillings as haddock Mornay, bacon and maple syrup (an American favourite), and chicken currry, all under £2, and a selection of 'cool crisp salads', cheeses, ham, chicken or egg, served with two thin pancakes, mayonnaise or pickle on a bed of lettuce, tomato or cucumber for around the same price. If you have enough room to spare (the menu does warn that all sweet pancakes can ruin your diet) try an 'American' – three sweet pancakes layered with butter and served with a jug of maple syrup for about £1.50. A couple of 'spoon size' pancakes topped with sliced banana and cream cost 80p.

Post House Hotel ☆☆☆
Corstorphine Road
(031-334 8221)
Open: Coffee Shop Mon–Sun 12.30–10pm

[C][P][S]

Very handy for the zoo, this bright and modern coffee shop serves anything from large and colourful double-decker

---

DESPERATE DAN'S

231 High Street, Edinburgh. Telephone: 031-225 7992
and
17a Frederick Street, Edinburgh. Telephone: 031-225 5697

WHY NOT TRY DESPERATE DAN'S SPECIAL COW PIE
OR A DANBERGER WITH ONE OF THE VARIOUS FILLINGS

Open: Monday - Sunday 12 noon - Midnight

Edinburgh

sandwiches to a three-course meal. Try soup at 75p, followed by an omelette, burger or salad at around £2.50, and finish with cheesecake or sherry trifle at 75p. Babies are well-catered for here with 'strained dinner' or boiled egg and buttered fingers – and everything consumed within earshot of the animals!

Sorrento, 15 Albert Place
(031-554 7282)
Open: Mon–Sat 12noon–2.30pm, Mon–Thu & Sun 5.30pm–12.30am, Fri & Sat 5.30pm–1am
C P S &

The infectious, cheery attitude of the owners in looking after their guests is alone worth a visit to this friendly Italian restaurant. The varied menu has all the popular dishes including a good selection of pastas and pizzas and is priced to satisfy all pockets. Minestrone soup at 65p followed by a pasta or pizza dish at around £2.50 leaves sufficient to indulge in a tasty sweet – try zabaglione (beaten egg, sugar and marsala) at £1.10. Veal and steak dishes are a bit more expensive (£3.50–£5). All main dishes (except pastas and pizzas) come suitably garnished and are served with chips; vegetables are around 65p a portion. The table d'hôte menu at £2.20 is particularly good value.

St John's Restaurant, 259 St John's Road, Corstophine
(031-334 2857)
Open: Mon–Sat 11am–10pm, Sun 3pm–10pm
P S &

This compact restaurant with Mexican-style décor is next door to a modern fish and chip shop which is part of the same operation. The à la carte menu offers a

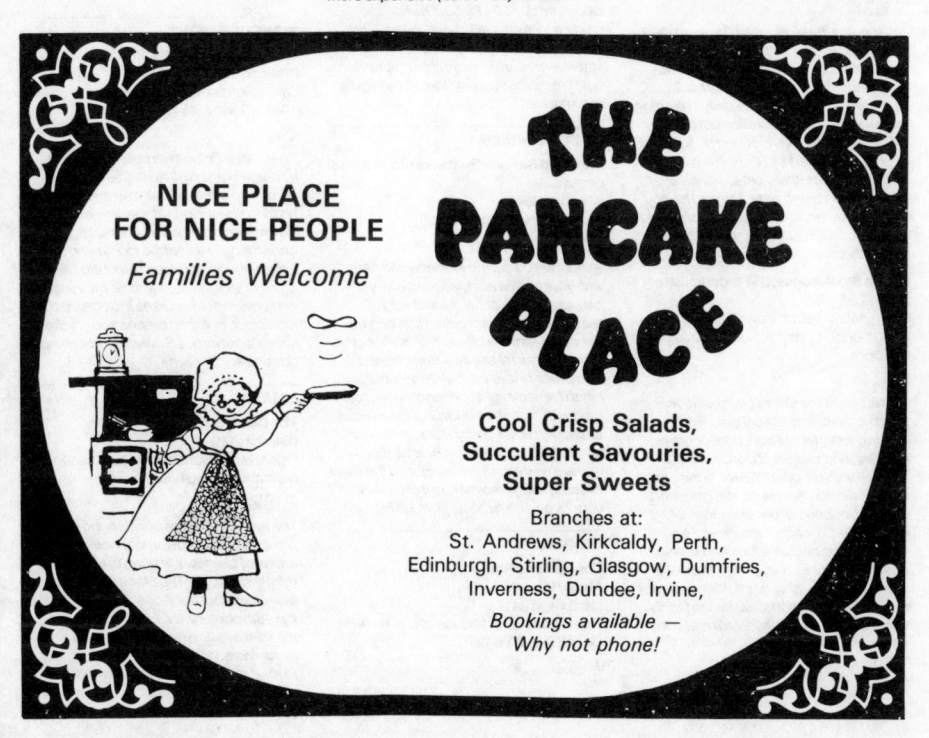

THE PANCAKE PLACE

NICE PLACE FOR NICE PEOPLE
Families Welcome

Cool Crisp Salads,
Succulent Savouries,
Super Sweets

Branches at:
St. Andrews, Kirkcaldy, Perth,
Edinburgh, Stirling, Glasgow, Dumfries,
Inverness, Dundee, Irvine.

*Bookings available —
Why not phone!*

Sorrento
RESTAURANT AND POMPEI ROOM

15 ALBERT PLACE, EDINBURGH (on Leith Walk)
Telephone: 031-554 7282

THE HEART OF NAPLES IN EDINBURGH
Pizzas for the connoisseur traditionally baked in a log fired oven
THE BEST IN ITALIAN CUISINE
FULLY LICENSED, OPEN 7 DAYS A WEEK
Restaurateurs. Mr B Gianni, Mr Z Remo

choice of dishes to suit even the tightest budget, with main courses such as haddock and chips and beefburger and chips both at around £1.50. Omelettes are around £1.35 and various steak dishes around £4. Vegetables are extra. Pastas and pizzas reflect the Italian influence and are priced at under £2. A three-course business lunch is £1.90. The restaurant should have a drinks license by the beginning of 1983.

The Stable Bar, Mortonhall Park, 30 Frogstone Road East
(031-664 0773)
Open normal licensing hours
Restaurant Mon–Sat 12noon–2pm

[A][P][&]

Adjacent to the Mortonhall Caravan Park but occupying an 18th-century coach house, this bar/restaurant is situated in an extremely pleasant environment. Open for lunches only, the daily changing menu offers a limited choice but good value for money. A typical lunch gives the choice of two starters, three main courses and two sweets, the most expensive combination being pâté, braised ham with vegetables and gâteau which would cost around £3.40. With the addition of coffee this meal will still be around £4.

Stakis Steakhouse, 26 Frederick Street
(031-225 2103)
Open: Mon–Sat 12noon–2.30pm, 5–10.30pm, 11pm Fri, Sun 12.30–2pm, 6–10pm

[C][&]

This is one of the Stakis Organisation steakhouses, and typical of its kind, offering a starter of soup, pâté or prawn cocktail, and sweets of peach melba, gâteau or apple pie inclusive in the cost of the main course. Haddock, gammon, chicken, or beefburger are under £4, steaks £5–£6, and all are served with jacket or chipped potatoes and peas. Lunchtime prices are £2–£4. It is in the heart of Edinburgh, just off Princes Street and is spacious, and ideal for the family, with a three-course children's menu for £1.45.

Gretna Green
—
Lauder

GRANTSHOUSE

Cedar Cafeteria, ¼m S off A1
(Grantshouse 270)
Open: Mon–Fri 7am–7pm, Sat–Sun 9am–6pm

[P][&]

A small, family-run roadside café which impressed our inspector with its spotlessness, and the fact that all food is freshly prepared on the premises. Main courses always available are roast beef, mixed grill, gammon steak and sirloin steak from £1.50–£2.50. The hot and cold sweets are well above the usual cafeteria standard, with fresh strawberries and ice cream or banana split firm favourites with the many regular customers.

GRETNA GREEN

The Auld Smiddy Restaurant, Headless Cross
(Gretna 365)
Open: Summer 8am–7pm

[P][S][&]

Although you can no longer elope here with your sweetheart, you can enjoy a pleasant snack or full meal at very reasonable prices. Tucked just behind the world-famous blacksmith's shop, this low-ceilinged restaurant is festooned with brass bric-à-brac. A three-course lunch (which might consist of soup, roast beef with Yorkshire pudding, followed by apple tart) is still under £3, so even with coffee (28p) and a glass of wine (55p) you are well within the budget. In the early evening a high tea menu offers a variety of grills and cold meats from £2.50.

JEDBURGH

The Carter's Rest ✕
Abbey Place
(Jedburgh 3414)
Open: Mon–Sun 12noon–2pm, 6–9pm, closed Sun in Winter

[A][P][&]

This restaurant is built of stone plundered from the nearby Abbey, whose ruins dominate the outlook, and was the local 'Penny' School for a hundred years or so from 1779, then a real Carter's Rest for patrons of Jedburgh's horse fair. Today it offers excellent grills, bar lunches and dinners. You can eat à la carte very well for around £6 here. There is a special menu in the evening consisting of a main course, coffee and a glass of wine for £6, or make do with bar snacks. Hot buffet lunch specials include beef olives with trimmings at about £2.40, a £1.20 ham omelette, American-style burgers made with Scotch beef or a fresh Eyemouth haddock fish platter.

KIRKCUDBRIGHT

The Coffee Pot, 5 Castle Street
(Kirkcudbright 30569)
Open: Summer only Mon–Sat 10am–5pm, 6.45–8.30pm

[C][S][&]

The Coffee Pot with its bow-windowed frontage is a snug little restaurant just across from the old castle in the centre of historic Kirkcudbright. George and Rona Bower have devised an interesting à la carte menu to tempt the tourist and shopper alike at prices of around £5. Starters include mushrooms provençale and seven main courses include fried local trout, seafood crêpes and chicken Kiev. Raspberries St Moritz and crêpes Suzette are desserts.

LAUDER

The Black Bull Hotel
(Lauder 208)
Open: Mon–Sun 8am–9.30pm and normal licensing hours

[A][P][&]

The jangle of harness and sound of posthorns no longer announces the arrival of travellers in need of rest and refreshment, yet The Black Bull retains the atmosphere of a coaching inn. Built in the 18th century, it survived the coming of the railways and has been revived and modernised to cope with the swing back to road transport. In the elegant dining room you can enjoy lunch and dinner at

---

The Cedar Cafeteria
Grantshouse, Berwickshire

Telephone: Grantshouse (036 15) 270

¼ mile south of Grantshouse on A1 in lay-by on old road
All home baking and local produce used, vegetables and meat etc.

Opening hours
Mon-Fri 7am-7pm
Sat-Sun 9am-6pm

Coaches by appointment only

Under the personal supervision of the Locke family;
Jean, Ray, Kevin & Adrian
Cooked meals served all day.

around £4.50 with five or six main dishes including roasts. For a cold meal or snack, try the Harness Room Grill, where you can feast your eyes on relics of coaching days whilst enjoying your choice from the bar menu. This includes a three-course lunch at around £2.55 and ploughman's at about £1.

LINLITHGOW

Lochside Larder, 286 High Street (Linlithgow 7275)
Open: Mon–Tue 9am–6pm,
Wed–Sat 9am–6pm, 7–9.30pm,
Sun 11am–6pm, 7–9.30pm

P S

Linlithgow
—
Musselburgh

This small, neatly decorated restaurant and adjoining take-away bar is situated in a small shopping and residential complex between the main road and the banks of Linlithgow Loch. Both snacks and full meals are available. The daily menu offers soup at 25p, pizza, scampi, a daily dish and salads are all under £2 and include chips and vegetables. Cheesecake and gâteaux are around 45p. The dinner menu has a good range of starters from 50p. The fish, chicken and pizza dishes are all under £4 and steaks are around £5. All main courses are served with sauté and new potatoes, but vegetables are extra. Sweets are mainly around £1. Coffee is 40p and wine 55p a glass.

MUSSELBURGH

Caprice, 198 High Street
(031-665 2991)
Open: Summer Mon–Sat 12noon–12mdnt, Sun 4pm–12mdnt, Winter Mon–Sat 12noon–2.30pm, 5.30–12mdnt, Sun 4pm–12mdnt

P S

'Our succulent pizzas are cooked in the traditional manner in a wood-fired oven to give them that extra taste of quality. Even

---

LOCHSIDE LARDER
Licensed Restaurant

286 HIGH STREET, LINLITHGOW
☎ **(050 684) 7275**
MORNING COFFEE 9am - Noon
AFTERNOON TEAS
MEALS ARE SERVED FROM Noon - 6pm
TAKE-AWAY PIZZAS, BAKED POTATOES
SOFT DRINKS AND ICE CREAM
ARE AVAILABLE ANYTIME
EVENING MEALS FROM WEDNESDAY - SUNDAY
7pm 'TILL LAST ORDERS AT 9.30pm
PHONE NOW FOR A RESERVATION

Caprice

Licensed Restaurant and Pizarama

**198 High Street,
Musselburgh
Tel: 031-665 2991**

Choose from the sixteen different home-made pizzas, table d'hôte lunch menu or the extensive à la carte menu. Children catered for. Entertainment.
Under the personal supervision of the proprietor Cavalier Victor Alongi and his sons Alfredo and Vito.

Newcastleton — Portpatrick

the wood used, Scottish pine, is chosen because it adds the required flavour....' That's how Cavalier Victor Alongi introduces his customers to his pizzeria cum Italian restaurant. The 16 different home-made pizza specialities have deservedly gained Victor and his son Alfredo a renowned reputation. A medium-sized pizza (12in diameter) provides a very generous meal for the average eater, but for those with voracious appetites the large pizza (15in) will prove a challenge. A choice from the extensive à la carte menu costs around £5 but two table d'hôte lunch menus offer good value at around £1.50 for three courses.

NEWCASTLETON

The Dormouse, Main Street, on B6357 (Liddesdale 694)
Open: Mon–Sat 10am–5pm, Sun 11am–6pm, Wed, Fri & Sat 7.30–8.30pm

[P] [&]

Home-cooking and baking at their best are the trademarks of this little country-cottage restaurant/tea-room. Whether you stop for morning coffee, afternoon tea with home-made scones and cakes, or a full lunch or dinner you'll find the quality second to none and the service friendly. For lunch, try the home-made soup (45p), a rainbow trout served with a selection of vegetables (£2) and profiteroles (65p). The dinner menu could include home-made pâté, pork fillets à la Dormouse (cooked in cream sauce, with wine, green peppers and herbs), whiskied oranges with brandy-snaps, and coffee – all for just £6. It is essential to book for dinner.

NORTH BERWICK

Searles, 1 Station Hill (North Berwick 3622)
Open: Mon–Thu 10am–6pm, Fri & Sat 10am–5pm (Dinners 7pm–9pm), Sun 11am–6pm, (During July & August open to 8pm)

[P] [&]

This small, street level coffee shop/restaurant is a family business specialising in home baking and freshly cooked meals; snacks are also available. The atmosphere changes on Fridays and Saturdays when a three-course dinner is served. The fixed price menu includes a sherry, coffee and VAT at £5.60 per person. A small selection of wines is available with meals.

PORTPATRICK

The Old Mill House (Portpatrick 358)
Open: Apr–Oct Mon–Sun 10.30am–11pm

[P] [&]

This picturesque, whitewashed old mill house, set amid beautiful gardens complete with trout stream and heated outdoor pool, ground its last barley in 1929 and the miller is said to haunt the premises still. Food includes a table d'hôte lunch menu of good British fare costing something over £3.25. A luscious Galloway steak can be sampled from the à la carte menu for about £5.25 and fresh Solway salmon is another tempting local dish. An interesting bar menu offers a wide selection of less pricey dishes including special children's meals for around 85p for such favourites as bangers, fish or pizza fingers with salad or chips. A three-course children's menu for younger hungers costs around £1.75. High teas range from around £3–£5.50 according to the main dish chosen, with cheese and egg salad at the lower end and grilled sirloin steak at the top. This price is inclusive of hot home-baked scones with butter and jam, home-baked cakes and tea. All hot meals are served up to 10.30pm.

Crown Hotel (Portpatrick 409)
Open: Mon–Sun 12noon–2pm, 6–10pm

[P] [S] [&]

Walk through the bars of this harbour-front hotel to a room at the back where the coffee house is decorated in art nouveau 1920s style, with oval tables and willow chairs. At the far end is a lovely small conservatory area with doors leading out into the garden. Service is informal and the food is excellent. A typical three-course meal could consist of hearty soup at 45p, beef hot pot at £2 and profiteroles at 85p. The restaurant also offers a selection of toasted sandwiches from 60p or Danish open sandwiches on brown bread from 60p.

Meals on wheels?

'Isn't it strange how the worst motorway accidents occur in the kitchens?'

DRIVE & TRAIL is the AA's monthly motoring magazine for everyone on the road — whether you're just a motorist with an insatiable hunger for the best car tests in the business, or a caravanning-camping fresh-air fiend with a taste for *al fresco* eating. You can have the full 12-course subscription by post for just £9.95 *service compris* direct from the AA, or buy it *à la carte* — 85p from your bookstall. *Bon appetit!*

drive AND TRAIL AA

MONTHLY

GLASGOW AND THE WEST

Strathclyde, as the administrative region of much of western Scotland is known, is enormous – not only the area, but also its contents. It has everything from agricultural land in Ayrshire to a mass of industry and commerce in and around Glasgow; from innumerable islands scattered haphazardly in the sea, to umpteen mountains (including one, Ben Cruachan, which has a power station inside it); from rivers and lochs galore, to a great deal of forest.

Glasgow is the birthplace of the great Cunarders, including the *QE2*. It is the city where everybody is supposed to get drunk in Sauchiehall Street on Saturday nights; the metropolis whose architecture is scorned by aesthetes. All of which is very unfair to it. There are some delightful streets and squares and most of its citizens are temperate and hardworking.

The Clyde is one of those rivers that get better and better as they approach the sea.

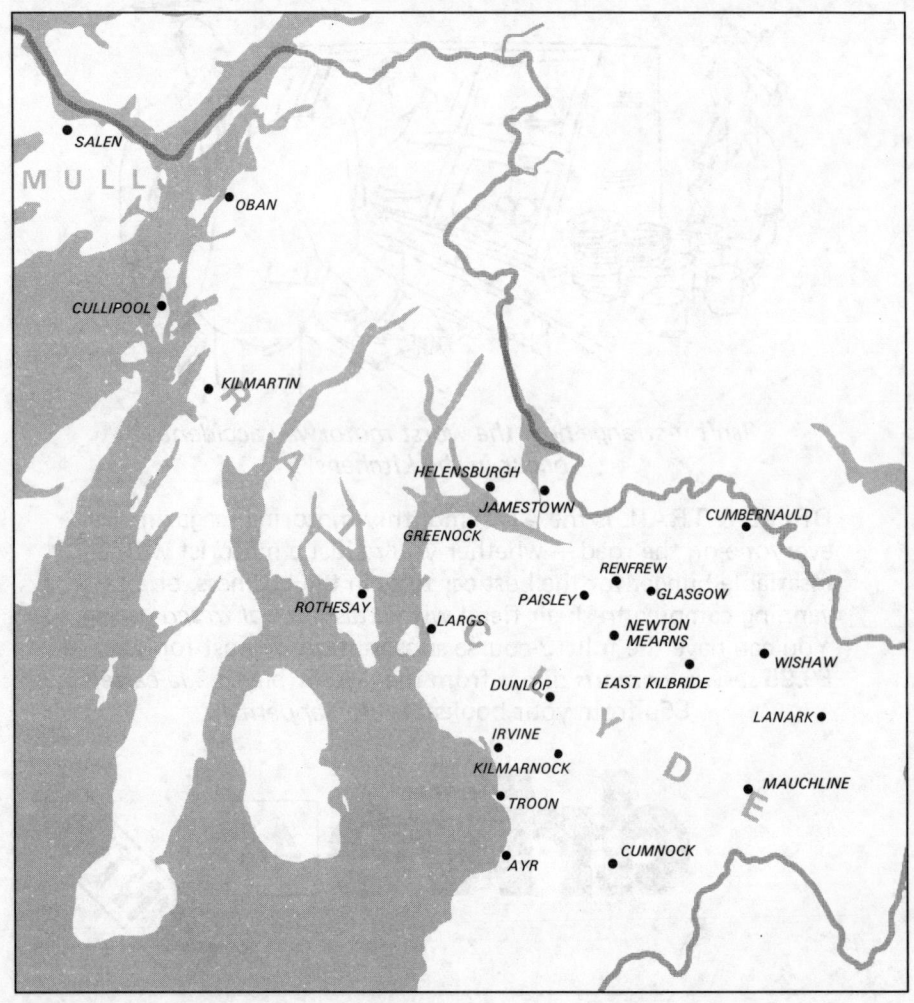

It used to be crowded with pleasure steamers. Now, alas, they are rarities. People, it seems, prefer to travel by car. North of the Clyde, nature goes wild and the mountains seem to multiply as you go north, and so do the lochs, especially those that have eaten deep into the coastline.

Among the litter of islands, Iona was the first foothold of Christianity in the northern parts of the future UK. The word was carried from Ireland in AD 563 by Saint Columba, who set up a base there. Another lozenge of land that has helped to ease the human predicament is Islay, where several distilleries produce fine malt whiskies.

The Gaelic for whisky is *uisge beatha*, meaning the 'water of life'. Originally, all whisky was malt. But, in 1830, a former excise officer named Coffey invented a new kind of still that produced 'grain whisky' – grain, that's to say, blended with malt. The advantages were that it needed only one distillation (malt requires two). Consequently, more of it was produced in less time at less cost. This should have been the cue for Scotch (as we should now call it) to become universally popular, but English law prohibited the import of it in bottles until Gladstone fathered the Spirit Act of 1860. After that, Scotch, properly packaged, went south and caught on; there are now about 3000 brands on the market. The malt whiskies are much finer and consequently more expensive. Each has a distinctive regional character and taste. It is well worth tasting as many kinds as possible to discover your favourite, though the experiment may take some time as there are more than 100 of them.

Whisky, of course, is an industry you find throughout Scotland. So, indeed, can you buy kippers more or less wherever you go, though few are finer than those that bear the name Loch Fyne, an arm of water that pierces the coast due north of the Island of Arran and pushes its way inland for about 35 miles.

Ayr — Cumbernauld

AYR

The Coffee Club, 37 Beresford Terrace
(Ayr 63239)
Open: Mon–Sat 10am–10pm

P S

This small and friendly establishment is situated near to Burns' Statue Square in the centre of Ayr. The clubby atmosphere extends to comfortable seating and low-level tables, making this a place to relax while you take your meal. An interesting variety of snacks, salads and light meals are served with a creative flair. Snacks range from pizza to substantial open sandwiches, clubhouse sandwiches, American beefburgers and savoury flan with salad. Sweets include pastries, and fruit flan at around 60p.

The Copperfield, 242 Prestwick Road
(Ayr 267095)
Open: Summer Mon–Sat 10am–8pm,
Winter Mon–Sat 10am–5pm

C P S 🍴

David himself would have felt quite at home amid the dark wooden beams of this pseudo-Dickensian eating house. Doubtless he would have tucked into home-baked goodies (proprietor Mrs Holland's forté) with relish. Menu prices, although alas a long way from Mr Micawber's ideas on costs, are very low indeed. A full three-course meal is still only around £2 – remarkable considering all prices include VAT. Meals are traditional – roast beef, potatoes and veg, haddock, chips and veg or ham and peach salad – the kind of choice to suit a whole family's tastes. Even sirloin steak with all the trimmings comes to under £5 with soup to start with and strawberry flan and cream to finish.

Olde Worlde Inn, 48 Newmarket Street
(Ayr 62392)
Open: Mon–Sat 12noon–2.30pm,
5–11pm, Sun 5–10pm

C 🎵 P S 🍴

Whether Robbie Burns, whose statue stands some 100 yards away, would have felt at home in this 'olde worlde inn' is debatable, but he would have been assured of a good basic meal at a fair price. This member of the Reo Stakis chain has panelled walls and beams, with a rough stone archway creating a break in the interior. Main course prices include a starter, but sweets are extra. However, haddock, chicken, gammon or beefsteak burger, all for around £4 should fill you up and keep you within the budget. The special lunchtime menu is particularly good value, at around £2, and includes in the main course choice scampi and prawn salad.

Plough Inn, 231 High Street
(Ayr 262578)
Open: Mon–Sun 11am–2.30pm,
5–11pm

C S 🍴

This Reo Stakis 'Olde Worlde' Inn is typical of the chain, with almost a North American flavour in its mellow lighting and unostentatious but comfortable furnishings. In the restaurant, a waitress-served meal of Scotch broth, prawn cocktail, pâté or fruit juice, followed by a main course such as steak, chicken or haddock costs around £4 (including appropriate vegetables, potatoes and a roll or chunky bread and butter). Apple pie and cream or Black Forest gâteau cost around 75p. There is a three-course children's menu too, for little more than £1, making this a good place to take the family. House wines are available by the carafe or glass.

The Tudor Restaurant, 6–8 Beresford Terrace
(Ayr 61404)
Open: Mon–Sat 9am–9pm

P S 🍴

The Tudor Restaurant may not be authentic 16th century, but for the family it offers a good wholesome meal at very reasonable prices. A table d'hôte lunch is still around £2.15 and includes soup or fruit juice, a main course such as beefsteak pie, cold meat with salad, or haddock and chips, and a sweet or cheese. There is a special children's menu at around £1.35. High tea, which comes with a pot of tea, bread, scone, jam and cake (all home-baked), gives a considerable choice, from eggs on toast at around £1.95 to entrecôte steak at around £3.80 and again there is a children's version for considerably less. The restaurant is not licensed.

CULLIPOOL

Longhouse Buttery, Isle of Luing
(Luing 209)
Open: Mon–Sun 11am–5pm, Thu–Sat 7.30–11pm

P

It's well worth the journey from the Scottish mainland across the Island of Seil and then the 90-second car ferry to this beautiful little island of Luing. The high spot of a visit must be this converted, whitewashed croft which incorporates a white and pine-clad restaurant with dispense bar and small gallery where partner Edna Whyte displays and sells gifts bearing her 'Old Rectory' designs. The other half of the partnership, Audrey Stone, is to be seen serving the delicious meals including such delicacies as buttery venison pâté, and fresh Luing prawns, served on wholemeal bread with crispy salad. Home-made sweets include the mouthwatering triple meringue with cream for £1.05. A three-course lunch with coffee and wine costs in the region of £4.95. Unfortunately, the special dinner, including fresh lobster or salmon, would over-stretch our pocket.

CUMBERNAULD

Old World Inn, Allanfauld Road
(Cumbernauld 27509)
Open: Mon–Sat 12noon–2.30pm,
5–11pm, Sun 12noon–2.30pm,
6.30–11pm

C P 🍴

Situated on the west side of Cumbernauld, on a hill overlooking the main Glasgow/Stirling road, this restaurant is typical of the Stakis Steakhouse chain to which it belongs. Decorated in mock-Tudor style with beams and dark-wood furnishings, the room exudes a restful, relaxing atmosphere. Each main course on the

---

Silver Moon

LICENSED CHINESE RESTAURANT
5-7 NEW KIRK LANE, BEARSDEN CROSS, GLASGOW.
Telephone: 041-942 4592

Supreme service with excellent surroundings.

Traditional Chinese cuisine now being served and a separate section for Take-Away service.

Orders by telephone are welcome.

menu incorporates in its price a choice of starters (farmhouse broth, country pâté, prawn cocktail or orange juice). Haddock, gammon steak and roast half chicken, all with suitable accompaniments, cost around £4.25, and for around £5.50 you could enjoy a ½lb prime Angus steak. To finish with there is a choice of dessert or the cheeseboard for about 75p, or a speciality ice cream for around 75p. Children get a good deal here with three courses, plus roll and butter and a choice of cola or orange drink, for less than £1.50.

CUMNOCK

The Royal Hotel ★★
1 Glaisnock Street
(Cumnock 20822)
Open: Mon–Sat 12noon–2pm, 5–6.30pm, 7–9pm, Sun 12.30–2.30pm, 5–6.30pm, 7–9pm

P S 🍴

It is a well-deserved compliment to this traditional and comfortable hotel that local business people are regular customers. In the attractively lit dining room, a conventional choice of dishes is very well presented, and very well priced. Three lunch courses focusing on roast sirloin (with perhaps banana fritters or green figs with cream to follow) will not cost much over £3.50, and even if you go for the fresh salmon, you'll still be spending well under £5. The very substantial high tea might cost £5 for a mixed grill, tea, scones, and cakes. Dinner will be around the £6 mark.

DUMFRIES

Kit's Place, 9 George St Meuse
(Dumfries 67450)
Open: Mon 9.30am–2.30pm, Tue–Sat 9.30am–2.30pm, 7–9pm

🎵 P S 🍴

This former stables and coach-house has been renovated and converted into a bistro restaurant. The décor is simple but effective, with natural stone walls, and various objets d'art; local artists and craftsmen exhibit their work here. Good home-cooking is the aim of the restaurant. A three-course meal of pâté maison, chili con carne, served with potatoes and a selection of vegetables and salads, followed by cheesecake would come to around £4.45.

DUNLOP

Burnhouse Manor Farm Hotel,
Burnhouse
(Dunlop 406)
Open: Tue–Sat 12noon–2pm, 5–9pm, Sun 5–9pm

P 🍴

Just off the A736 Paisley/Irvine Road, this large restaurant has tartan carpeting and modern furnishings. The menu offers many familiar items ranging from chicken, lamb cutlets, scampi and salads to duck in orange sauce and steaks. A three-course evening meal can come

Cumnock — Glasgow

within our budget, but the steak dishes are over our limit. A three-course lunch of soup, lasagne, apple pie and ice-cream and coffee is under £3.50. High teas from £2.20 for beefburgers to £5.50 for sirloin steak include chips, vegetables, tea, toast and cakes. There is also a children's menu.

EAST KILBRIDE

Hong Kong, 46–48 Kirkton Park
(East Kilbride 20112)
Open: Mon–Sat 12noon–12mdnt, Sun 2pm–12mdnt

C 🎵 P

A patio garden allows al fresco eating in summer, a touch which gives this Chinese restaurant a certain individuality. Inside, décor is unmistakably oriental with golden dragons set against black walls, and the à la carte is extensive and fairly typical, but it's the speciality teas, desserts and the extensive wine list which makes this restaurant stand out from the rest. Excellent value is the three-course business lunch at only £2.20, or the tasty salads and ploughman's at 80p–£1.30. You'll have to choose carefully if you're to keep within the limit on the à la carte menu but the set dinners, comprising six courses, coffee with cream and mint chocolate, offer excellent value at around £7. If you forgo the starter on the à la carte menu you might just afford a special sweet such as the Hong Kong Special – a delicate concoction of peaches, sparkling wine, soda water and angostura bitters costing £2.70 for two persons. Otherwise save your pennies for one of the 16 unusual teas such as 'gunpowder green tea' described as an 'attractive clear fragrant liquor' at £1 per pot for two, and a cocktail from the imaginative list of 29.
See advert on p. 188

GLASGOW

Ad-Lib (Mid Atlantic), 111 Hope Street
(041-248 7102)
Open: Mon–Sat 12noon–2am, Sun 6pm–1am

C 🎵 S 🍴

With stainless steel floor (yes floor), painted brick and hessian-hung walls covered with original movie posters of yesteryear, checked tablecloths and excellent service from friendly staff, this American diner, opposite Glasgow Central Sation, is a good place for a quick lunch or a leisurely evening meal. A selection of American hamburgers, served with chips, salad and a choice of pickles, is available. Hamburgers are available at prices from around £2.50. Main courses include kebabs, vegetarian pancakes, and Texas-style chili and prices range from £2 to around £6 – the latter for a T-bone steak with accompanying vegetables. Sweets

include pancakes with hot fudge and cream, and American cheesecake with fruit and cream, which explains perhaps, the diner's popularity with children. A business lunch of ¼lb hamburger with potatoes and salad, pancake, and coffee is available at the £2 mark – excellent value.

Bees Nees, 158–60 Main Street,
Alexandria
(Alexandria 51427/52530)
Open: Mon–Thu 10am–3pm, 5–11pm, Fri & Sat 10am–3pm, 5pm–1am

🎵 P 🍴

This modern Greek restaurant has a smart lounge bar and is furnished with banquette booths on a quarry-tiled floor, paintings of Greece are displayed on the walls. The day menu operates from 10am–3pm. Soup, a main course of haddock, chicken, hamburgers or a choice of the Greek dishes, such as moussaka, keftedes, pastitsio or dolmades, with a sweet, coffee and a glass of wine will cost around £4–£5. The dinner menu offers more variety and with care you can still keep within the budget. On Friday and Saturday evenings there is a disco dinner.

Le Bistro Metropolitain de Paris,
115 North Street, Charing Cross. Due to move to: 415 Sauchiehall Street (1st floor) early 1983
(041-221 2922)
Open: Mon–Fri 12noon–2.30pm, 5–11.30pm, Sat 12noon–11.30pm, Sun 7–11pm

🎵 P

Good, honest food is served here with, with the emphasis clearly on prix raisonables, you could well imagine yourself eating in a quiet corner of Paris. The gingham tablecloths, French posters and notices as well as the music of Edith Piaf all add to the atmosphere. Don't expect anything fancy, because this is not the objective. The food is simply cooked, often in traditional French style. Lunch-time prices are most reasonable and from the blackboard menu you could choose grilled pork chop for £1.60, carbonnade of beef at £3.15 or entrecôte au poivre at £3.65. For your sweet, cheese and patisserie aux pommes, both at 70p, are also good value. Wine is 60p a glass. There is a jazz guitarist on Tuesday evenings and occasionally an accordionist.

La Buca, 191 Hope Street
(041-332 7120)
Open: Mon–Sat 12noon–11pm

🍴

There is a definite Italian air to this pleasant pizzeria in the heart of Glasgow, accentuated by the Italian background music and the red-shirted Italian waiters. Pizzas are freshly prepared and range in price from around £1.10 for pizza Napolitana to £1.40 for pizza Quattro Stagioni, a delicious concoction of ham, olives, anchovies and mozzarella cheese. With a starter of insalata di mare

Savour Eastern Flavour

Savour delights suited to the taste of a mandarin in the Hong Kong restaurant.

Although a little off the main thoroughfare, the Hong Kong is heading in the direction for the connoisseur. It is a Chinese restaurant that is aiming for individuality.

The Hong Kong have concocted a menu that is easily on par with others and includes a few dishes special to themselves for European and Chinese tastes. What really distinguishes the Hong Kong from others is its astounding wine list, and inventive cocktails. You could be about to spoil yourself if you dine at the Hong Kong.

HONG KONG RESTAURANT

**46-48 KIRKTON PARK
EAST KILBRIDE
Telephone 20112**

Glasgow

(seafood salad) at about £1.50 and figs with fresh cream for dessert for around 65p, a satisfying three-course meal here need cost no more than £2.50. If you don't like pizza there are many other grills or pasta dishes to choose from such as sirloin steak with salad (more expensive at £3.80 or so) or lasagne all forno at £1.50.

Copra, 336 Argyle Street
(041-221 2460)
Open: Mon–Sat 9am–7pm
C S

Mr Joe Guidi has acquired a loyal and regular clientele since his family took over the Copra almost 20 years ago. Regular favourites such as lamb chops (two) and spaghetti bolognese appear on the otherwise varied menu each day, but there is also an extensive selection of entrées that changes daily offering such dishes as curried chicken, grilled rainbow trout with lemon or roast lamb. With both starters and sweets at around 50p it is not impossible to have a very satisfying meal here for around £2.50. Whilst this restaurant closes early, Mr Guidi also operates, and welcomes you to the Alhambra Restaurant, 350 Argyle Street, which stays open until 10.30pm and offers a similar menu.

Cul de Sac, 44 Ashton Lane, Hillhead
(041-334 4749)
Open: Mon–Sat 10am–12mdnt,
Sun 12noon–12mdnt
♫ P

This continental-style crêperie has an informal atmosphere and is popular with businessmen, shoppers and students alike. The menu is based on crêpes: savoury ones range from £2.15 for cheese and ham, to £2.75 for seafood and avocado and sweet crêpes (including bananas and rum) are around £1.25. Omelettes and tartes are under £2 and steaks just under £4. Coffee is 35p–45p and a glass of wine 65p.

Delta Restaurant, 283 Sauchiehall Street
(041-332 3661)
Open: Mon–Sat 10am–7.30pm
♫ S

Situated at the western end of Sauchiehall Street, this tartan-floored basement restaurant with pine-clad walls welcomes you with soft music for a three-course meal which includes such wholesome dishes as Loch Fyne herrings in oatmeal or sizzling roast pork with apple sauce at around £3. Smart waitresses serve morning coffee, lunch and, after three o'clock, high tea consists of a main dish such as fried fillet of haddock with French fried potatoes plus a pot of tea and buttered toast for about £2.40.

Epicures Bistro, 46 West Nile Street
(041-221 7488)
Open: Mon–Sat 8.30am–6pm
S

A first-floor restaurant usefully sited in the heart of the shopping centre, Epicures has an attractive tiled floor and director's chair seating. If you're lucky you can enjoy your meal in a window seat overlooking West Nile Street. Food is reasonably priced and the menu offers some interesting dishes. Try smoked haddock mousse, a delicately flavoured mousse made with fresh cream, eggs and smoked haddock, followed by crêpe poulet forestière, savoury pancakes filled with chicken, peppers, tomatoes, onions, bacon and other vegetables, and finish with Martian Moondust, chocolate ice-cream, banana, pineapples, fresh whipped cream, chocolate sauce, ground almonds, sprinkled cocoa and cherries, all for well under £5. Attentive and fast service.

Hansom Bar, The Fountain Restaurant, 2 Woodside Crescent
(041-332 6396)
Open: Mon–Fri 12noon–2.15pm,
5–9pm, Sat 5–9pm
C ♫ S

Not so much a bar, more a sort of bistro is the Hansom, downstairs in the elegant Georgian building which houses the upmarket Fountain Restaurant. There is always a good choice of cooked dishes available, such as mussel and onion stew at around £2.50 and Hansom Pie at about £2.95, for example. If you are hungry after 9pm then pâté and toast and cheese and biscuits are available. The Hansom is very popular and inclined to be crowded at lunchtime, but the atmosphere is friendly and relaxed nevertheless.

Massimo's, 465 Clarkston Road, Muirend
(041-637 8568)
Open: Mon–Sat 10am–8pm

This simple eating house on the south side of the city puts the emphasis on quality and value for money. All food is freshly prepared daily and this is a place where the proprietor always finds time to chat with his guests and thank them for their custom. The almost obligatory chianti-bottle lights stand on clean pine tables with benches which seat around 30 people. Minestrone soup is a 50p starter and roast beef salad (£1.60) is an example of the amazingly inexpensive main course. As there's no sweet above 50p you'll have a job to spend even £4 per head.

Moussaka House, 36 Kelvingrove Street
(041-332 2510)
Open: Mon–Sat 12noon–2.30pm,
6–12mdnt, Sun 6.30–11pm
C ♫ P

'The best value in town' is the claim made for this restaurant's lunchtime menu at about £2 – and they could be right. As the name suggests, a variety of moussaka dishes are the main feature, but kebab, stuffed pepper, or plainer dishes are also available. Soup and sweet are kept simple. It should be easy to choose an appetising meal of Greek specialities for about £5 from the à la carte. Try houmous (chick pea 'pâté') at about 75p, moussaka special (mince, aubergines, courgettes, potatoes, cheese and tomatoes) for about £2.75 and a sweet from the trolley for about 75p. A red and brown colour scheme, a plastic vine draped over a wooden archway and Greek music contribute to the Mediterranean atmosphere.

The Pancake Place, 8–12 Stockwell Street
(041-552 4528)
Open: Mon–Sat 9.30am–6.30pm,
Sun 12noon–5pm
♫ P S

Just around the corner from one of the city's busiest shopping streets is this attractive restaurant serving pancakes 'just like your mother's'. Full-size savoury pancakes are under £2 and snack-size just 90p. Try the Rocky Mountain Burger at £1.60 – two pancakes, layered with two beefburgers and topped with a cheese sauce. Sweet pancakes, for those not watching their waistlines are from £1.15 with smaller portions from 55p.

Pizza Park, 515 Sauchiehall Street
(041-221 5967)
Open: Mon–Sun 10am–11.30pm
P

At the western end of Sauchiehall Street this bright, airy restaurant attracts office workers and shoppers alike. There is a good selection of pizzas, from £1.50–£2.90, and also burgers, chilli, barbecue spare ribs and spaghetti bolognese all for less than £3. For starters and desserts, try corn on the cob and strawberry cheesecake, all around £1. There is a small selection of wines and beers.

Ramana, 427 Sauchiehall Street
(041-332 2528/2590)
Open: Mon–Sun 12noon–12mdnt
C ♫ P S

Never tried Indian food? Try Ramana then, for the well-designed menu explains what each dish contains and how it is cooked. The lounge bar, too, is well-designed with lush Kashmir furniture. Tandoori dishes (cooked in a charcoal-fired clay oven) are the house speciality – there's chicken tandoori with salad at around £4.25 or sheesh kebab Turkish (made with fillet steak) served with rice, salad and sauce at £5.25. And especially recommended for the 'beginner' are birianies and pillaus, priced between about £2.25 (for vegetable pillau) and £3.15 (for prawn birani). If you're still not convinced that Indian food is for you, there's a list of Western dishes too, so you can choose fish and chips or grilled steak if you must.

The business person's lunch at around £1.80 is very popular – doubtless for the oriental atmosphere which wafts the diner away from Glasgow for a little while, as well as for the good, low-priced food.

Secrets, 1487 Gt Western Road
(041-334 9491)
Open: Mon–Thu 12noon–11pm, Fri & Sat 12noon–12mdnt, Sun 6.30–10pm

C 🎵 P ✻

This ultra-modern restaurant diner is part of the Esquire House complex. The daytime menu offers soup at 60p, burgers (£1.95–£3.45), pizzas around £2 and chicken or sole goujons, just over £3, and a daily 'Chef's Special'. Steaks cost from £3.80. The extended evening menu offers a good variety of dishes – but take care or you will exceed the budget.

Silver Moon, 5 New Kirk Lane, Bearsden
(041-942 4592)

🎵 P ✻

This nicely-appointed Cantonese restaurant is tucked away in the middle of Bearsden's town centre. However, once you have found it you will not forget it. It is furnished with comfortably padded chairs and the walls are hung with Chinese paintings and embroidery. The staff are friendly and attentive and the food is interesting and good value for money. The business lunch is £2.20 and in the evening an extensive à la carte

Greenock
—
Helensburgh

menu includes grilled chicken Peking style at £2.80.
See advert on p. 186

Stakis Steakhouse, Great Western Road
(041-339 8811)
Open: Mon–Sat 12noon–2.30pm, Sun 12.30–2.30pm, Mon–Sun 5–11pm

C 🎵 P ✻

This steakhouse (part of a popular chain) is situated on the ground floor of the recently rebuilt Grosvenor Hotel which was destroyed in a fire in 1978. The steakhouse is decorated in the Victorian style, and the service is fast, friendly and attentive. The normal steakhouse menu is available, offering a wide choice of main courses, but for a three-course meal within our budget, with coffee and a glass of wine, you must choose something other than steak.

GREENOCK
Bangalore Indian Restaurant, 119 West Blackhall Street
(Greenock 84355/6)
Open: Mon–Wed 12noon–12mdnt, Thu–Sat 12noon–12.30am, Sun 5–12mdnt

C 🎵 P ✻

Just off the main Glasgow–Gourock road

is this modern Indian restaurant. Decorated in traditional style, the interior is dimly lit and the walls have dark flock wallpaper decorated with Asian paintings. There is seating for about 100 at white-clothed tables; some in cosy alcoves offer a more intimate dining place. An extensive menu of Indian dishes is offered with prices around £1.70 onwards per main dish; beef roghan josh, a spicy dish in tomato and onion sauce, is recommended. Tandoori specialities such as shaslik or tandoori chicken are about £3.50. Chicken jal frazy or chicken begum behar are only around £2.50. The business person's lunch is excellent value at around £2 for three courses.

HELENSBURGH
Sangam Indian Restaurant, 45 Sinclair Street
(Helensburgh 71650/4817)
Open: Sun–Thu 5pm–12.30am, Fri & Sat 12noon–1am

C P S ✻

You'll find this spacious, well-appointed restaurant on the first-floor of a corner site in Helensburgh's main shopping area. Maroon wallpaper and curtaining, plus imitation oil lamps, create a cosy, intimate atmosphere. A variety of typical Asian food (for instance, beef byriani or shami kebab with salad – both around £2.90) is agumented by 'western dishes' such as steak and chips (£5.10) or prawn

---

RESTAURANT
RAMANA

*Ramana was the Hindu God of Food —
What better name for
"the best Indian restaurant in town*"?
Now featuring also the Colonial Bar.
Vox Populi.

427 Sauchiehall Street, Glasgow.   Telephone 041-332-2590

BANGALORE INDIAN RESTAURANT
119 West Blackhall Street, Greenock.
Telephone Greenock 84355/6

Enjoy a superb Indian meal in traditional surroundings
TANDOORI SPECIALITIES

Open:
Monday - Wednesday 12 noon - midnight
Thursday - Saturday 12 noon - 12.30am
Sunday 5pm - Midnight

Irvine — Largs

omelette (£2.70). A midday feature is the special three-course lunch, which is very good value for money.

IRVINE
The Coffee Club, 142 High Street
Open: Mon – Sat 10am – 10pm

[S][&]

As in the other Ayrshire Coffee Clubs, this neat, modern restaurant with friendly waitress service offers an exciting selection of snacks, light meals and desserts at prices well within our budget. Fish and grills served with vegetables and chips are all under £2 and an assortment of flans and pies are served with a choice of salad and coleslaw, crunchy fried potatoes, or hot Vienna herb bread, for around £1.50 or so. Salads, omelettes, pizza or 'foreign foods' such as chili con carne with rice or moussaka and salad, are all under £2. For a meal on bread try one of the 14 'Danwiches' – open sandwiches with a mouthwatering variety of toppings starting from around 95p. In the 'children's corner', there is Paddington's Plateful (gammon, pineapple and chips) or Snoopy's Surprise (hamburger, beans and chips) for about 90p.

JAMESTOWN
Whitelaw's American Diner, 207 Main Street
(Alexandria 54864)
Open: Mon – Fri, Sun 7pm – 1.30am, Sat 5pm – 1.30am

[P][S]

If you like a friendly atmosphere in bright surroundings, this American diner is the answer. Portions are generous and the food is good. Starters such as soup of the day, stuffed peppers and a half portion of chili con carne are almost a meal in themselves. Prices range from 35p to just over £1. As well as the inevitable range of excellent budget burgers found in this style of operation, main dishes include gammon steak with pineapple rings and brown sugar (about £2.95), chicken served with honey (around £3.65) and scampi (less than £3). A selection of desserts include burnt almond parfait at 90p. A glass of wine costs 65p.

KILMARNOCK
The Coffee Club ✕
30 Bank Street
(Kilmarnock 22048)
Open: Mon – Sat 9.30am – 10pm

[♫][P][S][&]

Friendly, speedy service and a pleasant décor, with roughcast walls, alcoves and tiffany lamps make this a popular meeting and eating place. Snacks are served upstairs, while full meals may be enjoyed in the basement. Assorted starters are from 50p – for a choice of soup and fruit juices. Ravioli, corn-on-the-cob, pâté and pickled herrings are among more expensive items. A galaxy of grills from £1.75 – £4.95 offers a Scotsman's grill

(haggis, peas, carrots and chips) or Italian grills (meat balls, onion, tomato sauce and spaghetti) to name a few. Fish dishes and 'a few foreign foods' are also available. Ravioli, lasagne, chili con carne and spaghetti bolognese cost between £1.50 – £1.75. A three-course shopper's lunch costs around £1.75. A delicious selection of desserts is certain to tempt you – lemon meringue pie for only 55p is hard to resist.

KILMARTIN
Kilmartin Hotel
(Kilmartin 244/250)
Open: Mon – Sat 11.30am – 2pm, 6 – 9pm, Sun 12.30 – 2pm, 6.30 – 9pm

[P][&]

Situated some 30 miles south of Oban on the A816, this traditional roadside inn has built up a local reputation for its good food and friendly atmosphere. All items from the extensive light meal menu are served in a simple six-tabled dining area, after you've ordered at the lounge bar. A starter such as home-made soup is 40p, whilst fried, breaded scampi (£2.20) and sirloin steak with onion rings (£4.50) are two of the more popular main dishes. Pavlova is a recommended dessert at 70p. If you book in advance, a more formal meal can be had in an intimate, candlelit dining room, but at £7.15 it's stretching our budget.

LANARK
Silver Bell, 26 Bannatyne Street
(Lanark 3129)
Open: Mon – Sat 11am – 9pm, Sun 12.30 – 2.30pm, 4 – 8pm

[C][P][&]

Situated in the centre of a town that boasts its own racecourse, the Silver Bell takes this as its theme with prints of racehorses decorating the walls. Highbacked chairs and dark beamwork add character, and the warm, relaxed atmosphere is enhanced by the friendly local waitresses. A table d'hôte lunch menu is offered at around £3.25 for three courses such as home-made soup, beef steak pie, followed by pear belle Hélène. Tea or coffee is included in the price. Bar lunches and quick snacks are also available, soup and sweets are 40p, main courses £1.40, hamburgers and snacks are from 65p. The à la carte dinner menu is more extensive with sirloin steak (£6) and rainbow trout (£3.70) featuring on the menu, but be prepared to pay at least £2 more than lunch for your three courses. You may prefer high tea (around £2.70) which includes a main course such as farmhouse grill or French-fried chicken and bacon, tea, scones, cakes and bread.

The Tavern, Riverside Road, Kirkfieldbank
(Lanark 3163/2537)
Open: Mon – Sat 12noon – 3pm, 6.30 – 9pm

[C][♫][P]

Ideal for the motorist, this white-painted tavern has a very popular lounge bar with a small wood-panelled restaurant adjoining. The à la carte lunch and supper menus are very reasonably priced, with the emphasis on grills. French fries, garden peas and carrots are included in the price of all main courses. A plateful of mouth-watering beef steak pie comes at around £2.80. A really satisfying three-course meal can also be enjoyed at somewhere between £2.40 and £3. Basket meals are very popular at around £1.80.

LARGS
Green Shutter Tearoom, 28 Bath Street
(Largs 672252)
Open: Mon – Sun 10am – 6pm, Closed Oct – Mar

[P][&]

Just across the promenade from the sea, this restaurant commands a unique view of the beautiful Isle of Cumbrae. A three-course meal is excellent value – home-made soup of the day is around 45p and a wide selection of grills includes haddock with peas and chips (around £2) or gammon steak with peach (about £2.60). Sweets include home-made apple tart with cream, meringue with fruit and cream and brandy snaps with cream and ice cream – all less than 75p. A special 'Kiddies Corner' menu (for kids of 10 and under) offers beefburgers, sausages, or fish-fingers with peas and chips and ice cream novelties all for about £1.25.

Nardini's, Esplanade
(Largs 674555)
Open: Mon – Sun 12noon – 3pm, 3.30 – 8pm

[♫][P][&]

A popular seaside establishment catering mainly for holidaymakers in the season; but the enterprising proprietor of Nardini's keeps his winter trade going by offering a three-course meal at around £2. Just what you get for this money depends upon the day of the week – fish and chips on Monday, steak and kidney pie on Wednesday, lasagne on Thursday, for instance, but there is a selection of grills, omelettes, etc, if you do not fancy the 'dish of the day'. In the summer you can have a substantial lunch or high tea for well under £5. A variety of salads are on offer at £1.75 and the special children's menu offers smaller portions at smaller prices – for example tomato soup, sausage and beans, and knickerbocker glory (and what meal would please most children more?) would set you back about £1.50. Grown-ups in knickerbockers have to pay over £1.90 for their glory, but there are a number of other tempting sweets for about half that price. You can get dinner here too, served from 8pm to 10pm, but the bill would almost certainly exceed six pounds.

MAUCHLINE

La Candela, 5 Kilmarnock Road
(Mauchline 51015)
On the A76 to Dumfries
Open: Mon–Sun 12noon–2pm,
6.30–1am (last orders 10.30pm)

♬ P ♿

Despite the evident Italian influence, the extensive menu is quite cosmopolitan, with the French and English getting a decent look in. The décor is continental and romantic, with alcoves to ensure privacy. The lunchtime choice is adequate but fairly basic, its great advantage being cost at around £3. The dinner menu is à la carte.

NEWTON MEARNS

The Coffee Club, 114 Ayr Road
(041-639 6888)
Open: Mon–Sat 10am–10.30pm

♬ P S

You'll have to come early for lunch or dinner to this popular, cosy little coffee shop, as demand far outweighs the seating availability. Situated in a block of 10 shops on the main A77 road to Ayr, the soft brown interior with cork tiles and lots of pot plants offers shoppers and travellers alike a peaceful haven in which to relax and enjoy a meal such as soup of the day, egg, cheese and bacon flan served hot with salad and coleslaw, cheesecake and Viennese coffee for around £3.50. The Coffee Club is unlicensed but coffee is, of course, a speciality of the house.

OBAN

The Box Tree, 108 St George Street
(Oban 64641)
Open: Apr–Nov Mon–Sat 9am–10pm,
Sun 6–10pm

S

Simplicity is the attraction of this unlicensed restaurant. Uniformed staff give friendly, attentive service in a floral

Mauchline
—
Oban

wall-papered environment. Sit in your individual dining booth and choose from the short, simple menu. Lunch has an emphasis on salads (about £2), although fried Hebridean haddock (about £2.80) is also available. Dinner includes more expensive scampi and grilled gammon or steak but will still cost around £4 for the three courses. Pâté with oakcakes for a starter sounds a pleasant departure from the norm. Burger snacks and sandwiches are also served if you want to keep the total bill beneath a staggering £2.

The Gallery Restaurant, Gibraltar Street
(Oban 64641)
Open: Apr–Oct Mon–Sun
9.30am–10pm

P S ♿

Iain Reid is justly proud of his smart little restaurant situated in the busy town centre. Open all day, the Gallery offers hot or cold snacks and full three-course meals. In the evening the atmosphere is transformed as lights sparkle on the attractive watercolours adorning the cream walls. The special three-course 'farmhouse' dinner may cost about £4.95, with choices such as scampi or roast chicken. At lunchtime meals cost from £2 upwards. A selection of tempting cheesecakes and gâteaux are available for dessert.

McTavish's Kitchen, George Street
(Oban 63064)
Open: Restaurant Summer Mon–Sun
12noon–2.30pm, 6–10.30pm
Self-service Summer Mon–Sun
9am–10pm, Winter 9am–6pm

♬ S ♿

Oban lives for and by its visitors and no-one does more to provide good wholesome food and entertainment in comfortable and congenial surroundings than James and Jeremy Inglis at McTavish's Kitchen. Their large, modern, purpose-built premises overlooking the sea, houses a downstairs self-service food bar seating 150 and a clean and bright upstairs restaurant with room for

270, as well as the Laird's Bar and the predatorily named Mantrap Bar. Food in both restaurant and self-service is very good of its kind and not expensive. As you might expect, this is the place for Scottish specialities and you can have a three-course meal including 'haggis and neeps' for around £4.50. Table d'hôte lunch and evening meal menus enable you to select three courses and coffee for prices between £3.25 and £5. An added attraction during the summer are the Scottish Evenings featuring piping and highland dance. The unlicensed self-service restaurant offers no-nonsense eating-house fare at very reasonable prices. Helpings are generous and the dishes such as pork chop (£2.10) liver and bacon (£1.85) or haddock and chips (£1.95) are well-cooked and presented with flair.

Soroba House Hotel
(Oban 62628)
Open: Mon–Sun 12noon–2.30pm,
7–11pm

♬ P ♿

Take the A816 Lochgilpead road out of Oban for approximately 1 mile to David and Edyth Hutchinson's Soroba House Hotel, standing in nine acres of its own grounds with commanding views over Oban to Mull. Rebuilt after a fire, this hotel has an attractive restaurant and bar. The restaurant offers a good choice of well prepared and presented food. The lunch menu offers extremely good value and a meal consisting of iced melon, fresh salmon mayonnaise, a sweet from the trolley, a coffee and a glass of wine would cost £5.45. Only very careful choice from the dinner menu will keep you within our limit. Afternoon tea is served between 3.30 and 5pm; high tea between 5 and 6pm, and excellent bar meals are available from 7pm–11pm.

The Thistle Hotel, Restaurant,
Breadalbane Place
(Oban 63132)
Open: Apr–Sept Mon–Sun
12noon–2.30pm, 5–9.30pm

P ♿

The Gallery Restaurant

Proprietor: Iain Reid

**OPEN ALL DAY
AND EVERY DAY**

Hot or cold snacks and full three course meals always available.

CLOSED MID WINTER

Gibraltar Street, Oban, Argyll.
Telephone 64641

192

Paisley — Wishaw

Whatever you do, don't come to Oban without trying the excellent locally-landed seafood. And Robert Silverman's Thistle Restaurant is the place for it. The table d'hôte menu at £4.90 offers a good choice of starters and 14 main courses including fish, roast beef and chicken, minute steak and salads; and a variety of sweets. A two-course special light meal is available between 5–6.30pm with starters around 50p and main courses around £2.

PAISLEY

Cardosi's, 46 Causeyside Street
(041-889 5339)
Open: Mon–Thu 11am–7.30pm, 4.30–11pm

[F][P][S][&]

After about 20 years of running the same restaurant in the same town, the Cardosi family has had plenty of time to get to know its clientele and how to please them. They cater for all tastes by operating a café and take-away counter as well as the first-floor restaurant and dispense bar, where it's possible to get a good three-course business lunch for around £1.85. A typical choice of dishes from this menu would include cream of asparagus soup, 'haggis, neeps and tatties' and banana crumble and custard. A reasonably-priced à la carte menu is always available, along with its list of chef's specialities – Mexico steak, chicken Kiev or Napoli steak with all the trimmings – and yes, you will still get change from £5.

RENFREW

The Armoury Restaurant, Inchinnan Road
(041-886 4100)
Open: Jul–Aug 10am–3pm, 5–10.30pm, Sept–Jun 10am–10.30pm

[C][P][&]

Another of the Stakis steakhouses, but there's not the olde worlde décor here that you'd expect. This is very much an up-to-date restaurant, featuring a circular wood ceiling with ultra-modern lighting. Still, as a contrast, the armoury itself has several medieval wall-hangings and drawings. Starter choices here are country pâté, prawn cocktail, farmhouse broth or fruit juice, and are included in the price of the main course. Most of the favourites are on the menu, such as gammon steak (£3.95), half-chicken (£3.90) and fillet of haddock (£3.50). There's a very good deal for children, too. Soup, a choice of three main courses with ice-cream and strawberry sauce to follow, plus a fizzy drink costs just £1.25. Whichever dessert the adults decide on it will cost 75p, and a 30p cup of coffee should round things off satisfactorily and keep things within budget.

ROTHESAY

La Coloquinte, 63 Victoria Street
(Rothesay 2324)
Open: Summer Mon–Sat 12noon–2.30pm, 7–11pm, Sun 7–11pm, Winter: weekends, or check by phone for midweek opening

[C][&]

The time to sample the French cuisine of this small, but popular restaurant is when the seersucker cloths cover the tables at lunchtime. Stroll first along the pier, or in the public gardens opposite to whet your appetite. There's a choice of four or five starters, including home-made soup; main courses may be spaghetti or fish orientated (such as turbot with cheesy sauce), or pork with 'fines herbes', and a choice of three sweets. When the dinner-time linen cloths replace the seersucker, prices rise, and only careful and disciplined selection from the enticing à la carte will keep you within budget.

SALEN, ISLE OF MULL

The Puffer Aground ✕
Aros
(Aros 389)
Open: Easter–mid May Tue–Sat 12.30–2.30pm, 6.30–9pm, mid May–mid Oct Mon–Sun 12.30–2.30pm, 6.30–9pm, mid Nov–mid Jan, Fri–Sat (reservations only)

[P][&]

No need to find your sea-legs on this ship, though you may have doubts, as the restaurant's design is strikingly based on that of a Clyde 'Puffer', and maritime paintings line the walls. The restaurant shares its home in a row of converted roadside cottages with a craft shop. For about £5 you may sample a three-course meal (which could include local trout) and coffee. Excellent use is made of fresh local produce and as far as possible, each meal is individually prepared. Fisherman's pancake or shellfish soup with brandy and cream live side by side with more conventional, and cheaper starters. A main course salad or casserole will cost about £3.90, though you can spend more, and sweets such as baked sponge or fresh peach and cream roll, about 80p. Service is simple but very friendly.

TROON

Campbell's Kitchen, 3 South Beach
(Troon 314421)
Open: Thu–Sat 12noon–2pm, Tue–Sat 7–9.30pm

[P][S][&]

Opened during 1979, Campbell's Kitchen already has a homely atmosphere. Red and white floral décor and pinewood chairs give a pleasant ambience, but the main attraction is the delicious smell of home-baking. Home-made meringues and gâteaux around 50p per portion. A 'special meal', including a fruit juice or soup, and a hot dish of the day, is available at about £2. Alternatively there is a choice of salads or various omelettes at about £2. The French à la carte menu available in the evenings is outside the scope of this guide. Campbell's Kitchen welcomes disabled diners.

The Copper Kettle, 18 West Portland Street
(Troon 311394)
Open: Mon–Sat 10am–10pm

[F][P][S][&]

In this friendly, relaxed restaurant there is a good selection of appetising snacks and savoury dishes from which to choose. Imaginative, and presented with flair, the food available is excellent value for money – an omelette, breaded haddock or scampi and chips will not burn a hole in your pocket.

WISHAW

Anvil Steakhouse, 254 Main Street
(Wishaw 75546)
Open: Mon–Sat 12noon–2.30pm, 5–10pm, Sun 6.30–10pm

[C][F][S][&]

In Wishaw's main street, this member of the Stakis Steakhouse chain is a popular lunchtime venue for local business people. The emphasis is on convenience, with good value, standard menus of the chicken, gammon and steak variety. Accompaniments are chips or baked potato and peas, with salad garnish. A three-course meal will cost £3.20–£5.95.

CENTRAL, TAYSIDE AND FIFE

A stranger landing on the coast of Fife might think that he had arrived in a rather dull world. Industrious, perhaps, but without very much to boast about in the way of scenery. But if he persevered and journeyed westward, he would notice the view change from mundane to spectacular.

Callander is publicised as 'the natural gateway to the Highlands'. In fact, it bears more resemblance to a Lowland town (some of the sequences in TV's *Dr Finlay's Casebook* were filmed on location here). But Pitlochry is, for some people, the centre of the Highlands – commercially if not geographically. The tartan industry, never far beneath the surface in Scotland, explodes here. The town is crammed with shops selling this or that plaid and all the other mementoes that tourists seem to require.

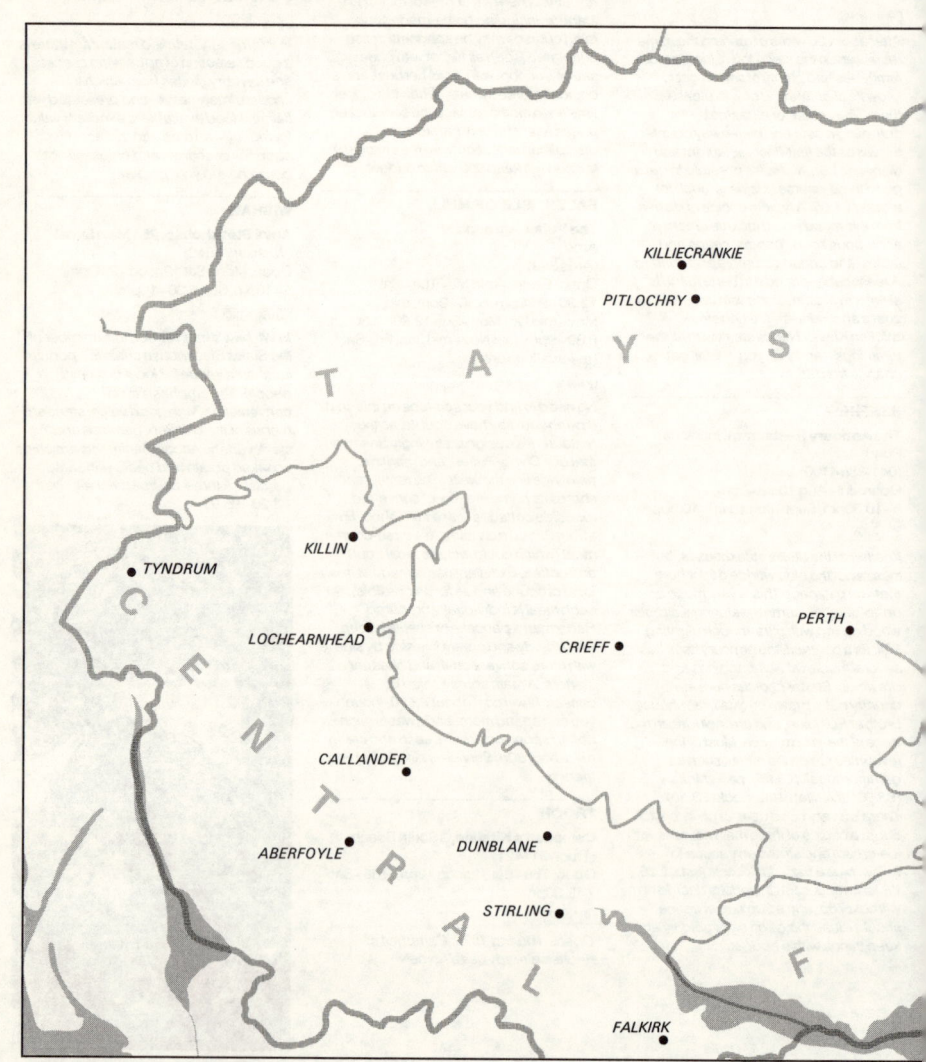

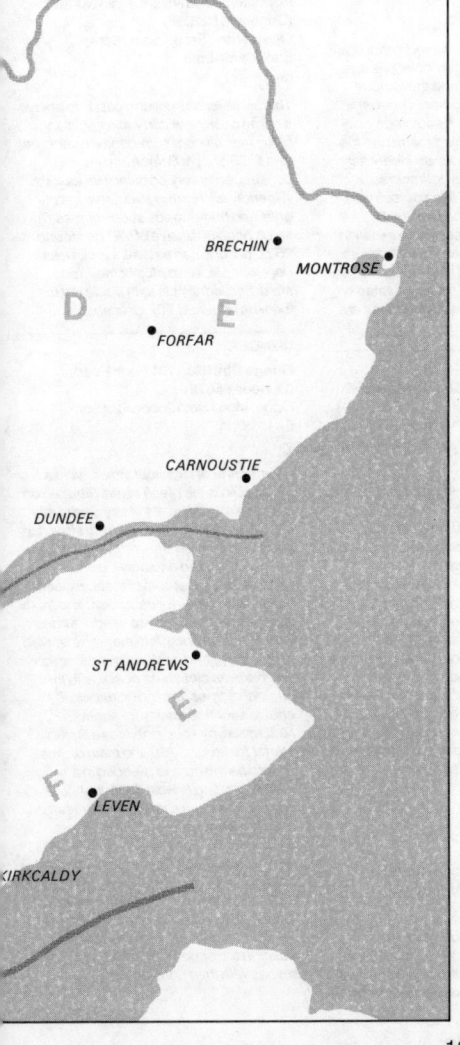

For many tourists, however, Perth is the actual gateway. Having travelled overnight by Motorail from London, they disembark from the train round about breakfast time (which is a good time to arrive in Scotland). The Scots are very capable breakfast cookers. If they patronise the Royal George Hotel, they may like to reflect that Queen Victoria slept here on her first railway journey from Balmoral to London. On her journeys from London to Balmoral, Victoria always used to alight at Perth for breakfast. Dundee, the town of jute and jam, is also associated with breakfast through its particularly delicious type of marmalade. Its other speciality is cake: a well-made rich Dundee cake will spoil the eater for other types of fruit cake.

As everyone knows (or ought to), Scotland invented golf. The first club was established at Leith in 1744. Its members called themselves the Honourable Company of Golfers. The course had only five holes and very little in the way of manicuring the greens and fairways was done. Nowadays, it is played with very much aplomb and 13 more holes all over Scotland. However, it is never attended by more style and reverence and, indeed, skill than at St Andrews and at Gleneagles – the one in Fife, the other in Tayside.

Arbroath's best known contribution to Scotland, in a gastronomical if not in an historic sense, is the Arbroath Smoky, which is a smoked haddock. It should not be confused – though it probably will be – with Finnan Haddies, which are also smoked haddocks. In this case, they come from Findon in Aberdeenshire.

Forfar Bridies are strips of steak in pastry; Fife broth is made from ribs of pork, and Kingdom of Fife pie is filled with rabbit and pork. Up in the Highlands, true haggis contains venison; but don't blame us if you cannot find a restaurant that serves it.

Aberfoyle – Dundee

ABERFOYLE
Old Coach House Restaurant, Main Street
(Aberfoyle 535)
Open: Mon–Sun 10am–11pm

♬ P ♨

In this white-walled restaurant, decorated in Austrian style, wild flowers and candles on green-and-white tables, create a pretty effect. The friendly staff contribute to a relaxing atmosphere. Meals are available throughout the day. For snacks, there is a selection of toasted sandwiches at around 70p, apple pie at around 65p, and coffee at 30p. A three-course meal consisting of home-made soup, grilled Glen Devon trout and fruit and ice-cream sundae, lavishly topped with cream would cost about £4.60. Children's portions are also available.

ANSTRUTHER
The Haven, 1 Shore Street, Cellardyke
(Anstruther 310574)
Open: Mon–Sun 12noon–10.30pm

P ♨

Wander along the quaint narrow streets that connect the better-known Anstruther to the old fishing village of Cellardyke and you will find The Haven overlooking the harbour. Bar-lunches, lunches, afternoon and high teas are available, as well as à la carte dinners. A three-course lunch costs around £4 and dinner around £6. Seafood is naturally popular and there is also a good choice of grills and salads. A children's menu is available.

BRECHIN
Northern Hotel ★★
2 Clerk Street
(Brechin 2156)
Open: Mon–Sun 12noon–2pm, 5–6.30pm, 7–8.30pm

C P ♨

For those who relish a proper 'sit down' meal within the realms of a tight budget, this hotel is the ideal place. A three-course dinner such as salami salad, farmhouse grill and vegetables of the day, followed by Drambuie pancake costs around £5.50. Snacks in the bar and satisfying high teas are also available, and cost, for the most part, around £2.

CALLANDER
Pips, 23 Ancaster Square
(Callander 30470)
Open: Summer Mon–Sat 9am–9pm, Sun 11am–6pm, Winter Mon–Tue 10am–5pm, Thu–Sun 10am–5pm

C P ♨

This eye-catching little restaurant snuggles in a corner of the Square. From the outside, attractive laboured brasswork, tinted windows and a sophisticated striped canopy invite further inspection. The interior is equally striking with white laminated tables and chairs and a bold décor with pictures mounted on hessian walls. Salads and home-baking are the specialities of the house, and desserts are served with lashings of cream. Great value at around £3 per head. During the summer a fixed-priced menu is available Mon–Sat 6–9pm featuring three or four hot dishes. Two courses and coffee is £3.45, three courses and coffee £3.95.

CARNOUSTIE
Glencoe Hotel ★★
Links Parade
(Carnoustie 53273)
Open: Mon–Sun 12noon–2pm, 7.30–9pm

C P

The name Carnoustie is synonymous with golf, and this neat, family hotel has the distinction of overlooking the famous championship golf-course. Table lamps and soft music create a soothing atmosphere in the dining room, and the patio extension provides an ideal eating place with views of the golf-course. A table d'hôte dinner of five courses with coffee incorporates the best local produce available. There is an excellent choice of tempting main course dishes such as grilled fillet of lemon sole Sorrento, cold baked gammon salad or beef and pheasant pie. Bar lunches are served.

CRIEFF
The Highlandman, East High Street
(Crieff 4265)
Open: Mon–Sat 10am–7pm, Sun 12noon–7pm

♨

The premises of The Highlandman, once a garage showroom and filling station, have been converted into a pleasant restaurant-cum-tearoom, where one can get anything from a cup of tea and a piece of home-made shortbread to a full three-course meal, anytime from morning to evening. Main dishes include sirloin steak or scampi at around £3, gammon steak at about £2.25, or various grills from around £1.25. Toasted sandwiches, hamburgers and salads exist for those who like a light lunch, and children's meals run from 40p for sausage and chips to £1.10 for fisherman's platter and chips. Incidentally, disabled persons will find access easy.

Star Hotel ★
East High Street
(Crieff 2632)
Open: Mon–Sun 12noon–2pm, 4.30–6pm (High Tea), 7–9pm

C P S ♨

The pleasant surroundings of the panelled dining room which overlooks the main street of this attractive Perthshire town provides an ideal venue for shoppers and tourists alike. Lunchtime specials such as fried fillet of haddock with lemon, grilled liver and onions or pizza – all served with French fried potatoes and two vegetables of the day – cost only £1.30. Starter, a sweet and coffee would add less than £1 extra to the bill. The à la carte menu is more extensive but still reasonable offering grilled Tay salmon, chicken Suedoise (sautéed in a delicious sauce of mushrooms, cream and white wine) or Wiener schnitzel for around £3.50. A high tea menu served from 4.30–6pm offers a selection of grills or cold meat salad with French fries and vegetables, tea, bread and butter, scones and cakes in a price range of £2.30–£4.50.

DUNBLANE
Fourways Restaurant, Main North Road
(Dunblane 822098)
Open: Mon–Sat 9.15am–6pm, Sun 10am–6pm

P ♨

This small restaurant and gift shop enjoys a prime position within walking distance of the magnificent 15th-century cathedral and the Bishop's Palace and is consequently very popular with tourists. A friendly and caring staff serve mainly grills and home-made soups or pies. Top lunch price (inclusive of VAT) is around £5.50 but one can eat well for a lot less (for example, soup plus home-made steak and kidney pie with apple tart to follow is under £3.50). Unlicensed.

DUNDEE
Gunga Din, 99c–101 Perth Road
(Dundee 65672)
Open: Mon–Sat 12noon–2.15pm, 6–11.30pm

C

For the lover of classical Indian dishes Gunga Din is the place to eat. Situated on the main road west of the city centre this attractive little Indian restaurant sits in the heart of the University area. All dishes are freshly-prepared and only the finest basmati rice, best cuts of meat, proper herbs and spices for each dish, and fresh seasonal vegetables are used. Patrons are asked to appreciate the time involved in preparing and cooking dishes, which are made as closely as possible to the original recipes, and not to expect the chef to sacrifice quality for speed. Mullagatawny soup provides a suitable starter for around 70p and main dishes should be mixed and blended in the Indian tradition (ideally friends should order dishes and share). Kofta (meatballs in curry sauce) or chicken curry costs around £2.50 as does sag gosh (meat with spinach) and a seafood muchi curry cost about £2.70. For £3.10 or so there is a speciality chicken tandoori masala or thaiti (a tray consisting of several Indian vegetarian dishes). Friendly staff will assist in the choosing and blending of dishes with their correct

accompaniments. For dessert you
should try kulfi, an Indian ice cream at
about 75p.

Olde Worlde Inn, 124 Seagate
(Dundee 21179)
Open: Mon–Sat 12noon–2.30pm,
5–10pm, Sun 6.30–9.30pm
C F S &

Handy for the new Wellgate shopping
centre and opposite the main bus station,
this is a typical Reo Stakis steakhouse,
serving items from the organisation's
standard menu. Main course items range
from about £3.75 for a fillet of haddock to
£5.50 for prime Angus steak and include
a choice of starters. A choice of sweets to
finish with will cost around 75p. Bar
lunches are served between 12noon and
2.15pm, and there is a special children's
menu for around £1.25.

Pizza Gallery, 3–7 Peter Street
(Dundee 21422)
Open: Mon–Sat 10am–11pm
S &

A bright and modern eatery situated in a
quiet lane off a pedestrianised precinct in
the city centre. The Gallery is on two
levels and is adorned by the
works of local artists, which are for sale.
Starters (they call them primers) are soup
(55p), spaghetti (85p) and fruit juice
(40p). The main-course pizzas are
named after famous artists (the Goya is
topped with anchovies, green pepper
and olives) and range from £1.45–£2.20.
Even if you finish off with apple pie and
fresh cream, all washed down with
coffee, you've probably only spent £4
altogether. So perhaps you could have
afforded that half-litre carafe of house
wine at £2.25.

FALKIRK

Hotel Cladhan, Kemper Avenue
(Falkirk 27421)
Open: Mon–Sat 12noon–2pm,
7–9.15pm, Sun 12noon–2pm
C F P &

This large, modern hotel is built on the site
of a Roman wall, and the personal touch
is provided by the owners Mr and Mrs
Reid, who serve modestly priced bar

Falkirk
—
Kirkcaldy

---

meals in the spacious lounge bars
(children's portions are available). The
dining room offers a good à la carte
menu, but many of the selections will take
you over our budget.

FORFAR

August Moon, 114 Castle Street
(Forfar 64105)
Open: Mon–Sat 11.30am–2pm,
5–11.30pm, Sun 4–11.30pm

For those who think that all Chinese
restaurants have a stereotyped
appearance with very little individuality, a
visit to August Moon will prove a pleasant
experience. No embossed wallpaper or
Chinese lanterns here. This little eating
place has a charm and character all of its
own, with white roughcast walls and
cosy Tudor-style banquettes. A
comprehensive à la carte menu offers the
usual complement of Oriental dishes plus
a selection of European ones. The price
of all main courses includes boiled rice,
and a heated stand is laid on your table to
keep the whole thing hot. Most dishes are
around the £2–£3 mark and, a set meal
for two of fried spring roll, sweet and sour
pork, chicken with cashew nuts and
vegetables, mixed vegetables, egg fried
rice plus coffee or tea offers excellent
value at just over £6.

KILLIECRANKIE

Killiecrankie Hotel, on the A9, 2m NW of
Pitlochry
(Pitlochry 3220)
Open: early Apr–mid Oct
12noon–2.30pm, 7–11pm
P &

This white-painted building with its well-
tended gardens is set in woodland close
to a National Trust beauty spot. Bar
lunches are very popular here and there's
a good range of food for you to sample.
After soup with roll and butter at 50p, two
of the options on offer are fried haddock
with chips and peas (£1.80) and tongue
salad (£1.90). A similar bar supper
service operates during the evenings.

The table d'hôte is a little expensive for
us, but if you stick to, say, game soup,
then Tayside trout or rump steak with
ice-cream to finish, you should see some
change from £6. A glass of wine is 55p.

KILLIN

**The Old Mill Restaurant and Lounge
Bar,** Glendochart, by Killin, Central, 4m
W of Killin on A85
(Killin 434)
Open: May–Oct Mon–Sun 9am–10pm
P &

An attractively modernised 17th-century
inn sits at the side of the A85. The wooden
beamed restaurant has recently been
extended and now has a lounge bar
offering a wide range of bar snacks.
Good home cooking is the speciality of
the restaurant, where the standard menu
for lunch and dinner offers a reasonably
priced selection of hot dishes and salads.
Try soup at 48p, steak pie at £2.80, and
fruit pie and cream at 65p, all home-
made. Morning coffee and afternoon tea
are also available.

KIRKCALDY

Green Cockatoo Restaurant,
275–277 High Street
(Kirkcaldy 263310)
Open: Mon–Sat 9am–5pm, closed Wed
C P S &

At the north end of the High Street, you'll
find a bakery and confectioner's shop.
Go through the shop and up some stairs
and on the first floor you will find the
Green Cockatoo, a traditional Scottish
tearoom with polished wood panelling,
fresh white linen on the tables, and
friendly service. Tea is obviously the meal
here, with all those delicious scones and
cakes downstairs, but the lunch menu is
good value too with the most expensive
dish – fresh salmon and salad – priced
about £3. Sweets include Bakewell tart
and custard, fresh cream gâteau and ice
creams. Coffee costs about 25p and a
glass of wine around 60p. On the second
floor is a grill room, the 'Drouthy Crony'
with a more limited menu at similarly
moderate prices.

Killiecrankie Hotel   AA★★

Nr. PITLOCHRY, PERTHSHIRE.
Telephone Pitlochry (0796) 3220 & 2144

★ Situated in the historic Pass of Killiecrankie alongside
the A9, near the Soldiers Leap.
★ Fully licensed 12 bedroom Hotel, offers the weary traveller
high quality Bar Lunches & Suppers up to 10.00pm.
★ Restaurant renowned for good food, serves Taste of
Scotland dishes & reasonably priced wines.
★ Non-residents, children & dogs made very welcome.

Resident Proprietors:
Duncan & Jennifer Hattersley Smith & Emma.

Olde Worlde Inn, Charlotte Street
(Kirkcaldy 65381)
Open: Mon–Fri 12noon–2.30pm,
5–10.30pm, Sun 6.30–10pm

The mid-19th-century building has come a long way from its days as a schoolhouse, to a Stakis Steakhouse. The big advantage of Olde Worlde Inns is that you can be confident of knowing exactly what to expect, in terms of standard, quantity and price. A simple starter followed by gammon steak or roast half-chicken with peas and chips or baked potato will cost under £4, and the sweets and cheeseboard are each under £1. The children's menu is good value, too, a three-course meal and soft drink costing around £1.50.

The Pancake Place, 28 Kirk Wynd
(Kirkcaldy 264982)
Open: Mon–Sat 10am–5.30pm
[F] [P] [S]

Housed in a converted stone building dating from 1779, this is a comfortable restaurant specialising in pancakes-with-everything. You can start with soup, but there is a choice of 12 snack-sized pancakes with intriguing fillings such as ham and peach, each costing around 95p. For your main course, large savoury pancakes such as chicken and pineapple (about £1.80) or Rocky Mountain Burger for less than £1.60 are recommended. Alternatively you can try one of seven crisp salads, served with two thin pancakes. There are a dozen varieties of sweet pancakes available for dessert. Costing around £1.30 'Pippin', a large spicy pancake with a delicious hot apple and cinnamon filling topped with cream is a gourmet's delight.

LEVEN

Osborne Lounge and Grill,
101 Commercial Road
(Leven 25626)
Open: Summer Mon–Sat
9.30am–12mdnt, Sun 3pm–12mdnt,
Winter Mon–Sat 9.30am–12mdnt
[F] [P] [⌕]

This smart, town-centre restaurant offers efficient friendly service with the owners, Mr and Mrs Herd always in attendance. At lunch-time, roast meat salads are around £2.75, and most of the grills cost less than £3. The dinner menu ranges from herring fillets in oatmeal at around £2.75 to steaks at over £5. Pâté as a starter is 95p, and there is a choice of sweets from the trolley.

LOCHEARNHEAD

Craigroyston, Lochside, Lochearnhead
(Lochearnhead 229)
Open: Apr–Oct Mon–Sun 10am–10pm
[P] [⌕]

Leven
—
Montrose

This hotel, situated on the edge of Loch Earn, allows diners to enjoy views of over the Loch, including the watersport activities which take place on the Loch. There are a variety of snacks and full meals available all day. Try the open sandwiches, served with salad at £1, or a baked potato with cheese filling at 65p. For a full meal, soup, steak pie and sherry trifle costs under £3.

MONTROSE

Corner House Hotel ★★
High Street
(Montrose 3126)
Open: Mon–Sun 12noon–2pm,
4.30–9pm
[P] [S] [⌕]

This attractive hotel-restaurant is run efficiently by friendly waitresses who will serve you a three-course lunch with coffee and a glass of wine for less than £3. The daily changing menu features the old favourites such as fried haddock, lasagne, roasts and omelettes for around £1.50. Later in the day a high tea menu is available with main courses such as gammon steak and chips or cold York ham salad at around £3.50 including a selection of vegetables, home-made scones, cakes and tea. The à la carte menu is rather more pricey but with careful selection a meal for around £5 is possible.

Osborne Lounge & Grill

101 Commercial Road, Leven.
Telephone: Leven 25626

Finest Eating House in town.

A warm welcome awaits you from the Proprietor and his wife,
Tom & Betty Herd.

CRAIGROYSTON
HOUSE and RESTAURANT

Lochearnhead, Perthshire, Scotland.
Telephone: Mrs. Stuart, Lochearnhead (056 73) 229

Dining-Room, Licensed Bistro Bar, Lounge and Terrace all face South with glorious views over Loch Earn to hills beyond.
We serve meals from 10am to 10pm: from Home Made Soup (.65p) and Open Sandwiches with Salad (£1.50), Chef's Special (£3.95) to Venison in Cream and Wine (£4.95) and Sirloin Steak (£6.95).
Relax and enjoy Scottish Hospitality at its best.

PERTH

Hunter's Lodge, Bankfoot
8m N of Perth off A9 at Bankfoot services turn-off
(Bankfoot 325)
Open: Mon–Sun 12noon–2pm, 5–9pm
C P ⌂

This country restaurant, only eight miles north of Perth on the main road to Inverness, makes a speciality of traditional Scottish fare, both in the à la carte and bar menus. The award-winning bar food features Hunter's Lodge pâté, home-made beef steak pie and curry – all firm favourites at around £1.60. Children's dishes (all under £1) are also available in the bar. In the dining room traditional Scottish high tea is nothing short of a slap-up dinner at around £4. An extensive à la carte menu lists main courses for as little as £3.50.

Kardomah, St John's Square
(Perth 25093)
Open: Mon–Sat 9.30am–6pm
C S ⌂

These Trusthouse Forte restaurants are favourites with many people. This one is certainly quick and convenient if you are shopping or sightseeing. Supplementing the usual THF menu of omelettes, grills and salads is a table d'hôte lunch (two courses at around £2.30, three £2.60) and a high tea (including tea and toast) at about £2.20.

Perth

Olde Worlde Inn, City Mill Hotel, West Mill Street
(Perth 28281)
Open: 12noon–2.30pm, 5–10.30pm
C P ⌂

Convenient, fast food of the steaks, chicken and haddock variety is served in a 19th-century mill which has been converted into a modern hotel of the Reo Stakis organisation. The mill stream and wheel can be seen through plated glass in the hotel's lounge bar and reception area. Main course prices, between £3.20 and £6 include a starter, but sweets or cheese are 75p extra.

The Pancake Place, 10 Charlotte Street
(Perth 28077)
Open: Summer Mon–Sat 10am–5.30pm, Sun 11.30am–5.30pm (open till later in the summer)
S ⌂

This specialised restaurant, with its informal tea-room atmosphere, was the first to pander to pancake fans in central Scotland (other sister restaurants have since opened at Edinburgh, Kirkcaldy and St Andrews). After fruit juice or soup of the day (around 35p), you can sample a giant burger (£1.80), chicken and pineapple (£1.80) or any one of six crispy salads from £1.50–£2. And to follow? How about 'Florida' – a large pancake topped with ice-cream, peaches and fresh whipped cream – just one of a dozen exotic desserts guaranteed to ruin your diet!

The Penny Post ✕
80 George Street
(Perth 20867)
Open: Mon–Sat 12noon–2pm, 7–10pm
C P S ⌂

A cosy little restaurant which should appeal to those who find historic connections of interest, for the 18th-century building that houses The Penny Post was one of the earliest post offices, dating back to 1773. The bar downstairs is, in fact, the old Post Office counter. The à la carte menu offers such dishes as home-made Scotch broth at around 50p, and the Penny Post Special (strips of beef cooked in red wine, mushrooms and cream and served on a bed of rice) at around £4.95 and this gives a good indication of the sort of prices prevailing. The cheaper lunch menu includes beefsteak, kidney and mushroom pie or fish at about £2.

Windsor Restaurant (Tudor Room),
38 St John Street
(Perth 23969)
Open: Mon–Sun 10am–7.30pm, closed Sun in winter
P ⌂

Hunters Lodge

Bankfoot — Perth
Telephone: Bankfoot 325

Restaurant   **Free House**

**A large selection of
BAR SNACKS**
avialable both mid-day and evenings until 9pm
HOME-MADE SOUP
OUR OWN PATE
CURRY
HOME-MADE PIE
A large selection of Salads
to mention just a few from our
EXTENSIVE BAR SNACK MENU
*Winner of the BBC Best Pub Grub
in Scotland Award*

Children most welcome

This is a first-floor restaurant in a complex of bars, restaurants and function rooms, with comfortable seating, and highly polished wooden tables. Home-made lentil soup at 40p, lasagne with green salad at £2, creamed chicken pie at £1.80 all served with boiled or french fried potatoes and vegetables of the day, offer good value for money. For dessert choose from peach condie at 50p or perhaps sherry trifle and cream at 75p. Children can choose from their own menu, cheeseburger with side salad, Windsor pizza, sausage, bacon and egg all priced at £1.20.

PITLOCHRY

Green Park Hotel ★★★
(Pitlochry 2537)
Open: Mar–Oct inclusive, Mon–Sun 8.30–9.30am, 12.30–2pm, 6.30–8pm and normal licensing hours

[P][&]

If you take pleasure in having your meal in beautiful surroundings, try the Green Park Hotel. This enlarged country house is set amongst lawns and fine trees, with a view across Loch Faskally. Inside, the dining room is very clean and bright. There are no à la carte meals, but the owners, Graham and Anne Brown, offer a good selection of dishes for a three-course lunch at around £4, including service and VAT. You could start with Salami and egg coupe, follow with grilled pork chop Normandi and finish with peach melba. Bar lunches generally cost around £2 (apart from steak which is £4). Lunch on Sunday features a mouth-watering cold buffet, with cold meats, fish and salad galore.

The Luggie, Rie-Achan Road
(Pitlochry 2085)
Open: Apr–early Nov Mon–Sun 10am–9pm

A 'luggie' is a milkmaid's bucket – appropriate since this quaint little restaurant was originally the byre of an old dairy farm. Inside, the raftered roof, white-painted rough-cast walls and stone fireplace are very welcoming. Ian and Diana Russell, the owners, ensure that home-baking and local produce are a main feature of all the fare. Lunchtime offers the choice of a self-service cold table and an excellent selection of cold meats, duck, salmon and smoked mackerel, accompanied by a variety of original salads, assorted gâteaux and fresh fruit salads, or hot dishes such as grills which are served at the table. The main course in either case will be between £3 and £4, with starters and sweets for about 60p–£2. The dinner menu offers a much wider choice of hot dishes but the price is likely to bring the full meal outside our budget.

Pitlochry — Tyndrum

ST ANDREWS

Pepita's, 11–13 Crails Lane
(St Andrews 74084)
Open: Mon–Sat 10am–4.45pm, 5.30–11pm, Sun 11.30am–4.45pm, 5.30–10pm

[&]

Stone-built cottages built in 1699, have been tastefully converted into a restaurant, situated in a narrow, paved lane in the centre of St Andrews, surrounded by ancient buildings. Start your meal with home-made soup, follow up with seafood risotto, beef in a paprika, cream and red wine sauce with rice, or lasagne, and finish with one of a wide variety of sweets and coffee, and you should still have change from a £5 note.

The Pancake Place, 177–179 South Street
(St Andrews 75671)
Open: Mon–Sat 10am–5.30pm, in Jul & Aug, 8am–9pm, Sun 11am–5.30pm

[♬][P][S]

The interior of this attractive speciality restaurant is surprisingly rural, with a beamed ceiling, natural stone and white-painted plaster walls. Pancakes may be sampled as a starter, main course or dessert. Soup of the day is about 35p, or you can start with a savoury pancake such as ham and peach or haddock Mornay for around 90p. For a main course you could choose a Rocky Mountain burger at about £1.60. A range of salads is also available including chicken, ham, cheese and egg, prices ranging from around £1.40–£2. There is a choice of a dozen sweet pancakes.

STIRLING

Boma Restaurant, Kingsgate Hotel ★
Kings Street
(Stirling 3944)
Open: Mon–Sun 8am–9pm

[S][&]

In their residential hotel, right in the town and handy for the railway station and Thistle shopping centre, Sandy and Jean Wallace have opened the 'Boma' Restaurant. Real zebra skins brought back from East Africa by the intrepid couple set the black-and-white theme of the décor. A lunch of soup or fruit juice, followed by a main course (from around £4 for chicken or ham salad, roast chicken or haddock fillet to around £5 for grilled sirloin steak garni) is available daily. Sweets, cheese and coffee are not included in the price. High tea includes a starter such as egg mayonnaise, prawn cocktail or pâté, a savoury dish with chips, scone, cake and tea at prices from about £4.60. Half portions of appropriate dishes are served for children and high chairs are available if required.

The Grubery, 25 Baker Street
(Stirling 70550)
Open: Mon–Sat 11am–3pm, Mon–Thu 6.30–11.30pm, Fri–Sun 6.30pm–12mdnt

[♬][P][&]

This recently-opened, modern restaurant is situated in the centre of town on the approach road to the castle. The proprietors are young and this is reflected in the décor. All types of meals are offered: morning coffee, self-service lunches, afternoon 'salad bowl', and waitress-service for evening meals. The menu offers something for everyone. The starters are all around £1 and include smoked mackerel mousse and taramasalata. Omelettes, served with salad and chips are £2.15 and savoury crêpes (try spiced seafood or ratatouille and gruyère) cost from £1.95. Main meals include chicken and tarragon pie at £2.75 and steak au poivre at £3.25. There is a delicious range of sweets available including sweet crêpes which are from £1.15. Adjoining is the 'Beanstalk' lounge bar which has waitress-service at lunchtime.

The Riverway Restaurant ✕
Kildean
(Stirling 5734)
Open: Mon–Wed 10.30am–3pm, Thu–Sun 10.30am–7pm

[♬][P][&]

Half a mile from the town centre, on the road to the Trossachs, just off the M9 motorway and yet enjoy a panoramic view of the River Forth, the Riverway Restaurant is well-known for its excellent cuisine at reasonable prices. The three-course table d'hôte lunch costs under £3 and is good nourishing food in ample portions. High tea, the main evening meal including grills, is about the same price. The Saturday night dinner-dance, with live music, costs about £6.

Station Hotel ★★
56 Murray Place
(Stirling 2017)
Open: Mon–Sun 12noon–2.30pm, 5–10pm

[C][&]

The Stakis Steakhouse at the Station Hotel offers their standard menu (as for 'The Plough' at Ayr). The wattle ceiling and dark oak settles may not be genuine antiques but the atmosphere is right for an enjoyable meal, with full waiter service, at very reasonable prices. Bar snacks run from around £1, and you might like to catch the Whistlestop Diner, also part of the Station Hotel.

TYNDRUM

Clifton Coffee House, A82/A85 junction
(Tyndrum 271)
Open: Apr–Oct Mon–Sun 8.30am–5.30pm

[C][P][S][&]

Tyndrum

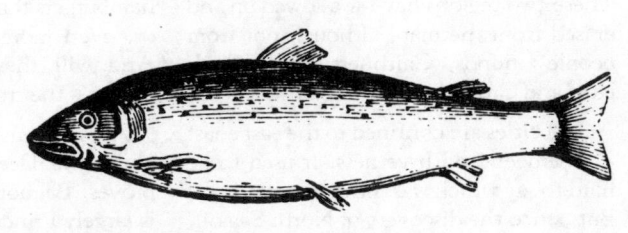

You'll be pleasantly surprised by the prices at this cheerful eaterie. It is part of a smoothly-run tourist complex that includes craft, book and whisky shops. Inside, the décor is predominantly white with strategically placed hanging baskets and hand-crafted pottery. There is an air of quality here, despite it being a self-service operation. A wide range of starters includes barley broth and cullen skink (the traditional fish-based soup). Various main courses are available throughout the day, such as beef in beer with mushrooms (£2.50), home-made chicken and ham pie (£2.20) and mushroom and prawn vol-au-vent (£2.10).

AA SELF CATERING IN BRITAIN

15000 AA-inspected self-catering holiday houses, chalets and cottages on which you can rely for a comfortable holiday.

Written description of each entry plus symbols and abbreviations for a wide range of facilities.

Hints for Self-Caterers

Maps to help you locate the holiday home of your choice.

On sale at AA shops and major booksellers

AA SUPERGUIDES

A Guide for every occasion at home or abroad — holidays in the sun, quiet weekends in the country, wining and dining out, fascinating places for day trips — family fun for everyone all backed by AA expertise.

HOTELS AND RESTAURANTS IN BRITAIN
CAMPING AND CARAVANNING IN BRITAIN
GUESTHOUSES, FARMHOUSES AND INNS IN BRITAIN
SELF CATERING IN BRITAIN
STATELY HOMES, MUSEUMS, CASTLES AND GARDENS IN BRITAIN
TRAVELLERS' GUIDE TO EUROPE
CAMPING AND CARAVANNING IN EUROPE
GUESTHOUSES, FARMHOUSES AND INNS IN EUROPE

All these Guides and many more AA publications are available from AA shops and major booksellers.

HIGHLAND AND GRAMPIAN

These two regions have swallowed up and erased from the map, although not from people's minds, Caithness, Sutherland, Ross and Cromarty, and five others.

The cities are confined to the east coast – Aberdeen and Inverness. It used to be hard to say which was the more attractive. But, since the discovery of North Sea oil, Aberdeen has changed. It is still the granite city but you are more likely to find hamburgers than haggis in its restaurants – or, even more probably, T-bone steaks. And will they be from the Aberdeen Angus – the true Scots beef?

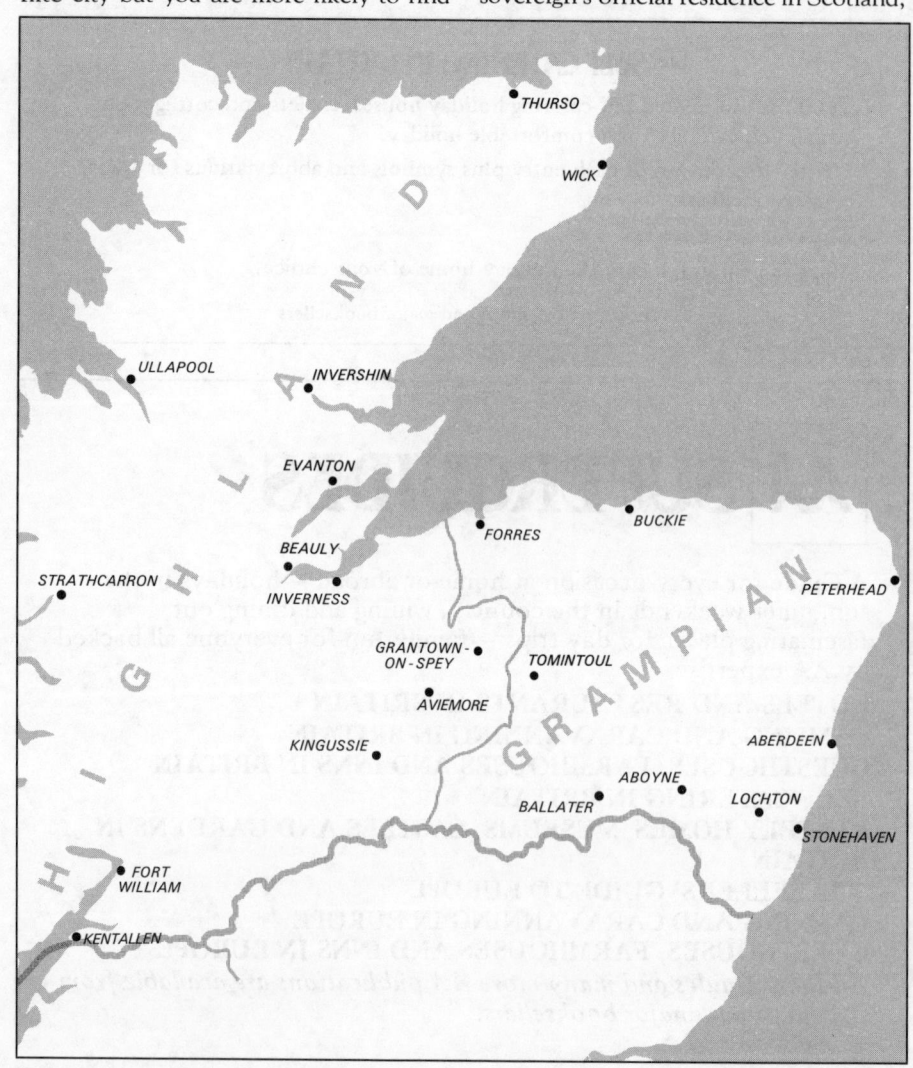

As you travel inland from Aberdeen along the Dee valley, the prospect improves. Balmoral, also built from granite, is largely Prince Albert's creation. Whilst Holyroodhouse in Edinburgh may be the sovereign's official residence in Scotland, this is the Queen's *real* Scottish home. It has been loved by a succession of monarchs: even Edward VII, inclined to prefer the social life of London to the more austere pleasures of mountains and forests, succumbed moderately to its charms. The Dee is of course famous not merely for royalty but for salmon. Fresh, smoked, even tinned, salmon from Scottish rivers finds its way not only nationwide but worldwide.

The Highlands breed not only sheep but many forms of game birds, notably the grouse. Venison is also becoming more popular, and the holidaymaker who arrives at the right season should have no difficulty in eating the sort of fare that Edwardian shooting parties feasted on.

Eating out in the Highlands, you are unlikely to find exotic dishes with subtle touches of herbs and garlic and wine-rich sauces. The cooking is plain, and often very, very good. Nowadays, it is rare indeed to find nettle broth on a menu; nor even on the coast, can you expect to experience Limpet Stovies (the instructions tell you to 'take out the eyes'). You may, however, come across Inky-Piny, even if not by name: it is carrots and roast beef warmed up.

Aberdeen — Buckie

ABERDEEN

Kardomah, 1 Union Bridge
(Aberdeen 50459)
Open: Mon–Sat 9am–6.30pm

[C][S][⌘]

This modern eating house provides a quick service for shoppers and holidaymakers, with a ground-floor self-service coffee shop and upstairs restaurant. The restaurant menu is reasonably priced (gammon steak around £2.95, steak and kidney pie around £2.10), with a waist-preserver menu for the figure-conscious and a children's menu including an exciting variety of ice creams.

The Lantern Restaurant, 101 Crown Street
(Aberdeen 55440)
Open: Mon–Fri 12noon–2pm,
Mon–Sat 7–10.30pm

[C][♫][P][S][⌘]

The Chef's Specialities menu is incredibly good value for lunch or dinner. Green bean salad is one of the delicious starters, costing around 75p. Casserole of kidney and sweetbreads (about £3) and poached salmon bonne femme (just over £3) are two of the main courses, both served with vegetables.

Stakis Steakhouse, Holburn Street
(Aberdeen 56442)
Open: Mon–Sun 12noon–2.30pm,
5–11pm, 10pm Sun

[C][P][S][⌘]

Stakis Steakhouses have a definite appeal for inveterate meat-eaters. Main course prices, from around £3.50–£7 and including haddock, chicken and various steaks, cover a starter as well as vegetables and a roll and butter. Sweets are about 75p.

Victoria Restaurant, 140 Union Street
(Aberdeen 28639)
Open: Mon–Sat 9am–7.30pm

[S][⌘]

Enjoy a nicely-presented yet inexpensive meal right here. The à la carte menu includes a selection of starters – soup, fruit juice or grapefruit cocktail all around 75p; main dishes such as omelettes,

grills, salads and fish which, with vegetables, are likely to cost between £1.75 and £4.20, and sweets at 50p or more. Very popular is a three-course lunch at around £2.70.

ABOYNE

The Boat Inn, Charleston Road
(Aboyne 2137)
Open: Mon–Sun 9am–11pm

[♫][P][S][⌘]

This large inn affords excellent views of Royal Deeside, and meals at thoroughly reasonable prices. At lunchtime try home-made soup and boat grill. High tea offers main dishes ranging from bacon and egg (about £3.60) to rump steak at around £5, all served with chips and vegetables and with toast, pancakes, cakes and a pot of tea included in the price. The dinner menu includes home-made pâté at about 90p.

AVIEMORE

Chieftain Grill, Colyumbridge Hotel
(Aviemore 810661)
Open: Mon–Sun 12.30–2pm,
5–10.15pm

[C][P][⌘]

The Colyumbridge Hotel occupies a heather-clad site on the road to the Cairngorm ski-slopes. The spacious grill-room, being part of one of the many hotels in the Reo Stakis chain, guarantees good food at competitive prices. Among the main courses (which include the price of a starter) are fried fillet of haddock (£3.75) and gammon steak (£3.95), but the sirloin and fillet steaks are, alas, out of our league. All sweets, including peach Melba and Black Forest gâteau, are 60p. During the summer various salads augment the menu, but a special children's three-course meal is available.

BALLATER

The Green Inn, 9 Victoria Road
(Ballater 55701)
Open: Tue–Sun 12noon–2pm, 7–10pm,
closed Jan & Feb and Mon–Thu Oct–Dec

[♫][P][⌘]

Built in 1840, this small pink granite house with colourful window canopies, has now been converted into a restaurant. Pine walls, tables and seating with wall prints and fresh flowers give it a cosy and restful atmosphere. A good three-course lunch can be enjoyed for £3. All main courses are served with potatoes, vegetables or salad. Sweets are home-made and the choice varies from day to day. Try the grilled venison with a port and redcurrant sauce at £3.75 if you feel like a change from ordinary restaurant fare.

BEAULY

The Skillet, The Square
(Beauly 2573)
Open: Apr–Oct, Mon–Sat 9.30am–8pm,
7pm Apr, May, Oct, Sun 11am–8pm

[P][S][⌘]

The Skillet is an ideal place for the hungry tourist. The simple but wholesome fare is reasonably priced at around £2.50 for a three-course table d'hôte lunch and from around £4.50 for a full dinner. The à la carte menu offers a good selection of grills, fish and salads at an average price of £2.75, with bread and butter or toast plus tea included.

BUCKIE

The Mill Motel ★★
Tynet
(Clochan 233)
Open: Mon–Sat 12.30–2pm, 7.30–9pm,
Sun 12.30–2pm

[C][♫][P]

This old mill was converted into a restaurant in 1970 and in recent years 15 letting bedrooms have been added. The original mill wheels form the entrance hall and the mill stones can be seen in the cocktail bar. The dining room offers lunch at around £3 and an evening meal at £6.50 consists of four courses with coffee

---

THE BOAT INN
ABOYNE – ON ROYAL DEESIDE
(Proprietors Victor & Audrey Sang)

Bed & Breakfast from £11.00 (private bath, showers).
Bar luncheon, High Teas, Dinners, Suppers.
Good Food Awards.
DON'T MISS THE BOAT
Telephone: 0339-2137

Evanton — Kentallen

and an excellent selection of fish and local meat.

EVANTON

Foulis Ferry, 1½m S of Evanton on A9
(Evanton 830535)
Open: Mon–Sat 10am–11pm,
Sun 12noon–6pm

P

Who pays the Ferryman? It's not important in this white-painted converted cottage restaurant where the ferryman once lived and where reasonably-priced meals are now served. Salads, quiches and simple, home-baked meals are available daily. Choose with care at dinner time and an exotic à la carte meal can work out at around £6.50.

FORRES

The Elizabethan Inn ××
Mondale
(Forres 72526)
Open: Mon, Tue, Thu–Sun 10.30am–3pm, 7.30–8.30pm, Wed 12.30–1.30pm

P

An authentic cottage atmosphere and honest-to-goodness home-cooked fare can be found about two miles west of Forres. Built of stone and close to the River Findhorn, the interior has brick and stone walls, Victorian and antique tables and chairs and a rare air of relaxation. Meals are table d'hôte and it is advisable to book for lunch. A three-course meal will cost around £8.

FORT WILLIAM

The Angus Restaurant, 66 High Street
(Fort William 2654)
Open: Summer Mon–Sat 10am–10pm

S

The Angus first-floor restaurant and ground-floor lounge bar has been strikingly created from former shop premises. Red is the colour theme of the well-appointed restaurant which offers a three-course meal from around £3. Grills predominate the à la carte lunch and dinner menus, and particularly recommended is the salmon steak, available in season for around £3.95.

McTavish's Kitchen, High Street
(Fort William 2406)
Open: Restaurant Easter and mid-May to end Sept Mon–Sun 12noon–2.30pm, 6–10.30pm
Self-service Mon–Sun Summer 9am–7.30pm or later

♪ P S

Excellent food, Scottish cabaret acts (summer evenings) and obliging staff are features here. Although prices in the main restaurant are rather near the limit, a three-course 'budget special' lunch will cost only £2.75, whereas a meal including 'A Tast of Scotland' dishes such as Tweed Kettle (a 19th-century Edinburgh dish of poached salmon fillet cooked in white wine, carrots and onion

topped with a light cream sauce) can be had for around £6.75. The ground-floor and self-service restaurant offer a less pricey selection of meals.

Mercury Motor Inn ☆☆
Achintore Road, 2m along the A85 to Glasgow
(Fort William 3117)
Open: Mon–Sun 12noon–2pm, for bar lunches, 6.30–9.30pm, 9pm Winter

C ♪ P

Panoramic views from the dining room over Loch Linnhe are a bonus here. The 'Taverners Table' lunch features a salad bowl selection at around £2.75 and various hot dishes and home-made soups in the comfortable lounge bar. The à la carte dinner menu offers a variety of creative dishes but a three-course meal is too expensive for this guide.

The Stag's Head Hotel ★★
High Street
(Fort William 4144)
Open: Restaurant Mon–Sun 12.30–2.30pm, 6.30–8.30pm
Bar snacks 12noon–5pm

C P S

A stag's head motif on the carpet and expensive dark oak furniture set the scene. The à la carte lunch and dinner menu is a little pricey for our needs but includes a good choice of reasonably-priced starters, and a selection of fish or meat dishes, all at under or around £3. But the bar lunches are the thing - chicken chasseur is around £1.20, fried scampi costs around £1.85 and a fresh salmon salad £3.50.

GRANTOWN-ON-SPEY

Craggan Mill Restaurant
(Grantown-on-Spey 2288)
Open: Summer Mon–Sun 12.30–2pm, 6–10pm, Winter Mon–Sun 7–10pm

P

A plain and rustic style is favoured by proprietors Bruno and Ann Bellini. Cuisine is a winning mixture of Italian and British, as the stylish menu reflects. A starter, such as mussels in wine or mushrooms and Stilton soup, should be followed by scampi provençale £4.90 or chicken in cream at £3.40. Interesting sweets are available.

INVERNESS

Crawfords Restaurant, 19 Queensgate
(Inverness 33198)
Open: Mon–Sat (also Sun Jul & Aug)
Self-service 8am–5.30pm
Restaurant 10am–7pm

S

Crawfords in Queensgate is a restaurant for all the family offering good food and friendly service both in the self-service and the restaurant. Self-service prices range from 50p for filled rolls to £2.50 for

gammon steak. A wide range of pure beef hamburgers and of course steak at £5 is available in the basement restaurant.

Crawfords Pizza Restaurant, Lombard Street
(Inverness 34328)
Open: Mon–Sat 10am–11pm,
Sun 12noon–6pm, Sun 8pm

S

This bright, modern pizzeria is conveniently situated in a pedestrianised shopping precinct. Inside, tiled floors and stucco walls with mirrors are in pleasant contrast to the city atmosphere outside. There are 19 varieties of pizza to choose from, as well as salads, open sandwiches, spaghetti bolognese and cannelloni.

Olde Worlde Inn, Bank Street
(Inverness 36577)
Open: Mon–Sat 12noon–2.30pm, 5–10.30pm, Sun 12.30–2.30pm, 5–10.30pm

C S

All the usual friendly, efficient service you'd expect from an establishment in the Reo Stakis chain makes this a popular Inverness eating-house. Main courses include the price of a starter and, apart from some steak options, are quite within the budget. Gammon steak with peach is an appealing choice at £3.50, and why not spoil yourself with hot apple pie and cream for 75p? Children are well catered for as well – their whole meal (that's three courses and a drink) costs only £1.45 in this charming restaurant.

INVERSHIN

Invershin Hotel ★
(Invershin 202)
Open: Mon–Fri 8am–9pm,
Sat 8am–10pm, Sun 9am–9.30pm

C P

You'll be encouraged to eat Scots at this traditional Highland hotel. Successful consumption of 'freshly-killed Highland haggis with tatties', roast ribs of Angus beef, and sweet little Cloutie dumplings, should leave you with a sense of achievement. And the old Scottish trait of getting good value for money holds true, too – lunch will be under £4, dinner around £5. Local fish features on all menus.

KENTALLEN

Holly Tree Restaurant, on A828, 3m SW of Ballachulish Bridge
(Duror 292)
Open: Restaurant 10am–2.30pm
Coffee Shop 10am–5.30pm

P

This restaurant is delightfully situated at the water's edge by Kentallen pier, allowing diners to gaze across the lovely Loch Linnhe to the misty mountains beyond. The eaterie is housed in a converted extension of the old Kentallen railway station and faithfully reproduces much of the original Edwardian-style décor. The coffee shop is open all day until 5.30pm and serves home baking, teas and light lunches. The menu is changed daily and might include venison pie at £2.25, lasagne at £1.50 or fresh salmon crêpes at £1.70. In the evening a large à la carte menu is offered, but with prices starting at £6 it's beyond our limit.

KINGUSSIE

Wood'N'Spoon Restaurant, 3–7 High Street
(Kingussie 488)
Open: Mon–Sat 10am–9.30pm, Sun 12.30–9.30pm

C F P S

The recently renovated restaurant has exposed stonework, a log fire, natural pine partitions and a self-service counter where home-made cakes, pies, quiches and other goodies are arrayed. Starters include smoked fish pâté at around £1. Chef's specials include game casserole and poached salmon, both served with baked potato and vegetables for around £3.75. Home-baked pies, fresh salads, cold roasts and venison burgers are always available. Sweets from the trolley are home-made and served with cream or ice-cream.

LOCHTON

T'Mast, Lochton House(A957, 6m SE of Banchory)
(Crathes 543/585)
Open: Summer Mon–Sun 12noon–2.30pm, 4.30–10.30pm

P

Formerly a grocer's shop, then a tearoom, this pub-cum-restaurant with its sun lounge extension now acts as a modern oasis for Grampian travellers. Lunchtime prices here are exceptionally low. For example, a simple starter, roast pork with apple sauce and peach Melba only comes to about £3. A typical high tea offering is gammon with pineapple (£3.75), including a hot drink, toast and cakes. Prices for dinner and supper are a little higher, with sirloin steak garni costing about £5.

Kingussie
—
Tomintoul

PETERHEAD

Coffee Shop, Fraserburgh Road
(Peterhead 71121)
Open: Mon–Sun 7.30am–11pm

C F P

Inside Peterhead's newest and most modern hotel, the Waterside Inn, you will find this glowing Coffee Shop. A variety of sandwiches are available otherwise a three-course meal of soup (60p), haddock (£1.85) and apple turnover (80p) are just a few of the dishes on the menu. A three-course evening meal is served from 6.30–11pm featuring a daily main course choice, soup as a starter and ice cream or cheese and biscuits for £4.95.

STONEHAVEN

Creel Inn, 1m E of A92, 5m S of Stonehaven
(Catterline 254)
Open: Tue–Sun 12.30–2.30pm

C P

James and Avril Young's attractive white-painted inn nestles on the clifftop above the tiny harbour of Catterline. In the short period that they've owned the restaurant, the Youngs have considerably enhanced its reputation. As you'd expect from an East Grampian eaterie the accent is on sea-food. After a home-made soup you can try home-cured ham salad for £2 or a fresh prawn salad at £2.50.

STRATHCARRON

Carron Restaurant, (On the A890, at the head of Lochcarron, between Achnasheen and Kyle of Lochalsh)
(Lochcarron 488)
Open: in season Mon–Sat 10.30am–9.15pm, out of season, Wed, Fri & Sat 7–9.15pm

A small restaurant that epitomises the best in careful attention and well-prepared food. Local paintings adorn brown hessian walls and, if you like the look of one of the paintings, you can take

---

it home with you as they are all for sale. The tiled floor and large windows, the pine tables, set with locally-made pottery all add to the homely atmosphere. The chicken-liver pâté at 75p is well recommended and the minute steak at £2.65 including salad and French fries is good value (all steaks are charcoal grilled). Choose from a selection of home-made sweets for 90p.

THURSO

Pentland Hotel ★★
Princes Street
(Thurso 3202)
Open: Mon–Thu 12noon–2pm, 6.30–8.30pm, Fri–Sat 12noon–2pm, 6.30–8.30pm, Sun 12.30–2pm, 6.30–8.30pm

S

In the bright, cheerful dining room of the Pentland, you can be tempted by an extensive à la carte lunch, dinner, or to combine the best of two meals, a high tea (5–6pm). A three-course lunch can easily cost under £4 and may include roast Caithness ribs of beef, or for 'a few dollars more', fresh Thurso salmon. Bar lunches served during the week are again very reasonably priced.

TOMINTOUL

Glenmulliach Restaurant, 2m SE of Tomintoul on A939 Braemar road
(Tomintoul 356)
Open: Mon–Sun 10am–8pm

P

The Lannagan family have built their dream restaurant from scratch. Father and sons did the building work, mum took over the decorating. The result is a pleasant, modern, cottage-style building set amongst forested hills. Inside, a wood-burning stove, red-pine fittings and a cheerful atmosphere defy the occasional Scottish mist. Food-wise, the emphasis is on home-baking and Scottish fare. A three-course lunch is available from £2.50–£4. In the evening soup, venison and home-made apple strudel is £5.75.

GLENMULLIACH RESTAURANT
TWO MILES SOUTH EAST OF TOMINTOUL
ON THE A939
TEL. TOMINTOUL 356
LUNCHES, SNACKS, TRADITIONAL SCOTTISH HIGH TEAS
WITH OUR OWN HOME BAKING.
CHILDRENS PLAY AREA
À LA CARTE MENU WITH SALMON, VENISON, STEAKS
AND OTHER SCOTTISH DISHES.
LARGE PRIVATE CAR PARK

ULLAPOOL

Far Isles, North Road
(Ullapool 2385)
Open: Mon–Sun 12noon–2.15pm,
5.30–9.30pm

P S

This attractively decorated, modern restaurant and bar on the northern outskirts of this picturesque little fishing village serves reasonably-priced wholesome food. Dishes include fresh Loch Broom scallops with savoury rice and salad, or escalope of pork Cordon Bleu, French fried and croquette potatoes with vegetables for £3.50.

Ullapool
—
Wick

WICK

Lamplighter, Wellington Guest House,
41–43 High Street
(Wick 3287)
Open: Summer Mon–Sat
11.30am–1.45pm, Thu–Sat 6–9pm (last orders), Winter
Mon–Sat 11.30am–1.45pm

P

This well-established house has been in operation for 50 years, and now John and Rhona Houston are at the helm to provide an excellent lunch or dinner at their first-floor restaurant, or a good range of snack meals in the ground-floor cafeteria. Lunch of melon boat at 60p, followed by Caithness salmon and mixed salad at around £2.70, plus home-made sweet from the trolley for about 60p is a satisfying meal.

WALES

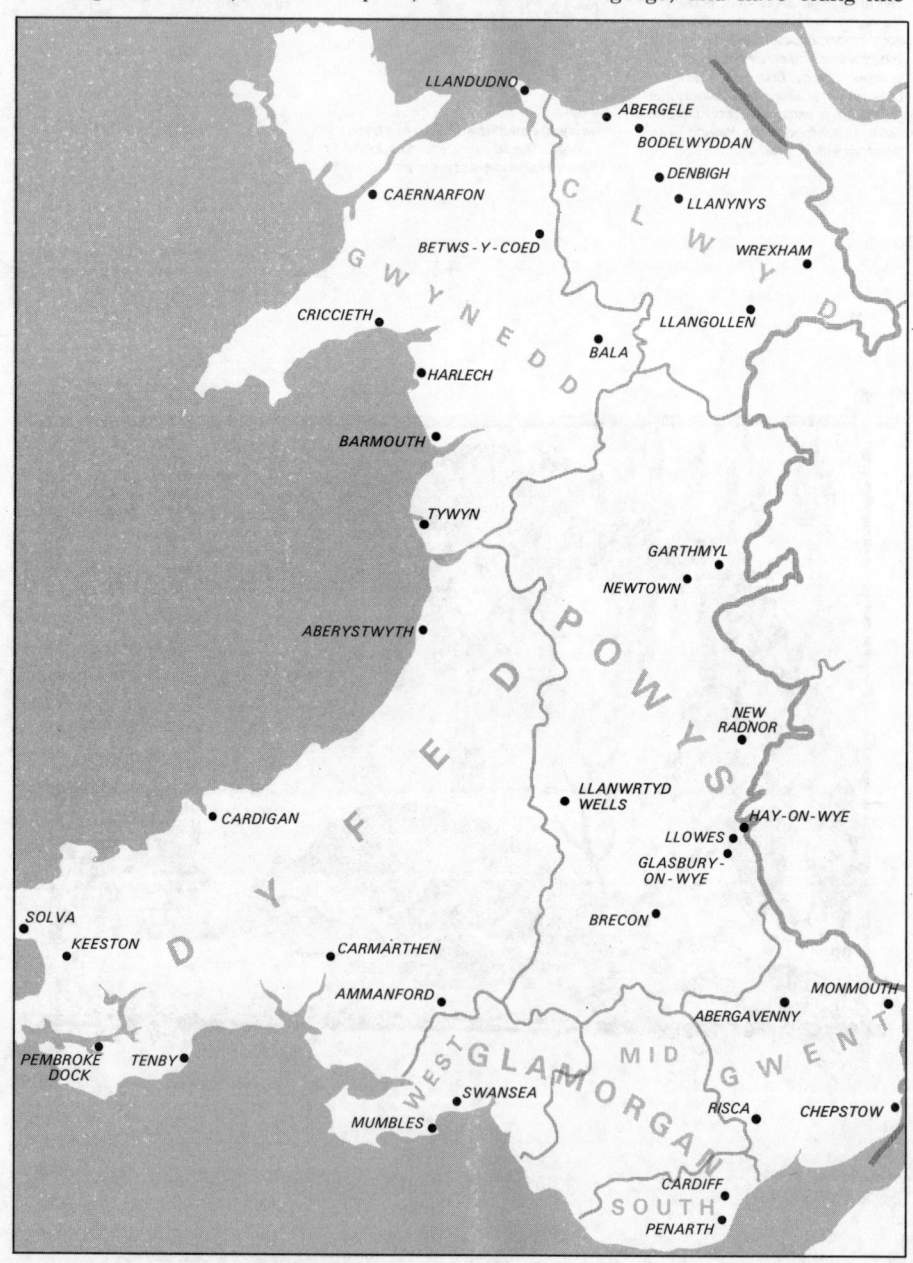

To an Englishman visiting Wales, the experience is not unlike going abroad. Although, ultimately, the Principality is governed from Westminster, it is undoubtedly another country. People speak a different language, and have clung like limpets to their identity. The Welsh have refused to be absorbed.

Offa's Dyke, that famous, though now fragmented, earthworks built by the King of Mercia at the end of the 8th century, helped in the early days. It may have kept the Welsh out of England; it also kept the land-hungry English out of Wales.

Edward I took a less liberal line. The castles that, nowadays, are obligatory viewing for sightseers, are testimony to his rule. But these are English castles. To the Welsh warriors of history, the ultimate fortress – and sanctuary – was Snowdonia. It was to here, amid the grey mountains with their peaks brushed by clouds, that they turned in times of trouble.

Since the Welsh are a race of individualists, one would expect to find a strong tradition of local dishes (some are naturally based on leeks, the national emblem) and so one does; leek porridge (the vegetable is boiled, cut into thin slices and served with toast fingers) and leek pie – to mention only two. Caerphilly cheese is rather less local than it used to be as it is now manufactured in Somerset, Devon and Dorset as well as in the town where it originated. Welsh rarebit really did originate in Wales, but, like Caerphilly cheese, its recipe escaped to England. That of Snowdon pudding did not; but there is nothing remarkable about it, and other places were probably content with their own puddings. Bara Brith is a type of currant cake; Bara Cressath and Brywes are all biscuits. Ham Cymraig is ham and tongue – though, it is stressed, the ham must be of a very high quality. Welsh lamb is second to none – unless you come from Devon, when you might well dispute the claim.

Laver bread causes much amusement among the non-Welsh. It is certainly a labour-intensive dish – first gather your seaweed. . . .

Abergavenny — Aberystwyth

ABERGAVENNY

Cartwheel, Monk Street
(Abergavenny 2692)
Open: Summer Mon & Wed–Fri
11am–2pm, 6–9.30pm,
Tue 10am–3pm, 6–9.30pm,
Sat 10am–10pm, Sun 12noon–9pm,
Winter Mon–Sat 12noon–2pm, Fri &
Sat 7–9.30pm

C ♫ P ☼

You will find this charming 17th-century restaurant in the centre of town on the main A40. The décor is pleasant and cosy with polished tables and wheel-back chairs. The restaurant offers à la carte menus with a good selection of dishes at sensible prices. Starters range from 45p for fruit juice to £1.65 for prawn cocktail. The main courses include roasts (£2.10), grills (steak costs £4.85) and pie (£1.95). Sweets range from 65p–85p. The dinner menu consists mainly of grills and, although more expensive, you can still enjoy a three-course meal well within our budget.

The Llanwenarth Arms Hotel, Brecon Road, Llanwenarth (2m W of Abergavenny off the A40)
Abergavenny 810550)
Open: Mon–Sun 12noon–2pm, 7–10pm

C P ☼

American hospitality and local culinary expertise welcome the visitor to D'Arcy and Janette McGregor's inn and restaurant. Lunch and dinner are available and although the à la carte menu may be beyond the limit of this guide, the bar meals are excellent and prove good value for money. Among the wide range of dishes, try the house specialities, pineapple prawn indienne (half a fresh pineapple with curried prawns and salad) £3.50, or steak and kidney pie £2.75. Other dishes on the menu, most at well under £4, include sirloin steak, quiche lorraine, cold meat salad platter, grilled trout with almonds and chili con carne. There is an extensive selection of home-made sweets priced from 95p–£1.50.

ABERGELE

Bull Hotel, Chapel Street
(Abergele 822115)
Open: Mon–Sun 12noon–2.30pm,
7–8.30pm

♫ P S

Emphasis is on good home cooking in this traditionally furnished inn with a friendly, relaxed atmosphere. The dining room menu operates for lunch and dinner and offers basic English fare, with three courses costing around £5.50. Home-made fruit pies or sherry trifle with cream are around 60p.

ABERYSTWYTH

The Cambrian Hotel ★★
Alexandra Road
(Aberystwyth 612446)
Open: Mon–Sun 12noon–2pm,
6.30–8pm, 10pm Thu–Sat, 7.30pm Sun

P

The atmosphere is warm and friendly and the food is home-cooked, hot and well served. Three-course table d'hôte lunch is around £4.25 and includes a choice of basic English roasts or salad. The four-course table d'hôte dinner has cheese and biscuits as the fourth course. Roast dinners are around £4.50, steak dinners around £5.

Caprice, 8–10 North Parade
(Aberystwyth 612084)
Open: Jun–Oct Mon–Sun 9am–8.30pm;
the rest of the year
Mon–Fri 9am–5.30pm, closed Winter Wed

C ♫ S ☼

Crabs straight from the harbour are a speciality at Jill and Alun Evans's cheerful restaurant. A three-course meal, with soup or fruit juice, a main course of roast, poultry or fish, and a sweet such as fruit tart and custard costs about £3.25. The à la carte menu is equally modestly priced, with starters from 35p for fruit juice to around £1.20 for prawn cocktail, main courses are up to about £4.

Gannets, St James Square
(Aberystwyth 617164)
Open: Tue–Sat 12noon–2pm,
6.30–10pm

♫ ☼

Previously a hairdresser's salon, now neatly converted into a popular, informal bistro, Gannets displays the work of local art graduates and students. Ann Jones and Gina Walpole, the proprietors, take turns in preparing the delicious home-made food. Typical dishes from the blackboard menu include carrot and mushroom bake, £1.85, stuffed marrow, £2.20, ratatouille, lasagne and chili con carne, all at £1.95. Home-made soups and sweets supplement the menu.

Marine Hotel, Marine Parade
(Aberystwyth 612444)
Open: Summer: Bar and dining room
Mon–Sun 12.30–2pm, 7–9.30pm,
Winter 12.30–2pm, 7pm onwards
Grill room Mon–Sat 7–9.30pm

C ♫ P S ☼

This Welsh hotel is Welsh owned, and the lamb on the menu is Welsh too. Lunch at around £3.50 cannot be bad value, and here one has a choice of four starters, a main course followed by a pudding or lighter sweet and coffee. The table d'hôte dinner offers a wider choice than the lunch menu at around £5.50. There is also a snack menu, with sandwiches and ploughman's lunch supplemented by sausage (about £1.30) and fish or chicken (about £1.30) all served with chips. Omelettes are priced from £1 with chips. A meal from the cold table is around £2.

Y Dewin Bistro, Ffordd Portland Road
(Aberystwyth 617738)
Open: Mon–Sat 12noon–2pm, 5–10pm

♫ S

The owner has succeeded in creating a Celtic atmosphere in the heart of Wales. Murals and paintings by a local artist enhance the effect with 'Lord of the Rings' themes. Menus are in Welsh and English, though no attempt has been made to translate pizza or quiche lorraine into either language! All food is home-cooked. Specialities are cawl and syllabub.

Cartwheel Restaurant

Monk Street
Abergavenny
Gwent NP75ND
Telephone 0873-2692

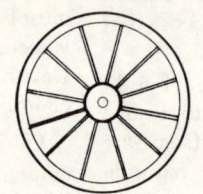

VEGETARIAN MENU

CHILDREN ALWAYS WELCOME

WELSH CREAM TEAS

BALA

Neuadd Y Cyfnod, High Street
(Bala 520262)
Open: Summer Mon–Sun 9am–9pm,
Winter Mon–Fri dinner only

C P S ⌖

In this imposing building, a long school hall, with its panelled walls and high ceilings, Gwyn and Ann Evans offer a taste or two of traditional Welsh cooking. Menus, with parallel text translations, include lunch at around £3 (half price for children), dinner at about £3.50 (again just over half price for children) and a particularly Welsh dinner, that includes a glass of mead, at just over £3.25. Welsh farmhouse soup, with local salmon and lamb figure among the alternatives in all three meals. A speciality of the house is an authentic Welsh tea at around £1 – unbeatable value.

BARMOUTH

The Angry Cheese, Church Street
(Barmouth 280038)
Open: Summer Mon–Sun 12noon–2pm,

Bala — Barmouth

6–10.30pm, Winter Fri–Sat 6–10.30pm

C P ⌖

Inside this attractive restaurant pine tables give a cosy, rustic effect. The three-course set menu costs around £5.50. There's a choice of six items in each course, featuring main dishes such as pork schnitzel with beurre noisette or home-made steak and kidney pie. Vegetarians are tempted by such dishes as fruit and vegetable kebabs or vegetarian cutlets. If you go à la carte, potatoes and fresh vegetables of the day are included in the price of the main course dish from that menu.

CAMBRIAN HOTEL
Alexandra Road, ABERYSTWYTH, Dyfed
Telephone 0970 612446

Excellent reputation for three-course meals, with roasts, steaks and fish from £4.25.

The 70 seater restaurant is charmingly decorated in keeping with the 150 year old Tudor-style building.

Food is also offered in both of the lively bars — including Chef's Special steak and kidney pie at £1.25.

14 comfortable bedrooms available.

Pat and Mike welcome you.

Caprice
... Licensed Restaurant

**OPEN EVERY DAY
9.00am - 8.30pm
JUNE to OCTOBER**

WE HAVE 3 GREAT SALES GIMMICKS
VALUE FOR MONEY
FRIENDLY SERVICE
PLEASANT SURROUNDINGS

WELSH TEAS A SPECIALITY

**8-10 NORTH PARADE, ABERYSTWYTH
Telephone: Aberystwyth (0970) 612084**

Betws-y-Coed — Caernarfon

BETWS-Y-COED
Park Hill Hotel ★★
Llanrwst Road
(Betws-y-Coed 540)
Open: Mon–Sun for dinner, beginning 7–7.30pm (booking essential

C P

If 'home-made and fresh' appeals to you then you'll like this hotel restaurant. Choice is necessarily limited as proprietors John and Jenny Waite do the cooking and serving themselves. The table d'hôte dinner at around £6 offers a choice between soup, fruit juice and two other starters (pâté perhaps), at least three main dishes (a roast, coq au vin, plaice meunière and baked gammon in cider are examples), three sweets (raspberry tart and cream, peach lorraine, blackcurrant cheesecake for instance) and cheese and biscuits, plus tea or coffee. Just one thing – it's advisable to book well in advance.

BODELWYDDAN
Cromwell's Bistro, Faenol Fawr Manor ××
(Rhuddlan 590784)
Open: Mon–Sun 12noon–2.30pm, 7.30–11pm (closed Sun in winter)

C ♫ P

Faenol Fawr is a restaurant (a bit expensive for us) in a manor house built in 1597, but Cromwell's is really old, dating back to the early part of the 13th century. Here, you can take a pleasant yet inexpensive meal chosen from the Supper Bar menu. Starters include home-made soup at around 40p and Arbroath smokies at about £1.50. There are casseroles – duck and blackberry at around £2.20 and local pheasant in red wine (around £3) and meat platters for about £2 – with help-yourself salad and jacket potato included in the price. A home-made sweet will add 75p or so.

BRECON
Red Lion Inn, Llangorse
(Llangorse 238)
Open: Mon–Sun 12noon–2pm, 7–9.30pm

P ♫

A warm Welsh welcome is assured in this two hundred-year-old inn close to the famous Llangorse lake. Situated deep in the heart of the Brecon Beacons National Park, it is an ideal holiday stopping-place. Meals in the bar include snacks such as Chef's terrine, roll and butter at about 75p, beef kebabs at £1.30 and tipsy cake at £1.15. More substantial dishes such as chicken Red Lion style, veal Cordon Bleu or beef chasseur cost around £3.25. An à la carte meal may be had in the dining room and could include seafood pancake, Hungarian pork, a sweet from the trolley and coffee for £6.25.

CAERNARFON
Plas Bowman, High Street
(Caernarfon 5555)
Open: Mon–Sat 12noon–2.30pm, 6–9.30pm, Sun 12noon–1.30pm, 6–10pm

S ♫

Built in 1334 for the High Sheriff, Thomas Bowman, this three-storey property now houses Posi Williams, North Wales Chef of the Year 1980, who cooks fresh meats, fish and vegetables for a brilliantly imaginative menu which changes daily. Just under £6 will get you three courses, coffee or tea and a glass of wine for lunch or dinner. The set menu offers about four choices for each course. Appetisers could include celery and ham with a cheese sauce, seafood vol-au-vent or stuffed courgettes. Lasagne and Welsh lamb are examples of main dishes, and vegetarians are catered for here. It is advisable to book in advance as Plas Bowman is deservedly popular with the locals of Caernarfon.

The Red Lion Inn
Llangorse, Brecon.
AA ★

This delightful Country Inn has 10 Bedrooms (5 with bath and 5 with shower).
The restaurant, open to residents, serves an à la carte menu every evening, Monday to Saturday, from 7-9.30pm and also offers an extensive wine list.
Bar snacks and meals are served in the bar every lunchtime and evening from 7-9.30pm.
Cold buffet is served in the bar every Sunday lunchtime, between 12.00 noon and 2pm.
Telephone Llangorse 238

Himalaya TANDOORI Restaurant

Tandoori Cooking is a traditional Indian method of preparing food in a charcoal fired clay pot using a large range of oriental spices which gives a distinctive and delicious flavour to the dishes.

Our Specialities

Himalaya Special

(This is a two course meal, started with Tandoori Chicken, spiced, marinated and barbecued on a skewer in "Charcoal Clay Oven" and also served with Salad and mint sauce. Followed by authentically cooked spicy chicken and prawn curries, pillou rice, freshly baked Nan Bread and spiced Papadam.)

Murghi Mussala

(A traditional Indian Dish prepared authentically with spring chicken marinated, spiced and barbecued on a skewer in "Charcoal Clay Oven" seasoned with spicy minced meat sauted in Gee, with finely chopped onions and pimentoes etc. also garnished with tomatoes, eggs and almonds and salad served with pillou rice and spiced papadam.)

Chef's Special

(This is a two course meal with various combinations of Onion, Pakura, Tandoori Chicken, Rogon gushth vegetable curry, Rice and Nan.) Main dishes include Tandoori Chicken (Full whole chicken with salad), Tandoori Tikka Mashalla (with thick sauce), Tandoori Chicken Tikka with Salad (dry) as well as many others — also a large range of starters, sundries and side dishes.

FULLY LICENSED

24 WELLFIELD ROAD
CARDIFF
Telephone: Cardiff 491722

26 HOLTON ROAD
BARRY
Telephone: Barry 746623

The Stables Restaurant and Hotel ☆☆☆
(Llanwnda 830711/830213)
Open: Mon–Sun 12noon–1.45pm,
7–9.45pm

C 🎵 P ♿

Some of the best food that Caernarfon has to offer is to be found at Mrs Jenny Howarth's Stables Restaurant, some three miles outside the town, on the A317 road to Pwllheli. Formerly the stables to Plas Fynnon, the building was very cleverly and tastefully converted for its present use in 1972. The menu is a long and impressive one but the locals, who ought to know, swear by the barbecued spare ribs starter, ham and asparagus mornay, grilled trout with almonds, local lamb chops in wine sauce and pineapple flambé, all around £4.85. A table d'hôte menu is also available for around £6.50 and about £5.50 at lunchtimes. Live entertainment is frequently provided in the evenings.

CARDIFF

The Himalaya Restaurant, 24 Wellfield Road
(Cardiff 491722)
Open: Mon–Sun 12noon–3pm,
6pm–2am

C 🎵 S ♿

The best Indian food in Cardiff is the local verdict on Bakshi Suleman's restaurant. The Himalaya has a vaguely Oriental décor. Biraini dishes, chicken curries and meat or prawn curries cost from around £2.50–£2.75. Be warned: the helpings are enormous.

See advert on p. 213

Savastano's, 302 North Road
(Cardiff 30270)
Open: Mon–Sat 12noon–2.30pm, 7–11.30pm, Thu–Sat 12mdnt

Giacomo Savastano's restaurant doesn't strike one as particularly Italian, for the décor is plain and the furniture pine. But his food is very Italian, very good and – as Italian restaurants go – extremely reasonably priced, with soups around 80p, pastas at about £2.60, a number of fish, chicken or veal dishes at around £3.50 and steaks from about £4.05. Service is very efficient at this restaurant.

Cardiff
—
Carmarthen

Ye Olde Wine Shoppe, Wyndham Arcade, St Mary Street
(Cardiff 29876)
Open: Mon–Sat 12noon–2.30pm,
7–11pm

🎵 P S

Don't be put off by the name. This must be the best-stocked wine bar in Cardiff and well worth a visit, for its friendly bars and bright little bistro. The downstairs bar and bistro serve the same food at the same prices – the menu features three-course meals from 10 different countries ranging in price from £4.45–£6.85. The Hungarian meal at £5.60 consists of mixed salamis and pickles, lamb goulash, and cream cheese and nut pancake. The Italian meal of minestrone soup, lasagne, and cassata ice-cream costs £4.45. Whilst the above full meals are served in the restaurant any single dish can be served as a snack in the bar.

Yr Ystafell Gymraeg, 74 Whitchurch Road
(Cardiff 42317)
Open: Mon–Fri 12noon–2pm,
7–11.30pm, Sat 7–11.30pm

C ♿

Yr Ystafell Gymraeg (The Welsh Room to you) is just that, with its Welsh-weave drapes, Welsh tapestry posters, Welsh Tourist Board posters, the Welsh dresser and a Welsh menu (with English subtitles). The owners sound Italian and, indeed, proprietor Umberto Palladino is, but his wife is just about as Welsh as it is possible to be. Starters include Penclawdd Cockles at around £1.10. Poultry dishes range in price from around £3 for chicken Snowdonia. Home-made fruit pies, gâteaux and trifle range from between 70p–£1.20.

CARDIGAN

The Bell Hotel, Pendre
(Cardigan 612629)
Open: Mon–Sat 12noon–2pm, 7–9pm

P S ♿

Malcolm and Jenny Wood have a good lunchtime trade at The Bell. A range of basket and plate meals are all under £2. The evening menu gives a considerable choice of three-course meals for £5.25 (main courses include scampi, lamb chops and trout).

The Black Lion Hotel, High Street
(Cardigan 612532)
Open: Mon–Sat 12noon–2.30pm,
8–10pm

🎵 S ♿

Inglenook fireplaces, exposed beams and stone walls set the scene at the Black Lion. For about £5 you can have a satisfying three-course meal in the Linenfold Bar (rounded off by a speciality ice-cream) and perhaps even try a cocktail or two. Drivers are catered for with non-alcoholic wine and lager, and tea, coffee or hot chocolate served at the bar. Try the meals in baskets at prices from £2.55 upwards, served in the lounge.

Cliff Hotel ☆☆☆
Gwbert-on-Sea
(Cardigan 613241/613242/612517)
Open: Mon–Sun 12.45–2pm, 7–9pm

C 🎵 P ♿

This restaurant offers an interesting choice of menu but unfortunately, the à la carte is beyond our reach but the table d'hôte lunch and dinner at around £6 and £7 respectively are just within our limit. For starters hot consommé with profiteroles, main course – hot crab Gwbert style with new potatoes and tomato provençale, and a choice of sweets from the trolley. In the newly-opened buttery it is possible to dine in style on a meal of locally-caught sewin, plus starter and sweet, for under or around the £5 mark.

CARMARTHEN

The Old Curiosity, 20A King Street
(Carmarthen 32384)
Open: Mon–Sat 10am–5pm, Fri & Sat 7.30–10.30pm

🎵 S ♿

Black Lion Hotel
Cardigan
Telephone: 612532

FREE HOUSE

WEST WALES' PREMIER INN

". . . a return to gracious living"

The Old Curiosity is much, much more than a convenient place for a coffee, a snack, or a meal. The Indian salad contains brown rice, not white, and vegetarians may choose from a number of appetising dishes. The seafood salad at around £2.75 is excellent, and omelettes include mushroom, ham or chicken all at around £1.70. 'Gap fillers' at around £1.30 include curry butter prawns and bacon-wrapped bananas. Various quiches cost about 95p a slice.

Queensway Restaurant, Queen Street (Carmarthen 5631)
Open: Mon-Sat 10am-2.30pm, 6.30-11pm

Chepstow

C

This ground-floor restaurant and first-floor wine bar opens on to a sun-trap roof garden. Steaks are popular in the restaurant, where the à la carte menu includes Chef's specials priced about £3. Meals served from the wine bar include plaice and chips or roast beef and Yorkshire pudding at around £4 or steak and chips at under £4.

CHEPSTOW
Castle View Hotel ★★
Bridge Street
(Chepstow 70349)
Open: Mon-Sat 12.15-2pm, 6.30-9pm, Sun 12.15-1.45pm, 6.30-8.30pm and normal licensing hours

C P S ⌖

As its name suggests this charming, ivy-clad hotel is opposite Chepstow Castle. Meals in the bar include imaginative home-made soup at 75p. Prawns au gratin is a popular main course choice at £2.25 so is fresh Wye salmon at £3.40 with salad. Lemon syllabub costs around

---

BROOK HOUSE MILL TAVERN
Lower Ruthis Road, Denbigh, Clwyd.
Telephone: Denbigh 3377

Visit the Restored Mill which retains the Old Watermill Workings.

Much of the produce used in our kitchen is bought at local markets and there are many fresh and seasonal dishes on the menu.

Sunday lunch is available, which is followed by a children's disco from 2-3pm.

Open: Monday-Friday noon - 3pm, Sunday noon - 2pm, Monday - Sunday 7pm - 11pm.

Family run hotel with an excellent food reputation both with the "locals" and tourists. Service, good food and wine our aim. We serve traditional and continental food in the bar and also in our restaurant. Built in 1730 as a coaching inn and situated on the main Manchester to Swansea road (A483). Residential, real ale, snacks, bar meals and restaurant.
Open: Mon-Sat 10.30-2.30pm, 6.00-10.30pm.
Sun 12.00 noon-2.00 pm, 7-10.30pm.

THE NAG'S HEAD HOTEL — GARTHMYL
MONTGOMERY — POWYS — WALES
Telephone: Berriew 287 & 537

LLWYNAUBACH LODGE
Glasbury-on-Wye Hereford HR3 5PJ

AA ★★

COUNTRY HOTEL & RESTAURANT

Inter-Hotel

LUNCHES · DINNERS
DINNER DANCES
CARVERS'S TABLE
À LA CARTE and
SPECIALITY EVENINGS
CONFERENCES and
WEDDING RECEPTIONS

Telephone Glasbury 473

Criccieth — Hay-on-Wye

80p. The restaurant serves two- and three-course lunches with coffee and has a good variety of starters, grills, home-cooked dishes and sweets, but they are out of our price range. The three-course vegetarian meal, with a choice of dishes, is around £6.50.

The First Hurdle, 9 Upper Church Street (Chepstow 2189)
Open: Mon–Sat 12noon–9pm

C P S &

Just off Chepstow's town centre is this small hotel, immediately attractive because of its Edwardian furniture and pretty soft furnishings. At lunchtime, roast joints carved hot from the oven represent good value, as well as Welsh lamb chops and daily specials such as home-made steak and kidney pie or curry. In the evening diners can choose from the French menu, where a good choice would be French onion soup (70p), followed by trout with almonds and fresh vegetables (£3.60), and a sweet from the trolley, or the grill menu where prawn cocktail, gammon with pineapple, salad, peas and chips and a sweet costs about £6.

CRICCIETH

Bron Eifion Country Hotel ★★★
(Criccieth 2385)
Open: Mon–Sun 8.30–9.30am, 1–2pm, 7.30–9pm

P &

Bron Eifion was built in the 1870s as the summer residence of slate master John Greaves. Its main hall boasts superb wall panelling and a magnificent central gallery of pitch pine. The hotel's three-course lunch is about £5 (including service) and gives a tempting choice of starters and desserts.

The Moelwyn Restaurant, Mona Terrace
(Criccieth 2500)
Open: Mon–Sun 12.30–2pm, 7–9.30pm, closed Mon all day and Sun pm in winter

C P &

Mr and Mrs Peter Booth worked for the previous owners for four years before purchasing the Moelwyn Restaurant, a creeper-clad Victorian house with panoramic views over Cardigan Bay and the Cambrian Range, five years ago. Tasty lunch offerings include a good quality home-made soup for around 65p, smoked mackerel or lasagne verdi at about £1.85, fresh crab salad (when available) at £2.95, a choice of sweet or cheeseboard for 80p or so and Cona coffee at 50p. A children's menu offers three courses for about £2 and, on Sundays, a traditional roast lunch table d'hôte costs under £5. A special three-course dinner (available at £6.25) could include home-made soup, Welsh lamb cutlets and a choice of sweets from the trolley.

DENBIGH

Brook House Mill Tavern, 2m E of Denbigh on the A525
(Denbigh 3377)
Open: Mon–Fri 12noon–3pm, Sun 12noon–2pm, Mon–Sun 7–11pm

月 P &

The mill is run by David Hall whose family also runs the Faenol Fawr Manor (Cromwell's Bistro) at Bodelwyddan (see p. 212. The mill has been well restored and retains the old watermill workings. Much of the produce used in the kitchen is bought at local markets and there are many fresh and seasonal dishes listed on the blackboard menu. Prawn cocktail, pâté, and melon are 95p, chicken curry and fresh fish are £2.40 and sweets are around £1. Cooked snack meals are around £1.60. Sunday lunch, available at £2.95, is followed by a children's disco from 2–3pm.
See advert on p. 215

DOLGELLAU

Paris House Steak Bar, Smithfield Street (Dolgellau 422585)
Open: Easter to Oct Mon–Sat 6–9pm, high season 6–10pm

C P S &

This steak bar was converted from a 'Paris' fashion house and has attractive oak panels taken from a nearby chapel. Starters include pâté at 90p and hot mussels in white wine and garlic at £1.75. Main courses range from a quarter chicken at £2.50 to steak at £4.50. Sweets are around £1, coffee 45p and a glass of wine 70p. There is a children's menu, and small portions can be ordered from the main menu.

GARTHMYL

The Nag's Head Hotel
(Berriew 287/537)
Open: Mon–Sat 10.30am–2.30pm, 6–10.30pm, Sun 12noon–2pm, 7–10.30pm

C 月 P &

Modern, colourful décor is the hallmark of the small restaurant at The Nag's Head, where Mr and Mrs Emilio Moreno attend personally to your needs. The atmosphere is cosy and intimate in the small bar where you can drink while you wait for your excellent meal. Particularly recommended is the table d'hôte – for example, you can eat Spanish omelette, roast chicken Cuban style and apple pie for under £5, or pick a 'main course special' which comes preceded by soup at £2.80.
See advert on p. 215

GLASBURY

Llwynaubach Lodge ★★
(Glasbury 473)
Open: Mon–Sun 12noon–2.30pm, 7.30–10.30pm

C 月 P &

Llwynaubach Lodge enjoys a peaceful situation in the Wye Valley with 10 acres of grounds including its own trout-filled lake and an outdoor swimming pool. At lunchtime during the week, hot and cold bar snacks and salads are available from £1–£3 – sandwiches even cheaper. Chef's carving table offers hot roast joints in the evenings and for Sunday lunch.
See advert on p. 215

HARLECH

Castle Cottage
(Harlech 780479)
Open: Summer Mon–Sun 10.30am–2pm, 6.30–9pm, Winter Fri–Sun 10.30am–2pm, 6.30–8.30pm (closed Sun eve)

C &

Castle Cottage had a variety of uses before it became a restaurant and guest house some 25 years ago; it was once a farm, a smithy, a butcher's shop and originally, a gin shop. Jim and Betty Yuill cater for up to 35 people in their 16th-century beamed cottage which can be found adjacent to Harlech Castle. Simple lunch dishes include cottage pie, smoked haddock kedgeree and plaice and chips all at around £1.50 (all home-made). A special three-course table d'hôte menu is excellent value at £2.50. At dinner time the table d'hôte menu is more adventurous and includes starters such as New Orleans prawn or eggs Florentine, with main course of haddock in cream, and coffee granita for dessert, you have a substantial meal for a fixed price of just over £5. There is an extensive and modestly priced wine list.

HAY-ON-WYE

The Old Barn Inn, Three Cocks, on A438 (Glasbury 500)
Open: Mon–Sat 12noon–2.30pm, 6.30–9.30pm, Sun 12noon–1.30pm, 7–9.30pm

C P &

This old barn was converted about three years ago and still retains the original high ceilings and beams. The dining area is suitable for children and is furnished with old oak tables and wheelback chairs. There is a small cold counter display and the dish of the day is chalked on the blackboard. The standard menu lists typical pub fare, soup at 70p, cottage pie topped with cheese at £1.60, scampi and chips at £2.85 and a range of sweets around 60p. The children's menu contains the ever popular fish fingers, chips, sausages, etc and when they have finished eating there is a play area with swings and climbing frames. Sunday lunch is £2.35 (£1.85 for children).

LLANDUDNO

Coffee Shop and Poolside Bar, Empire Hotel ★★★
Church Walks
(Llandudno 79955)
Open: Mon–Sun 11am–3pm, 6–10pm
C P

The range of five different starters (predominantly fishy!) cost from 70p–£1.50. A variety of salads, fresh Conwy plaice and barbequed chicken are just some of the main courses that enable you to keep within the budget. Desserts are around 75p and include fresh fruit salad and cherry brandy cake.

Plas Fron Deg Hotel, 48 Church Walks
(Llandudno 77267)
Open: Mon–Sun 12.30–2pm, 6.30–7.30pm
C

Lunch and dinner menus priced from around £4.50–£6 offer a real choice, with dishes such as salmon mousse, coq au vin and ratafia trifle to tempt the taste buds. 'A Taste of Wales' dishes are a feature of Plas Fron Deg, too, and well worth trying. The à la carte menu is likely to be out of our price range.

LLANGOLLEN

Gale's Wine and Food Bar, 18 Bridge Street
(Llangollen 860089)

Llandudno
—
Llowes

Open: Mon–Sat 12noon–1.45pm, 6–10pm (also Sun Jun–Oct)
P S

There are more than a hundred wines on offer at Richard and Jill Gale's Wine and Food Bar, including one vintage port. The atmosphere is very friendly and welcoming, the menu written on a blackboard behind the bar. The food is outstandingly good for this kind of operation and very reasonable, with home-made soups at around 60p, a choice of pâtés at around 95p and a hot dish of the day from around £2.30. Very popular are pork and apple Stroganoff at around £2.10 and beef in Guinness at about £2.20.

Royal Hotel ★★★
Bridge Street
(Llangollen 860202)
Open: Mon–Sun 12.30–2.15pm, 7–9.30pm, 10pm Sat
C P S ♠

There are views of the River Dee from the restaurant of this Trusthouse Forte hotel. The à la carte menu is on the expensive side, but the three-course table d'hôte lunch at about £5.25 and dinner at around £6 are excellent value. A good, more modest bar lunch or evening meal is possible at around £2.

LLANYNYS

The Lodge, L'lanrhaeadr, near Denbigh
(Llanynys 370)
Open: Mon–Sat 9am–5.30pm
C P ♠

The Lodge combines the display of fashions (from many parts of the world) and objets d'art with the provision of tasty inexpensive food. The accent is on light meals with filled baps, Welsh rarebit, hamburger, and several other items, all at under £2, but there are more substantial dishes including salads (cheese, ham, prawn or chicken) for between £1.60–£2.50 and savoury pancakes or omelettes for less than £2. Sweets and pastries are home-made. A wide variety of beverages is available – but the Lodge is not licensed.

LLOWES

Radnor Arms
(Glasbury 460)
Open: Mon–Sat 12noon–3pm, 7–10.30pm
P ♠

This small, pleasant country pub is a converted house with white-painted walls. The atmosphere in the dining area with its high, beamed ceiling, is informal and relaxed. A good selection of food is chalked up on the blackboard menu with home-made soups at about 90p, quiches

The Empire Hotel
Coffee Shop and pool side bar

Indoor heated swimming pool

The Empire hotel is an independent, first-class hotel, which has been in the same family since 1947. Beautiful setting overlooking indoor heated swimming pool, where one can buy a drink of wine or coffee, and eat toasted sandwiches, home-made soup or a more complicated grill meal. Charcoal cooked steaks or fresh local fish. Welsh lamb steaks served with crispy salad and chips.
Home-made gateaux and pies.
Open all year (except Christmas and New Year) normal bar hours.
**Llandudno, Gwynedd
Telephone 0492 79955
Telex 617161**

Monmouth — Newtown

at around £2, lasagne or Cheshire pork and apple pie, both around £2.50 and mackerel in white wine costing a little more. There is a good selection of sweets at around £1.

MONMOUTH

King's Head Hotel ★★★
Agincourt Square
(Monmouth 2177)
Open: Mon–Fri 12.30–2pm, 7–9pm,
Sat 12.30–2pm, 7–10pm,
Sun 12.30–1.45pm, 7–9pm
Coach House Mon 6.30–11pm,
Tue–Sat 12noon–3pm, 6.30–11pm,
Sun 12noon–2pm, 7–10pm

[P][S]

Table d'hôte lunch costs around £6.50 but the dinner menu is £8 or more. Other informal lunches well within the budget are served in the cocktail bar – a cold buffet selection with interesting, fresh salads costs about £2.50 and hot dish of the day might be a casserole, pasta dish or steak and kidney pie. To the rear of the main hotel, is the Coach House. Colourful plants are arranged on the very pleasant patio area. Prices on the pub-snack menu range between 65p and £2. In the grill room, the usual selection of grills is enlivened by Barnsley chop at £3.50 or Polynesian prawn and pineapple curry at about £5.

MUMBLES

La Gondola, 590 Mumbles Road
(Swansea 62338)
Open: Tue–Sun 12noon–2.30pm,
6.30–11pm

[C][P]

Apart from his native Italian, Proprietor Aldo Grattarola speaks English very well, and gets by in French and German so it follows that he should keep a cosmopolitan menu. À la carte choices include veal dishes, fillet Stroganoff, Dover sole meunière and lasagne verdi al forno – a pretty cosmopolitan bag, you'll agree! More modest is the set lunch menu offering four choices of roast, plaice, trout or steak and kidney pie with vegetables and potatoes, plus a sweet and starter, around £3.

NEW RADNOR

Red Lion Inn, Llanfihangel Nant Melan
(New Radnor 220)
Open: Mon–Sun 12noon–2pm, 7–11pm

[P][&]

A warm welcome always awaits visitors to this 300-year-old roadside inn. Situated on the A44 between Leominster and Rhayader, the building retains its olde-worlde character and charm while also benefiting from modern comforts inside such as the cosy wood-burning stove in the lounge. Dennis and Pauline, the proprietors, pride themselves in offering homely fare and for only £4.75 or so, you can sit down to a wholesome lunch of soup, an 8oz sirloin steak with trimmings followed by ice-cream or cheese and biscuits. Sunday lunch costs around £1 less – so you can afford to treat the family. Tasty bar snacks, served day or evening, include scampi or steak and kidney pie at around £1.70 and a cold buffet, served from the verandah, is a big attraction at £2.50 per head.

NEWTOWN

Bear Hotel ★★★
Broad Street
(Newtown 26964)
Open: Mon–Sun 12noon–2pm,
6.30–9.30pm

[C][♫][P][S]

Formerly a coaching inn, the Bear has all the atmosphere anyone could wish for. Food is available in the bar and in two grill rooms: the Spinning Wheel and the Severn. Bar snacks are served in the evening and are mainly substantial, including steak and kidney pie or chicken and chips. The restaurant serves an excellent three-course dinner with a large

---

The Red Lion Inn

**Llanfihangel-Nant-Melan
New Radnor
Powys**

Set among the mountains of mid Wales on the direct route to the beautiful Elan Valley and Dams. We are close to the beautiful River Wye which is the principle salmon and trout river in mid Wales. The area abounds with breath-taking scenery for both hikers and motorists. Pony trekking is close by. Local beauty spots are Hergest Croft, Offa's Dyke, Water Break-its-Neck and many more.

La Gondola

590 Mumbles Rd., Mumbles,
Swansea
Telephone: Swansea 62338

Aldo Grattarola

Open: 12-2.30 6.30-11

Closed all day Mon

choice for each course, including fresh goujons of sole in tomato sauce or chicken Marengo at around £6.25 including coffee.

PEMBROKE DOCK

Hill House Inn, Cosheston
(Pembroke 64352)
Open: Mon–Sun 12noon–2pm, 7–10.30pm, 11pm in Summer

C P

There's a touch of Welsh patriotism at this early Georgian inn, which offers a comfortable, welcoming atmosphere along with several real ales. The bar meals are good value at around £5 for a three-course meal and charcoal-grilled steaks and kebabs are the speciality of the house.

PENARTH

Rabaiotti's, Caprice Restaurant ✕✕✕
The Esplanade
(Penarth 702424)
Open: Mon–Sat 10.30am–2.30pm, 7–10.30pm, Sun 10.30am–2.30pm

C 🎵 P S

Situated below the Caprice Restaurant (superb cuisine but too expensive for us!) Rabaiotti's operates from the same kitchen and offers good, unpretentious food at very reasonable prices. Starters include home-made soup of the day at around 40p, potted shrimps at about

Pembroke Dock

Solva

£1.20 and mixed hors d'oeuvres at around £2. Dishes include lamb cutlets, peas and chips, at just over £3, and fillet steak garni with chips, at about £4.50. Sweets include a choice of gâteaux and fruit tart with cream in the 50p–80p range. The three-course Sunday lunch is very good value, the price list for the main course being inclusive of starter and sweet and costing about £4.65. Starters offer a choice of soup, fruit juice or Florida cocktail, the third course can be a fresh cream dessert or cheese and biscuits. Rabaiotti's also boasts an interesting cocktail bar open to non-diners which proves popular.

RISCA

Michael's, 39–41 Tredegar Street
(Risca 614300)
Open: Tue–Sat 9.30am–4pm, 7.30pm–12mdnt, Sun 12noon–2pm

C 🎵 P S

The restaurant seats about 50 people and also has a snack bar. Two-course lunches are around £2 and three courses are from £3.20–£5.60. In the evening the 'Chef's Specials' offer three courses with coffee for £5.95 (main course choices are trout, scampi, sirloin steak and chicken

chasseur). The extensive à la carte menu is generally outside the scope of this guide.
See advert on p. 220

SOLVA

Harbour House, Solva
(St Davids 721267)
Open: Summer Mon–Sun 12noon–2.30pm, Mon–Sat 7–9.30pm, Winter Thu–Sat only – telephone to determine times

P

The Canby-Lewis family run this small hotel with obvious enjoyment. For lunch you could do no better than to try the home-made cawl, a large bowl of steaming hot soup which comes served with a tasty cheese roll and butter at £1.15. Individual steak and kidney pies are made on the premises, the trout and mackerel come from local waters, and the steaks are cut from local beef. The speciality of the house is tournedos Maximillian – fillet steak wrapped in bacon, served on a croute and covered in mushroom and Madeira sauce, but it's out of our price range. However, plenty of other dishes – such as Krispy Prawns with tartare sauce – are under £3. Sweets include home-made gâteau, cheesecake and chocolate mousse Basquaise. Children under 12 have their own Junior Menu with old favourites such as fish finger or sausage and chips, ice cream and lemonade.

EAGLE HOTELS
A welcome through Wales

Hotels conveniently situated in north, mid and south Wales offering comfortable facilities, most rooms with bath, shower en-suite, and attractive restaurants offering traditional Welsh cooking.

For bookings, details of weekend packages and longer breaks, please contact our central reservation office:
EAGLE HOTELS LIMITED
Shortbridge Street, NEWTOWN, Powys.
Tel: (0686) 26639

Rabaiotti's Grill Room
PENARTH
SOUTH GLAMORGAN
Telephone: 702424

Proprietor: Mr. Eddie Rabaiotti.

Attractive views of shipping in the Bristol Channel can be gained from this attractive lounge where one may enjoy a casual drink whilst contemplating the wide selection of food available in the most pleasant surroundings.
There is a delightful cold buffet as well as a range of starters, hot and cold main courses and sweets — all prepared from the same kitchen as the exclusive Caprice Restaurant.

SWANSEA
The Dragon Hotel ☆☆☆☆
Kingsway Circle
(Swansea 51074)
Open: The Birch Room Mon–Sun
12.30–2.30pm, 7–9.30pm
The Dragon Coffee Shop Mon–Sat
10am–11pm

C F P S ♦

The Birch Room Restaurant offers a 'Town and Country Luncheon' selection, two courses from £4.95 and in the evening there is a three-course 'Carvery' from £6.95. An à la carte menu featuring local Welsh dishes is also on offer. The

---

Swansea
—
Tenby

Coffee Shop prices are extremely competitive for a quick meal or snack throughout the day. Bar salads are served in both bars.

TENBY
Hoi San Restaurant, Tudor Square
(Tenby 2025)
Open: Apr–Sept Mon–Sun
12noon–11.45pm, Oct–Dec, Mar
Thu–Fri 6–11.45pm,

Sat–Sun 12noon–11.45pm

C F S ♦

A friendly, enthusiastic Cantonese atmosphere is to be found here in the centre of Tenby. Chopsticks are laid out to test your dexterity and help is at hand should you fail the test. Special home cooking evenings are laid on when unusual family-style dishes are available. The choice of special dinners is impressive. A four-course dinner and coffee will cost about £5.15 per person, but two can share the £4.90 menu which offers three courses (a choice of four main dishes) and coffee. Particularly recommended are hot and sour soup and

---

Michael's Restaurant
FULLY LICENSED

Open daily for lunches and evening meals — Table d'hote and à la carte.
Sunday lunches a speciality
(Not open on Monday)

**Tredegar Street, Risca, Gwent. (3 miles from M4)
Telephone: Risca (0633) 614300**

The Coffee Shop where you can enjoy an intimate and informal meal with prices starting from £2.75 for a Farmhouse Platter or a Cheese and Bacon Burger with French Fries.

Open daily Monday/Saturday from 10.00 a.m. until 10.45 p.m.

Enjoy a quiet drink in the Dragon and Viking Bar, adjacent to the Coffee Shop.

DRAGON HOTEL
**Kingsway Circle
Swansea
Telephone: (0792) 51074**

thf Hotels

海山酒樓

HOI SAN RESTAURANT
TUDOR SQUARE, TENBY
Telephone (0834) 2025

A FULLY LICENSED, TRADITIONAL, CHINESE RESTAURANT
FOR FAMILY CELEBRATIONS SMALL PARTIES
OR ROMANTIC DINNER FOR TWO

Personal service and a friendly atmosphere

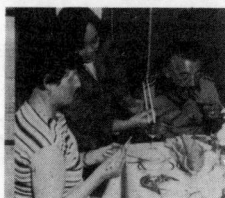

Comprehensive menu and a full range of wines and drinks

British food is also served and a take-away service is available.

Open:
Monday to Friday — 6 p.m. - 11.45 p.m.
Saturday and Sunday — Noon - 11.45 p.m.
Peak Season — Monday to Sunday — Noon - 11.45 p.m.

We also do Cookery Demonstrations

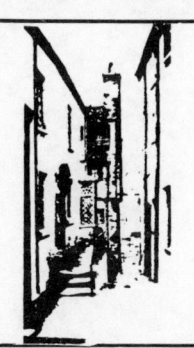

Plantagenet House
Licensed Restaurant

Quay Hill, Tenby. Telephone 2350

Enjoy good wholesome food and see a superb example of a 'Flemish Chimney' in this XV Century House.
Morning coffee, luncheons, afternoon teas, evening meals.
Vegetarian meals a speciality.
Meals also served in our

QUAY ROOM
(Originally the cellars with a wealth of old beams and stonework).
Salads and home made wholemeal pizzas a speciality
— sandwiches and other light meals available.
Last orders 10.00pm

THE LIONS DEN

Situated on the seafront, in the centre of West Wales's premier holiday resort, this below ground restaurant is the ideal rendezvous for holidaymakers.

A varied, reasonably priced, menu is available, including one for children.
The small intimate bar is the meeting place for visitors and locals alike. Many of the guests from the Royal Lion Hotel, situated directly above, often pop down to the "Den" to savour the atmosphere.

Open daily 12pm to 2.30pm and 7.00pm to 11.00pm

High Street, Tenby, Dyfed. Telephone Tenby (0834) 2127

char siu – honey roast pork with Cantonese roast and boiled rice. Special facilities exist for mothers with young babies.

The Lion's Den, Royal Lion Hotel ★★
High Street
(Tenby 2127)
Open: Summer Mon–Sun
12noon–2.30pm, 7–11pm

C &

The Lion's Den restaurant and bar, with its dark oak settles and intimate atmosphere provides a perfect venue for a relaxing meal. The lunch menu ranges from salads, hot snacks and full meals from £1.50–£3.50. The à la carte evening menu specialises in local home-produced food. Seafood is the house speciality, mackerel, plaice and bass are all £5 fully garnished. The sweet trolley at 80p provides a good variety of choice to conclude your meal.
See advert on p. 221

Tywyn — Wrexham

Plantagenet House, Quay Hill
(Tenby 2350)
Open: Etr–Oct Mon–Sun
10am–10.30pm

C ♫ S &

This 15th-century house boasts a superb example of a Flemish chimney. As well as the more traditional meals, Barney and Tina Stone also offer an interesting selection of vegetarian and wholemeal-based dishes. Prices range from around £1 for a slice of vegetarian quiche to around £4 for local crab or salmon in season with a large mixed salad. Home-made chili con carne with brown rice or a large home-made wholemeal pizza can be enjoyed for around £2. A lighter meal of open sandwiches or burgers can be had in the downstairs Quay Room. This historical restaurant welcomes families. Children are well-catered for.
See advert on p. 221

TYWYN

Greenfield Restaurant, High Street
(Tywyn 710354)
Open: May–Oct Mon–Sun
12noon–2pm, 4–9pm

P S &

This small restaurant with bay windows is attached to the Greenfield guesthouse (AA listed) and they are both run by Brian and Cynthia Elson. There are two lunch menus – the 'special', at £1.60, offering soup or juices followed by steak and kidney pie or fish, and the 'fixed price' at £2.75 (£1.95 for children) which has a choice of seven main dishes, mostly grills and fried dishes, and a choice of sweets. A similar menu is available in the evening at £2.95 (children £1.95), along with a more expensive à la carte menu. Sunday lunch is £2.75 (£1.95 children).

WREXHAM

The Welsh Kitchen, 7–9 Church Street
(Wrexham 263302)
Open: Mon–Sat 10am–2.30pm

C ♫ S

Ann Evans owns and runs this tranquil restaurant in a 14th-century listed building – the oldest in Wrexham. Exposed roof timbers set the scene and there is a good choice from any one of 13 home-made main courses, all for around £2.50. Home-made desserts such as fruit pie and cream cost about 65p each.

INDEX

TOWN	PAGE
Aberdeen	204
Aberfoyle	196
Abergele	210
Aberystwyth	210
Aboyne	204
Alcester	120
Alderley Edge	142
Aldershot	44
Alnwick	168
Alresford	44
Altrincham	142
Alveston	14
Ambleside	168
Amersham	72
Anstruther	196
Arreton	61
Ashbourne	110
Ashburton	14
Ashton-under-Lyne	142
Aviemore	204
Aylesbury	72
Ayr	186
Bala	211
Baldock	72
Ballater	204
Bakewell	110
Barking	94
Barmouth	211
Barnet	94
Barnsley	157
Barnstaple	14
Basingstoke	44
Bath	15
Beauly	204
Berwick-upon-Tweed	168
Betws-y-Coed	212
Bewdley	120
Bideford	17
Billingshurst	64
Birmingham	120
Bishops Stortford	72
Blackburn	142
Blackpool	143
Blandford Forum	45
Bleadney	17
Bodelwyddan	212
Bodmin	17
Bognor Regis	64
Bolton	143
Bolton-le-Sands	143
Boroughbridge	157
Borrowdale	169
Boston	110
Botesdale	100
Bourne	111
Bournemouth	45
Bovey Tracey	17
Bowes	169
Bowness-on-Windermere	169
Bradford	157
Braintree	100
Brechin	196
Brecon	212
Brentwood	100
Bridgnorth	126
Bridlington	157
Bridport	47
Brighouse	157
Brighton	64
Bristol	17
Brixham	19
Broadstairs	64
Broadway	126
Bromley	94
Bromsgrove	127
Bromyard	127
Broughton	143
Buckfastleigh	19
Buckie	204
Bude	20
Budleigh Salterton	20
Burbage	47
Burford	72
Burnley	143
Bury St Edmunds	100
Buxton	111
Caernarfon	212
Callander	196
Cambridge	100
Camelford	20
Cannington	20
Cannock	127
Canterbury	65
Cardigan	214
Carlisle	169
Carmarthen	214
Carnoustie	196
Castleton	111
Chelmsford	101
Cheltenham	73
Chepstow	215
Chester	143
Chichester	65
Chippenham	47
Chipping Sodbury	20
Chudleigh	21
Chulmleigh	21
Church Stretton	127
Cinderford	73
Cleethorpes	157
Clent	127
Clevedon	21
Cleveleys	145
Colchester	101
Coleford (Devon)	21
Coleford (Glos)	73
Congleton	145
Cookham	74
Corsham	47
Coventry	128
Creetown	176
Crewe	145
Crewkerne	22
Criccieth	216
Crieff	196
Croydon	95
Cullipool	186
Cumbernauld	186
Cumnock	187
Dalkieth	176
Darlington	169
Dartmeet	22
Dartmouth	22
Datchet	74
Deal	65
Denbigh	216
Derby	111
Disley	145
Doddiscombleigh	22
Dolgellau	216
Doncaster	157
Dorchester	48
Downham Market	102
Droitwich	128
Dumfries	176, 187
Dunblane	196
Dundee	196
Dunlop	187
Dunsford	23
Durham	170
Eastbourne	65
East Kilbride	187
Edinburgh	176
Egham	65
Ellesmere	128
Enfield	95
Enville	128
Epping	102
Esher	66
Eton	74
Evanton	205
Evesham	128
Ewell	66
Ewhurst Green	66
Exeter	23
Exmouth	24
Fakenham	102
Falkirk	197
Falmouth	24
Fareham	48
Farnham	66
Faversham	66
Felixstowe	103
Fenny Bridges	24
Fiddleford	48
Folkestone	66
Folkingham	112
Forfar	197
Forres	205
Fort William	205
Fossebridge	74
Foxt	129
Framlingham	103
Freckleton	145
Garthmyl	216
Gateshead	170
Gisburn	146
Glasbury	216
Glasgow	187
Glossop	112
Gloucester	74
Godalming	66
Godshill	61
Goldstone	129
Grantham	112
Grantown-on-Spey	205
Grantshouse	180
Grasmere	170
Great Yarmouth	103
Greenock	190
Gretna Green	180
Guildford	66
Guiseley	158
Hale	146
Halifax	158
Halstead	103
Halwell	24
Hambledon	48
Hampton Court	95
Harlech	216
Harleston	103
Harrogate	158
Harrow	95
Hartley Wintney	49
Hastings	66
Hatfield	74
Hathersage	112
Hay-on-Wye	216
Haywards Heath	67
Helensburgh	190
Hemel Hempstead	74
Henley-in-Arden	129
Hereford	129
Hexham	170
Honiton	24
Hook	49
Horsham	67
Hounslow	95
Huddersfield	160
Hull	160
Hungerford	74
Hythe	67
Ilchester	25
Ilford	95
Ilkley	160
Inverness	205
Invershin	205
Ipswich	103
Ironbridge	129
Irvine	191
Jamestown	191
Jedburgh	180
Keenthorne	25
Keighley	161
Kendal	170
Kenilworth	129
Kennford	25
Kentallen	205
Keswick	170
Kew	96
Keynsham	26
Kilkhampton	26
Killiekrankie	197
Killin	197
Kilmarnock	191
Kilmartin	191
Kingsbridge	26

Kingston-upon-Thames	96	
Kingswinford	130	
Kingussie	206	
Kinver	131	
Kirby Misperton	161	
Kirkaldy	197	
Kirk Langley	112	
Kirkcudbright	180	
Knaresborough	161	
Knottingley	161	
Knowle	131	
Knowstone	26	
Knutsford	146	
Lanark	191	
Lancaster	146	
Largs	191	
Lauder	180	
Leamington Spa	131	
Ledbury	131	
Leeds	161	
Leek	131	
Leicester	112	
Leighton Buzzard	75	
Leven	198	
Lincoln	114	
Linlithgow	181	
Little Chalfont	75	
Liverpool	146	
Llandudno	217	
Llangollen	217	
Llanynys	217	
Llowes	217	
Lochearnhead	198	
Lochton	206	
London (Inner)	84–93	
Lostwithiel	26	
Lowestoft	103	
Ludlow	132	
Lydford	27	
Lydney	75	
Lymm	147	
Lyndhurst	49	
Lynton	27	
Lytham	147	
Macclesfield	148	
Maidenhead	75	
Maidstone	67	
Manchester	148	
Marlborough	49	
Marlow	76	
Marple	150	
Martock	27	
Matlock	114	
Mauchline	192	
Melksham	49	
Melton Mowbray	114	
Mere	49	
Mevagissey	27	
Milford-on-Sea	50	
Milnthorpe	171	
Minehead	27	
Monmouth	218	
Montrose	198	
Morecambe	150	
Moretonhampstead	28	
Mousehole	28	
Mumbles	218	
Musselburgh	181	
Nesscliffe	132	
Newbury	76	
Newcastleton	182	
Newcastle-upon-Tyne	172	
Newport (IOW)	61	
Newquay	29	
New Radnor	218	
Newton Abbot	30	
Newton Mearns	192	
Newtown (Powys)	218	
Northampton	114	
North Berwick	182	
Northleach	76	
North Petherton	30	
Norwich	104	
Nottingham	114	
Nutbourne	67	
Oakford	30	
Oban	192	
Okehampton	30	
Oldham	151	
Ollerton	116	
Olney	76	
Ormskirk	151	
Otterbourne	50	
Ottery St Mary	31	
Oundle	116	
Oxford	76	
Paignton	31	
Painswick	77	
Paisley	193	
Pateley Bridge	162	
Pembroke Dock	219	
Penarth	219	
Penrith	173	
Penzance	32	
Pershore	132	
Perth	199	
Peterborough	105	
Peterhead	206	
Petersfield	50	
Petworth	68	
Pewsey	50	
Piddletrenthide	51	
Pinner	96	
Pitlochry	200	
Plymouth	32	
Pocklington	162	
Polegate	68	
Polperro	33	
Porlock Weir	33	
Portishead	33	
Portpatrick	182	
Portscatho	33	
Portsmouth	51	
Poynton	151	
Prestbury	151	
Preston	151	
Princetown	33	
Ralegh's Cross	33	
Reading	77	
Redbourne	78	
Redruth	34	
Reigate	68	
Renfrew	193	
Richmond-upon-Thames	96	
Richmond (N Yorks)	162	
Rickmansworth	78	
Ringwood	51	
Risca	219	
Rochdale	152	
Romsey	51	
Ross-on-Wye	133	
Rothesay	193	
Rugby	133	
Rye	68	
Saffron Walden	105	
St Albans	79	
St Andrews	200	
St Austell	34	
St Michaels-on-Wyre	152	
Salen, Isle of Mull	193	
Salisbury	52	
Sampford Peverell	35	
Sandwich	68	
Seaford	68	
Shanklin	61	
Sheffield	162	
Sherborne	52	
Shoeburyness	105	
Shrewsbury	133	
Sidmouth	35	
Skegness	117	
Skipton	163	
Sleaford	117	
Solihull	134	
Solva	219	
Southampton	52	
Southend-on-Sea	106	
South Petherton	36	
Southport	153	
South Zeal	36	
Stafford	134	
Stamford	117	
Stanmore	297	
Stirling	200	
Stockport	153	
Stoke-on-Trent	134	
Stonehaven	206	
Stow-on-the-Wold	79	
Stratford-upon-Avon	135	
Strathcarron	206	
Street	36	
Stretton	117	
Sudbury	97	
Sunderland	173	
Surbiton	97	
Sutton Coldfield	137	
Sutton-on-Sea	117	
Swansea	220	
Swindon	56	
Taunton	36	
Tenbury Wells	137	
Tenby	220	
Thame	79	
Theale	79	
Thorverton	37	
Thrapston	117	
Thurso	206	
Tideswell	117	
Tomintoul	206	
Topsham	37	
Tormarton	37	
Torquay	37	
Torrington	39	
Totnes	39	
Troon	193	
Trumpet	137	
Tunbridge Wells	68	
Turvey	80	
Tyndrum	200	
Tywyn	222	
Ullapool	207	
Upminster	97	
Uppingham	117	
Upton-upon-Severn	137	
Ventnor	61	
Veryan	40	
Wakefield	163	
Waltham Cross	80	
Wareham	56	
Warminster	57	
Warwick	138	
Waterhouses	138	
Wellington	40	
Wells	40	
Welwyn Garden City	80	
Wembley	97	
Westbury	57	
Westerham	68	
West Kirkby	153	
Weston-super-Mare	40	
Weymouth	57	
Whitby	163	
Whitchurch (Herefs and Worcs)	138	
Whittington	138	
Wick	207	
Wigan	153	
Wilmslow	153	
Wilton	58	
Wimborne	58	
Winchester	58	
Windermere	173	
Windsor	80	
Wingfield	81	
Winscombe	40	
Winslow	81	
Wisbech	106	
Wishaw	193	
Wiveliscombe	40	
Wivenhoe	106	
Wolverhampton	139	
Woolhampton	81	
Worcester	139	
Worthing	68	
Wrexham	222	
Yarmouth, Great	103	
Yarmouth (IOW)	61	
Yeovil	41	
York	164	